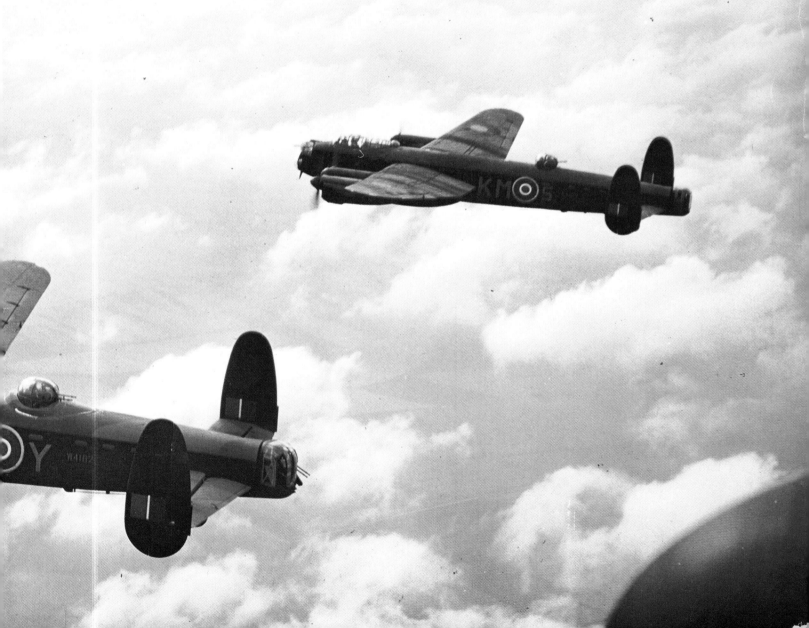

The Encyclopedia of the World's

COMBAT AIRCRAFT

The Encyclopedia of the World's
COMBAT AIRCRAFT

a Salamander book

Published by
Hamlyn
London, New York, Sydney, Toronto

A Salamander Book

This edition published 1976 by
The Hamlyn Publishing Group Ltd
London · New York · Sydney · Toronto
Astronaut House, Feltham,
Middlesex, England

ISBN 0 600 33144 X

© Salamander Books Ltd 1976
52 James Street
London W1
United Kingdom

All correspondence concerning the content of this volume should be addressed to Salamander Books Limited. Trade enquiries should be addressed to the publisher.

Credits

Editor: Iain Parsons
Design: Chris Steer,
            Malcolm Little

Line drawings of aircraft: © Pilot Press. Colour drawings of aircraft: John W. Wood, County Studios Limited and © Pilot Press

Photographs: Ministry of Defence London, and Richard Riding

Filmset by
SX Composing, Leigh-on-Sea, Essex, United Kingdom

Colour reproduction by
City Engraving Limited, Hull, North Humberside, United Kingdom

Printed in Belgium by
Henri Proost, Turnhout, Belgium

Author's Introduction

This is the first book ever to tackle the daunting task of illustrating and describing in depth all the important or significant types of combat aircraft there have ever been. Choosing the right types for inclusion was by no means easy. Obviously it was desirable not to present an unbalanced picture by giving undue prominence to particular periods of time, particular nations, particular manufacturers or particular classes of aircraft. For instance, how should one equate a fighter built in small numbers, yet which made a significant contribution to somebody's distant war, with a transport aircraft made in vast numbers and used for 40 years? Even more fundamentally, are transport aircraft combat aircraft? If so, what about assault gliders?

One basic principle followed throughout is that combat aircraft do not have to go to war. Some of the most famous machines built their reputations in peacetime, and—fortunately for the human race—this has never been so true as today. Not many of the modern aircraft in this book have proved themselves in actual combat, though there is not much doubt about how they would perform. The hardware of today has a wealth of experience and refinement behind it and if its performance falls short it is probably because of inadequate training, manning levels, spares holdings or plain bad management. We do not have many modern equivalents of the World War I fighters whose wings came off in a dive, or the World War II bomber that caught fire so readily in combat it was called "the one-shot lighter".

In fact, the whole business has become very serious, very professional, and so expensive that thousand-bomber raids, or even hundred-bomber raids, have gone for ever. And one thing history makes clear about combat aircraft is that the belief that air forces, armies, navies, procurement officials or manufacturers have at last hit on the ultimate machine is nonsense. There have been many times in the past when it seemed that, like the breech-

loading rifle and the *Dreadnought*, combat aircraft had reached a plateau of development that was going to suffice indefinitely. Such plateaux were real enough at the time, but it is difficult to think of any that have lasted longer than a dozen years.

The first combat aircraft were balloons. Then came kites, followed by primitive flying machines (aeroplanes) exactly like those flown for fun by civilians. Gradually bold spirits fired pistols and aimed bombs by hand—incidentally finding that accurate aiming was impossible—and by the start of World War I the combat aircraft proper had been born. Some had pusher engines, so that a machine-gunner could occupy the front cockpit. Today we

can see that it might have been better to put the engine in the nose and the machine gunner behind the tail, joining the two by an ordinary fuselage. Oddly, nobody in authority ever sat down and thought about the problem, because these cart-before-horse aeroplanes lasted right through World War I.

To get high performance in those days of feeble engines generally meant making aircraft small, with only one occupant. Holding a control column in one hand and aiming a machine gun with the other was not easy, though thousands of early fighter pilots tried it. It did not need a great mental leap to see that a better answer might be to fix one or even two machine guns to fire directly ahead so that the whole aircraft could be aimed at the enemy and that, with the aid of a Bowden cable, the trigger could be on the control column. This is precisely what several people suggested, in Britain, Germany, France and Russia, and probably in other countries also, in 1912-13. The Edwards brothers took out a patent for a method of synchronizing the bullets with the propeller speed so that machine guns could fire safely past a tractor propeller. They sent the idea to the War Office, which showed no interest. In Germany the Swiss engineer Franz Schneider had the same experience, and so did Lt Poplavko in Russia. French aircraft builder Raymond Saulnier actually tested a synchronizing gear, but got nowhere. Later Saulnier's test pilot, Roland Garros, went into action with V-shaped deflector channels on his propeller. He almost inevitably racked up an unprecedented tally of victories, becoming famous in a matter of days—without any interest being shown in the reason. Then Garros was forced down in German hands and, not for the first time, an idea instantly looked marvellous because the enemy used it. A few months later Allied pilots had become mere "Fokker fodder", shot down in droves by the Fokker monoplane with its more sophisticated interrupter gear.

Between the wars almost every fighter had two machine guns synchronized to fire through the propeller disc. Then came World War II, which opened to the roar of batteries of eight machine guns and closed to the formidable sound of quartets of 30mm cannon and the thunder of guided missiles and rockets. By the 1950s the gun had been almost forgotten and British bombers were thought capable of flying so fast and high that they would need no defensive armament at all. They were given none, but American bombers kept tail guns, even if they could fly at Mach 2, while Soviet jet bombers bristled with 23mm cannon from stem to stern. It took many years for the experts to learn that the bomber that flies fast and high is much easier to shoot down than the one that flies more slowly low down, and that the gun is as vital to the fighter today as it has ever been.

Undoubtedly the most difficult parameter to give

in a meaningful way is range. In some early aircraft the only available figure is endurance, the time it could fly at cruise power and still land with a few drops of petrol left. Such a figure is important today in the case of ocean patrol aircraft, but for most combat aircraft it is more usual to cite range (distance it can fly) or radius of action (which, common sense suggests, ought to be about half the range). In modern supersonic aircraft the ferry range, cruising at high altitude with maximum fuel, may be 20 times the radius of action with external weapons when flying a combat profile (hi-lo-hi means the attack is hugging the ground, while the rest of the flight is at high altitude) at supersonic speed; this makes it difficult to give a meaningful picture of how far such an aircraft can fly. Even with World War II machines a manufacturer may publish a range that represents all fuel and no bombs, while another may be more honest; it is often difficult to interpret such figures today.

All the text was deliberately set in small type in the belief that most readers would prefer more information. Even so, one often had a choice between giving a technical history of design features and sub-types and a combat history of people and events. Despite the problems, I believe we have included more information on the important combat aircraft of history than has ever before appeared between two covers.

But that is not to suggest that nothing has changed. Perhaps the most fundamental change of all has been the cost, due to inflation and ever-increasing complexity. Early combat aircraft were simple. One of the first machines bought by the Royal Flying Corps cost £368 7s, though this was considered quite enough until war came. By 1939 costs had multiplied many times. Early Wellington bombers were priced at about £26,000 and during World War II they were built in great numbers. One Wellington was built each day at the old Vickers factory at Brooklands, near Weybridge; then a factory was built at Chester that turned out 50 a month, followed by a third at Blackpool that added another 30 a month. But this is insignificant when compared with the industry of the United States. The hastily built factory at Willow Run, Michigan, very nearly achieved its popular target of making the large and extremely complicated B-24 Liberator at the rate of one an hour.

The Liberator, the most advanced and costly warplane of its day, was designed in the summer of 1939. It first flew in December 1939, and by mid-1945 the number of Liberators and closely related aircraft that had been delivered exceeded 20,000. Things are different today. The modern equivalent of the Liberator is the Rockwell B-1. This was studied in 1964, studied in more detail until 1968, studied in very great detail for two further years, designed in the early 1970s, and finally, in December 1974, a single aircraft was flown. By the late 1970s three more may be completed. Production aircraft may follow in the 1980s but, as the expected price tag is $76,000,000 each, the number built is likely to be fewer than the 241 the US Air Force needs.

There is only one country that continues to have no difficulty in finding huge sums to buy advanced combat aircraft, possibly because its general public has no say in the matter. In the Soviet Union, each year brings a new crop of formidable and impressive warplanes, which mature swiftly and take their place in the operational inventory while Western nations argue and fumble. In the old days the arguing and fumbling used to stop when a threat loomed, but in the modern world that would be approximately five to ten years too late. Today's combat aircraft are those designed ten years ago and put into production about seven years ago—except for types such as the Skyhawk, MiG-21 and Phantom where one can go back ten years earlier.

Today's combat aircraft work much harder than their predecessors. In Vietnam an F-100 Super Sabre force averaging 245 in number flew more missions than were flown by nearly 16,000 P-51 Mustangs in World War II. The average combat lifetime of a Spitfire was about 65 flying hours, whereas quite a few Lightnings have over 3,000 hours in their log books. Between the wars hardly any combat aircraft flew 200 hours a year; today many exceed 2,000 hours a year. Before 1945 it was unusual to come across a combat aircraft in the active inventory more than five years old—half lasted less than 15 months. In Vietnam many of the American warplanes were older than the pilots that flew them, and some of today's aircraft are expected to have an active life longer than 30 years. New types emerge less and less frequently, and can be afforded by fewer and fewer nations. To counter escalating costs the trend is for the building of new combat aircraft to be undertaken as huge international projects, completed in very small numbers and lasting an increasingly longer time. Really good aircraft have the ability to undergo a continual process of development, being utterly transformed over many years. This makes it hard to quote concise data, but ensures that this book will not look out of date for quite a while.

Aircraft are grouped under manufacturers, which are arranged in alphabetical order. However, this system leads to inevitable complications; the names of manufacturers tend to change within the production lifetime of individual aircraft. Aircraft appear in the text under their most likely title but are listed in the index under all relevant titles. For example, the C-119 appears in the text under Fairchild but can be found in the index under AC-119, Boxcar, C-82, C-119, Fairchild, Fairchild Hiller, Flying Boxcar, Gunship and Packet.

The treatment accorded each type varies with its diversity or importance. Most occupy a third of a page and are illustrated by one or more beautiful drawings in full colour, though some have a monochrome drawing, or drawings showing contrasting sub-types, and some of the most important have a cutaway drawing. These last occupy two pages and this has prevented a rigid alphabetical order being followed throughout, but any departure is noted in the text. The data and text are intended to convey the most useful information. Though the data generally follow a standard format this has been varied to suit either common sense or the available figures. Most is self-explanatory, but a few points need elaboration. Where engine power or thrust is given the figure is the highest that can be attained. For a piston engine this means maximum power at sea level or full-throttle rated height, with water injection or other boost, if fitted. For a jet it means with full afterburner, if fitted. Unless otherwise stated, dimensions are overall, including nose probes, wing-tip tanks or other projections; in the case of helicopters it is usually assumed that the rotors are turning. Loaded weight (clean) means with maximum internal fuel and ammunition but no external stores; maximum loaded weight means the greatest weight allowable, with external load if carried. Most of the maximum speeds are those at the best height, but many modern jets can fly so much faster at altitude (36,000 feet and above) than at sea level that both speeds are given. Unless otherwise stated, all speeds, climbs and ceilings are for the aircraft in clean condition. Fuel capacities are in Imperial gallons (1.2 US gal).

Bill Gunston

AEG bombers

K.I, G.IV, G.IVb and G.V
(data for G.IV)
Type: day and night bomber and reconnaissance aircraft.
Engines: two 260 hp Mercedes D.IVa water-cooled six-cylinder.
Dimensions: span (upper wing) 60 ft 3 in (18·35 m); length 32 ft 4 in (9·85 m); height 12 ft 9½ in (3·90 m).
Weights: empty, equipped 4410 lb (2000 kg); maximum 8,003 lb (3630 kg).
Performance: maximum speed 90 mph (145 km/h); ceiling 13,120 ft (4000 m); endurance about 4 hr 30 min.
Armament: see text.
History: first flight in Germany January 1916; remained in production to late 1918.

In 1914 the Allgemeine Elektrizitäts Gesellschaft, a huge German electrical combine, began to design a large twin-engine warplane. This went into service the following year as the K.I (*Kampfflugzeug*, fighting aircraft). Over the years it was enlarged and developed, the final and biggest version being the G.V of 1918, some of which served after the Armistice as airliners. By far the most important AEG bomber was the G.IV, of which about 400 were built. This had a crew of three or four, was defended by two Parabellum

machine guns and could carry up to 772 lb (350 kg) of bombs. In comparison with the Gotha and Zeppelin Staaken the G.IV was smaller and less powerful, and could not be used on missions longer than about 435 miles (700 km), except when carrying only fuel and cameras for long-range reconnaissance. It could not raid Britain.

Though not an outstanding design, and one marking an unusual intermediate class between single-engined bombers and huge multi-engined designs, the G.IV was pleasant to fly and reputedly able to take a lot of punishment. The direct-drive engines were notably reliable, and G.IV bombers operated by day and night on the Western Front, on the Italian front, in the

AEG G.IV (lozenge camouflage)

Balkans and as far afield as Salonika, and Macedonia. The experimental G.IVb and the final production version, the G.V, had increased wing span in order to carry a heavier load of bombs and fuel. Both the G.IV and G.V remained in front-line service to the end of the war, by which time their design was obsolescent.

Aérospatiale 321 Super Frelon

321F, G, Ja and L
Type: anti-submarine and offshore patrol helicopter.
Engines: three 1,630 hp Turboméca Turmo IIIC turboshafts.
Dimensions: diameter of main (six-blade) rotor 62 ft (18·9 m); length (rotors turning) 75 ft 7 in (23 m); height (tail rotor turning) 21 ft 10 in (6·66 m).
Weights: empty, equipped 14,607 lb (6626 kg); maximum 28,660 lb (13,000 kg)
Performance: maximum speed 171 mph (275 km/h) (a Super Frelon prototype in racing trim set a record at 212 mph in 1963); maximum rate of climb 1312 ft (400 m)/min (three engines), 479 ft (146 m)/min (two engines); service ceiling 10,325 ft (3150 m); endurance in ASW role 4 hr.
Armament: see text.
History: first flight, SA.3210 Super Frelon December 1962; SA 321G November 1965.

The biggest and heaviest helicopter yet produced in quantity to a West European design, the Super Frelon first flew in 1962 at the Marignane (Marseilles) plant of what was then Sud-Aviation. It was derived from the SA.3200 Frelon with the assistance of Sikorsky Aircraft whose technology and experience were used in the lifting and tail rotors and drive systems. Fiat of Italy assisted with the main gearbox and power transmission and continue to make these parts. The Super Frelon has been made in three versions: SA 321F civil airliner; SA 321G anti-submarine; and SA 321Ja utility. The 321Ja is the most numerous version and has been sold to several air forces. A sub-variant called SA 321L serves in quantity with the South African Air Force, and Israel used Super Frelons to carry commando raiders to Beirut Airport. The 321G is a specialised ASW aircraft, which equips Flotille 32F of the

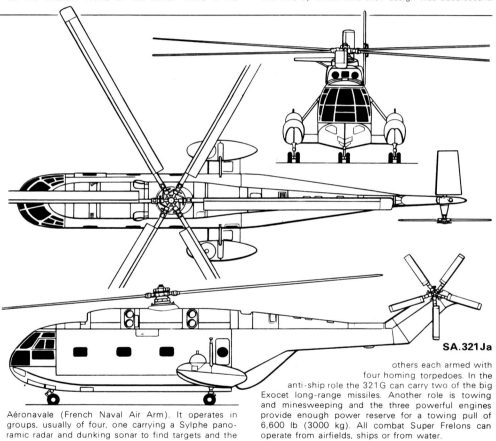

SA.321Ja

others each armed with four homing torpedoes. In the anti-ship role the 321G can carry two of the big Exocet long-range missiles. Another role is towing and minesweeping and the three powerful engines provide enough power reserve for a towing pull of 6,600 lb (3000 kg). All combat Super Frelons can operate from airfields, ships or from water.

Aéronavale (French Naval Air Arm). It operates in groups, usually of four, one carrying a Sylphe panoramic radar and dunking sonar to find targets and the

Agusta Bell

204, 205 and 212 (data for 205)
Type: multi-role combat helicopter.
Engine: Lycoming T5313 turboshaft, flat-rated at 1,250 hp (212, PT6T Twin Pac of 1,800 hp).
Dimensions: diameter of main (twin-blade) rotor 48 ft (14·63 m); length (rotors turning) 57 ft 1 in (17·4 m); height (rotors turning) 14 ft 8 in (4·48 m).
Weights: empty 5,195 lb (2356 kg); maximum 9,500 lb (4310 kg); maximum with slung external load 10,500 lb (4762 kg).
Performance: maximum speed 138 mph (222 km/h); maximum rate of climb 1,800 ft (548 m)/min; service ceiling 12,600 ft (3840 m); maximum endurance about 3½ hours.
Armament: see text.
History: Bell YUH-1D first flew August 1961; Italian Agusta versions from 1966, with 212 deliveries from 1971.

These helicopters are of American Bell design, further developed and made under licence by Agusta at Gallarate, Italy. It was in 1952 that Agusta obtained a licence for the little Bell 47, which is still in production

AB 205 (Heyl Ha'Avir, Israel)

at Gallarate though not by Bell. The much bigger turbine-powered 204B, a version of the well-known "Huey", entered production at Agusta in 1961 and has been supplied to at least eight air forces as well as civil operators. The 204AS is an all-Agusta development carrying APN-195 search radar, automatic all-weather flying aids and two Mk 44 homing torpedoes. Many are in use, the latest versions being equipped with anti-ship missiles for use against fast missile boats. The larger 205, corresponding to the Bell UH-1D and -1H, has been built in slightly larger numbers, over 400

being in use with many air forces. The illustration shows one of the multi-role 205 helicopters that played so big a role with the Israeli Heyl Ha'Avir during the war of October 1973, mainly in moving front-line troops and evacuating casualties. Unlike many 205s the Israeli examples have powered hoists. Next on the production line came the more powerful 212ASW, a much modified development of the Bell 212 and likewise powered by a United Aircraft of Canada PT6T-3 Twin Pac (with two separate engine units) rated at up to 1,800 hp. Capable of carrying a 5,000 lb (2270 kg) load, the 212ASW has a new search radar, AQS-13B variable depth sonar and many other devices, as well as two Mk 44 or 46 torpedoes.

Aichi D3A

D3A1 and D3A2
Type: two-seat carrier dive bomber.
Engine: 1,075 hp Mitsubishi Kinsei 44 14-cylinder radial (D3A2, 1,200 hp Kinsei 54).
Dimensions: span 47 ft 1½ in (14·365 m); (D3A2) 47 ft 8 in (14·53 m); length 33 ft 5½ in (10·2 m); (D3A2) 33 ft 7 in (10·25 m); height 11 ft (3·35 m); (D3A2 same).
Weights: empty 5,309 lb (2408 kg) (D3A2) 5,772 lb (2618 kg); loaded 8,047 lb (3650 kg); (D3A2) 8,378 lb (3800 kg).
Performance: maximum speed 242 mph (389 km/h); (D3A2) 281 mph (450 km/h); service ceiling 31,170 ft (9500 m); (D3A2) 35,700 ft (10,880 m); range with bomb 1,131 miles (1820 km); (D3A2) 969 miles (1560 km).
Armament: two fixed 7·7 mm guns in wings, one pivoted in rear cockpit; centreline bomb of 551 lb (250 kg), plus two bombs under wings each of 66 lb (30 kg); (D3A2: wing bombs 132 lb, 60 kg).
History: first flight August 1936; (D3A2) probably 1941; termination of production 1944.

In World War II the proper designations of Japanese aircraft were difficult to remember and often unknown to the Allies, so each major type was allotted a code-

name. Even today "Aichi D3A" may mean little to a grizzled veteran to whom the name "Val" will evoke memories of terrifying dive-bombing attacks. Aichi began this design for the Imperial Navy in 1936, its shape showing the influence of Heinkel who were secretly advising the Navy at that time. A total of 478 D3A1, also called Model 11 or Type 99, were built by August 1942, when production switched to the D3A2, Model 22. The D3A1 was the dive bomber that attacked Pearl Harbor on 7 December 1941. In April 1942 Aichis confirmed their bomb-hitting accuracy of 80–82% by sinking the British carrier *Hermes* and heavy cruisers *Cornwall* and *Dorsetshire*. They were extremely strong and manoeuvrable, and until 1943 were effective dogfighters after releasing their bombs. But loss of skilled pilots in the great battles of 1943–44, especially Midway and the Solomons, reduced bomb-

ing accuracy to 10% and the Aichis ceased to be the great threat they were in 1942. Production of the D3A2 was stopped in January 1944 at the 816th example of this cleaner and better-looking version. Some Aichis were converted as trainers or as over-loaded Kamikaze aircraft. Nakajima developed a smaller version with retractable landing gear, the D3N1, but this was not adopted.

Aichi D3A1 Model 11

Airspeed AS.51 Horsa

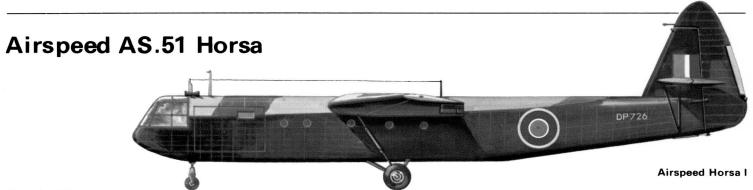

Airspeed Horsa I

Horsa I and II
Type: assault glider.
Engine: none.
Dimensions: span 88 ft (26·84 m); length 67 ft (20·43 m); height 19 ft 6 in (5·9 m).
Weights: empty 7,500 lb (3402 kg); loaded 15,250 lb (6917 kg).
Performance: Typical towing speed 127 mph (204 km/h); gliding speed 100 mph (161 km/h).
History: prototype (DG597) flew 12 September 1941; first delivery (DP279) May 1942.

Germany's success with airborne assault in the Low Countries in May 1940 was so self-evident the British decided to emulate and, if possible, improve on it. Urgent work went ahead with a number of types of training, troop-carrying and cargo glider and of these

by far the most important was the Airspeed AS.51 Horsa, designed to specification X.26/40 as a multi-role assault aircraft. It was the biggest glider that could reasonably be towed by available twin-engined tugs. At first training proceeded with Whitley V tugs, with Horsas camouflaged above and painted below with the diagonal black/yellow stripes first seen on target-towing aircraft. By 1943, the usual tug was the Albemarle and the operational gliders had black sides and undersurfaces. Very large orders were placed, not only with Airspeed at Christchurch but also with the Harris Lebus furniture firm, Austin Motor Co and Tata Industries of India. The Indian contract was cancelled but in Britain 3,655 Horsas were built and most saw action. In flight the Horsa creaked loudly and smelled of the wood from which it was made. The Mk I had

towing brackets on the wings, necessitating a bifurcated rope. The Mk II had a single socket under the nose for a rope which by 1944 was often springy nylon. The rear fuselage could be jettisoned, and there was a large door on the left side; the whole nose of the Mk II could also swing open. With its huge flaps lowered by compressed air and air brakes above and below the wings, the Horsa could almost stand on its nose and swoop quietly into small fields, carrying up to 25 troops. Halifaxes towed two on a special mission to Norway in November 1942. The same type of tug was used in the invasion of Sicily. Hundreds of Horsas took nearly a quarter of the air-supplied loads in the Normandy invasion and, in March 1945, 440 carried the 6th Airborne Division across the Rhine. Many also served with the US Army.

Albatros D.V

D.IV, V and Va (data for D.V)
Type: single-seat fighting scout.
Engine: 170/185 hp Mercedes D.IIIa six-cylinder water-cooled.
Dimensions: span 29 ft 8 in (9·05 m); length 24 ft (7·33 m); height 9 ft 4¼ in (2·85 m).
Weights: empty 1,511 lb (687 kg); loaded 2,066 lb (937 kg).
Performance: maximum speed 116 mph (187 km/h); service ceiling about 20,500 ft (6250 m); endurance 2 hr.
Armament: two synchronised 7·92 mm Spandau machine guns.
History: first flight spring 1917; first delivery May 1917; full production until Armistice.
This was the result of the efforts of Albatros Werke to improve the splendid D.III (overleaf) to maintain supremacy in the face of more formidable Allied fighters. The D.IV, of early 1917, was powered by the troublesome geared engine that was abandoned in AEG bombers, and the D.V reverted to the D.IIIa

engine but with higher compression ratio and a more streamlined installation than in the D.III. In fact the D.V can claim to have been the most perfectly stream-lined fighter of the pre-1920 period, with a completely new plywood-skinned fuselage of oval section and a pugnacious appearance that was heightened by the appearance of these aircraft in brightly coloured swarms. Nevertheless, by the time of the huge battles of March 1918 the D.V and very similar D.Va were no longer superior to the Allied fighting scouts, and had to rely on numerical superiority instead. Although the D.Va was strengthened it still sometimes broke in combat, the lower wing being especially weak and leading in 1918 to prohibition of prolonged diving. As 1,512 D.V and Va aircraft served on the Western Front

Albatros D.V
(aircraft of Manfred von Richthofen)

total production probably exceeded 3,000, a pro-portion coming from Ostdeutsche Albatros Werke at Schneidermühl.

Albatros D.I, II and III see page 10

Albatros D.III

D.I, II and III (data for D.III)

Type: single-seat fighting scout.
Engine: 160/175 hp Mercedes D.IIIa six-cylinder water-cooled.
Dimensions: span 29 ft 8 in (9·05 m); length 24 ft (7·33 m); height 9 ft 9 in (2·98 m).
Weights: empty 1,450 lb (661 kg); loaded 1,953 lb (886 kg).
Performance: maximum speed 109 mph (175 km/h); service ceiling 18,000 ft (5500 m); endurance 2 hr.
Armament: two synchronised 7·92 mm Spandau machine guns.

History: first flight probably October 1916; first delivery December 1916; production terminated early 1918.

This was one of the truly great fighting scouts of World War I, though it was produced largely by trying to copy features of an Allied design, and the Albatros design team, led by Robert Thelen, never succeeded in following it up with a major new fighter capable of maintaining supremacy in the sky over the Western Front. Thus the D.III was largely fortuitous; but for all that it was the chief means whereby the Idflieg, the Imperial German Air Service, did gain undisputed air superiority over the RFC and French Aviation Militaire throughout the first half of 1917. Indeed, so one-sided did the situation become in the spring of that year that "Bloody April" will forever be remembered in the annals of British military aviation.

Thelen's first production design, the D.I, appeared in 1916. It had the usual 160 hp Mercedes engine but twin 7·92 mm Spandau guns and it was notable for its streamlined fuselage and rounded tail, the tailplane and elevators being almost in the shape of a circular disc. The D.I was soon replaced in production by the D.II, with water radiator mounted flush in the upper wing to give less drag, and some 600 were made by Albatros Werke, LVG and the Austrian Oeffag. To produce the D.II, Thelen, on request from the Idflieg, redesigned the wings along the lines of the Nieuport series of scouts. As several extremely successful fighters, such as the SE.5, had upper and lower wings of equal size it is not clear why the Germans should have been so keen to copy the French formula, but the result was that the D.III emerged in October 1916 with a lower plane of much reduced size, braced by V interplane struts. The D.III also introduced a higher-compression engine, for better performance at altitude, and numerous minor changes.

The result was undoubtedly an improvement over the D.II, though the single-spar lower wing occasionally broke in pulling out from steep dives. D.IIIs entered service in January 1917, and by Bloody April equipped all the 37 Jagdgeschwader Staffeln (hunting squadrons, abbreviated to Jasta) then operational on the Western Front. No record survives of production,

though when it finally gave way to the D.Va in February or March 1918 the total was probably in excess of 2,000, not including the many hundreds of Albatros 53, 153 and 253 made by Oeffag with Austro-Daimler engines. Quite early in production, before February 1917, the flush radiator was moved well to the right of the centreline so that, if punctured by bullets, the boiling water missed the pilot.

Though Goering's D.III was sombrely painted, most were lividly hued and, with their shark-like appearance, started combat with a visible superiority in performance, firepower and, usually, numbers. Throughout 1917 the great "circuses", formed by such aces as Boelke and Richthofen and gathering all the outstanding fighter pilots of the Idflieg, demolished opposition wherever they operated. This was at the expense of the other squadrons, but the Allies were so hard pressed this was of small consequence. Thanks mainly to the D.III the life expectancy of RFC pilots on the Western Front in 1917 could be measured in days.

Albatros, D.IV, V and Va see page 9

Albatros D.Va cutaway drawing key:

1 Propeller boss
2 Laminated wooden propeller
3 Metal tips
4 Front fuselage frame
5 Bracing-wire anchor point
6 Engine mounting structure
7 Access panel
8 Bracing wire
9 Lower longeron
10 Upper longeron
11 Centre-section N-strut
12 Mercedes D.IIIa six-cylinder water-cooled engine (170–185 hp)
13 Water pipe to radiator
14 Auxiliary bracing strut (modification)
15 Aileron control cables
16 Starboard wingtip bracing wire
17 Interplane struts
18 Composite wood/metal leading edge member
19 Drift wires
20 Wing rib stations
21 Steel compression tube (strut anchorage)
22 Leading edge carry-round
23 Aileron crank
24 Aileron actuating cables
25 Welded-steel aileron frame
26 Steel wire trailing edge
27 Auxiliary spar
28 Rear spar
29 Steel compression tube
30 Teeves und Braun radiator
31 Radiator header tank
32 Copper exhaust pipe (starboard side)
33 Steel-tube centre-section strut
34 Twin Spandau 7·92 mm machine guns
35 Spent cartridge chute
36 Support frame
37 Ammunition box
38 Gun support bar
39 Open cockpit
40 Windshield
41 Rear-view mirror (sometimes on cockpit coaming)
42 Trailing-edge cut-out
43 Padded cockpit coaming
44 Fuselage frames (plywood former)
45 Fuselage skin
46 'X'-tube bracing strut
47 Upper longeron (spruce)
48 Starboard tailplane
49 Fin structure
50 Rudder balance
51 Rudder frame (metal)
52 Rudder hinges
53 Rudder post
54 Elevator control horns
55 Elevator frame (metal)
56 Elevator balance
57 Tailplane structure (wooden framed)
58 Under-fin
59 Steel shoe
60 Ash tailskid
61 Elastic cord shock-absorber
62 Tailplane stub attachment
63 Control cables (rudder)
64 Lower longeron (spruce)
65 Control cables (elevator)
66 Aileron crank
67 Wooden hinge blocks
68 Welded-steel aileron frame
69 Rear spar
70 Plywood wing ribs
71 Strut anchorage
72 Entry step
73 Plywood bulkhead
74 Pilot's seat
75 Control column
76 Rudder pedals
77 Interplane bracing wires
78 Fuel tank
79 Wing stub
80 Starboard wheel
81 700 mm x 100 mm tyre
82 Axle
83 Compression strut
84 Undercarriage bracing
85 Port tyre
86 Metal retaining strap
87 Access panel
88 Elastic cord shock-absorber
89 Forward section compression struts (3)
90 Wing spar
91 Aileron cables
92 Upper mainplane front spar
93 Interplane bracing wire
94 False rear spar (not anchored)
95 Interplane strut
96 Aileron control cables
97 Port wingtip bracing wire
98 Aileron control pulley housing
99 Auxiliary bracing strut (modification)
100 Lower wing structure

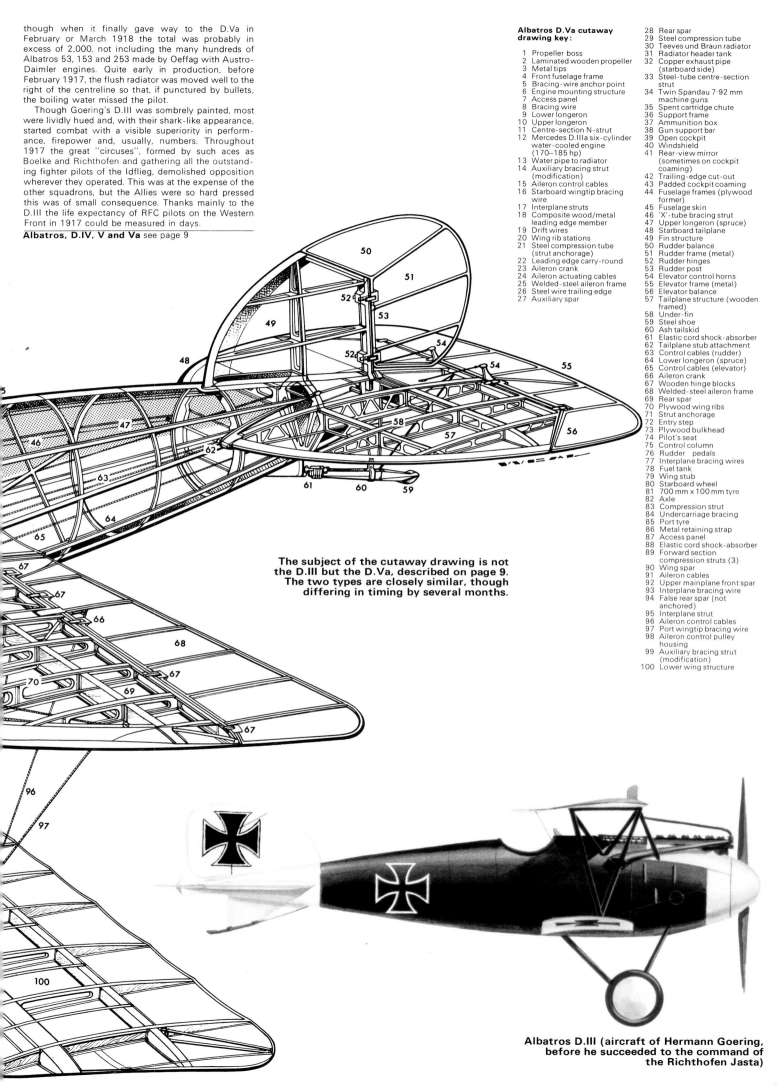

The subject of the cutaway drawing is not the D.III but the D.Va, described on page 9. The two types are closely similar, though differing in timing by several months.

Albatros D.III (aircraft of Hermann Goering, before he succeeded to the command of the Richthofen Jasta)

Amiot 143

143M (B-5)
Type: five-seat reconnaissance bomber.
Engines: two 900 hp Gnome-Rhône 14K Mistral Major 14-cylinder air-cooled radials.
Dimensions: span 80 ft 6 in (24·53 m); length 59 ft 11 in (18·25 m); height 18 ft 7¾ in (5·65 m).
Weights: empty 13,448 lb (6100 kg); loaded 19,568 lb (8876 kg); maximum overload 21,385 lb (9700 kg).
Performance: Maximum speed 193 mph (310 km/h) at 13,120 ft (4000 m); maximum cruising speed 168 mph (270 km/h); normal range 746 miles (1200 km); service ceiling 25,930 ft (9000 m).
Armament: four 7·5 mm machine guns; up to 1,764 lb (800 kg) of bombs internally and same weight on external wing racks.
History: prototype flew April 1931; production aircraft flew April 1935; first delivery July 1935.

Between the world wars French bombers were invariably aesthetic monstrosities. Fortunately few were built in numbers, but the 143, produced by SECM-Amiot and flown (as the 140) at Villacoublay in April 1931, had a long and varied operational career. Designed to a 1928 Multiplace de Combat specification, the 140 progressed through serveral stages to become the production 143, which entered service with GB 3/22 at Chartres in August 1935. The last of 138 was delivered in March 1937. At first the guns were all World War I Lewises, with drum magazines, but at the 41st aircraft they changed to the belt-fed MAC 1934

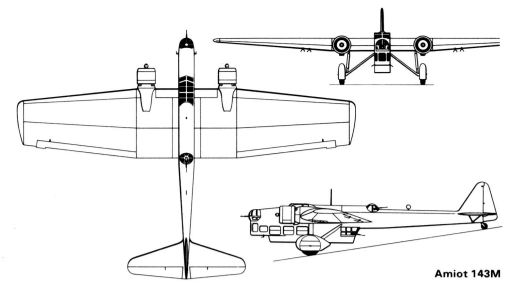

(though with only one gun at each rear position instead of two). The structure was all-metal, and the wing was so thick the engines could be reached in flight. Main wartime units were GB 34 at Dugny, GB 35 at Bron and GB 38 at Metz (which took the Amiots from GB 22). After leaflet raiding, operations began in earnest with the invasion of the Low Countries on

Amiot 143M

10 May, and in 197 night operations the rugged Amiots dropped 338,626 lb (153 tonnes) of bombs for the loss of four aircraft. But in a desperate day assault on the Sedan bridges only one came back from GB I/38 and II/38. These lumbering bombers served Vichy France and then the Allies as transports in Tunisia until 1944.

Antonov An-12

An-12
Type: Paratroop, passenger and freight transport.
Engines: four 4,000 ehp Ivchenko AI-20K single-shaft turboprops.
Dimensions: span 124 ft 8 in (38 m); length 121 ft 4½ in (37 m); height 32 ft 3 in (9·83 m).
Weights: empty 61,730 lb (28,000 kg); loaded 121,475 lb (55,100 kg).
Performance: maximum speed 482 mph (777 km/h); maximum cruising speed 416 mph (670 km/h); maximum rate of climb 1,970 ft (600 m)/min; service ceiling 33,500 ft (10,200 m); range with full payload 2,236 miles (3600 km).
Armament: powered tail turret with two 23 mm NR-23 cannon.
History: first flight (civil An-10) 1957; (An-12) believed 1958.

With the big An-2 biplane Oleg K. Antonov, previously noted mainly for his smaller glider designs, established himself as pre-eminent supplier of utility transport and freight aircraft in the Soviet Union. In 1958 he flew a large twin-turboprop which owed something to German designs of World War II and the C-130. From this evolved the An-10 airliner and the An-12, which since 1960 has been a standard transport with many air forces. Fully pressurised, the An-12 has an excep-

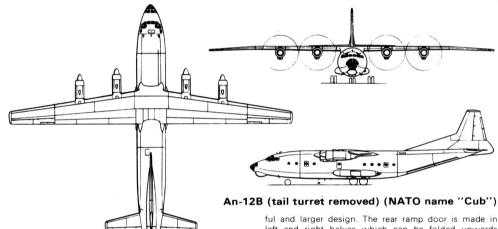

tionally high performance yet can operate from unpaved surfaces. At least one was fitted with large skis with shallow V planing surfaces equipped with heating (to prevent sticking to ice or snow) and brakes. Nearly all have the tail turret, and under the transparent nose is a weather and mapping radar, which in most Soviet Air Force An-12s has been changed to a more power-

An-12B (tail turret removed) (NATO name "Cub")

ful and larger design. The rear ramp door is made in left and right halves which can be folded upwards inside the fuselage, either for loading heavy freight with the aid of a built-in gantry or for the dispatch of 100 paratroops in less than one minute. Huge numbers of these capable logistic transports have taken part in manoeuvres of Warsaw Pact forces, and others have been supplied to the air forces of India, Egypt, Indonesia, Poland, Iraq, Algeria and Bangladesh, and to many other operators. The total number built almost certainly exceeds 1,000.

Arado Ar 68

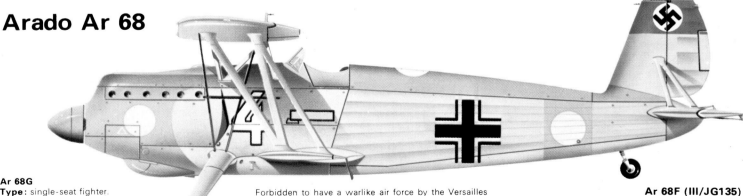

Ar 68G
Type: single-seat fighter.
Engine: 750 hp BMW VI 12-cylinder vee liquid-cooled.
Dimensions: span 36 ft (11 m); length 31 ft 2 in (9·5 m); height 10 ft 10 in (3·3 m).
Weights: empty 3,307 lb (1500 kg); loaded 4,410 lb (2000 kg).
Performance: maximum speed 192 mph (310 km/h) at 13,125 ft (4000 m); service ceiling 24,280 ft (7400 m); range with service load 342 miles (550 km).
Armament: two 7·92 mm MG 17 machine guns above engine; racks for six 110 lb (50 kg) bombs.
History: first flight November 1933; (Ar 68G) December 1935; termination of production, probably 1937.

Forbidden to have a warlike air force by the Versailles Treaty, Germany produced no combat aircraft in the 1920s and early 1930s, though German design teams did produce important prototypes in Spain, Sweden and Switzerland. By the time the Nazi party seized power in 1933 there was a useful nucleus of talent and industrial strength and the Arado Werke was, with Heinkel, charged with urgently building a first-line fighter for the new Luftwaffe. The result was the Ar 68V1 prototype, powered by the trusty BMW VI engine, rated at 660 hp and constructed of welded steel tube and wood, with fabric covering except over the forward and upper fuselage. Like all Arado aircraft of the period it had a tailplane well behind the fin and rudder, and the single-strut cantilever landing gear was distinctive. Two prototpes flew in 1934 with the 610 hp

Ar 68F (III/JG135)

Jumo 210 engine and this was selected for the production Ar 68E which entered service with the newly formed Luftwaffe in 1935. But the Ar 68F reverted to the BMW engine, uprated to 675 hp, and the main production centred on the still more powerful Ar 68G. Despite good engines the Ar 68 was never an outstanding machine. It ran second in timing and performance to its great rival the He 51 and, apart from a few used as night fighters, had been relegated to training before World War II. One example of the Ar 68H, with BMW 132Dc radial and enclosed cockpit, was flown and a development, the Ar 197, would have been used aboard the carrier *Graf Zeppelin* had the vessel been commissioned.

Arado Ar 196

Ar 196A-1 to A-5 (data for A-3)
Type: two-seat maritime reconnaissance aircraft.
Engine: 960 hp BMW 132K nine-cylinder radial.
Dimensions: span 40 ft 8 in (12·4 m); length 36 ft 1 in (11 m); height 14 ft 4½ in (4·4 m).
Weights: empty 6,580 lb (2990 kg); loaded 8,223 lb (3730 kg).
Performance: Maximum speed 193 mph (310 km/h) at 13,120 ft (4000 m); initial climb 980 ft (300m)/min; service ceiling 23,000 ft (7020 m); range 670 miles (1070 km) at 158 mph (253 km/h).
Armament: two MG FF 20 mm cannon in wings outboard of propeller disc, one MG 17 7·92 mm in top decking and twin MG 17 on pivoted mounting aimed by observer. Rack under each wing for 110 lb (50 kg) bomb.
History: first flight (196V1) May 1938; first operational service 1 August 1939.

One of the very few float seaplanes to be used in World War II outside the Pacific area, the Ar 196 was designed as a replacement for the He 60 biplane on the catapults of all the German Navy's capital ships. Its duties were thus primarily reconnaissance and shadowing of surface vessels, but in comparison with such Allied types as the Curtiss Seagull and Fairey Seafox it had a much higher performance and eventually was given formidable armament. Four prototypes, powered by the 880 hp BMW 132Dc engine (derived in Germany from the Pratt & Whitney Hornet), were flown in 1938, two

with twin floats and the others with a large central float. The following year, 26 Ar 196A-1s were built, entering service in August aboard the battle cruisers *Gneisenau* and *Scharnhorst*, and at shore bases on the North Sea. In 1940 the Ar 196A-3 entered service, and this type made up the bulk of the 401 aircraft built. Though quite outclassed by the best fighters, the A-3 was a versatile multi-role aircraft which actually spent most of the war operating on sea patrols

from coastal bases, mainly on the Bay of Biscay and islands in the Mediterranean. Batches were built by Vichy-France at Saint Nazaire and, in a slightly modified A-5 form, by Fokker at Amsterdam in 1943—44. About 50 served with co-belligerent Balkan air forces in the Adriatic and Black Sea. The type was never developed as an effective anti-submarine search and strike machine, despite its obvious potential.

Ar 196A-3 (II/Aufk. 125)

Arado Ar 234 Blitz

Ar 234B-1 and B-2 Blitz (Lightning)
Type: single-seat reconnaissance bomber.
Engines: two 1,980 lb (900 kg) thrust Junkers Jumo 004B axial turbojets.
Dimensions: span 46 ft 3½ in (14·2 m); length 41 ft 5½ in (12·65 m); height 14 ft 1¼ in (4·3 m).
Weights: empty 11,464 lb (5200 kg); loaded 18,541 lb (8410 kg); maximum with rocket takeoff boost 21,715 lb (9850 kg).
Performance: maximum speed (clean) 461 mph (742 km/h); service ceiling 32,800 ft (10,000 m); range (clean) 1,013 miles (1630 km), (with 3,300 lb bomb load) 684 miles (1100 km).
Armament: two fixed MG 151 20 mm cannon in rear fuselage, firing to rear and sighted by periscope; various combinations of bombs slung under fuselage and/or engines to maximum of 3,300 lb (1500 kg).
History: first flight (Ar 234V1) 15 June 1943, (Ar 234V9 with landing gear) March 1944 (Ar 234B-0 pre-production) 8 June 1944; operational delivery September 1944.

As the first jet reconnaissance bomber, the Ar 234 Blitz (meaning Lightning) spearheaded Germany's remarkably bold introduction of high-performance turbojet aircraft in 1944. Its design was begun under Walter Blume in 1941, after long studies in 1940 of an official specification for a jet-propelled reconnaissance aircraft with a range of 1,340 miles. The design was neat and simple, with two of the new axial engines slung under a high wing, and the single occupant in a pressurised cockpit forming the entire nose. But to achieve the required fuel capacity no wheels were fitted. When it flew on 15 June 1943 the first 234 took off from a three-wheel trolley and landed on retractable skids. After extensive trials with eight prototypes the ninth flew with conventional landing gear, leading through 20 pre-production models to the operational 234B-1, with ejection seat, autopilot and drop tanks under the engines. Main production centred on the

234B-2, made in many sub-variants, most of them able to carry a heavy bomb load. Service over the British Isles with the B-1 began in September 1944, followed by a growing force of B-2s which supported the Battle of the Bulge in the winter 1944–45. In March 1945 B-2s of III/KG76 repeatedly attacked the vital Remagen bridge across the Rhine with 2,205 lb (1,000 kg) bombs, causing its collapse. Though handicapped by fuel shortage these uninterceptable aircraft played a significant role on all European fronts in the closing months of the war, 210 being handed over excluding the many prototypes and later versions with four engines and an uncompleted example with a crescent-shaped wing.

Ar 234B-2 (9/KG 76)

Armstrong Whitworth F.K.8

F.K.3 and 8
Type: two-seat reconnaissance bomber.
Engine: usually 160 hp Beardmore six-cylinder water-cooled.
Dimensions: span 43 ft 4 in (13·23 m); length 31 ft 5 in (9·55 m); height 11 ft (3·35 m).
Weights: empty 1,916 lb (869 kg); loaded 2,811 lb (1275 kg).
Performance: maximum speed 95 mph (153 km/h); rate of climb 330 ft (100 m)/min; ceiling 13,000 ft (3960 m); endurance 3 hr.
Armament: one synchronised 0·303 in Vickers firing forward; one 0·303 in Lewis aimed by observer; bomb load of 160 lb (72·6 kg).
History: first flight May 1916; first service delivery, end of 1916; production termination July 1918.

Dutchman Fritz Koolhoven came, like his compatriot Fokker, to the British Air Ministry in 1914 and asked if he could build aeroplanes. Unlike Fokker he stayed, and his F.K.3 was accepted in August 1915 as a replacement for the somewhat dated B.E.2c. Though not an outstanding performer, the 90 hp F.K.3 was easy to fly and many of the 498 built served as trainers (but RFC No 47 Sqn used them as bombers until 1918, often having to leave the observer behind to carry a 112 lb bomb load)! The F.K.8 was made in even larger numbers and, thanks to its greater power could lift both men and the full bomb load – and the massive steel maker's nameplate screwed on each side of the nose in best heavy engineering fashion! Called "Big Ack", to distinguish it from the F.K.3 "Little Ack", it was strong and reliable, and often got

away from seemingly impossible combat situations. The classic case was when 2nd Lt A. A. McLeod and his observer Lt A. W. Hammond got back alive, but both sorely wounded, after shooting down four of the eight Fokker Triplanes which attacked them on 27

Armstrong Whitworth F.K. 8

March 1918 when they were flying alone and carrying full bomb load. AWA delivered 650 Big Acks, and Angus Sanderson at least 750 of an order for 900. Throughout the last two years of the war the F.K.8 did every kind of reconnaissance, bombing and straffing mission on the Western Front, in Macedonia and in Palestine. At the Armistice it equipped 2, 8, 10, 35 and 82 Sqns of the RAF, as well as 17, 47 and 142 overseas.

Armstrong Whitworth Siskin

Siskin III and IIIA (data for IIIA)
Type: single-seat fighter.
Engine: 450 hp Armstrong Siddeley Jaguar IV 14-cylinder two-row radial.
Dimensions: span (upper) 33 ft 2 in (10·1 m); length 25 ft 4 in (7·72 m); height 10 ft 2 in (3·1 m).
Weights: empty 2,061 lb (935 kg); loaded 3,012 lb (1366 kg).
Performance: maximum speed 156 mph (251 km/h); climb to 15,000 ft (4572 m) 10½ min; service ceiling 27,000 ft (8230 m).
Armament: two fixed synchronised 0·303 in Vickers machine guns; provision for four 20 lb (9 kg) Cooper practice bombs under wings.
History: first flight (IIIA) 20 October 1925; entry to service March 1927; production termination March 1931.

The first Siddeley S.R.2 Siskin, by the Siddeley-Deasy Motor Car Co, was ready in May 1918, but it was unable to fly until 1919 because of hopeless trouble with its ABC Dragonfly engine (the engine on which most British military aviation for the future had rashly been based). After the Armistice the infant RAF had no new fighters until 1924, when orders were placed for Gloster Grebes and Siskin IIIs, the latter from the Sir W. G. Armstrong Whitworth Aircraft Ltd at Coventry. The Siskin III had the new Jaguar engine, a structure that was no longer all-wood but partly made of rolled steel strip, and followed the old Nieuport idea of having V struts bracing a very small lower wing. The 62 Mk III Siskins equipped 41 Sqn at Northolt and 111 at

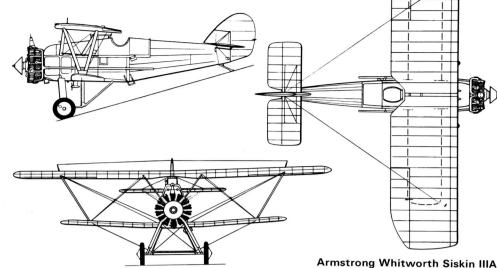

Duxford. In March 1927 No 41 became the first of ten home-defence squadrons to have the Siskin IIIA, with the much more powerful supercharged Jaguar IVS (the first supercharged engine in service in the world) and several structural changes. Altogether 360 single-seat Siskin IIIAs were delivered by AWA, Bristol,

Armstrong Whitworth Siskin IIIA

Vickers, Gloster and Blackburn, as well as 47 DC (dual control) two-seat trainers. These superb aerobatic aircraft, which performed tied-together at Hendon in 1930, actually outnumbered the later Bulldog, but they ceased to be the No 1 RAF fighter from 1929 and faded swiftly in the 1930s.

Armstrong Whitworth A.W.38 Whitley

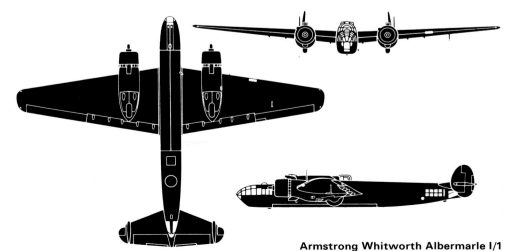

Whitley I to VIII (data for V)
Type: five-seat heavy bomber.
Engines: two 1,145 hp Rolls-Royce Merlin X vee-12 liquid-cooled.
Dimensions: span 84 ft (25·6 m); length 70 ft 6 in (21·5 m); height 15 ft (4·57 m).
Weights: empty 19,330 lb (8768 kg); maximum 33,500 lb (15,196 kg).
Performance: maximum speed 222 mph (357 km/h); cruising speed, about 185 mph (297 km/h); initial climb 800 ft (244 m)/min; service ceiling from 17,600–21,000 ft (5400–6400 m); range with maximum bomb load 470 miles (756 km); range with 3,000 lb (1361 kg) bombs 1,650 miles (2650 km).
Armament: one 0·303 in Vickers K in nose turret; four 0·303 in Brownings in tail turret; up to 7,000 lb (3175 kg) bombs in cells in fuselage and inner wings.
History: first flight (prototype) 17 March 1936; first delivery (Mk I) January 1937; first flight (Mk V) December 1938; first delivery (Mk V) August 1939; production termination June 1943.

Designed to Specification B.3/34, this heavy bomber was at least an all-metal monoplane with retractable

landing gear, but the original Mk I was still primitive. Its thick wing, which in the first batch had no dihedral, was set at a marked positive incidence, so that at normal cruising speeds the long sl(b-sided Whitley flew in a characteristic nose-down attitude. Powered by 795 hp Armstrong Siddeley Tiger IX radials, the Mk I was soon replaced by the Mk II, and then by the III with the 920 hp Tiger VIII. In 1938 production switched to the greatly improved Mk IV, with Merlin engines and a power-driven rear turret mounting four machine guns. The Mk IVA had a more powerful Merlin, and this was retained in the Mk V which was 15 in longer and had straight-edged fins. AWA made 1,466 Whitley Vs, the last in June 1943, and also delivered 146 longer-range GR.VIII patrol aircraft with ASV radar for Coastal Command. Whitleys bore the

Armstrong Whitworth Whitley V (102 Sqn)

brunt of long leaflet raids, starting on the first night of the war. On 19 March 1940 Whitleys dropped the first bombs to fall on Germany since 1918, and during the next two years these tough and capable aircraft made missions as far as Turin and Pilsen, often in terrible conditions, highlighting deficiencies in navigation and equipment the hard way. Coastal's first U-boat kill was U-206, sunk by a Whitley VII in November 1941. From 1942 the Whitley served mainly as a trainer for paratroops, as a glider tug and with 100 Group as a carrier of experimental or special-purpose radars and countermeasures. Total production was 1,737.

Armstrong Whitworth A.W.41 Albemarle

Albemarle I to VI
Type: Four-crew special transport and glider tug.
Engines: two 1,590 hp Bristol Hercules XI 14-cylinder sleeve-valve.
Dimensions: span 77 ft (23·47 m); length 59 ft 11 in (18·25 m); height 15 ft 7 in (4·75 m).
Weights: empty (GT.VI) 22,600 lb (10,260 kg); maximum 36,500 lb (16,570 kg).
Performance: maximum speed 265 mph (426 km/h); initial climb 980 ft (299 m)/min; service ceiling 18,000 ft (5490 m); typical range 1,350 miles (2160 km).
Armament: none except in Mk I/1 (Boulton Paul dorsal turret with four 0·303 in Brownings and powered ventral turret with two 0·303 in Brownings) and ST.I (manual dorsal installation with various guns).
History: first flight 20 March 1940; (production aircraft) December 1941; final delivery December 1944. After Bristol had proposed the Type 155 bomber with a nosewheel landing gear (never used in Britain except experimentally) the Air Ministry issued Specification B.18/38 which was notable for its insistence on minimal use of light alloys, which were likely to be in short supply in event of war. Instead the design was to be made mainly of steel and wood, even though this would increase weight. Bristol dropped the 155, and the specification was met by the AW.41, first flown on 20 March 1940. Production was entirely subcontracted to firms outside the aircraft industry, and parts were brought to a plant at Gloucester for which

Hawker Siddeley formed a company called A. W. Hawksley Ltd. Thus, not only did the Albemarle conserve strategic materials (with very small penalty, as it turned out) but it had no parent factory or design organization. Delivery began in October 1941, but only 32 were completed as bombers and these were converted as transports. Altogether 600 were de-

Armstrong Whitworth Albermarle I/1

livered by the end of 1944, in many versions grouped into two main families: ST, or Special Transport, used all over Europe and North Africa; and GT, Glider Tug, used in Sicily, Normandy and at Arnhem. Glider towing needed high power at low airspeeds, and the Hercules overheated and poured oil smoke, but the Albemarle was otherwise pleasant to fly.

Avia 534

534-III and -IV
Type: single-seat fighter.
Engine: 760/860 hp Avia-built Hispano-Suiza 12
Ydrs 12-cylinder vee liquid-cooled.
Dimensions: span 30 ft 10 in (9·4 m);
length 26 ft 7 in (8·1 m); height 10 ft 2 in (3·1 m).
Weights: empty 3,218 lb (1460 kg); loaded 4,364 lb
(1980 kg).
Performance: maximum speed 249 mph (400 km/h);
initial climb 2,953 ft (900 m)/min; service ceiling
34,770 ft (10,600 m); range 373 miles (600 km).
Armament: four 7·92 mm Mk 30 (modified Vickers)
machine guns.
History: first flight (B 34) late 1931; (B 534) August
1933; final delivery, not known but after 1938.

In 1930 the Avia works at Prague-Letnany, a subsidiary
of the great Czech Skoda company, appointed a new
chief designer, F. Nowotny. His first design was the
B 34 fighter, which in 1932 was studied with a series
of radial and vee engines and eventually gelled as the
B 534. This was probably the finest fighter of its day,
having outstanding speed and manoeuvrability, no
vices and the heavy armament of four guns. Originally
two were in the lower wing, as in Britain's Gloster
Gladiator of two years later. Wing vibration when the
guns were fired led to all four being put in the fuselage,

with a bulge over the belt feed and case boxes. In 1935
the type went into large-scale production and at the
time of the Munich crisis in September 1938 over 300
of the eventual total of 445 had been delivered, so the
Czech Army was actually stronger in fighters than the
Luftwaffe. Many of the aircraft were B 534-IIIs with
enclosed cockpit and -IVs with more powerful 12Y
engine. A batch of 35, designated Bk 534, were to

Avia B.534-IV (Slovakian AF, 1941)

have had a 20 mm cannon firing through the propeller hub; only a few had the big gun, most having a
mere machine gun, with one more on each side.
Slovak Air Force fighter squadrons 11, 12 and 13
operated on the Russian front from July 1941, but
morale was low and many Avias deserted to the Soviet
side. Three aircraft survived to fight against the
Germans in the Slovak revolt of 1944.

Aviatik

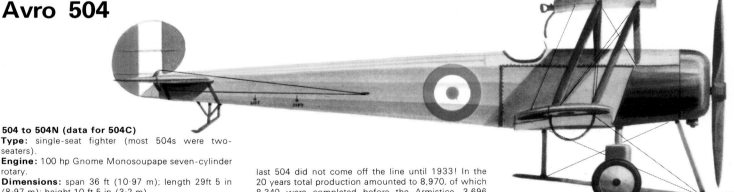

B.I, II and II (data for B.I)
Type: two-seat reconnaissance aircraft.
Engine: 100 hp Mercedes D.I six-cylinder
water-cooled.
Weights: empty about 1,300 lb (590 kg); loaded
1,900 lb (860 kg).
Dimensions: span 45 ft 11 in (14 m); length 26 ft 3in
(8 m); height 10 ft 6 in (3·2 m).
Performance: maximum speed 65 mph (105 km/h);
ceiling about 8,200 ft (2500 m); endurance 4 hr.
Armament: see text.
History: first flight, believed November 1914; first
service delivery, 1914; effort then transferred to B.II
from Austrian subsidiary.

One of the earliest purpose-designed combat aircraft
was the B.I produced in late 1914 by the Automobil
und Aviatik AG, of Leipzig. In the following year a
subsidiary of this company, the O-U F Aviatik (Austro-
Hungarian Aircraft Works), of Vienna, went into production on a rather larger scale on a development
called B.II. Though still a delicate "stick and string"
machine, with performance very low by standards of

even a year later, the B.II had an extremely good range
and endurance and served for a strategic reconnaissance over wide sectors of the Russian front. None
was originally built with armament, though crew-
members invariably carried revolvers which were often
used in the air. Some observers carried rifles, and
many B.IIs were later modified to carry a heavy
Schwarzlose 7·92 mm machine gun either on a tripod
or a spigot behind the rear cockpit. The B.II was also
one of the early bombers, with racks for two 22 lb

Aviatik B.I

(10 kg) bombs. Before mid-1915 the B.II had been
succeeded in production by the 160 hp B.III, with a
different airframe, a large communal cockpit (with
Schwarzlose as standard) and racks for three bombs.
Unfortunately it did not handle as well as the pleasant
B.II, and so the older aircraft was put back into production with the B.III's engine, machine gun and
extra bomb rack. This second batch, called B.II Series
34, were able to fly 50% faster and twice as high as
the original version.

Avro 504

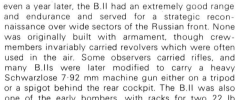

504 to 504N (data for 504C)
Type: single-seat fighter (most 504s were two-
seaters).
Engine: 100 hp Gnome Monosoupape seven-cylinder
rotary.
Dimensions: span 36 ft (10·97 m); length 29ft 5 in
(8·97 m); height 10 ft 5 in (3·2 m).
Weights: empty about 1,240 lb (562 kg); loaded
1,800 lb (816 kg).
Performance: maximum speed 82 mph (132 km/h);
climb, 10,000 ft (3050 m) in 19 minutes; ceiling
13,000 ft (3960 m); endurance 3 hr.
Armament: one 0·303 in Lewis gun on upper plane,
aimed by pilot.
History: first flight (first 504) July 1913; first 504C
flew early 1916; completion of production (504N)
mid-1933.

When young A. V. Roe built his first 504, in the
pioneer days more than a year before World War I, he
thought he would be lucky to sell six. In fact the

last 504 did not come off the line until 1933! In the
20 years total production amounted to 8,970, of which
8,340 were completed before the Armistice, 3,696
being built by Avro. These figures do not include
quantities built in the Soviet Union in the 1920s which
are believed to bring the total above 10,000. There
were many versions. At first the standard engine was
the 80 hp Gnome, and the 504A achieved the
double distinction of being the first Allied aircraft shot
down (22 August 1914) and first to make a bombing
raid on Germany (the daring Royal Naval Air Service
attack on Zeppelin sheds at Friedrichshafen, when two
airships were destroyed). The RNAS 504B had racks
for four 20 lb (9 kg) bombs, and the observer in the
front cockpit had a Lewis gun. The 504C and D were
single-seat anti-Zeppelin fighters. By early 1917 the
504J was the standard British trainer, and as the K

Avro 504C (single-seat anti-Zeppelin)

(equipped with any of several engines) it continued in
use until 1930. Final version was the 504N, or Lynx-
Avro (because of its Lynx radial giving from 160
to 215 hp), which entered production in 1927. These
had no skid (formerly fitted to prevent nosing over)
and looked much more modern. The Lynx-Avros of the
Central Flying School were the first aircraft in the
world used to teach blind flying on instruments alone.
694 Lincoln and 696 Shackleton see page 18

Avro 683 Lancaster

Lancaster I to MR.7 (data for I)

Type: seven-seat heavy bomber.

Engines: four 1,460 hp Rolls-Royce or Packard Merlin 20 or 22 (Mk II only: four 1,650 hp Bristol Hercules VI, 14 cylinder two-row, sleeve-valve radials).

Dimensions: span 102 ft (31·1 m); length 69 ft 4 in (21·1 m); height 19 ft 7 in (5·97 m).

Weights: empty 36,900 lb (16,705 kg); loaded 68,000 lb (30,800 kg); overload with 22,000 lb bomb 70,000 lb (31,750 kg).

Performance: maximum speed 287 mph (462 km/h) at 11,500 ft (3500 m); cruising speed 210 mph (338 km/h); climb to 20,000 ft (6095 m) 41 minutes; service ceiling 24,500 ft (7467 m); range with 14,000 lb (6350 kg) bombs 1,660 miles (2675 km).

Armament: nose and dorsal turrets (sometimes also ventral) with two 0·303 in Brownings (some, including Mk VII, had Martin dorsal turret with two 0·5 in), tail turret with four 0·303 in Brownings, 33 ft (10·06 m) bomb bay carrying normal load of 14,000 lb (6350 kg) or 22,000 lb (9979 kg) bomb with modification.

History: first flight 9 January 1941; service delivery September 1941; last delivery from new 2 February 1946.

Undoubtedly one of the major influences on World War II, and one of the greatest aircraft of history, the "Lanc" came about because of the failure of its predecessor. In September 1936 the Air Staff issued specification P.13/36 for a twin-engined bomber of exceptional size and capability to be powered by one of the very powerful engines then under development: the Rolls-Royce Vulture 24-cylinder X engine was preferred. Handley Page switched to four Merlins with the Halifax, but A. V. Roe adhered to the big-twin formula and the first Type 679 Manchester flew on 25 July 1939. Altogether 209 Manchesters were delivered by November 1941, but the type was plagued by the poor performance and unreliability of its engine. Though it equipped eight Bomber Command squadrons, and parts of two others plus a flight in Coastal Command, the Manchester was withdrawn from service in June 1942 and survivors were scrapped.

Nevertheless the basic Manchester was clearly outstandingly good, and in 1940 the decision was taken to build a longer-span version with four Merlin engines. The first Lancaster (BT 308) flew as the Manchester III at the beginning of 1941. So outstanding was its performance that it went into immediate large-scale production, and Manchesters already on the line from L7527 onwards were completed as Lancasters (distinguished from later aircraft by their row of rectangular windows in the rear fuselage). Deliveries

began in early 1942 to 44 Sqn at Waddington, and on 17 April 1942 a mixed force of 44 and 97 Sqns made a rather foolhardy daylight raid against the MAN plant at Augsburg, whereupon the new bomber's existence was revealed.

From then until the end of World War II Lancasters made 156,000 sorties in Europe and dropped 608,612 long tons of bombs. Total production, including 430 in Canada by Victory Aircraft, was 7,377. Of these 3,425 were Mk I and 3,039 the Mk III with US Packard-built engines. A batch of 300 was built as Mk IIs with the more powerful Bristol Hercules radial, some with bulged bomb bays and a ventral turret. The Mk I (Special) was equipped to carry the 12,000 lb (5443 kg) light-case bomb and the 12,000 lb and 22,000 lb (9979 kg) Earthquake bombs, the H S radar blister under the rear fuselage being removed. The Mk I (FE) was equipped for Far East operations with Tiger Force. The aircraft of 617 (Dambusters) Sqn were equipped to spin and release the Wallis skipping drum bomb. The Mk VI had high-altitude Merlins and four-blade propellers and with turrets removed served 635 Sqn and 100 Grp as a countermeasure and radar spoof carrier. Other marks served as photo-reconnaissance and maritime reconnaissance and air/sea rescue aircraft, the last leaving RAF front-line service in February 1954.

Lancasters took part in every major night attack on Germany. They soon showed their superiority by dropping 132 long tons of bombs for each aircraft lost, compared with 56 (later 86) for the Halifax and 41 for the Stirling. They carried a heavier load of bigger bombs than any other aircraft in the European theatre. The 12,000 lb AP bomb was used to sink the *Tirpitz*, and the 22,000 lb weapon finally shook down the stubborn viaduct at Bielefeld in March 1945. Around Caen, Lancasters were used en masse in the battlefield close-support role, and they finished the war dropping supplies to starving Europeans.

Avro Lancaster III

1 Two 0·303in Browning machine guns
2 Frazer-Nash power-operated nose turret
3 Nose blister
4 Bomb-aimer's (optically flat) panel
5 Bomb-aimer's control panel
6 Side windows

7 External air temperature thermometer
8 Pitot head
9 Bomb-aimer's chest support
10 Fire extinguisher
11 Parachute emergency exit
12 F.24 camera
13 Glycol tank and step
14 Ventilator fairing
15 Bomb-door forward actuating jacks
16 Bomb-bay forward bulkhead
17 Control linkage
18 Rudder pedals
19 Instrument panel
20 Windscreen de-icer sprays
21 Windscreen
22 Dimmer switches
23 Flight-engineer's folding seat
24 Flight-engineer's control panel
25 Pilot's seat
26 Flight-deck floor level
27 Elevator and rudder control rods (underfloor)
28 Trim-tab control cables
29 Main floor/bomb-bay support longeron
30 Fire extinguisher
31 Communications radio and (if fitted) electronic jammers
32 Navigator's seat
33 Canopy vision blister
34 Pilot's head armour
35 Emergency escape hatch
36 D/F loop
37 Aerial mast support
38 Electrical services panel
39 Navigator's window
40 Navigator's desk
41 Aircraft and radio compass receiver
42 Wireless-operator's desk
43 Wireless-operator's seat
44 Wireless-operator's window
45 Front spar carry-through/ fuselage frame
46 Astrodome
47 Inboard section wing ribs
48 Spar join
49 Aerial mast
50 Starboard inner engine nacelle
51 Spinner
52 Three-blade de Havilland constant-speed propellers
53 Oil-cooler intake
54 Oil-cooler radiator
55 Carburettor air intake
56 Radiator shutter
57 Engine bearer frame
58 Exhaust flame-damper shroud

59 Packard-built Rolls-Royce Merlin 28 liquid-cooled engine
60 Nacelle/wing fairing
61 Fuel tank bearer ribs
62 Intermediate ribs
63 Leading-edge structure
64 Wing stringers
65 Wingtip skinning
66 Starboard navigation light
67 Starboard formation light
68 Aileron hinge fairings
69 Wing rear spar
70 Starboard aileron
71 Aileron balance tab

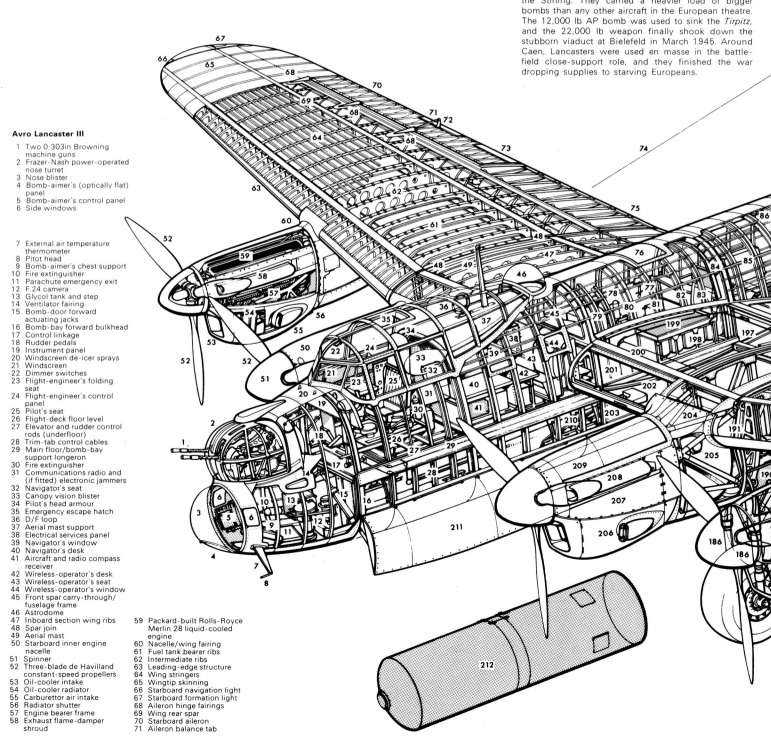

Avro Lancaster B.1 (aircraft of 467 Sqn, then operating from WaddinYton, which coOpleted 137 operational sorties, the second-hiYhest total for any RAF "heavy")

The cutaway shows a standard Mk III Lancaster, with twin-tread tailwheel tyre. The most common load was incendiaries, plus a 4,000 lb "cookie"

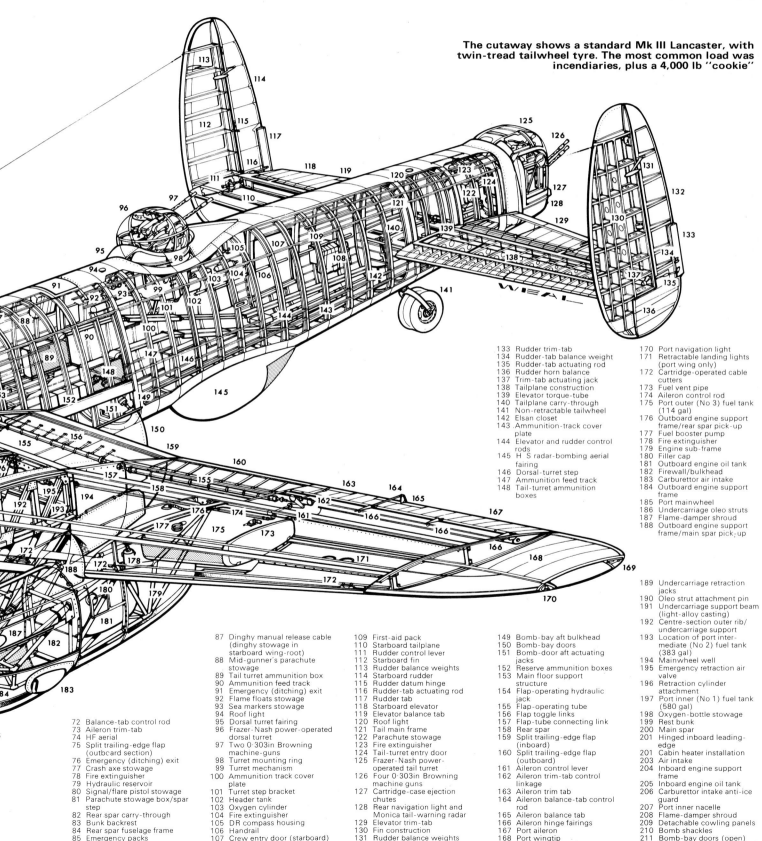

133 Rudder trim-tab
134 Rudder-tab balance weight
135 Rudder-tab actuating rod
136 Rudder horn balance
137 Trim-tab actuating jack
138 Tailplane construction
139 Elevator torque-tube
140 Tailplane carry-through
141 Non-retractable tailwheel
142 Elsan closet
143 Ammunition-track cover plate
144 Elevator and rudder control rods
145 H S radar-bombing aerial fairing
146 Dorsal-turret step
147 Ammunition feed track
148 Tail-turret ammunition boxes

170 Port navigation light
171 Retractable landing lights (port wing only)
172 Cartridge-operated cable cutters
173 Fuel vent pipe
174 Aileron control rod
175 Port outer (No 3) fuel tank (114 gal)
176 Outboard engine support frame/rear spar pick-up
177 Fuel booster pump
178 Fire extinguisher
179 Engine sub-frame
180 Filler cap
181 Outboard engine oil tank
182 Firewall/bulkhead
183 Carburettor air intake
184 Outboard engine support frame
185 Port mainwheel
186 Undercarriage oleo struts
187 Flame-damper shroud
188 Outboard engine support frame/main spar pick-up

189 Undercarriage retraction jacks
190 Oleo strut attachment pin
191 Undercarriage support beam (light-alloy casting)
192 Centre-section outer rib/ undercarriage support
193 Location of port inter-mediate (No 2) fuel tank (383 gal)
194 Mainwheel well
195 Emergency retraction air valve
196 Retraction cylinder attachment
197 Port inner (No 1) fuel tank (580 gal)
198 Oxygen-bottle stowage
199 Rest bunk
200 Main spar
201 Hinged inboard leading-edge
201 Cabin heater installation
203 Air intake
204 Inboard engine support frame
205 Inboard engine oil tank
206 Carburettor intake anti-ice guard
207 Port inner nacelle
208 Flame-damper shroud
209 Detachable cowling panels
210 Bomb shackles
211 Bomb-bay doors (open)
212 8,000 lb bomb

72 Balance-tab control rod
73 Aileron trim-tab
74 HF aerial
75 Split trailing-edge flap (outbcard section)
76 Emergency (ditching) exit
77 Crash axe stowage
78 Fire extinguisher
79 Hydraulic reservoir
80 Signal/flare pistol stowage
81 Parachute stowage box/spar step
82 Rear spar carry-through
83 Bunk backrest
84 Rear spar fuselage frame
85 Emergency packs
86 Roof light

87 Dinghy manual release cable (dinghy stowage in starboard wing-root)
88 Mid-gunner's parachute stowage
89 Tail turret ammunition box
90 Ammunition feed track
91 Emergency (ditching) exit
92 Flame floats stowage
93 Sea markers stowage
94 Roof light
95 Dorsal turret fairing
96 Frazer-Nash power-operated dorsal turret
97 Two 0·303in Browning machine-guns
98 Turret mounting ring
99 Turret mechanism
100 Ammunition track cover plate
101 Turret step bracket
102 Header tank
103 Oxygen cylinder
104 Fire extinguisher
105 DR compass housing
106 Handrail
107 Crew entry door (starboard)
108 Parachute stowage

109 First-aid pack
110 Starboard tailplane
111 Rudder control lever
112 Starboard fin
113 Rudder balance weights
114 Starboard rudder
115 Rudder datum hinge
116 Rudder-tab actuating rod
117 Rudder tab
118 Starboard elevator
119 Elevator balance tab
120 Roof light
121 Tail main frame
122 Parachute stowage
123 Fire extinguisher
124 Tail-turret entry door
125 Frazer-Nash power-operated tail turret
126 Four 0·303in Browning machine guns
127 Cartridge-case ejection chutes
128 Rear navigation light and Monica tail-warning radar
129 Elevator trim-tab
130 Fin construction
131 Rudder balance weights
132 Port rudder frame

149 Bomb-bay aft bulkhead
150 Bomb-bay doors
151 Bomb-door aft actuating jacks
152 Reserve ammunition boxes
153 Main floor support structure
154 Flap-operating hydraulic jack
155 Flap-operating tube
156 Flap toggle links
157 Flap-tube connecting link
158 Rear spar
159 Split trailing-edge flap (inboard)
160 Split trailing-edge flap (outboard)
161 Aileron control lever
162 Aileron trim-tab control linkage
163 Aileron trim tab
164 Aileron balance-tab control rod
165 Aileron balance tab
166 Aileron hinge fairings
167 Port aileron
168 Port wingtip
169 Port formation light

Avro 694 Lincoln

Avro Lincoln B.2 (57 Sqn, in Tiger Force tropical colour scheme).

Lincoln B.1 and B.30

Type: Long-range bomber with crew of seven.
Engines: four 1,750 hp Rolls-Royce Merlin 85 (alternatively Packard Merlin 68A or 300).
Dimensions: span 120 ft (36·6 m); length 78 ft 3½ in (23·85 m) (RAAF Mk 31(MR), 84 ft 4 in); height 17 ft 3½ in (5·26 m).
Weights: empty 44,188 lb (20,044 kg); loaded 82,000 lb (37,194 kg).
Performance: maximum speed 295 mph (475 km/h) at 20,000 ft (6096 m); initial climb 660 ft (200 m)/min; service ceiling 22,000 ft (6710 m) (at 75,000 lb, 30,500 ft); range with maximum bomb load at 230 mph (370 km/h) 2,250 miles (3620 km).
Armament: twin 0·50 in Browning guns in nose, dorsal and tail turrets (B.2 dorsal turret, two 20 mm Hispano cannon) and, in many aircraft, one manually aimed ventral 0·50 in (from 1948 dorsal turrets often removed); bomb load up to 14,000 lb (6350 kg) in fuselage.

History: first flight (prototype) 9 June 1944; (production B.1) April 1945; operational service August 1945; first flight (Australian B.30) 17 March 1946.

Designed to specification B.14/43 and originally called Lancaster IV and V, the Lincoln was a natural extension of the basic Lancaster formula to carry heavier loads further. Though in technology a generation more primitive than the B-29, which ran earlier in timing, the Lincoln was extremely efficient and cost/effective. Major changes from the Lancaster included: increased span for operation at greater heights with heavier loads of bombs and fuel; high-altitude Merlin engines with two-stage blowers and four-blade propellers; longer fuselage; new nose with turret controlled from sighting station below it; new dorsal and tail turrets with twin 0·5 in Brownings or (dorsal) two 20 mm Hispano cannon; and a major rework of systems and equipment. Development went fast and plans were made for huge production in Britain, some marks using US-built Packard Merlin engines, and for the Mk XV by Victory Aircraft at Toronto and the Mk 30 by the Beaufort Division of the Department of Supply at Melbourne. Deliveries began to 57 Sqn in July 1945 and the following month the first aircraft were about to fly out to Tiger Force in the Far East when Japan capitulated. So production was limited to 528, all in Britain, plus 54 Mk 30s in Australia. Avro built only 168, the rest being by Armstrong Whitworth (281) and Metropolitan-Vickers (79). Lincolns operated against terrorists in Malaya, against the Mau-Mau in Kenya and served in Signals Command until 1963. The RAAF and Argentine Air Force pensioned off their Lincolns by 1965.

Avro 696 Shackleton

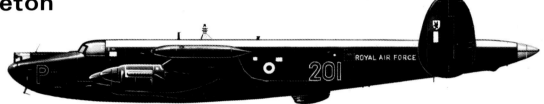

Avro Shackleton MR. 3 (201 San, Coastal Command, 1960–68).

Shackleton MR.1 and 1A, MR.2 and AEW.2, MR.3 and 3 series 3, T.4.

Type: (MR) maritime reconnaissance and ASW, with usual crew of ten; (AEW) airborne early warning; (T) crew trainer.
Engines: 'four 2,455 hp Rolls-Royce Griffon 57A vee-12 liquid-cooled; (MR.3 Series 3), in addition two 2,500 lb (1134 kg) thrust Rolls-Royce Viper 203 single-shaft turbojets.
Dimensions: span (1,. 2, 4) 120 ft (36·58 m); (3) 119 ft 10 in (36·53 m); length (1, 4) 77 ft 6 in (23·6 m); (2) 87 ft 3 in (26·59 m); (3) 92 ft 6 in (28·19 m); height (1, 2, 4) 16 ft 9 in (5·1 m); (3) 23 ft 4 in (7·11 m).
Weights: empty (1) about 44,000 lb (20,000 kg); (3) 57,800 lb (26,218 kg); maximum loaded (1, 4) 86,000 lb (39,000 kg); (2) 98,000 lb (44,450 kg); (3) 100,000 lb (45,360 kg).

Performance: maximum speed (2) 272 mph (439 km/h); '(3) 302 mph (486 km/h); initial climb (typical) 850 ft (260 m)/min; service ceiling (typical) 20,000 ft (6100 m); range (typical for MR.3) 4,215 miles (6780 km).
Armament: (1) two 20 mm Hispano cannon in dorsal turret; at least 10,000 lb (4540 kg) depth charges, torpedoes or other ordnance carried in weapon bay; (2) as MR.1 plus two 20 mm cannon in nose, aimed by gunner seated above, with bomb aimer below; (3) as (2) without dorsal turret; (4) none.
History: first flight (Mk 1 prototype) 9 March 1949; service delivery (MR.1) 28 September 1950; (MR.2) October 1952; (MR.3) October 1957; final delivery June 1959.

Derived from the Lincoln to Specification R.5/46, the Shackleton MR.1 had contra-rotating propellers, large single-wheel main gears and a chin radome. After delivering 77, many of which were converted into T.4 trainers after 1956, Avro delivered 69 MR.2 with redesigned fuselage of better form with semi-retractable rear-ventral radar. In 1962 many were updated as MR.2C with better navaids and survivors now serve as the UK airborne early-warning aircraft with APS-20 radar (taken from Skyraiders and Gannets) and extra fuel. The 42 MR.3 introduced twin-wheel tricycle landing gear and tip tanks. Eight were supplied to the South African AF. To ease strain on the engines most RAF MR.3 were updated to Series 3 standard with Viper turbojets in the inner nacelles to assist during take-off and initial climb.

Avro Canada CF-100

CF-100 Mk 1 to 5 (data for 5)

Type: two-seat all-weather interceptor.
Engines: two 7,275 lb (3300 kg) thrust Orenda 11 turbojets.
Dimensions: span 58 ft (17·7 m); length 54 ft 1 in (16·5 m); height 15 ft 7 in (4·72 m).
Weights: empty about 18,000 lb (8200 kg); loaded 37,000 lb (16,780 kg).
Performance: maximum speed 650 mph (1045 km/h); climb to 30,000 ft (9144 m) in 5 min; maximum range 2,000 miles (3200 km).
Armament: 58 or 106 Mighty Mouse 2·75 in spin-stabilised air-to-air rockets.
History: first flight (prototype) 19 January 1950; first flight (production Mk 4) 24 October 1953; (Mk 5) 1956; completion of production 1957.

Often dubbed the Canuck, this excellent long-range all-weather fighter was the first combat aircraft of all-Canadian design. Work began in 1946, at a time when the RAF had no money to think about jet night fighters, to meet an obvious need by the RCAF for a night and all-weather fighter having great range, fast climb and the ability to operate from small Arctic airstrips. The newly formed Avro Canada design team showed brilliance in completing this challenging project quickly, and the first prototype, painted black and powered by Avon engines, flew in January 1950. The first production model was the unarmed Mk 2 (one a dual trainer), powered by the home-grown Orenda engine, followed by 124 Mk 3 fighters with the more powerful Orenda 8 and fitted with Hughes APG-33 radar and a belly pack containing eight 0·5 in Browning guns. Mk 3 production was cut short to make way for the Mk 4, which followed USAF ideas in rejecting guns

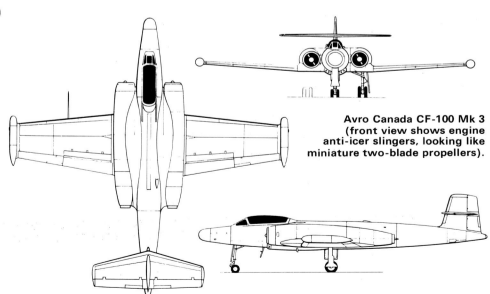

Avro Canada CF-100 Mk 3 (front view shows engine anti-icer slingers, looking like miniature two-blade propellers).

in favour of wing-tip pods each housing 29 Mighty Mouse air-to-air rockets, fired automatically by an interception system incorporating APG-40 radar and collision-course autopilot computer. A further 48 rockets, or eight 0·5 in or four 30 mm guns, could be carried in the belly. In 1953 a Mk 4 was dived to beyond Mach 1. Final production version was the Mk 5, with a 3 ft untapered extension on each wing tip and the more powerful engines of the Mk 4B. With 53 Mk 5s for the Belgian Air Force the total production of this big and formidable aircraft came to 645. The Mk 6 was to have had afterburning engines and Canadian Sparrow 2 missiles, but did not proceed beyond experimental prototypes.

BAC (English Electric) Canberra

Canberra 1 to 24 (data for B(I).12)
Type: two-seat interdictor.
Engines: two 7,500 lb (3402 kg) thrust Rolls-Royce Avon 109 single-shaft turbojets.
Dimensions: span 63 ft 11½ in (19·5 m); length 65 ft 6 in (19·95 m); height 15 ft 7 in (4·72 m).
Weights: empty 23,173–27,950 lb (10,400–12,700 kg); loaded 43,000 lb (19,504 kg); maximum permissible 56,250 lb (25,515 kg).
Performance: maximum speed 580 mph (933 km/h) at 30,000 ft (9144 m) or Mach 0·83; initial climb at maximum weight 3,400 ft (1036 m)/min; service ceiling 48,000 ft (14,630 m); range (typical mission at low level) 805 miles (1295 km); ferry range 3,630 miles (5,842 km).
Armament: four 20 mm Hispano cannon; three 1,000 lb (454 kg) bombs or sixteen 4·5 in flares internally; two AS.30 missiles or two 1,000 lb bombs or two packs of 37 rockets externally.
History: first flight (prototype) 13 May 1949; first service delivery October 1950; first flight of B(I) series 23 July 1954.

When W. E. W. "Teddy" Petter joined English Electric at Preston as chief engineer he already had a scheme for a jet bomber. To meet specification B.3/45 he eventually planned a straightforward unswept aircraft with a broad wing for good behaviour at great heights, with two of the new axial jet engines centred on each wing giving a total of 15,000 lb thrust. Like the Mosquito, the A.1 bomber was to be fast enough to escape interception, whilst carrying a 6,000 lb bomb load over a radius of 750 nautical miles. It was to have a crew of two and a radar bomb sight for blind attacks in all conditions. The prototype amazed everyone with its low-level manoeuvrability, and the A.1, named Canberra, was a superb flying machine from the start. But the radar bombing system lagged years in development, and a new specification, B.5/47, had to be raised to cover a simpler visual bomber with a transparent nose and crew of three. This entered production without much more trouble and became the first axial-jet aircraft in the RAF. First Canberra B.2s were painted black on sides and undersurfaces, but this changed in 1952 to grey-blue, and the white serial number was painted extra-large to serve as a "buzz number" visible to fighter pilots from a safe distance. In February 1951 a B.2 set a transatlantic record flying out to Baltimore to serve as pattern aircraft for the Martin B-57 programme (p. 145). The Korean war caused a sudden jump in orders, and Canberra B.2s were made by EECo and by Handley Page (75), Avro (75) and Short (60). The PR.3 was a reconnaissance version with longer fuselage for more fuel. The T.4 had side-by-side dual controls. The Mk 5 prototype introduced Avon 109 engines and integral wing tanks, and was to be a visual target marker. It led to the B.6, the heavier and more powerful replacement for the B.2. The corresponding reconnaissance version was the PR.7, from which was derived the much more powerful, long-span PR.9 developed and built by Short. Most versatile Canberra was the B(I).8, with offset pilot canopy and nav/bomb position in the nose. With four 20 mm cannon (and ammunition for 55 seconds continuous firing) the Mk 8 also carried a wide range of underwing missiles, bombs, tanks and special pods, and, like earlier versions, proved an export winner, particularly the B(I).12. Until they were ready the B(I).6 served in Germany in the multi-role tasks and also dashed to Kuwait in 1961. Later mark numbers include special trainers, electronic-warfare versions, target tugs, pilotless targets and, as one-off conversions, platforms for testing almost every British postwar engine, missile and airborne device. Total Canberra production was 925 in Britain, including exports to India, Venezuela, Peru, Rhodesia, New Zealand, South Africa, Sweden, France and (second-hand) other countries. Australia made 49 B.20s for the RAAF.

BAC Lightning

Lightning F.1 to 6 and export versions (data for F.6)
Type: single-seat all-weather interceptor.
Engines: two 15,680 lb (7112 kg) thrust Rolls-Royce Avon 302 augmented turbojets.
Dimensions: span 34 ft 10 in (10·6 m); length 53 ft 3 in (16·25 m); height 19 ft 7 in (5·95 m).

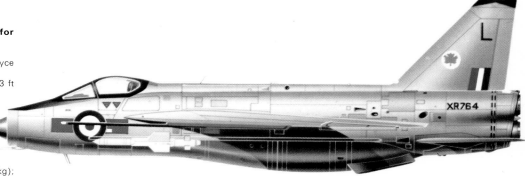

BAC Lightning F.6 (5 Sqn, RAF)

Weights: empty about 28,000 lb (12,700 kg); loaded 50,000 lb (22,680 kg).
Performance: maximum speed 1,500 mph (2415 km/h) at 40,000 ft (12,200 m); initial climb 50,000 ft (15,240 m)/min; service ceiling over 60,000 ft (18,290 m); range without overwing tanks 800 miles (1290 km).
Armament: interchangeable packs for two all-attitude Red Top or stern-chase Firestreak guided missiles; option of two 30 mm Aden cannon in forward part of belly tank; export versions up to 6,000 lb (2722 kg) bombs or other offensive stores above and below wings.
History: first flight (P.1B) 4 April 1957; (first production F.1) 30 October 1959; (first F.6) 17 April 1964. As he had been with the Canberra, "Teddy" Petter was again moving spirit behind the award, in 1947, of a study contract for a supersonic research aircraft. Later this was built and flown as the P.1 of August 1954, exceeding Mach 1 on two crude unaugmented Sapphire engines mounted one above and behind the other and fed by a plain nose inlet. In mid-1949 specification F.23/49 was issued for a supersonic fighter, and after complete redesign the P.1B was produced and flown in 1957. This had a new fuselage with a two-shock intake, the central cone being intended to house Ferranti Airpass radar. The Avon engines were fitted with primitive afterburning, allowing a speed of Mach 2 to be attained on 25 November 1958. Helped by 20 pre-production aircraft, the Lightning F.1 was cleared for service in 1960. Though relatively complicated, so that the flying rate and maintenance burden were terrible in comparison with more modern aircraft, these supersonic all-weather interceptors at last gave the RAF a modern fighter with radar, guided missiles (heat-homing Firestreaks) and supersonic performance. Production was held back by the belief that all manned fighters were obsolete (as clearly set forth in the Defence White Paper of April 1957), but the Treasury were persuaded to allow the improved F.2 to be built in 1961 with fully variable afterburner and all-weather navigation. Eventually, as the error of

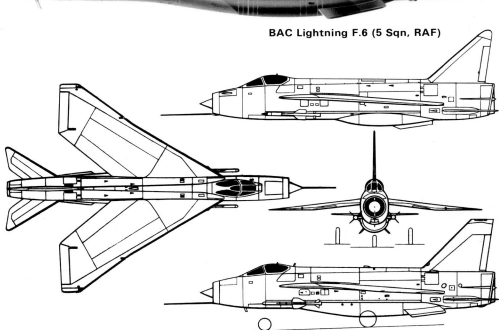

BAC Lightning F.6 (upper side view, F.1)

the 1957 doctrine became apparent, the Mk 3 was allowed in 1964, with more powerful engines, more fuel, bigger fin, collision-course fire-control and all-attitude Red Top missiles; but it was decided to fit no guns, earlier marks having had two 30 mm Aden cannon. Finally, in 1965, the belated decision was taken to follow the advice of BAC and almost double the fuel capacity and also fit the kinked and cambered wing (first flown in 1956) to improve operation at much increased weights. The T.4 and T.5 are dual conversion trainers equivalent to the F.2 and F.3. For Saudi Arabia and Kuwait, BAC paid for development of the Lightning as a multi-role fighter and attack aircraft, adding 57 to the production total to bring it up to 338.

BAC 145 and Strikemaster

BAC 145 and Strikemaster
Type: two-seat light tactical aircraft and trainer.
Engine: 3,410 lb (1547 kg) thrust Rolls-Royce Viper 535 turbojet.
Dimensions: span 36 ft 10 in (11·23 m); length 33 ft 8½ in (10·27 m); height 10 ft 11½ in (3·34 m).
Weights: empty 6,270 lb (2840 kg); loaded (clean) 9,200 lb (4170 kg); maximum 11,500 lb (5210 kg).
Performance: maximum speed 481 mph (774 km/h); maximum speed at sea level 450 mph (726 km/h); initial climb (max fuel, clean) 5,250 ft (1600 m)/min; service ceiling 44,000 ft (13,410 m); ferry range 1,615 miles (2600 km); combat radius with 3,300 lb weapon load 145 miles (233 km).
Armament: two 7·62 mm FN machine guns fixed firing forwards with 550 rounds each; very wide range of stores to maximum of 3,000 lb (1360 kg) on four underwing strongpoints.
History: first flight (Jet Provost) 16 June 1954; (Strikemaster) 26 October 1967; first delivery 1968.

The Percival Provost basic trainer flew in February 1950. Hunting then produced a jet version, and flew this in June 1954. Subsequently the Hunting (later BAC) Jet Provost became a successful basic trainer made in great numbers for the RAF and many overseas countries, and more powerful pressurised versions are still one of BAC's current products. From this was developed the BAC.145 multi-role trainer/attack aircraft, which in turn was developed into the highly refined Strikemaster. With a more powerful Viper engine,

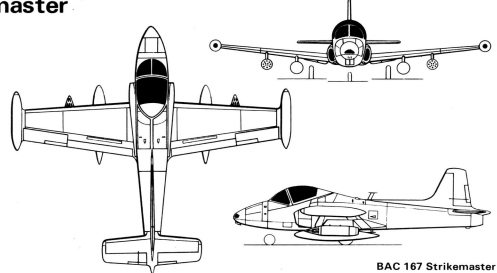

BAC 167 Strikemaster

the Strikemaster proved to be a great worldwide success. It had side-by-side ejection seats, and the ability to operate from the roughest airstrip whilst carrying a combat load three times a typical bomber's load in the 1930s and any desired equipment fit. The first customers were Saudi Arabia, South Yemen People's Republic, Sultanate of Oman, Kuwait, Singapore, Kenya, New Zealand and Ecuador; and it is remarkable that nearly all these countries have come back for one or more repeat orders. Doubtless a more capable version will soon be offered with the 4,000 lb thrust Viper 632 engine.

B.E.2

(Royal Aircraft Factory) B.E.2 to 2e
Type: two-seat reconnaissance and bombing aircraft.
Engine: 70 hp Renault vee-8 water-cooled.
Dimensions: span 35 ft 0½ in (10·68 m) (sometimes 38 ft 7½ in, 11·75 m); length 29 ft 6½ in (9 m); height 10 ft 2 in (2·1 m).
Weights: empty 1,274 lb (578 kg); loaded 1,600 lb (726 kg).
Performance: maximum speed 70 mph (113 km/h); service ceiling about 10,000 ft (3048 m); endurance 3 hr.
Armament: crew's small arms; sometimes 100 lb (45 kg) bomb.
History: first flight February 1912; service delivery (2) February 1913; (2c) October 1914; (2d) March 1916; (2e) July 1916.

Britain's first military aircraft designed as such was the first B.E. (Bleriot Experimental, though having nothing to do with Bleriot), designed by Geoffrey de Havilland and F. M. Green at the Royal Aircraft Factory in August 1911. It was the first aircraft to have a military serial number (B1, later 201). From it emerged the B.E.2 of

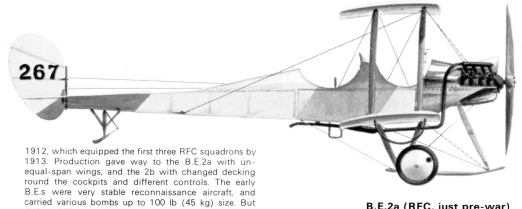

1912, which equipped the first three RFC squadrons by 1913. Production gave way to the B.E.2a with unequal-span wings, and the 2b with changed decking round the cockpits and different controls. The early B.E.s were very stable reconnaissance aircraft, and carried various bombs up to 100 lb (45 kg) size. But their stability was lethal in aerial combat, and losses were very high when Fokkers came on the scene. The B.E.2c, 2d and 2e were redesigned with ailerons instead of wing-warping, more powerful engines and many other changes, but they continued in production

B.E.2a (RFC, just pre-war)

much longer than they should. As the first product of the official establishment the B.E. was built by at least 22 firms, and many more were built than the 3,535 for which records survive.

Bell P-39 Airacobra

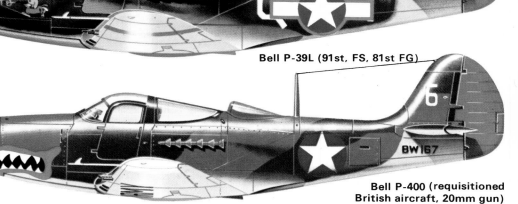

Bell P-39L (91st, FS, 81st FG)

Bell P-400 (requisitioned British aircraft, 20mm gun)

P-39 to P-39Q Airacobra (data for P-39L)
Type: single-seat fighter.
Engine: 1,325 hp Allison V-1710-63 vee-12 liquid-cooled.
Dimensions: span 34 ft (10·37 m); length 30 ft 2 in (9·2 m); height (one prop-blade vertical) 11 ft 10 in (3·63 m).

Weights: empty 5,600 lb (2540 kg); loaded 7,780 lb (3530 kg).
Performance: maximum speed 380 mph (612 km/h); initial climb 4,000 ft (1220 m)/min; service ceiling 35,000 ft (10,670 m); ferry range with drop tank at 160 mph (256 km/h) 1,475 miles (2360 km).
Armament: one 37 mm cannon with 30 rounds (twice as many as in first sub-types), two synchronised 0·5 in Colt-Brownings and two or four 0·30 in outer wings.
History: first flight of XP-39 August 1939; (P-39F to M-sub-types, 1942); final batch (P-39Q) May 1944. First flown as a company prototype in 1939, this design by R. J. Woods and O. L. Woodson was unique

in having a nosewheel-type landing gear and the engine behind the pilot. The propeller was driven by a long shaft under the pilot's seat and a reduction gearbox in the nose, the latter also containing a big 37 mm cannon firing through the propeller hub. Other guns were also fitted in the nose, the first production aircraft, the P-39C of 1941, having two 0·30 in and two 0·5 in all synchronised to fire past the propeller. Britain ordered the unconventional fighter in 1940 and in June 1941 the first Airacobra I arrived, with the 37 mm gun and 15 rounds having been replaced by a 20 mm Hispano with 60. Two 0·303 in Brownings in the nose

and four more in the wings completed the armament. No 601 Sqn did poorly with it and failed to keep the unusual aircraft serviceable, but the US Army Air Force used it in big numbers. Altogether 9,588 were built and used with fair success in the Mediterranean and Far East, some 5,000 being supplied to the Soviet Union, mainly through Iran. Biggest production version was the P-39Q, of which over 4,900 were built. The P-39 was succeeded in production in 1944 by the P-63 Kingcobra, first flown on 7 December 1942, which had longer wing and tail surfaces and improved performance; 3,603 were built by January 1946.

Bell P-59 Airacomet

YP-59, P-59A and XF2L-1
Type: single-seat jet fighter trainer.
Engines: two 2,000 lb (907 kg) thrust General Electric J31-GE-3 turbojets.
Dimensions: span 45 ft 6 in (13·87 m); length 38 ft 1½ in (11·63 m); height 12 ft (3·66 m).
Weights: empty 7,950 lb (3610 kg); loaded 12,700 lb (5760 kg).
Performance: maximum speed 413 mph (671 km/h); service ceiling 46,200 ft (14,080 m); maximum range with two 125 Imp gal drop tanks 520 miles (837 km) at 289 mph (465 km/h) at 20,000 ft (6096 m).
Armament: usually none, but some YP-59A fitted with nose guns (eg one 37 mm cannon and three 0·5 in) and one rack under each wing for bomb as alternative to drop tank.
History: first flight (XP-59A) 1 October 1942; (production P-59A) 7 August 1944.

In June 1941 the US government and General "Hap" Arnold of the Army Air Corps were told of Britain's development of the turbojet engine. On 5 September 1941 Bell Aircraft was requested to design a jet

Bell P-59A (without armament)

fighter and in the following month a Whittle turbojet, complete engineering drawings and a team from Power Jets Ltd arrived from Britain to hasten proceedings. The result was that Bell flew the first American jet in one year from the start of work. The Whittle-type centrifugal engines, Americanised and made by General Electric as the 1,100 lb (500 kg) thrust I-A, were installed under the wing roots, close to the centreline and easily accessible (two were needed to

fly an aircraft of useful size). Flight development went extremely smoothly, and 12 YP-59As for service trials were delivered in 1944. Total procurement amounted to 66 only, including three XF2L-1s for the US Navy, and the P-59A was classed as a fighter-trainer because it was clear it would not make an effective front-line fighter. But in comparison with the British E.28/39 it was a remarkable achievement, being very similar to that attained with the early Meteors.

Bell 209 HueyCobra

AH-1G and -1J HueyCobra (data for -1G)
Type: two-seat combat helicopter.
Engine: 1,100 shp Lycoming T53-L-13 turboshaft.
Dimensions: main-rotor diameter 44 ft (13·4 m); overall length (rotors turning) 52 ft 11½ in (16·14 m); length of fuselage 44 ft 5 in (13·54 m); height 13 ft 5½ in (4·1 m).
Weights: empty 6,073 lb (2754 kg); maximum 9,500 lb (4309 kg).
Performance: maximum speed 219 mph (352 km/h); maximum rate of climb (not vertical) 1,230 ft (375 m)/min; service ceiling 11,400 ft (3475 m); hovering ceiling in ground effect 9,900 ft (3015 m); range at sea level with 8% reserve 357 miles (574 km).
Armament: typically one 7·62 mm multi-barrel Minigun, one 40 mm grenade launcher, both in remote-control turrets, or 20 mm six-barrel or 30 mm three-barrel cannon, plus four stores pylons for 76 rockets of 2·75 in calibre or Minigun pods or 20 mm gun pod, or (TOWCobra) eight TOW missiles in tandem tube launchers on two outer pylons, inners being available for other stores.
History: First flight 7 September 1965; combat service June 1967 (TOWCobra January 1973).

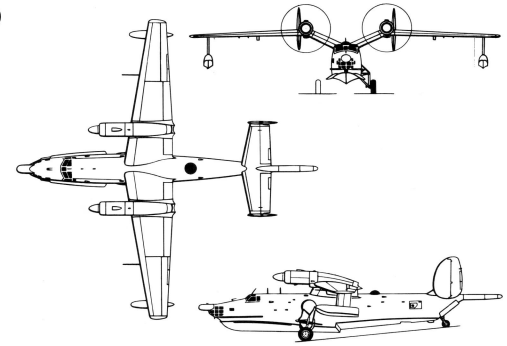

Bell AH-1G

First flown in 1965 after only six months of development, the HueyCobra is a combat development of the UH-1 Iroquois family (see Agusta-Bell). It combines the dynamic parts — engine, transmission and rotor system — of the original Huey with a new streamlined fuselage providing for a gunner in the front and pilot above and behind him and for a wide range of fixed and power-aimed armament systems. The first version was the US Army AH-1G, with 1,100 hp T53 engine,

of which 1,124 were delivered, including eight to the Spanish Navy for anti-ship strike and 38 as trainers to the US Marine Corps. The AH-1Q is an anti-armour version often called TOWCobra because it carries eight TOW missile pods as well as the appropriate sighting system. The AH-1J SeaCobra of the Marine Corps and Iranian Army has twin engines, the 1,800 hp UAC Twin Pac having two power sections driving one shaft. All Cobras can have a great variety of armament.

Beriev Be-12 (M-12)

Type: ocean reconnaissance and utility amphibian.
Engines: two 4,190 ehp Ivchenko AI-20D single-shaft turboprops.
Dimensions: span 97 ft 6 in (29·7 m); length overall 99 ft 0 in (30·2 m); height on land 22 ft 11½ in (7 m).
Weights: empty approximately 48,000 lb (21,772 kg); maximum approximately 66,140 lb (30,000 kg).
Performance: maximum speed about 380 mph (612 km/h); cruising speed 199 mph (320 km/h); service ceiling 38,000 ft (11,582 m); range with full equipment 2,485 miles (4000 km).
Armament: at least 6,600 lb (3000 kg) sonobuoys and AS bombs in internal weapon bay; one to three external hard points for stores under each outer wing.
History: first flight 1960 or earlier; combat service probably about 1962; set many world records in 1964, 1968, 1972 and 1973.

The bureau of Georgi M. Beriev, at Taganrog on the Azov Sea, is the centre for Soviet marine aircraft. The Be-6, powered by two 2,300 hp ASh-73TK radial engines and in the class of the Martin PBM or P5M, served as the standard long-range ocean patrol flying boat from 1949 until about 1967. In 1961 Beriev flew a remarkable large flying boat, the Be-10, powered by two Lyulka AL-7PB turbojets, but though this set world records it never entered major operational service. Instead a more pedestrian turboprop aircraft, first seen at the 1961 Moscow Aviation Day at the same time as the swept-wing Be-10, has fast become the Soviet Union's standard large marine aircraft. The Be-12 Tchaika (Seagull) is an amphibian, with retractable tailwheel-type landing gear. Its twin fins are unusual and the gull wing, which puts the engines high above the spray, gives an air of gracefulness. The Be-12 is extremely versatile. The search and

mapping radar projects far ahead of the glazed nose, and a MAD (magnetic anomaly detector) extends 15 ft behind the tail. Much of the hull is filled with equipment and there is a weapon and sonobuoy bay aft of the wing with watertight doors in the bottom aft of the

Be-12 (M-12) Tchaika (NATO name, "Mail")

step. Be-12s, known as M-12s in service with the Soviet naval air fleets, have set many class records for speed, height and load-carrying. They are based all around the Soviet shores and in Egypt and, possibly, other countries.

Bloch MB-152C-1

MB-150 to 157 (data for 152)
Type: single-seat fighter.
Engine: 1,080 hp Gnome-Rhône 14N-25 14-cylinder radial.
Dimensions: span 34 ft 6¾ in (10·5 m); length 29 ft 10 in (9·1 m); height 13 ft (3·95 m).
Weights: empty 4,453 lb (2020 kg); loaded 5,842 lb (2650 kg).
Performance: maximum speed 323 mph (520 km/h); climb to 16,400 ft (5000 m) in 6 minutes; service ceiling 32,800 ft (10,000 m); range 373 miles (600 km).
Armament: two 20 mm Hispano 404 cannon (60-round drum) and two 7·5 mm MAC 1934 machine guns (500 rounds each); alternatively four MAC 1934.
History: first flight (MB-150) October 1937; (MB-151) 18 August 1938; (MB-152) December 1938; (MB-155) 3 December 1939; (MB-157) March 1942.

Like so many French aircraft of the time, the Bloch monoplane fighter story began badly, got into its stride just in time for the capitulation and eventually produced outstanding aircraft which were unable to be used. The prototype 150 was not only ugly but

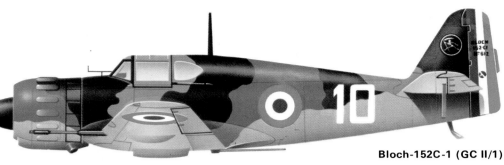

Bloch-152C-1 (GC II/1)

actually failed to fly, the frightened test pilot giving up on 17 July 1936. It was only after redesign with more power and a larger wing that the aircraft finally left the ground. Bloch had been absorbed into the new nationalised industry as part of SNCASO and five of the new group's factories were put to work making 25. But the detail design was difficult to make, so the MB-151 was produced with the hope that 180 would be made each month from late 1938. Orders were also placed for the more powerful MB-152, but by the start of World War II only 85 Blochs had been de-

livered and not one was fit for use; all lacked gunsights and most lacked propellers! Eventually, after overcoming desperate problems and shortages, 593 were delivered by the capitulation, equipping GC I/1, II/1, I/8, II/8, II/9, II/10, III/10 and III/9. The Germans impressed 173 surviving Bloch 151 and 152 fighters, pasing 20 to Rumania. The MB-155 had a 1,180 hp engine and was used by Vichy France. The ultimate model was the superb MB-157, with 1,580 hp 14R-4 engine and 441 mph (710 km/h) speed, never put into production. By this time the firm's founder had changed his name to Dassault.

Bloch 174

Bloch 174A-3 (GR II/33)

174 A3, 175 B3 and T
Type: three-seat reconnaissance, target marker and light bomber.
Engines: two 1,140 hp Gnome-Rhône 14N 14-cylinder radials.
Dimensions: span 58 ft 9½ in (17·9 m); length 40 ft 1½ in (12·23 m); height 11 ft 7¾ in (3·59 m).
Weights: empty 12,346 lb (5600 kg); maximum 15,784 lb (7160 kg).
Performance: maximum speed 329 mph (529 km/h) at 17,060 ft (5200 m); cruising speed 248 mph (400 km/h); climb to 26,250 ft (8000 m) 11 min; service ceiling 36,090 ft (11,000 m); maximum range with 880 lb (400 kg) bomb load 800 miles (1,450 km).
Armament: Two 7·5 mm MAC 1934 fixed in wings, three fixed at different angles below and to the rear, and two manually aimed from rear cockpit; internal bay for eight 110 lb (50 kg) bombs, wing racks for light bombs or flares.
History: first flight (170-01) 15 February 1938;

(174-01) 5 January 1939; (first production 174 A3) 5 November 1939; first delivery to combat unit (GR II/33) 19 March 1940.

Under chief designer Henri Deplante the Bloch 170 was planned as a bomber and army co-operation machine in 1936–37. As a result of indecision by the Armée de l'Air this took three years to evolve into the Bloch 174 A3 reconnaissance and target-marking aircraft, with secondary capability as a bomber. By the time production of the 174 stopped in May 1940 a total of 50 had been delivered. The first sortie was flown in March 1940 by the famed Capitaine Antoine de Saint-Exupéry. As it had an insignificant bomb load the 174 made little impact on the Blitzkrieg – it was

only in 1942, in Tunisia, that the survivors were fitted to conduct shallow dive-bombing with bombs of up to 500 kg (1,102 lb) – but the performance and handling were so outstanding and made such a difference to the casualty-rate among squadrons equipped with the type, that the Bloch 175 was hurriedly planned as a purpose-designed bomber. Altogether 25 Bloch 175 B3s were completed before France collapsed, with more than 200 on the production line, and had France been able to resist longer the 175 would have been a potent weapon. A few 174 and 175 aircraft saw service with the Luftwaffe, but most served Vichy-France in North Africa and many survived the war. Indeed the torpedo-carrying 175T remained in production for the Aéronavale until 1950.

Blohm und Voss Bv 138

Bv 138C-1 (III F/SAGr 125)

Bv 138A-1, B-1 and C-1 (data for C-1)
Type: six-crew reconnaissance flying boat.
Engines: three 880 hp Junkers Jumo 205D diesels with 12 opposed pistons in six cylinders.
Dimensions: span 88 ft 7 in (27 m); length 65 ft 1½ in (19·85 m); height 19 ft 4¼ in (5·9 m).
Weights: empty 24,250 lb (11,000 kg); loaded 34,100 lb (15,480 kg); (rocket assist) 39,600 lb (16,480 kg).
Performance: maximum speed 171 mph (275 km/h); climb to 10,000 ft (3050 m) in 24 min; service ceiling 16,400 ft (5000 m); maximum range 2,500 miles (4023 km).
Armament: 20 mm MG 151 cannon in front and rear

turrets; 13 mm MG 131 in cockpit behind centre engine; four 331 lb (150 kg) depth charges or other stores under inner right wing.
History: first flight (Ha 138V-1) 15 July 1937; first delivery (A-1) January 1940; (C-1) 1941.

Originally designated Ha 138, reflecting the fact that the aircraft subsidiary of the Blohm und Voss shipyard is (even today) Hamburger Flugzeugbau, the 138 was designed by Richard Vogt and took a long time to reach its final form. Major changes had to be made to the hull, wing, tail and tail booms, though none of the alterations were due to the unusual layout. The first 25 Bv 138A-1 boats were intended to be ocean re-

connaissance platforms, but were not a success and ended up as transports in the Norwegian campaign and thereafter. They were underpowered with three 600 hp Jumo 205 C diesel engines, the fuel oil being carried inside the tubular main spar of the wing. In late 1940 the Bv 138B-1 entered service with 880 hp Jumo 205D engines, further modified tail and a 20 mm turret at each end of the hull. After building 21, production was switched to the final Bv 138C-1, of which 227 were delivered in 1941–43. This had improved propellers, added a dorsal turret and was greatly improved in equipment. Throughout 1942–45 the 138C gave good front-line service in the Arctic, the Baltic, the North Atlantic and Mediterranean.

Boeing F4B/P-12

F4B-1 to -4, P-12 to P-12F (data F4B-4, P-12E)
Type: single-seat pursuit (day fighter).
Engine: 500 hp Pratt & Whitney SR-1340 direct-injection Wasp nine-cylinder radial.
Dimensions: span 30 ft (9·14 m); length 20 ft 1 in to 20 ft 8 in (6·1–6·3 m); height 9 ft 3 in (2·8 m).
Weights: empty about 2,100 lb (952 kg); loaded 2,557 to 2,750 lb (1160–1240 kg).
Performance: maximum speed 169 to 180 mph (272–304 km/h); cruising speed 150 mph (241 km/h); service ceiling 27,000 ft (8230 m); range 371 miles (F4B-1) to 520 miles (P-12E) (597–837 km).
Armament: two 0·30 in Colt-Browning machine guns in top decking.
History: first flight (Model 83) 25 June 1928; (first production F4B-1) 6 May 1929; (first P-12E) 15 October 1931; last delivery (an F4B-4) 28 February 1933.

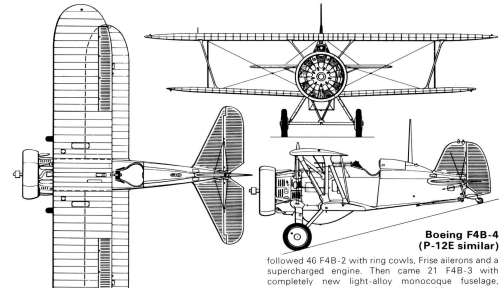

Boeing F4B-4 (P-12E similar)

Known in their commercial forms as the Boeing 100, these were extremely widely used American fighters of the period between the world wars. The prototype was built as a company venture, largely because Boeing could see a pursuit aircraft could be created that was much better than anything at that time asked for by the Army or Navy (and also because the new Pratt & Whitney company had obviously scored a great success with their Wasp engine which Boeing had fitted to the F2B and F3B). Apart from an odd switch from welded steel tube to riveted and bolted square-section aluminium tube for the fuselage, the only major advantage of the new design was that it was smaller and lighter than its predecessors. As a result its per-formance was higher. The Navy tested it and soon bought 27 F4B-1 fighter dive-bombers. In 1931

followed 46 F4B-2 with ring cowls, Frise ailerons and a supercharged engine. Then came 21 F4B-3 with completely new light-alloy monocoque fuselage, followed by 92 F4B-4 with wider fin; 23 were added for Brazil. Army buys started with ten P-12s, after which came 90 P-12B, 96 P-12C, 35 P-12D, 110 P-12E, 25 P-12F and a long string of specials. Painted in glorious squadron markings the Navy and Army Boeings droned on until World War II and several are still in existence (one of them flying, in the markings of VF-5B, the Navy "Red Rippers").

Boeing P-26

Model 281, P-26 to P-26C (data for -26C)
Type: single-seat pursuit (day fighter).
Engine: 600 hp Pratt & Whitney SR-1340-33; Wasp direct-injection nine-cylinder radial.
Dimensions: span 27 ft 11½ in (8·82 m); length 23 ft 9 in (7·28 m); height 10 ft 0½ in (3·1 m).
Weights: empty about 2,200 lb (998 kg); loaded 3,075 lb (1395 kg).
Performance: maximum speed 235 mph (378 km/h); cruising speed 200 mph (322 km/h); initial climb, 2,500 ft (762 m)/min; service ceiling, over 28,000 ft (8530 m); range 635 miles (1100 km).
Armament: one or two 0·30 in Colt-Brownings; optional underwing racks for light bombs.
History: first flight (Model 248) 20 March 1932; (first production P-26A) 10 January 1934; (P-26C) late 1934.

Having firmly switched from biplane to monoplane with the Monomail, the Model 247 airliner and the B-9 bomber, it was natural for Boeing to design a monoplane fighter. However, when the company-funded Model 248 first flew, care was taken not to make it too advanced for the conservative Army Air Corps. It had an

open cockpit, wire-braced wing and fixed landing gear. Indeed the design was undertaken in partnership with the Air Corps, who provided such expensive hardware as engine, instruments and guns. Three prototypes were built, tested by the Army and — despite the landing speed of 73 mph, which was extremely high for 1932 — adopted for production. In January 1933 the Air Corps ordered 111 P-26As, and these soon became known as "peashooters". In service they received radio, flotation gear and deeper headrest fairings. Boeing also built two P-26B with fuel-injection engines and split flaps on the wings, plus 23 P-26C with just the flaps. As the Model 281, eleven aircraft were exported, one to Spain and the rest to

Boeing P-26A

China. In the latter country the Boeings fought Japanese air power and in Philippine Army colours they did so again in 1941–42. In Guatemala these distinctive machines soldiered on until 1955.

Boeing Stearman

Model 75 Kaydet, PT-13, -17, -18, -27, N2S
Type: dual-control primary trainer.
Engine: 215 hp Lycoming R-680-5 (PT-13, N2S-2, -5); 220 hp Continental R-670-5 (PT-17, PT-27, N2S-1, -3, -4); 225 hp Jacobs R-755 (PT-18) radials, R-680 having nine cylinders, others seven.
Dimensions: span 32 ft 2 in (9·8 m); length 25 ft 0¼ in (7·63 m); height 9 ft 2 in (2·79 m).
Weights: empty about 1,936 lb (878 kg); loaded 2,717–2,810 lb (1232–1275 kg).
Performance: maximum speed 120–126 mph (193–203 km/h); initial climb 840 ft (256 m)/min; service ceiling 11,200 ft (3413 m); range 440–505 miles (708–812 km).
Armament: only on Model 76D export versions, typically two 0·30 in machine guns in lower wings and single 0·30 in aimed by observer in rear cockpit. Optional racks for light bombs under fuselage.
History: first flight (Model 70) December 1933; (Model 75) early 1936; final delivery February 1945.

When the monopolistic United Aircraft and Transport combine was broken up by the government in 1934, the Stearman Aircraft Co remained a subsidiary of Boeing and in 1939 the Wichita plant lost the Stearman

name entirely. Yet the family of trainers built by Boeing to Floyd Stearman's design have always been known by the designer's name rather than that of the maker. The Model 70 biplane trainer was conservative and, as it emerged when biplanes were fast disappearing from combat aviation, it might have been a failure — especially as Claude Ryan had a trim monoplane trainer competing for orders. Yet the result was the biggest production of any biplane in history, as the standard primary trainer in North America in World War II. The Model 70 flew on a 220 hp Lycoming but the Navy, the first customer, bought 61 NS-1 primary trainers (Model 73) with surplus 225 hp Wright Whirl-winds drawn from storage. By 1941 Boeing had delivered 17 similar aircraft and 78 Model 76s (with various engines) for export. But the biggest production was the Model 75, ordered by the Army Air Corps after evaluating the first example in 1936. The first were

Boeing Stearman PT-13 Kaydet

PT-13s of various models, with Lycoming engines of 215 to 280 hp, but the biggest family was the PT-17. The 300 built for the RCAF were named Kaydets, a name unofficially adopted for the entire series. A few Canadian PT-27 Kaydets and similar Navy N2S-5s had enclosed cockpits. Total production, including spares, was 10,346, of which several hundred are still flying, mainly as glider tugs and crop dusters.

Boeing B-17 Fortress

Model 299, Y1B-17 and B-17 to B-17G (basic data for G)

Type: high-altitude bomber, with crew of six to ten.
Engines: four 1,200 hp Wright R-1820-97 (B-17C to E, R-1820-65) Cyclone nine-cylinder radials with exhaust-driven turbochargers.
Dimensions: span 103 ft 9 in (31·6 m); length 74 ft 9 in (22·8 m); (B-17B, C, D) 67 ft 11 in; (B-17E) 73 ft 10 in; height 19 ft 1 in (5·8 m); (B-17B, C, D) 15 ft 5 in.
Weights: empty 32,720–35,800 lb (14,855–16,200 kg); (B-17B, C, D) typically 31,150 lb; maximum loaded 65,600 lb (29,700 kg) (B-17B, C, D) 44,200–46,650 lb; (B-17E) 53,000 lb.
Performance: maximum speed 287 mph (462 km/h); (B-17C, D) 323 mph; (B-17E) 317 mph; cruising speed 182 mph (293 km/h); (B-17C, D) 250 mph; (B-17E) 210 mph; service ceiling 35,000 ft (10,670 m); range 1,100 miles (1,760 km) with maximum bomb load (other versions up to 3,160 miles with reduced weapon load).
Armament: twin 0·5 in Brownings in chin, dorsal, ball and tail turrets, plus two in nose sockets, one in radio compartment and one in each waist position. Normal internal bomb load 6,000 lb (2724 kg), but maximum 12,800 lb (5800 kg).
History: first flight (299) 28 July 1935; (Y1B-17) January 1937; first delivery (B-17B) June 1939; final delivery April 1945.

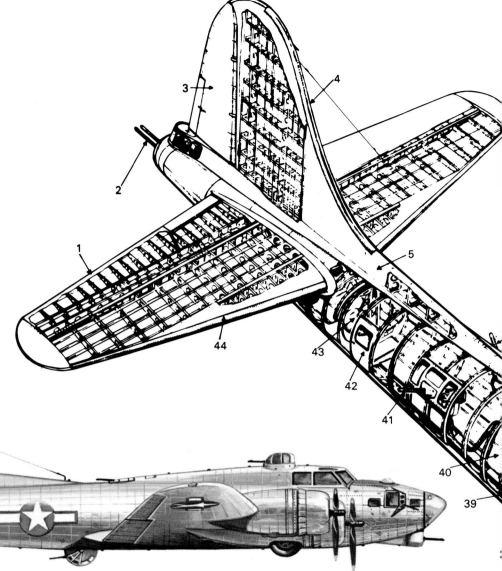

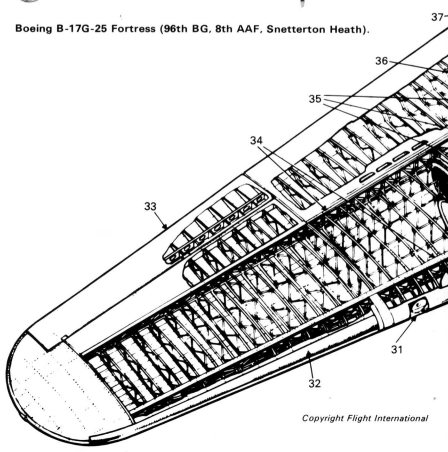

Boeing B-17G-25 Fortress (96th BG, 8th AAF, Snetterton Heath).

In May 1934 the US Army Air Corps issued a specification for a multi-engined anti-shipping bomber to defend the nation against enemy fleets. The answer was expected to be similar to the Martin B-10, but Boeing proposed four engines in order to carry the same bomb load faster and higher. It was a huge financial risk for the Seattle company but the resulting Model 299 was a giant among combat aircraft, with four 750 hp Pratt & Whitney Hornet engines, a crew of eight and stowage for eight 600 lb (272 kg) bombs internally. On delivery to Wright Field it crossed the nation at 232 mph, causing editors to think of the Flying Fortress in a new light. With the service-test batch of 13 Y1B-17 the Wright Cyclone engine was adopted, later versions all being turbocharged for good high-altitude performance. The production B-17B introduced a new nose and bigger rudder and flaps, though the wing loading was conservative and an enduring characteristic of every "Fort" was sedate flying.

With the B-17C came a ventral bathtub, flush side guns, armour and self-sealing tanks. In return for combat data 20 were supplied to the RAF, which used them on a few high-altitude daylight raids with 90 Sqn of Bomber Command. It was found that the Norden sight tended to malfunction, the Browning guns to freeze at the high altitude and German fighters to attack from astern in a defensive blind spot. While surviving Fortress Is operated with coastal and middle east forces, the improved B-17D joined the US Army and bore the brunt of early fighting in the Pacific. But extensive combat experience led to the redesigned B-17E, with powered dorsal, ventral (ball) and tail turrets, a huge fin for high-altitude bombing accuracy and much more armour and equipment. This went into huge production by Boeing, Lockheed-Vega and Douglas-Tulsa. It was the first weapon of the US 8th Bomber Command in England, and on 17 August 1942 began three gruelling years of day strategic bombing in Europe.

Copyright Flight International

Soon the E gave way to the B-17F, of which 3,405 were built, with many detail improvements, including a long Plexiglas nose, paddle-blade propellers and provision for underwing racks. At the end of 1942 came the final bomber model, the B-17G, with chin turret and flush staggered waist guns. A total of 8,680 G models were made, Boeing's Seattle plant alone turning out 16 a day, and the total B-17 run amounted to 12,731. A few B-17Fs were converted to XB-40s, carrying extra defensive guns to help protect the main Bomb Groups, while at least 25 were turned into BQ-7 Aphrodite radio-controlled missiles loaded with 12,000 lb of high explosive for use against U-boat shelters. Many F and G models were fitted with H_2X radar with the scanner retracting into the nose or rear fuselage, while other versions included the F-9 reconnaissance, XC-108 executive transport, CB-17 utility transport, PB-1W radar early-warning, PB-1G lifeboat-carrying air/sea rescue and QB-17 target drone. After the war came other photo, training, drone-director, search/rescue and research versions, including many used as engine and equipment testbeds. In 1970, 25 years after first flight, one of many civil Forts used for agricultural or forest-fire protection was re-engined with Dart turboprops!

Boeing B-17G- Fortress (305th BG, 8th AAF, Chelveston).

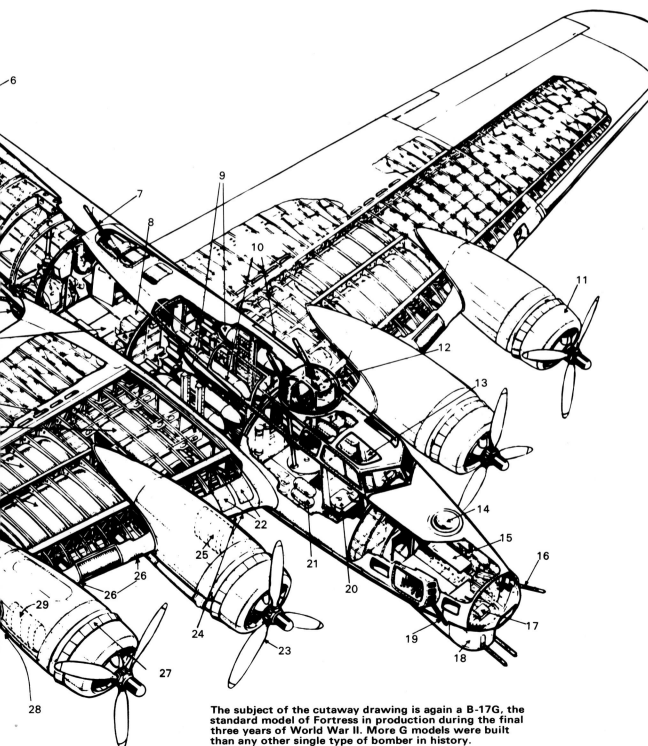

Boeing B-17 Fortress cutaway key

1 Fabric covered elevator
2 Remote control tail guns
3 Fabric covered rudder
4 De-icer on fin
5 Dorsal fin
6 Port waist gun
7 Dorsal gun manned by radio operator
8 Radio operator
9 Horizontal bombs in vertical racks
10 Life rafts stowed
11 1,000 hp Wright 9-cylinder radial engines. 12,000 hp for take-off
12 Upper turret
13 Pilot's seat
14 Astrodome
15 Navigator's table
16 Optional gun
17 Bombardier's seat
18 Remotely controlled chin turret
19 Navigator's gun
20 Co-pilot's seat
21 Oxygen bottles
22 Battery covers
23 Hamilton hydromatic airscrews
24 Air ducts to aircharger and cooler
25 Oil tank
26 Air ducts to oil radiators
27 Cooling control gills
28 G.E. turbochargers in each nacelle
29 Oil tank
30 Air ducts to supercharger and cooler
31 Landing light
32 De-icer on leading edge
33 Fabric covered aileron
34 Main spars
35 Self-sealing fuel tanks
36 Ventilating slots for hot air from oil radiators and supercharger cooler
37 Camera well
38 Ball turret
39 Catwalk
40 Ammunition
41 Starboard waist gun
42 Door
43 Housing for retractable tail wheel
44 De-icer on leading edge

The subject of the cutaway drawing is again a B-17G, the standard model of Fortress in production during the final three years of World War II. More G models were built than any other single type of bomber in history.

Boeing B-29 Superfortress

Boeing B-29-45 Superfortress modified to drop Hiroshima bomb (393rd BS, 315 BW)

Model 345, B-29 to -29C

Type: high-altitude heavy bomber, with crew of 10–14.
Engines: four 2,200 hp Wright R-3350-23 Duplex Cyclone 18-cylinder radials each with two exhaust-driven turbochargers.
Dimensions: span 141 ft 3 in (43·05 m); length 99 ft (30·2 m); height 27 ft 9 in (8·46 m).
Weights: empty 74,500 lb (33,795 kg); loaded 135,000 lb (61,240 kg).
Performance: maximum speed 357 mph (575 km/h) at 30,000 ft (9144 m); cruising speed 290 mph (467 km/h); climb to 25,000 ft (7620 m) in 43 min; service ceiling 36,000 ft (10,973 m); range with 10,000 lb (4540 kg) bombs 3,250 miles (5230 km).
Armament: four GE twin-0·50 in turrets above and below, sighted from nose or three waist sighting stations; Bell tail turret, with own gunner, with one 20 mm cannon and twin 0·50 in; internal bomb load up to 20,000 lb (9072 kg). Carried first two nuclear

bombs. With modification, carried two 22,000 lb British bombs externally under inner wings.
History: first flight 21 September 1942; (pre-production YB-29) 26 June 1943); squadron delivery July 1943; first combat mission 5 June 1944; last delivery May 1946.

Development and mass production of the B-29, the Boeing Model 345, was one of the biggest tasks in the history of aviation. It began with a March 1938 study for a new bomber with pressurised cabin and tricycle landing gear. This evolved into the 345 and in August 1940 money was voted for two prototypes. In January 1942 the Army Air Force ordered 14 YB-29s and 500 production aircraft. By February, while Boeing engineers worked night and day on the huge technical problems, a production organisation was set up involving Boeing, Bell, North American and Fisher

(General Motors). Martin came in later and by VJ-day more than 3,000 Superforts had been delivered. This was a fantastic achievement because each represented five or six times the technical effort of any earlier bomber. In engine power, gross weight, wing loading, pressurisation, armament, airborne systems and even basic structure the B-29 set a wholly new standard. First combat mission was flown by the 58th Bomb Wing on 5 June 1944, and by 1945 20 groups from the Marianas were sending 500 B-29s at a time to flatten and burn Japan's cities. (Three aircraft made emergency landings in Soviet territory, and Tupolev's design bureau put the design into production as the Tu-4 bomber and Tu-70 transport.) The -29C had all guns except those in the tail removed, increasing speed and altitude. After the war there were 19 variants of B-29, not including the Washington B.I supplied to help the RAF in 1950–58.

Boeing B-50 Superfortress

B-50 to KB-50J (data for -50D)

Type: strategic bomber with crew of 11.
Engines: four 3,500 hp Pratt & Whitney R-4360-35 Wasp Major 28-cylinder four-row radials each with one CH-7A turbocharger.
Dimensions: span 141 ft 3 in (43·05 m); length 100 ft (30·48 m); height 34 ft 7 in (10·5 m).
Weights: empty 81,000 lb (36,741 kg); loaded 173,000 lb (78,471 kg).
Performance: maximum speed 400 mph (640 km/h); cruising speed 277 mph (445 km/h); service ceiling 38,000 ft (11,580 m); range with maximum bomb load 4,900 miles (7886 km).
Armament: four remote-control turrets above and below, forward upper with four 0·50 in guns and remainder with two; tail gunner in turret with three 0·50 in; maximum internal bomb load 28,000 lb (12,701 kg); exceptionally, can substitute bombs for drop tanks.
History: first flight 25 June 1947; last delivery (a TB-50H unarmed bomb/nav trainer) March 1953.

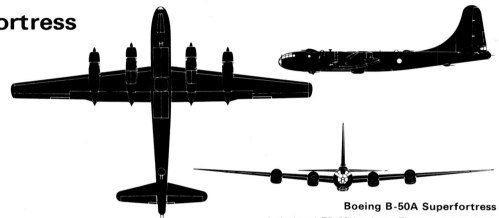

When Japan surrendered in 1945, 5,092 B-29 bombers were cancelled at the stroke of a pen. However, one batch of 200 B-29Ds was merely cut back to 60. The D model was to be powered by a completely new and very powerful engine, the Wasp Major, then giving 3,250 hp and expected ultimately to yield 4,000 hp in

a Turbo-Compound version. The new bomber was also to have an airframe in lighter yet stronger alloy and many other detail changes, including a taller fin for better stability with the longer engines and paddle-blade propellers. Redesignated B-50A, this became the standard front-line aircraft of Strategic Air Command. All of the 371 B-50s were built by Boeing, there being 80 A models, 45 Bs (increased gross weight), 222 Ds (moulded nose and 4,000 lb (1814 kg) outer-wing attachments for bombs or 700 gal drop tanks) and 24

Boeing B-50A Superfortress

dual-control TB-50H trainers. These were very soon being rebuilt in a score of variants, major families being RB reconnaissance versions, WB weather reconnaissance, and KB tanker conversions using either the British hose-reel system or the Boeing Flying Boom. The KB-50J, of which 112 were converted for Tactical Air Command, had triple hose reels and under-wing J47 turbojet pods to boost speed and height to improve contacts with high-performance tactical aircraft. The final WB-50D, WB-50H and KB-50J aircraft were not withdrawn until 1968.

Boeing C-97 Stratofreighter/Stratotanker

C-97 to KC-97L (data for -97G)

Type: air refuelling tanker and logistic transport with crew of six or seven.
Engines: four 3,500 hp Pratt & Whitney R-4360-59B Wasp Major 28-cylinder four-row radials (KC-97L, in addition two 5,200 lb, 2359 kg thrust GE J47 turbojets).
Dimensions: span 141 ft 3 in (43·05 m); length 117 ft 5 in (35·8 m); height 38 ft 3 in (11·7 m).
Weights: empty 85,000 lb (38,560 kg); loaded 175,000 lb (78,980 kg).
Performance: maximum speed 370 mph (595 km/h); service ceiling 30,000 ft (9144 m); range at 300 mph (482 km/h) without using transfer fuel 4,300 miles (6920 km).
Armament: normally, none.
History: first flight (XC-97) 15 November 1944; (production C-97A) 28 January 1949; (KC-97G) 1953; final delivery July 1956.

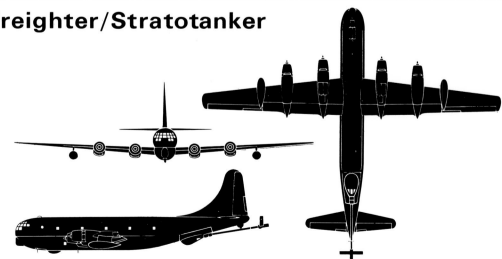

Big as the B-29 Superfortress was, it was dwarfed by the transport derived by adding on top of the existing fuselage a second fuselage of much greater diameter so that the final whale-like body had a section like a figure 8 (called "double bubble"). The Army Air Force had ordered three of these monster XC-97s in January 1942 when it first bought the B-29, but their development took second place behind the vital bomber programmes. But when the first did fly it soon startled everyone; on 9 January 1945 it flew non-stop from Seattle to Washington in 6 hr 4 min, at an average of

383 mph (616 km/h), whilst carrying a payload of ten tons. Only a few years earlier the transcontinental journey had required three days (air by day, rail by night). The YC-97A was even more capable, for it had the Wasp Major engine. Eventually 50 C-97As were built, with nose radar and extra outer-wing tankage, plus 14 aeromedical C-97Cs for casualty evacuation in Korea. But it was Strategic Air Command's need for a refuelling tanker that made the C-97 a giant pro-

Boeing KC-97G Stratofreighter

gramme. By July 1956 Boeing had delivered 60 KC-97Es, carrying nearly double the original fuel load, plus 159 KC-97F and no fewer than 592 KC-97G with underwing tanks and the capability of serving as a heavy cargo aircraft without removing the refuelling gear. Many Gs were converted to jet-boosted Ls, and several have served with the Israeli Heyl Ha'Avir.

Boeing B-47 Stratojet

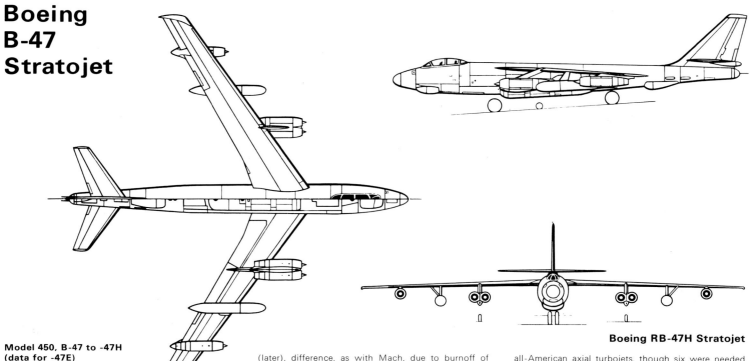

Model 450, B-47 to -47H (data for -47E)
Type: three-seat medium bomber.
Engines: six 5,970 lb (2707 kg) thrust (7,200 lb (3266 kg) with water injection for takeoff) General Electric J47-25A single-shaft turbojets.
Dimensions: span 116 ft (35·36 m); length 109 ft 10 in (33·5 m); height 27 ft 11 in (8·52 m).
Weights: empty 78,200 lb (36,281 kg); loaded 206,700 lb (93,760 kg); maximum permissible 220,000 lb (99,790 kg).
Performance: maximum speed 606 mph (980 km/h); combat speed 557 mph (994 km/h); cruise Mach number 0·75 (early) to 0·82 (later); service ceiling 32,000 ft (9754 m) (early) to 38,000 ft (11,582 m)

(later), difference, as with Mach, due to burnoff of fuel; range with maximum bomb load 3,600 miles (5794 km).
Armament: remotely controlled tail turret with twin 20 mm cannon. Internal bomb load of up to 22,000 lb (9979 kg), all free-fall.
History: first flight (XB-47) 17 December 1947; (B-47A) 25 June 1950; (B-47E) 30 January 1953; final delivery February 1957.

Boeing began studies of jet bombers in 1943 but it was the discovery of swept wings in Germany that spurred the Model 450, which the Army Air Force rather dubiously bought in prototype form in 1945. As flight test results with this dramatically futuristic design began to come in it was clear that it was an unprecedented technical success. Drag was 25 per cent lower than estimate and, though it could not fly the very long missions Strategic Air Command wanted, the B-47A was ordered in quantity in 1949. It introduced the new

all-American axial turbojets, though six were needed for adequate performance and even then rocket boost was provided for maximum-weight takeoff with early versions. The podded engine installation was novel in 1947, and swept wings and tail, a remote-control tail turret and bicycle landing gear were other advanced features. The first major service version was the B-47B, which the Korean War pitchforked into a vast production programme involving Boeing-Wichita, Lockheed-Georgia and Douglas-Tulsa. In 1951 production switched to the more powerful B-47E, with 20mm guns, new radar bombing system, refuelling boom receptacle, ejection seats and huge drop tanks. Despite a very high wing-loading the B-47E was a delight to fly. Throughout the perilous 1950s it equipped 28 SAC Bomb Wings, each with 45 combat-ready aircraft, and there were over 300 RB-47E and ERB-47H reconnaissance and countermeasures aircraft. More than 19 other test, weather, electronic and drone versions existed, several still being in use.

Boeing C-135/KC-135

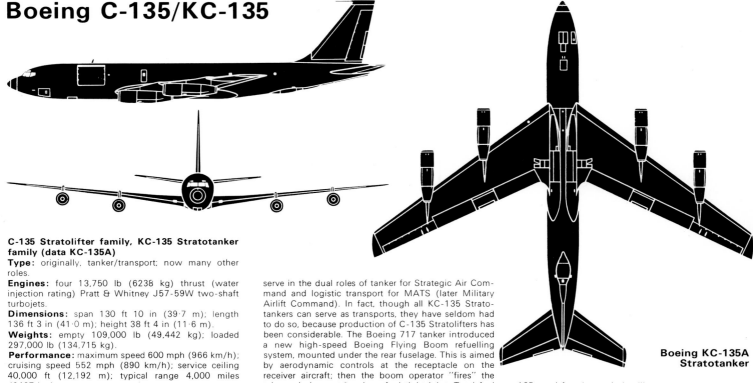

C-135 Stratolifter family, KC-135 Stratotanker family (data KC-135A)
Type: originally, tanker/transport; now many other roles.
Engines: four 13,750 lb (6238 kg) thrust (water injection rating) Pratt & Whitney J57-59W two-shaft turbojets.
Dimensions: span 130 ft 10 in (39·7 m); length 136 ft 3 in (41·0 m); height 38 ft 4 in (11·6 m).
Weights: empty 109,000 lb (49,442 kg); loaded 297,000 lb (134,715 kg).
Performance: maximum speed 600 mph (966 km/h); cruising speed 552 mph (890 km/h); service ceiling 40,000 ft (12,192 m); typical range 4,000 miles (6437 km).
Armament: none.
History: first flight (civil 367–80) 15 July 1954; (KC-135) 31 August 1956; final delivery (RC-135S) mid-1966.

Boeing jet transports all stemmed from a company-funded prototype, the 367-80, flown in July 1954. After evaluation of this aircraft the US Air Force decided in October 1954 to buy 29 developed versions to

serve in the dual roles of tanker for Strategic Air Command and logistic transport for MATS (later Military Airlift Command). In fact, though all KC-135 Stratotankers can serve as transports, they have seldom had to do so, because production of C-135 Stratolifters has been considerable. The Boeing 717 tanker introduced a new high-speed Boeing Flying Boom refuelling system, mounted under the rear fuselage. This is aimed by aerodynamic controls at the receptacle on the receiver aircraft; then the boom operator "fires" the telescopic boom to make a fuel-tight joint. Total fuel capacity on the KC-135A is about 26,000 Imp gal (118,000 litres), leaving the upper fuselage free for cargo. Between June 1957 and January 1965 no fewer than 732 were delivered to SAC. Another 88 Model 739 aircraft have been supplied as various models of C-135, most having 18,000 lb (8165 kg) thrust TF33 fan engines. At least 28 species of modifications are in USAF service, including VC-135 VIP aircraft, command posts, and more than 21 types of

135 used for electronic intelligence, countermeasures and special research. Twelve KC-135F tankers were supplied to refuel the nuclear Mirage IVA *force de frappe* of the Armée de l'Air, these having booms modified for probe/drogue refuelling. Though not armed with guns or bombs, the huge and varied fleets of 135s are very much "combat" aircraft in the context of an electronically based form of warfare and will continue to pry, probe and spoof — and feed fuel to thirsty fighters "below bingo" — for many years.

Boeing B-52 Stratofortress

Boeing B-52G (as originally built)

B-52 to B-52H

Type: strategic bomber and ECM platform with crew of six.

Engines: (B-52F, G) eight 13,750 lb (6238 kg) thrust (water-injection rating) Pratt & Whitney J57-43W two-shaft turbojets; (B-52H) eight 17,000 lb (7711 kg) thrust Pratt & Whitney TF33-3 two-shaft turbofans.

Dimensions: span 185 ft (56·4 m); length 157 ft 7 in (48 m); height 48 ft 3 in (14·75 m); (B-52G, H) 40 ft 8 in (12·4 m).

Weights: empty 171,000–193,000 lb (77,200–87,100 kg); loaded 450,000 lb (204,120 kg) (B-52G, 488,000 lb, 221,500 kg; B-52H, 505,000 lb 229,000 kg).

Performance: maximum speed about 630 mph (1014 km/h) at over 24,000 ft (7315 m); service ceiling 45,000–55,000 ft (13,720–16,765 m); range on internal fuel with maximum weapon load (C, D, E, F) 6,200 miles (9978 km); (G) 8,500 miles (13,680 km); (H) 12,500 miles (20,150 km).

Armament: remotely directed tail mounting for four 0·50 in (B-52H, 20 mm six-barrel ASG-21 cannon). Normal internal bomb capacity 27,000 lb (12,247 kg) including all SAC special weapons; (B-52D) internal and external provision for up to 70,000 lb (31,750 kg) conventional bombs; (B-52G and H) external pylons for two AGM-28B Hound Dog missiles or 12 AGM-69A SRAM missiles, with optional rotary dispenser for eight SRAM internally.

History: first flight (YB-52) 15 April 1952; (B-52A) 5 August 1954; combat service with 93rd BW, 29 June 1955; final delivery (H) June 1962.

Biggest, heaviest and most powerful bomber ever to be built, the mighty B-52 was planned in 1946 as a straight-winged turboprop. At that time no jet engine existed capable of propelling an intercontinental bomber, because fuel consumption was too high. It was Pratt & Whitney's development of a more efficient turbojet, the two-shaft J57, that tipped the scales and led to the new bomber being urgently redesigned in October 1948 as a swept-wing jet. In some ways it resembled a scaled-up B-47, but in fact the wing was made quite different in section and in construction and it housed most of the fuel, which in the B-47 had been in the fuselage. Although the J57, with an expected rating of 10,000 lb (4536 kg), was the most powerful engine available, an unprecedented four double pods were needed. The two prototypes had pilots in tandem, as in the B-47, but the production B-52A had side-by-side pilots with an airline-type flight deck. The crew of six included a rear gunner in the extreme tail to look after his four radar-directed 0·5 in guns. The B-52B had provision for 833 Imp gal (3800 litre) underwing tanks and could carry a two-crew camera or countermeasures capsule in the bomb bay. As the first true service version it encountered many problems, especially with the accessory power systems driven by high-speed air turbines using hot air bled from the engines. The four two-wheel landing gear trucks swivelled for cross-wind landings, the lofty fin could fold to enter hangars and normal bomb load was 10,000 lb (4536 kg) carried for 8,000 miles (12,875 km). The B-52C had much more fuel, the D was similar but used for bombing only (not reconnaissance) and the E and F introduced completely new nav/bombing systems. The G had an integral tank "wet wing" housing far more fuel, more powerful engines driving the accessories directly, as on the F, and many other changes including shorter fin, Quail countermeasures vehicles and a pair of Hound Dog stand-off missiles. Final model was the B-52H, the 102 of which brought the total to 744. Powered by TF33 fan engines the H got rid of engine water injection, greatly extended range and performance, had a new tail stinger (a 20 mm "Gatling" with operator up front as in the G) and in recent years has grown many new sensor and defensive avionics systems. In Vietnam D to F models carried up to 70,000 lb (31,750 kg) of "iron bombs", most of which were rained down without precision aiming (because targets were seldom seen), while the G and H remained in SAC service as multi-role low-level strategic systems pending the introduction of the Rockwell B-1.

Boeing E-3A

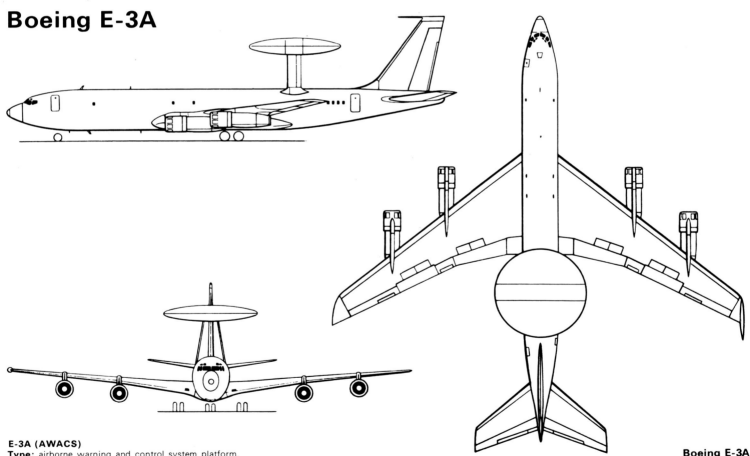

Boeing E-3A

E-3A (AWACS)

Type: airborne warning and control system platform, with crew of 17.

Engines: four 21,000 lb (9525 kg) thrust Pratt & Whitney TF33-100A turbofans.

Dimensions: span 145 ft 9 in (44·42 m); length 152 ft 11 in (46·61 m); height 42 ft 5 in (12·93 m).

Weights: empty at least 175,000 lb (7938 kg); maximum, probably about 350,000 lb (158,760 kg).

Performance: maximum speed, about 600 mph (966 km/h) at high altitude (about 300 mph, 483 km/h at low levels); normal operating height, over 40,000 ft (12,190 m); endurance, at least 12 hr on station without refuelling.

Armament: none.

History: first flight (EC-137D test aircraft) 9 February 1972; (E-3A) before March 1976.

Developments in radars and airborne data processing led first to the basic early-warning aircraft, exemplified by the Douglas EA-1 series and Grumman E-1B, and then, around 1965, to the concept of the Airborne Warning And Control System (AWACS). This is a flying surveillance and management station from which the entire air situation of a small nation, or part of a large one, can be controlled. Carrying an extremely powerful surveillance radar, a mass of sensing and data-processing systems and advanced displays both for the crew and for transmission to the ground, an AWACS can maintain perfect watch on every kind of aerial vehicle, hostile and friendly, over a radius exceeding 200 miles (322 km). This facilitates the most efficient handling of every situation, right down to air traffic control at a beach-head or the best route for helicopters to rescue a friendly pilot. The first AWACS is the Boeing E-3A. Derived from the 707-320B airliner, it was to have had eight TF34 engines but owing to their fantastic overall cost these aircraft now retain the TF33 and have emerged somewhat less complex than once planned. Trials with rival Hughes and Westinghouse radars were held with EC-137D test aircraft; the Westinghouse was chosen, with aerial rotating at six times a minute in a 30 ft (9·14 m) dome high above the rear fuselage. Except for the E-4A, the E-3A, of which 42 may be built, is probably the world's most costly combat aircraft.

Boeing E-4A

E-4A (AABNCP)
Type: airborne command post,
with crew/staff of 28–60.
Engines: four 52,500 lb (23,815 kg) thrust General
Electric F103-100 turbofans.
Dimensions: span 195 ft 8 in (59·64 m); length
231 ft 4 in (70·5 m); height 63 ft 5 in (19·33 m).
Weights: empty, probably 380,000 lb (172,370 kg);
loaded 803,000 lb (364,230 kg).
Performance: maximum speed 608 mph (978 km/h)
at 30,000 ft (9144 m); maximum Mach number 0·92;
normal operational ceiling 45,000 ft (13,715 m);
normal unrefuelled range about 6,500 miles (10,460
km).
Armament: none.
History: first flight (747) 9 February 1969; (E-4)
January 1973.

Since the late 1950s the United States has created a
growing fleet of various kinds of EC-135 aircraft as
airborne command posts. Operated by the National
Military Command System and SAC, these are the
platforms carrying the national strategic and economic
command and decision-taking machinery, with perfect
unjammable communications to all government and
military organizations and the capacity to survive even
a nuclear war. Since 1965 the EC-135 has become
restrictive, and to meet future needs and provide for a
larger staff in greater comfort, with the capability of
more flexible action and response, the 747B airframe

Boeing E-4A

was adopted to carry the Advanced Airborne National
Command Post (AABNCP). The first two were fitted
with Pratt & Whitney JT9D engines, but the standard
was later adopted as that of the fourth E-4A, bought
for $39 million in December 1973 with GE engines
and later equipment. Much of the special equipment
has been taken from the EC-135A, H, J, K, L and P
force. There are three decks, the main deck being a
mixture of executive offices and luxurious living
quarters and the rest being packed with advanced
electronics. All E-4As are based in the United States.

Boeing T-43A

T-43A
Type: navigational trainer.
Engines: two 14,500 lb (6575 kg) thrust Pratt &
Whitney JT8D-9 two-shaft turbofans.
Dimensions: span 93 ft (38·35 m); length 100 ft
(30·48 m); height 37 ft (11·28 m).
Weights: empty, about 62,000 lb (28,123 kg);
maximum 115,500 lb (52,390 kg).
Performance: maximum speed 586 mph (943 km/h);
maximum cruising speed 576 mph (927 km/h) at
22,600 ft (6890 m); economical cruise, Mach 0·7 at
35,000 ft (10,670 m); initial rate of climb at gross
weight 3,750 ft (1143 m)/min; range with military
reserves 2,995 miles (4820 km); endurance 6 hr.
Armament: none.
History: first flight (/37-100) 9 April 1967; (T-43A)
10 April 1973.

Derived from the commercial 737-200, the T-43A is
the world's most advanced navigational trainer. Though
the "baby" of current Boeing production aircraft, it is
nevertheless much larger and more powerful than any
Superfortress, and the fleet of 19 used at Mather Air
Force Base, California, have replaced 77 Convair T-29
crew trainers previously used. This has been possible
because of the T-43's much higher utilisation and
ability to carry 12 trainee navigators (each with a
complete aircraft instrument and systems station),
four proficiency students and three instructors, apart
from the T-43A crew. In addition the T-43A is used in
conjunction with a comprehensive computer-based

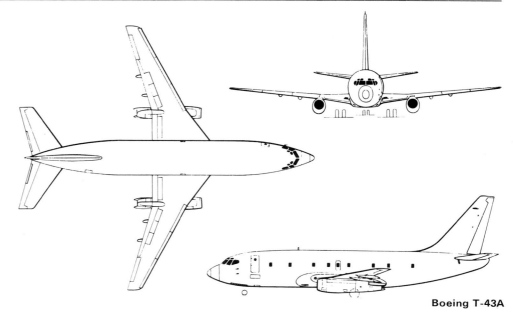

mission simulation system which enables every kind of
combat mission up to Mach 2 at 70,000 ft (21,340 m)
altitude to be "flown" on the ground. Each T-43A
carries complete inertial navigation systems, Loran and

Boeing T-43A

other radio systems, and provision for celestial and
even dead-reckoning navigation techniques. Mission
endurance is increased by a 667 gal (3027 litre) tank
in the rear cargo compartment.

Boeing YC-14

YC-14
Type: advanced military transport.
Engines: two 51,000 lb (23,133 kg) thrust General
Electric F103 turbofans.
Dimensions: span 129 ft (39·32 m); length 131 ft 8 in
(40·13 m); height 48 ft 8 in (14·83 m).
Weights: empty, about 85,000 lb (38,555 kg);
loaded (STOL) 172,000 lb (78,020 kg); loaded (long
runway) 216,000 lb (97,975 kg).
Performance: maximum speed 460 mph (740 km/h)
at 30,000 ft (9144 m); takeoff and landing to and from
50 ft (15 m) 2,000 ft (610 m); range approximately
1,250 miles (2000 km) with STOL payload of 27,000 lb
(12,247 kg) or conventional payload of 65,000 lb
(29,500 kg).
Armament: none, though gunship versions may be
developed.
History: first flight early 1976.
In early 1972 the USAF requested proposals for an
Advanced Medium STOL (short take-off and landing)
Transport (AMST), primarily as a replacement for the
C-130 but also to gather all the diverse new technology of increasing wing lift at low airspeeds and
the possibility of integrating wings and propulsion
systems to achieve better short-field performance. The
two finalists were the McDonnell Douglas YC-15 and
Boeing YC-14. The former, first flown in 1975, has
four JT8D engines hung on pylons close below the
leading edge of the wing so that, in STOL regimes,
their efflux blows straight into the two-segment flaps.
The YC-14 has a relatively small supercritical wing
carrying the two large engines in a high position so that

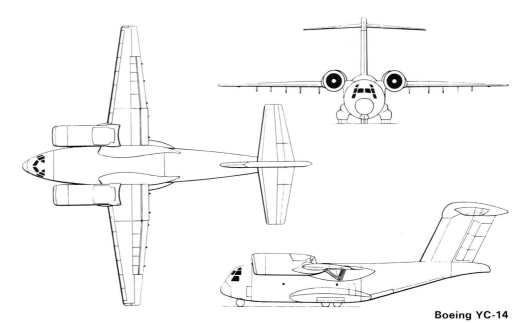

they blow the upper surface. This offers many benefits,
including efficient thrust-reverse, uncluttered under-
surface for carrying stores or Remotely-Piloted Vehicles,
less infra-red signature to ground-based detectors, and

Boeing YC-14

reduced noise footprint. Some of these assets would
apply to future commercial versions for serving remote
or minor airstrips. It is anticipated that many hundreds
of YC-14s will be built before 1990.

Vertol (Boeing) Model 44 (H-21) Work Horse

H-21 to H-21C (data for C)

Type: transport and rescue helicopter with crew two to four.

Engine: 1,425 hp Wright R-1820-103 Cyclone nine-cylinder radial.

Dimensions: diameter of main rotors 44 ft (13·42 m); fuselage length 54 ft (16·47 m); height 15 ft 1 in (4·6 m).

Weights: 9,000 lb (4082 kg); loaded 15,000 lb (6804 kg).

Performance: maximum speed 120 mph (192 km/h); initial climb 800 ft (245 m)/min; normal range 300 miles (482 km).

Armament: normally, none (experimentally, pivoted machine guns and cannon and launchers for rockets).

History: first flight (HRP-2 Rescuer) 1949; (YH-21) 11 April 1952.

Frank N. Piasecki was one of a group of American engineers interested in helicopters who met in their spare time and then formed a company in August 1940.

They flew their first helicopter in April 1943 and followed it in March 1945 with the biggest then flown, the HRP-1 Rescuer built for the Navy. Powered by a 600 hp Pratt & Whitney R-1340 Wasp, it had tandem lifting rotors to avoid the need for a giant rotor and to cancel out torque without a tail rotor. The arrangement also allowed heavy loads to be carried anywhere in a 400 cubic foot (11·32 m³) cabin. From this came the important HRP-2 and H-21 families with the R-1820 engine. Eighteen YH-21 were followed by 32 H-21A Arctic rescue, 153 H-21B Work Horse and 85 H-21C Shawnee for the Army. These had 22 seats instead of

Boeing Vertol 44A (Royal Swedish Navy)

16, and the more powerful engine allowed weight to rise from 11,500 lb to 15,000. Many Model 44 helicopters of the same basic type were then exported, including four for the Royal Swedish Navy and many for West Germany, France and Canadian forces. Though obsolescent by 1965, these were among the most useful helicopters of their day and led to the turbine-engined Model 107 and Chinook.

Boeing Vertol Model 114 Chinook

CH-47A, B and C Chinook (data for C)

Type: medium transport helicopter with normal crew of two/three.

Engines: two 3,750 shp Lycoming T55-L-11A free-turbine turboshafts.

Dimensions: diameter of main rotors 60 ft (18·29 m); length, rotors turning, 99 ft (30·2 m); length of fuselage 51 ft (15·54 m); height 18 ft 7 in (5·67 m).

Weights: empty 20,616 lb (9351 kg); loaded (condition I) 33,000 lb (14,969 kg); (overload condition II) 46,000 lb (20,865 kg).

Performance: maximum speed (condition I) 189 mph (304 km/h); (II) 142 mph (229 km/h); initial climb (I) 2,880 ft (878 m)/min; (II) 1,320 ft (402 m)/min; service ceiling (I) 15,000 ft (4570 m); (II) 8,000 ft (2440 m); mission radius, cruising speed and payload (I) 115 miles (185 km) at 158 mph (254 km/h) with 7,262 lb (3294 kg); (II) 23 miles (37 km) at 131 mph (211 km/h) with 23,212 lb (10,528 kg).

Armament: normally, none.

History: first flight (YCH-47A) 21 September 1961; (CH-47C) 14 October 1967.

Development of the Vertol 114 began in 1956 to meet the need of the US Army for a turbine-engined all-weather cargo helicopter able to operate effectively in the most adverse conditions of altitude and temperature. Retaining the tandem-rotor configuration, the first YCH-47A flew on the power of two 2,200 shp Lycoming T55 turboshaft engines and led directly to the production CH-47A. With an unobstructed cabin 7½ ft (2·29 m) wide, 6½ ft (1·98 m) high and over 30 ft (9·2 m) long, the Chinook proved a valuable vehicle, soon standardised as US Army medium helicopter and deployed all over the world. By 1972 more

Boeing Vertol CH-47B Chinook

than 550 had served in Vietnam, mainly in the battle-field airlift of troops and weapons but also rescuing civilians (on one occasion 147 refugees and their belongings were carried to safety in one Chinook) and lifting back for salvage or repair 11,500 disabled aircraft valued at more than $3,000 million. The A model gave way to the CH-47B, with 2,850 hp engines and numerous improvements and, finally, to the much more powerful CH-47C. Over 800 Chinooks were built, all at Boeing Vertol at Philadelphia (successor to Piasecki). Small numbers of C models continue in licence-production by Meridionali of Italy. Work is now concentrated on the Model 179, with single lifting rotor, and the huge XCH-62 heavy-lift helicopter for the US Army.

Boeing Paul P.82 Defiant

Defiant I and II (data for I)

Type: two-seat fighter.

Engine: I, 1,030 hp Rolls-Royce Merlin III vee-12 liquid-cooled; II, 1,260 hp Merlin 20.

Dimensions: span 39 ft 4 in (12 m); length 35 ft 4 in (10·75 m); height 12 ft 2 in (3·7 m).

Weights: empty 6,000 lb (2722 kg); loaded 8,350 lb (3787 kg).

Performance: maximum speed 303 mph (488 km/h); initial climb 1,900 ft (579 m)/min; service ceiling 30,500 ft (9300 m); range, probably about 500 miles (805 km).

Armament: hydraulically operated dorsal gun turret with four 0·303 in Browning machine guns, each with 600 rounds.

History: first flight (prototype) 11 August 1937; (production Mk I) 30 July 1939; first delivery December 1939.

By 1933 military staffs were intensely studying the enclosed gun turret, manually worked or power-driven, either to defend a bomber or to arm a fighter. A primitive

form was seen on the Hawker Demon in 1936, while in France the *Multiplace de Combat* class of aircraft were huge fighters with turrets all over. The Defiant was a bold attempt to combine the performance of the new monoplanes with a powered enclosed turret carrying four 0·303 in Brownings, each with 600 rounds. The gunner, behind the pilot, had a control column moved left/right for rotation, fore/aft for depression and elevation and with a safety/firing button on top. The Defiant itself was a clean and pleasant aircraft, not terribly degraded in performance by carrying a crew of two and the heavy turret. No 264 Sqn went into action on 12 May 1940 in desperate fights over the Low Countries. On the 13th six escorted

Boulton Paul Defiant II (night fighter without AI radar)

Battle bombers, and only one returned; it seemed the Defiant was a failure against the Bf 109E. But seven days later remnants of 264 shot down "17 Messerschmitts without loss" and later on the same day destroyed eleven Ju 87s and 88s. Once the enemy were familiar with the Defiant it had had its day by daylight, but fitted with AI radar did well in 1940–41 as a night fighter. Most of the 1,064 built served as night fighters, target tugs and in air/sea rescue in Britain, the Middle East and Far East. Defiants carried the Mandrel jamming system to confuse German defences.

Breguet 14 (XIV)

Breguet Bre. 14A-2, B-2, BN-2 and 16
Type: two-seat day bomber.
Engine: 300 hp Renault 12 Fe or 12 Fcx 12-cylinder vee water-cooled.
Dimensions: span 48 ft 11½ in (14·91 m); length 29 ft 1¼ in (8·87 m); height 10 ft 9¾ in (3·3 m).
Weights: empty 2,513 lb (1140 kg); loaded 3,858–4,144 lb (1750–1880 kg).
Performance: maximum speed 112 mph (180 km/h); climb to 16,400 ft (5000 m) in 39 minutes; service ceiling 18,290 ft (6000 m); range with bomb load 435 miles (700 km).
Armament: normally one 0·303 in (7·7 mm) fixed Vickers firing forward and twin 0·303 in Lewis on pivoted mount for observer. Some had pivoted Lewis on upper wing in place of Vickers; some had one Lewis at rear; some had ventral Lewis in floor of rear cockpit. Racks under lower wings for 32 bombs of 17·6 lb (8 kg) or 22 lb (10 kg).
History: first flight (AV) 21 November 1916; termination of production, mid-1926.

Louis Breguet himself flew this extremely advanced new prototype, which contravened official regulations in having the engine in front (the rule was decreed so

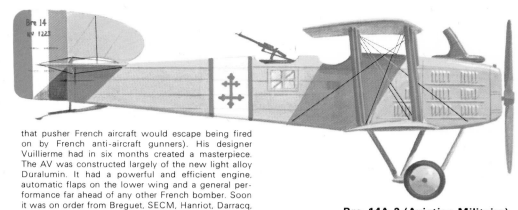

that pusher French aircraft would escape being fired on by French anti-aircraft gunners). His designer Vuillierme had in six months created a masterpiece. The AV was constructed largely of the new light alloy Duralumin. It had a powerful and efficient engine, automatic flaps on the lower wing and a general performance far ahead of any other French bomber. Soon it was on order from Breguet, SECM, Hanriot, Darracq, Renault, Bellanger, Schmitt and Michelin, different versions being the 14A-2 for reconnaissance, the B-2 bomber, the B-1 single-seat bomber and the BN-2 two-seat night bomber. The 14 (often written XIV) served with 71 French Escadrilles on the Western Front, five in Serbia, six in Morocco, eight in Macedonia and three in Greece and with Allied air forces, notably Belgium and the USA. This impressive aircraft swiftly

Bre. 14A-2 (Aviation Militaire)

built a mighty reputation, and 5,500 were ordered during the war. But that was only the start of a great worldwide career and by 1926 total deliveries had reached at least 8,370. With the long-span Bre. 16B-2, the 14 remained in service until 1930 and many of the 17 post-war versions were seaplanes and civil transports.

Breguet 19

19A-2 and B-2
Type: two-seat bomber.
Engine: 375–800 hp vee-12 water-cooled, most common being 450 hp Lorraine, 475–580 hp Renault or 450–600 hp Hispano-Suiza.
Dimensions: span 48 ft 8 in (14·85 m); length 31 ft 2½ in (9·52 m); height 10 ft 11½ in (3·34 m).
Weights: empty 2,645 lb (1200 kg); loaded 4,850 lb (2200 kg).
Performance: maximum speed, typically 137 mph (220 km/h); service ceiling (450 hp) 22,970 ft (7000 m); range with bomb load 497 miles (800 km).
Armament: if fitted, typically one fixed rifle-calibre machine gun and one or two pivoted for observer. Provision for underwing bomb load of 1,543 lb (700 kg).
History: first flight May 1922; service delivery 1925; termination of production (France) 1928, (other countries) after 1930.

Designed as a natural successor to the Bre. 14, the 19 (often written XIX) was built even more widely and in even more versions, though it was denied the impetus of being launched in wartime. It emerged into a world littered with discarded military aircraft, being displayed before having flown at the Paris Salon of 1921.

Breguet 19-7 (Turkish AF)

Points in its favour were its outstanding structure, entirely of Duralumin apart from parts of wing ribs and the fabric covering, and its very clean design with single streamlined interplane struts and landing gear legs. Compared with the 14, it had an almost identical empty weight yet could carry a load of fuel and bombs 60 to 80 per cent greater. Soon the prototype was setting a series of world records and by the end of 1926 Breguet had delivered 1,100 A-2 reconnaissance and

B-2 bomber versions to the Armée de l'Air and nine other air forces. Licence-production continued in Belgium, Greece, Japan, Spain, Turkey and Yugoslavia. The 19 was in major front-line Armée de l'Air service until 1939 and the Turkish example illustrated survived World War II. Most famous 19 of all was the long-range "Question Mark" which was the first aircraft to cross the North Atlantic westbound and made many great flights longer than 5,000 miles.

Breguet 691

Bre. 690, 691, 693 and 695
Type: two-seat light attack bomber.
Engines: two 640/700 hp Hispano-Suiza 14AB10/11 14-cylinder radials (693 two 680/700 hp Gnome-Rhône 14M6/7 14-cylinder radials).
Dimensions: span 50 ft 4¾ in (15·3 m); length 33 ft 7 in (10·22 m); height 10 ft 3¾ in (3·4 m).
Weights: empty 6,834 lb (3100 kg) (693: 6,636 lb, 3010 kg); maximum loaded 11,023 lb (5000 kg) (693: 10,800 lb, 4900 kg).
Performance: (very similar for both) maximum speed 300 mph (483 km/h); time to climb to 13,120 ft (4000 m) 7 minutes; service ceiling 27,885 ft (8500 m); range 840 miles (1350 km).
Armament: one 20 mm Hispano 404 cannon with 60-round drum and two 7·5 mm MAC 1934 machine guns (500 rounds each) all fixed firing forward (pilot could tilt all three 15° down for ground strafing); one MAC 1934 fixed firing obliquely down at rear (late-model 693 also had two more MAC 1934 oblique in nacelles); single MAC 1934 fed by 100-round drums on pivoted mount in rear cockpit; racks for eight 110 lb (50 kg) bombs in bomb bay.
History: first flight (Bre. 690) 23 March 1938; (Bre. 691) 22 March 1939; (Bre. 693) 25 October 1939; (Bre. 695) 23 April 1940.

In 1934 designers in seven countries began work on what were to become significant members of a new breed of fighter having two engines. These were hoped to be in no way inferior in performance to other, smaller, fighters and to be superior in navigation, long-range escort and ground attack. It was also considered they would be superior if fighting should ever be necessary at night. One of the best designs was Breguet's 690. It was finished in March 1937 but then had to wait almost a year for engines, because Breguet had not joined the newly nationalised French industry and

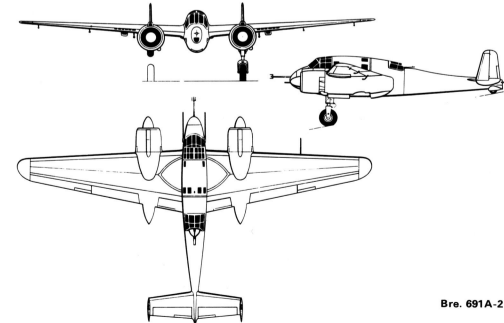

Bre. 691A-2

Potez had priority for engines for the 630 family. But once it was able to fly it could outclass even the MS.406 single-seater, adopted as future Armée de l'Air fighter. With all haste, the Bre. 691 light attack version was put into production, all but the first 50 having imported Hamilton propellers because of a shortage of the Ratier type. At aircraft No 78 production switched to the Bre. 693, with more reliable G-R engines of even

smaller diameter. By the capitulation 224 had been delivered, plus 50 Bre. 695 hastily put into production with the American P&W Twin Wasp Junior engine, which was lighter and more powerful but actually harmed flight performance, handling and pilot view. Breguet escadrilles fought valiantly, especially GBA I/54 and II/54. The Luftwaffe took engines from 693s to power Hs 129 and Me 323 aircraft, and some dozens of 693s served Italy in 1942–43.

Breguet Alizé

Br.1050
Type: three-seat carrier anti-submarine search and strike.
Engine: 1,975 shp Rolls-Royce Dart RDa.21 single-shaft turboprop.
Dimensions: span 51 ft 2 in (15·6 m); length 45 ft 6 in (13·86 m); height 15 ft 7 in (4·75 m).
Weights: empty 12,566 lb (5700 kg); loaded 18,190 lb (8250 kg).
Performance: maximum speed 285 mph (460 km/h) at sea level, about 295 mph (475 km/h) at altitude; initial climb (gross weight with landing gear down) 1,380 ft (420 m)/min; service ceiling 20,500 ft (6250 m); endurance at 144 mph (235 km/h) patrol speed at low level 5 hr 12 min; ferry range with auxiliary fuel 1,785 miles (2850 km).
Armament: weapon bay for acoustic torpedo or three 353 lb (160 kg) depth charges; underwing racks for two Nord SS.11M or AS.12 missiles, or various combinations of rockets, bombs or depth charges.
History: first flight (Br 960) 3 August 1951; (Br 1050 aerodynamic prototype) 26 March 1955; (Br 1050 prototype) 6 October 1956; (Br 1050 production model) 22 June 1957; first delivery 26 March 1959.

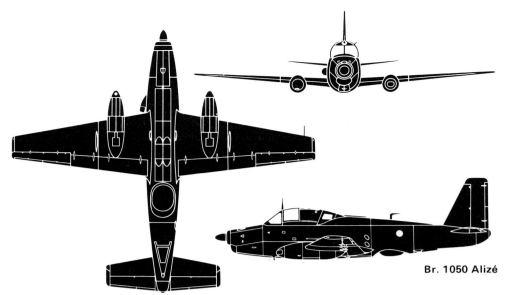

Br. 1050 Alizé

In 1948 the Breguet company began work on a design to meet a requirement of the Aéronavale for a carrier-based strike aircraft. The resulting Br.960 Vultur (vulture) looked conventional, but in fact had a speed of 559 mph (900 km/h) on the thrust of a Rolls-Royce Nene jet at the back and an AS Mamba turboprop in the nose. With the jet shut down it had a long range and endurance. This never went into production, though it was very successful and pleasant to fly. Instead, in 1954, the long task began of turning the Vultur into an anti-submarine aircraft carrying both search radar and weapons. So different did it become that it was renamed Alizé (tradewind). The retractable radome replaced the turbojet, the main landing gears retracted forwards into nacelles also housing sonobuoys and the cockpit was arranged for the pilot on the left, a radar operator on the right and a second sensor operator behind. Flottilles 4F, 6F and 9F still deploy most of the 75 built for the carriers *Foch* and *Clémenceau*, and a further 12 were supplied for 310 Sqn Indian Navy aboard the carrier *Vikrant*.

Breguet Atlantic

Br.1150 Atlantic
Type: maritime patrol and anti-submarine aircraft with normal crew of 12.
Engines: two 6,106 ehp Rolls-Royce Tyne 21 two-shaft turboprops.
Dimensions: span 119 ft 1 in (36·3 m); length 104 ft 2 in (31·75 m); height 37 ft 2 in (11·33 m).
Weights: empty 52,900 lb (24,000 kg); maximum 95,900 lb (43,500 kg).
Performance: maximum speed (above 16,400 ft/ 5000 m) 409 mph (658 km/h); patrol speed 199 mph (320 km/h); initial climb at gross weight 2,450 ft (746 m)/min; service ceiling 32,800 ft (10,000 m); patrol endurance 18 hours; maximum range 5,592 miles (9000 km).
Armament: unpressurised weapon bay carries all NATO standard bombs, 385 lb (175 kg) depth charges, four homing torpedoes (or nine acoustic torpedoes) and HVAR rockets. Underwing racks for up to four AS.12, Martel or other missiles with nuclear or conventional warheads.
History: first flight 21 October 1961; (production aircraft) 19 July 1965; service delivery 10 December 1965.

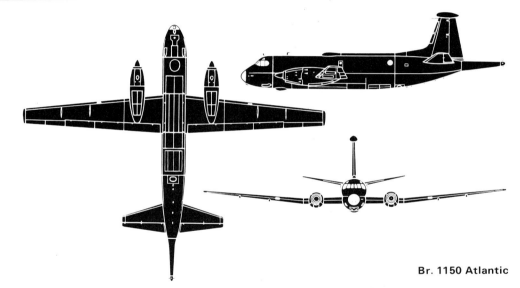

Br. 1150 Atlantic

The history of NATO shows the almost continual failure of its members to agree on weapon standardization, especially in aircraft. One of the few real attempts to do better was the 1958 decision to procure a standard aircraft to replace the Lockheed P-2. The French Br.1150 was selected from 25 designs submitted and in December 1959 two prototypes were ordered from NATO funds. Though most NATO members refused to have anything to do with it – often because their own design had not been chosen – the programme was launched by France and Germany, which ordered 40 and 20 respectively. Subsequently the Netherlands Navy bought nine and the Italian Navy 18, so that finally the airframe was being built in all four countries, with avionics partly supplied from the USA and Britain. The engines were made by a British/Belgian/ German/French/Italian consortium, with assembly by SNECMA of France. The Atlantic proved a most comfortable and efficient machine, with pressurization above the floor of the double-bubble fuselage and a great amount of room. The airframe is skinned mainly in metal honeycomb sandwich. Five of the German Atlantics bristle with special electronic countermeasures, and in 1976 plans were continuing to be studied for a heavier Atlantic II with M45 turbofan pods under the wings to allow operation at weights as high as 110,000 lb (50,000 kg).

Brewster F2A Buffalo

Model 339, F2A-1, -2 and -3 (data for -2)
Type: single-seat carrier or land-based fighter.
Engine: 1,100 hp Wright R-1820-40 (G-205A) Cyclone nine-cylinder radial.
Dimensions: span 35 ft (10·67 m); length 26 ft 4 in (8 m); height 12 ft 1 in (3·7 m).
Weights: empty 4,630 lb (2100 kg); loaded 7,055 lb (3200 kg) (varied from 6,848–7,159 lb).
Performance: maximum speed 300 mph (483 km/h); initial climb 3,070 ft (935 m)/min; service ceiling 30,500 ft (9300 m); range 650–950 miles (1045–1530 km).
Armament: four machine guns, two in fuselage and two in wing, calibre of each pair being 0·30 in, 0·303 in or, mostly commonly, 0·50 in.
History: first flight (XF2A-1) January 1938; first service delivery April 1939; termination of production 1942.

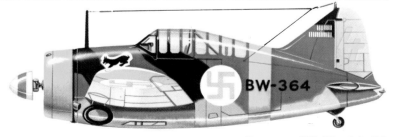

Brewster 239 (Finnish AF)

The Brewster company was established in 1810 to build carriages. In 1935 it plunged into planemaking and secured an order for a US Navy scout-bomber. It also entered a competition for a carrier-based monoplane fighter and won. Not surprisingly, it took almost two years – a long time in those days – to fly the first prototype. Yet one must give the team their due, for the F2A-1 was confirmed as the Navy's choice for its first monoplane fighter even after Grumman had flown the G.36 (Wildcat). In June 1938 a contract was placed for 54 of these tubby mid-wingers, then armed with one 0·50 in and one 0·30 in machine guns. Only 11 reached USS *Saratoga*; the rest went to Finland, where from February 1940 until the end of World War II they did extremely well. The US Navy bought 43 more powerful and more heavily armed F2A-2 (Model 339), and then 108 F2A-3 with armour and self-sealing tanks. Of these, 21 in the hands of the Marine Corps put up a heroic struggle in the first Battle of Midway. In 1939 bulk orders were placed by Belgium and Britain, and the RAF operated 170 delivered in 1941 to Singapore. Another 72 were bought by the Netherlands East Indies. All fought valiantly against the Japanese, but were outclassed as well as outnumbered. Brewster gave up planemaking in July 1944.

Bristol Types 1-5 Scout

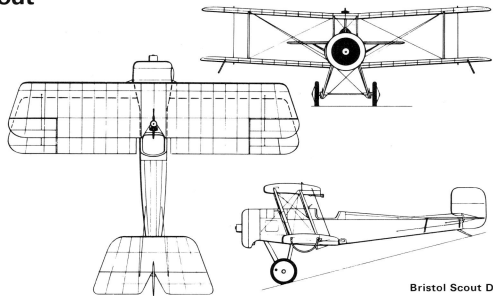

Scout A to D
Type: single-seat scout (reconnaissance).
Engine: 80 hp, 100 hp or 110 hp Gnome, Le Rhône or Clerget nine-cylinder rotary.
Dimensions: span 24 ft 7 in (7·5 m); length 20 ft 8 in (6·3 m); height 8 ft 6 in (2·6 m).
Weights: empty 760 lb (345 kg) with 80 hp to 925 lb (420 kg) with 110 hp engines; loaded, most 1,200 lb (544 kg); (Scout D with 110 hp, 1,440 lb, 653 kg).
Performance: maximum speed 100–110 mph (161–177 km/h) depending on engine; initial climb 1,100 ft (335 m)/min; service ceiling 14,000 ft (4267 m); endurance 2½ hours (thus, range about 200 miles).
Armament: see text.
History: first flight (Scout A) 23 February 1914; (production Scout C) February 1915 (Scout D) November 1915.

In 1914 the prototype Bristol Scout was almost unique: it was a modern, clean, fast aeroplane that was soundly built and flew very well indeed. Although officially committed to Royal Aircraft Factory designs the War Office was impressed and fought the Admiralty to get first deliveries. The production Scout C broke more new ground in combat aviation than any other type, because it carried guns from the start. Maj W. G. Moore fixed three Webley-Fosbery revolvers to his, Capt Vesey Holt shot down two of the enemy with a pistol (the Mauser was preferred, for its accuracy) and in 1915 it was not untypical to find one of these baby aircraft carrying an SMLE rifle (stock sawn off and the gun screwed to the fuselage obliquely) plus a Mauser and five rifle grenades. Some had a Lewis machine gun and many had two. In February 1916 one

Bristol Scout D

of the aerodynamically improved Scout D models was at the front with the first synchronizing gear on the Allied side, a Vickers design controlling a fixed gun of the same make. RNAS Scouts often carried two canisters of Ranken darts, to set fire to Zeppelins, and others carried bombs under the nose. Though only

161 C and 210 D models were delivered they accomplished an amazing amount on the Western Front (RFC), in Macedonia (47 Sqn), Mesopotamia (30 and 63), Palestine (14, 111 and Australian 67) and with the RNAS from the carrier *Vindex* and many shore bases in Britain and the Dardanelles.

Bristol Types 14-17 Fighter

Fighter F.2A and 2B
Type: two-seat fighter.
Engine: 275 hp Rolls-Royce Falcon III (data below apply) vee-12 water-cooled, or any of 16 other engines of 120–400 hp from R-R, Hispano, Liberty, Sunbeam, Beardmore, RAF, Siddeley or Wolseley.
Dimensions: span 39 ft 3 in (11·9 m); length 25 ft 10 in (7·9 m); height 9 ft 9 in (2·98 m).
Weights: empty 1,930 lb (875 kg); loaded 2,800 lb (1280 kg).
Performance: maximum speed 125 mph (201 km/h); climb to 10,000 ft (3048 m) in 11½ minutes; service ceiling 20,000 ft (6096 m); endurance 3 hours.
Armament: one 0·303 in Vickers machine gun fixed on top centreline with C.C. synchronizing gear; single or twin 0·303 in Lewis on Scarff ring on rear cockpit; provision for up to twelve 20 lb (9·1 kg) bombs (final Mk IV, two 112 lb (51 kg) bombs).
History: first flight (F.2A) 9 September 1916; service delivery 20 December 1916; final deliveries (RAF) December 1926, (Mexico) 1927; final withdrawal from service (RNZAF) 1938.

By 1916 the popular image of the RFC being Fokker fodder was literally true. Bristol's designer Capt Frank Barnwell could see the need for something better than the obsolete machines from the Royal Aircraft Factory (his own firm was making the "B.E. replacement", the R.E.8), and in the Fighter he provided it. In every way this splendid design was right. It was planned around a new and powerful, yet reliable, engine and a properly developed scheme of armament. Pilot and observer could talk to each other, had a fine view and unobstructed field of fire. The F.2A began fighting on 5 April 1917. The first few days were disastrous until crews suddenly realised that they had speed and manoeuvrability previously found only in single-seaters. Henceforward the pilot flew aggres-

Bristol F.2B

sively and aimed his front gun, while the observer could still aim as well as in straight and level flight. The result was now disaster for the enemy, compounded by the fact that the Fighter could withstand immense punishment and could dive vertically faster than anything else on the Front. Fighters of many sub-types were made by ten factories in Britain and three in the USA. Excluding later versions with the new Jupiter engine, 5,252 were built by 1927, serving 14 foreign air forces. One still flies in Britain.

Bristol Type 20 M.1 series

M.1A, B and C
Type: single-seat scout (reconnaissance).
Engine: 110 hp Le Rhône nine-cylinder rotary (see text).
Dimensions: span 30 ft 9 in (9·4 m); length 20 ft 5 in (6.25 m); height 7 ft 10 in (2·4 m).
Weights: empty 900 lb (408 kg); loaded 1,350 lb (613 kg).
Performance: maximum speed 130 mph (209 km/h); service ceiling 20,000 ft (6096 m); endurance 1¾ hours.
Armament: one Vickers 0·303 in machine gun on upper centreline, with Sopwith-Kauper synchronizing gear.
History: first flight (Type A) 14 July 1916; (production M.1C) September 1917; service delivery 19 September 1917.

The degree of incompetence of those in positions of authority in the British World War I machine is today difficult even to comprehend. In aircraft procurement it was taken for granted that no monoplane was acceptable, a blanket rule dating from 1912. In defiance of this Bristol's Capt Barnwell decided to design a superior scout as a monoplane and the M.1A flew as a private venture on a 110 hp Clerget. It was the fastest

and most delightful machine in the sky and after prolonged argument the War Office ordered four M.1Bs with a Vickers gun in the left wing root and a cut-out in the right wing to improve downward view. These had 130 hp Clerget or 150 hp Bentley engines. By this time the RFC was wild with excitement, because here at last was a fighting scout that could gain what in later years was to be called air superiority. But the squadrons on the Western Front waited in vain. The War Office ordered a mere 125, called M.1C, claiming the landing speed of 49 mph was dangerously high (ignoring the fact that the little monoplanes had become the most coveted mounts for senior officers). All were relegated to Mesopotamia, Salonika, Palestine and Basra, where they ran rings round the opposition and

Bristol M.1C
(No. 2 School of Aerial Fighting, RFC)

once caused a complete Kurdish tribe to desert to the Allies. Six served with the Chilean Air Force from 1917, making the first flights across the Andes (the second such double-crossing being an unauthorised flight by a pupil!).

Bristol Type 105 Bulldog

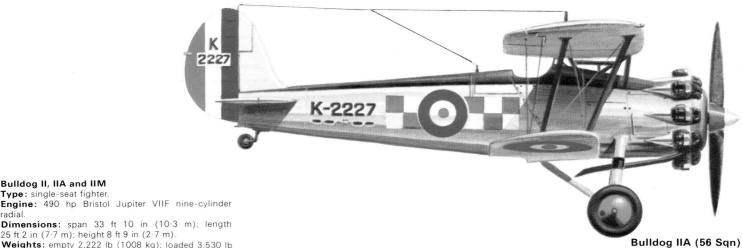

Bulldog IIA (56 Sqn)

Bulldog II, IIA and IIM

Type: single-seat fighter.

Engine: 490 hp Bristol Jupiter VIIF nine-cylinder radial.

Dimensions: span 33 ft 10 in (10·3 m); length 25 ft 2 in (7·7 m); height 8 ft 9 in (2·7 m).

Weights: empty 2,222 lb (1008 kg); loaded 3,530 lb (1601 kg) (later 3,660 lb, 1660 kg).

Performance: maximum speed 174 mph (280 km/h); climb to 20,000 ft (6096 m) in 14½ minutes; service ceiling 29,300 ft (8940 m); range/endurance, never published but about 300 miles (482 km)/2 hours.

Armament: two 0·303 in Vickers machine guns in fuselage sides, each with 600 rounds; provision for underwing racks for four 20 lb (9·1 kg) bombs.

History: first flight (Type 105) 17 May 1927; (Mk II) 21 January 1928; first delivery 8 May 1929; final deliveries (Finland) February 1935.

To meet Specification F.9/26 for a day and night fighter for the RAF, no fewer than nine competing prototypes were tested, most of them using the powerful and reliable Jupiter engine. After a close battle with Camm's Hawker Hawfinch, the Bulldog was finally selected. Points in its favour were good pilot view, single-bay wings, easy changing of fuel tanks in the upper wing and robust structure of rolled stainless-steel strip, with aluminium skinning back to the rear of the cockpit and fabric elsewhere. The Bulldog II became the standard fighter of the RAF, 312 being supplied, of which most were IIAs with bigger fin,

**Above, Bulldog II
(Estonian AF supporting Basques)**

wider track gear and bigger tyres, tailwheel and improved oil system. A further 131 were exported, usually with Gnome-Rhône Jupiter engine, to Estonia, Denmark, Sweden, Latvia, Siam and (two) the US Navy. Numerous research Bulldogs and smaller Bullpups tested new engines and equipment, and 58 dual trainer Bulldog IIMs were also supplied to the RAF. In the 1930s this popular fighter provided 70 per cent of the air defence of Britain, serving in fighter squadrons until 1938.

Bristol Blenheim

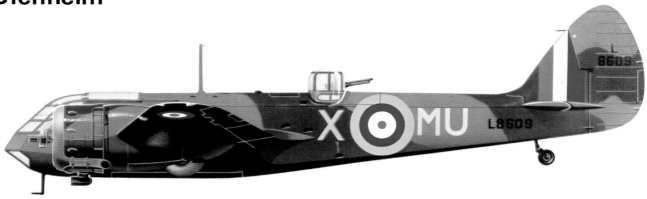

Bristol Blenheim I (60 Sqn, Lahore, 1940)

Types 142 M, 149 and 160 Blenheim/Bisley/Bolingbroke (data for Blenheim IVL)

Type: three-seat light bomber (IF, IVF, fighter versions).

Engines: two 920 hp Bristol Mercury XV (I, Bolingbroke I, II, 840 hp Mercury VIII; Bolingbroke IV series, 750–920 hp Twin Wasp Junior, Cyclone or Mercury XX; Blenheim V, 950 hp Mercury XXX)

Dimensions: span 56 ft 4 in (17·17 m) (V, 56 ft 1 in); length 42 ft 9 in (13 m) (I, 39 ft 9 in; Bolingbroke III, 46 ft 3 in; V, 43 ft 11 in); height 12 ft 10 in (3·91 m) (Bolingbroke III, 18 ft).

Weights: empty 9,790 lb (4441 kg) (I, Bolingbroke III, 8,700 lb; V, 11,000 lb); loaded 14,400 lb (6531 kg) (I, 12,250 lb; Bolingbrokes 13,400 lb; V, 17,000 lb).

Performance: maximum speed 266 mph (428 km/h); (I) 285 mph; (early IV) 295 mph; (Bolingbrokes and V) 245–260 mph; initial climb 1,500 ft (457 m)/min (others similar); service ceiling 31,500 ft (9600 m) (others similar except Bolingbroke III, 26,000 ft); range 1,950 miles (3138 km); (I) 1,125 miles; (Bolingbrokes) 1,800 miles; (V) 1,600 miles.

Armament: one 0·303 in Vickers K in nose, two 0·303 in Brownings in FN.54 chin turret and two

0·303 in Brownings in dorsal turret; (I) single fixed Browning and single Vickers K in dorsal turret; (IF, IVF) four fixed Brownings under fuselage; bomb load 1,000 lb (454 kg) internal (non-standard aircraft had underwing 500 lb racks).

History: first flight (Type 142) 12 April 1935; (142M Blenheim I) 25 June 1936; service delivery November 1936; termination of production (VD) June 1943; withdrawal from service (Finland) 1956.

It was the newspaper magnate Lord Rothermere who asked the Bristol company to build him a fast executive aircraft to carry a pilot and six passengers at 240 mph, appreciably faster than any RAF fighter in 1934. The result was the Type 142, the first modern stressed-skin monoplane in Britain with retractable landing gear, flaps and, after a wait, imported American variable-pitch propellers. Its performance staggered even the designer, Barnwell, for on Air Ministry test it reached 307 mph. The inevitable result was the Blenheim bomber, to produce which Barnwell designed a new fuselage with mid-wing and bomb bay beneath it. Pilot and nav/bomb-aimer sat in the neat glazed nose, and a part-retractable dorsal turret was added behind

the wing. The Blenheim I was ordered in what were huge quantities to a company almost devoid of work. Ultimately 1,134 were built, many of which made gallant bombing raids early in the war and were then converted to IF fighter configuration (some having the AI Mk III, the first operational fighter radar in the world). The fast new bomber excited intense foreign interest and many were exported to Finland, Turkey, Yugoslavia, Lithuania, Rumania and Greece. To provide a nav/bomb-aimer station ahead of the pilot the nose was then lengthened 3 ft and this type was named Bolingbroke, a name retained for all the variety of Blenheims built in Canada (the Bolingbroke Mk III being a twin-float seaplane). A revised asymmetric nose was adopted for production in the speedy Mk IV, which later acquired a fighter gun pack (IVF) or a manual rear-firing chin gun (IVL), finally having a two-gun chin turret. Made by Bristol, Avro and Rootes, like the Mk I, the IV was the main combat version with the RAF, 3,297 being delivered and making many daylight missions in many theatres. The heavily armed and armoured two-seat Bisley attack aircraft did not go into production, but the three-seat equivalent did, as the Blenheim Mk V. Heavy and underpowered the 902 VDs served in North Africa and the Far East.

Bristol Type 152 Beaufort

Beaufort I to VIII
Type: four-seat torpedo bomber.
Engines: two 1,130 hp Bristol Taurus VI 14-cylinder sleeve-valve radials (most other marks, two 1,200 hp Pratt & Whitney Twin Wasp).
Dimensions: span 57 ft 10 in (17·63 m); length 44 ft 2 in (13·46 m); height 14 ft 3 in (4·34 m).
Weights: empty 13,107 lb (5945 kg); loaded 21,230 lb (9629 kg).
Performance: maximum speed 260 mph (418 km/h) clean, 225 mph (362 km/h) with torpedo; service ceiling 16,500 ft (5030 m); range 1,600 miles (2575 km).
Armament: various, but typically two 0·303 in Vickers K in dorsal turret and one fixed forward-firing in left wing, plus one 0·303 in Browning in remote-control chin blister. Alternatively four 0·303 in Brownings in wing, two Brownings manually aimed from beam windows and (Mk II) twin Brownings in dorsal turret (final 140 Australian Mk VIII, two 0·50 in Brownings in dorsal turret). One 18 in torpedo semi-external to left of centreline or bomb load of 2,000 lb (907 kg).
History: first flight 15 October 1938; first delivery October 1939; first flight of Australian aircraft (Mk V) August 1941; last delivery (Australia) August 1944.

Derived from the Blenheim, the torpedo-carrying Beaufort was inevitably heavier because the Air Staff demanded a crew of four. Performance on Mercury

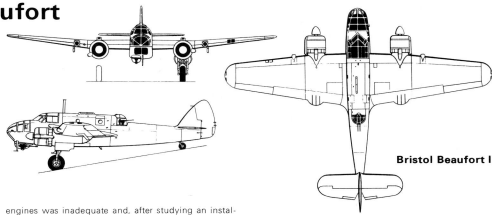

Bristol Beaufort I

engines was inadequate and, after studying an installation of the sleeve-valve Perseus, the choice fell on the Taurus, an extremely neat two-row engine only 46 in in diameter. A clever installation was schemed for this but it overheated and various engine troubles held the programme back in the early days, but 22 and 42 Sqns of Coastal Command were fully operational by August 1940. As well as laying hundreds of mines they bombed the battlecruiser *Scharnhorst*, torpedoed the *Gneisenau* and sank numerous smaller ships. In 1939 plans were laid for Beaufort production in Australia and, because of the difficulty of supplying engines from Britain, the Australian Mks V-VIII had

Twin Wasp engines, most of them made in Australia. A large batch of British Beauforts (Mk II) had this engine, but a Merlin-Beaufort was abandoned and from No 165 the Mk II reverted to later models of Taurus. The total built was 2,080, including 700 built in Australia for duty in the Southwest Pacific. Australian models had a bigger fin and progressed through four series with different equipment, ending with transport and trainer versions. The finest RAAF missions were against Japanese fleets at Normanby Island, in the Timor Sea and around New Guinea and the Solomons.
Type 156 Beaufighter see page 36

Bristol Type 163 Buckingham

Buckingham B.I and Buckmaster
Type: four-seat day bomber (later transport).
Engines: two 2,520 hp Bristol Centaurus VII 18-cylinder sleeve-valve radials.
Dimensions: span 71 ft 10 in (21·8 m); length 46 ft 10 in (14·2 m); height 17 ft 7 in (5·36 m).
Weights: empty 24,042 lb (10,910 kg); loaded 38,050 lb (17,270 kg).
Performance: maximum speed 330 mph (528 km/h); high-speed cruise 285 mph (460 km/h); speed for best range 195 mph (315 km/h); initial climb 1,700 ft (516 m)/min; service ceiling 25,000 ft (7620 m); range at 195 mph 3,180 miles (5120 km).
Armament: four fixed 0·303 in Brownings in nose, four in Bristol B.12 dorsal turret and two in B.13 ventral turret; internal bomb capacity 4,000 lb (1814 kg).
History: first flight 4 February 1943; (production B.1) 12 February 1944; termination (Buckmaster) 1946.

This aircraft offers a good example of the shortcomings of the official procedure of issuing a specification and then trying to design an aeroplane to meet it. Throughout 1939 and 1940 the Air Staff studied layouts for bombers developed from the Beaufighter and, in October 1940, Bristol chief designer Leslie Frise (he succeeded Barnwell, killed in 1938) proposed an enlarged aircraft named Beaumont. Eventually specification B.2/41 emerged and it was almost impossible

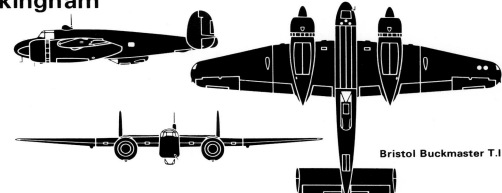

Bristol Buckmaster T.I

to meet. It called for a 370 mph bomber with three seats, a range of 1,000 miles with a 2,000 lb bomb load and many other attributes including a ceiling of 15,000 ft in the most adverse climate after failure of either engine. Unlike the Mosquito, it was also to bristle with defensive guns. Fortunately the Bristol engine king, Roy Fedden, had produced the much more powerful Centaurus and this would have provided the answer; but the Air Staff then called for a 1,600 mile range and crew of four. The need for heavy nose armament meant the bomb aimer had to be placed in a

ventral bath under the rear fuselage and difficulties mounted while a big scheme was planned for mass production. Rapid production was arranged with components made by dispersed subcontractors being assembled at the main Bristol plant, which was cleared of Beaufort and Beaufighter work for the purpose. Yet the result, the Buckingham, never saw action, and the last 65 of the 119 built were delivered as transports. From it emerged the Type 166 Buckmaster, of which 112 were built as dual-control trainers.

Bristol Type 164 Brigand

Brigand B.1 to T.5
Type: three-seat attack bomber.
Engines: two 2,810 hp (methanol/water injection) Bristol Centaurus 57 18-cylinder sleeve-valve radials.
Dimensions: span 72 ft 4 in (21·9 m); length 46 ft 5 in (14·1 m); height 17 ft 6 in (5·33 m).
Weights: empty 25,598 lb (11,612 kg); loaded 39,000 lb (17,690 kg).
Performance: maximum speed 360 mph (575 km/h); initial climb 1,500 ft (456 m)/min; service ceiling 26,000 ft (7925 m); range 1,980 miles (3168 km) (with drop tanks 2,800 miles, 4506 km).
Armament: four fixed 20 mm Hispano cannon in forward fuselage; centreline racks for torpedo or up to 2,000 lb (907 kg) bombs; underwing hardpoints for 16 rocket projectiles or other ordnance.
History: first flight 4 December 1944; first delivery (Coastal) June 1946; (B.1) December 1948; last delivery (T.4) 1950; withdrawal from service (T.5) 1958.

So successful was the Beaufighter as a torpedo carrier that the Air Staff decided to investigate aircraft related to it that were specifically designed for the job. First, a Buckingham II was studied with two torpedoes and then a smaller aircraft, derived from the Beaufighter, called Brigand. This carried only one torpedo but had a crew of three seated close together for good communication. Eventually it was discovered this needed

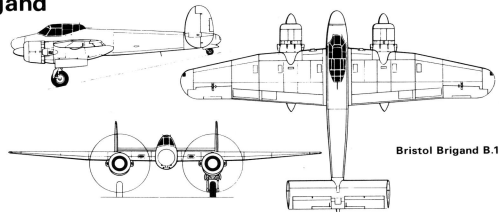

Bristol Brigand B.1

the more powerful Centaurus engine and in this form four prototypes were ordered in March 1943. The aircraft went into production behind the Buckingham, using most of the same jigs, but with a 6 in wider centre section, stronger tail and completely new fuselage. Deliveries were made of the Brigand TF.1 (torpedo fighter) to 36 and 42 Sqns, but with the war over the RAF had a major rethink. The aircraft were recalled and rebuilt as bombers for tropical duty, with clear-view canopies and many detail changes. Altogether

147 Brigands were built, 143 being delivered to the RAF. Most were B.1s, operated with immense skill and daring under gruelling conditions against terrorists in Malaya and the Mau Mau in Kenya. The Met.3 was a weather reconnaissance version, 16 of which made daily penetrations of tropical storms. The T.4 and T.5 were radar trainers. These tough and powerful aircraft served in places unsuited to the wooden Mosquito and worked hard until the arrival of the Canberra.

Bristol Type 156 Beaufighter

Beaufighter I to TF.X (data mainly Mk X)

Type: two-seat torpedo strike fighter (other marks, night fighters, target tugs).

Engines: two 1,770 hp Bristol Hercules XVII 14-cylinder sleeve-valve radials; (Mk II) 1,250 hp R-R Merlin XX; (other marks) different Hercules; (one-offs had R-R Griffons and Wright GR-2600 Cyclones).

Dimensions: span 57 ft 10 in (17·63 m); length 41 ft 8 in (12·6 m) (II, 42 ft 9 in); height 15 ft 10 in (4·84 m).

Weights: empty 15,600 lb (7100 kg) (I, II, 13,800 lb; VI, XI, 14,900 lb); loaded 25,400 lb (11,530 kg) (most other marks, 21,000 lb, 9525 kg).

Performance: maximum speed 312 mph (502 km/h) (fighter marks, 330 mph, 528 km/h); initial climb 1,850 ft (564 m)/min; service ceiling 26,500 ft (8077 m) (fighters, 30,000 ft, 9144 m); range 1,540 miles (2478 km).

Armament: four 20 mm Hispano cannon fixed in underside of forward fuselage (initially hand loaded with 60-round drums, later with belt feed), and one 0·303 in Vickers K aimed by observer (fighters, also six 0·303 in Brownings, two fixed in outer left wing and four in right. One 1,605 lb (728 kg) torpedo on centreline or 2,127 lb (954 kg) and wing racks for eight rocket projectiles or two 1,000 lb (454 kg) bombs.

History: first flight (Type 156 prototype) 17 July 1939; (production Mk I) May 1940; service delivery 27 July 1940; first flight (Mk 21, Australia) 26 May 1944; last delivery from new (UK) September 1945, (Australia) October 1945.

During the critical years 1935–39 the most glaring gap in the RAF's armoury was the lack of any long-range fighter, any cannon-armed fighter and any fighter capable of effective bomber escort and night fighting. Leslie Frise and engine designer Fedden talked at length of the possibility of creating a single type out of the Blenheim and Beaufort families that could meet all demands, but no official requirement was forthcoming — other than the strange F.11/37 Specification for a fighter with a heavily armed cannon turret. Eventually the two Bristol leaders did the obvious thing: they proposed a new twin-Hercules two-seater carrying enough armament to blast anything in front of it out of the sky. By using the wing, tail, landing gear, systems and jigs of the Beaufort it could be put into production quickly. The Air Ministry was enthusiastic and the first of what was to be an historic war-winning aeroplane took the air only six months later. A snub-nosed battleship, it was immensely strong, surprisingly manoeuvrable and a great basis for development. Almost its only operational shortcoming was a tendency to swing on takeoff, which later addition of a large dorsal fin and dihedral tailplane did not cure.

Early models barely exceeded 300 mph with low-power Hercules and, in the absence of Griffon engines, 450 were fitted with Merlins, but these were less powerful and accentuated instability. Speed was soon judged less important when the need for night fighters to beat the Blitz became urgent. Equipped with AI Mk IV radar the early deliveries to 25 and 29 Sqns were a major reason for the Luftwaffe giving up the Blitz on Britain. Eventually the "Beau" served on all fronts, having thimble-nose AI Mk VII in 1942, torpedoes in 1943, rockets in 1944 and a spate of special installations in 1945. A total of 5,564 were built in England and 364 in Australia, the last fighter and torpedo versions serving with Coastal Command, the Far East Air Force and the RAAF until 1960. To the Luftwaffe it was the most feared opponent even 500 miles out in the Atlantic; to the Japanese it was "Whispering death", so named because of the quietness of the sleeve-valve engines. It was sheer luck the "Beau" could be produced in time.

Type 163 Buckingham and Type 164 Brigand see page 35

The cutaway shows the basic Mk I fighter, without AI radar

Bristol Beaufighter I cutaway drawing key:

1 Starboard navigation light (forward) and formation-keeping light (rear)
2 Wing structure
3 Aileron adjustable tab
4 Starboard aileron
5 Four Browning 0·303in machine guns
6 Machine gun ports
7 Starboard outer fuel tank (87 gal/395 litres)
8 Split trailing-edge flaps, hydraulically actuated
9 Fixed trailing edge
10 Flap operating jack
11 Starboard nacelle tail fairing
12 Oil tank (17 gal/77 litres)
13 Starboard inner fuel tank (188 gal/855 litres)
14 Cabin air duct
15 Hinged leading-edge for access
16 Engine bulkhead
17 Engine bearers
18 Auxiliary intake
19 Supercharger air intake
20 Cooling gills
21 Bristol Hercules III 14-cylinder sleeve-valve radial engine, 1,650 hp
22 De Havilland Hydromatic propeller
23 Spinner
24 Lockheed oleo-pneumatic shock-absorber
25 Starboard mainwheel, Dunlop brakes
26 Forward identification lamp in nose cap
27 Rudder pedals
28 Control column
29 Cannon ports
30 Seat adjusting lever
31 Pilot's seat
32 Instrument panel
33 Clear-vision panel
34 Flat bullet-proof windscreen
35 Fixed canopy (sideways-hinged on later aircraft)
36 Spar carry-through step
37 Nose/centre section attachment
38 Fuselage/centre section attachment
39 Pilot's entry/emergency escape hatchway
40 Underfloor cannon blast tubes
41 Fuselage/centre section attachment
42 Centre section attachment longeron reinforcement
43 Cabin air duct
44 Cannon heating duct
45 Rear spar carry-through
46 Bulkhead cut-out (observer access to front hatch)
47 Bulkhead
48 Hydraulic header tank
49 Aerial mast
50 Monocoque fuselage construction
51 Starboard cannon (two Hispano 20mm)
52 Floor level
53 Steps
54 Observer's swivel seat (normally forward-facing)
55 Radio controls and intercom
56 Observer's cupola
57 Hinged panel
58 Aerial
59 Oxygen bottles
60 Vertical control cable shaft
61 Sheet metal bulkhead
62 Control cables
63 Tailplane structure
64 Elevator
65 Elevator balance tab
66 Fin (extended forwards in dorsal fin on later aircraft)
67 Rudder balance
68 Rudder framework
69 Tail lights: formation-keeping (upper) and navigation (lower)
70 Rudder
71 Rudder trim tab
72 Elevator trim tab
73 Elevator balance tab
74 Elevator structure
75 Port tailplane (12 deg dihedral on later aircraft)

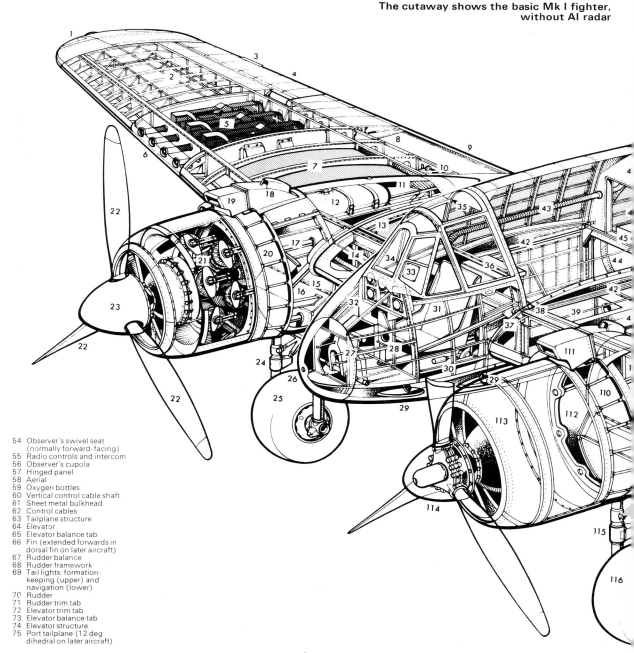

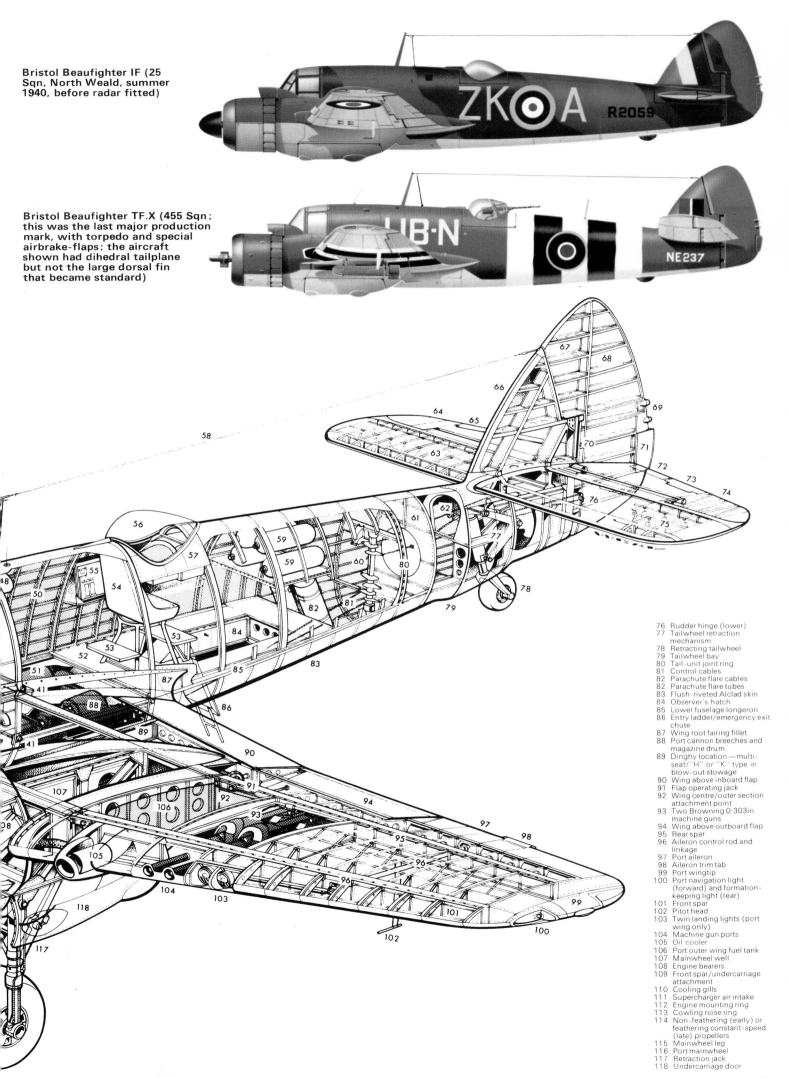

Bristol Beaufighter IF (25 Sqn, North Weald, summer 1940, before radar fitted)

Bristol Beaufighter TF.X (455 Sqn; this was the last major production mark, with torpedo and special airbrake-flaps; the aircraft shown had dihedral tailplane but not the large dorsal fin that became standard)

76 Rudder hinge (lower)
77 Tailwheel retraction mechanism
78 Retracting tailwheel
79 Tailwheel bay
80 Tail-unit joint ring
81 Control cables
82 Parachute flare cables
82 Parachute flare tubes
83 Flush-riveted Alclad skin
84 Observer's hatch
85 Lower fuselage longeron
86 Entry ladder/emergency exit chute
87 Wing root fairing fillet
88 Port cannon breeches and magazine drum
89 Dinghy location—multi-seat/"H" or "K" type in blow-out stowage
90 Wing above inboard flap
91 Flap operating jack
92 Wing centre/outer section attachment point
93 Two Browning 0·303in machine guns
94 Wing above outboard flap
95 Rear spar
96 Aileron control rod and linkage
97 Port aileron
98 Aileron trim tab
99 Port wingtip
100 Port navigation light (forward) and formation-keeping light (rear)
101 Front spar
102 Pitot head
103 Twin landing lights (port wing only)
104 Machine gun ports
105 Oil cooler
106 Port outer wing fuel tank
107 Mainwheel well
108 Engine bearers
109 Front spar/undercarriage attachment
110 Cooling gills
111 Supercharger air intake
112 Engine mounting ring
113 Cowling nose ring
114 Non-feathering (early) or feathering constant-speed (late) propellers
115 Mainwheel leg
116 Port mainwheel
117 Retraction jack
118 Undercarriage door

Britten-Norman Defender

BN-2A Defender
Type: multi-role light military aircraft.
Engines: two 300 hp Lycoming IO-540-K1B5 six-cylinder direct-injection horizontally-opposed.
Dimensions: span (extended raked tips) 53 ft (16·15 m); length 35 ft 8 in (10·86 m); height 13 ft 8¾ in (4·18 m).
Weights: empty 3,708 lb (1682 kg); loaded 6,600 lb (2993 kg).
Performance: maximum speed (clean) 176 mph (283 km/h), (pylons loaded) 168 mph (270 km/h); initial climb (clean) 1,300 ft (5180 m)/min; service ceiling 17,000 ft (5180 m); range (maximum combat load) 375 miles (603 km), (maximum fuel) 1,723 miles (2772 km).
Armament: weapons normally all carried on four underwing hardpoints, inner pair stressed to 700 lb (318 kg) and outers to 450 lb (204 kg). Typical loads include 7·62 mm Minigun pods, twin 7·62 mm machine guns, bombs up to 500 lb (227 kg), Matra or SURA rocket dispensers, wide variety of grenades and markers, loud hailers, guided missiles or 50 gal (227 litre) drop tanks.
History: first flight (civil Islander) 13 June 1965; (Defender) March 1971.

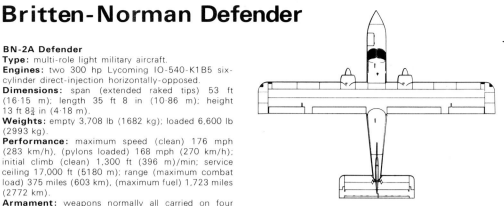

BN-2A Islander/Defender

The Britten-Norman Islander has become one of the dominant light utility transports all over the world and it was natural that the enterprising company should have produced a military version. Roles for which the Defender has been planned include internal security, long-range patrol, search/rescue, forward air control, battlefield supply and casualty evacuation, recon-naissance and mapping, and indeed all forms of light limited-war combat, including ground attack, anti-ship and psy-war (psychological) operations. One of the major options is nose-mounted weather radar, providing a marine search capability. Within a year of first flight the Defender had been cleared for most kinds of ordnance dropping, rocket launching and gun firing, including firing of beam guns in the fuselage. Among the first operators of this versatile and efficient aircraft are the Abu Dhabi Defence Force, Ghana Air Force, Guyana Defence Force, Jamaica Defence Force, Malagasy Air Force, Royal Hong Kong Auxiliary Air Force and Sultan of Oman's Air Force.

Canadair CP-107 (CL-28) Argus

CP-107 Argus 2 (415 Sqn)

Argus Mk 1 and 2
Type: Maritime patrol and anti-submarine aircraft with normal crew of 15.
Engines: four 3,700 hp (water-injection rating) Wright R-3350-32W (TC18-EA1) Turbo-Compound 18-cylinder piston engines with exhaust turbines geared to crankshaft.
Dimensions: span 142 ft 3½ in (43·37 m); length 128 ft 3 in (39·1 m); height 36 ft 9 in (11·2 m).
Weights: empty 81,500 lb (36,967 kg); loaded 148,000 lb (67,130 kg).
Performance: maximum speed 288 mph (463 km/h) at sea level, 315 mph (507 km/h) at 20,000 ft (6096 m); initial climb 1,700 ft (518 m)/min; service ceiling 29,000 ft (8840 m); range at 190 mph (306 km/h) at low level 5,900 miles (9495 km); endurance 30 hours.
Armament: two 18 ft 6 in (5·65 m) internal bays accommodate all normal large sonics, depth bombs,

acoustic torpedoes, homing torpedoes, mines and other stores, to total weight of 8,000 lb (3629 kg). Additional 7,600 lb (3450 kg) can be carried on two underwing racks.
History: first flight 29 March 1957; (33rd and last aircraft) 13 July 1960.

In the early 1950s the Royal Canadian Air Force examined ways of replacing the Lancaster MR.10 and Catalina as standard ocean patrol aircraft. It needed great endurance and the ability to carry comprehensive ASW (anti-submarine warfare) search and attack equipment. It eventually adopted the solution of Canadair Ltd, which like its US parent, General Dynamics, was anxious to produce developed versions of the British Britannia turboprop airliner. To meet the RCAF need the CL-28 was produced by replacing the Britannia's turboprops by Turbo-Compound engines

giving maximum range and endurance at low level, together with a new unpressurised fuselage incorporating weapon bays ahead of and behind the low wing. Comprehensive equipment was installed including APS-20 radar in the nose, desks for seven sensor operators and, in the rear fuselage, batteries of sonobuoys dropped or fired through dispensers. MAD equipment resulted in the long tail "stinger". At the 13th aircraft production switched to the Mk 2 with a more advanced British radar with smaller scanner and completely rearranged communication and navigation equipment plus ECM gear requiring two small dorsal aerials. The wing pylons were planned for the defunct Petrel missile and have seldom been used. Arguses have served well for almost 20 years with four squadrons of the Canadian Armed Forces and will eventually be replaced by the far more costly Lockheed P-3C Orion.

CRDA Cant Z.1007 Alcione

Z.1007 bis (230a Squadriglia, 95o Gruppo)

Z.1007, 1007 bis and 1018
Type: four/five-seat medium bomber.
Engines: three 1,000 hp Piaggio P.XIbis RC40 14-cylinder two-row radials.
Dimensions: span 81 ft 4 in (24·8 m); length 60 ft 4 in (18·4 m); height 17 ft 1½ in (5·22 m).
Weights: empty 19,000 lb (8630 kg); loaded 28,260–30,029 lb (12,840–13,620 kg).
Performance: maximum speed 280 mph (448 km/h); initial climb 1,550 ft (472 m)/min; service ceiling 26,500 ft (8100 m); range 800 miles (1280 km) with maximum bombs, 3,100 miles (4989 km) with maximum fuel.
Armament: (first 25) four 7·7 mm Breda-SAFAT machine guns in dorsal turret, two beam hatches and ventral position; (remainder) as before except dorsal and ventral guns 12·7 mm Breda-SAFAT; internal

bomb capacity 4,410 lb (2000 kg); alternatively two 1,000 lb (454 kg) torpedoes and four bombs up to 551 lb (250 kg) each on underwing racks.
History: first flight May 1937; (first production aircraft) 1939; entry to service 1939.

A famous Italian naval yard, the Cantieri Monfalcone (Trieste), entered the aircraft construction business in 1923, forming a subsidiary called Cantieri Riuniti dell' Adriatico (always shortened to Cant). Their first products were seaplanes and flying boats and the most important of these was the three-engined Z.506B Airone (Heron) twin-float seaplane used in large numbers in World War II. Designer Filippo Zappata then produced a landplane bomber version, powered by three 840 hp Isotta-Fraschini Asso inverted-vee liquid-cooled engines. Like the seaplane this new

bomber, the Z.1007, was built entirely of wood. It received a generally favourable report from the Regia Aeronautica's test pilots and after modifications went into production, two other firms – Meridionali and Piaggio – later being brought in to increase rate of output. Nearly all the several hundred production Alciones were powered by the much better Piaggio radial engine, and this version, the Z.1007bis, also had longer fuselage, bigger wings and stronger landing gear. Almost half also had twin tail fins. Though easy meat for RAF fighters, Alciones were bravely operated throughout the Mediterranean, and many even served on the Russian front. Various developments culminated in the excellent twin-engined Z.1018 Leone (Lion), with metal airframe and 1,350 hp engines, but few of these had been delivered when Italy surrendered in 1943.

Caproni Ca 1 to Ca 5

Ca 30 to Ca 47 (military designations)
(data for 33)
Type: four-seat heavy day bomber.
Engines: three 150 hp Isotta-Fraschini V-4B six-cylinder water-cooled.
Dimensions: span 72 ft 10 in (22·2 m); length 35 ft 9 in (10·9 m); height 12 ft 2 in (3·7 m).
Weights: empty, 5,512 (2500 kg); loaded 7,302 lb (3315 kg);
Performance: maximum speed 94 mph (151 km/h); service ceiling 13,450 ft (4100 m); range with bomb load 280 miles (450 km).
Armament: gunner's cockpit in nose with 6·5 mm Revelli machine gun (sometimes, 20 mm or other calibre of cannon) and gunner's platform at rear with one, two or three 6·5 mm Revelli; external racks for 1,543 lb (700 kg) bombs.
History: first flight (Ca 30) 1913; (Ca 31) late 1914; (production Ca 32) May 1915; (Ca 33) mid-1916; last delivery (Ca 33) 1918; (Ca 36M) after 1925.

Apart from Sikorsky's great series of four-engined aircraft in Czarist Russia, Italy was the first nation in the world to produce heavy bombers. This was entirely due to the Società di Ing Caproni, the first of what was to become the biggest group of industrial companies in Italy. In 1913, at a time when the British had no explicit military aircraft at all and generally doubted

that flying machines would even be much help for reconnaissance, Caproni designed, built and flew the Ca 30 bomber. It had a short central nacelle in which were the three 80 hp Gnome rotary engines, one driving a pusher screw and the others being geared to tractor propellers on the tail booms. With the Ca 31 the tractor screws were driven by engines mounted directly on the front of the tail booms, while the Ca 32 had 100 hp or 120 hp Fiat engines. This went into operational service, a total of 164 being delivered by 1917. The Ca 32, called Ca 2 by the Corpo Aeronautica Militare, established a proud tradition of arduous bombing missions on the Austro-Hungarian front over most difficult mountainous terrain. The Ca 33 (Ca 3)

Ca 3 (Ca 33)

was the most important Caproni bomber, 269 being built and giving rise to many later versions. Its rear gunner had to stand for up to six hours in freezing slipstream within inches of the rear propeller. The 36M was a post-war version produced in the first years of Mussolini's regime. Later Capronis were bigger, the largest (Ca 40–43) being triplanes. The final wartime family, the 44-47 (Ca 5), were made in France and the USA.

Caproni Ca 133

Ca 133 (Fleigerregiment 2, Austrian AF)

Ca 101, 111 and 133 (data for 133)
Type: colonial bomber and transport.
Engines: three 450/460 hp Piaggio P.VII RC14 Stella seven-cylinder radials.
Dimensions: span 69 ft 8 in (21·3 m); length 50 ft 4¾ in (15·35 m); height 13 ft 1 in (4 m).
Weights: empty 8,598 lb (3900 kg); loaded 14,330 lb (6500 kg).
Performance: maximum speed 174 mph (280 km/h); initial climb 940 ft (286 m)/min; service ceiling 21,325 ft (6500 m); range 839 miles (1350 km).
Armament: one or two 7·7 mm or one 12·7 mm machine gun on pivoted mounting in roof at trailing edge of wing; one machine gun in sliding hatchway in

floor of rear fuselage; often one 7·7 mm on each side in aft window-openings; bomb load (up to 2,200 lb, 1000 kg) carried in internal bay and on external racks under fuselage.
History: first flight (Ca 101) 1932; (Ca 111) 1933; (Ca 133) 1935; end of production, prior to 1938.

As Mussolini restored "the lost colonies" and Italy forcibly built up an overseas empire, so did the need arise for "colonial" type aircraft similar to the British Wapiti and Vincent. Caproni produced the Ca 101 to meet this need, at least 200 being delivered in the early 1930s to serve as bomber, troop carrier, reconnaissance aircraft, ground attack machines and, most of all, to

supply forward troops with urgent stores. Powered by three 235 hp Alfa Romeo engines, it was made of robust welded steel tube with fabric covering. The Ca 111, powered by a single 950 hp Isotta-Fraschini engine, gave even better service and survived the Albanian and Ethiopian campaigns in World War II. The Ca 133 was the most important of all and many hundreds were built. When Italy entered the war in 1940 it equipped 14 Squadriglie di Bombardimento Terrestri (bomber squadrons), nearly all in East or North Africa. Though scorned by the RAF and easy meat on the ground or in the air, these versatile STOL machines worked hard and well and finished up as ambulances and transports in Libya, on the Russian Front and in Italy (on both sides after the 1943 surrender).

Caproni Ca 135

Ca 135bis (4/III Bomb Group, Hungarian AF)

Ca 135 and 135bis (data for 135bis)
Type: five-seat medium bomber.
Engines: two 1,000 hp Piaggio P.XIbis RC40 14-cylinder two-row radials.
Dimensions: span 61 ft 8 in (18·75 m); length 47 ft 1 in (14·4 m); height 11 ft 2 in (3·4 m).
Weights: empty 9,921 lb (4500 kg); loaded 18,740 lb (8500 kg).
Performance: maximum speed 273 mph (440 km/h); initial climb 1,435 ft (437 m)/min; service ceiling 22,966 ft (7000 m); range with bomb load 746 miles (1200 km).
Armament: three Breda-SAFAT turrets, each mounting one 12·7 mm or two 7·7 mm guns, in nose, dorsal and ventral positions (dorsal and ventral retractable); bomb cells in fuselage and inner wings for up to 3,527 lb (1600 kg) weapon load.

History: first flight (135) 1 April 1935; (135bis) about November 1937.

When the great Caproni combine took on Breda's designer Cesare Pallavicino it embarked on a series of modern aircraft of higher performance. The most important appeared to be the Ca 135 medium bomber, designed in the summer of 1934 to meet a Regia Aeronautica specification. A curious blend of wooden wings, light-alloy monocoque forward fuselage and steel tube plus fabric rear fuselage and tail, the prototype had two 800 hp Isotta-Fraschini Asso engines but no guns. After over a year of testing the government ordered 14 as the Tipo Spagna to serve in the Spanish civil war; Peru bought six Tipo Peru, eventually

purchasing 32. Yet the Ca 135 was not as good as the S.M.79 and Z.1007 by rival makers and the Regia Aeronautica kept delaying a decision. More powerful Fiat A.80 RC41 radials improved behaviour but at the expense of reliability and a good 135 did not appear until the Milan Aero Show in October 1937, when the Piaggio-engined 135bis was displayed. Though never adopted by the Regia Aeronautica it was frequently identified as having been used against Malta, Yugoslavia and Greece! The real raiders in these cases were probably BR.20s, but the 135 bis did find a customer: the Hungarian Air Force. Several hundred were operated by that service whilst attached to Luftflotte IV in the campaign on the Eastern Front in 1941–43.

Caudron G. series

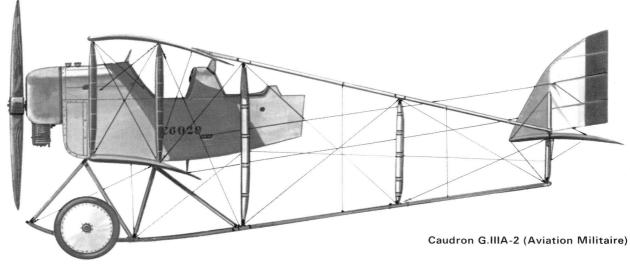

Caudron G.IIIA-2 (Aviation Militaire)

Caudron G. III and IV (data for G.IVB-2)
Type: two-seat reconnaissance bomber.
Engines: two 80 hp Le Rhône 9C nine-cylinder rotaries (alternatively, 100 hp Anzanis).
Dimensions: span 56 ft 5 in (17·2 m); length 23 ft 7½ in (7·2 m); height 8 ft 6 in (2·6 m).
Weights: empty 2,425 lb (1100 kg); loaded 2,932 lb (1330 kg).
Performance: maximum speed 82 mph (132 km/h); service ceiling 14,760 ft (4500 m); range 249 miles (400 km).
Armament: one 0·303 in Lewis or Vickers machine gun on pivoted mount in observer's (front) cockpit; sometimes second similar gun on top wing aimed by same observer; underwing racks for bomb load of 220 lb (100 kg).
History: first flight (G.III) 1914; (G.IV) March 1915; termination of production (G.IV) May 1918.

In the early war years the Caudron brothers, Gaston and René, were among the most successful of Allied planemakers. So great was the demand for their aircraft that they allowed them to be built by any rival company without any royalty payment. As a result the G.III (often written G.3) was made in vast quantities by many firms and used at first as the G.IIIA-2 reconnaissance machine on the Western Front by the RFC, French and Belgian Air Forces and by the forces of Italy and Russia. This two-seater had an 80 hp rotary on the nose but a curious tail-boom layout as if it were a pusher. The bigger G.IV had twin engines and greater span. Though still slow and primitive, the G.IV was as reliable and easy to fly as its predecessor and was very popular. Precise production totals are not known; though fewer than for the G.III, the total was many hundreds, about half having the 100 hp Anzani engine and rather higher performance. The final batch were trainers ordered in 1918 for the American Expeditionary Force. The French Aviation Militaire equipped 38 escadrilles with the Caudron G series aircraft and at least as large a number served with Allied nations.

Caudron R.11

Caudron R.11A-3 (Aviation Militaire)

R.11A-3
Type: three-seat reconnaissance and escort fighter.
Engines: two 215 hp (alternatively, 200, 235 or 300 hp) Hispano-Suiza vee-8 water-cooled.
Dimensions: span 58 ft 9 in (17·9 m); length 36 ft 9½ in (11·22 m); height 9 ft 2¼ in (2·8 m).
Weights: empty 3,130 lb (1422 kg); loaded 4,773 lb (2167 kg).
Performance: maximum speed 114 mph (183 km/h); climb to 6560 ft (2000 m) in 8 min 10 sec; ceiling (presumably absolute) 19,520 ft (5950 m); endurance 3 hours.
Armament: two 0·303 in Lewis machine guns in gunner's cockpits at front and rear, from October 1917 additionally with one extra gun in floor of either or both cockpits (thus total five or six); external bomb load possible up to 660 lb (300 kg) but seldom carried.

History: first flight (R.4) June 1915; (R.11) March 1917; service delivery December 1917.

Gaston Caudron was killed in December 1915 flying a production R.4, a development of the G.4 that transformed the "stick and string" machine into a streamlined and formidable combat aircraft. Brother René then went one better with the R.11, a much more powerful successor to the R.4 intended to carry heavier bomb loads. The R.11 was a fine-looking three-seater, with the pilot between the two gunners. It could have been one of the most important aircraft of the war, had it not been for persistent and serious trouble with the geared Hispano engines. Even as it was the R.11 was made in big numbers (certainly 500 and possibly 1,000) and, despite the engine problem, entered service in a trickle from the end of 1917. Though intended as a bomber, the R.11 really found its niche as an escort for such bombers as the Bre.XIV. Unlike single-seat scouts the three-seat Caudrons could hold their formation tight alongside the bombers while their gunners swept the sky with five or six guns. The R.11 was strong and fully aerobatic and as delightful to fly as the G series. Had the war continued, this excellent fighting machine would have replaced the Letord 1, 2 and 4 as standard French reconnaissance aircraft.

Cessna Model 318, A-37

A-37, -37A and -37B (Model 318E) (data for -37B)
Type: two-seat light strike aircraft.
Engines: two 2,850 lb (1293 kg) thrust General Electric J85-17A single-shaft turbojets.
Dimensions: span (over tip tanks) 35 ft 10½ in (10·93 m); length (not including refuelling probe) 29 ft 3 in (8·92 m); height 8 ft 10½ in (2·7 m).
Weights: empty 6,211 lb (2817 kg); loaded 14,000 lb (6350 kg).
Performance: maximum speed 507 mph (816 km/h) at 16,000 ft (4875 m); initial climb at gross weight 6,990 ft (2130 m)/min; service ceiling 41,765 ft (12,730 m); range (maximum weapons) 460 miles (740 km), (maximum fuel) 1,012 miles (1628 km).
Armament: one 7·62 mm GAU-2B/A six-barrel Minigun in nose; eight wing pylon stations, two inners for up to 870 lb (394 kg), intermediate for 600 lb (272 kg) and outers for 500 lb (227 kg); maximum ordnance load 5,680 lb (2576 kg).
History: first flight (XT-37) 12 October 1954; (YAT-37D) 22 October 1963; (A-37B) September 1967.

The Cessna Model 318 was the first American jet trainer. With two 920 lb (417 kg) thrust Continental J69 (Turboméca Marboré licence) engines and side-

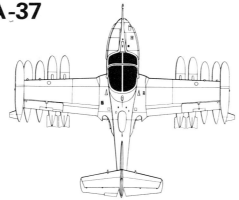

Cessna A-37B

by-side seats it was a very attractive machine. With more powerful J69 engines it remained in production in 1975 with more than 1,300 delivered to the USAF and seven other air forces. It was logical to fit the much more powerful J85 engine and restress the airframe to carry greater loads in arduous combat duties. The work began in 1960 at the time of the upsurge of interest in Co-In (counter-insurgency) aircraft to fight "brushfire wars". Deliveries of A-37A aircraft converted from T-37 trainers began in May 1967 and a squadron of 25 had flown 10,000 combat missions in Vietnam in an extensive evaluation by early 1968. The slightly more powerful A-37B is the definitive production version and by 1975 deliveries had reached about 600, mainly to the USAF, Air Reserve and Air National Guard, but also to South Vietnam, Peru and Guatemala. The A-37B is not pressurised, nor does it have ejection seats, but the dual pilots are protected by layered nylon flak curtains. The wealth of nav/com avionics and possible underwing stores is impressive and nearly all B models have a fixed nose refuelling probe.

Commonwealth Boomerang

CA-12 to CA-19 Boomerang (data for CA-12)
Type: single-seat fighter.
Engine: 1,200 hp Pratt & Whitney R-1830-S3C4G Twin Wasp 14-cylinder two-row radial.
Dimensions: span 36 ft 3 in (11 m); length 25 ft 6 in (7·77 m); height 11 ft 6 in (3·5 m).
Weights: empty 5,450 lb (2474 kg); loaded 7,600 lb (3450 kg).
Performance: maximum speed 296 mph (474 km/h); service ceiling 29,000 ft (8845 m); range at 190 mph (304 km/h) 930 miles (1490 km).
Armament: normally, two 20 mm Hispano cannon and four 0·303 in Browning machine guns in wings.
History: first flight 29 May 1942; first delivery August 1942; final deliveries, early 1944.

When Australia suddenly found itself in the front line, in December 1941, it had no modern fighters save a few Buffaloes supplied to the RAAF in Singapore. To try to produce a stop-gap quickly the Commonwealth Aircraft Corporation at Fishermen's Bend, Melbourne, decided to design and build their own. But the design

team, under Wing Commander Laurence J. Wackett, was severely restricted. The new fighter had to be based on the familiar North American trainer series, which since 1938 had served as the basis for the excellent Wirraway general-purpose combat machine and trainer, of which 755 were made by CAC by 1946. Moreover the only powerful engine available was the 1,200 hp Twin Wasp, judged by 1942 to be much too low-powered for first-line fighters elsewhere. Despite these restrictions the resulting machine was tough, outstandingly manoeuvrable and by no means out-

classed by the Japanese opposition. Wackett's team worked day and night to design the CA-12 in a matter of weeks and build and fly the prototype in a further 14 weeks. Testing and production went ahead together and, as there were no real snags, the first of 105 CA-12s were soon fighting in New Guinea. There followed 95 CA-13s with minor changes and 49 CA-19s, as well as a CA-14 with turbocharged engine and square tail. Boomerangs did not carry bombs but often marked targets for "heavies" and undertook close support with their guns.

CA-13 Boomerang (5 Sqn, RAAF)

Consolidated Vultee Model 28 Catalina

PBY-1 to PBY-5A Catalina (data for -5)
Type: maritime patrol flying boat with normal crew of seven.
Engines: two 1,200 hp Pratt & Whitney R-1830-92 Twin Wasp 14-cylinder two-row radials.
Dimensions: span 104 ft (31·72 m); length 63 ft 11 in (19·5 m); height 18 ft 10 in (5·65 m).
Weights: empty 17,465 lb (7974 kg); loaded 34,000 lb (15,436 kg).
Performance: maximum speed 196 mph (314 km/h); climb to 5,000 ft (1525 m) in 4 min 30 sec; service ceiling 18,200 ft (5550 m); range at 100 mph (161 km/h) 3,100 miles (4960 km).
Armament: US Navy, typically one 0·30 in or 0·50 in Browning in nose, one 0·50 in in each waist blister and one in "tunnel" in underside behind hull step; RAF typically six 0·303 in Vickers K (sometimes Brownings) arranged one in nose, one in tunnel and pairs in blisters; wing racks for 2,000 lb (907 kg) of bombs and other stores.
History: first flight (XP3Y-1) 21 March 1935; first delivery (PBY-1) October 1936; (Model 28–5 Catalina) July 1939; final delivery, after December 1945.

Consolidated of Buffalo battled with Douglas of Santa Monica in 1933 to supply the US Navy with its first cantilever monoplane flying boat. Though the Douglas was good, its rival, designed by Isaac M. Laddon, was to be a classic aircraft and made in bigger numbers than any other flying boat before or since. Its features included two 825 hp Twin Wasps mounted close together on a wide clean wing, on the tips of which were to be found the retracted stabilising floats. The XP3Y-1, as it was called, clocked a speed of 184 mph, which

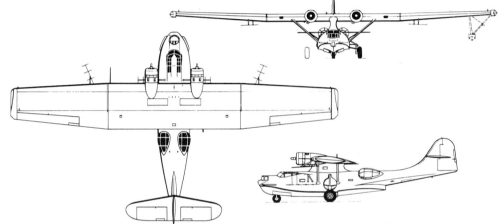

was high for a 1935 flying boat. The order for 60 was huge for those days, but within a decade the total had topped a fantastic 4,000! In 1938 three were bought by the Soviet Union, which urgently tooled up to build its own version, called GST, with M62 engines. In 1939 one was bought by the RAF, which soon placed large orders and called the boat Catalina, a name adopted in the USA in 1942. In December 1939 came the PBY-5A (OA-10) with retractable landing gear, which was named Canso by the RCAF. Many hundreds of both the boat and the amphibian were built by Canadian Vickers (as the PBV-1) and Boeing Canada

(PB2B-1) and revised tall-fin versions were made at New Orleans (PBY-6A) and by the Naval Aircraft Factory at Philadelphia (PBN-1). The "Cat's" exploits are legion. One found the *Bismarck* in mid-Atlantic; one attacked a Japanese carrier in daylight after radioing: "Please inform next of kin"; in 1942 Patrol Squadron 12 started the Black Cat tradition of stealthy night devastation; and one had both ailerons ripped off by a storm but crossed the Atlantic and landed safely. Hundreds served in many countries for long after World War II.

Consolidated Vultee PBY-5A

Model 32 Liberator see page 42

Consolidated Vultee Privateer

PB4Y-2 (P4Y-2) Privateer
Type: maritime patrol bomber with normal crew of 11.
Engines: four 1,200 hp Pratt & Whitney R-1830-94 Twin Wasp 14-cylinder two-row radials.
Dimensions: span 110 ft (33·5 m); length 74 ft (22·6 m); height 26 ft (7·9 m).
Weights: empty 41,000 lb (18,600 kg); loaded 65,000 lb (29,484 kg).
Performance: maximum speed 247 mph (399 km/h); initial climb 800 ft (244 m)/min; service ceiling 19,500 ft (5970 m); range with maximum ordnance load 2,630 miles (4230 km).
Armament: Consolidated nose and tail turrets, two Martin dorsal turrets and two Erco blister-type waist turrets each armed with two 0·50 in Brownings; internal bomb bay similar to B-24 accommodating up to 6,000 lb (2725 kg) bombs, depth charges and other stores. In PB4Y-2B provision to launch and control two ASM-N-2 Bat air-to-surface missiles.
History: first flight (XPB4Y-2) 20 September 1943; first production delivery July 1944; final delivery September 1945.

In May 1943 the US Navy placed a contract with Convair (Consolidated Vultee Aircraft) for a long-range oversea patrol bomber derived from the B-24 Liberator. Three B-24Ds were taken off the San Diego line and largely rebuilt, with fuselages 7 ft longer and completely different interior arrangements, radically altered defensive armament and many airframe changes,

such as hot-air de-icing and engine cowlings in the form of vertical ovals instead of flattened horizontal ones. The distinctive vertical tail was similar to that adopted on the final Liberator transport versions (C-87C, RY-3 and RAF C.IX) and much taller than that of the Liberator B-24N. The Navy bought a straight run of 739, of which 286 were delivered in 1944 and 453 in 1945. From the start performance was lower than that of Liberators of equal power because

of the bigger and heavier airframe, extra equipment and emphasis on low-level missions. Over the ten years of service the Privateer — called P4Y from 1951 — grew more and more radar and secret countermeasures and finally made long electronic probing flights round (and probably over) the edges of the Soviet Union, at least one being shot down in the process. Over 80 served with the French Aéronavale and Chinese Nationalist Air Force.

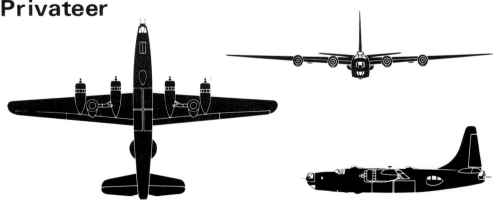

PB4Y-2 Privateer

Consolidated Vultee Model 32 Liberator

For variants, see text (data for B-24J Liberator B.VI)

Type: long-range bomber with normal crew of ten.

Engines: four 1,200 hp Pratt & Whitney R-1830-65 Twin Wasp 14-cylinder two-row radials.

Dimensions: span 110 ft (33·5 m); length 67 ft 2 in (20·47 m); height 18 ft (5·49 m).

Weights: empty 37,000 lb (16,783 kg); loaded 65,000 lb (29,484 kg).

Performance: maximum speed 290 mph (467 km/h); initial climb 900 ft (274 m)/min; service ceiling 28,000 ft (8534 m); range at 190 mph (306 km/h) with 5,000 lb (2268 kg) bomb load, 2,200 miles (3540 km).

Armament: ten 0·50 in Brownings arranged in four electrically operated turrets (Consolidated or Emerson in nose, Martin dorsal, Briggs-Sperry retractable ventral "ball" and Consolidated or Motor Products tail) with two guns each plus two singles in manual waist positions; two bomb bays with roll-up doors with vertical racks on each side of central catwalk for up to 8,000 lb (3629 kg); two 4,000 lb (1814 kg) bombs may be slung on inner-wing racks instead of internal load.

History: first flight (XB-24) 29 December 1939; first delivery (LB-30A) March 1941; first combat service Liberator I) June 1941; first combat service with US Army (B-24C) November 1941; termination of production 31 May 1945; withdrawal from service (various smaller air forces) 1955–56.

This most distinctive aircraft was one of the most important in the history of aviation. Conceived five years after the B-17 it did not, in fact, notably improve on the older bomber's performance and in respect of engine-out performance and general stability and control it was inferior, being a handful for the average

pilot. It was also by far the most complicated and expensive combat aircraft the world had seen — though in this it merely showed the way things were going to be in future. Yet it was built in bigger numbers than any other American aircraft in history, in more versions for more purposes than any other aircraft in history, and served on every front in World War II and with every Allied nation. In terms of industrial effort it transcended anything seen previously in any sphere of endeavour.

It had a curious layout, dictated by the slender Davis wing placed above the tall bomb bays. This wing was efficient in cruising flight, which combined with great fuel capacity to give the "Lib" longer range than any other landplane of its day. But it meant that the main gears were long, and they were retracted outwards by

electric motors, nearly everything on board being electric. Early versions supplied to the RAF were judged not combat-ready, and they began the Atlantic Return Ferry Service as LB-30A transports. Better defences led to the RAF Liberator I, used by Coastal Command with ASV radar and a battery of fixed 20 mm cannon. The RAF Liberator II (B-24C) introduced power turrets and served as a bomber in the Middle East. The first mass-produced version was the B-24D, with turbocharged engines in oval cowls, more fuel and armament and many detail changes; 2,738 served US Bomb Groups in Europe and the Pacific, and RAF Coastal Command closed the mid-Atlantic gap, previously beyond aircraft range, where U-boat packs lurked.

Biggest production of all centred on the B-24G, H and J (Navy PB4Y and RAF B.VI and GR.VI), of

which 10,208 were built. These all had four turrets, and were made by Convair, North American, Ford and Douglas. Other variants included the L and M with different tail turrets, the N with single fin, the luridly painted CB-24 lead ships, the TB-24 trainer, F-7 photo-reconnaissance, C-109 fuel tanker and QB-24 drone. There was also a complete family of Liberator Transport versions, known as C-87 Liberator Express to the Army, RY-3 to the Navy and C.VII and C.IX to the RAF, many having the huge single fin also seen on the PB4Y-2 Privateer. Excluding one-offs such as the redesigned R2Y transport and 1,800 equivalent aircraft delivered as spares, total production of all versions was a staggering 19,203. Their achievements were in proportion.

Model 28 Catalina and Privateer see page 42
For later Convair aircraft see General Dynamics

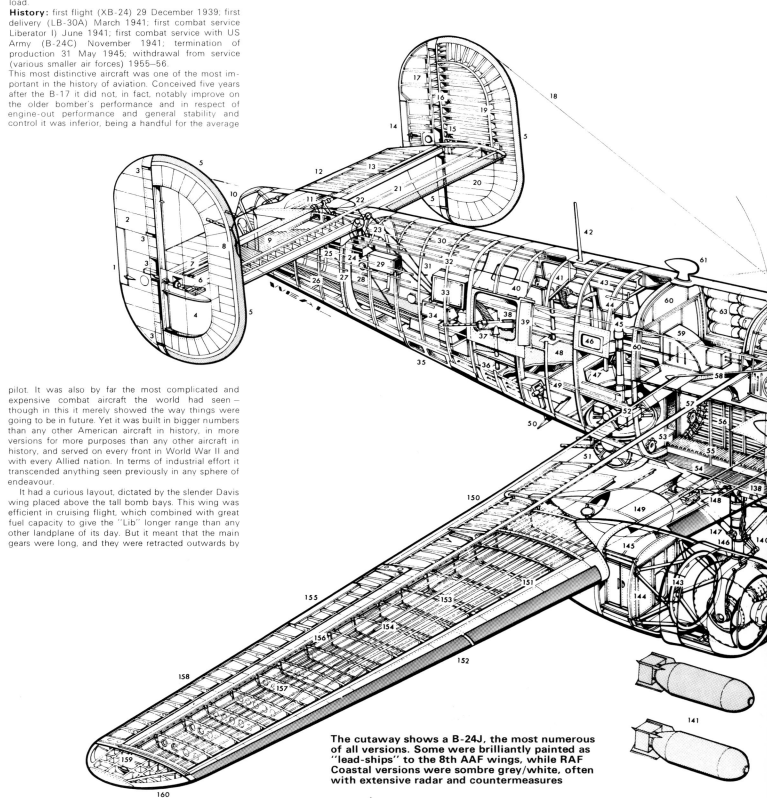

The cutaway shows a B-24J, the most numerous of all versions. Some were brilliantly painted as "lead-ships" to the 8th AAF wings, while RAF Coastal versions were sombre grey/white, often with extensive radar and countermeasures

Consolidated B-24J Liberator cutaway key:

1. Rudder trim tab
2. Fabric-covered rudder
3. Rudder hinges (metal leading-edge)
4. Starboard fin
5. Leading-edge de-icer boot
6. Starboard rudder horn
7. Rudder push-pull tube
8. Rear navigation light
9. Tailplane stringers
10. Consolidated (or Motor Products) electrically-operated turret (two 0·5in)
11. Elevator torque tube
12. Elevator trim tab
13. Elevator frame (fabric-covered)
14. Rudder trim tab
15. Tab control linkage
16. Rudder post
17. Light-alloy rudder frame
18. HF aerial
19. Fin construction
20. Metal-covered fixed surfaces
21. Tailplane front spar
22. Port elevator push-pull tube
23. Elevator drive quadrant
24. Elevator servo unit
25. Rudder servo unit
26. Ammunition feed track (tail turret)
27. Fuselage aft main frame
28. Walkway
29. Signal cartridges
30. Longitudinal Z-section stringers
31. Control cables
32. Fuselage intermediate secondary frames
33. Ammunition box
34. Aft fuselage camera installation
35. Lower windows
36. Waist gun mounting
37. Starboard manually-operated waist gun (0·5in)
38. Waist position (open)
39. Wind deflector plate
40. Waist position hinged cover

Consolidated B-24J-105 (392nd Bombardment Group, 2nd Air Division, 8th AAF)

41. Port manually-operated waist gun (0·5in)
42. Dorsal aerial
43. Ball-turret stanchion support beam
44. Ammunition box
45. Ball-turret stanchion
46. Midships window
47. Turret well
48. Cabin floor
49. Tail-bumper operating jack
50. Tail-bumper fairing
51. Briggs-Sperry electrically-operated ball turret (two 0·5in)
51. Turret actuation mechanism
53. Bomb-door actuation sprocket (hydraulically operated)
54. Bomb-door corrugated inner skin
55. Bomb-bay catwalk (box keel)
56. Bomb-bay catwalk vertical channel support members (bomb-release solenoids)
57. Bomb-door actuation track and rollers
58. Wing rear spar
59. Bomb-bay access tunnel
60. Fuselage main frame/bulkhead
61. D/F loop housing
62. Whip aerial
63. Oxygen cylinders
64. Aileron cable drum
65. Starboard flap extension cable
66. Wing rib cut-outs
67. Wing centre-section carry-through
68. Two 5-man inflatable dinghies
69. Flap hydraulic jack
70. Flap/cable attachments
71. Hydraulically-operated Fowler flap
72. Wing rear spar
73. Port mainwheel well and rear fairing
74. Engine supercharger waste-gate
75. Three auxiliary self-sealing fuel cells (port and starboard)
76. Wing outer section
77. Aileron gearboxes
78. Flush-riveted smooth metal wing skinning
79. Port statically-balanced aileron (fabric covered)
80. Port wingtip
81. Port navigation light
82. Wing leading-edge de-icer boot
83. Hopper-type self-sealing oil tank (27·4 gal/ 125 litres)
84. Engine nacelle

85. 1,200 hp Pratt & Whitney Twin Wasp R-1830-65 fourteen-cylinder two-row radial engine
86. Hamilton Standard Hydromatic constant-speed propeller (11ft 7in)
87. Landing/taxiing light
88. Nacelle structure
89. Supercharger duct
90. Self-sealing inter-rib fuel cells (12)
91. Martin electrically-operated dorsal turret (two 0·5in)
92. Turret mechanism
93. Fuselage main frame/ bulkhead
94. Radio compartment starboard window
95. Bomb-bay catwalk access trap
96. Radio-operator's position
97. Sound-insulation wall padding
98. Emergency escape hatch
99. Pilot's seat
100. Co-pilot's seat
101. Co-pilot's rudder pedals
102. Instrument panel
103. Windscreen panels
104. Compass housing
105. Control wheel
106. Control wheel mounting
107. Control linkage chain
108. Fuselage forward main frame/bulkhead
109. Pitot heads
110. Navigator's chart table
111. Navigator's compartment starboard window
112. Chart table lighting
113. Astro-dome
114. Consolidated (or Emerson) electrically-operated nose turret (two 0·5in)
115. Turret seating
116. Optically-flat bomb-aiming panel
117. Nose side glazing
118. Bombardier's prone couch
119. Ammunition boxes
120. Navigator's swivel seat
121. Navigator's compartment entry hatch (via nosewheel well)
122. Nosewheel well
123. Nosewheel door
124. Forward-retracting free-castoring nosewheel (self-aligning)
125. Mudguard
126. Torque links
127. Nosewheel oleo strut
128. Cockpit floor structure
129. Nosewheel retraction jack
130. Angled bulkhead
131. Smooth Alclad fuselage skinning
132. Underfloor electrics bay
133. 'Roll-top desk' bomb doors (four)
134. Supercharger nacelle 'cheek' intakes
135. Ventral aerial (beneath bomb-bay catwalk)
136. Nacelle/wing attachment cut-out
137. Wing front spar nacelle support
138. Undercarriage front pivoting shaft
139. Drag strut
140. Bendix scissors
141. Internal bomb load (max 8,000 lb/3,629 kg)
142. Starboard mainwheel
143. Engine-mounting ring
144. Firewall
145. Monocoque oil tank
146. Mainwheel oleo (Bendix 'pneudraulic' strut)
147. Side brace (jointed)
148. Undercarriage actuating cylinder
149. Starboard mainwheel well and rear fairing
150. Fowler flap structure
151. Wing front spar
152. Wing leading-edge de-icer boot
153. All-metal wing structure
154. Spanwise wing stringers
155. Aileron trim tab (starboard only)
156. Wing rear spar
157. Wing ribs (pressed and built-up former)
158. Statically-balanced aileron (metal frame)
159. Starboard navigation light
160. Wing-tip structure

Consolidated Liberator B.VI (356 Sqn RAF, operating on the Burma front from Salbani, India)

Curtiss H series ("Large America")

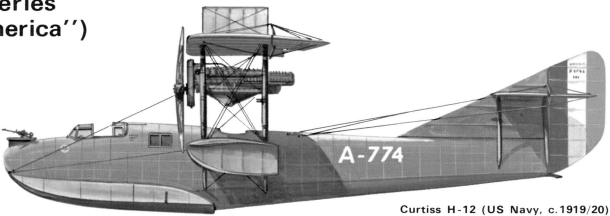

Curtiss H-12 (US Navy, c. 1919/20)

H.8 to H.16 (data for H.12)
Type: maritime patrol flying boat with crew of four.
Engines: two 330 hp Liberty 12 12-cylinder vee water-cooled.
Dimensions: span 92 ft 8 in (28·25 m); length 46 ft (14 m); height 16 ft 9 in (5·1 m).
Weights: empty 5,800 lb (2631 kg); loaded 7,989 lb (3624 kg).
Performance: maximum speed 85 mph (137 km/h); climb to 5,000 ft (1524 m) in 15 minutes; service ceiling 10,800 ft (3292 m); range at 75 mph (121 km/h) 450 miles (724 km).
Armament: two 0·30 in or 0·303 in Lewis machine guns in bow cockpit, single Lewis in rear gunner's cockpit between wing spars; racks under lower wing for four 100 lb (45 kg) or two 236 lb (107 kg) bombs.
History: first flight (H.8) probably July 1916; (H.12)

probably late 1916; first delivery (H.12) February 1917; final delivery (H.16) October 1918.

Cdr John C. Porte, one of the pioneer pilots of the Royal Naval Air Service, resigned his commission in 1913 and joined the American Curtiss company, a pioneer of flying boats. His immediate objective was to fly the special flying boat, "America", being built to try to win the £10,000 prize offered by the Daily Mail for a flight across the Atlantic. War prevented the flight and Porte rejoined the RNAS. He soon persuaded the Admiralty to order two Curtiss boats similar to "America", and eventually 64 were bought, 58 made in Britain; all eventually had the 100 hp Anzani instead of the original Curtiss OX-5. Even so, they were nothing like powerful enough and so Curtiss was

asked to build what became the "Large America" boats. The first was the H.8, with 160 hp engines, delivered in July 1916. In Britain 275 hp Rolls-Royce Eagles were substituted and a batch of 50 was ordered. Though still bad sea boats, the H.12s were excellent in the air and soon established a great reputation. On 14 May 1917 one shot down a Zeppelin over the North Sea, the first aircraft ever to fall to an attack by a US-built machine. Six days later another H.12 scored the first aerial victory against a submarine. In January 1918 the RNAS began to receive improved H.12Bs and 20 were supplied to the US Navy, the final engine being the Liberty. Best Curtiss of all was the H.16, with efficient two-step hull and more guns and bombs. The RNAS had 75 with 345 hp Eagle engines and the US Navy 74 with the 400 hp Liberty.

Curtiss Hawk

Curtiss BF2C-1 Hawk (VB-5, USS Ranger)

Variants, see text (data for BF2C-1/Hawk III)
Type: single-seat fighter-bomber.
Engine: 750 hp Wright R-1820F-53 Cyclone nine-cylinder radial.
Dimensions: span 31 ft 6 in (9·59 m); length 23 ft 6 in (7·16 m); height 10 ft (3·05 m).
Weights: empty 3,100 lb (1406 kg); loaded (Hawk III) 4,317 lb (1958 kg), (BF2C-1) 5,086 lb (2307 kg).
Performance: maximum speed (Hawk III) 240 mph (386 km/h); (BF2C-1) 228 mph (368 km/h); initial climb 2,200 ft (671 m)/min; service ceiling 27,000 ft (823 m); range (Hawk III) 575 miles (925 km); (BF2C-1) 797 miles (1282 km).
Armament: (basic) two 0·30 in machine guns (usually Colt-Browning) in fuselage (often changed or increased locally); underwing racks for four 116 lb (52·5 kg) bombs, plus one 474 lb (215 kg) on centre-line in place of extra fuel tank.
First flight: (XPW-8) June 1923; (production PW-8) May 1924; (P-1 Hawk and F6C-1 Hawk) both April 1925; (XF11C-3) May 1933; final export delivery, after 1936.

Curtiss Hawk III (25th Sqn, Chinese AF, defending Hankow).

Transcending even the Hawker Hart family for variety and longevity, the Curtiss Hawk series covered such a span that early and late models bore virtually no relation to each other. Nevertheless the Hawks were among the most important of all combat aircraft of the 1920s and 1930s and served as front-line fighters (later fighter-bombers) of the US Army and Navy and many other countries. In the early 1920s Curtiss had developed an excellent new water-cooled engine, the D-12, which gave fighters a new shape of streamlined nose. He used this as the basis for the XPW-8, in which the traditional wooden fuselage was rejected in favour of steel tube. In June 1924 Army Lt Russell Maughan used one of the first production machines to fly from Mineola, Long Island, to Crissy Field, San Francisco, between dawn and dusk in one day (21 hr 48 min,

travelling with the sun). There followed 260 Hawk biplanes built for the Army, most having the Curtiss V-1570 Conqueror vee-12 engine (some with turbo-chargers). The final production version was the P-6E with cantilever landing gear with spats, 46 being delivered in 1932. Navy Hawks began with duplicates of the P-1 called F6C. By 1927 the air-cooled Wasp engine had been made standard, and in 1932 the XF11C-2 introduced the new Goshawk family with metal wing, Cyclone engine and a 500 lb bomb. In 1933 appeared the XF11C-3 (later redesignated BF2C-1) with new fuselage and retractable main gear to compete with the Grumman FF. These distinctive

aircraft were not adopted by the Army but found wide acceptance in the Navy and also in overseas air forces. The Hawk I and II were export versions of the BFC-2 (fixed-gear F11C-2) with fuel capacities of 50 and 94 gallons respectively. The Hawk III was the re-tractable-gear model, which was the most important type of fighter used by the Chinese to try to defend their land against the Japanese. Over 100 Hawk IIs and IIIs were bought by China, as well as a licence to make the Hawk III. Turkey bought 24 and nine other nations were major customers, the final batches for Spain and Siam in 1936 having enclosed cockpits and being called Hawk IVs.

Curtiss Condor

BT-32 Condor

Type: reconnaissance bomber and transport with crew of six.
Engines: two 710 hp Wright R-1820F-2 Cyclone nine-cylinder radials.
Dimensions: span 82 ft (25 m); length 49 ft 6 in (15·05 m); height 16 ft 4 in (4·98 m).
Weights: empty 11,233 lb (5090 kg); loaded 17,500 lb (7940 kg).
Performance: maximum speed 180 mph (290 km/h); climb to 10,000 ft (3048 m) 15 min; service ceiling 22,000 ft (6710 m); range 840 miles (1352 km).
Armament: normally single Colt-Browning or other 0·30 in machine guns in nose, two dorsal positions, floor mounting and beam windows (total five or six guns); bomb load of up to 3,968 lb (1800 kg) carried mainly in internal bay under wing but also on underwing racks.
History: first flight (civil Condor) February 1932; (BT-32) May 1934; service delivery late 1934.

The last large biplane built in the United States, the Curtiss-Wright Corporation's Condor, is best remembered as a civil airliner. It was the yardstick against which the new cantilever monoplane transports,

Curtiss BT-32 Condor (Chinese AF, personal aircraft of Chiang Kai-Shek).

notably the Boeing 247, were judged. It was neither designed as a military aircraft nor considered as such by the US Army, but in 1933 the BT-32 was developed as a multi-role warplane for the Chinese government. Records of the number built and when they were delivered are few, but a small number were delivered as twin-float seaplanes; the normal Condor was a landplane, all later versions having retractable landing gear (unusual in a large biplane). One of the greatest assets of the BT-32 was its excellent lifting power and even with the full 1800 kg bomb load it could still operate from airstrips only 1,800 ft in length. Most of those supplied to China operated as bombers, transports and strategic reconnaissance machines, but one was permanently equipped as the personal vehicle of General Chiang Kai-Shek himself.

Curtiss SB2C/A-25 Helldiver

SB2C-1 to -5 (data for -1)

Type: two-seat carrier-based dive bomber.
Engine: 1,700 hp Wright R-2600-8 Cyclone 14-cylinder two-row radial.
Dimensions: span 49 ft 9 in (15·2 m); length 36 ft 8 in (11·2 m); height 16 ft 11 in (5·1 m).
Weights: empty 11,000 lb (4990 kg); loaded 16,607 lb (7550 kg).
Performance: maximum speed 281 mph (452 km/h); service ceiling 24,700 ft (7530 m); range 1,110 miles (1786 km).
Armament: two 20 mm or four 0·50 in guns in wings and two 0·30 in or one 0·50 in in rear cockpit; provision for 1,000 lb (454 kg) bomb load internally (later versions added wing racks).
History: first flight (XSB2C-1) 18 December 1940; (production SB2C-1) June 1942; termination of production 1945.

During World War II, by far the most successful Allied dive bomber was the Helldiver, which perpetuated a Curtiss trade-name established with a biplane dive

Curtiss SB2C-1 Helldiver (VB-8, US Navy, Saipan).

bomber used by the US Navy as the SBC series and, briefly, by the RAF as the Cleveland. The new monoplane was a totally different design, with very powerful engine, large folding wing and internal bomb bay. Yet development took a long time, partly because the prototype crashed but mainly because the US services asked for 880 further major design changes after the SB2C-1 had been frozen for production in November 1941. This was partly for Army/Navy/Marine Corps standardization, the Army/Marines aircraft being called A-25 Shrike or SB2C-1A. Eventually production rolled ahead at Curtiss, at Fairchild (who built SBFs) and Canadian Car & Foundry (who made SBWs). Althogether 7,200 Helldivers were delivered, roughly equally divided between the -1, -3, -4 and -5 subtypes. The -2 was a twin-float seaplane. From Rabaul in November 1943 Helldivers fought hard and effectively in every major action of the Pacific war.

Curtiss Hawk 75, 81 and 87

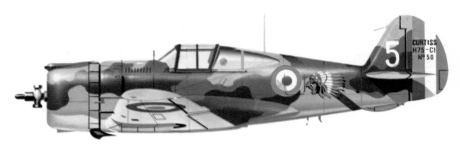

Tomahawk IIA (349 Belgian Sqn, RAF, Ikeja, W. Africa)

A: Hawk 75A, P-36A, Mohawk IV
B: Hawk 81A, P-40C, Tomahawk IIB
C: Hawk 87D, P-40F, Kittyhawk II
D: Hawk 87M, P-40N, Kittyhawk IV

Type: (A) single-seat fighter; (B) single-seat fighter, reconnaissance and ground attack; (C, D) single-seat fighter bomber.
Engine: (A) P-36A, 1,050 hp Pratt & Whitney R-1830-13 Twin Wasp 14-cylinder two-row radial; Hawk 75A and Mohawk, 1,200 hp Wright GR-1820-G205A Cyclone nine-cylinder radial; (B) 1,040 hp Allison V-1710-33 vee-12 liquid-cooled; (C) 1,300 hp Packard V-1650-1 (R-R Merlin) vee-12 liquid-cooled; (D) 1,200 hp Allison V-1710-81, -99 or -115 vee-12 liquid-cooled.
Dimensions: span 37 ft 3½ in (11·36 m); length (A) 28 ft 7 in (8·7 m), (B) 31 ft 8½ in (9·7 m); (C) 31 ft 2 in (9·55 m) or 33 ft 4 in (10·14 m); (D) 33 ft 4 in (10·14 m); height (A) 9 ft 6 in (2·89 m), (B, C, D) 12 ft 4 in (3·75 m).
Weights: empty (A) 4,541 lb (2060 kg), (B) 5,812 lb (2636 kg), (C) 6,550 lb (2974 kg), (D) 6,700 lb (3039 kg); loaded (A) 6,662 lb (3020 kg), (B) 7,459 lb (3393 kg), (C) 8,720 lb (3960 kg), (D) 11,400 lb (5008 kg).

Hawk 75C-1 (1er Escadrille, GC II/5, Armée de l'Air)

Performance: maximum speed (A) 303 mph (488 km/h), (B) 345 mph (555 km/h), (C) 364 mph (582 km/h), (D) 343 mph (552 km/h); initial climb (A) 2,500 ft (762 m)/min, (B) 2,650 ft (807 m)/min, (C) 2,400 ft (732 m)/min, (D) 2,120 ft (646 m)/min; service ceiling (all) about 30,000 ft (9144 m); range on internal fuel (A) 680 miles (1,100 km), (B) 730 miles (1175 km), (C) 610 miles (976 km), (D) 750 miles (1207 km).

continued on page 46

Curtiss Hawk 75, 81 and 87 (continued)

Armament: (A) P-36A, one 0·50 in and one 0·30 in Brownings above engine; P-36C, as P-36A with two 0·30 in in wings; Hawk 75A/Mohawk IV, six 0·303 in (four in wings); (B) six 0·303 in (four in wings); (C, D) six 0·50 in in wings with 281 rounds per gun (early P-40N, only four); bomb load (A) underwing racks for total of 400 lb (181 kg); (B) nil; (C) one 500 lb on centreline and 250 lb (113 kg) under each wing; (D) 500 or 600 lb (272 kg) on centreline and 500 lb under each wing.

History: first flight (Model 75 prototype) May 1935; (first Y1P-36) January 1937; (first production P-36A) April 1938; (XP-40) October 1938; (P-40) January 1940; (P-40D) 1941; (P-40F) 1941; (P-40N) 1943; final delivery (P-40N-40 and P-40R) December 1944. In November 1934 Curtiss began the design of a completely new "Hawk" fighter with cantilever monoplane wing, backwards retracting landing gear (the wheels turning 90° to lie inside the wing) and all-metal stressed-skin construction. After being tested by the Army Air Corps this design was put into production as the P-36A, marking a major advance in speed though not in firepower. Successive types of P-36 and its export counterpart, the Hawk 75A, had different engines and additional guns and the Hawk 75A was bought in huge numbers by many countries and made under licence in several. Biggest customer was the French Armée de l'Air, which began to receive the

H75A in March 1939. Five groups – GC I/4, II/4, I/5, II/5 and III/2 – wrote a glorious chapter over France in May 1940, invariably outnumbered and usually outperformed, but destroying 311 of the Luftwaffe, more than the total H75A strength when France fell. The rest of the French orders were supplied to the RAF as Mohawks, serving mainly on the Burma front.

More than 1,300 radial-engined models were delivered, but the real story began with the decision in July 1937 to build the P-40, with the liquid-cooled Allison engine. This was a novel and untried engine in a land where aircraft engines had become universally air-cooled, and teething troubles were long and severe. Eventually, towards the end of 1940, the P-40B and RAF Tomahawk I were cleared for combat duty and the process of development began. The rest of the aircraft was almost unchanged and in comparison with the Bf109 or Spitfire the early P-40 showed up badly, except in the twin attributes of manoeuvrability and strong construction. Eventually the RAF, RAAF and SAAF took 885 of three marks of Tomahawk, used as low-level army co-operation machines in Britain and as ground attack fighters in North Africa. Many hundreds of other P-40Bs and Cs were supplied to the US Army, Soviet Union, China and Turkey.

With the P-40D a new series of Allison engines allowed the nose to be shortened and the radiator was

deepened, changing the appearance of the aircraft. The fuselage guns were finally thrown out and the standard armament became the much better one of six "fifties" in the wings. The RAF had ordered 560 of the improved fighters in 1940, and they were called Kittyhawk I. When the US Army bought it the name Warhawk was given to subsequent P-40 versions. The Merlin engine went into production in the USA in 1941 and gave rise to the P-40F; none of the 1,311 Merlin P-40s reached the RAF, most going to the Soviet Union, US Army and Free French. Most Fs introduced a longer fuselage to improve directional stability. Subsequent models had a dorsal fin as well and reverted to the Allison engine. Great efforts were made to reduce weight and improve performance, because the whole family was fundamentally outclassed by the other front-line fighters on both sides; but, predictably, weight kept rising. It reached its peak in the capable and well-equipped P-40N, of which no fewer than 4,219 were built. Some of the early Ns had all the weight-savings and could reach 378 mph (608 km/h), but they were exceptions. Altogether deliveries of P-40 versions to the US government amounted to 13,738. Though it was foolhardy to tangle with a crack enemy fighter in close combat the Hawk family were tough, nimble and extremely useful weapons, especially in close support of armies.

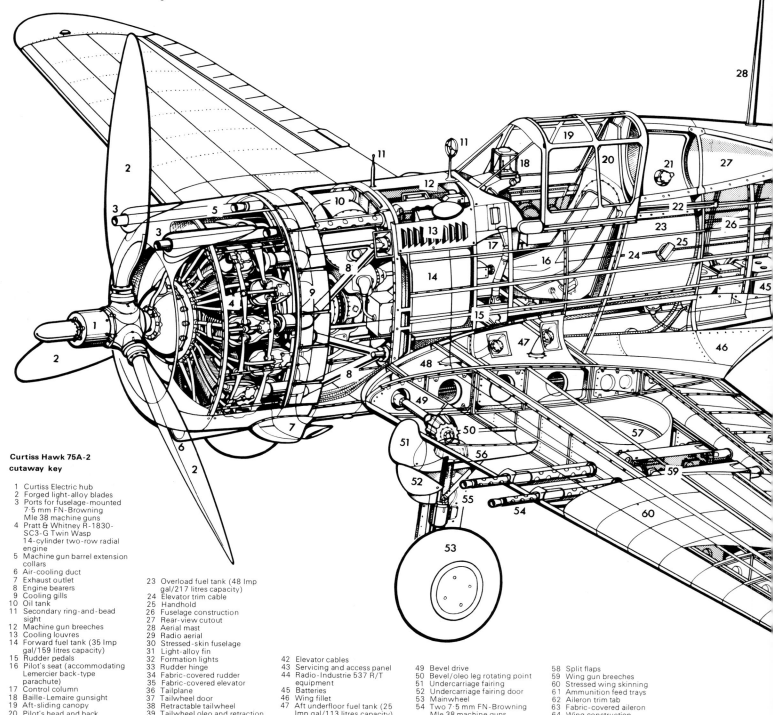

**Curtiss Hawk 75A-2
cutaway key**

1 Curtiss Electric hub
2 Forged light-alloy blades
3 Ports for fuselage-mounted 7·5 mm FN-Browning Mle 38 machine guns
4 Pratt & Whitney R-1830-SC3-G Twin Wasp 14-cylinder two-row radial engine
5 Machine gun barrel extension collars
6 Air-cooling duct
7 Exhaust outlet
8 Engine bearers
9 Cooling gills
10 Oil tank
11 Secondary ring-and-bead sight
12 Machine gun breeches
13 Cooling louvres
14 Forward fuel tank (35 Imp gal/159 litres capacity)
15 Rudder pedals
16 Pilot's seat (accommodating Lemercier back-type parachute)
17 Control column
18 Baille-Lemaire gunsight
19 Aft-sliding canopy
20 Pilot's head and back armour
21 Fuel filler cap
22 Canopy track
23 Overload fuel tank (48 Imp gal/217 litres capacity)
24 Elevator trim cable
25 Handhold
26 Fuselage construction
27 Rear-view cutout
28 Aerial mast
29 Radio aerial
30 Stressed-skin fuselage
31 Light-alloy fin
32 Formation lights
33 Rudder hinge
34 Fabric-covered rudder
35 Fabric-covered elevator
36 Tailplane
37 Tailwheel door
38 Retractable tailwheel
39 Tailwheel oleo and retraction jack
40 Lift point
41 Rudder trim cable
42 Elevator cables
43 Servicing and access panel
44 Radio-Industrie 537 R/T equipment
45 Batteries
46 Wing fillet
47 Aft underfloor fuel tank (25 Imp gal/113 litres capacity)
48 Forward underfloor fuel tank (27 Imp gal/125 litres capacity)
49 Bevel drive
50 Bevel/oleo leg rotating point
51 Undercarriage fairing
52 Undercarriage fairing door
53 Mainwheel
54 Two 7·5 mm FN-Browning Mle 38 machine guns
55 Mainwheel leg
56 Retraction actuator rod
57 Wheel well
58 Split flaps
59 Wing gun breeches
60 Stressed wing skinning
61 Ammunition feed trays
62 Aileron trim tab
63 Fabric-covered aileron
64 Wing construction
65 Port navigation lamps (upper and lower)
66 Pitot tube

Curtiss P-40C (77th Fighter Sqn, 20th Pursuit Group,
US Army Air Corps, Hamilton Field).

Kittyhawk III (250 Sqn, RAF, S. Italy)

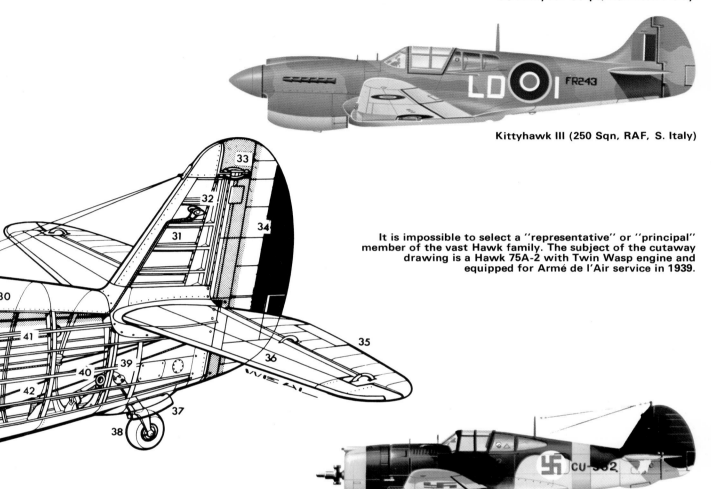

It is impossible to select a "representative" or "principal"
member of the vast Hawk family. The subject of the cutaway
drawing is a Hawk 75A-2 with Twin Wasp engine and
equipped for Armé de l'Air service in 1939.

Curtiss Hawk 75A-2 (32 Sqn, Finnish AF, Suulajärvi)

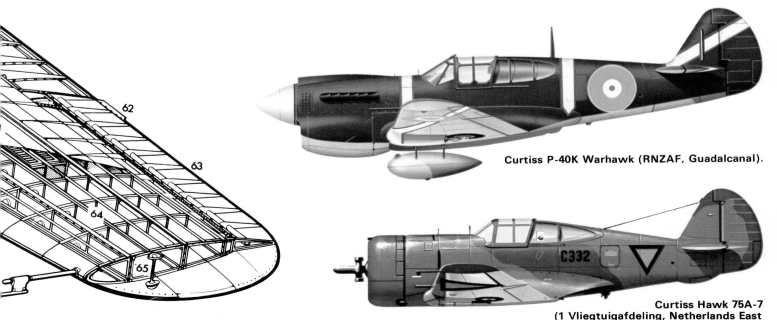

Curtiss P-40K Warhawk (RNZAF, Guadalcanal).

Curtiss Hawk 75A-7
(1 Vliegtuigafdeling, Netherlands East
Indies AF, Madioen).

Dassault Ouragan

MD.450 Ouragan C1
Type: single-seat fighter.
Engine: 5,070 lb (2300 kg) thrust Hispano-Suiza Nene 104B single-shaft turbojet.
Dimensions: span (over tip tanks) 43 ft 2 in (13·2 m); length 35 ft 3 in (10·74 m); height 13 ft 7 in (4·15 m).
Weights: empty 9,150 lb (4150 kg); loaded 14,991 lb (6800 kg).
Performance: maximum speed 584 mph (940 km/h); initial climb 7,874 ft (2400 m)/min; service ceiling 49,210 ft (15,000 m); range 620 miles (1000 km).
Armament: four 20 mm Hispano 404 cannon; underwing load of two 1,100 lb (500 kg) bombs or 16 rockets.
History: first flight (MD.450-01) 28 February 1949; (first production aircraft) June 1951; final delivery January 1955.

After World War II the French aircraft industry had to be almost rebuilt from scratch, whilst at the same time learning the new technology of jet propulsion. Most companies in the nationalised groups failed to see any of their new jet designs built in quantity, but the private

Dassault MD.450 Toofani (Indian AF)

firm of Dassault — created after VE-day by the former Marcel Bloch, who, as a member of the Resistance, changed his name to Dassault — strode confidently ahead with what has become one of the pre-eminent families of jet combat aircraft in the entire world. The whole line of Mirages, Etendards and Mystères stemmed from the extremely simple and conventional Ouragan (Hurricane) of 1949. Sensibly, the French, to iron out the bugs, ordered not only three prototypes

but also 12 pre-production aircraft and they also built the British Nene engine under licence in order to have a powerful and reliable turbojet. The Armée de l'Air received 350 Ouragans, the Indian Air Force 104 (known in India as Toofanis) and Israel 12 new aircraft and 42 from French storage. Highly manoeuvrable, the Ouragan was cheap and effective and established a sound reputation for Marcel Dassault and his design team.

Dassault Mystère II

MD.452 Mystère IIC
Type: single-seat fighter bomber.
Engine: 6,600 lb (3000 kg) thrust SNECMA Atar 101D3 single-shaft turbojet.
Dimensions: span 42ft 9¾ in (13·1 m); length 38 ft 6¼ in (11.7 m); height 13 ft 11¾ in (4·25 m).
Weights: empty 11,514 lb (5250 kg); loaded 16,442 lb (7450 kg).
Performance: maximum speed 658 mph (1060 km/h); initial climb 8,460 ft (2545 m)/min; service ceiling 42,650 ft (13,000 m); range 745 miles (1200 km).
Armament: two 30 mm Hispano 603 cannon, each with 150 rounds; provision for underwing bomb or rocket load not used.
History: first flight (MD.452-01) 23 February 1951; (production IIC) 1954.

Dassault's philosophy is always to try to progress in easy steps and the first Mystère was merely an Ouragan with 30° of sweep on wings and tail. Flown in April and July of 1952, there followed eight further prototypes, built in 1952–53, powered by the Hispano-Suiza Tay 250, of 6,280 lb (2850 kg) thrust, and also introducing a new armament of 30 mm guns. At the tenth the engine changed dramatically: the new French Atar axial engine was substituted, marking the first use of any French gas turbine for military aircraft propulsion. In April 1953 the Armée de l'Air ordered 150 of the new all-French fighters; ultimately 180 were built, 156 for France and 24 for Israel, though the latter

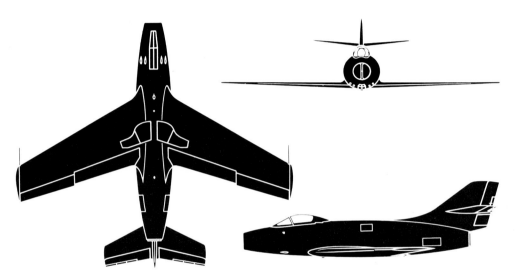

Dassault MD.452 Mystère IIC

were never delivered. For several reasons the service career of the IIC was fairly short, but it is significant on several counts. It was the first swept-wing aircraft to go into production in Western Europe, it was the first all-French jet fighter and it was also the first West

European fighter to be dived faster than sound (a feat first demonstrated by a USAF test pilot on 28 October 1952, during an evaluation of European aircraft that might be subjects for US-funded "offshore procurement").

Dassault Mystère IV

Mystère IVA
Type: single-seat fighter bomber.
Engine: (first 50) 6,280 lb (2850 kg) thrust Hispano-Suiza Tay 250A; (remainder) 7,716 lb (3500 kg) thrust Hispano-Suiza Verdon 350 single-shaft turbojet.
Dimensions: span 36 ft 5¾ in (11·1 m); length 42 ft 2 in (12·9 m); height 14 ft 5 in (4·4 m).
Weights: empty 12,950 lb (5875 kg); loaded 20,950 lb (9500 kg).
Performance: maximum speed 696 mph (1120 km/h) (Mach 0·913) at sea level, 615 mph (990 km/h) (Mach 0·94) at height; initial climb 8,860 ft (2700 m)/min; service ceiling 45,000 ft (13,750 m); range on internal fuel 820 miles (1320 km).
Armament: two 30 mm DEFA 551 cannon, each with 150 rounds; four underwing hardpoints for tanks or up to 2,000 lb (907 kg) bombs or rocket pods.
History: first flight (MD.454-01) 28 September 1952; (production Mystère IVA) December 1954; service delivery May 1955; final delivery October 1958.

Though superficially similar to the Mystère IIC, the IVA was a totally different aircraft, with hardly a single structural part being common to both. The wing of the new fighter was thinner (7½% instead of 9%), more

Dassault Mystère IVA (Indian AF)

sharply swept (41° instead of 30°) and much stronger. Fuselage and tail were completely new, flight controls were fully powered and the tailplane was a primary control surface. In this, as in so many features, Dassault followed the pioneering of North American and he likewise boldly made the wing skins from tapered sheet which had never before been produced in Europe. The US Air Force thoroughly tested the prototype — which in fact was an intermediate aircraft nothing like the final IVA — and in April 1953 placed an off-shore contract for 225. With a follow-up order from the

French government, Dassault added 67 for India and 50 for Israel. Aircraft from the French buy were then sold to India to make the total for that country 110 and the total run 425. In addition there were several advanced prototypes, including the two-seat, radar-equipped IVN night fighter (based on the F-86D Sabre) and the supersonic IVB that led to the Super Mystère B2. French IVAs fought at Suez in 1956, Israeli examples have been on active duty 20 years and the big Indian batch have also had an active career. in 1975 all were at last being phased out.

Dassault Super Mystère

Super Mystère B2 (SMB.2)
Type: single-seat fighter bomber.
Engine: 9,920 lb (4500 kg) thrust (with afterburner) SNECMA Atar 101G single-shaft augmented turbojet.
Dimensions: span 34 ft 5¾ (10·5 m); length 46 ft 1¼ in (14 m); height 14 ft 10¾ in (4·53 m).
Weights: empty 15,400 lb (6985 kg); loaded 22,046 lb (10,000 kg).
Performance: maximum speed 686 mph (1104 km/h) (Mach 0·9) at sea level, 743 mph (1200 km/h) (Mach 1·125) at altitude; initial climb 17,500 ft (5333 m)/min; service ceiling 55,750 ft (17,000 m); range (clean) at altitude 540 miles (870 km).
Armament: two 30 mm DEFA cannon; internal Matra launcher for 35 SNEB 68 mm rockets; two wing pylons for tanks or weapons up to total of 2,000 lb (907 kg).
History: first flight (Mystère IVB) 16 December 1953; (Super Mystère B1) 2 March 1955; (pre-production SMB.2) 15 May 1956; (production SMB.2) 26 February 1957; final delivery October 1959.

Dassault's policy of progression by logical low-risk steps often makes it difficult to see where one type ends and another begins. The Mystère IVB, flown before 1953 was out, was a major leap ahead, with

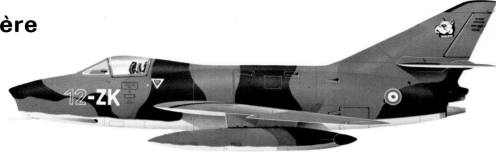

Dassault Super Mystère B2 (Escad. 2/12)

tapered, milled and chem-milled sheets, integral tanks, flush aerials and a radar gunsight in a new nose. It also introduced the much more powerful and more highly developed Atar 101G with variable afterburner. But it proved to be only a stepping-stone to the bigger, heavier and more formidable SMB.2, which introduced yet another new wing with 45° sweep and aerodynamics copied from the F-100 (but with outboard ailerons, inboard flaps and a dogtooth leading edge). The flattened nose was also derived from the North American supersonic fighter, but Dassault bravely kept the tailplane well above the fuselage. After success-

ful but prolonged development Dassault made a production run of 180, all powered by the Atar 101G, though the first SMB.2 had flown on an Avon RA.7R and a later Avon had been considered as the production engine. On its fourth flight, SMB.2-01, with Avon, easily exceeded Mach 1 on the level, to make this the first supersonic aeroplane to go into production, or in service, in Europe (the first Mystère IVB having gone supersonic on the level on 24 February 1954). Israel took 20 SMB.2s and in 1975 several remained in front-line use. The Atar 9 would have powered an SMB.4 had it not been for the success of the Mirage.

Dassault Etendard

Etendard IVM and IV P
Type: single-seat carrier strike fighter.
Engine: 9,700 lb (4400 kg) thrust SNECMA Atar 8B single-shaft turbojet.
Dimensions: span 31 ft 5¾ in (9·6 m); length 47 ft 3 in (14·4 m); height 14 ft (4·26 m).
Weights: empty 12,786 lb (5800 kg); loaded 22,486 lb (10,200 kg).
Performance: maximum speed 683 mph (1099 km/h) at sea level, 673 mph (1083 km/h) (Mach 1·02) at altitude; initial climb 19,685 ft (6000 m)/min; service ceiling 49,215 ft (15,000 m); range (clean) at altitude 1,056 miles (1700 km).
Armament: two 30 mm DEFA cannon each with 150 rounds; four wing pylons carrying variety of stores up to total weight of 3,000 lb (1360 kg).
History: first flight (Etendard II) 23 July 1956; (Etendard IV-01) 24 July 1956; (Etendard VI) 13 March 1957; (pre-production IVM) 21 May 1958; (production IVM) July 1961; final delivery 1964.

Dassault planned the Etendard (standard, or national flag) to meet a NATO need for a light strike fighter capable of high-subsonic speed and operation from unpaved forward airstrips. NATO specified that the engine should be the 4,850 lb thrust Bristol Orpheus and this aircraft took shape as the Etendard VI. Previously Dassault had been working on a variant, powered by two of the range of very small French

Dassault Etendard IVM

turbojets then under development to meet an Armée de l'Air proposal for a light interceptor, and this, though never pressed with enthusiasm, was first to fly (Etendard II, with two 2,420 lb thrust Turboméca Gabizos). Dassault scorned both. He was certain such light and underpowered aircraft would be useless and risked company money to build an Atar-powered Etendard IV. In fact, the Armée de l'Air dropped the light interceptor and the NATO contest was won by the Fiat G91. But Dassault's private-venture IV

attracted the attention of the Aéronavale and, after long development, went into production in two forms. The IVM, of which 69 were built, became the standard strike fighter aircraft of the carriers Foch and Clémenceau (Flotilles 11F and 17F), while the IVP, of which 21 were ordered, is the corresponding reconnaissance aircraft serving with 16F. The IVM has Aida nose radar and a folding refuelling probe, while the camera equipped IVP has a fixed nose probe.

Dassault-Breguet Super Etendard

Super Etendard
Type: single-seat carrier strike fighter.
Engine: 11,265 lb (5110 kg) thrust SNECMA Atar 8K-50 single-shaft turbojet.
Dimensions: span 31 ft 6 in (9·6 m); length 46 ft 11½ in (14·31 m); height 12 ft 8 in (3·85 m).
Weights: empty 13,889 lb (6300 kg); loaded 25,350 lb (11,500 kg).
Performance: maximum speed 745 mph (1200 km/h) at sea level, Mach 1 at altitude; initial climb 24,600 ft (7500 m)/min; service ceiling 52,495 ft (16,000 m); range (clean) at altitude, over 1,243 miles (2000 km).
Armament: two 30 mm DEFA cannon; mission load up to 9,921 lb (4500 kg) carried on five pylons.
History: first flight (converted Etendard) 28 October 1974; first delivery, summer of 1977.

During the late 1960s it had been expected that the original force of Etendards would be replaced, in about 1971, by a specially developed version of the Jaguar, the M version with single main wheels, full carrier equipment and specially fitted for the naval strike role. A Jaguar M completed flight development and carrier compatibility, but for various reasons, mainly concerned with politics and cost, this was rejected by the Aéronavale and a search began for an alternative. After studying the A-4 Skyhawk and A-7 Corsair, the Aéronavale chose Dassault-Breguet's proposal for an improved Etendard. This has a substantially redesigned structure, for operation at higher indicated airspeeds and higher weights; a new and more efficient engine, obtained by removing the afterburner from the Atar

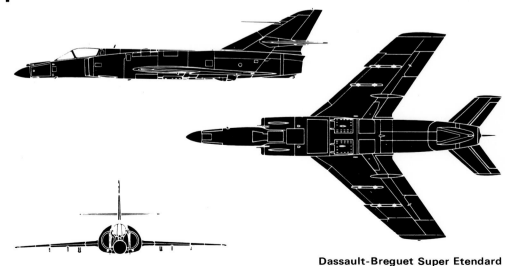

Dassault-Breguet Super Etendard

9K-50 of the Mirage F1.C; completely new inertial navigation system, produced mainly by SAGEM with American help; new multi-mode nose radar, produced jointly by Thomson-CSF and Electronique Marcel Dassault, with especially good performance in surface vessel detection and attack; and much greater and

more varied mission load. The SE is planned to begin replacing the earlier Etendard aboard the two French carriers in mid-1977. In August 1973 a batch of 100 were ordered and the first was expected to fly in 1975, flight development having been previously carried out with two converted Etendards.

Dassault-Breguet Mirage delta fighters

Dassault-Breguet Mirage IIICJ (Heyl Ha'Avir, Israel; this was the original export version, J standing for Jew).

Dassault-Breguet Mirage IIIEP (longer—note relative position of canopy and engine inlet—with attack avionics; 5 Sqn, Royal Pakistani AF).

Mirage III and 5

Type: single-seat or two-seat interceptor, tactical strike, trainer or reconnaissance aircraft (depending on sub-type)

Engine: (IIIC) 13,225 lb (6000 kg) thrust (maximum afterburner) SNECMA Atar 9B single-shaft turbojet; (all other versions – apart from IAI Kfir, page 119) 13,670 lb (6200 kg) Atar 9C.

Dimensions: span 27 ft (8·22 m); length (IIIC) 50 ft 10¼ in (15·5 m); (IIIB) 50 ft 6¼ in (15·4 m), (5) 51 ft (15·55 m); height 13 ft 11½ in (4·25 m).

Weights: empty (IIIC) 13,570 lb (6156 kg); (IIIE) 15,540 lb (7050 kg); (IIIR) 14,550 lb (6600 kg); (IIIB) 13,820 lb (6270 kg); (5) 14,550 lb (6600 kg); loaded (IIIC) 19,700 lb (8936 kg); (IIIE, IIIR, 5) 29,760 lb (13,500 kg), (IIIB) 26,455 lb (12,000 kg).

Performance: maximum speed (all models, clean) 863 mph (1390 km/h) (Mach 1·14) at sea level, 1,460 mph (2350 km/h) (Mach 2·2) at altitude; initial climb, over 16,400 ft (5000 m)/min (time to 36,090 ft, 11,000 m, 3 min); service ceiling (Mach 1·8) 55,775 ft (17,000 m); range (clean) at altitude about 1,000 miles (1610 km); combat radius in attack mission with bombs and tanks (mix not specified) 745 miles (1200 km); ferry range with three external tanks 2,485 miles (4000 km).

Armament: two 30mm DEFA 5-52 cannon, each with 125 rounds (normally fitted to all versions except when IIIC carries rocket-boost pack); three 1,000 lb (454 kg) external pylons for bombs, missiles or tanks (Mirage 5, seven external pylons with maximum capacity of 9,260 lb, 4200 kg).

History: first flight (MD.550 Mirage I) 25 June 1955; (prototype Mirage III-001) 17 November 1956; (pre-production Mirage IIIA) 12 May 1958; (production IIIC) 9 October 1960; (IIIE) 5 April 1961; (IIIR) 31 October 1961; (IIIB) 19 July 1962; (Australian-assembled IIIO) 16 November 1963; (Swiss-assembled IIIS) 28 October 1965; (prototype 5) 19 May 1967; (Belgian-assembled 5BA) May 1970.

The Mirage, which has come to symbolise modern aerial combat and to bring additional trade to France and incalculable prestige, especially in defence hardware, began in a most uncertain fashion. It was conceived in parallel with the Etendard II to meet the same Armée de l'Air light interceptor specification of 1952 and was likewise to be powered by two small turbojets (but, in this case, boosted by a liquid-propellant rocket engine in addition). As the small French engines were not ready, Dassault fitted the Mirage I with two British Viper turbojets and before the rocket was fitted this small delta was dived to Mach 1·15. With the rocket it reached Mach 1·3 in level flight. But Dassault had no faith in the concept of such low-power aircraft and after some work on the twin-Gabizo Mirage II took the plunge and produced a bigger and heavier Mirage III, powered by the 8,820 lb thrust Atar 101G. From this stemmed the pre-production IIIA, with larger but thinner wing and completely redesigned fuselage housing the new Atar 9 engine. On 24 October 1958 Mirage IIIA-01 became the first West European aircraft to attain Mach 2 in level flight.

This clinched the decision of the Armée de l'Air to buy 100 of a slightly developed interceptor called Mirage IIIC, fitted either with guns or with a boost rocket for faster climb and better combat performance at heights up to 82,000 ft. Normally the SEP 844 rocket was fitted to the IIIC, the sole armament being air-to-air missiles, such as Sidewinders and the big Matra R.530 used in conjunction with the CSF Cyrano radar, fitted to permit the new fighter to operate in all weather. Altogether 244 C models were delivered, large batches also going to South Africa and Israel (a nation which did much to develop and promote both the III and the 5). From the IIIC emerged the dual-control IIIB trainer, the longer and heavier IIIE for ground attack (with Marconi doppler radar for blind low-level navigation, new fire-control and navigation computer, and increased internal fuel) and the IIIR

family of camera-equipped reconnaissance aircraft. By 1975 about 1,500 of the Mirage III family had been sold, including a fairly standard version made in Australia and an extremely non-standard version made in Switzerland after painful development problems which inflated the price and reduced the numbers bought.

In 1965 Israel suggested that Dassault should produce a special VFR (clear weather) version for ground attack in the Middle East, with the radar and fire control avionics removed and replaced by an extra 110 gallons of fuel and more bombs. The result was the Mirage 5 and Israel bought 50 of the first production batch of 60. It can be distinguished by its longer and much more pointed nose, devoid of radar unless the small Aida II is fitted. For political reasons the French refused to deliver the paid-for Mirages to Israel but more than 500 have been sold to many other countries and 106 were assembled, and partly constructed, in Belgium. Largely as a result of the French action, Israel developed its own improved version of the Mirage (page 119).

In addition to production aircraft there have been many experimental or unsold variants. One of the latter was the Spey-powered Mirage IIIW jointly proposed by Dassault and Boeing as a rival to the F-5 as a standard simple fighter for America's allies. Another non-starter was the Milan (Kite), fitted with retractable "moustache" foreplanes for shorter field-length and better manoeuvrability (this excellent idea is available on the Mirage 5). By far the biggest development programme concerned the enlarged and far more powerful Mirage IIIV V/STOL fighter with a 19,840 lb thrust SNECMA TF306 augmented turbofan for propulsion and eight 5,500 lb thrust Rolls-Royce RB.162-31 lift jets. The IIIT was a non-VTOL of the same size and the equally large F2 led to the smaller (Atar-size) F1 (pages 52–53).

Mirage F1 see page 52

Dassault Mirage IV

Dassault-Breguet Mirage IVA (Escadron I/91 Gascogne, Mont-de-Marsan).

Mirage IVA

Type: limited-range strategic bomber with crew of two.

Engines: two 15,432 lb (7000 kg) thrust (maximum afterburner) SNECMA Atar 9K single-shaft augmented turbojets.

Dimensions: span 38 ft 10½ in (11·85 m); length 77 ft 1 in (23·5 m); height 17 ft 8½ in (5·4 m).

Weights: empty 31,967 lb (14,500 kg); loaded 73,800 lb (33,475 kg).

Performance: maximum speed (dash) 1,454 mph (2340 km/h) (Mach 2·2) at 40,000 ft (13,125 m), (sustained) 1,222 mph (1966 km/h) (Mach 1·7) at 60,000 ft (19,685 m); time to climb to 36,090 ft (11,000 m), 4 min 15 sec; service ceiling 65,62 ft (20,000 m); tactical radius (dash to target, hi-subsonic return) 770 miles (1240 km); ferry range 2,485 miles (4000 km).

Armament: no defensive armament other than ECM; one 60 kiloton free-fall bomb recessed in under-

side of fuselage; alternatively, up to 16,000 lb (7257 kg) of weapons on hard points under wings and fuselage.

History: first flight (Mirage IV-001) 17 June 1959; (production IVA) 7 December 1963; first delivery 1964; final delivery March 1968.

When the French government decided in 1954 to create a national nuclear deterrent force the most obvious problem was to choose a delivery system for the bombs. The likely enemy appeared to be the Soviet Union and this involved a long mission flown at high speed. After studying developments of the Vautour – a type used to form the nucleus of the *Force de Frappe* – Dassault began work on a bomber derived from a 1956 project for a twin-engined night fighter. After a year the design had to be scaled up to be powered by two Pratt & Whitney J75B engines, to meet more severe demands on speed, load and the range sufficient to reach desirable targets and then fly to places outside the Soviet Union. The final choice was to adopt extensive

flight refuelling, which allowed the design to shrink again to an intermediate level. As a result the force of 62 bombers that was eventually created relies totally upon Boeing KC-135F tankers, with booms fitted for probe/drogue refuelling, and also upon the "buddy technique" whereby aircraft would fly a mission in pairs, one carrying a bomb and the other spare fuel and a refuelling hose-reel for transfer to its partner. Even so, the initial planning of the Commandement des Forces Aériennes Stratégique presupposed that most

missions would be one-way (or at least would not return to France). Dispersal has been maximised, with the force divided into three Escadres (91 at Mont de Marsan, 93 at Istres and 94 at Avord), which in turn are subdivided into three four-aircraft groups, two of which are always dispersed away from Escadrille HQ. Despite being a heavy and "hot" aircraft, the IVA has also been rocket-blasted out of short unpaved strips hardened by quick-setting chemicals sprayed on the soil.

Dassault-Breguet/Dornier Alpha Jet

Alpha Jet
Type: two-seat trainer and light strike/reconnaissance aircraft.
Engines: two 2,976 lb (1350 kg) thrust SNECMA/Turboméca Larzac 04 two-shaft turbofans.
Dimensions: span 29 ft 11 in (9·12 m); length (excluding any probe) 40 ft 3¾ in (12·29 m); height 13 ft 9 in (4·2 m).
Weights: empty 6,944 lb (3150 kg); loaded (clean) 9,920 lb (4500 kg), (maximum) 15,432 lb (7000 kg).
Performance: (clean): maximum speed 576 mph (927 km/h) at sea level, 560 mph (900 km/h) (Mach 0·85) at altitude; climb to 39,370 ft (12,000 m), less than 10 minutes; service ceiling 45,930 ft (14,000 m); typical mission endurance 2 hr 30 min; ferry range with two external tanks 1,510 miles (2430 km).
Armament: optional for weapon training or combat missions, detachable belly fairing housing one 30 mm DEFA or 27 mm Mauser cannon, with 125 rounds, or two 0·50 in Brownings, each with 250 rounds; same centreline hardpoint and either one or two under each wing (to maximum of five) can be provided with pylons for maximum external load of 4,850 lb (2200 kg), made up of tanks, weapons, reconnaissance pod, ECM or other devices.
History: first flight 26 October 1973; first production delivery originally to be early 1976, now to be in 1978.

Realization that the Jaguar was too capable and costly to be a standard basic trainer led to the Armée de l'Air issuing a requirement for a new trainer in 1967. The chosen design was to be capable of use in the light ground attack role, in which the Luftwaffe had a parallel need for an aircraft. On 22 July 1969 the two governments agreed to a common specification and to adopt a common type of aircraft produced jointly by the two national industries. After evaluation against

the Aérospatiale (Nord)/MBB E650 Eurotrainer, the Alpha Jet was selected on 24 July 1970. Aircraft for the two partners are nearly identical. France makes fuselage and centre section and Germany the rear fuselage, tail and outer wings. SABCA of Belgium makes minor portions. Engines, originally shared by two French companies (see above), are being pro-

duced in partnership with MTU and KHD of Germany, plus a small share by FN of Belgium. Trainer aircraft are assembled at Toulouse (France) and attack versions at Oberpfaffenhofen (Germany). Decision to go ahead with production was reached on 26 March 1975. Total orders at that time were 200 for France, 200 for Germany and 33 for Belgium.

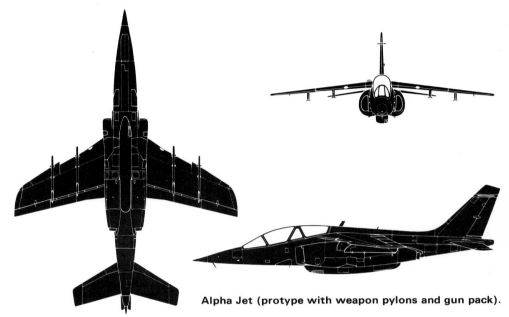

Alpha Jet (protype with weapon pylons and gun pack).

Dassault-Breguet Super Mirage and Delta 2000

Super Mirage (ACF)
Type: single-seat multi-role combat aircraft.
Engines: two 18,740 lb (8500 kg) thrust (maximum afterburner) SNECMA M53 single-shaft augmented by-pass turbojets.
Dimensions (provisional): span 36 ft 1 in (11 m); length 65 ft 8 in (20 m); height 19 ft 8 in (6 m).
Weights (provisional): empty 22,050 lb (10,000 kg); maximum 44,100 lb (20,000 kg).
Performance: maximum speed at 36,090 ft (11,000 m) or above, 1,650 mph (Mach 2·5, 2650 km/h); initial climb 61,000 ft (20,000 m)/min; service ceiling, greater than 59,000 ft (18,000 m); radius of action (low-level, with eight 882 lb, 400 kg bombs) 334 miles (537 km), (interception, with external fuel) 536 miles (861 km).
Armament: two fixed internal 30 mm DEFA 553 cannon; provision for external load of up to 13,200 lb (6000 kg) including Matra Super 530 and Matra 550 Magic air-to-air guided missiles, wide range of air-to-ground weapons or multi-sensor reconnaissance pod.
History: start of detailed study May 1972; start of prototype construction early 1975; first flight was scheduled for end of 1976 and combat service for 1978.

During the 1960s Dassault tried to develop a larger fighter as a replacement for the Mirage III and eventually flew the Mirage F2, powered by a 20,000 lb thrust TF306 engine, on 12 June 1966. From this was developed an improved version with variable-sweep wings, the Mirage G, flown on 18 November 1967. In late 1968 the French government ordered two prototypes of a further revised version with two Atar 9K-50 engines; the first of these, called Mirage G8, flew on 8 May 1971. The second, a single-seater, flew on 13 July 1972. In May 1972 the Armée de l'Air finally completed a specification for what it called Avion de Combat Futur (ACF) – future combat aircraft – for service late in the decade. To meet this Dassault

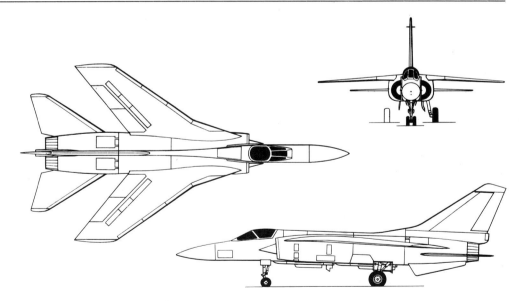

This drawing shows the Super Mirage, abandoned in early 1976. The design of the Delta 2000 is not yet final.

went back to the drawing board and developed a refined and slightly smaller study called Mirage G8A, with a wing of different form having a fixed sweep angle of 55°. By 1975 this was being translated into an aircraft intended for combat service, renamed Super Mirage to avoid confusion with the USAF ACF (Air Combat Fighter). The Super Mirage represents the only example of a modern multi-role aircraft being funded wholly by a single nation other than the two super-powers. It will require development of completely new systems, including inertial navigation and an advanced pulse-doppler radar, using technology not available without foreign help. There are to be two versions, one a fighter and the other a ground attack and reconnaissance machine (as in the case of the

existing MRCA, which meets all the same requirements). It will be the first French aircraft with a folding flight-refuelling probe, zero/zero seat and other devices found on aircraft of other nations. The programme, frozen in September 1975, was obviously vulnerable on grounds of cost and inflation.

Since the above was written, the last sentence has been proved true; the Super Mirage was cancelled in early 1976. In its place the Armé de l'Air hopes to buy the Mirage Delta 2000, a light and relatively cheap interceptor derived from the Mirage III and powered by one M53. For export, Dassault-Breguet hopes to build the Delta Super Mirage (two M53), with unspecified foreign funding.

Dassault-Breguet Mirage F1

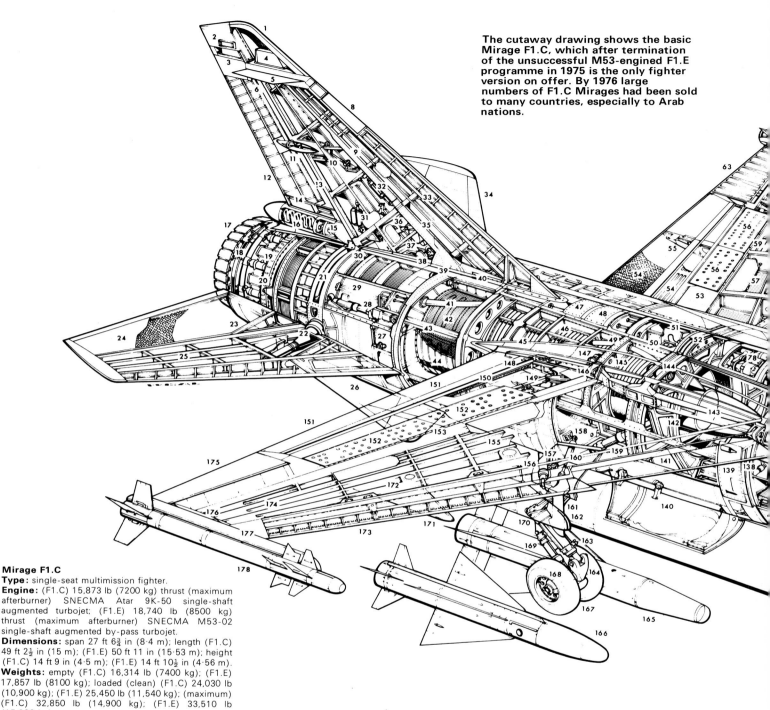

The cutaway drawing shows the basic Mirage F1.C, which after termination of the unsuccessful M53-engined F1.E programme in 1975 is the only fighter version on offer. By 1976 large numbers of F1.C Mirages had been sold to many countries, especially to Arab nations.

Mirage F1.C

Type: single-seat multimission fighter.

Engine: (F1.C) 15,873 lb (7200 kg) thrust (maximum afterburner) SNECMA Atar 9K-50 single-shaft augmented turbojet; (F1.E) 18,740 lb (8500 kg) thrust (maximum afterburner) SNECMA M53-02 single-shaft augmented by-pass turbojet.

Dimensions: span 27 ft 6¾ in (8·4 m); length (F1.C) 49 ft 2½ in (15 m); (F1.E) 50 ft 11 in (15·53 m); height (F1.C) 14 ft 9 in (4·5 m); (F1.E) 14 ft 10½ in (4·56 m).

Weights: empty (F1.C) 16,314 lb (7400 kg); (F1.E) 17,857 lb (8100 kg); loaded (clean) (F1.C) 24,030 lb (10,900 kg); (F1.E) 25,450 lb (11,540 kg); (maximum) (F1.C) 32,850 lb (14,900 kg); (F1.E) 33,510 lb (15,200 kg).

Performance: maximum speed (clean, both versions) 915 mph (1472 km/h) (Mach 1·2) at sea level, 1,450 mph (2335 km/h) (Mach 2·2) at altitude (with modification to cockpit transparency and airframe leading edges F1.E capable of 2·5); rate of climb (sustained to Mach 2 at 33,000 ft) (F1.C) 41,930–47,835 ft (12,780–14,580 m)/min; (F1.E) above 59,000 ft (18,000 m)/min; service ceiling (F1.C) 65,600 ft (20,000 m); (F1.E) 69,750 ft (21,250 m); range with maximum weapons (hi-lo-hi) (F1.C) 560 miles (900 km); (F1.E) 621 miles (1000 km); ferry range (F1.C) 2,050 miles (3300 km); (F1.E) 2,340 miles (3765 km).

Armament: (both versions), two 30 mm DEFA 5-53 cannon, each with 135 rounds; five Alkan universal stores pylons, rated at 4,500 lb (2000 kg) on centreline, 2,800 lb (1350 kg) inners and 1,100 lb (500 kg) outers; launch rails on tips rated at 280 lb (120 kg) for air-to-air missiles; total weapon load 8,820 lb (4000 kg). Typical air combat weapons, two Matra 550 Magic or Sidewinder on tips for close combat, one/two Matra 530 with infrared or radar homing, and one/two Matra Super 530 for long-range homing with large changes in height. Wide range of weapons for surface attack, plus optional reconnaissance pod containing cameras, SAT Cyclope infrared linescan and EMI side-looking radar.

History: first flight (F1-01) 23 December 1966; (pre-production F1-02) 20 March 1969; (production F1.C) 15 February 1973; (F1-M53, prototype for F1.E) 22 December 1974; first delivery (F1.C) 14 M (rch 1973.

Recognising that the Mirage III family would eventually have to be replaced, the French government awarded Dassault a development contract for a successor in February 1964. This aircraft was the large Mirage F2, in the 20 ton (clean) class and powered by a TF306 turbofan engine. It broke away from the classic Mirage form in having a high-mounted conventional swept wing with efficient high-lift slats and flaps, used in conjunction with a slab tailplane. It flew on 12 June 1966. Dassault, however, had privately financed a smaller version of the F2, called F1, sized to be powered by a single Atar engine. This became increasingly attractive and effort was progressively transferred to it from the F2. It went supersonic on its fourth flight and, though it later crashed, the Armée de l'Air decided to buy 100 as replacements for the original Mirage IIIC interceptor and Vautour IIN. Thus

was launched an aircraft which in most ways marks a tremendous advance on the tailless delta.

Thanks to the far higher efficiency of the new wing the field lengths and take-off and landing speeds are lower than for the delta Mirages, even though the weights are greater and the wing area much less. Increased thrust comes from the latest Atar engine and among the many less obvious advances are the Cyrano IV multi-mode radar and integral tankage for 45 per cent more fuel (trebling patrol endurance and doubling ground-attack mission radii). Combat manoeuvrability in many situations was increased by as much as 80 per cent and the all-round performance of the new fighter was outstanding. Sales to Israel were prohibited, but orders were soon placed by South Africa and Spain, the former also buying a manufacturing licence. More recently the F1 was chosen by several Middle East countries and many more sales seem certain.

In 1967 the French engine company, SNECMA, began the design of a completely new engine for the Super Mirage. To test the engine the F1 was an obvious

Dassault-Breguet Mirage F1.C (30me Escadre, Armée de l'Air, Reims)

Dassault-Breguet Mirage F1C cutaway drawing key:

1 Dielectric tip
1 Dielectric tip antenna housings
2 Rear navigation light
3 IFF aerial
4 VHF 1 aerial
5 VOR/LOC aerial
6 Rudder upper hinge
7 Fin structure
8 UHF aerial
9 Main fin spar (machined)
10 Rudder control linkage
11 Rudder central hinge fairing
12 Rudder
13 Fin rear spar
14 VHF 2 aerial
15 Parachute release mechanism
16 Braking parachute
17 Variable nozzle
18 Cooling annulus
19 Pneumatic nozzle actuators
20 Jet pipe mounting link
21 Fuselage aft support frame (tailplane trunnion/fin rear spar)
22 Tailplane trunnion
23 Trunnion frame
24 Honeycomb-stabilized structure
25 Multi-spar box structure
26 Ventral fin (port and starboard)
27 Control input linkage
28 Tailplane power unit
29 Hydraulic lines
30 Fin rear spar attachment
31 Rudder trim actuator
32 Rudder power unit
33 Fin leading-edge structure
34 Port tailplane
35 main spar lower section
36 Spring rod
37 Servo control quadrant
38 Rudder pulley bellcranks and cables
39 Fin main spar
39 Fin main spar attachment
40 Fin root fittings
41 Sealed-sheath hydraulic line
42 Afterburner
43 Engine mounting rail
44 Chem-milled tank inner skin
45 Wing root fairing
46 Rear lateral fuselage fuel tanks
47 Engine mounting access panel
48 Control run access panel
49 Filler/cross-feed system (rear/forward lateral tanks)
50 Aileron linkage
51 Compressor bleed-air pre-cooler
52 Main wing/fuselage mounting frame
53 Machined wing skins
54 Inboard flap composite-honeycomb structure
55 Flap tracks

56 Perforated spoilers
57 Spoiler actuator
58 Wing tank fuel lines
59 Aileron trimjack
60 Aileron servo control
61 Aileron operating rod
62 Aileron inboard hinge
63 Port aileron
64 Aileron outboard hinge
65 Missile attachment points
66 Missile ignition box
67 Matra 550 Magic air-to-air missile
68 Missile adapter shoe
69 Hinged, powered leading-edge
70 Leading-edge actuation system
71 Pylon mount (outboard)
72 Pylon mount (inboard)
73 Port inboard weapon pylon
74 Matra 530 air-to-air missile (infra-red homing)
75 Inboard leading-edge actuator
76 Forged high-tensile steel root fitting
77 IFF aerial
78 Engine duct ventilation
79 Central fuselage fuel tank
80 Aileron control rod
81 Avionics bay
82 Electrical/hydraulic leads
83 Inverted-flight accumulator
84 Amplifier
85 Main radio/electronics bay
86 Water separator and air-conditioning turbo-compressor
87 Canopy hinge
88 Canopy actuating jack
89 Martin-Baker Mk 4 ejection seat
90 Clamshell jettisonable canopy
91 Gunsight
92 One-piece cast windshield frame
93 Instrument panel
94 Control column
95 Instrument panel shroud/gunsight mounting
96 Heated, bird-strike proof windshield
97 Pitot heads
98 Radar attachment points
99 Thomson-CSF Cyrano IV fire-control radar
100 Radar scanner
101 Glass-reinforced plastic radome
102 Tacan aerial
103 Front pressure bulkhead
104 Rudder pedals
105 Aileron control bellcrank
106 Control column base
107 Elevator control bellcrank
108 Retraction jack fairing
109 Nosewheel retraction jack
110 Oleo-pneumatic shock-absorber
111 Twin nosewheels
112 Nose gear forging
113 Guide link
114 Steering/centering jack
115 Nose gear door
116 Pilot's seat
117 Nose gear trunnion
118 Elevator linkage
119 Angled rear pressure bulkhead

120 Battery (24 volt)
121 Gun trough
122 Air intake shock-cone
123 Heat exchanger
124 Shock-cone electric motor
125 Boundary-layer bleed
126 Shock-cone guide track
127 Screw jack
128 Starboard air intake
129 DEFA cannon barrel
130 Auxiliary air intake door
131 Starboard airbrake
132 Starboard DEFA 30mm cannon
133 Forward fuselage integral fuel tank
134 Wing root fillet
135 Fuel pipes
136 Machined frame
137 Wing forward attachment point
138 Landing gear door actuator/linkage
139 Ammunition magazine (125 rounds)
140 Pre-closing landing gear door (lower)
141 Main landing gear well (starboard)
142 Main wing/fuselage mounting frame
143 SNECMA Atar 9K50 turbojet (15,870 lb/7,200 kg with afterburner)
144 Main wing attachment
145 Machined frame
146 Wing rear attachment
147 Engine mounting trunnion
148 Inboard flap track
149 Flap actuator and linkage
150 Honeycomb trailing-edge structure
151 Double-slotted flaps
152 Perforated spoilers
153 Spoiler leading-edge piano hinge
154 Multi-spar integral tank structure
155 Pylon mount (inboard)
156 Main gear actuator
157 Leg door link
158 Main gear trunnion
159 Landing gear hydraulic truss jack
160 Landing gear rocking bellcrank and actuator
161 Messier main leg
162 Starboard inboard weapon pylon
163 Up-lock
164 Rocker beam
165 Matra Super 530 air-to-air missile
166 Matra 530 air-to-air missile (semi-active radar guidance)
167 Twin mainwheels
168 Hydraulic multi-plate disc brakes
169 Oleo-pneumatic shock-absorber
170 Main landing gear bogie beam
171 Starboard outboard weapon pylon
172 Pylon mount (outboard)
173 Powered leading edge
174 Auxiliary spars
175 Starboard aileron
176 Machined end rib
177 Missile adapter shoe
178 Matra 550 Magic air-to-air missile
179 Drop tank (264 gal/1,200 litres)

choice, and the combination could not fail to be of interest in its own right. The M53 engine confers benefits in acceleration, climb, manoeuvrability and range and, to make up a more modern package, Dassault-Breguet proposed the fully modular Cyrano IV-100 radar and the SAGEM-Kearfott SKN 2603 inertial navigation system, as well as the SFENA 505 digital autopilot of the F1.C. The result is the F1.E, which from early 1974 was strongly, but unsuccessfully, pressed on overseas customers, particularly Belgium, the Netherlands, Denmark and Norway (which agreed a common objective in replacing their F-104Gs). The Armée de l'Air did not want the F1.E, but had agreed to buy a limited quantity had it been chosen by the four NATO nations. Two M53-powered prototypes are flying, and Dassault-Breguet also propose the simple F1.A (corresponding to the Mirage 5, with fuel replacing avionics), and the tandem-seat F1.B (Atar) and F1.D (M53 and Cyrano IV-100).

Mirage IVA, Alpha Jet and Super Mirage see page 51

Dewoitine D 500 series

D 500, D 501 and D 510

Type: single-seat fighter.

Engine: (D 500) one 690 hp Hispano-Suiza 12 Nbrs-1, (D 501) one 690 hp Hispano-Suiza 12 Xcrs, (D 510) one 860 hp Hispano-Suiza 12 Ycrs, all engines being vee-12 water-cooled.

Dimensions: span 39 ft 8 in (12·1 m); length (D 500) 25 ft 3½ in (7·7 m); (D 501) 25 ft 1¼ in; (D 510) 26 ft 0¾ in; height 8 ft 10½ in (2·7 m).

Weights: empty (D 510) 2,870 lb (1300 kg); loaded (D 500) 3,792 lb (1720 kg); (D 501) 4,193 lb (1902 kg); (D 510) 4,235 lb (1920 kg).

Performance: maximum speed (D 500, 501) 224 mph (360 km/h); (D 510) 249 mph (400 km/h); service ceiling (D 500, 501) 35,400 ft (10,790 m); (D 510) 34,500 ft (10,500 m); range (D 500, 501) 530 miles (853 km); (D 510) 435 miles (700 km).

Armament: (D 500) two 7·5 mm or 7·7 mm machine guns above engine (Vickers, Darne, Colt or MAC 1934) and, in later aircraft, two 7·5 mm or 7·7 mm guns in wings (Darne); (D 501) as D 500 plus 20 mm Hispano-Suiza cannon firing through hub of propeller; (D 510) as D 501; certain aircraft (eg Turkish D 510T) fitted with underwing racks for four 110 lb (50 kg) bombs.

History: first flight (D 500) 19 June 1932; (production D 500) early 1934; final delivery, early 1938.

During the 1920s French fighters had generally been biplanes (though not exclusively, as was the case with the RAF and US Army and Navy). By 1930 the monoplane was fast coming into the ascendant, especially in France. Most were of the parasol type, with the wing carried above the fuselage, but in the D 500 Dewoitine broke away from this tradition and designed the most modern-looking fighter of its day. Designed

to meet a French specification of 1930, the new fighter was especially notable in being made entirely of light alloy, with stressed skin covering. After encouraging flight testing an order for 57 was placed in November 1933 for the Armée de l'Air, the last 12 being of the D 501 type. These were not the first cannon-armed fighters — in fact the earlier D 371 had often carried two cannon in its parasol wing — but the installation firing through the propeller hub was extremely neat and attracted widespread attention.

By 1934 foreign governments were practically queueing up to buy the fast and attractive Dewoitines. Among them were Turkey, Lithuania, the Soviet Union, the Hedjaz (these were sold to Republican Spain), China and Japan; even Britain bought one to evaluate it at Martlesham against British fighters. Meanwhile production continued at an increasing rate for the Armée de l'Air. By the spring of 1938 a total of 352 of the three sub-types had been delivered to the Armée de l'Air and Aéronavale and these represented about 60 per cent of the total front-line French strength in fighters. But they were swiftly becoming obsolescent in Europe and by the start of World War II had dwindled to a mere three groups and a few odd squadrons. Only in China did the Dewoitine low-wingers continue to give battle until at least the end of 1941. Like the Boeing P-26 and Soviet I-16, they made the transition between the fabric-covered biplane with open cockpit and the fighters that dominated World War II.

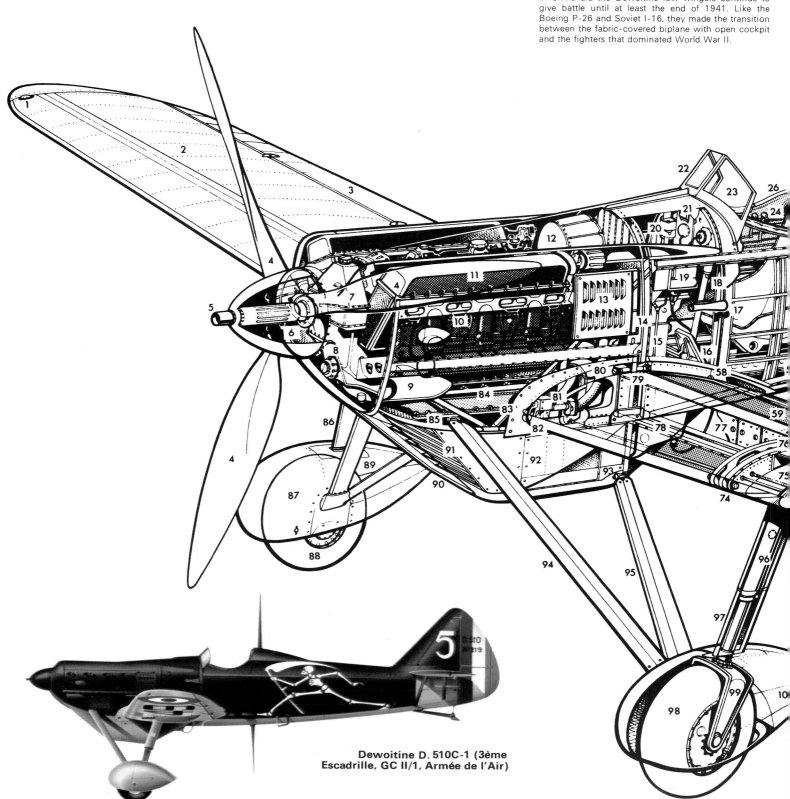

Dewoitine D. 510C-1 (3ème Escadrille, GC II/1, Armée de l'Air)

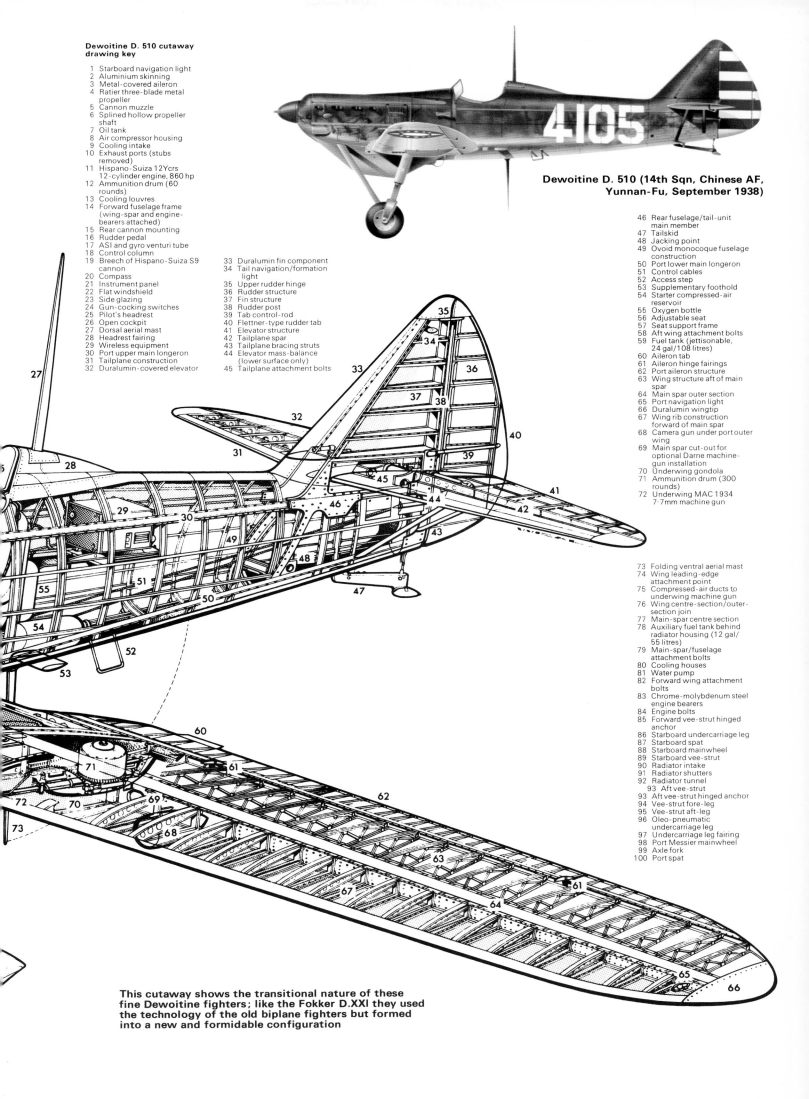

Dewoitine D. 510 cutaway drawing key

1 Starboard navigation light
2 Aluminium skinning
3 Metal-covered aileron
4 Ratier three-blade metal propeller
5 Cannon muzzle
6 Splined hollow propeller shaft
7 Oil tank
8 Air compressor housing
9 Cooling intake
10 Exhaust ports (stubs removed)
11 Hispano-Suiza 12Ycrs 12-cylinder engine, 860 hp
12 Ammunition drum (60 rounds)
13 Cooling louvres
14 Forward fuselage frame (wing-spar and engine-bearers attached)
15 Rear cannon mounting
16 Rudder pedal
17 ASI and gyro venturi tube
18 Control column
19 Breech of Hispano-Suiza S9 cannon
20 Compass
21 Instrument panel
22 Flat windshield
23 Side glazing
24 Gun-cocking switches
25 Pilot's headrest
26 Open cockpit
27 Dorsal aerial mast
28 Headrest fairing
29 Wireless equipment
30 Port upper main longeron
31 Tailplane construction
32 Duralumin-covered elevator

33 Duralumin fin component
34 Tail navigation/formation light
35 Upper rudder hinge
36 Rudder structure
37 Fin structure
38 Rudder post
39 Tab control-rod
40 Flettner-type rudder tab
41 Elevator structure
42 Tailplane spar
43 Tailplane bracing struts
44 Elevator mass-balance (lower surface only)
45 Tailplane attachment bolts

Dewoitine D. 510 (14th Sqn, Chinese AF, Yunnan-Fu, September 1938)

46 Rear fuselage/tail-unit main member
47 Tailskid
48 Jacking point
49 Ovoid monocoque fuselage construction
50 Port lower main longeron
51 Control cables
52 Access step
53 Supplementary foothold
54 Starter compressed-air reservoir
55 Oxygen bottle
56 Adjustable seat
57 Seat support frame
58 Aft wing attachment bolts
59 Fuel tank (jettisonable, 24 gal/108 litres)
60 Aileron tab
61 Aileron hinge fairings
62 Port aileron structure
63 Wing structure aft of main spar
64 Main spar outer section
65 Port navigation light
66 Duralumin wingtip
67 Wing rib construction forward of main spar
68 Camera gun under port outer wing
69 Main spar cut-out for optional Darne machine-gun installation
70 Underwing gondola
71 Ammunition drum (300 rounds)
72 Underwing MAC 1934 7·7mm machine gun

73 Folding ventral aerial mast
74 Wing leading-edge attachment point
75 Compressed-air ducts to underwing machine gun
76 Wing centre-section/outer-section join
77 Main-spar centre section
78 Auxiliary fuel tank behind radiator housing (12 gal/55 litres)
79 Main-spar/fuselage attachment bolts
80 Cooling houses
81 Water pump
82 Forward wing attachment bolts
83 Chrome-molybdenum steel engine bearers
84 Engine bolts
85 Forward vee-strut hinged anchor
86 Starboard undercarriage leg
87 Starboard spat
88 Starboard mainwheel
89 Starboard vee-strut
90 Radiator intake
91 Radiator shutters
92 Radiator tunnel
93 Aft vee-strut
93 Aft vee-strut hinged anchor
94 Vee-strut fore-leg
95 Vee-strut aft-leg
96 Oleo-pneumatic undercarriage leg
97 Undercarriage leg fairing
98 Port Messier mainwheel
99 Axle fork
100 Port spat

This cutaway shows the transitional nature of these fine Dewoitine fighters; like the Fokker D.XXI they used the technology of the old biplane fighters but formed into a new and formidable configuration

Dewoitine D 520

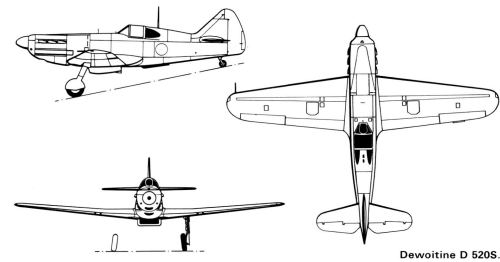

D 520S
Type: single-seat fighter.
Engine: one 910 hp Hispano-Suiza 12Y-45 vee-12 liquid-cooled.
Dimensions: span 33 ft 5⅝ in (10.2 m); length 28 ft 8½ in (8.75 m); height 11 ft 3 in (3.4 m).
Weights: empty 4,630 lb (2100 kg); loaded 6,173 lb (2800 kg).
Performance: maximum speed 329 mph (530 km/h); initial climb 2,362 ft (720 m)/min; service ceiling 36,090 ft (11,000 m); range 777 miles (1240 km).
Armament: one 20 mm Hispano-Suiza 404 cannon, with 60 rounds, firing through the propeller hub, and four 7.5 mm MAC 1934 machine guns, each with 500 rounds, in wings.
History: first flight (520-01) 2 October 1938; (production, 520-2) 3 December 1939; service delivery 1 February 1940.

Dewoitine D 520S.

Few people have ever disputed that this neat little fighter was the best produced in France prior to the Armistice; it was certainly the best to reach the squadrons. Unlike so many other hopeful types which just failed to be ready in time, the D 520 made it – but only just. The great Marcel Doret did not help when, having made a splendid first test flight, he forgot about the retractable landing gear on 27 November 1938 and put the first prototype out of action. The new fighter was a direct development of the 500 series and though it was very small it was hoped to fit an engine of 1,300 hp – but nothing suitable was available. The first prototype had an open cockpit and the second still had a curved windscreen, tailskid and two drum-fed machine guns, as did the first production machine. But the second was up to production standard. The Dewoitine plants had vanished into the nationalised SNCA du Midi under the law of 1936 and these were meant to deliver ten in September 1939 and 30 in October. Actually timing ran about three months late, but with the panic in 1940 industry went mad. In May 1940 101 were delivered and by June the output had reached ten per day, a figure seldom exceeded by any aircraft plant in history. GC I/3 was first to go into action, followed in late May by GC II/3, with III/3, III/6 and II/7 following before the capitulation. These groups were credited with 147 kills for the loss of 85 fighters and 44 pilots. Subsequently the Vichy government restored the D 520 to production, 740 being built in all. In 1942 the Luftwaffe seized 411, passing many to Italy, Rumania and Bulgaria. But in 1944 GC I/8 was re-formed under Doret and, after painting out the German insignia, went into action against the last German pockets in southern France.

D.H.2

Airco D.H.2
Type: single-seat scout.
Engine: one pusher 100 hp Gnome Monosoupape nine-cylinder rotary.
Dimensions: span 28 ft 3 in (8.61 m); length 25 ft 2 in (7.68 m); height 9 ft 6 in (2.9 m).
Weights: empty 1,145 lb (520 kg); loaded 1,441 lb (654 kg).
Performance: maximum speed 93 mph (150 km/h); service ceiling 14,500 ft (4420 m); range 220 miles (354 km).
Armament: one 0.303 in Lewis machine gun manually aimed by pilot, mounted on bracket to left or right of windscreen.
History: first flight (prototype) spring 1915; first delivery (same aircraft) July 1915.

Geoffrey de Havilland's first aircraft dated from 1909 and 1910. From the second he developed the F.E.2 for the Royal Aircraft Factory and carried the idea of a pusher scout further with the D.H.1, the first of his designs for Airco (the Aircraft Manufacturing Co), of which 100 were built in 1915–16. The D.H.2 was a smaller single-seat edition. The idea of the pusher was to get around the problem of fitting a machine gun, because at this time the British had no interrupter or synchronising gear and so could not fire ahead through a tractor propeller. But in the D.H.2 the obvious step of fitting one (or more) fixed guns was not taken. Instead, the pilot had to aim and fire the gun whilst flying the aircraft with the other hand! On production D.H.2s the traverse was eliminated and eventually most squadrons found ways of fastening down the rear of the gun. Though tricky to fly, mainly because of its sensitive controls, the D.H.2 was very manoeuvrable in skilled hands and for its day had adequate performance – though the Monosoupape (single-valve) Gnome tended to blow off its cylinders whilst running. Indeed it was soon the master of the once-dreaded Fokker E.III and curtly ended the RFC's period as

Airco D.H.2 (24 Sqn, RFC).

"Fokker Fodder". When 24 Sqn went to France with 12 of the pusher fighters in February 1916 it was the first unit on the Allied side to be equipped with single-seat fighters. Altogether 450 of these aircraft were built, about 300 serving in France and the rest in the Middle East.

de Havilland (Airco) D.H.4.

D.H.4
Type: two-seat bomber.
Engine: one 375 hp Rolls-Royce Eagle VIII vee-12 water-cooled (alternatively, 200 hp RAF 3a, 230 hp Siddeley Puma, 260 hp Fiat A-12 or 400 hp Liberty).
Dimensions: span 42 ft 5 in (12.95 m); length 30 ft 8 in (9.35 m) (slightly different with other engines); height 11 ft (3.35 m).
Weights: empty 2,300 lb (1043 kg); loaded 3,472 lb (1575 kg).
Performance: maximum speed 136 mph (219 km/h); initial climb 1,042 ft (306 m)/min; service ceiling 20,000 ft (6096 m); range 420 miles (676 km).
Armament: (RFC) one fixed 0.303 in Vickers and single or twin 0.303 in Lewis manually aimed in rear cockpit; (RNAS) as above but two fixed Vickers; (AEF) two fixed 0.30 in Marlin and twin manually aimed 0.30 in Lewis. Bomb load up to 460 lb (209 kg), on external racks under fuselage and wings.
History: first flight (prototype) August 1916; (first production aircraft) December 1916; first squadron delivery (55 Sqn RFC) March 1917; withdrawal from service (US Army) late 1932.

Designed by de Havilland around the 160 hp BHP (Beardmore-Halford-Pullinger) engine, the D.H.4 was Airco's response to an Air Ministry request for a new day bomber and was the first British aircraft to be designed for such a purpose. Unlike so many British aircraft of its day it had a clean tractor layout and broke away from the use of a rotary engine. These facts allowed it to be later developed for use at greater weights and higher speeds with much more powerful engines. Its most controversial feature was the wide separation of pilot and observer, to give the former the best view and the latter the best field of fire. This made it difficult for them to communicate and the petrol tank between them was also judged a safety hazard which by 1918 was being strongly criticised by the Americans, who made it their most important warplane. But in its first year, even with less-powerful engines, the D.H.4 had things all its own way because it foreshadowed de Havilland's later Mosquito in outflying even the opposing fighters. In Britain 1,449 were built by seven companies and used for many purposes

Airco D.H.4. (5 Wing, RNAS).

in addition to bombing, two having tanks for 14 hour flights to the Kiel Canal on photo missions and two others carrying upward-firing COW 1½-pounder guns on anti-Zeppelin sorties. In the United States vast production was urgently planned as the Liberty Plane (the name derived from the engine) and though production did not begin until the end of 1917 no fewer than 4,846 were soon built. After 1918 both British and US examples were sold to many air forces, and also served as the basis for civil airliners.

de Havilland (Airco) D.H.9

D.H.9a, USD-9, Mpala
Type: two-seat bomber (later, overseas multi-role).
Engine: (D.H.9) 230, 240 or 290 hp Siddeley Puma,
250 hp Fiat A-12, 430 hp Napier Lion, 400 hp Liberty
or (SAAF Mpala) 540 hp Bristol Jupiter; (D.H.9A),
standard engine 400 hp Liberty vee-12 water-cooled
(alternatively 360 or 375 hp Rolls-Royce Eagle VIII,
300 hp Hispano or 450 hp Napier Lion.
Dimensions: span 45 ft 11½ in (14 m); length
(Liberty) 30 ft 3 in (9·22 m); height 11 ft 4 in (3·45 m).
Weights: empty 2,695 lb (1223 kg); loaded 4,645 lb
(2107 kg).
Performance: maximum speed (1917) 123 mph
(198 km/h), (1927, with extra equipment) 114 mph
(183 km/h); initial climb 595 ft (181 m)/min; service
ceiling 16,750 ft (5105 m); endurance 5 hr 30 min.
Armament: one fixed 0·303 in Vickers, one manually
aimed 0·303 in Lewis; bomb load 450 lb (204 kg).
History: first flight July 1917; production delivery
December 1917; first flight (USD-9) November 1918;
final delivery (Westland and Parnall) 1928; withdrawal
from service (Mpala) 1937.

In 1917 German raids on Britain prompted the British
government to authorise a doubling of the size of the
RFC in France, with most of the new squadrons being
equipped with day bombers. The D.H.4 was the
expected type, but this was soon replaced by the new
D.H.9 as a result of the obvious improvements this
offered. Planned specifically for fast mass-production,

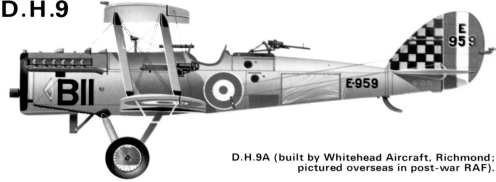

**D.H.9A (built by Whitehead Aircraft, Richmond;
pictured overseas in post-war RAF).**

the D.H.9 moved the pilot behind the fuel tank close to
the observer; it also had a Germanic engine installation with exposed cylinders and a retractable ventral
radiator. The only thing wrong was persistent failure
of the BHP engine. The prototype, a converted D.H.4,
flew with a Galloway Adriatic, but the standard engine
was the Siddeley Puma, derived from the BHP, which
had to be reduced in power and made the early examples dangerously underpowered. Thus it suffered in
having a low ceiling and poor manoeuvrability, compared with its predecessor, but officialdom had
planned vast production and soon one was coming
off the line every 40 minutes. No fewer than 14,000

were ordered in the USA as USD-9s, with the Liberty
engine, but only four were completed at the Armistice.
After 3,204 had been built in Britain the 9 was replaced
by the much improved 9A, or "Nine-Ack", developed
and made by Westland Aircraft with much more
powerful engines. Westland built 885 by the Armistice,
and during the 1920s a further 1,600 were built by
12 companies as the standard RAF overseas utility
machine. Many more were made with various engines
in the USSR, Spain and other countries. Hundreds
survived into the 1930s festooned with bombs, guns,
cameras, extra tanks, rations, bicycles, dinghies and
spare wheels.

de Havilland (Airco) D.H.10

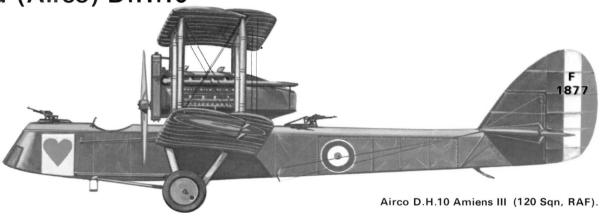

Airco D.H.10 Amiens III (120 Sqn, RAF).

D.H.10 Amiens I to IIIA (data for IIIA)
Type: three-seat (sometimes four-seat) day bomber.
Engines: two 400 hp Liberty 12 vee-12 water-
cooled (Amiens I and II, see text).
Dimensions: span 65 ft 6 in (19·96 m); length
39 ft 7 in (12·1 m); height 14 ft 6 in (4·4 m).
Weights: empty 5,585 lb (2533 kg); loaded 9,000 lb
(4082 kg).
Performance: maximum speed 126 mph (203 km/h);
initial climb 550 ft (168 m)/min; service ceiling
17,000 ft (5180 m); range 600 miles (966 km).
Armament: single or twin 0·303 in manually aimed
Lewis machine guns in cockpits in nose and behind
wings; bomb load 900 lb (408 kg) in internal bay and
on underwing racks.

History: first flight 4 March 1918; service delivery
September 1918; termination of production, probably
1920.

In 1916 Capt de Havilland produced his first twin-
engined aircraft, a bomber powered by two pusher
120 hp Beardmore engines mounted midway between
the biplane wings which were arranged to fold. The
two main landing wheels were supplemented by two
smaller ones nearer the nose. This D.H.3 was not put
into production, but during 1917 de Havilland redesigned it for greater power and the first D.H.10
Amiens I flew in March 1918 with pusher 230 hp
BHP engines. On 20 April the second aircraft, called
Amiens II, flew with tractor 360 hp Rolls-Royce Eagle
VIIIs. As it carried twice the bomb load of the mass-

produced D.H.9, and flew faster and had better defensive armament, a series of production orders were
quickly placed for a total of 1,291 to be built by seven
manufacturers. Deliveries began shortly before the
Armistice and several production machines, called
Amiens III and with the Libery engines, reached
Independent Air Force squadrons in the final month of
the war. Contracts were cut back or terminated but at
least 220 were delivered, more than half these being
of the improved D.H.10A, or Amiens IIIA, type in
which the Liberty engines were mounted on the lower
wings. A small final batch were Eagle-powered Amiens
IIIAs. Four squadrons in Britain, Egypt and India used
this fine aircraft until about 1927, one of its lasting
contributions being the pioneering of service communications and postal routes in all three areas.

de Havilland Mosquito

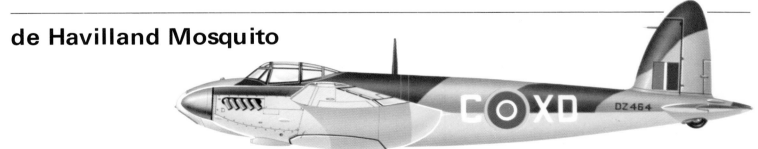

D.H. Mosquito IV (139 Sqn, Marham, 1942).

D.H.98 Mosquito I to 43
Type: designed as high-speed day bomber; see text
for subsequent variants.
Engines: (Mks II, III, IV and early VI) two 1,230 hp
Rolls-Royce Merlin 21 or (late FB.VI) 1,635 hp
Merlin 25; (Mk IX) 1,680 hp Merlin 72; (Mk XVI)
Merlin 72 or 1,710 hp Merlin 73 or 77; (Mk 30) 1,710 hp
Merlin 76; (Mk 33) 1,640 hp Merlin 25; (Mks 34, 35,
36) 1,690 hp Merlin 113/114. Many other variants
had corresponding Merlins made by Packard.

Dimensions: span (except Mk XV) 54 ft 2 in (16·5 m);
length (most common) 40 ft 6 in (12·34 m); (bombers)
40 ft 9½ in; (radar-equipped fighters and Mks 34–38)
typically 41 ft 9 in; (Mk 39) 43 ft 4 in); height (most
common) 15 ft 3½ in (4·66 m).
Weights: empty (Mks II–VI) about 14,100 lb;
(Mks VIII–30) about 15,200 lb; (beyond Mk 30) about
15,900–16,800 lb; maximum gross (Mks II and III)
around 17,500 lb; (Mks IV and VI) about 22,500 lb;
(later night fighters) about 20,500 lb but (HF.XV)

only 17,395 lb; (Mks IX, XVI and marks beyond 30)
typically 25,000 lb (11,340 kg).
Performance: maximum speed, from 300 mph
(TT.39 with M4 sleeve) to 370 mph (595 km/h) for
early night fighters, 380 mph (612 km/h) for III, IV and
VI, 410 mph (660 km/h) for IX, XVI and 30, and 425 mph
for 34 and 35; service ceiling, from 30,000 ft (9144 m)
for low-rated naval versions to 34,500 ft (10,520 m) for

continued on page 58

de Havilland Mosquito (continued)

most marks, to around 40,000 ft (12,190 m) for high-blown versions, with Mk XV reaching 44,000 ft (13,410 m); combat range, typically 1,860 miles (2990 km), with naval TFs down at 1,260 miles and PR.34 up at 3,500 miles.

Armament: see text.
History: see text.

The de Havilland Aircraft Co planned the Mosquito in October 1938 as a high-speed unarmed day bomber, with the added attraction of wooden construction to ease the strain on Britain's hard-pressed materials suppliers. The Air Ministry showed no interest, suggesting instead the Hatfield plant should make wings for existing heavy bombers. In 1940, with extreme reluctance, it was agreed to allow the firm to proceed, the only role thought possible for an unarmed aircraft being reconnaissance. The first prototype, built secretly at Salisbury Hall by a team which grew from 12 in January 1940 to 30 in the summer, was flown painted yellow on 25 November 1940. From it stemmed 7,781 aircraft, built in Britain, Canada and Australia, of the following types:

PR.I Unarmed photo-reconnaissance, with span lengthened from 52 ft 6 in of prototype to 54 ft 2 in but still with short engine nacelles.

F.II Night fighter, with pilot and observer side by side, flat bullet-proof windscreen, extended nacelles (as in all subsequent aircraft, with flaps divided into inner and outer segments) and armament of four 20 mm Hispano cannon with 300 rounds each under the floor and four 0·303 in Brownings with 2,000 rounds each in the nose. First flew 15 May 1941; subsequently fitted with AI Mk IV or V radar or Turbinlight searchlight.

T.III Dual-control trainer, first flown January 1942 but produced mainly after the war (last delivery 1949).

B.IV Unarmed bomber, carrying four 500 lb (227 kg) bombs internally; first delivered to 105 Sqn at Swanton Morley November 1941, making first operational sortie (Cologne, the morning after the first 1,000-bomber night attack) on 31 May 1942. Some later fitted with bulged bomb bays for 4,000 lb (1814 kg) bomb.

FB.VI Fighter-bomber and intruder, by day or night; same guns as F.II but two 250 lb (113 kg) bombs in rear bay and two more (later two 500 lb) on wing racks; alternatively, 50 or 100 gal drop tanks, mines, depth charges or eight 60 lb rockets. Some fitted with AI radar. Total production 2,584, more than any other mark.

B.VII Canadian-built Mk IV, used in North America only.

PR.VIII Reconnaissance conversion of B.IV with high-blown Merlin 61.

Mk IX important advance in bomber (B.IX) and reconnaissance (PR.IX) versions; high-blown two-stage engines, bulged bomb bay for 4,000 lb bomb or extra fuel, much increased weight, paddle-blade propellers and new avionics (Rebecca, Boozer, Oboe or H2S Mk VI).

NF.XII Conversion of F.II fitted with new thimble nose containing AI Mk VIII centimetric radar in place of Brownings.

NF.XIII Similar to Mk XII but built as new, with thimble or bull nose and same wing as Mk VI for drop tanks or other stores; flew August 1943.

NF.XV High-altitude fighter with wings extended to 59 ft, pressurised cockpit, lightened structure, AI Mk VIII in nose and belly pack of four 0·303 in Brownings to combat Ju 86P raiders.

Mk XVI Further major advance with two-stage Merlins, bulged bomb bay and pressurised cockpit. PR.XVI flew July 1943; B.XVI in January 1944, over 1,200 of latter being used for high-level nuisance raids with 4,000 lb bombs.

NF.XVII Night fighter with new AI Mk X or SCR.720 (some with tail-looking scanner also); four 20 mm each with 500 rounds.

FB.XVIII Dubbed Tse-Tse Fly, this multi-role Coastal Command fighter had low-blown engines and carried a 57 mm six-pounder Molins gun with 25 rounds plus four Brownings, as well as eight 60 lb rockets or bombs.

NF.XIX Mk XIII developed with AI.VIII or X or SCR.720 in bulged Universal Nose and low-blown Merlin 25s.

B.XX Canadian-built B.IV (USAAF designation F-8).

FB.21 to T.29, Canadian marks with Packard V-1650 (Merlin) engines, not all built.

NF.30 Night fighter with two-stage engines, paddle blades, AI Mk X and various sensing, spoofing or jamming avionics; based on Mk XIX.

PR.32 Extended-span reconnaissance version with Merlin 113/114.

Mk 33 First Royal Navy Sea Mosquito version, with power-folding wings, oleo main legs (in place of rubber in compression), low-blown engines driving four-blade propellers, arrester hook, four 20 mm cannon, torpedo (or various bomb/rocket loads), American ASH radar and rocket JATO boost.

PR.34 Strategic reconnaissance version, with 113/114 engines, extra-bulged belly for 1,269 gal fuel (200 gal drop tanks) and pressure cabin.

B.35 Equivalent bomber version, with PR and target-tug offshoots.

NF.36 Postwar fighter, with 113/114 engines and AI Mk X.

TF.37 Naval torpedo-fighter; basically Mk 33 with AI/ASV Mk XIII.

NF.38 Final fighter, mainly exported; AI Mk IX, forward cockpit.

TT.39 Complete rebuild by General Aircraft as specialised target tug.

FB.40 Australian-built Mk VI, with PR.40 as conversions.

PR.41 Australian-built derivative of PR.IX and Mk 40.

T.43 Australian trainer; all Australian production had Packard engines.

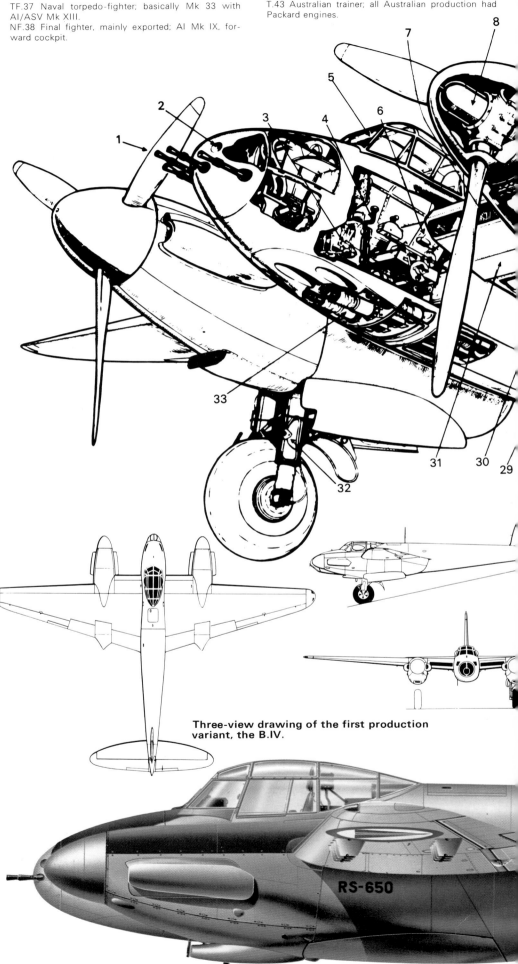

Three-view drawing of the first production variant, the B.IV.

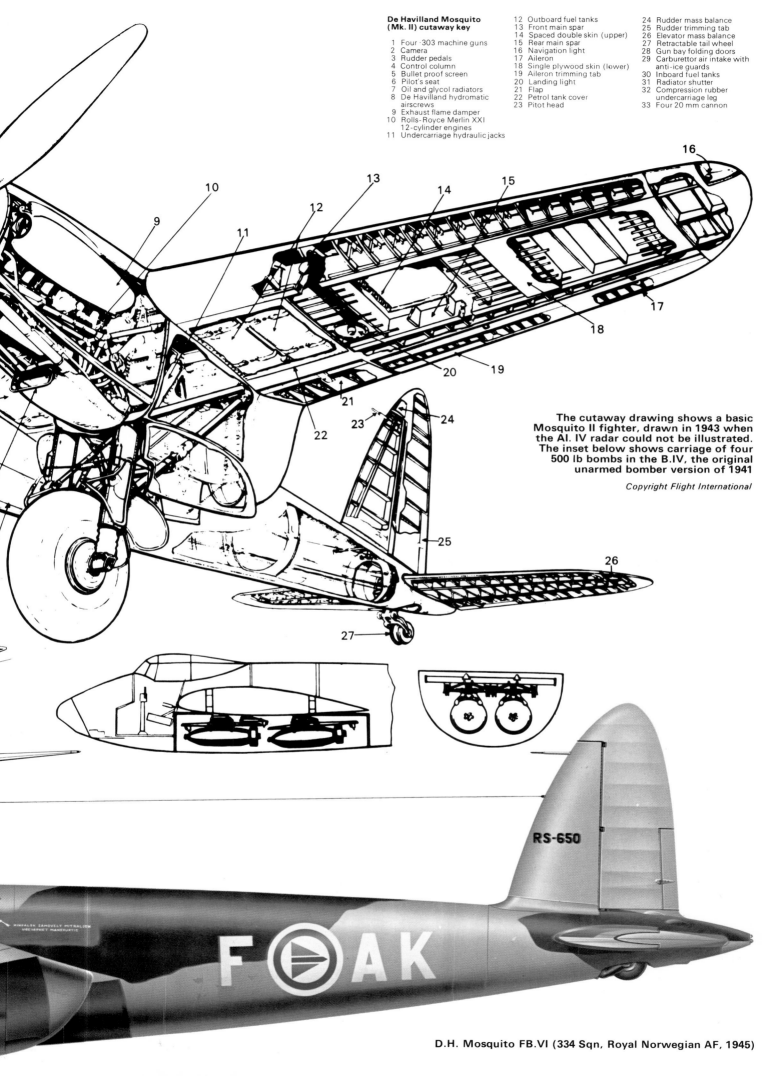

De Havilland Mosquito (Mk. II) cutaway key

1 Four ·303 machine guns
2 Camera
3 Rudder pedals
4 Control column
5 Bullet proof screen
6 Pilot's seat
7 Oil and glycol radiators
8 De Havilland hydromatic airscrews
9 Exhaust flame damper
10 Rolls-Royce Merlin XXI 12-cylinder engines
11 Undercarriage hydraulic jacks
12 Outboard fuel tanks
13 Front main spar
14 Spaced double skin (upper)
15 Rear main spar
16 Navigation light
17 Aileron
18 Single plywood skin (lower)
19 Aileron trimming tab
20 Landing light
21 Flap
22 Petrol tank cover
23 Pitot head
24 Rudder mass balance
25 Rudder trimming tab
26 Elevator mass balance
27 Retractable tail wheel
28 Gun bay folding doors
29 Carburettor air intake with anti-ice guards
30 Inboard fuel tanks
31 Radiator shutter
32 Compression rubber undercarriage leg
33 Four 20 mm cannon

The cutaway drawing shows a basic Mosquito II fighter, drawn in 1943 when the AI. IV radar could not be illustrated. The inset below shows carriage of four 500 lb bombs in the B.IV, the original unarmed bomber version of 1941

Copyright Flight International

RS-650

F◉AK

D.H. Mosquito FB.VI (334 Sqn, Royal Norwegian AF, 1945)

de Havilland Hornet/ Sea Hornet

D.H.103 Hornet F.1 to FR.4 and Sea Hornet F.20 to PR.22
Type: F.3 single-seat day fighter-bomber; Sea Hornet 21, two-seat naval all-weather fighter.
Engines: two 2,030 hp Rolls-Royce Merlin (Mk 3, one Mk 130, one 131; Mk 21, one 134, one 135).
Dimensions: span 45 ft (13·72 m); length (Mk 3) 36 ft 8 in (11·1 m), (Mk 21) 37 ft (11·3 m); height 14 ft 2 in (4·26 m).
Weights: empty (Mk 3) 12,880 lb (5842 kg); (Mk 21) 14,230 lb (6454 kg); loaded (Mk 3) 20,900 lb (9481 kg); (Mk 21) 19,530 lb (8858 kg).
Performance: maximum speed (Mk 3) 472 mph (760 km/h); (Mk 21) 430 mph (692 km/h); initial climb (Mk 3) 4,600 ft (1400 m)/min; (Mk 21) 3,600 ft (1100 m)/min; service ceiling (Mk 3) 35,000 ft (10,670 m); (Mk 21) 37,000 ft (11,280 m); maximum range (Mk 3) 3,000 miles (4830 km), (Mk 21) 1,500 miles (2415 km).
Armament: four fixed 20 mm Hispano cannon under floor; provision for wing racks for two 1,000 lb (454 kg) bombs or eight 60 lb (27 kg) rockets.
History: first flight (D.H.103 prototype) 28 July 1944; first service delivery (F.1) 7 February 1945; first flight of semi-navalised Hornet, 19 April 1945; first Sea Hornet deliveries, October 1946; final delivery (NF.21) November 1950, (FR.4) June 1952.

Like the Mosquito, the Hornet was proposed by de Havilland; this time there was no opposition, as the need for a long-range strike fighter for the Pacific war was inescapable. Specification F.12/43 was written round it and design and construction proceeded rapidly. Much smaller than the Mosquito, it actually had more powerful Merlin engines, the left and right four-blade propellers rotating in opposite directions (hence the different engine mark numbers) to improve handling. The structure was part-wood and part-metal, with the new Redux bonding (hot-glueing) method used in production for the first time. The prototype was delightful to handle, offered a perfect pilot view and achieved the phenomenal speed of 485 mph (faster than the contemporary Meteor jet). Deliveries of the F.1 single-seat fighter began just too late for squadrons to see action. This was followed by the F.3 with much increased tankage and large dorsal fin and, finally, the FR.4 with added cameras. Most of the 204 RAF Hornets were Mk 3s, used with great effect against Malayan bandits until 1955. They were the last piston-engined RAF fighters. It was obvious that

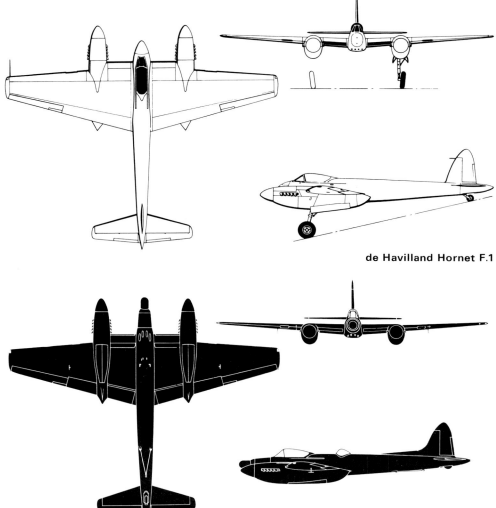

de Havilland Hornet F.1

de Havilland Sea Hornet F.21

the Hornet would be an ideal Fleet Air Arm fighter and, after specification N.5/44 had been written, the Heston Aircraft Co designed a conversion to the Sea Hornet, carrier trials beginning in August 1945. The Sea Hornet F.20 was very like a navalised F.3, equipping 801 Sqn at Ford in June 1947. The Sea Hornet

NF.21, to specification N.21/45, was a night fighter with a second cockpit for a radar observer behind the wing, and ASH radar in a thimble nose. Tailplane span was increased and flame-damped exhausts were fitted. There were 78 NF.21s and 24 unarmed Sea Hornet PR.22 reconnaissance machines.

de Havilland Vampire (single-seat)

D.H.100 Vampire F.1 to FB.30 and SNCASE Mistral
Type: single-seat fighter (FB.6 fighter-bomber).
Engine: one de Havilland Goblin centrifugal turbojet rated at 3,100 lb (1420 kg) thrust; (FB.6) Goblin 3, rated at 3,300 lb (1498 kg).
Dimensions: span (Mk 1) 40 ft (12·19 m); (FB.6) 38 ft (11·6 m); length 30 ft 9 in (9·37 m); height 8 ft 10 in (2·7 m).
Weights: empty (F.1) 6,372 lb (2890 kg); (FB.6) 7,200 lb (3266 kg); loaded (F.1) 8,578 lb (3890 kg), (FB.6 with drop tanks) 12,290 lb (5600 kg).
Performance: maximum speed (F.1) 540 mph (869 km/h); (FB.6) 548 mph (883 km/h); initial climb (F.1) 4,200 ft (1280 m)/min; (FB.6) 4,800 ft (1463 m)/min; service ceiling (F.1) 41,000 ft (12,500 m); (FB.6) 44,000 ft (13,410 m); range at height (F.1) 730 miles (1175 km), (FB.6 with drop tanks) 1,400 miles (2253 km).
Armament: four fixed 20 mm Hispano cannon each with 150 rounds (FB.6, in addition, underwing racks for two 1,000 lb bombs or eight 60 lb rockets).
History: first flight (D.H.100) 20 September 1943; (first production F.1) 20 April 1945; service delivery, December 1945; final delivery of British-built fighter (FB.9) December 1953.
The D.H.100 was the first aircraft designed with the appreciation that the turbojet made possible, and might demand, a completely new arrangement of the parts of an aeroplane. Maj. Frank Halford had designed a single-entry turbojet, the de Havilland H.1 (later named Goblin), giving a thrust of about 2,500 lb. The aircraft side of the firm reasoned that, if the installation was carefully done, this would be enough for a small single-engined jet fighter. The final answer was a short central nacelle, built of wood, containing the pressurised cockpit ahead of the engine, with wing-root inlets and short jet pipe. The tail was carried on twin

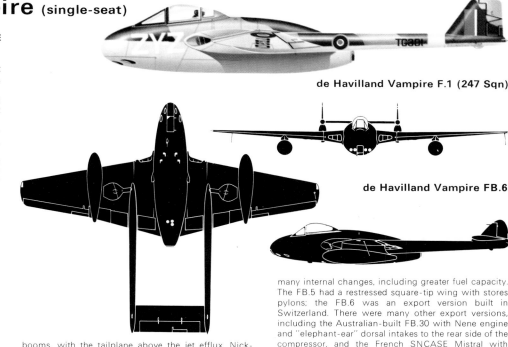

de Havilland Vampire F.1 (247 Sqn)

de Havilland Vampire FB.6

booms, with the tailplane above the jet efflux. Nicknamed the "Spider Crab", the prototype soon became the first Allied aircraft to exceed 500 mph, but the production Mk 1 fighter — entrusted to English Electric at Samlesbury, because the parent firm had no spare capacity — failed to reach squadrons in time for the war. It was replaced by the F.3, with traditional DH-shape fins and rudders and lowered tailplane, and

many internal changes, including greater fuel capacity. The FB.5 had a restressed square-tip wing with stores pylons; the FB.6 was an export version built in Switzerland. There were many other export versions, including the Australian-built FB.30 with Nene engine and "elephant-ear" dorsal intakes to the rear side of the compressor, and the French SNCASE Mistral with Hispano Nene fed by enlarged wing-root ducts. The final RAF version was the tropicalised FB.9. In addition the Sea Vampire F.20 was made in small numbers. Including the two-seat night fighters and trainers, the total production of all variants of Vampire was 4,206, greater than that for any other British post-war aircraft of any type.

de Havilland Vampire (two-seat)

D.H.113 Vampire NF.10 and D.H.115 Vampire Trainer

Type: D.H.113, two-seat night fighter; D.H.115, dual-control trainer.

Engine: one de Havilland Goblin centrifugal turbojet; (NF) 3,350 lb (1520 kg) thrust Goblin 3; (T) 3,500 lb (1589 kg) thrust Goblin 35.

Dimensions: span 38 ft (11·6 m); length 34 ft 7 in (10·55 m); height (NF) 6 ft 7 in (2 m); (T) 6 ft 2 in (1·86 m).

Weights: empty (NF) 6,984 lb (3172 kg); (T) 7,380 lb (3347 kg); loaded (NF) 11,350 lb (5148 kg); (T) 11,150 lb (5060 kg) clean or 12,920 lb (5860 kg) with drop tanks.

Performance: maximum speed (NF and T) 549 mph (885 km/h); initial climb (NF and T) 4,500 ft (1372 m)/min; service ceiling (NF and T) 40,000 ft (12,200 m); range (NF) 780 miles (1255 km) clean, 1,220 miles (1964 km) with drop tanks; (T) 853 miles (1370 km) clean, 1,300 miles (2092 km) with drop tanks.

Armament: (NF) four fixed 20 mm Hispano cannon; (T) two 20 mm Hispanos (four in most T.55 export versions), plus two 500 lb (227 kg) bombs or other stores.

History: first flight (D.H.113) 28 August 1949; (D.H.115) 15 November 1950; first service delivery (NF) September 1951, (T) February 1952; withdrawal from service (T) 1967 (but continuing in many'overseas air forces).

The RAF was amazingly slow to order jet night fighters. De Havilland planned the D.H.113 as a private venture,

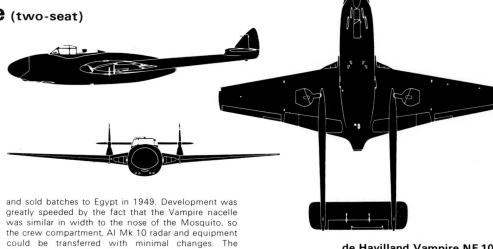

de Havilland Vampire NF.10

and sold batches to Egypt in 1949. Development was greatly speeded by the fact that the Vampire nacelle was similar in width to the nose of the Mosquito, so the crew compartment, AI Mk 10 radar and equipment could be transferred with minimal changes. The biggest snag was that the pilot and observer sat close together in ordinary seats, with sole entry and exit by the hinged roof, which was judged inadequate for emergency escape. Nevertheless, when exports of arms to Egypt were banned in 1950 the RAF took over the contract and received 95 aircraft, which were first used by 25 Sqn at West Malling from late 1951. This rapid development reflected the fact that the type did not have to meet an official specification. The trainer was an equally obvious development which sold in large numbers to many customers. Soon after pro-

duction began, at Hatfield and Chester, ejection seats were fitted, the cockpit canopy was changed to a frameless upward-hinged hood, the vertical tail surfaces were redesigned and provision was made for tanks or stores under the wings. Main model was the RAF's T.11, of which 731 were delivered; other versions were the Australian-built T.33 and T.35, and T.34 for the RAN, and the 55 T.55s assembled from British parts by Hindustan Aircraft (India). In 1976 large numbers were still in use around the world.

---

de Havilland Venom (single-seat)

D.H.112 Venom FB.1 to FB.50

Type: single-seat day fighter-bomber.

Engine: one 4,850 lb (2200 kg) thrust Rolls-Royce (formerly de Havilland, then Bristol Siddeley) Ghost 103 centrifugal turbojet.

Dimensions: span (over tanks) 41 ft 8 in (12·7 m); length 31 ft 10 in (9·7 m); height 6 ft 2 in (1·9 m).

Weights: empty 8,100 lb (3674 kg); loaded 15,310 lb (6945 kg).

Performance: maximum speed 640 mph (1030 km/h) clean, 595 mph (857 km/h) with external stores; initial climb 9,000 ft (2743 m)/min clean, 7,200 ft (2195 m)/min at full load; service ceiling 45,000 ft (13,720 m) clean.

Armament: four fixed 20 mm Hispano Mk 5 cannon; two underwing pylons each cleared for 1,000 lb (454 kg) plus attachments further outboard for eight 60 lb (27 kg) rockets.

History: first flight (prototype) 2 September 1949; first service delivery (FB.1) December 1951; withdrawal from RAF service June 1962 (continuing in other nations).

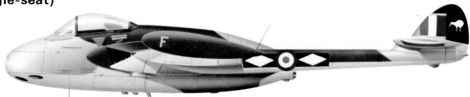

de Havilland Venom FB.1 (on hire to RNZAF, 14 Sqn)

As a natural successor to the Vampire the D.H.112 was designed to specification 15/49 (written around the company's proposal) and was originally to have been the Vampire FB.8. Use of the more powerful Ghost engine, however, called for extensive airframe changes, including a new wing of 10% thickness (compared with 14%) and very slight sweep, a new and thinner main landing gear and a longer-span tailplane. Despite lack of an ejection seat and a very poor rate of roll, the Venom was chosen for production on a huge scale at de Havilland and at Bristol and in four continental

countries. Fortunately this plan was abandoned, but 373 FB.1s were supplied to the RAF (at first striped in red to denote a temporary manoeuvre restriction) followed by 150 of the much-improve FB.4 type with ejection seat, powered ailerons and redesigned vertical tail surfaces. Export single-seat Venoms were supplied to Iraq and Venezuela and no fewer than 250 FB.50s were constructed, with their engines, under licence in Switzerland in 1952–55. Nearly all the Swiss aircraft have been remanufactured with improved equipment and longer fatigue life.

---

de Havilland Venom (two-seat)

D.H.112 Venom NF.2, 3 and 51, Sea Venom FAW.20 to 53 and SNCASE Aquilon.

Type: two-seat night and all-weather fighter (Sea Venom and Aquilon for naval use).

Engine: one 4,950 lb (2245 kg) thrust de Havilland (later Bristol Siddeley, but withdrawn before Rolls-Royce) Ghost 104 centrifugal turbojet.

Dimensions: (NF.3) span (over tanks) 41 ft 9 in (12·8 m); (FAW.21 and Aquilon) 42 ft 10 in (13·05 m); length (NF.3) 36 ft 8 in; (FAW.21) 36 ft 7 in; (Aquilon) 36 ft 10 in; height 8 ft 6 in (2·59 m).

Weights: empty, not released (about 8,800 lb, 4000 kg); loaded (typical) 15,800 lb (7167 kg).

Performance: maximum speed (NF.3) 630 mph (1014 km/h); (FAW.21) 590 mph (950 km/h); initial climb (NF.3) 8,762 ft (2840 m)/min; service ceiling 49,200 ft (15,000 m); range (typical) 1,000 miles (1610 km).

Armament: four fixed 20 mm Hispano Mk 5 cannon; Sea Venom and Aquilon, provision for two, 1,000 lb stores and eight 60 lb rockets; Sea Venom FAW.22 only, two Firestreak air-to-air missiles; Aquilon only, two Sidewinder and two Nord 5103 air-to-air missiles.

History: first flight (private venture prototype) 22 August 1950; (Sea Venom 20) February 1951; (production NF.2) 1952; (NF.3) 22 February 1953; (prototype FAW.21) 10 March 1954; (Aquilon) 25 March 1954.

Following very closely on the single-seat Venom, the two-seat radar-equipped night fighter was flown as a private venture without equipment for combat use. Official assessment found it good to handle, except for the very poor rate of roll, and agreed that it would also

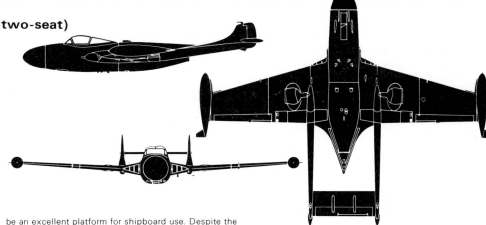

de Havilland Sea Venom FAW.21

be an excellent platform for shipboard use. Despite the fact that there were no provisions for emergency escape, production of the NF.2 for the RAF began in 1952. Pilot and navigator were huddled together, the navigator being just behind and to the right, and the roof of the heavily framed canopy had to be lifted manually. After building 60 (excluding a batch built for Sweden as the NF.51) the Chester factory switched to the NF.3 with the old AI.10 radar replaced by a US APS-57 supplied under the Mutual Defence Assistance Programme, and with a redesigned tail, powered ailerons and quick-jettison frameless canopy. Production of the NF.3 totalled 129. The Sea Venom FAW.20, with Ghost 103 engine was an interim machine, of which 50 were built; features included finned tip tanks, power-folding wings, catapult spools and arrester hook. The FAW.21, with US radar, had

the redesigned tail and other NF.3 improvements and 36 were exported as the Mk 53 to Australia. Final batches had Martin-Baker Mk 4 seats, which were retro-fitted to many early Sea Venoms. The last variant was the FAW.22 with provision for Firestreak guided missiles and powered by a 5,300 lb (2404 kg) Ghost 105. The Aquilon (North Wind) was a considerably redesigned version made by SNCASE in France for the Aéronavale, powered by a Fiat-built Ghost and with sliding canopy and Westinghouse APQ-65 radar. Nearly half the 114 Aquilons were single-seaters.

For later de Havilland aircraft see under Hawker Siddeley

de Havilland Canada Caribou

DHC-4 Caribou (C-7A and CC-108)
Type: STOL tactical transport.
Engines: two 1,450 hp Pratt & Whitney R-2000-D5ror-7M2 fourteen-cylinder two-row radials.
Dimensions: span 95 ft 7½ in (29·15 m); length 72 ft 7 in (22·13 m); height 31 ft 9 in (9·7 m).
Weights: empty, equipped, 18,260 lb (8283 kg); normal gross 28,500 lb (12,928 kg); maximum 31,300 lb (14,197 kg).
Performance: maximum speed 216 mph (347 km/h); initial climb 1,355 ft (413 m)/min; service ceiling 24,800 ft (7560 m); range, 242 miles (390 km) with maximum payload of 8,740 lb (3965 kg), 1,307 miles (2103 km) with maximum fuel; take-off run to 50 ft (15 m) and landing distance from same height, both 1,200 ft (366 m).
Armament: not normally fitted.
History: first flight 30 July 1958; service delivery (evaluation) August 1959; service delivery (inventory) 1961.

Designed to combine the carrying capacity of a C-47 (DC-3) with the STOL (short take-off and landing) performance of the company's earlier Beaver and Otter, the Caribou was a company venture undertaken in partnership with the Canadian Department of Defense Production. One was ordered by the RCAF (later Canadian Armed Forces), designated CC-108. Five, designated YAC-1, were delivered for evaluation by the US Army and subsequently 159 of a heavier version were delivered to that service in 1961–65; at first called AC-1, they were redesignated CV-2A and CV-2B. In 1967, when many were serving in SE Asia, this force was transferred to the US Air Force and restyled C-7A. Meanwhile, production continued for 12 other air forces around the world, as well as the United Nations and several civilian organizations. By

1975 over 330 had been built. Carrying up to 32 equipped troops, 22 stretchers (litters) or two small combat vehicles, the Caribou's main attribute is its ability to operate from short rough strips inaccessible to other fixed-wing aircraft. One C-7A, equipped with nine separate communications stations along the fuselage, served in Vietnam as an airborne command post with the 1st (Air) Cavalry Division.

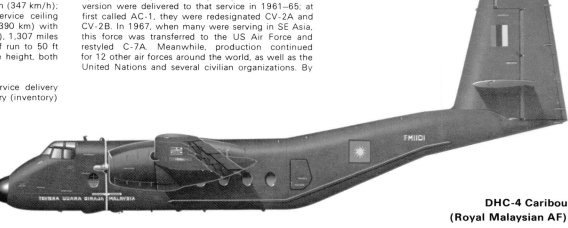

**DHC-4 Caribou
(Royal Malaysian AF)**

---

de Havilland Canada Buffalo

DHC-5 Buffalo (C-8A, CC-115)
Type: STOL tactical transport.
Engines: two 2,850 ehp General Electric T64-10 single-shaft turboprops (CC-115, 3,060 ehp T64-CT-820).
Dimensions: span 96 ft (29·26 m); length (C-8A) 77 ft 4 in (23·57 m), (CC-115) 79 ft (24·1 m); height 28 ft 8 in (8·73 m).
Weights: empty, equipped, 23,157 lb (10,505 kg); loaded 41,000 lb (18,598 kg).
Performance: maximum speed 271 mph (435 km/h), which is also maximum continuous cruising speed; initial climb 1,890 ft (575 m)/min; service ceiling 30,000 ft (9145 m); range, 507 miles (815 km) with maximum payload of 13,843 lb (6279 kg), 2,170 miles (3490 km) with maximum fuel and full allowances; take-off and landing distances, in order of 1,100 ft (335 m).
Armament: not normally fitted.
History: first flight 9 April 1964; service delivery (evaluation) April 1965; final delivery (Peru) 1972.
Unlike the Caribou, the Buffalo was designed to meet a customer requirement, winning, against 24 other contenders, an order from the US Army for a new STOL transport specified in May 1962. Obviously based on the Caribou, the Buffalo has an even higher maximum lift coefficient, T-tail, advanced turboprop

engines and considerably increased gross weight. Development costs were shared one-third each by DHC, the US Army and the Canadian government. Four aircraft, designated CV-7A, were supplied to the US Army for evaluation, but a change of policy terminated the whole programme. DHC were rescued by an order for 15 CC-115s, with uprated engines and nose radar, for the Canadian Armed Forces. Subsequently the Brazilian Air Force bought 24 and Peru 16 and alto-

gether 59 were built. One of the US aircraft, redesignated C-8A by the US Air Force, was converted into an experimental augmentor-wing machine powered by blown and deflected Spey turbofans, while a CC-115 has conducted successful trials with the Bell Air-Cushion Landing Gear (ACLG) for operations from any kind of surface. As an assault transport the Buffalo can carry 41 troops, a 105 mm gun or Pershing missile.

DHC-5 (with nose radar)

Dornier Do 17

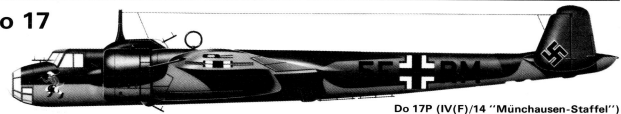

Do 17P (IV(F)/14 "Münchausen-Staffel")

Do 17E, F, K and P
Type: three-seat medium bomber (17F, reconnaissance).
Engines: two 750 hp BMW VI 7·3 12-cylinder vee liquid-cooled; 17P, two 1,000 hp BMW 132N nine-cylinder radials.
Dimensions: span 59 ft 0½ in (18 m); length (17E, F) 53 ft 3¾ in (16·25 m); (17P) 52 ft 9¾ in (16·1 m); height (17E, F) 14 ft 2 in (4·3 m); (17P) 14 ft 11 in (4·57 m).
Weights: empty (17E, F) 9,921 lb (4500 kg) (17P) 10,140 lb (4600 kg); loaded (17E) 15,520 lb (7050 kg); (17F) 15,430 lb (7000 kg) (17P) 16,887 lb (7660 kg).
Performance: maximum speed (17E, F) 220 mph (355 km/h); (17P) 249 mph (400 km/h); service ceiling (17E) 16,730 ft (5100 m); (17F) 19,685 ft (6000 m); (17P) 20,340 ft (6200 m); typical range (17E) 620 miles (1000 km); (17F) 994 miles (1600 km); (17P) 745 miles (1200 km).
Armament: (17E, F) one 7·92 mm MG 15 manually aimed from rear ventral hatch and one manually aimed to rear from dorsal position, with internal bomb load of 1,650 lb (750 kg); (17P) three MG 15s, one (nor-

mally fixed to fire ahead) in right windscreen, one in ventral hatch and one in dorsal position, with internal bomb load of 2,205 lb (1000 kg).
History: first flight (single-fin V1 prototype) autumn 1934; (Do 17E) 7 November 1936; (Do 17F) 10 November 1936; (Do 17P) late 1937.

Popularly dubbed "the flying pencil" in both Germany and Britain, the Do 17 was not planned as a bomber and secretly tested as a civil transport; its history was the other way round. Deutsche Luft Hansa decided its slender body left much too little room for the six passengers, but the Reischsluftfahrtministerium eventually decided the Do 17 was worth developing as a bomber. Numerous prototypes were built with different noses and engines and eventually the Do 17E-1 and the F-1 reconnaissance machine went into large-scale, and widely subcontracted, production for the embryo Luftwaffe. As early as March 1937 both were in combat service, with one Staffel of 17Fs being in Spain with the Legion Kondor (there to prove virtually immune to

interception by the Republican forces). In the spring of 1937 a Do 17M prototype with powerful DB 600 engines walked away from all the fighter aircraft at the International Military Aircraft Competition at Zurich. This caused a great sensation and the first nation to buy the new bomber was Yugoslavia, receiving 20 from Germany plus a construction licence. The Yugoslav Do 17Kb-1 had a very early nose profile (the same, in fact, as the Zurich demonstrator) and Gnome-Rhône 14N radial engines. They had a 20 mm Hispano cannon and three 7·92 mm Brownings. About 70 were on strength when the Germans invaded Yugoslavia in April 1941, two escaping to Greece with cargoes of gold bullion. The several hundred E and F models formed the biggest portion of the Luftwaffe bomber and reconnaissance force up to 1939, but by the end of that year had been relegated to operational training. The later Do 17M-1 (Bramo Fafnir radials of 1,000 hp) and Do 17P succeeded the E and F in production during 1937 and saw combat during World War II. They were the final types to retain the slender "flying pencil" shape and hemispherical nose-cap.

Dornier Do 17Z and 215

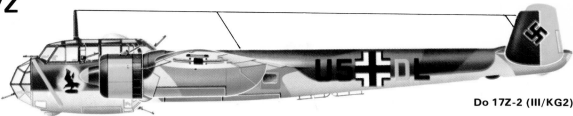

Do 17Z-2 (III/KG2)

Do 17Z-1 and -2 and Do 215A-1, B-1 and B-5

Type: four-seat medium bomber and reconnaissance.
Engines: (Do 17Z-2) two 1000 hp Bramo Fafnir 323P nine-cylinder radials; (Do 215B-1) two 1075 hp Daimler-Benz DB 601A 12-cylinder inverted-vee liquid-cooled.
Dimensions: (both) span 59 ft 0½ in (18 m); length 51 ft 9½ in (15·79 m); height 14 ft 11½ in (4·56 m).
Weights: empty (Do 17Z-2) 11,484 lb (5210 kg); (Do 215B-1) 12,730 lb (5775 kg); loaded (both) 19,841 lb (9000 kg).
Performance: maximum speed (Do 17Z-2) 263 mph (425 km/h); (Do 215B-1) 280 mph (450 km/h); service ceiling (Do 17Z-2) 26,740 ft (8150 m); (Do 215B-1) 31,170 ft (9500 m); range with half bomb load (Do 17Z-2) 721 miles (1160 km); (Do 215B-1) 932 miles (1500 km).

Armament: normally six 7·92 mm Rheinmetall MG 15 machine guns, one fixed in nose, remainder on

manually aimed mounts in front windscreen, two beam windows, and above and below at rear; internal bomb load up to 2205 lb (1000 kg).
History: first flight (Do 17S prototype) early 1938; (Do 17Z-2) early 1939; (Do 215V1 prototype) late 1938; first delivery (Do 17Z-1) January 1939, (Do 215A-1) December 1939; termination of production (Do 17Z series) July 1940, (Do 215 series) January 1941.

Whereas the slenderness of the first families of Do 17 bombers had earned them the nickname of "Flying Pencil", the Do 17S introduced a completely new front end with much deeper cabin and extensive window area all round. Such a change had been obvious from the inadequate defensive armament of the earlier models, revealed in the Spanish Civil War, and the penalty of increased weight and drag was to some degree countered by a search for more powerful engines. The S prototype had DB 600 liquid-cooled

engines, as did the Do 17U five-seat pathfinder, of which 12 were delivered to the nine Bomber Groups already using earlier Do 17s. The Do 17Z, powered by the Bramo radial engine, was at first underpowered and full bomb load had to await the more powerful Fafnir 323P of the 17Z-2. Between late 1939 and the summer of 1940 about 535 Do 17Z series bomber and reconnaissance machines were delivered and, though they suffered high attrition over Britain, they did much effective work and were the most popular and reliable of all Luftwaffe bombers of the early Blitzkrieg period. The Do 215 was the Do 17Z renumbered as an export version, with the more powerful DB 601 engine. The Do 215A-1 for Sweden became the Do 215B-0 and B-1 for the Luftwaffe and altogether 101 were put into service for bomber and reconnaissance roles; 12 were converted as Do 215B-5 night intruders, with a "solid" nose carrying two cannon and four machine guns, and operated by night over Britain before transfer to Sicily in October 1941.

Dornier Do 217

Do 217E-2/R-19 (9/KG2, Gilze-Rijen)

Do 217E-2, K-2, M-1, J-2/N-2, P-1

Type: (E, K, M) four-seat bomber; (J, N) three-seat night fighter; (P) four-seat high-altitude reconnaissance.
Engines: (E-2, J-2) two 1580 hp BMW 801A or 801M 18-cylinder two-row radials; (K-2) two 1700 hp BMW 801D; (M-1, N-2) two 1750 hp Daimler-Benz DB 603A 12-cylinder inverted-vee liquid-cooled; (P-1) two 1860 hp DB 603B supercharged by DB 605T in the fuselage.
Dimensions: span 62 ft 4 in (19 m); (K-2) 81 ft 4½ in (24·8 m); (P-1) 80 ft 4 in (24·4 m); length 56 ft 9¼ in (17·3 m); (E-2 with early dive brakes) 60 ft 10½ in (18·5 m); (K-2 and M-1) 55 ft 9 in (17 m); (J and N) 58 ft 9 in (17·9 m); (P) 58 ft 11 in (17·95 m); height 16 ft 5 in (5 m) (all versions same within 2 in).
Weights: empty (E-2) 19,522 lb (8850 kg); (M-1) 19,985 lb (9000 kg); (K-2, J and N) all about 21,000 lb (9450 kg); (P) about 23,000 lb (10,350 kg); loaded (E-2) 33,070 lb (15,000 kg); (K-2, M-1) 36,817 lb (16,570 kg); (J and N) 30,203 lb (13,590 kg); (P) 35,200 lb (15,840 kg).
Performance: maximum speed (E-2) 320 mph (515 km/h); (K-2) 333 mph (533 km/h); (M-1) 348 mph (557 km/h); (J and N) about 311 mph (498 km/h); (P) 488 mph (781 km/h); service ceiling (E-2) 24,610 ft (7500 m); (K-2) 29,530 ft (9000 m); (M-1) 24,140 ft (7358 m); (J and N) 27,560 ft (8400 m); (P) 53,000 ft (16,154 m); range with full bomb load, about 1,300 miles (2100 km) for all versions.
Armament: (E-2) one fixed 15 mm MG 151/15 in nose, one 13 mm MG 131 in dorsal turret, one MG 131 manually aimed at lower rear, and three 7·92 mm MG 15 manually aimed in nose and beam windows; maximum bomb load 8818 lb (4000 kg), including 3307 lb (1500 kg) external; (K-2) defensive armament similar to E-2, plus battery of four 7·92 mm MG 81 fixed rearward-firing in tail and optional pair fixed rearward-firing in nacelles (all sighted and fired by pilot), and offensive load of two FX 1400 radio controlled glide bombs and/or (K-3 version) two Hs 293 air-to-surface rocket guided missiles; (M-1) as E-2 except MG 15s replaced by larger number of MG 81; (J-2 and N-2) typically four 20 mm MG FF cannon and four 7·92 mm MG 17 in nose plus MG 131 for lower rear defence (N-2 often had later guns such as MG 151/20 in nose and MG 151/20 or MK 108 30 mm in Schräge Musik upward-firing installation); (P) three pairs of MG 81 for defence, and two 1102 lb bombs on underwing racks.
History: first flight (Do 217V1) August 1938; (pre-production Do 217A-0) October or November 1939; first delivery of E series, late 1940; termination of production, late 1943.

Superficially a scaled-up Do 215, powered at first by the same DB 601 engines, the 217 was actually considerably larger and totally different in detail design. Much of Dornier's efforts in 1938–40 were devoted to

Dornier Do 217N-2 night fighter

finding more powerful engines and improving the flying qualities, and when the BMW 801 radial was available the 217 really got into its stride and carried a heavier bomb load than any other Luftwaffe bomber of the time. Early E models, used from late 1940, had no dorsal turret and featured a very long extension of the rear fuselage which opened into an unusual dive brake. This was soon abandoned, but the 217 blossomed out into a prolific family which soon included the 217J night fighter, often produced by converting E-type bombers, and the N which was likewise produced by converting the liquid-cooled M. Several

series carried large air-to-surface missiles steered by radio command from a special crew station in the bomber. Long-span K-2s of III/KG 100 scored many successes with their formidable missiles in the Mediterranean, their biggest bag being the Italian capital ship *Roma* as she steamed to the Allies after Italy's capitulation. The pressurised high-altitude P series had fantastic performance that would have put them out of reach of any Allied fighters had they been put into service in time. From 1943, Dornier devoted more effort to the technically difficult Do 317, which never went into service.

Dornier Do 24

Do 24T
Type: reconnaissance flying boat (typical crew, six).
Engines: three 1,000 hp Bramo Fafnir 323R-2 nine-cylinder radials.
Dimensions: span 88 ft 7 in (27 m); length 72 ft 2 in (22 m); height 17 ft 10 in (5·45 m).
Weights: empty 29,700 lb (13,500 kg); loaded 40,565 lb (18,400 kg).
Performance: maximum speed 211 mph (340 km/h); service ceiling 19,360 ft (5900 m); maximum range 2,950 miles (4750 km).
Armament: one 7·92 mm MG 15 machine gun in bow turret, one MG 15 in tail turret and one 20 mm MG 151/20 or 30 mm MK 103 cannon in dorsal turret behind wing; underwing racks for 12 110 lb (50 kg) bombs or other stores.
History: first flight (Do 24V3) 3 July 1937; service delivery (Do 24K) November 1937; withdrawal from service (Spain) 1967.

This excellent trimotor flying boat was one of the very few aircraft of the Nazi period to be designed for a foreign government. The customer was the Netherlands and by 1940 a total of 11 had been built by Weserflugzeugbau and flown out to the Dutch East Indies naval air service (MLD). In addition, 26 more had been supplied by the Dutch de Schelde and Aviolanda companies, under a government-purchased licence. After the invasion of the Low Countries production was continued in Holland for the Luftwaffe,

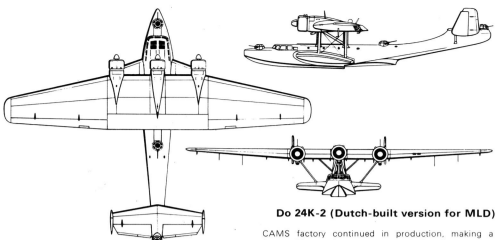

with the French Potez-CAMS factory at Sartrouville also assigned to Do 24 production in 1941. Production for the Luftwaffe amounted to 170 in Holland and 48 in France and the type was met all round the European coasts. One force-landed in Sweden in 1944, was impressed into RSAF service as the Tp 24 and not surrendered to the USSR until 1951. After VE-day the

Do 24K-2 (Dutch-built version for MLD)

CAMS factory continued in production, making a further 20 aircraft to augment ex-Luftwaffe machines for a force of more than 60 in Aéronavale service until 1955. The remaining aircraft were sold to Spain to augment an original force of 12 purchased from Germany in 1944. Designated HR-5, the Do 24T-3 in Spain and the Spanish Mediterranean and Atlantic islands was the last type of large military flying boat operating in Europe. Since 1969 Dornier has been seeking markets for the proposed Do 24/72 development, powered by three 1,800 hp Lycoming turboprops.

Dornier Do 335 Pfeil

Do 335A-1 and A-6
Type: (A-1) single-seat fighter, (A-6) two-seat night fighter.
Engines: two 1,900 hp Daimler-Benz DB 603G 12-cylinder inverted-vee liquid-cooled, in push/pull arrangement.
Dimensions: span 45 ft 4 in (13·8 m); length 45 ft 6 in (13·87 m); height 16 ft 4 in (4 m).
Weights: empty (A-1) 16,314 lb (7400 kg); (A-6) 16,975 lb (7700 kg); maximum loaded (both) 25,800 lb (11,700 kg).
Performance: maximum speed (A-1) 413 mph (665 km/h) sustained; 477 mph (765 km/h) emergency boost (A-6 about 40 mph slower in each case); initial climb (A-1) 4,600 ft (1400 m)/min; service ceiling (A-1) 37,400 ft (11,410 m); (A-6) 33,400 ft (10,190 m); maximum range (both) 1,280 miles (2050 km) clean, up to 2,330 miles (3750 km) with drop tank.
Armament: typical A-1, one 30 mm MK 103 cannon firing through front propeller hub and two 15 mm MG 151/15 above nose; underwing racks for light stores and centreline rack for 1,100 lb (500 kg) bomb; A-6 did not carry bomb and usually had 15 mm guns replaced by 20 mm MG 151/20s.
History: first flight (Do 335V1) autumn 1943; (production A-1) late November 1944.

Dornier took out a patent in 1937 for an aircraft powered by two engines, one behind the other, in the fuselage, driving tractor and pusher propellers. In 1939–40

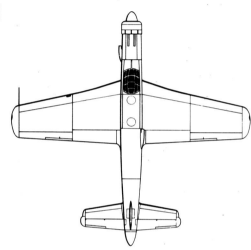

Schempp-Hirth built the Gö 9 research aircraft to test the concept of a rear propeller driven by an extension shaft and in 1941 work began on the Do 231 fighter-bomber. This was replaced by the Do 335 and by first flight Dornier had orders for 14 prototypes, ten pre-production A-0s, 11 production A-1s and three dual-control trainer A-10 and A-12 with stepped tandem cockpits. At high speed the 335 was prone to unpleasant porpoising and snaking, but production continued

Do 335A-0 (pre-production)

tinued on the A-1, the A-4 reconnaissance batch and the A-6 with FuG 220 radar operated by a rear-seat observer. Though heavy, the 335 was strong and very fast and was notable in having the first production type of ejection seat (for obvious reasons). By VE-day about 90 aircraft had been rolled out, more than 60 flown and about 20 delivered to combat units. Work was also well advanced on a number of versions of the Do 335B heavy fighter, with added 30 mm MK 108 cannon in the wings (some having two-stage engines and long-span wings), the Do 435 with various very powerful engines, and the twinned Do 635 with two Do 335 fuselages linked by a new parallel centre-section. The 635, which was being designed and produced by Junkers as the 8-635, would have weighed 72,000 lb as a reconnaissance aircraft, and flown 4,050 miles cruising at 398 mph. Pfeil means "arrow".

Douglas B-18

B-18, B-18A Bolo and Digby I
Type: heavy bomber (later maritime patrol) aircraft, with normal crew of six.
Engines: two 930 hp Wright R-1820-45 or -53 Cyclone nine-cylinder radials.
Dimensions: span 89 ft (27·3 m); length 57 ft 10 in (17·63 m); height 15 ft 2 in (4·62 m).
Weights: empty 19,700 lb (8936 kg); loaded 27,673 lb (12,550 kg).
Performance: maximum speed 215 mph (349 km/h); service ceiling 23,900 ft (7285 m); range with maximum bomb load 1,180 miles (1900 km).
Armament: normally one 0·30 in Browning machine gun in nose, dorsal and retractable ventral positions, all aimed manually; internal bomb load of up to 4,000 lb (1814 kg).
History: first flight (DB-1) October 1935; service delivery (B-18) 1937; (B-18A) 1939.

In 1934 the United States Army issued a requirement for a new bomber to replace the Martin B-10. Martin entered an improved B-10, Boeing the four-engined Model 299 and Douglas the DB-1 (Douglas Bomber

Douglas B-18A Bolo (as delivered)

1). It was the last-named which won and nobody at the time expected that, whereas the Douglas would have a short career and soon be forgotten, the controversial Boeing giant would become perhaps the most famous bomber in history. Douglas were awarded an immediate contract for the unprecedented number (since 1918, at least) of 133 aircraft, designated B-18. Based on the DC-2 transport, the B-18 had a fat body bulged under the wing to accommodate an internal bomb bay. Orders were later placed for a further 217 modified aircraft designated B-18A, plus a further 20 for the Royal Canadian Air Force called Digby (after the British bomber airfield). In 1937–40

this family was the most important heavy warplane in North America, but after that it faded rapidly. No big orders were placed by France or Britain, as was the case with all the newer American bombers, and the B-17 gradually replaced the B-18 in US Army bombardment squadrons. In 1941 122 B-18As were converted as anti-submarine patrol aircraft, with a large nose radome and the first MAD installation projecting behind the tail, for use in the Caribbean and off the east coast of the United States. The Digbys were also used for maritime duties until 1943. A few B-18s were later converted for use as business aircraft and several even remain in various types of civilian use.

Douglas military DC-3

C-47 and AC-47,
R4D, C-53, Dakota, C-117, L2D and Li-2
Type: utility transport (formerly also paratroop/glider tug); AC-47 air/ground weapon platform.
Engines: usually two 1,200 hp Pratt & Whitney R-1830-90D or -92 Twin Wasp 14-cylinder two-row radials; (C-117D) two 1,535 hp Wright R-1820-80 Cyclone nine-cylinder radials; (Li-2) two 1,000 hp M-62IR (Cyclone-derived) nine-cylinder radials; (L2D) two 1,050 or 1,300 hp Mitsubishi Ki-43 or Ki-51 Kinsei 14-cylinder radials.
Dimensions: span 95 ft (28·96 m); length 64 ft 5½ in (19·64 m); height 16 ft 11 in (5·16 m).
Weights: empty, about 16,970 lb (7700 kg); loaded, about 25,200 lb (11,432 kg); overload limit 33,000 lb (14,969 kg).
Performance: maximum speed, about 230 mph (370 km/h); initial climb, about 1,200 ft (366 m)/min; service ceiling 23,000 ft (7000 m); maximum range 2,125 miles (3420 km).
Armament: (AC-47) usually three 7·62 mm Miniguns; many other types of armament in other versions,

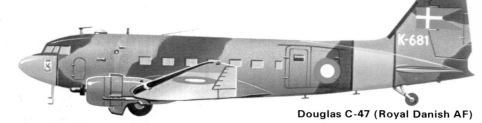

Douglas C-47 (Royal Danish AF)

but none usually fitted.
History: first flight (DST) 17 December 1935; first service delivery (C-41) October 1938.
When, in 1935, Douglas designer Arthur E. Raymond planned the Douglas Sleeper Transport (DST) as an enlarged and improved DC-2, he little thought that, as well as becoming the worldwide standard airliner of its day, it would be by far the most widely used military transport in history. During World War II there were numerous versions, some civil aircraft impressed into military use, some paratroopers and tugs and the vast majority utility C-47 versions with a strong cargo floor and large double doors. Oddities included a glider and a twin-float amphibian. US military production totalled

10,048 by June 1945, followed by small batches of redesigned Super DC-3 versions including the R4D-8 and C-117. Showa and Nakajima in Japan built about 571 of the L2D family and in the Soviet Union production is estimated to have exceeded 2,700. Many hundreds of these aircraft, most of them C-47s, remain in daily use in almost every air force (the RAF retired its last in 1970). Many serve as platforms for research projects and countermeasures and in Vietnam the AC-47 — called "Puff the Magic Dragon" — was developed in several versions to deliver suppressive fire against ground targets. Other important variants are the EC-47 series used for multi-spectral sensing and electronic reconnaissance.

Douglas DB-7 family

A-20, Boston, Havoc, BD-2, F-3 and P-70
Type: two-seat fighter and intruder, three-seat bomber or two-seat reconnaissance aircraft.
Engines: early DB-7 versions (Boston I, II, Havoc II) two 1,200 hp Pratt & Whitney R-1830-S3C4-G Twin Wasp 14-cylinder two-row radials; all later versions, two 1,500, 1,600 or 1,700 hp Wright GR-2600-A5B, -11, -23 or -29 Double Cyclone 14-cylinder two-row radials.
Dimensions: span 61 ft 4 in (18·69 m); length varied from 45 ft 11 in to 48 ft 10 in (A-20G, 48 ft 4 in, 14·74 m); height 17 ft 7 in (5·36 m).
Weights: early Boston/Havoc, typically empty 11,400 lb (5171 kg), loaded 16,700 lb (7574 kg); (A-20G, typical of main production), empty 12,950 lb (5874 kg), loaded 27,200 lb (12,340 kg).
Performance: maximum speed, slowest early versions 295 mph (475 km/h); fastest versions 351 mph (565 km/h); (A-20G) 342 mph (549 km/h); initial climb 1,200–2,000 ft (366–610 m)/min; service ceiling typically 25,300 ft (7720 m); range with maximum weapon load typically 1,000 miles (1,610 km).
Armament: (Havoc I) eight 0·303 in Brownings in nose, one 0·303 in Vickers K manually aimed in rear cockpit; (Havoc II) twelve 0·303 in in nose, (Havoc intruder), four 0·303 in in nose, one Vickers K, and 1,000 lb (454 kg) bomb load; (A-20B) two fixed 0·5 in Brownings on sides of nose, one 0·5 in manually aimed dorsal, one 0·30 in manually aimed ventral, 2,000 lb (907 kg) bomb load; (Boston III bomber) four fixed 0·303 in one sides of nose, twin manually aimed 0·303 in dorsal, twin manually aimed 0·303 in ventral, 2,000 lb (907 kg) bomb load; (Boston III intruder) belly tray of four 20 mm Hispano cannon, 2,000 lb (907 kg) bomb load; (A-20G) four 20 mm and two 0·5 in or six 0·5 in in nose, dorsal turret with two 0·5 in, manually aimed 0·5 in ventral, 4,000 lb (1814 kg) bomb load. Many other schemes, early A-20s having fixed rearward firing 0·30 in in each nacelle.
History: first flight (Douglas 7B) 26 October 1938; (production DB-7) 17 August 1939; service delivery (France) 2 January 1940; termination of production September 1944. Designed by Jack Northrop and Ed Heinemann, the DB-7 family was one of the great combat aircraft of all time. Originally planned to meet a US Army Air Corps attack specification of 1938, it was dramatically altered and given more powerful Twin Wasp engines and a nosewheel-type landing gear (for the first time in a military aircraft). In February 1939 the French government ordered 100 of a further modified type, with deeper but narrower fuselage and other gross changes. This model, the DB-7, went into production at El Segundo and Santa Monica, with 1,764 lb (800 kg) bomb load and armament of six 7·5 mm MAC 1934 machine guns. Delivery took place via Casablanca and about 100 reached the Armée de l'Air, beginning operations on 31 May 1940. Much faster than other bombers, the DB-7 was judged "hot", because it was a modern aircraft in an environment of small unpaved airfields and because it was very different, and more complex, than contemporary European machines. One unusual feature was the emergency control column in

Below, Havoc I (RAF intruder for bombing, 23 Sqn, RAF, Ford)

Below, Boston III (22 Sqn, RAAF)

Below, Boston IIIA (88 Sqn, 2nd TAF)

Below, A-20G-20 Havoc (US 9th AAF)

the rear gunner's cockpit for use if the pilot should be killed. A few DB-7s escaped to Britain, where most of the French order was diverted (increased to 270 by 1940), and over 100 were converted at Burtonwood, Lancs, into Havoc night fighters. Many Havocs had 2,700-million candlepower "Turbinlites" in the nose for finding enemy raiders by night, while 93 Sqn towed Long Aerial Mine charges on steel cables. In February 1942 the RAF began operations with the much more powerful Boston III; making daring daylight low-level raids over Europe, while production of the first US

Army A-20s got into its stride. By far the most important model was the A-20G, with heavier bomb load, dorsal turret and devastating nose armament. Among other important US Army versions were the P-70 night fighters and the transparent-nosed A-20J and K, often used as bombing lead ships by the 9th and 15th Air Forces (respectively in Northwest Europe and Italy). The RAF counterparts of the J and K were the Boston IV and V, of the 2nd Tactical Air Force and Desert AF (Italy). Total production of this hard-hitting aircraft was 7,385, of which 3,125 were supplied freely to the Soviet Union.

Douglas Devastator

TBD-1 Devastator
Type: three-seat carrier-based torpedo bomber.
Engine: one 850 hp Pratt & Whitney R-1830-64 Twin Wasp 14-cylinder two-row radial.
Dimensions: span 50 ft (15·24 m); length 35 ft 6 in (10·82 m); height 15 ft 1 in (4·6 m).
Weights: empty 7,195 lb (3264 kg); maximum loaded 10,194 lb (4622 kg).
Performance: maximum speed 206 mph (332 km/h); initial climb at maximum weight 900 ft (274 m)/min; service ceiling 19,700 ft (6000 m); range with full weapon load 435 miles (700 km).
Armament: one 0·30 in Colt-Browning fixed on right side of nose, one 0·5 in manually aimed in rear cockpit, single 21 in (1,000 lb, 454 kg) Bliss-Leavitt torpedo recessed into belly, light bomb racks under wings for total additional load of 500 lb (227 kg).
History: first flight (XTBD-1) January 1935; production delivery 25 June 1937.

In the early 1930s the US Navy ordered new aircraft carriers, the *Ranger, Yorktown* and *Enterprise*. Among their complement were to be squadrons of torpedo bombers and on 30 June 1934 orders were placed for two prototypes of rival designs. One was the Great Lakes XTBG-1, rather similar to the later British Swordfish. The other was the first cantilever monoplane designed for such a duty, the Douglas XTBD-1. The monoplane started with the drawback of being radically new, though the wing was very thick, the retracted main wheels protruded far enough for safe landings and the landing speed was only 59 mph. The large canopy over the pilot, radio operator and gunner opened into six sections for "open cockpit" vision, and the all-round performance of the monoplane was superior. Despite competition from another monoplane contender, on 3 February 1936, the Douglas won the production order for 110 aircraft, then the largest peacetime order for aircraft placed by the US Navy. The

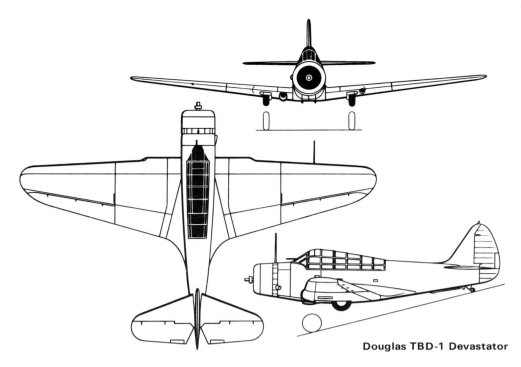

Douglas TBD-1 Devastator

production TBD had a taller canopy with crash pylon, power-folding wings and other changes. Altogether 129 were delivered, and over 100 were still the only carrier-based torpedo bombers in US service at the time of Pearl Harbor. Named Devastator, they immediately went into violent action, bombing and torpedoing almost on a round-the-clock basis. The

middle crewmember aimed the torpedo, sighting through doors in the belly from a prone position. In the Marshalls and Gilberts these aircraft proved formidable, but they were obsolescent and in the Battle of Midway 35 were shot down by flak and Zeros in a single action. The Devastator was soon afterwards replaced by the Avenger.

Douglas Dauntless

SBD, A-24 Dauntless
Type: two-seat carrier-based (SBD) or land-based (A-24) dive bomber.
Engine: one 1,000 hp Wright R-1820-32 or -52 or 1,200 hp R-1820-60 or -66 Cyclone nine-cylinder radial.
Dimensions: span 41 ft 6 in (12·65 m); length 33 ft (10·06 m); height 12 ft 11 in (3·94 m).
Weights: empty, typically 6,535 lb (2970 kg); loaded 9,519–10,700 lb (4320–4853 kg).
Performance (SBD-5): maximum speed 252 mph (406 km/h); initial climb 1,500 ft (457 m)/min; service ceiling 24,300 ft (7400 m); range (dive bomber) 456 miles (730 km), (scout bomber) 773 miles (1240 km).
Armament: one (later invariably two) 0·5 in Browning machine guns fixed in nose, one (later two) 0·30 in Brownings manually aimed from rear cockpit; one bomb or other store of up to 1,000 lb (454 kg) on swinging crutch under belly, outer-wing racks for two 100 lb (45 kg) bombs or, sometimes, two 250 lb (113 kg) bombs or depth charges.
History: first flight (XBT-1) July 1935; service delivery (XBT-1) 12 December 1935; (BT-1) 15 November 1937 to 19 October 1938; (XBT-2, Dauntless prototype) 23 July 1938; (SBD-1) 4 June 1940; termination of production 22 July 1944.

In 1932 John K. Northrop set up his own company to specialise in the new technique of all-metal stressed-skin construction, though he retained close links with his former employer, Douglas Aircraft. His brilliant designer, Ed Heinemann, started in 1934 to develop a carrier-based dive-bomber for the new Navy carriers, basing the design on the established Northrop A-17A. The resulting Northrop BT-1 was ordered in quantity (54) in February 1936. It featured perforated split flaps and main gears folding backwards into large fairings. The last BT-1 was delivered in a greatly modified form, as the BT-2, with inward-retracting mainwheels, a 1,000 hp Cyclone engine and many refinements. By this time Northrop had become the El Segundo division of Douglas and in consequence the production BT-2 was redesignated SBD-1. From June 1940 until four years later this was one of the most important US combat aircraft; indeed, in the first half of 1942 it saw more action than any other American type. After the 57 SBD-1s came 87 SBD-2s with greater fuel capacity, 584 SBD-3s with armour and self-sealing tanks (and 168 more for the Army with pneumatic tailwheel and no hook), 780 SBD-4 (24V electrics) plus 170 for the Army, 3,024 SBD-5s with 1,200 hp engine (including 615 as Army A-24Bs) and 451 SBD-6 (1,350 hp), to make the total 5,936. Dauntlesses sank more Japanese shipping than any other Allied weapon, stopped the Imperial Fleet at Midway and played a major role at the Coral Sea and Solomons actions.

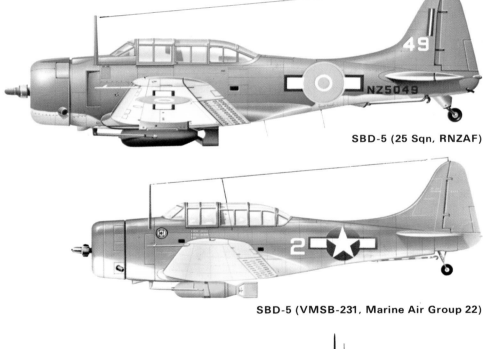

SBD-5 (25 Sqn, RNZAF)

SBD-5 (VMSB-231, Marine Air Group 22)

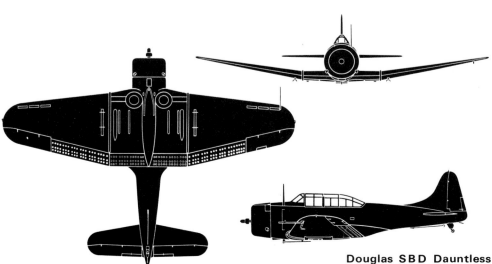

Douglas SBD Dauntless

Douglas Globemaster

C-74 Globemaster I, C-124 Globemaster II
Type: strategic transport.
Engines: (C-74) four 3,000 hp Pratt & Whitney R-4360-49 Wasp Major 28-cylinder four-row radials; (C-124A) four 3,500 hp R-4360-20WA; (C-124C) four 3,800 hp R-4360-63A.
Dimensions: span 173 ft 3 in (52·78 m); (C-124A and C) over tip heater pods 174 ft 1½ in (53·08 m); length (C-74) 124 ft 1½ in (37·83 m); (C-124) 130 ft 5 in (39·75 m); height (C-74) 43 ft 8 in (13·31 m); (C-124) 48 ft 3½ in (14·7 m).
Weights: C-74, empty 92,000 lb (41,731 kg), loaded 165,000 lb (74,910 kg); C-124, empty 101,165 lb (45,887 kg), maximum loaded 194,500 lb (88,223 kg).
Performance: maximum speed (C-74) 325 mph (523 km/h); (C-124) 304 mph (489 km/h); initial climb 760 ft (232 m)/min; service ceiling 21,800 ft (6645 m); range with maximum fuel (C-74) 7,800 miles (12,553 km); (C-124) 6,820 miles (10,975 km); range with maximum 56,000 lb (25,400 kg) payload (both) about 1,200 miles (1931 km).
History: first flight (XC-74) 5 September 1945; (YC-124) 27 November 1949; service delivery (C-124A) May 1950.

The Douglas Long Beach division drew up plans during World War II for a giant transport resembling a scaled-

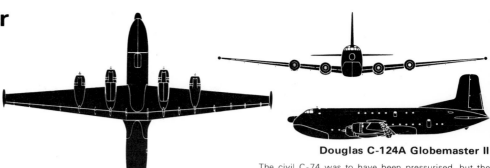

Douglas C-124A Globemaster II

up DC-4 and secured a military (Army Air Force) order for a prototype in 1942. The main emphasis was placed on post-war civil transoceanic use and Pan American ordered 26, with the designation DC-7, in 1945. The first (military) prototype flew in that year, but PanAm cancelled its order and the planned Army Air Force contract was cut back to 14. These were delivered in 1946-7, the C-74 having curious twin bug-eye pilot canopies above the nose, full-span Fowler flaps and an almost circular-section fuselage.

The civil C-74 was to have been pressurised, but the large doors and freight hoists in the C-74 made this impractical with 1945 technology. Advantage was taken of deletion of pressurisation to redesign the C-74 with a huge fuselage offering twice the volume and capable of being fitted with two passenger decks. The vast nose had a normal flight deck above and large left and right clamshell doors for loading vehicles and heavy freight. This aircraft was the C-124A, flown as a prototype by converting the fifth C-74 before delivery. Ultimately 204 C-124As were delivered, while the earlier C-74s made their presence felt on the Berlin Airlift. There followed one turboprop C-124B and 243 C-124Cs. One of the tasks of these lumbering monsters was to airlift the Thor ballistic missile installations to England in 1959-61.

Douglas Invader

A-26 (later B-26) and JD-1 Invader; rebuilt as B-26K, redesignated A-26A
Type: three-seat attack bomber; FA-26 reconnaissance, JD target tug.
Engines: two 2,000 hp Pratt & Whitney R-2800-27, 71 or 79 Double Wasp 18-cylinder two-row radials; On Mark B-26K, 2,500 hp R-2800-103W.
Dimensions: span 70 ft (21·34 m) (B-26K, 75 ft, 22·86 m, over tip tanks); length 50 ft (15·24 m); height 18 ft 6 in (5·64 m).
Weights: empty, typically 22,370 lb (10,145 kg); loaded, originally 27,000 lb (12,247 kg) with 32,000 lb (14,515 kg) maximum overload, later increased to 35,000 lb (15,876 kg) with 38,500 lb (17,460 kg) maximum overload.
Performance: maximum speed 355 mph (571 km/h); initial climb 2,000 ft (610 m)/min; service ceiling 22,100 ft (6736 m); range with maximum bomb load 1,400 miles (2253 km).
Armament: (B-26B) ten 0·5 in Brownings, six fixed in nose and two each in dorsal and ventral turrets; internal bomb load of 4,000 lb (1814 kg), later supplemented by underwing load of up to 2,000 lb (907 kg); (B-26C) similar but only two 0·5 in in nose; (B-26K, A-26A) various nose configurations with up to eight 0·5 in or four 20 mm, plus six 0·30 in guns in wings and total ordnance load of 8,000 lb (3629 kg) in bomb bay and on eight outer-wing pylons.
History: first flight (XA-26) 10 July 1942; service delivery December 1943; final delivery 2 January 1946; first flight of B-26K, February 1963.

The Douglas Invader has a unique history. It was one of very few aircraft to be entirely conceived, designed, developed, produced in quantity and used in large

Douglas B-26K Invader (rebuilt by On Mark)

numbers all during World War II. The whole programme was terminated after VJ-day and anyone might have judged the aircraft finished. With new jets under development, Douglas made no effort to retain any design team on Invader development, neither did the Army Air Force show any interest. Yet this aircraft proved to be of vital importance in the Korean war and again in Vietnam and, by 1963, was urgently being remanufactured for arduous front-line service. Many remain in combat units 30 years after they were first delivered, a record no other kind of aircraft can equal. The design was prepared by Ed Heinemann at El Segundo as a natural successor to the DB-7 family, using the powerful new R-2800 engine. The Army Air Corps ordered three prototypes in May 1941, one with 75 mm gun, one with four 20 mm forward-firing cannon and four 0·5 in guns in an upper turret, with radar nose, and the third as an attack bomber with optical sighting station in the nose and two defensive turrets. In the event it was the bomber that was bought first, desig-

nated A-26B. Much faster than other tactical bombers with the exception of the Mosquito, it was 700 lb lighter than estimate, and capable of carrying twice the specified bomb load. It was the first bomber to use a NACA laminar-flow airfoil, double-slotted flaps and remote-control turrets (also a feature of the B-29). Combat missions with the 9th AF began on 19 November 1944 and these aircraft dropped over 18,000 tons of bombs on European targets. A total of 1,355 A-26Bs were delivered, the last 535 having -79 engines boosted by water injection. The A-26C, in service in January 1945, had a transparent nose, lead-ship navigational equipment and was often fitted with H_2S panoramic radar. In 1948 the B-26 Marauder was retired from service and the Invaders were redesignated B-26. Over 450 were used in Korea, and in Vietnam these fine aircraft were one of the most favoured platforms for night attack on the Ho Chi Minh trail and in other interdiction areas. Though top speed was depressed to about 350 mph, the A-26A (as the rebuilt B-26K was called) could carry up to 11,000 lb (4990 kg) of armament and deliver it accurately and, with 2 hr over target, over a wide radius. In 1976 eight air forces retained Invader squadrons.

Douglas C-133 Cargomaster

C-133A and -133B
Type: heavy logistic freighter.
Engines: C-133A, four 7,000 ehp Pratt & Whitney T34-7 single-shaft axial turboprops; C-133B, 7,500 ehp T34-9W.
Dimensions: span 179 ft 8 in (54·75 m); length 157 ft 6½ in (48·02 m); height 48 ft 3 in (14·7 m).
Weights: empty 120,263 lb (54,550 kg); maximum loaded 286,000 lb (129,727 kg).
Performance: maximum speed 359 mph (578 km/h); initial climb 1,280 ft (389 m)/min; service ceiling at gross weight 29,950 ft (9140 m); range with 44,000 lb (19,960 kg) payload, 4,300 miles (6920 km).
Armament: none.
History: first flight (first production C-133A) 23 April 1956; service delivery 29 August 1957; first flight of C-133B 31 October 1959.

Designed to meet a US Air Force requirement for a logistic transport capable of carrying indivisible bulky loads which could not easily be loaded into the C-124, the C-133 was a bold, clean design with four of the powerful single-shaft turboprops developed at Pratt & Whitney since 1944. These engines had powered C-97, R7V-2 (Navy Super Constellation) and YC-124B aircraft and were fully developed in time for the

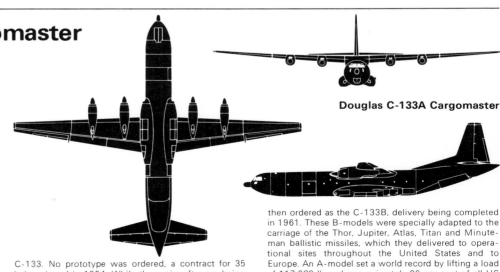

Douglas C-133A Cargomaster

C-133. No prototype was ordered, a contract for 35 being signed in 1954. While these aircraft were being delivered, from the Long Beach plant, changes were made in the shape of the rear fuselage and freight door arrangement and the final three introduced clamshell rear doors. A further 15 more powerful aircraft were

then ordered as the C-133B, delivery being completed in 1961. These B-models were specially adapted to the carriage of the Thor, Jupiter, Atlas, Titan and Minuteman ballistic missiles, which they delivered to operational sites throughout the United States and to Europe. An A-model set a world record by lifting a load of 117,900 lb and approximately 96 per cent of all US military equipment could be carried by these capable machines. The C-133 will be retired from Military Airlift Command before 1980, after about 20 years of service.

Douglas Skyraider

Douglas (later McDonnell Douglas) BT2D, AD, A-1 Skyraider
Type: initially, naval torpedo and dive bomber; later, many roles (see text).
Engine: one 3,020 hp Wright R-3350-26W or 3,050 hp R-3350-26WB Cyclone 18-cylinder two-row radial.
Dimensions: span 50 ft (A-1J, 50 ft 9 in) (15·24 m); length 38 ft 2 in to 40 ft 1 in (A-1J 38 ft 10 in, 11·84 m); height 15 ft 5 in to 15 ft 10 in (A-1J, 15 ft 8¼ in, 4·77 m).
Weights: empty 10,090-12,900 lb (A-1J, 12,313 lb, 5585 kg); maximum loaded 18,030—25,000 lb (A-1J, 25,000 lb, 11,340 kg).
Performance: maximum speed 298—366 mph; (A-1J) 318 mph (512 km/h); initial climb (typical) 2,300 ft (700 m)/min; service ceiling (typical) 32,000 ft (9753 m); range, from 900 miles with maximum ordnance to 3,000 miles (4828 km) with maximum external fuel.
Armament: varies with sub-type, but attack variants generally four 20 mm cannon in outer wings and 15 pylons for total ordnance/fuel load of 8,000 lb (3630 kg).
History: first flight (XBT2D-1) 18 March 1945; service delivery (AD-1) November 1946; termination of production February 1957.

Like so many of Ed Heinemann's designs the Skyraider simply refused to grow obsolete. Planned in 1944 as the first combined torpedo/dive bomber to be a single-seater, the XBT2D competed against three rival designs and, due to Martin's protracted detailed development of the more powerful AM-1 Mauler, soon became the favoured type. Its obvious versatility led to modifications for additional missions, explored in 1946 with prototypes fitted with various kinds of radar, search-lights and countermeasures. Of 242 AD-1s, 35 were AD-1Q ECM aircraft with a countermeasures operator in the rear fuselage. The AD-2 was strengthened and given greater fuel capacity and several were equipped for drone control and target towing. The AD-3 branched out into anti-submarine detection/strike and, with a vast belly radome, airborne early-warning. The further refined AD-4 was built in the largest number (1,032), of which 40 were supplied to the Royal Navy in 1952. Still in their USN "midnight blue" these AD-4W early-warners equipped 849 Sqn. Much larger numbers were used from land airfields by the Armée de l'Air. In the redesigned AD-5 (later redesignated A-1E) the wider fuselage allowed some versions to have side-by-side seating, with a rear cabin for 12 seats or four stretchers. None of the A-1E variants were single-seaters, but the A-1H (AD-6) reverted to the single seat and 713 were built for multi-role operations. The final A-1J (AD-7) version had strengthened wings for low-level tactical attack. Altogether 3,180 of this amazingly versatile aircraft were built. Whereas it was almost terminated in 1946, by 1962 the Skyraider was fast becoming one of the most important weapon platforms in the US inventory with the renewed outbreak of warfare in Vietnam. Eventually more than 1,000 Skyraiders were sent to Vietnam, operated not only by the Navy and Marines but also by the US Air Force and the air force of the Republic of Vietnam (ARVN). It proved one of the most effective combat types, as it had done

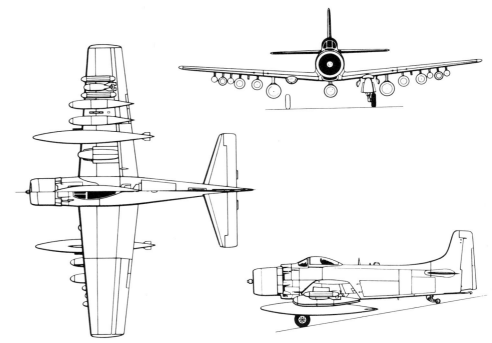

Douglas A-1J with assorted stores

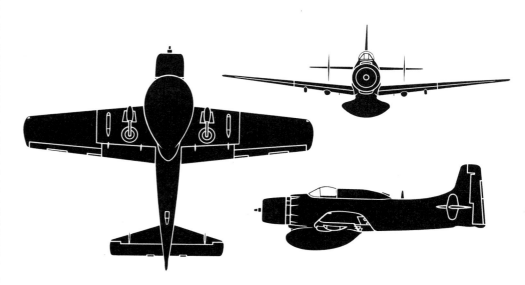

Douglas AD-3w Skyraider

earlier in Korea, with huge weight-lifting ability, ten-hour endurance and ability to survive severe flak damage. Universally called the "Spad", it bore a heavy burden of combat in Southeast Asia until 1973 and in 1976 many were still in front-line service with smaller air forces.

Douglas Skyray

F4D (F-6) Skyray
Type: carrier-based interceptor and attack.
Engine: one 16,000 lb (7257 kg) thrust Pratt & Whitney J57-8 two-shaft turbojet with afterburner.
Dimensions: span 33 ft 6 in (10·2 m); length 45 ft 8 in (13·9 m); height 13 ft (3·96 m).
Weights: empty 16,030 lb (7250 kg); loaded 27,000 lb (12,250 kg).
Performance: maximum speed 725 mph (1167 km/h); initial climb 18,000 ft (5300 m)/min; service ceiling 55,000 ft (16,760 m); typical range 950 miles (1530 km).
Armament: four 20 mm cannon in outer wings; six pylon attachments for total external load of 4,000 lb (1814 kg).
History: first flight (XF4D-1) 23 January 1951; service delivery 16 April 1956; last delivery December 1958.

Based in part on the wartime projects of Alex Lippisch, this unusual fighter was planned by Heinemann to have a large wing, for good combat manoeuvrability, with minimum structure weight. From the start it was

Douglas F4D-1 Skyray (VFAW-3)

planned for possible supersonic performance and when it first flew it was much more advanced in concept than any other naval fighter. One of its features was powered flying controls with manual reversion, the stick being unclipped and extended by the pilot to give more leverage. Another was the double skin, with a very light outer sheet stiffened by an inner "waffle plate"; this was not wholly successful, because it was prone to being dented, with degraded flight performance. On 3 October 1953 a prototype gained the world speed record at 753 mph — a great shock to the Air Force — but the programme was severely hurt by the technical

failure of the Westinghouse J40 engine. After a delay of three years the J57 was adopted instead and then the Skyray never looked back. A straight run of 419 were delivered to Navy and Marine Corps squadrons for use from carriers and NAS *Alameda*, with equipment for "buddy" refuelling. A service Skyray took world time-to-height records, reaching 50,000 ft in 2·6 minutes from a standing start. A development, the highly supersonic F5D Skylancer with thicker skin, was cancelled after four had flown very successfully. In 1962 the F4D-1 was redesignated F-6A, squadrons progressively re-equipping with the Phantom.

Douglas Skywarrior and B-66

Douglas (later McDonnell Douglas) A-3 (previously A3D) Skywarrior and B-66 Destroyer
Type: originally (A3D) carrier-based strategic bomber, (B-66) tactical attack bomber; later, different roles (see text).
Engines: (A-3) two 12,400 lb (5625 kg) thrust Pratt & Whitney J57-10 two-shaft turbojets; (B-66) two

10,000 lb (4536 kg) thrust Allison J71-13 single-shaft turbojets.
Dimensions: span 72 ft 6 in (22·1 m); length, typical (EA-3B) 76 ft 4 in (23·3 m); (EB-66E) 75 ft 2 in–78 ft 9 in (22·9–24 m); height 23 ft 6 in (7·16 m).
Weights: empty (A-3B) 39,409 lb (17,875 kg); (B-66B) 42,369 lb (19,218 kg); maximum loaded (A-3B) 82,000 lb (37,195 kg); (B-66B) 83,000 lb (37,648 kg).
Performance: (typical) maximum speed 610 mph (982 km/h); initial climb 3,600 ft (1100 m)/min; service ceiling 43,000 ft (13,110 m); range with maximum fuel 2,000 miles (3220 km).
Armament: normally none; as built, most bomber A-3s and B-66s had two remotely controlled 20 mm cannon in a tail turret and internal provision for 12,000 lb (5443 kg) bombs (15,000 lb, 6804 kg, in the B-66).
History: first flight (XA3D-1) 28 October 1952; (RB-66A) 28 June 1954, service delivery (A3D-1) December 1954 (first squadron, March 1956); (RB-66B) March 1956; last delivery of new aircraft (A3D-2Q) January 1961, (WB-66D) September 1958. The Douglas El Segundo design team under Heinemann produced the A3D as the world's first carrier-based strategic bomber, matching the design both to the predicted size and mass of future thermonuclear bombs and to the deck length and strength of the super-carriers of the *Forrestal* class in 1948. The bomb bay dictated a high wing, which in turn meant the landing gears had to retract into the fuselage. Outer wings and vertical tail folded hydraulically and the nose was filled with an advanced blind-bombing radar. Unfortunately Westinghouse, supplier of both the engines and the radar, succeeded in delivering only the Aero-21B tail turret. Redesigned with the J57 engine the A3D-1 finally equipped VAH-1 (Heavy Attack Squadron 1) in 1956. Soon the Skywarriors on the catapults of giant carriers of the 6th Fleet in the Mediterranean and the 7th Fleet in the Pacific were playing a central role in the balance of power in the Cold War, and giving a new global dimension to naval air power. Eventually, though only 280 Skywarriors were built (not enough, as it turned out), the changing scene called for numerous completely different versions mainly achieved by rebuilding bombers. Major production was of the A3D-2 bomber, restyled A-3B. From this evolved the A3D-2P (RA-3B) reconnaissance, A3D-2Q (EA-3B) electronic countermeasures and A3D-2T (TA-3B) radar/nav trainer, followed by rebuilds for the KA-3B tanker, EKA-3B ECM/tanker and various special-mission and test versions.

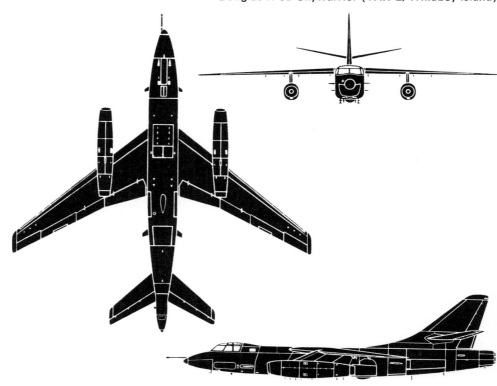

Douglas A-3B Skywarrior (VAH-2, Whidbey Island)

Douglas EB-66E Destroyer

The B-66 Destroyer was produced by the Long Beach plant to meet the needs of the US Air Force. What had begun as a minimum modification of the Skywarrior turned into a totally different aircraft. Though it looked similar, hardly a single airframe part or item of equipment was common and the B-66 proved difficult and expensive. After building five RB-66As for indoctrination, Long Beach and a re-opened wartime plant at Tulsa built 145 RB-66B reconnaissance aircraft as well as 72 B-66B bombers. There followed 36 RB-66C electronic reconnaissance aircraft with four-man crew and 36 WB-66Ds for weather reconnaissance. Modified further over the years for many clandestine special ferreting missions, a number of EB-66E aircraft served throughout the Vietnam war.
For later Douglas aircraft see under McDonnell Douglas.

Etrich Taube

Taube, licence-built by many companies (see text)
Type: two-seat military aircraft.
Engine: one 100 hp Mercedes-Benz D1 six-cylinder water-cooled; alternatively Mercedes, Argus or Austro-Daimler engines of 78–120 hp.

Dimensions: span 47 ft 1 in (14·35 m); length 32 ft 3¾ in (9·85 m); height 10 ft 4 in (3·15 m).
Weights: empty 1,323 lb (600 kg); maximum loaded 1,918 lb (870 kg).
Performance: maximum speed 71·5 mph (115 km/h); initial climb, about 200 ft (60 m)/min; service ceiling 9,840 ft (3000 m); endurance, about 4 hr, or 240 miles (386 km).
Armament: not fitted to aircraft, but invariably carried by crew.
History: first flight August 1910; first flight of Rumpler production for German Army late 1912; termination of production 1915.

One of the pioneers of aircraft design was Austrian Dr Igo Etrich, who built and flew his first aircraft in 1908. Like Bleriot he advocated the tractor monoplane and when his graceful Taube design appeared in 1910 it attracted wide attention. He negotiated a licence for its production by the Rumpler company and many were in use by both private individuals and the Imperial

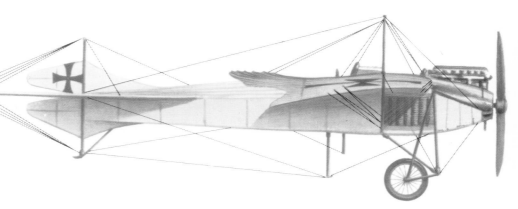

Etrich Taube (typical of 1913 production)

German forces in August 1914. At the Battle of Tannenberg Taubes were of vital use in warning of Russian movements, while later in August 1914 Lt von Hiddesen flew all the way from the Marne front to Paris and dropped a succession of hand-held grenades, in what is believed to have been the first bombing attack on a city. But the Taube's main claim to fame lies in its use as the principal trainer aircraft for the Central Powers until after 1915. Many hundreds were built, not only by Rumpler but also by DFW, Albatros, Gotha, Halberstadt, Kondor, Lübeck, Jeannin, Krieger and Travemunde, the DFW and Jeannin Taubes having fuselages of welded steel tubes. At least nine kinds of engine were fitted and there were countless minor variations in Taube airframes.
For F+W and Fairchild C-119 see p. 72.

Fairchild Republic A-10A

A-10A

Type: single-seat close-air-support aircraft.
Engines: two 9,275 lb (4207 kg) thrust General Electric TF34-100 two-shaft turbofans.
Dimensions: span 55 ft (16·76 m); length 53 ft 4 in (16·26 m) including FR probe; height 14 ft 8 in (4·47 m).
Weights: empty 21,300 lb (9660 kg); maximum loaded 45,825 lb (20,786 kg).
Performance: maximum speed, 500 mph (805 km/h) clean, 380 mph (612 km/h) at maximum weight; initial climb 1,000 ft (328 m)/min at maximum weight; take-off distance (at maximum weight) 3,850 ft (1173 m), (at forward-airstrip weight with six Mk 82 bombs), 1,130 ft (344 m); steady speed in 45° dive with full airbrake 299 mph (481 km/h); close-air-support radius with reserves 288 miles (463 km); ferry range 2,723 miles (4382 km).
Armament: 30 mm high-velocity GAU-8/A cannon in forward fuselage; 11 pylons for total external ordnance load of 16,000 lb (7257 lb) (exceptionally, 18,500 lb, 8392 kg).
History: first flight 10 May 1972; service delivery for inventory December 1974.

Despite the more overt attractions of Mach 2 aircraft the US Air Force was forced to consider the CAS (close air support) mission because of the total unsuitability of its existing equipment. In both the wars it had had to fight since World War II – Korea and Vietnam – its aircraft had been worldbeaters but planned for a totally different kind of war. What was needed, it appeared, was something like an up-to-date Skyraider that could carry a heavy load of ordnance, had good endurance and could survive severe damage from ground fire. Between 1963–69 extensive studies gradually refined the AX specification, which had begun by presupposing a twin-turboprop and ended with a larger aircraft powered by two turbofans. After an industry-wide competition the Northrop A-9A and Fairchild A-10A were chosen for prototype fly-off evaluation, which took place with two of each type at Edwards in October–December 1972. The A-10A was announced winner and GE the winner of the contest to produce the 30mm tank-busting gun, the most powerful ever fitted to any aircraft, with very high muzzle velocity and rate of fire, and muzzle horsepower 20 times that of the 75 mm gun fitted to some B-25s in World War II. Underwing load can be made up of any stores in the Tactical Air Command inventory, the landing gears (which protrude when retracted for damage-free emergency landing) and all tail surfaces are interchangeable, the cockpit is encased in a "bath" of thick titanium armour, and the engines are hung above the rear fuselage where their infra-red signature is a minimum. Up to 600 A-10As are to be bought by 1981, making a dramatic difference to Tactical Air Command's ability to fight limited wars.

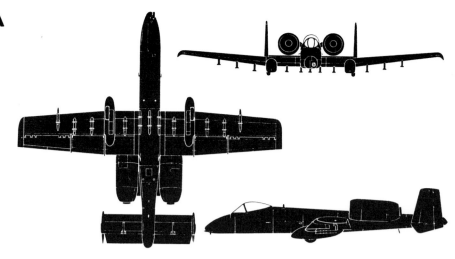

Fairchild A-10 cutaway drawing key:

1. Flight refuelling probe (removable)
2. Universal aerial refuelling receptacle slipway (UARRSI) for drogue or boom
3. Nosewheel (retracted) position
4. Forward electrical compartment
5. Battery
6. Gun muzzle
7. Nosewheel door
8. Nosewheel leg (offset to starboard)
9. Twin landing/taxying lamps
10. Forward retracting nose-wheel
11. Nosewheel linkage
12. General Electric GAU-8A 30mm Gatling-type gun
13. Forward gun support pallet
14. Gun recoil pack
15. Linkless feed chutes
16. Hydraulic pump
17. Pave Penny laser target-seeker pod (offset to starboard)
18. Integral titanium armour (lower cockpit area and vital controls)
19. Rubber pedals
20. Control column
21. Head-up display
22. Bullet-resistant glass windscreen
23. Upward-hinged canopy
24. Headrest
25. Pilot's zero-zero ejection seat
26. Electrical and avionics equipment bays
27. Forward fuselage structure
28. Ammunition drum (1,350 rounds)
29. Ammunition chute inter-change
30. Heavy skin panelling area (HE shell triggering)
31. LB warning aerial
32. Fuselage fuel cells forward wall (fire retardant foam filling)

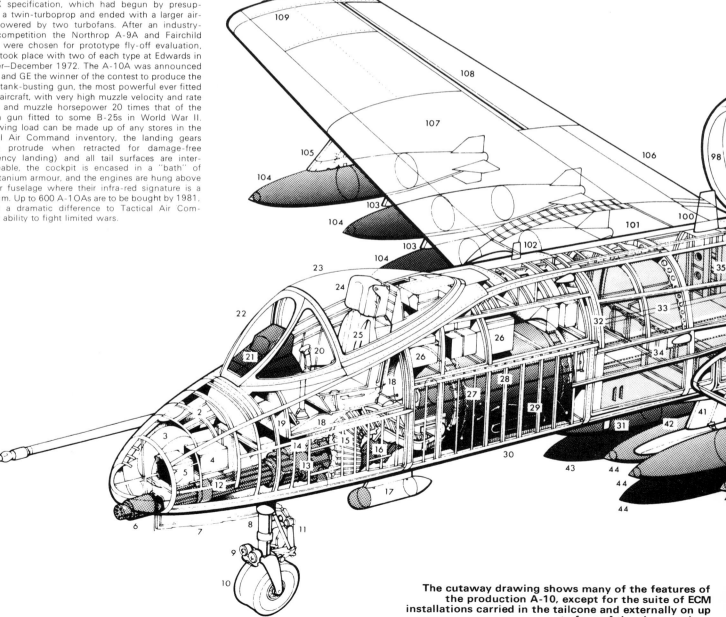

The cutaway drawing shows many of the features of the production A-10, except for the suite of ECM installations carried in the tailcone and externally on up to four of the eleven pylons

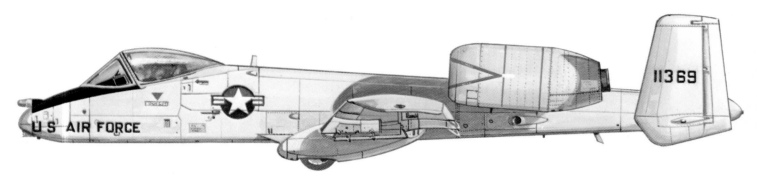

Fairchild Republic A-10A (prototype, in form evaluated at Edwards in 1972)

33 Fuselage forward fuel cell
34 Fuselage 'notch' (wing centre-section carry-through)
35 Centre bulkhead
36 Fuselage aft fuel cell
37 Control runs/plumbing/wiring service trough
38 Port wing fuel cell (wing break to fuselage centreline)
39 Front spar
40 Leading edge structure
41 Fuselage port bomb pylon
42 Triple bomb-rack shoe
43 Fuselage starboard triple bomb cluster
44 Fuselage port triple bomb cluster
45 Wing centre-section bomb pylon
46 Mk 82 bomb (nominal 500 lb/227 kg)

47 Mainwheel gear door
48 Landing gear fairing
49 Wing strengthening
50 Wing centre/outer section break
51 Main landing gear (port and starboard identical)
52 Wing outer-section bomb pylons
53 Single Mk 82 bombs
54 Port mainwheel
55 Outboard pylon (extended forward)
56 Front spar (outer section)
57 Centre spar
58 Rear spar
59 Wing structure
60 Drooped wingtip
61 Port navigation light
62 Port aileron
63 Flaps
64 Port engine nacelle
65 X-band beacon
66 Hydraulic reservoirs (2)
67 Auxiliary power unit
68 Environmental control

system
69 Aerials
70 APU exhaust
71 VHF Tacan
72 Port nacelle forward attachment
73 Port nacelle aft attachment
74 Control runs
75 Tailplane centre-section
76 IFF aerial (beneath fuselage)
77 Tailplane structure
78 Tailplane/fin bolt attachments
79 Rudder lower hinge
80 Port rudder (same as 91)
81 Port fin (same as 92)
82 Rudder upper hinge
83 Port elevator (same as 88)
84 Elevator hinge fairing
85 Rear navigation light
86 Tail cone
87 Elevator actuation system
88 Starboard elevator
89 Tailplane stringers
90 Starboard tailplane (same as 77)

91 Starboard rudder
92 Starboard fin
93 Upward canted exhaust pipe
94 Nacelle module installation fairing
95 Steel engine bearers
96 General Electric TF34-100 turbofan (9,065 lb/4,112 kg thrust, identical port and starboard)
97 Centrebody
98 Engine intake
99 VHF/AM aerial
100 VHF/FM aerial
101 Starboard wing centre-section
102 VHF Tacan aerial
103 Starboard bomb pylons
104 Single Mk 82 bombs
105 Outboard pylon (extended forward)
106 Flaps
107 Wing skinning
108 Starboard aileron
109 Drooped wingtip
110 Starboard navigation light

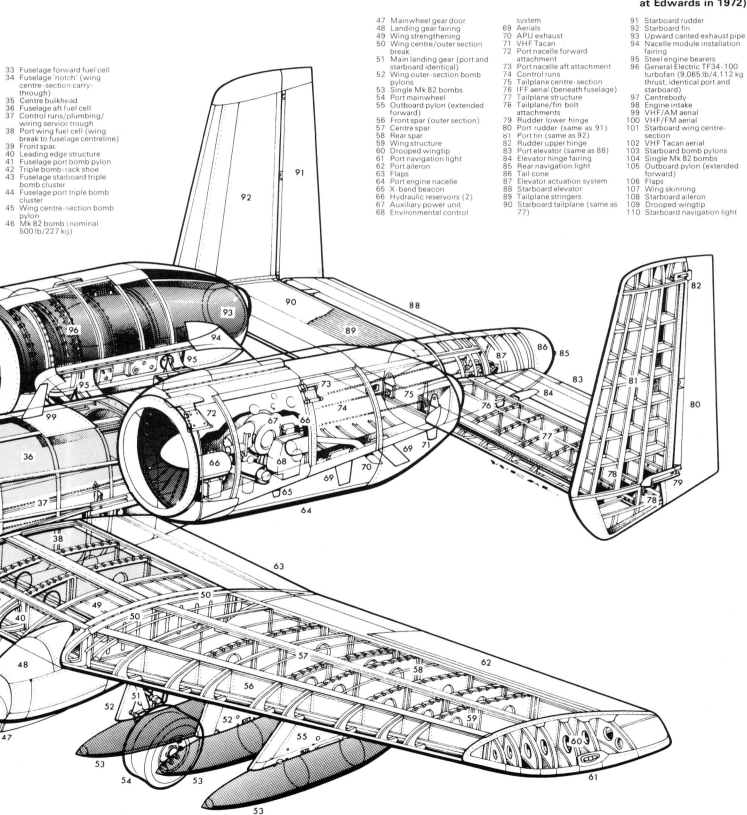

F+W C-3603

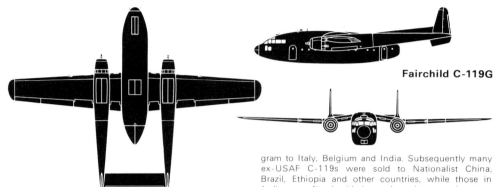

F+W C-3603 (Flugwaffe)

F+W (previously EFW or EKW) C-3603 and 3605

Type: 3603, two-seat attack bomber and reconnaissance; 3605, two-seat target tug.

Engine: (3603) one 1,000 hp Hispano-Suiza 12Y-51 vee-12 liquid-cooled made under licence by Saurer/SLM; (3605) one 1,100 shp Lycoming T53-7 free-turbine turboprop.

Dimensions: span 45 ft 1 in (13·74 m); length, (3603) 33 ft 6¾ in (10·2 m); (3605) 39 ft 5¾ in (12 m); height, (3603) 11 ft (3·35 m); (3605) 13 ft 3½ in (4·05 m).

Weights: empty, (3603) 5,009 lb (2272 kg); (3605) 5,806 lb (2634 kg); maximum loaded, (3603) 7,600 lb (3450 kg); (3605) 8,192 lb (3716 kg).

Performance: maximum speed (3603) 295 mph (475 km/h); (3605) 268 mph (432 km/h); initial climb (both) about 2,400 ft (732 m)/min; service ceiling (both) about 32,800 ft (10,000 m); range on internal fuel (both) about 620 miles (1000 km).

Armament: 3603, one 20 mm Oerlikon cannon firing through propeller hub, two 7·5 mm machine guns in outer wings and two 7·5 mm manually aimed in rear cockpit; wing racks for up to four 220 lb (100 kg) bombs or ten rocket projectiles. C-3605, nil.

History: first flight (C-3601) 23 February 1939; (C-3603) 23 November 1941; termination of production 1944 (four more built in 1947); first flight (C-3605) 19 August 1968; final C-3605 delivery 1972.

In 1934 the Swiss government issued a specification for a new two-seat reconnaissance bomber. The Federal Aircraft Factory at Emmen, then called EKW, designed the C-35 biplane and C-36 monoplane. The biplane was chosen for production, but was so obviously obsolescent that within three years of go-ahead it had to be replaced by the C-36. The latter, a clean monoplane with twin fins, was first built as the C-3601, but in 1941—44 160 were built of the C-3603 production version which served extremely well for more than 20 years — even after introduction of the Venom jet and the Hunter. Only 13 were made of the more powerful C-3604 with three forward-firing cannon, and the 3603 continued with very few modifications until, in 1965, the decision was taken to refit some as target tugs. Following successful trials of a prototype 3605 in 1968—69, conversion went ahead on 23 aircraft, the main structure being left unaltered. The much lighter turboprop necessitated a great extension of the nose, balanced by a central fin being added. The target and winch are housed under the rear cockpit.

Fairchild C-119

Fairchild Hiller C-119 to -119K Boxcar and AC-119 Gunship

Type: C-119 tactical transport; AC-119 multi-sensor armed interdiction.

Engines: in most variants two 3,350 hp Wright R-3350-85WA or 3,700 hp R-3350-89B Turbo-Compound 18-cylinder two-row radials (older versions, two 3,250 hp Pratt & Whitney R-4360-20WA Wasp Major 28-cylinder four-row radials); (AC-119K) two additional underwing booster pods each containing 2,850 lb (1293 kg) thrust General Electric J85-17 turbojets; (Indian AF C-119) one dorsal booster pod containing HAL Orpheus of 4,700 lb, 2132 kg thrust, or Westinghouse J34 of 3,400 lb, 1542 kg thrust.

Dimensions: span 109 ft 3 in (34·3 m); length 86 ft 6 in (26·36 m); height 26 ft 6 in (8·07 m).

Weights: empty (C-119B) 37,691 lb (15,981 kg); (C-119K) 44,747 lb (20,300 kg); (AC-119K) 60,955 lb (27,649 kg); maximum loaded (C-119B) 74,000 lb (33,600 kg); (C-119K) 77,000 lb (34,925 kg); (AC-119K) 80,400 lb (36,468 kg).

Performance: maximum speed (all versions) 243—250 mph (391—402 km/h); initial climb (all) 1,100—1,300 ft (335—396 m)/min; service ceiling, typically 24,000 ft (7315 m); range with maximum payload 990—1,900 miles (1595—3060 km).

Armament: transport versions, none; (AC-119K) two 20 mm and four 7·62 mm multi-barrel rapid-fire guns firing laterally, with over 100,000 rounds total ammunition. For sensors, see text.

History: first flight (XC-82) 10 September 1944;

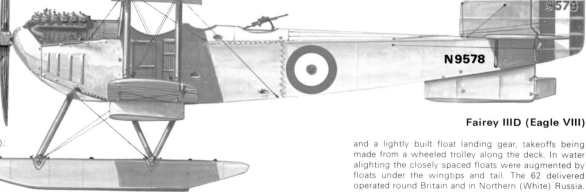

Fairchild C-119G

(C-119A) November 1947; service delivery (C-119B) December 1949; (AC-119) 1967.

Fairchild began the design of a purpose-built cargo and troop transport — the first specialised transport ever designed for the Army Air Corps — in 1941. This flew in 1944 as the XC-82 Packet and 220 C-82s were delivered by 1948. The C-119 introduced a new nose, with the flight deck ahead of the cargo compartment instead of on top. Fuselage width was increased, engine power was greatly increased and the wings were strengthened for operation at higher weights. By 1955, when production of new aircraft ceased 946 C-119s had been delivered to US forces, plus 141 supplied under the Mutual Defense Assistance Program to Italy, Belgium and India. Subsequently many ex-USAF C-119s were sold to Nationalist China, Brazil, Ethiopia and other countries, while those in India were fitted with jet pods to improve the near-zero engine-out rate of climb from hot-and-high airstrips. Many earlier 119s were converted to the C-119J configuration with a rear beaver-tail openable in flight, instead of a hinged rear end that could be opened only on the ground. The AC-119G and jet-boosted AC-119K are extremely heavily armed interdiction aircraft formerly used by night in Southeast Asia. Fitted with batteries of Gatling guns, 26 AC-119Gs were delivered with night illumination systems, image intensifiers, computer fire-control, various gunsights, flare launchers, crew armour and other gear. The 26 AC-119Ks, with underwing jets, added 20 mm Gatlings, forward looking infra-red (FLIR), forward and side-looking radar (SLAR) and precision nav/com equipment.

Fairchild Republic A-10A see pp. 70—1.

Fairey Campania and early III series

F.16 and F.22 Campania and IIIA, B, C and D

Type: two- or three-seat naval reconnaissance aircraft.

Engine: (Campania) 250 hp Sunbeam Maori, 275 hp R-R Eagle V or 345 hp Eagle VIII; (IIIA and IIIB) 260 hp Maori; (IIIC) 375 hp Eagle VIII; (IIID) 450 hp Napier Lion IIB, V or VA (a few had Eagle VIII).

Dimensions: span (Campania) 61 ft 7 in (18·75 m); (IIIA, B, C, D) 46 ft 1¼ in (14·1 m); length (Campania) 43 ft 1 in (13·2 m); (IIIA) 31 ft (9·45 m); (IIIC) 36 ft (10·98 m); (IIID) 37 ft (11·28 m); height (Campania) 15 ft 1 in (4·6 m); (IIIA) 10 ft 8 in (3·3 m); (IIIC) 12 ft 2 in (3·7 m); (IIID) 11 ft 4 in (3·5 m).

Weights: empty (Campania (Eagle VIII)) 3,850 lb (1746 kg); (IIIA) 2,532 lb; (IIIB) 3,258 lb; (IIIC) 3,392 lb; (IIID) 3,248 lb (1473 kg); loaded (Campania) 5,657 lb (2566 kg); (IIIA) 3,945 lb; (IIIB) 4,892 lb; (IIIC) 4,800 lb; (IIID) 4,918 lb (2240 kg).

Performance: maximum speed (Campania) 80·5 mph (130 km/h); (IIIA) 97 mph; (IIIB) 95 mph; (IIIC) 110 mph; (IIID) 120 mph (193 km/h); service ceiling (Campania) 5,500 ft (1675 m); (IIIA) 13,000 ft; (IIIB) 16,000 ft; (IIIC) 15,000 ft; (IIID) 17,000 ft (5182 m); typical endurance (Campania) 3 hr, IIIA-IIID 5 hr.

Armament: one manually aimed 0·303 in Lewis in rear cockpit — (IIIC and IIID) in addition one fixed synchronised 0·303 in Vickers; underwing racks for two 100 lb (45 kg) bombs.

History: first flight (Campania) 16 February 1917; (IIIA) July 1917; (IIIB) early 1918; (IIIC) September 1918; final delivery (IIID) 1925.

Fairey IIID (Eagle VIII)

The Fairey Campania took its name from the former Cunard passenger liner which the Admiralty converted into a seaplane carrier in 1915—16. The neat Fairey product was the first aircraft ever designed for carrier operation. Like the clumsier Short naval aircraft of the same era, the Campania had a considerable wing span and a lightly built float landing gear, takeoffs being made from a wheeled trolley along the deck. In water alighting the closely spaced floats were augmented by floats under the wingtips and tail. The 62 delivered operated round Britain and in Northern (White) Russia. The smaller IIIA, of which 50 were delivered to the Royal Naval Air Service in 1918, was a replacement for the Sopwith 1½-Strutter. The bigger IIIB bomber (25 built) was another seaplane, this time discarding the rear float. The 35 IIIC seaplanes were faster and introduced a fixed gun. They were soon replaced by the IIID, of which 207 were built in the six years following the Armistice. Landplane and twin-float versions operated all over the Far East and in many other areas from the carriers *Argus* and *Vindictive* and from RAF airfields (the RAF operated the Fleet Air Arm between the wars). In 1925 IIIDs flew from Heliopolis to Cape Town and back to Britain without mechanical failure of any kind.

Fairey III derivatives

IIIF, Gordon and Seal

Type: three-seat (RAF IIIF and Gordon, two-seat) GP reconnaissance and bombing.

Engine: (IIIF) one 570 hp Napier Lion XIA broad-arrow 12-cylinder water-cooled; (Gordon and Seal) one 525 hp Armstrong Siddeley Panther IIA 14-cylinder two-row radial.

Dimensions: span 45 ft 9 in (13·9 m); length (IIIF) 34 ft 4 in (10·4 m); (Gordon and Seal landplane) 36 ft 8¾ in (11·2 m); height (all landplanes) 14 ft 3 in (4·35 m).

Weights: empty (IIIF) 3,880 lb; (typical Gordon/Seal landplane) 3,500 lb; loaded (IIIF Mk IV) 6,041 lb (2740 kg); (Gordon/Seal) 5,906 lb (2680 kg).

Performance: maximum speed (IIIF Mk IV) 120 mph (193 mph); (Gordon/Seal) 145 mph (233 km/h); initial climb (all) 1,000 ft (305 m)/min; service ceiling (all) 22,000 ft (6700 m); range with military load (IIIF) 400 miles (644 km); (Gordon/Seal) 600 miles (966 km).

Armament: one fixed 0·303 in Vickers, one manually aimed 0·303 in Lewis; bomb load under lower wings of 500 lb (227 kg); (Gordon/Seal) 460 lb (210 kg).

History: first flight (IIIF) 19 March 1926; (Gordon) 1930; (Seal) 11 September 1930; final delivery 1936.

Though derived from the IIID, the IIIF, built to Specification 19/24, was a completely new design. Though not as famed as, say, the Fury or Bulldog, the IIIF was built in larger numbers than any other military aircraft between the wars. The total was 622, of which 340 were delivered to the Fleet Air Arm as three-seat

Fairey Gordon

spotter and utility aircraft and 215 were of the more streamlined, all-metal, two-seat Mk IV GP and communications version for the RAF. Until 1940 the IIIF served all over the world and from the carriers *Glorious* and *Hermes.* The Gordon, designed to Specification 18/30, was basically a redesigned IIIF with Panther radial engine, one of the odd features being that the fixed Vickers was mounted externally on the left side instead of firing through a blast trough. Altogether 207 were delivered to the RAF, the final 24 being Mk IIs with shorter and more rounded vertical tails; a further 64 were produced by rebuilding IIIFs. The Seal, to Specification 12/29, was the Fleet Air Arm version of the Gordon, with the Mk II tail. Most were twin-float seaplanes, as were many Gordons including the batch sold to Brazil. Seal production totalled 92, of which most survived until 1941.

Fairey Fox

Fox I and IA and Avions Fairey Fox family

Type: two-seat day bomber.

Engine: (Fox I) one 480 hp Fairey Felix; (Fox IA) 490 hp R-R Kestrel IB; (Fox VI) 860 hp Hispano-Suiza 12 Ydrs; all vee-12 water-cooled.

Dimensions: span 38 ft (11·58 m); length (Fox I, IA) 31 ft 2 in (9·5 m); (Fox VI) 29 ft 11 in (9·12 m); height 10 ft 9 in (3·3 m).

Weights: empty (Fox I, IA) about 2,700 lb (1225 kg); (Fox VI) 3,000 lb (1361 kg); loaded (Fox I, IA) 4,117 lb (1867 kg); (Fox VI) 4,800 lb (2177 kg).

Performance: maximum speed (Fox I) 156 mph (250 km/h); (Fox IA) 160 mph (257 km/h); (Fox VI) 230 mph (370 km/h); initial climb (Fox I, IA), 1,300 ft (396 m)/min; (Fox VI) 2,700 ft (823 m)/min; service ceiling (Fox I) 17,000 ft (5182 m); (Fox IA) not published; (Fox VI) 29,000 ft (8840 m); range with bomb load (Fox I, IA) 500 miles (805 km); (Fox VI) 466 miles (750 km).

Armament: (Fox I, IA), one fixed 0·303 in Vickers and one manually aimed 0·303 in Lewis; (Fox VI) two fixed 7·5 mm FN and one manually aimed Lewis; underwing racks for bomb load of up to 460 lb (208 kg); (Fox VI) 528 lb (240 kg).

History: first flight (prototype) 3 January 1925; Fox I, 10 December 1925; Fox VI, 1934; final delivery (UK) January 1927, (Belgium) 1939.

The Fox was one of the classic combat aircraft which, conceived by a private company which combined design freedom with enthusiasm and good direction from above, far outclassed all existing machines and acutely embarrassed the government officials and Service chiefs. It stemmed from Richard Fairey's visit to America in 1923, when he was struck by the Curtiss D.12 engine and the finely streamlined nose cowling it permitted. He purchased British marketing and manufacturing rights, built it as the Fairey Felix and designed the Fox around it (Marcel Lobelle and P. A. Ralli

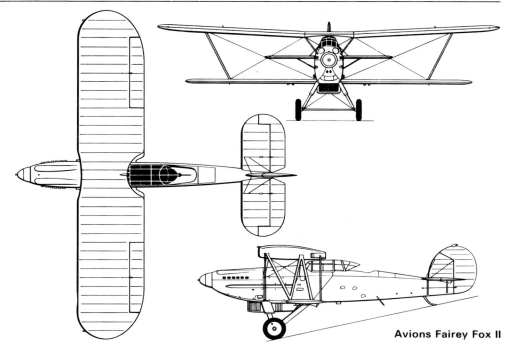

headed the design team). The Air Staff were shocked to find this bomber not only 50 mph faster than any RAF bomber but 30 mph faster than the standard fighting scout. Trenchard at once ordered ''a complete squadron'' (No 12 Sqn) and 28 were delivered, about 12 later being re-engined with the Kestrel as the Fox IA. In 1929 the all-metal Fox II reached 190 mph, and though beaten by the Hart for RAF orders it gained foreign acceptance. Avions Fairey was set up in

Avions Fairey Fox II

Belgium after a thrilling programme of competitive fly-offs with rival designs and manufacture began at Gosselies in 1933. The following year the vastly more powerful Fox VI appeared, with three-blade propeller, spatted wheels and enclosed cockpits, and this formidable new model accounted for the last 94 of the 178 Foxes built in Belgium. The Aéronautique Militaire Fox squadrons fought virtually to the last man in May 1940.

Fairey Hendon

Hendon II

Type: five-seat night bomber.

Engines: two 600 hp Rolls-Royce Kestrel VI vee-12 water-cooled.

Dimensions: span 101 ft 9 in (31 m); length 60 ft 9 in (18·5 m); height 18 ft 8 in (5·7 m).

Weights: empty 12,773 lb (5793 kg); loaded 20,000 lb (9072 kg).

Performance: maximum speed 155 mph (250 km/h); initial climb 940 ft (286 m)/min; service ceiling 21,500 ft (6580 m); range with bomb load 1,360 miles (2188 km).

Armament: single manually aimed 0·303 in Lewis in nose turret, mid-upper and tail cockpits; bomb load of up to 1,660 lb (755 kg) accommodated in cells in inner wing.

History: first flight (prototype) November 1931; re-engined 1932; production Mk I, September 1936; last delivery March 1937.

Designed to Specification B.19/27, the Fairey Night

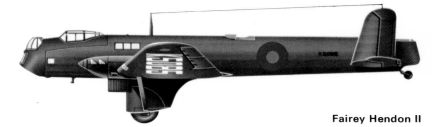

Fairey Hendon II

Bomber was a dark horse. Painted deep olive, it had the temerity to be a monoplane, at a time when monoplanes were not even considered for fighters. Powered by Jupiter radials, it unfortunately suffered damage and was rebuilt in 1932 with different engines. It could have been in production by that year, but its advanced design caused the Air Staff to wait until four further years had gone by before ordering production as the Hendon, to revised Specification 20/34. The Heyford, to the original requirement 19/27, had meanwhile been built in quantity. Features of the basic

design included all-metal structure with fabric covering, a huge deep-section wing, trousered and braced landing gear and twin fins. The production Hendon II had an enclosed cockpit, enclosed front gunner's cockpit (not a powered turret) and three-blade Fairey-Reed metal propellers. The Hendon equipped 38 Sqn, with a detached flight forming the nucleus of 115 Sqn. Only 14 were delivered, a second batch of 60 being cancelled (after the extraordinary delay in placing an order, hardly surprising). Hendons were withdrawn in January 1939, when some were less than two years old.

Fairey Battle

Battle I to IV (data for II)
Type: three-seat light bomber.
Engine: one 1,030 hp Rolls-Royce Merlin II vee-12 liquid-cooled.
Dimensions: span 54 ft (16·46 m); length 42 ft 1¾ in (12·85 m); height 15 ft 6 in (4·72 m).
Weights: empty 6,647 lb (3015 kg); loaded 10,792 lb (4895 kg).
Performance: maximum speed 241 mph (388 km/h); initial climb 920 ft (280 m)/min; service ceiling 25,000 ft (7620 m); range with bomb load at economical setting 900 miles (1448 km).
Armament: one 0·303 in Browning fixed in right wing and one 0·303 in Vickers K manually aimed in rear cockpit; bomb load up to 1,000 lb (454 kg) in four cells in inner wings.
History: first flight (prototype) 10 March 1936; production Mk I, June 1937; final delivery January 1941; withdrawal from service 1949.

The Battle will forever be remembered as a combat aeroplane which seemed marvellous when it appeared and yet which, within four years, was being hacked out of the sky in droves so that, ever afterward, aircrew think of the name with a shudder. There was nothing faulty about the aircraft; it was simply a sitting duck for modern fighters. Designed to Specification P.27/32 as a replacement for the biplane Hart and Hind, this clean cantilever stressed-skin monoplane epitomised modern design and carried twice the bomb load for twice the distance at 50 per cent higher speed. It was the first aircraft to go into production with the new Merlin engine, taking its mark number (I, II, III or IV) from that of the engine. Ordered in what were previously unheard-of quantities (155, then 500 and then 863 from a new Austin 'shadow factory'), production built up faster than for any other new British aircraft;

15 RAF bomber squadrons were equipped between May 1937 and May 1938. When World War II began, more than 1,000 were in service and others were exported to Poland, Turkey and Belgium (where 18 were built by Avions Fairey). On 2 September 1939 ten Battle squadrons flew to France as the major offensive element of the Advanced Air Striking Force. They were plunged into furious fighting from 10 May 1940 and suffered grievously. On the first day of the Blitzkrieg in the West two members of 12 Sqn won posthumous VCs and four days later, in an all-out attack on German pontoon bridges at Sedan, 71 Battles attacked and 31 returned. Within six months all Battles were being replaced in front-line units and the survivors of the 2,419 built were shipped to Canada or Australia as trainers (many with separate instructor/pupil cockpits) or used as target tugs or test beds.

Fairey Swordfish

Swordfish I–IV
Type: basic role, two-seat torpedo carrier and three-seat spotter reconnaissance; later many other duties.

Engine: (Mk I and early II) one 690 hp Bristol Pegasus IIIM3 nine-cylinder radial (later II onwards) 750 hp Pegasus 30.
Dimensions: span 45 ft 6 in (13·87 m); length (landplane) 35 ft 8 in (10·87 m); height 12 ft 4 in (3·76 m).
Weights: empty 4,700 lb (2134 kg); loaded 7,510 lb (3410 kg).
Performance: maximum speed 138 mph (222 km/h); initial climb 1,220 ft (372 m)/min; service ceiling 19,250 ft (5867 m); range with full ordnance load 546 miles (879 km).
Armament: one fixed 0·303 in Vickers, one manually aimed 0·303 in Browning or Vickers K in rear cockpit; crutch for 18 in 1,610 lb torpedo (or 1,500 lb mine or 1,500 lb of bombs). (Mk II–IV) underwing racks for eight 60 lb rockets or other stores.
History: first flight (TSR.II) 17 April 1934; production Mk I December 1935; service delivery February 1936; final delivery June 1944.

One of the great combat aircraft of history, the well-loved "Stringbag" looked archaic even when new, yet outlasted the aircraft intended to replace it and served

valiantly and successfully from countless carriers and rough airstrips from start to finish of World War II. Designed to Specification S.38/34, it derived from an earlier prototype which got into an uncontrollable spin. Designated TSR.II the revised aircraft had a longer, spin-proof body, necessitating sweeping back the upper wing slightly. All-metal, with fabric covering, pre-war Swordfish were often twin-float seaplanes, these usually serving in the three-seat spotter role. Most, however, equipped the Fleet Air Arm's 13 land-

plane torpedo squadrons and during World War II a further 13 were formed. Stories of this amazingly willing aircraft are legion. One aircraft made twelve minelaying sorties in 24 hours. Another torpedoed an enemy ship in a round trip taking ten hours. A handful based in Malta sank an average of 50,000 tons of enemy vessels (most very heavily armed with flak) every month in 1941–43. The highlight of the Swordfish's career was the attack on the Italian naval base of Taranto, on 10–11 November 1940, when two Swordfish were lost in exchange for the destruction of three battleships, a cruiser, two destroyers and other warships. The Mk II had metal-skinned lower wings for rocket-firing, the III had radar and the IV an enclosed cockpit. From 1940 all production and development was handled by Blackburn, which built 1,699 of the 2,391 delivered.

Fairey Barracuda

Type 100 Barracuda I, II, III and V
Type: three-seat (Mk V, two-seat) naval torpedo/dive bomber.
Engine: (I) one 1,260 hp Rolls-Royce Merlin 30 vee-12 liquid-cooled; (II and III) one 1,640 hp Merlin 32; (V) one 2,020 hp R-R Griffon 37.
Dimensions: span (I–III) 49 ft 2 in (15 m); (V) 53 ft (16·15 m); length (I–III) 39 ft 9 in (12·12 m); (V) 41 ft 1 in (12·5 m); height (I–III) 15 ft 1 in (4·6 m); (V) 13 ft 2 in (4 m).
Weights: empty (I) 8,700 lb (3946 kg); (II, III) 9,407 lb (4267 kg); (V) 9,800 lb (4445 kg); loaded (I) 13,500 lb (6125 kg); (II, III) 14,100 lb (6395 kg); (V) 16,400 lb (7450 kg).
Performance: maximum speed (I) 235 mph; (II) 228 mph (367 km/h); (III) 239 mph; (V) 264 mph (422 km/h); initial climb 950 ft (290 m)/min; (V) 2,000 ft (610 m)/min; service ceiling (I) 18,400 ft; (II) 16,600 ft (5060 m); (III) 20,000 ft (6096 m); (V) 24,000 ft; range with full weapon load (I, II) 524 miles (845 km); (III) 686 miles (1104 km); (V) 600 miles.
Armament: (I–III) two 0·303 in Vickers K manually aimed in rear cockpit; (V) one fixed 0·50 in Browning in wing, no rear guns; one 18 in torpedo (1,610 or 1,620 lb) or bomb load up to 2,000 lb (907 kg) under fuselage and wings (including mines or depth charges).
History: first flight 7 December 1940; production Mk I, 18 May 1942; service delivery, 10 January 1943; first Mk V (converted II) 16 November 1944; final delivery January 1946.

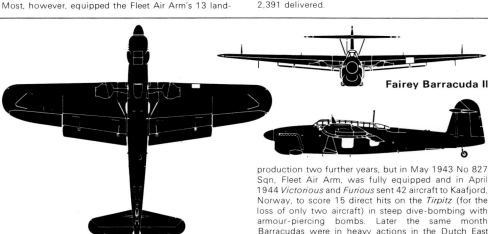

The Barracuda was designed to Specification S.24/37 to replace the Albacore, which in turn had been designed to replace the venerable Swordfish. The Albacore was withdrawn from production in 1943, after 800 had been built, while manufacture of Swordfish continued. The Barracuda, however, was in a different class and might have played a greater part in World War II had it not been so severely delayed. The first delay, from 1938–40, was due to abandonment of the proposed Rolls-Royce Exe engine, and the low-rated Merlin was only marginally powerful enough as a substitute. Pressure of other programmes held back

production two further years, but in May 1943 No 827 Sqn, Fleet Air Arm, was fully equipped and in April 1944 *Victorious* and *Furious* sent 42 aircraft to Kaafjord, Norway, to score 15 direct hits on the *Tirpitz* (for the loss of only two aircraft) in steep dive-bombing with armour-piercing bombs. Later the same month Barracudas were in heavy actions in the Dutch East Indies, and others were equipped to para-drop secret agents (from underwing nacelles) to occupied Europe. The II had more power and four-blade propeller, later receiving ASV.IIN radar, while the III had ASV.10 in an under-fuselage radome. Wartime output of "Barras" was: Fairey 1,131, Blackburn 700, Boulton Paul 692 and Westland 18 (mostly IIs). In 1945 production began on the much more powerful Mk V, later called TF.5, with redesigned structure and accommodation. Radar was housed in a left-wing pod, and later Mk Vs had a tall pointed tail and other changes, but only 30 were built and used mainly for training.

Fairey (later Westland) Firefly

Firefly I to 7 and U.8 to 10

Type: originally two-seat naval fighter; later, see text.
Engine: I, up to No 470, one 1,730 hp Rolls-Royce Griffon IIB vee-12 liquid-cooled; from No 471, 1,990 hp Griffon XII; Mks 4–7, 2,245 hp Griffon 74.
Dimensions: span (I–III) 44 ft 6 in (13·55 m), (4–6) 41 ft 2 in (12·55 m), (7) 44 ft 6 in (13·55 m); length (I–III) 37 ft 7 in (11·4 m); (4–6) 37 ft 11 in (11·56 m); (7) 38 ft 3 in (11·65 m); height (I–III) 13 ft 7 in (4·15 m); (4–7) 14 ft 4 in (4·37 m).
Weights: empty (I) 9,750 lb (4422 kg); (4) 9,900 lb (4491 kg); (7) 11,016 lb (4997 kg); loaded (I) 14,020 lb (6359 kg); (4) 13,927 lb (6317 kg) clean, 16,096 lb (7301 kg) with external stores; (7) 13,970 lb (6337 kg).
Performance: maximum speed (I) 316 mph (509 km/h); (4) 386 mph (618 km/h); initial climb (I) 1,700 ft (518 m)/min; (4) 2,050 ft (625 m)/min; service ceiling (I) 28,000 ft (8534 m); (4) 31,000 ft (9450 m); range on internal fuel (I) 580 miles (933 km); (4) 760 miles (1223 km).
Armament: (I) four fixed 20 mm Hispano cannon in wings; underwing racks for up to 2,000 lb (907 kg) of weapons or other stores; (4 and 5) usually similar to I in most sub-types; (6) no guns, but underwing load increased to 3,000 lb and varied; (7) no guns, but underwing load remained at 3,000 lb and equipment changed.
History: first flight 22 December 1941; first production F.I 26 August 1942; production FR.4, 25 May 1945; final delivery of new aircraft May 1955.

Before World War II Fairey designed a light bomber, P.4/34, from which evolved the Fulmar naval two-seat fighter to Specification O.8/38. A total of 600 of these slender carrier-based aircraft served during the war with various equipment and roles. The Firefly followed the same formula, but was much more powerful and useful. Designed to N.5/40 – a merger of N.8/39 and N.9/39 – it was a clean stressed-skin machine with

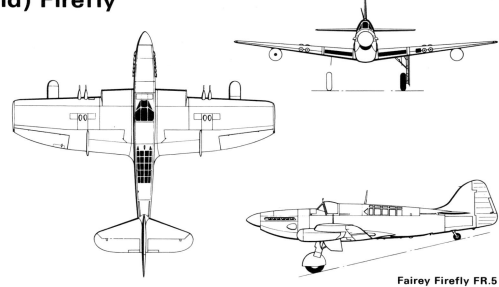

folding elliptical wings housing the four cannon and with the trailing edge provided with patented Young-man flaps for use at low speeds and in cruise. Unlike the installation on the Barracuda, these flaps could be recessed into the wing. The pilot sat over the leading edge, with the observer behind the wing. The main wartime version was the Mk I, widely used from the end of 1943 in all theatres. Fairey and General Aircraft built 429 F.Is, 376 FR.Is with ASH radar and then 37 NF.2 night fighters. There followed the more powerful Mk III, from which derived the redesigned FR.4 with two-stage Griffon and wing-root radiators. There were

Fairey Firefly FR.5

160 of these, 40 going to the Netherlands and the rest serving in Korea, with the 352 Mk 5s with folding wings. There were FR, NF and AS (anti-submarine) Mk 5s, and they were followed by the 133 specialised AS.6 versions with all role equipment tailored to anti-submarine operations. The 151 AS.7s rounded off production, this being a redesigned three-seater, with new tail and wings and distinctive beard radiator. More than 400 Fireflies were rebuilt in the 1950s as two-cockpit T.1s, or armed T.2s, or as various remotely piloted drone versions (U.8, U.9, U.10). Some Fireflies were converted as target tugs and for other civil duties.

Fairey (later Westland) Gannet

GR.17, Gannet Mks 1-7

Type: three-seat naval anti-submarine or airborne early-warning aircraft.
Engine: (AS.1 and T.2) one 2,950 ehp Armstrong Siddeley (later Bristol Siddeley, then Rolls-Royce) Double Mamba 100 double turboprop with two single-shaft power sections; (AEW.3) 3,875 ehp Double Mamba 102; (AS.4 and T.5) 3,035 ehp Double Mamba 101.
Dimensions: span 54 ft 4 in (16·5 m); (AEW.3) 54 ft 6 in; length 43 ft (13.1 m); (AEW.3) 44 ft; height 13 ft 8 in (4·16 m); (AEW.3) 16 ft 10 in.
Weights: empty 14,069 lb (6382 kg); (AEW.3) 16,960 lb; loaded 22,506 lb (10,208 kg); (AEW.3) 24,000 lb.
Performance: maximum speed (clean) (AS.1) 311 mph (500 km/h); (AS.4) 299 mph; (AEW.3) 250 mph; initial climb (all), 2,200 ft (670 m)/min; service ceiling (AEW.3) 25,000 ft (7625 m); range with full armament load (AS.1) 662 miles (1066 km) at sea level; (AEW.3) about 800 miles (1287 km) at altitude.
Armament: (AS versions) typical load of two torpedoes in weapon bay (or 2,000 lb of bombs, depth charges or mines) plus 16×5 in or 24×3 in rockets on wing racks.
History: first flight (GR.17) 19 September 1949; production AS.1, 9 July 1953; AS.4, 13 April 1956; AEW.3, 20 August 1958 (aerodynamic prototype), 2 December 1958 (production aircraft); final delivery 1961.

Designed to the challenging Specification GR.17/45, of October 1945, the Gannet was the successful answer to the problem of building a small carrier-based aircraft combining anti-submarine search and strike capability and using gas-turbine engines running on ship's diesel fuel. The central feature of the design was the engine, in which two power sections could run independently, each driving one of a pair of co-axial propellers. Both power sections were used for take-off and during tactical attack, one being shut down in cruising flight to improve specific consumption (and also extend engine life). A year after first flight the customer could not make up his mind how the Gannet should be designed, but eventually a third seat had to be added, together with two auxiliary tail fins, and the radar was put in a retractable bin under the rear fuselage. No sonobuoy or MAD equipment was fitted, but there was a large weapon bay. The wings power-folded into five sections. Fleet Air Arm No 826 Sqn equipped with the radical new type by January 1955. Following 181 AS.1s came 38 dual-control T.2s, 75 AS.4s and 8 T.5s, including 40 Gannets for Australia, 16 for West Germany and 18 for Indonesia.

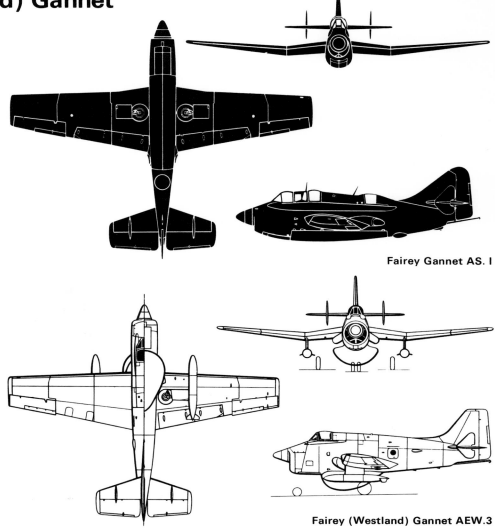

Many Mk 4s were converted to AS.6 and AS.7 standard with additional and updated avionics and ECM and five were turned into COD (Carrier On-board Delivery) transports, supporting *Ark Royal*. The 44 AEW.3

Fairey Gannet AS. I

Fairey (Westland) Gannet AEW.3

Gannets were completely redesigned early-warners with giant APS-20 surveillance radome underneath. The pilot sat alone up front and the two radar plotters occupied a rear cabin, as in corresponding Skyraiders.

Farman Longhorn

MF.7 (British S.7),
and MF.11
Shorthorn (British S.11)
Type: (MF.7) trainer and general
utility; (MF.11) bombing
and reconnaissance.
Engine: (MF.7) usually 70 hp Renault
(S.7, alternative 75 hp R-R Hawk); (MF.11)
usually 100 hp Renault (alternatively 100 hp Fiat
A-10, 100 hp Colombo or 80 hp Gnome). These
engines were mostly water-cooled vee-8s.
Dimensions: span (MF.7) 51 ft (15·54 m); (MF.11)
57 ft 9 in (17·6 m); length (MF.7) 28 ft 10 in (8·75 m);
(MF.11) typically 30 ft (9·2 m); height (MF.7)
11 ft 4 in (3·45 m); (MF.11) 12 ft 9 in (3·9 m).
Weights: empty (MF.7) about 1,300 lb (590 kg);
(MF.11) about 1,700 lb (769 kg); loaded (MF.7)
1,885 lb (855 kg); (MF.11) 2,620 lb (1188 kg).
Performance: maximum speed (MF.7) 59 mph
(95 km/h); (MF.11) 66 mph (106 km/h); service
ceiling (MF.7) 13,123 ft (4000 m); (MF.11) 12,470 ft
(3800 m); endurance (MF.7) 3½ hr; (MF.11) 3¾ hr.
Armament: (MF.7) none; (MF.11m) usually one
machine gun manually aimed by observer; (MF.11bis)
factory-built installation with Lewis or Hotchkiss
mounted to fire either from pillar on front cockpit,
covering forward hemisphere, or from bracket on
upper wing, covering upper hemisphere; On the
MF.11 in addition, light bombs could be carried

under lower wing or on sides of nacelle, eg 18 16 lb
bombs.
History: first flight (MF.7) February 1913; (MF.11)
1914; service delivery (MF.7) about July 1913;
(MF.11) May 1915.

Designed by Maurice Farman (hence the initials), these
extremely widely used aircraft were built in both his
own factories and that of his brother Henry and both
were also constructed in large numbers in plants of
other Allied countries, including Britain, Italy and
(probably) Russia. The Longhorn, so-called because
of the long "horns" carrying the canard elevator in
front, was the most widely used of all Allied trainers
before and during the first half of World War I, and
several squadrons were also equipped with it for
operational use as an observation machine over the
Western Front. It was reliable, sluggish and rather

Farman MF.7 Longhorn (S.7, REC)

unstable, though the latter quality was held to make it
a good trainer. The more powerful Shorthorn had no
front elevator, but a single rear tailplane carrying twin
fins. Until at least mid-1915 it was the main Allied
combat aircraft, flying not only armed reconnaissance
missions but also carrying out night bombing. Cdr
Samson of the RNAS made a daring single-handed
night bombing raid against U-boats at Ostend on
21 December 1914 using an S.11, with eighteen 16 lb
bombs, a signal Very pistol and a torch! About one-
fifth of the MF.11s built in Italy and the S.11s built in
Britain were float seaplanes suitable for operation
from calm water. The Shorthorn remained in use as a
trainer until 1918.

Farman F 220 family

F 221, 222 and 223 series
Type: all, basically, five-seat heavy bombers.
Engines: (F 221) four 800 hp Gnome-Rhône
GR14Kbrs 14-cylinder two-row radials; (F 222) four
860 hp GR14Kdrs; (F 222/2) four 950 hp GR14N
11/15 or Kirs; (F 223) four 1,100 hp Hispano-Suiza
HS14Aa08/09 vee-12 liquid-cooled; NC 223.3,
four 910 hp HS12Y29; (NC 223.4) four 1,050 hp
HS12Y37.
Dimensions: span (F 221, 222, 222/2) 118 ft 1½ in
(36 m); (F 223, NC 223) 110 ft 2¾ in (33·5 m);
length (F 221–222/2) 70 ft 8¾ in (21·5 m); (F 223,
NC 223) 72 ft 2 in (22 m); (NC 223.4) 77 ft 1 in
(23·5 m); height (all) 16 ft 9 in to 17 ft 2¼ in (5·22 m).
Weights: empty (F 222/2) 23,122 lb (10,488 kg);
(NC 223.3) 23,258 lb (10,550 kg); (NC 223.4)
22,046 lb (10,000 kg); loaded (F 221) 39,242 lb
(17,800 kg); (F 222/2) 41,226 lb (18,700 kg);
(NC 223.3) 42,329 lb (19,200 kg); (NC 223.4)
52,911 lb (24,000 kg).
Performance: maximum speed (F 221) 185 mph
service ceiling (F 221) 19,700 ft (6000 m); (F 222/2)

26,250 ft (8000 m); (NC 223.3 at maximum weight)
24,606 ft (7500 m); (NC 223.4 at maximum weight)
13,120 ft (4000 m); range with maximum bomb load
(300 km/h); (F 222/2) 199 mph (320 km/h); (NC
223.3) 248 mph (400 km/h) (264 mph as unarmed
prototype); (NC 223.4) 239 mph (385 km/h);

(F 221) 745 miles (1200 km); F 222/2)
1,240 miles (2000 km); (NC 223.3) 1,490 miles
(2400 km); (NC 223.4) 3,107 miles (5000 km).
Armament: (F 221) three manually aimed 7·5 mm
MAC 1934 machine guns in nose turret, dorsal and
ventral positions; bomb load seldom carried; (F 222/2)
same guns as 221; normal bomb load of 5,510 lb, with
maximum internal capacity of 9,240 lb (4190 kg);
(NC 223·3) one MAC 1934 manually aimed in nose,
one 20 mm Hispano 404 cannon in SAMM 200 dorsal
turret, one 20 mm Hispano 404 in SAMM 109 ventral
turret; internal bomb load of 9,240 lb. NC 223·4, one
manually aimed 7·5 mm Darne machine gun in entry
door; internal bomb load of 4,410 lb (eight 250 kg
bombs).
History: first flight (F 211) October 1931; (F 221)
1933; (F 222) June 1935; (F 222/2) October 1937;
(NC 223) June 1937; (NC 223·3) October 1938;
(NC 223·4) 15 March 1939.

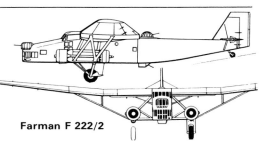

Farman F 222/2

This distinctive family formed the backbone of the
Armée de l'Air heavy bomber force from 1935 until the
collapse in 1940. It began with the F 210 of 1930,
which set the pattern in having an angular box-like
body, high-mounted wing and four engines slung on
braced struts from the wing and fuselage in push/pull
double nacelles. By way of the 220 came the 221,
which served mainly as a 20-seat troop transport. The
222 introduced retractable landing gear, and the
36 F. 222/2 bombers of GBI/15 and II/15 served tire-
lessly in the dark months of 1940, often flying bombing
missions by night over Germany and even Italy and as
transports in North Africa until late 1944.

F.E.2

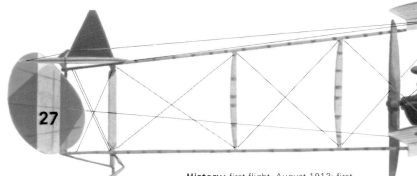

27

F.E.2b (G. & J. Weir-built)

Royal Aircraft Factory F.E.2a, 2b and 2d
Type: two-seat combat aircraft.
Engine: (F.E.2b) one 120 hp or 160 hp Beardmore
six-cylinder water-cooled, driving pusher propeller.
Dimensions: span 47 ft 9 in (14·55 m); length
32 ft 3 in (9·83 m); height 12 ft 7 in (3·8 m).
Weights: empty (120 hp) 2,550 lb (1160 kg);
loaded (120 hp) 2,967 lb (1346 kg); (160 hp) 3,037 lb
(1378 kg).
Performance: maximum speed (120 hp) 81 mph
(130 km/h); (160 hp) 91 mph (146 km/h); service
ceiling (120 hp) 9,000 ft (2743 m); (160 hp) 11,000 ft
(3353 m); endurance (both) 2 hr 30 min, equivalent
to a range of about 180 miles.
Armament: various, depending on production batch
and operating unit. Invariably one 0·303 in Lewis
manually aimed in front cockpit covering forward
hemisphere; often a second Lewis on pillar between
cockpits covering upper hemisphere and upper rear;
for other guns see text; underwing racks for total
bomb load of 336 lb (153 kg).

History: first flight, August 1913; first
production aircraft, January 1915;
final delivery (F.E.2d), probably October 1916.

Viewed from 60 years later, the "Fee" appears to be a
tale of official procrastination and delay. Certainly this
fine aircraft, the first successful Fighter Experimental
design by the Royal Aircraft Factory at Farnborough,
could have given the Royal Flying Corps a world-
beating combat aircraft at a time when it was desperately needed. Instead, a whole year was allowed to
elapse before a production order was even placed and
by this time the concept of the slow pusher was due for
fairly swift obsolescence, except for night bombing. The
layout was due to the need to fire a machine gun,
there being in 1913 no way of safely firing ahead
through a tractor propeller. The gunner (observer)
therefore occupied the front cockpit, though in the
later F.E.2c night operations were made easier by the
crew changing places. The first order, for 12 F.E.2a aircraft, was placed in August 1914 and deliveries took
place in the first three months of 1915. This version,

with the 100 hp Green engine, was swiftly supplanted
by the Beardmore-engined F.E.2b. Until the end of
World War I the "Fee" acquitted itself very well,
moving into night bombing after the daytime scene
became too hot in September 1916. Had they been
available in numbers in late 1916 they would have
dominated the sky over the Western Front and been a
match for the Fokkers of 1915 that became such a
dreaded scourge. As late as June 1916 "Fees" were
still doughty foes, one shooting down the great Max
Immelmann in that month. Altogether 1,939 were
built, as well as 386 long-span F.E.2d models with
250 hp R-R Eagle engines. Many of both types had
Vickers 1-pdr or 0·45 in Maxim guns, as well as
forward-firing Lewises.

Felixstowe flying boats

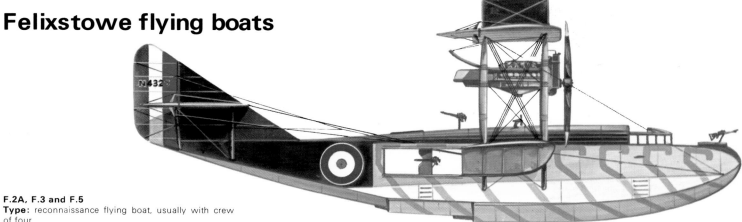

F.2A, F.3 and F.5

Type: reconnaissance flying boat, usually with crew of four.
Engines: (F.2A) two 345 hp Rolls-Royce Eagle VIII vee-12 water-cooled; (F.3) same; (F.5) same or 375 hp Eagle VIII.
Dimensions: span (F.2A) 95 ft 7 in (29·15 m); (F.3) 102 ft 8 in (31·6 m); length (F.2A) 46 ft 3 in (14·1 m); (F.3, F.5) 49 ft 2 in (15 m); height (F.2A) 17 ft 6 in (5·33 m); (F.3, F.5) 18 ft 9 in (5·7 m).
Weights: empty (F.2A) 7,900 lb (3583 kg); (F.3) about 9,500 lb (4310 kg); (F.5) 9,100 lb (4128 kg); loaded (F.2A) 10,978 lb (4980 kg); (F.3) 13,281 lb (6024 kg).
Performance: maximum speed (F.2A) 95·5 mph (154 km/h), (F.3, F.5) about 89 mph (143 km/h); climb to 6,500 ft (F.2A) 20 min, (F.5) 30 min; service ceiling (F.2A) 9,600 ft (2926 m), (F.3) 6,000 ft (1829 m), (F.5) 6,800 ft (2073 m); endurance (F.2A) 6 hr, (F.3) 7 hr 30 min, (F.5) 7 hr.
Armament: standard defensive armament for all, four 0·303 in Lewis machine guns manually aimed from bow cockpit, dorsal cockpit and left and right

beam positions; bomb load, carried below wings, 460 lb (209 kg) for F.2A, 920 lb (417 kg) for F.3 and F.5.
History: first flight (F.1) 1916; (production F.2A) November 1917; (F.3) late 1917 (prototype February 1917); (F.5) May 1918.

Credit for the excellent series of flying boats used by the Royal Naval Air Service in World War I belongs to John Porte, who had earlier instigated the Curtiss boats described on p. 44. Returning to Britain to take part in the war, in September 1915 he assumed command of RN Air Station Felixstowe, where he operated H.4 Small America boats on patrol over the North Sea. Appreciating their shortcomings he set to work to design an improved hull, and after testing a successful design with the Porte I (F.1) scaled this up to fit the H.12 "Large America". The result was the F.2A, the standard RNAS boat of the war. About 100 were de-

Felixstowe F.3

livered by S. E. Saunders of Cowes and ten by Aircraft Manufacturing Co of Hendon. Though slow and ponderous, they were well armed and fought many battles against Brandenburg seaplanes, the biggest battle being on 4 June 1918 when three, circling over a fourth that had landed on the sea after fuel failure, were set upon by 14 German W.29 seaplanes, shooting down six without loss to themselves! Zeppelins and U-boats were also attacked successfully by these prickly boats, which in 1918 were painted in individual dazzle schemes to facilitate recognition. The long-span F.3 carried a much heavier bomb load further, while the completely redesigned F.5 was the standard boat of the post-war RAF. A Short-built F.5 of 1924 had an all-metal hull, the first in the world.

Fiat C.R.32

C.R.30, 32 and 32bis

Type: single-seat fighter.
Engine: (C.R.30) one 600 hp Fiat A.30 vee-12 water-cooled, (C.R.32) one 600 hp Fiat A.30 RAbis.
Dimensions: span (C.R.30) 34 ft 5½ in (10·45 m); (C.R.32) 31 ft 2 in (9·5 m); length (30) 25 ft 8¼ in (7·83 m); (32) 24 ft 5½ in (7·45 m); height (30) 8 ft 7½ in (2·62 m); (32) 7 ft 9 in (2·4 m).
Weights: empty (both) about 3,100 lb (1400 kg); loaded (both) about 4,150 lb (1900 kg).
Performance: maximum speed (30) 217 mph (350 km/h), (32) 233 mph (375 km/h); initial climb (both) 2,000 ft (907 m)/min; service ceiling (both) about 29,530 ft (9000 m); range (30) 528 miles (850 km), (32) 466 miles (750 km).
Armament: (C.R.30) two fixed Breda-SAFAT 7·7 mm or 12·7 mm machine guns above engine; (C.R.32) two 12·7 mm; (C.R.32bis), two 12·7 mm above engine and two 7·7 mm above lower wings, with provision for single 220 lb (100 kg) or two 110 lb bombs.
History: first flight (C.R.30) 1932; (C.R.32) August 1933; final delivery, about October 1939.

In 1923 Ing Celestino Rosatelli supervised his first C.R. (Caccia Rosatelli) fighter. From it stemmed an

unbroken line which reached its climax in the 1930s. The C.R.30 offered a considerable jump in performance, for it had much more power without increase in aircraft drag. The lusty Fiat vee-12 drove a metal propeller and was cooled by a prominent circular radiator in a duct in the chin position below the crankcase. The all-metal structure was notable for continuing the scheme of Warren (W-form) interplane bracing. The tail was also braced and the main gears had large wheel spats. The C.R.32 was a general refinement, built in larger numbers and forming the major part of the Regia Aeronautica fighter force in 1935–40. In August 1936 some were sent to form La

Fiat C.R.32 (Spanish Nationalist ace Morato)

Cucuracha squadron fighting for the Spanish Nationalist forces and this grew to become by far the largest of Franco's fighter units. Spain built many under licence as the Hispano HA-132-L Chirri, and more than 150 were exported by Fiat to China, Hungary and South American countries. The nimble little Fiats were compact, robust and highly manoeuvrable and gave impressive displays all over Europe in the hands of the Pattuglie Acrobatiche. Total Fiat output amounted to at least 1,212, the final 500 being mainly four-gun 32bis fighter-bombers and a few 32ter and 32quater versions with small modifications. The Regia Aeronautica did its best with the C.R. 32 until 1942, finally using it for night tactical operations in Greece, Eritrea and Libya.

Fiat C.R.42 Falco

C.R.42, 42bis, 42ter, 42AS and 42N

Type: single-seat fighter.
Engine: one 840 hp Fiat A.74 RC38 14-cylinder two-row radial.
Dimensions: span 31 ft 10 in (9·7 m); length 27 ft 1¼ in (8·25 m); height 11 ft (3·35 m).
Weights: empty, 3,790 lb (1720 kg); loaded 5,070 lb (2300 kg).
Performance: maximum speed 267 mph (430 km/h); initial climb 2,400 ft (732 m)/min; service ceiling 34,450 ft (10,500 m); range 481 miles (775 km).
Armament: (early C.R.42) one 7·7 mm and one 12·7 mm Breda-SAFAT machine guns mounted above forward fuselage; (C.R.42bis) two 12·7 mm; (C.R.42ter) two 12·7 mm and two more 12·7 mm in fairings beneath lower wing; (C.R.42AS) two/four 12·7 mm and underwing racks for two 220 lb (100 kg) bombs.
History: first flight (C.R.41) 1936; (C.R.42) January 1939; first service delivery, November 1939; termination of production, early 1942.

In the mid-1930s the Fiat company made a firm move away from liquid-cooled vee engines and concentrated on air-cooled radials. Rosatelli prepared a fighter, the C.R.41, to take one of these, but only the prototype was built. Other nations were by this time (1936) giving up the open-cockpit, fabric-covered

Fiat C.R.42bis (95 Squadriglia, 18o Gruppo)

December 1939–June 1940) and Sweden (72, delivered 1940–41). Total production, including the AS close support and N night fighter versions, amounted to 1,784. One group of 50 C.R.42bis provided the fighter element of the Corpo Aereo Italiano which operated from Belgium against England in October 1940–January 1941 – with conspicuous lack of success. The rest persevered in the Mediterranean and North African areas, acting as both fighters and ground attack aircraft, a few being converted as dual trainers. One was built in 1940 as a twin-float seaplane and the final fling was a C.R.42B with 1,010 hp DB 601A inverted-vee engine. The German power unit made it, at 323 mph, the fastest biplane fighter but no production was attempted.

biplane in favour of the stressed-skin monoplane with retractable landing gear, but Rosatelli persisted with his C.R. family and developed the C.R.41 into the C.R.42. Though a robust, clean and very attractive design, it was really obsolete at the time of its first flight. Despite this – and perhaps confirming that Fiat knew the world market – the C.R.42 found ready acceptance. It went into large-scale production for the Regia Aeronautica and for Belgium (34, delivered January–May 1940), Hungary (at least 40, delivered

Fiat B.R.20 Cicogna

Fiat B.R.20 (1st Chutai, 12th Hikosentai, Imperial Japanese Army)

B.R.20, 20M and 20 bis
Type: heavy bomber, with normal crew of five or six.
Engines: (B.R.20) two 1,000 hp Fiat A.80 RC41 18-cylinder two-row radials; (B.R.20M) as B.R.20 or two 1,100 hp A.80 RC20; (B.R.20bis) two 1,250 hp A.82 RC32.
Dimensions: span, 70 ft 9 in (21·56 m); length, (B.R.20) 52 ft 9 in (16·2 m); (B.R.20M, 20bis) 55 ft (16·78 m); height, 15 ft 7 in (4·75 m).
Weights: empty (all), about 14,770 lb (6700 kg); loaded (B.R.20) 22,046 lb (10,000 kg); (B.R.20M) 23,038 lb (10,450 kg).
Performance: maximum speed, (B.R.20) 264 mph (425 km/h); (B.R.20M) 267 mph (430 km/h); (B.R.20bis) 292 mph (470 km/h); initial climb (all) about 902 ft (275 m)/min; service ceiling, (B.R.20, 20M) 22,145 ft (6750 m); (B.R.20bis) 26,246 ft (8000 m); range, (B.R.20, 20M) 1,243 miles (2000 km); (B.R.20bis) 1,710 miles (2750 km).
Armament: (B.R.20) four 7·7 mm Breda-SAFAT machine guns in nose turret (one), dorsal turret (two) and manual ventral position; bomb load 3,527 lb

(1600 kg); (B.R.20M) as B.R.20 except nose gun 12·7mm; (B.R.20bis) as B.R.20M with two extra 12·7 mm guns manually aimed from lateral blisters; bomb load 5,511 lb (2500 kg).
History: first flight (prototype) 10 February 1936; service delivery, September 1936; first flight (B.R.20M) late 1939; first B.R.20bis, December 1941.

Ing Rosatelli was responsible for a great series of B.R. (Bombardamento Rosatelli) designs from 1919 onwards. Most were powerful single-engined biplanes, but in the mid-1930s he very quickly produced the B.R.20, a large monoplane with stressed-skin construction and other modern refinements. Despite its relative complexity the original aircraft was put into production within six months of the first flight and by the end of 1936 the B.R.20-equipped 13° Stormo was probably the most advanced bomber squadron in the world. Fiat also built two civil B.R.20L record-breakers, and also offered the new bomber for export, soon gaining a valuable order for 85, not from the expected China but from Japan, which needed a

powerful bomber to bridge the gap caused by a delay with the Army Ki-21. In June 1937 the B.R.20 figured prominently in the Aviazione Legionaria sent to fight for the Nationalists in Spain and, with the He 111, bore the brunt of their very successful bomber operations. Spain purchased a manufacturing licence, which was not taken up, and purchased at least 25 from Fiat. An additional number were bought by Venezuela. In 1940, when Italy entered World War II, some 250 had been delivered to the Regia Aeronautica, the last 60 being of the strengthened and much more shapely M (Modificato) type. In October 1940 two groups of 37 and 38 of the M model operated against England, but they were hacked down with ease and were recalled in January 1941. During 1942 the B.R.20 began to fade, becoming used for ocean patrol, operational training and bombing where opposition was light. A large force supported the Luftwaffe in Russia, where casualties were heavy. By the Armistice only 81 of all versions were left out of 606 built. The much improved B.R.20bis never even got into bulk production.

Fiat G.50 Freccia

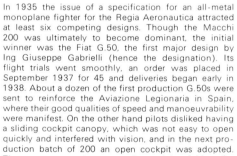

Fiat G.50 (1o Gruppo Sperimentale, Spain)

G.50, 50bis, 50ter and 55 Centauro
Type: single-seat fighter.
Engine: (G.50, G.50bis) one 840 hp Fiat A.74 RC38 14-cylinder two-row radial; (G.50ter) 1,000 hp A.76 RC40S; (G.55) 1,475 hp Daimler-Benz DB 605A inverted-vee-12 liquid-cooled.
Dimensions: span, (G.50) 36 ft (10·97 m); (G.55) 38 ft 10½ in (11·85 m); length, (G.50) 25 ft 7 in (7·79 m); (G.55) 30 ft 9 in (9·37 m); height (G.50) 9 ft 8 in (2·9 m); (G.55) 10 ft 3¼ in (3·15 m).
Weights: empty (G.50) 4,188 lb (1900 kg); (G.55) 6,393 lb (2900 kg); loaded (G.50) 5,966 lb (2706 kg); (G.55) 8,179 lb (3710 kg).
Performance: maximum speed (G.50) 293 mph (471 km/h); (G.55) 385 mph (620 km/h); initial climb (G.50) 2,400 ft (731 m)/min; (G.55) 3,300 ft (1000 m)/min; service ceiling (G.50) 32,810 ft (10,000 m); (G.55) 42,650 ft (13,000 m); range (G.50) 621 miles (1000 km); (G.55) 994 miles (1600 km).
Armament: (G.50, G.50bis) two 12·7 mm Breda-SAFAT machine guns above front fuselage; (G.55/0) as above, plus one 20 mm Mauser MG 151 cannon firing through propeller hub; (G.55/I) as G.55/0 plus two 20mm MG 151 in outer wings.
History: first flight 26 February 1937; (G.50bis) September 1940; (G.55) 30 April 1942.

In 1935 the issue of a specification for an all-metal monoplane fighter for the Regia Aeronautica attracted at least six competing designs. Though the Macchi 200 was ultimately to become dominant, the initial winner was the Fiat G.50, the first major design by Ing Giuseppe Gabrielli (hence the designation). Its flight trials went smoothly, an order was placed in September 1937 for 45 and deliveries began early in 1938. About a dozen of the first production G.50s were sent to reinforce the Aviazione Legionaria in Spain, where their good qualities of speed and manoeuvrability were manifest. On the other hand pilots disliked having a sliding cockpit canopy, which was not easy to open quickly and interfered with vision, and in the next production batch of 200 an open cockpit was adopted. The poor armament was not changed, but fairings for the retracted wheels were added. Production from the CMASA plant at Marina di Pisa got under way in 1939,

with deliveries replacing the C.R.32 in Regia Aeronautica fighter squadrons (not always to the pilots' delight), and a further 35 being flown to Finland in 1940 where they gave admirable service. The main production version was the G.50bis, with reprofiled fuselage giving improved pilot view, armour and self-sealing tanks. About 450 were built, mainly by CMASA. Other versions included the tandem-seat G.50B trainer, of which 139 were built; the G.50ter with more powerful engine; and prototypes of the G.50bis-A, with four 12·7 mm guns and racks for two bombs, and of the DB 601A-powered G.50V. The latter led to the G.55, a much more formidable fighter, of which 105 were produced by the end of the war. The G.55A and G.55B advanced fighter/trainers were built in 1949–54, mainly for export, and led to the Merlin-powered G.59 family.

Fiat G91

Fiat G91R/3 (LKG 43, Luftwaffe)

Fiat (Aeritalia) G91R, G91T, G91PAN and G91Y
Type: G91R and Y, single-seat tactical reconnaissance/fighter; G91T, two-seat weapon trainer; G91PAN, single-seat aerobatic display fighter.
Engine(s): (G91R, T and PAN) one 5,000 lb (2268 kg) thrust Rolls-Royce (previously Bristol, then Bristol Siddeley) Orpheus 80302 single-shaft turbojet; (G91Y) two General Electric J85-13A single-shaft augmented turbojets each rated at 4,080 lb (1850 kg) with full afterburner.
Dimensions: span (G.91R, T, PAN) 28 ft 1 in (8·57 m); (G91Y) 29 ft 6½ in (9·01 m); length (G91R, PAN) 33 ft 9¼ in (10·31 m); (G91T, Y) 38 ft 3½ in (11·67 m); height (G91R, PAN) 13 ft 1½ in (4 m); (G91T, Y) 14 ft 6 in (4·43 m).
Weights: empty (G91R) typically 7,275 lb (3300 kg); (G91Y) 8,598 lb (3900 kg); maximum loaded (G91R) 12,500 lb (5695 kg); (G91Y) 19,180 lb (8700 kg).
Performance: maximum speed (G91R) 675 mph (1086 km/h); (G91Y) 690 mph (1110 km/h); initial climb (G91R) 6,000 ft (1829 m)/min; (G91Y) 17,000 ft (5180 m)/min; service ceiling (G91R) 43,000 ft (13,106 m); (G91Y) 41,000 ft (12,500 m); combat radius at sea level (G91R) 196 miles (315 km); (G91Y) 372 miles (600 km); ferry range (G91R) 1,150 miles (1850 km); (G91Y) 2,175 miles (3500 km).
Armament: (G91R/1) four 0·5 in Colt-Browning machine guns, each with 300 rounds, and underwing racks for ordnance load up to 500 lb (227 kg); (G91R/3) two 30 mm DEFA 552 cannon, each with

125 rounds, and underwing racks for ordnance up to 1,000 lb (454 kg); (G91Y) two DEFA 552, underwing load up to 4,000 lb (1814 kg).
History: first flight 9 August 1956; (G91R) December 1958; (G91Y prototype) 27 December 1966; (production G91Y) June 1971.

In December 1953 the North Atlantic Treaty Organisation (NATO) announced a specification for a light tactical strike fighter. It was to be robust, simple to maintain and capable of operation from rough advanced airstrips, yet had to reach Mach 0·92 and be able to deliver conventional or tactical nuclear weapons. There were three French contenders and the G91 from Italy. On the first flight the test pilot lost control and had to eject, but orders had already been placed by the Italian government and production was put in hand. As

the design had been based on that of the F-86, but on a smaller scale, the tail problem of the first prototype was soon rectified; but the French refused to have anything to do with the G91 and the original customers — intended to be all the Continental NATO nations — were only Germany and Italy. Italy took 98 G91R/1, 1A and 1B plus 76 G91T/1, while Germany chose 50 R/3, 44 T/3 and 50 R/4, also building a further 294 R/3 under licence by Messerschmitt (later MBB), Heinkel (later VFW-Fokker) and Dornier. The Orpheus was built by a further European consortium. Among many other sub-variants is the PAN version of the Pattuglia Acrobatica Nazionale. The completely re-designed G91Y has much greater thrust, better navigation aids and can fly fighter, attack or reconnaissance missions. Aeritalia, the company formed in 1969 jointly by Fiat and Finrmeccanica-IRI, delivered 45 to the Regia Aeronautica in 1971–75.

FMA IA 58 Pucará

IA 50 GII, IA 58 and Astafan Trainer

Type: IA 58, tactical attack and counter-insurgency; IA 50, utility transport and survey; Trainer, trainer and light attack.

Engines: (IA 58) two 1,022 ehp Turboméca Astazou XVIG single-shaft turboprops; (IA 50) two 1,000 ehp Turboméca Bastan VIC single-shaft turboprops; (Trainer) two 2,710 lb (1230 kg) thrust Turboméca Astafan geared turbofans.

Dimensions: span (IA 58 and Trainer) 47 ft 6¾ in (14·5 m); (IA 50) 64 ft 3¼ in (19·59 m); length (IA 50 and Trainer) 46 ft 3 in (14·1 m); (IA 50) 50 ft 2½ in (15·3 m); height (IA 58 and Trainer) 17 ft 7 in (5·36 m); (IA 50) 18 ft 5 in (5·61 m).

Weights: empty (IA 58) 8,900 lb (4037 kg); (IA 50) 8,650 lb (3924 kg); (Trainer) 8,377 lb (3800 kg); loaded (IA 58) 14,300 lb (6486 kg); (IA 50) 17,085 lb (7750 kg); (Trainer) 14,330 lb (6500 kg).

Performance: maximum speed (IA 58) 323 mph (520 km/h); (IA 50) 310 mph (500 km/h); (Trainer) about 400 mph (643 km/h); initial climb (IA 58) 3,543 ft (1080 m)/min; (IA 50) 2,640 ft (805 m)/min; service ceiling (IA 58) 27,165 ft (8280 m); (IA 50) 41,000 ft (12,500 m); range with maximum fuel (IA 58) 1,890 miles (3042 km); (IA 50) 1,600 miles (2575 km).

Armament: IA 58, and optional for Trainer, two 20 mm Hispano cannon and four 7·62 mm FN machine guns in forward fuselage; pylons under fuselage and outer wings for up to 3,307 lb (1500 kg) of stores or tanks.

History: first flight (IA 50) 23 April 1963; (IA 58) 20 August 1969.

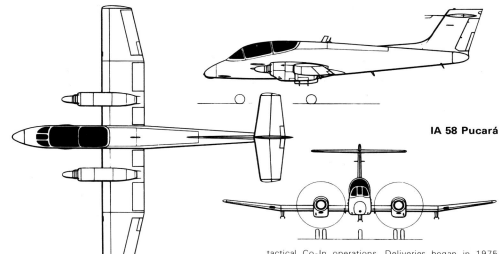

IA 58 Pucará

The unusual but effective Pucará was derived from the larger IA 50 GII (Guarani II) multi-role transport, noted for its slender unswept wings but sharply swept fin and rudder. The first production batch of GII's comprised 18 to the Argentine Air Force for communications and seating for up to 15 passengers, four as photo survey aircraft with the Military Geographic Institute and one as a VIP transport for the President of Argentina. Many others were ordered later, some having ski gear for use in the Antarctic. The smaller IA 58 seats pilot and observer in tandem Martin-Baker ejection seats and is well equipped for all-weather

tactical Co-In operations. Deliveries began in 1975 on the first batch of 30 for the Argentine Air Force, with further batches up to a predicted total of 100 being discussed. Interest has been expressed by several other nations in this versatile and cost/effective aircraft, which can operate from rough strips down to about 2,000 ft in length. The Trainer uses the IA 58 airframe restressed to have two turbofan engines on the sides of the fuselage, the twin-wheel main gears retracting forwards into wing pods in the same locations as the engine nacelles on the IA 58. It was expected that this project would lead to a tactical Co-In version, but inflation has thrown all Argentinian programmes into chaos.

Focke-Wulf Fw 189

Fw 189 A-1, -2 and -3

Type: three-seat reconnaissance and close support.
Engines: two 465 hp Argus As 410A-1 12 cylinder inverted-vee air-cooled.
Dimensions: span 60 ft 4½ in (18·4 m); length 39 ft 4½ in (12 m); height 10 ft 2 in (3·1 m).
Weights: empty 5930 lb (2690 kg); loaded 8708 lb (3950 kg).
Performance: maximum speed 217 mph (350 km/h); climb to 13,120 ft (4000 m) in 8 min 20 sec; service ceiling 23,950 ft (7300 m); range 416 miles (670 km).
Armament: (A-2) one 7·92 mm MG 17 machine gun in each wing root, twin 7·92 mm MG 81 manually aimed in dorsal position and (usually) twin MG 81 in rear cone with limited field of fire; underwing racks for four 110 lb (50 kg) bombs.
History: first flight (Fw 189V1) July 1938; first delivery (pre-production Fw 189A-O) September 1940; final delivery August 1944.

Today the diversity of aircraft layout makes us forget how odd this aircraft seemed. It looked strange to the customer also, but after outstandingly successful flight

Fw 189A-1 (Nahaufklärungsgruppe I)

trials the 189 Uhu (Owl) was grudgingly bought in quantity as a standard reconnaissance aircraft. Though it flew in numbers well before the war — no two prototypes being alike — it was unknown by the Allies until it was disclosed in 1941 as "the Flying Eye" of the German armies. On the Eastern front it performed beyond all expectation, for it retained its superb handling (which made it far from a sitting duck to fighters) and also showed great toughness of structure and more than once returned to base with one tail shot off or removed by Soviet ramming attack. Attempts to produce special attack versions with small heavily armoured nacelles were not so successful, but 10

Fw 189B trainers were built with conventional nacelle having side-by-side dual controls in a normal cockpit, with an observer above the trailing edge. The Fw 189A-3 was another dual-control version having the normal "glasshouse". Eventually the sole source became French factories with assembly at Bordeaux-Mérignac (today the Dassault Mirage plant), which halted as Allied armies approached. There were many different versions and several developments with more powerful engines, but the basic A-1, A-2 (better armament) and A-3 were the only types built in numbers, the total of these versions being 846.

Fw 190 see page 80

Focke-Wulf Fw 200 Condor

Fw 200C-0 to C-8

Type: maritime reconnaissance bomber and (C-6 to -8) missile launcher, many used as transports.
Engines: usually, four 1,200 hp BMW-Bramo Fafnir 323R-2 nine-cylnder radials.
Dimensions: span 107 ft 9½ in (30·855 m); length 76 ft 11½ in (23·46 m); height 20 ft 8 in (6·3 m).
Weights: (C-3/U-4) empty 28,550 lb (12,951 kg); loaded 50,045 lb (22,700 kg).
Performance: maximum speed (C-3) 224 mph (360 km/h); (C-8) 205 mph (330 km/h); initial climb, about 656 ft (200 m)/min; service ceiling 19,030 ft (5800 m); range with standard fuel, 2,206 miles (3550 km).
Armament: typical C-3/C-8, one forward dorsal turret with one 15 mm MG 151/15 (or 20 mm MG 151/20 or one 7·92 mm MG 15), one 20 mm MG 151/20 manually aimed at front of ventral gondola, three 7·92 mm MG 15 manually aimed at rear of ventral gondola and two beam windows (beam guns sometimes being 13 mm MG 131) and one 13 mm MG 131 in aft dorsal position; maximum bomb load of 4,626 lb (2100 kg) carried in gondola and beneath outer

Fw 200C-3 (II/KG 40)

wings (C-6, C-8, two Hs 293 guided missiles carried under outboard nacelles).
History: first flight (civil prototype) 27 July 1937; (Fw 200C-0) January 1940; final delivery (C-8) February 1944.

Planned solely as a long-range commercial transport for the German airline Deutsche Luft Hansa, the pre-war Fw 200 prototypes set up impressive record flights to New York and Tokyo and attracted export orders from Denmark, Brazil, Finland and Japan. Transport prototype and production versions were also used by Hitler and Himmler as VIP executive machines and several later variants were also converted as special transports. In 1938 the Japanese asked for one Condor converted for use as a long-range ocean reconnaissance machine. The resulting Fw 200V-10 prototype introduced a ventral gondola and led to the Fw 200C-0 as the prototype of a Luftwaffe aircraft

which had never been requested or planned and yet which was to prove a most powerful instrument of war. Distinguished by long-chord cowlings, twin-wheel main gears (because of the increased gross weight) and a completely new armament and equipment fit, the C-0 led to the C-1, used operationally from June 1940 by KG 40 at Bordeaux-Merignac. By September 1940 this unit alone had sunk over 90,000 tons of Allied shipping and for the next three years the C-series Condors were, in Churchill's words, "the scourge of the Atlantic". But, though the Fw 200 family continued to grow in equipment and lethality, the Allies fought back with long-range Coastal Command aircraft, escort carriers and CAM (Catapult-Armed Merchantman) fighters and by mid-1944 surviving Condors were being forced into transport roles on other fronts. Total production was 276 and one of the fundamental failings of the Condor was structural weakness, catastrophic wing and fuselage failures occurring not only in the air but even on the ground, on take-off or landing.

Focke-Wulf Fw 190

Fw 190A series, D series, F series and Ta 152H
Type: single-seat fighter bomber.
Engine: (A-8, F-8) one 1700 hp (2100 hp emergency boost) BMW 801Dg 18-cylinder two-row radial; (D-9) one 1776 hp (2240 hp emergency boost) Junkers Jumo 213A-1 12-cylinder inverted-vee liquid-cooled; (Ta 152H-1) one 1880 hp (2250 hp) Jumo 213E-1.

Dimensions: span 34 ft 5½ in (10·49 m); (Ta 152H-1) 47 ft 6¾ in (14·5 m); length (A-8, F-8) 29 ft (8·84 m); (D-9) 33 ft 5¼ in (10·2 m); (Ta 152H-1) 35 ft 5½ in (10·8 m); height 13 ft (3·96 m); (D-9) 11 ft 0¼ in (3·35 m); (Ta 152H-1) 11 ft 8 in (3·55 m).
Weights: empty (A-8, F-8) 7055 lb (3200 kg); (D-9) 7720 lb (3500 kg); (Ta 152H-1) 7940 lb (3600 kg); loaded (A-8, F-8) 10,800 lb (4900 kg); (D-9) 10,670 lb (4840 kg); (Ta 152H-1) 12,125 lb (5500 kg).
Performance: maximum speed (with boost) (A-8, F-8) 408 mph (653 km/h); (D-9) 440 mph (704 km/h); (Ta 152H-1) 472 mph (755 km/h); initial climb (A-8, F-8) 2350 ft (720 m)/min; (D-9, Ta 152) about 3300 ft (1000 m)/min; service ceiling (A-8, F-8) 37,400 ft (11,410 m); (D-9) 32,810 ft (10,000 m); (Ta 152H-1) 49,215 ft (15,000 m); range on internal fuel (A-8, F-8 and D-9) about 560 miles (900 km); (Ta 152H-1) 745 miles (1200 km).
Armament: (A-8, F-8) two 13 mm MG 131 above engine, two 20 mm MG 151/20 in wing roots and two MG 151/20 or 30 mm MK 108 in outer wings; (D-9) as above, or without outer MG 151/20s, with provision for 30 mm MK 108 firing through propeller hub; (Ta 152H-1) one 30 mm MK 108 and two inboard MG 151/20 (sometimes outboard MG 151/20s as well); bomb load (A-8, D-9) one 1100 lb (500 kg) on centreline; (F-8) one 3968 lb (1800 kg) on centreline; (Ta 152H-1) none normally carried.
History: first flight (Fw 190V1) June 1, 1939, (production Fw 190A-1) September 1940, (Fw 190D) late 1942.

Though flown well before World War II this trim little fighter was unknown to the Allies and caused a nasty surprise when first met over France in early 1941. Indeed, it was so far superior to the bigger and more sluggish Spitfire V that for the first time the RAF felt not only outnumbered but beaten technically. In June 1942 an Fw 190A-3 landed by mistake in England, and the Focke-Wulf was discovered to be even better than expected. It was faster than any Allied fighter in service, had far heavier armament (at that time the standard was two 7·92 mm MG 17s over the engine, two of the previously unknown Mauser cannon inboard and two 20 mm MG FF outboard), was immensely strong, had excellent power of manoeuvre and good pilot view. It was also an extremely small target, much lighter than any Allied fighter and had a stable wide-track landing gear (unlike the Bf 109). Altogether it gave Allied pilots and designers an inferiority complex. Though it never supplanted the 109, it was subsequently made in a profusion of different versions by many factories.

continued on page 82

Focke-Wulf Fw 190A-8 cutaway drawing key:

1 Pitot head
2 Starboard navigation light
3 Detachable wingtip
4 Pitot tube heater cable
5 Wing lower shell 'floating rib'
6 Aileron hinge
7 Wing lower shell stringers
8 Leading-edge ribs
9 Front spar
10 Outboard 'solid rib'
11 Wing upper shell stringers
12 Aileron trim tab
13 Aileron structure
14 Aileron control linkage
15 Ammunition box (125 rounds)
16 Starboard 20mm Mauser MG 151/20E cannon (sideways mounted)
17 Ammunition box rear suspension arm
18 Flap structure
19 Wing flap upper skinning
20 Flap setting indicator peep-hole
21 Rear spar
22 Inboard wing construction
23 Undercarriage indicator
24 Wing rib strengthening
25 Ammunition feed chute
26 Static and dynamic air pressure lines
27 Cannon barrel
28 Launch tube bracing struts
29 Launch tube carrier strut
30 Mortar launch tube (auxiliary underwing armament)
31 Launch tube internal guide rails
32 21cm (WfrGr.21) spin-stabilized Type 42 mortar shell
33 VDM three-blade constant-speed propeller propeller
34 Propeller boss
35 Propeller hub
36 Starboard undercarriage fairing
37 Starboard mainwheel
38 Oil warming chamber
39 Thermostat
40 Cooler armoured ring (6·5mm)
41 Oil tank drain valve
42 Annular oil tank (12·1 gal/55 litres)
43 Oil cooler
44 Twelve-blade engine cooling fan; 3·17 times propeller speed
45 Hydraulic-electric pitch control unit

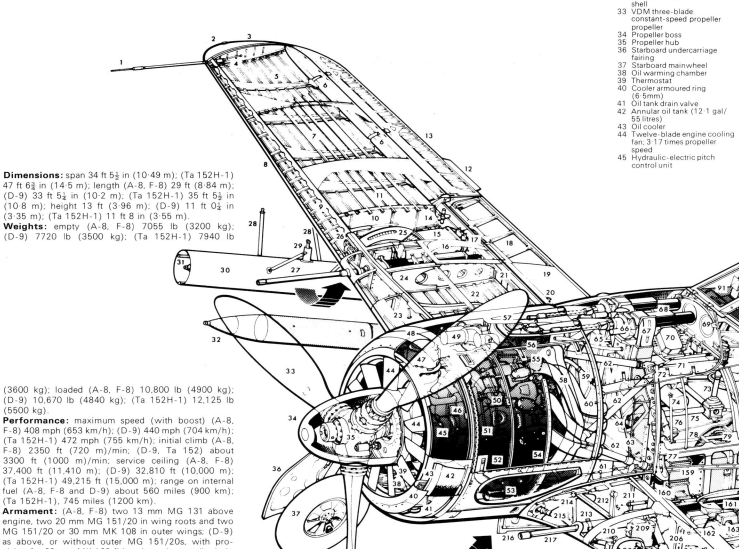

The Fw 190A-8, the subject of the cutaway, was introduced in late 1943. All had 25 gal more internal fuel, and there were many sub-types with differing armament and equipment

46 Primer fuel line
47 Bosch magneto
48 Oil tank armour (5·5mm)
49 Supercharger air pressure pipes
50 BMW 801D-2 fourteen-cylinder radial engine
51 Cowling support ring
52 Cowling quick-release fasteners
53 Oil pump
54 Fuel pump (engine rear face)
55 Oil filter (starboard)
56 Wing root cannon synchronization gear
57 Gun troughs/cowling upper panel attachment
58 Engine mounting ring
59 Cockpit heating pipe
60 Exhaust pipes (cylinders 11–14)
61 MG 131 link and case chute
62 Engine bearer assembly
63 MG 131 ammunition boxes (400 rpg)
64 Fuel filter recess housing
65 MG 131 ammunition cooling pipes
66 MG 131 synchronization gear
67 Ammunition feed chute
68 Twin fuselage 13mm Rheinmetall MG 131 guns
69 Windscreen mounting frame
70 Emergency power fuse and distributor box

71 Rear-hinged gun access panel
72 Engine bearer/bulkhead attachment
73 Control column
74 Transformer
75 Aileron control torsion bar
76 Rubber pedals (EC pedal unit with hydraulic wheel-brake operation)
77 Fuselage/wing spar attachment
78 Adjustable rudder push rod
79 Fuel filler head
80 Cockpit floor support frame
81 Throttle lever

82 Pilot's seat back plate armour (8mm)
83 Seat guide rails
84 Side-section back armour (5mm)
85 Shoulder armour (5mm)
86 Oxygen supply valve
87 Steel frame turnover pylon
88 Windscreen spray pipes
89 Instrument panel shroud
90 30mm armoured glass quarterlights
91 50mm armoured glass windscreen
92 Revi 16B reflector gunsight
93 Canopy

94 Aerial attachment
95 Headrest
96 Head armour (12mm)
97 Head armour support strut
98 Explosive-charge canopy emergency jettison unit
99 Canopy channel slide

Fw 190F-8 (I/JG 54 "Grünherz" on Eastern Front central sector)

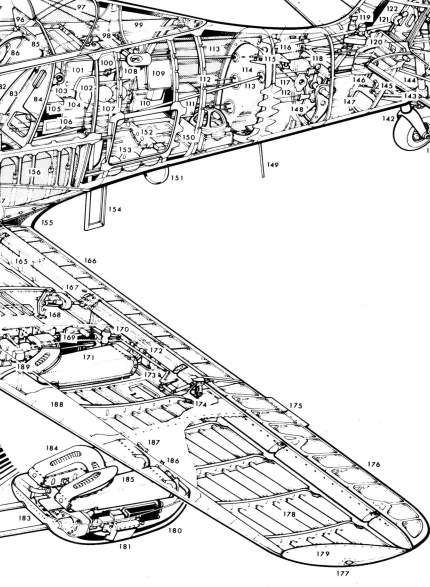

100 Auxiliary tank: fuel (25·3 gal/115 litres) or GM-1 (18·7 gal/85 litres)
101 FuG 16ZY radio trans-mitter-receiver
102 Handhold cover
103 Primer fuel filler cap
104 Autopilot steering unit (PKS 12)
105 FuG 16ZY power transformer
106 Entry step cover plate
107 Two tri-spherical oxygen bottles (starboard fuselage wall)
108 Auxiliary fuel tank filler point
109 FuG 25a transponder unit
110 Autopilot position integration unit
111 FuG 16ZY homer bearing converter
112 Elevator control cables
113 Rudder control DUZ-flexible rods
114 Fabric panel (Bulkhead 12)
115 Rudder differential unit
116 Aerial lead-in
117 Rear fuselage lift tube
118 Triangular stress frame
119 Tailplane trim unit
120 Tailplane attachment fitting
121 Tailwheel retraction guide tube
122 Retraction cable lower pulley
123 Starboard tailplane
124 Aerial
125 Starboard elevator
126 Elevator trim tab
127 Tailwheel shock strut guide
128 Fin construction
129 Retraction cable upper pulley
130 Aerial attachment stub
131 Rudder upper hinge
132 Rudder structure
133 Rudder trim tab
134 Tailwheel retraction mechanism access panel

135 Rudder attachment/actuation fittings
136 Rear navigation light
137 Extension spring
138 Elevator trim tab
139 Port elevator structure
140 Tailplane construction
141 Semi-retracting tailwheel
142 Forked wheel housing
143 Drag yoke
144 Tailwheel shock strut
145 Tailwheel locking linkage
146 Elevator actuation lever linkage
147 Angled frame spar
148 Elevator differential bellcrank
149 FuG 25a ventral aerial
150 Master compass sensing unit
151 FuG 16ZY fixed loop homing aerial
152 Radio compartment access hatch
153 Single tri-spherical oxygen bottle (port fuselage wall)
154 Retractable entry step
155 Wing-root fairing
156 Fuselage rear fuel tank (64·5 gal/293 litres)
157 Fuselage/rear spar attachment
158 Fuselage forward fuel tank (51 gal/232 litres)
159 Port wing root cannon ammunition box (250 rounds)
160 Ammunition feed chute
161 Wing root MG 151/20E cannon
162 Link and case chute
163 Cannon rear mount support bracket
164 Upper and lower wing shell stringers
165 Rear spar
166 Spar construction
167 Flap position indicator scale and peep-hole
168 Flap actuating electric motor
169 MG 151/20E cannon (sideways mounted)
170 Aileron transverse linkage
171 Ammunition box (125 rounds)
172 Ammunition box rear suspension arm
173 Aileron control linkage
174 Aileron control unit
175 Aileron trim tab
176 Port aileron structure
177 Port navigation light
178 Outboard wing stringers
179 Detachable wingtip
180 A-8/R1 variant underwing gun pack (in place of out-board wing cannon)
181 Link and case chute
182 Twin unsynchronized MG 151/20E cannon
183 Light metal fairing (gondola)
184 Ammunition feed chutes
185 Ammunition boxes (125 rpg)
186 Carrier frame restraining cord
187 Ammunition box rear suspension arms
188 Leading-edge skinning
189 Ammunition feed chute
190 Ammunition warming pipe
191 Aileron bellcrank
192 Mainwheel strut mounting assembly
193 EC-oleo shock strut
194 Mainwheel leg fairing
195 Scissors unit
196 Mainwheel fairing
197 Axle housing
198 Port mainwheel
199 Brake lines
200 Cannon barrel
201 FuG 16ZY Morane aerial
202 Radius rods
203 Rotating drive unit
204 Mainwheel retraction electric motor housing
205 Undercarriage indicator
206 Sealed air-jack
207 BSK 16 gun-camera
208 Retraction locking hooks
209 Undercarriage locking unit
210 Armament collimation tube
211 Camera wiring conduits
212 Wheel well
213 Cannon barrel blast tube
214 Wheel cover actuation strut
215 Ammunition hot air
216 Port inboard wheel cover
217 Wing root cannon barrel
218 ETC 501 carrier unit
219 ETC 501 bomb rack
220 SC 500 bomb (500 kg, 1,102 lb)

Focke-Wulf Fw 190 (continued)

The A series included many fighter and fighter bomber versions, some having not only the increasingly heavy internal armament but also two or four 20 mm cannon or two 30 mm in underwing fairings. Most had an emergency power boost system, using MW 50 (methanol/water) or GM-1 (nitrous oxide) injection, or both. Some were two-seaters, and a few had auto-pilots for bad weather and night interceptions. The F series were close-support attack aircraft, some having the Panzerblitz array of R4M rockets for tank-busting (also lethal against heavy bombers). The G was another important series of multi-role fighter/dive bombers, but by 1943 the main effort was devoted to what the RAF called the "long-nosed 190", the 190D. This was once more the fastest fighter in the sky and late in 1943 it was redesignated Ta 152 in honour of the director of Focke-Wulf's design team, Prof Kurt Tank. The early 152C series were outstandingly formidable, but the long-span H sacrificed guns for speed and height. Tank himself easily outpaced a flight of P-51D Mustangs which surprised him on a test flight; but only ten of the H sub-type had flown when the war ended. Altogether 20,051 Fw 190s were delivered, plus a small number of Ta 152s (67, excluding development aircraft). It is curious that the Bf 109, a much older and less attractive design with many shortcomings, should have been made in greater quantity and flown by nearly all the Luftwaffe's aces.

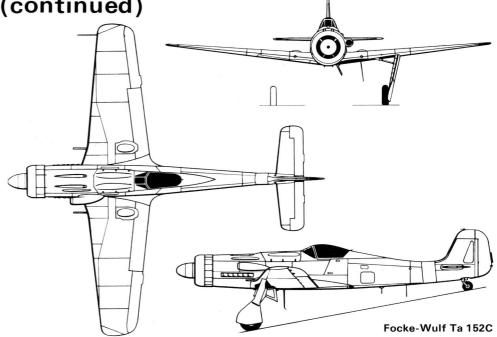

Focke-Wulf Ta 152C

Fokker E

E.I, E.II, E.III and E.IV
Type: single-seat fighting scout.
Engine: E.I, one 80 hp Oberursel U.O. seven-cylinder rotary; E.II and E.III, 100 hp Oberursel U.I; E.IV, 160 hp Oberursel 14-cylinder two-row rotary.
Dimensions: span (E.I) 28 ft (8·53 m), (E.II) 26 ft 2¾ in (8·00 m); (E.III) 31 ft 2¾ in (9·52 m); length (E.I) 22 ft 2 in (6·75 m); (E.II) 23 ft 2 in (7·1 m); (E.III) 23 ft 11½ in (7·3 m); height (E.I) 9 ft 6 in (3·12 m); (E.II) 7 ft 10 in (2·6 m); (E.III) 9 ft 1¾ in (2·79 m).
Weights: empty (all), about 1,100 lb (500 kg); loaded (E.I) 1,239 lb (562 kg); (E.II) 1,340 lb (609 kg); (E.III) 1,400 lb (635 kg).
Performance: maximum speed (E.I) 82 mph (132 km/h); (E.II) 87 mph (140 km/h); (E.III) 83 mph (134 km/h); service ceiling (E.I) 10,170 ft (3100 m); (E.II) 12,000 ft (3650 m); (E.III) 11,500 ft (3500 m); endurance (E.III) 2 hr 45 min.
Armament: one 7·92 mm Spandau machine gun (some E.III, two guns), fixed with synchronization gear for firing past the propeller blades.
History: first flight (M.5) 1913; (E.I) late May 1915; (E.II) July 1915; (E.III) September 1915.

Young Dutchman Anthony Fokker built and flew his first aircraft in 1912. It was a tandem-seat monoplane with considerable dihedral but no lateral control. Offered to Britain, it was judged "badly made", though there is no evidence that the rejection had any other basis than British official dislike of monoplanes. Fokker thereupon threw in his lot with the Central Powers and saw his M.5 monoplane produced in quantity in various versions. In April 1915 the French ace Garros was shot down and the crude bullet deflector he had used was inspected by the Germans. Fokker's design staff were convinced they could do better by devising an interrupter (synchronization) gear, and this was perfected in a matter of two weeks. Fitted to a short-span M.5K scout the result was the E.I, E signifying Eindecker (monoplane). Though a quick "bodge", it was far superior to any Allied fighter and E.I successes began to pile up from June 1915. Within a further month the refined E.II had appeared and after 65 of these had been delivered production switched to the definitive E.III. This restored the good handling qualities lost in cutting down the wing of the E.II and soon became a dreaded foe in the hands of

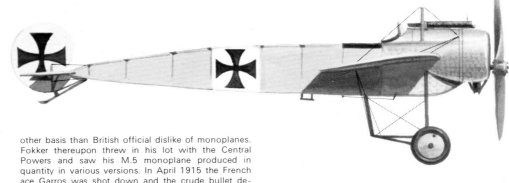

**Fokker E.III "Eindecker"
(as shot down in April 1916)**

such pilots as Boelcke and Immelmann. Though only about 300 E.IIIs were built they shot down at least 1,000 Allied aircraft. Those in Austro-Hungarian service had a Schwarzlose machine gun, and a very few had two Spandaus. The E.IV, with more power, was designed with two guns (and was flown for a time by Immelmann with three) but few were built. By 1916 the "Fokker Scourge" began to fade, as better Allied combat aircraft reached the Western Front.

Fokker Dr.I Triplane

Dr.I
Type: single-seat fighting scout.
Engine: usually one 110 hp Le Rhône (licence-built by Thulin) nine-cylinder rotary; alternatively, 110 hp Oberursel UR.II, 110 hp Goebel Goe.II, 145 hp Oberursel UR.III, 160 hp Goe.III, 160 hp Siemens u Halske Sh.III or 200 hp Goe.IIIa.
Dimensions: span 23 ft 7½ in (7·17 m); length 18 ft 11 in (5·77 m); height 9 ft 8 in (2·95 m).
Weights: empty 904 lb (410 kg); loaded 1,289 lb (585 kg).
Performance: maximum speed 103 mph (165 km/h); initial climb 720 ft (220 m)/min; service ceiling 20,013 ft (6100 m); endurance 1 hr 30 min (about 130 miles).
Armament: two 7·92 mm Spandau machine guns above forward fuselage.
History: first flight June 1917; service delivery August 1917; termination of production, late May 1918.

Though the triplane (three superimposed wings) was no magical formula, the impressive combat performance of the Sopwith Triplane so startled the German authorities that they immediately issued a request for triplane fighters and no fewer than 14 designs were quickly built. Far ahead in timing came the Dr.I, Dr signifying Dreidecker (triplane), of the Fokker Flugzeugwerke, because Fokker had seen the Sopwith in action in April 1917 and did not need to wait for the captured specimen in July. His brilliant chief designer, Rheinhold Platz, did not believe in the triplane layout, but nevertheless quickly produced the V.3 prototype. This had stubby, deep unbraced wings, the only struts being those carrying the top wing. Flight trails revealed undesirable buffet and interference, so Platz redesigned the wings with slightly shallower section, different wing locations and single interplane struts. The tail was improved, balanced ailerons were fitted and production began at once against an order for 350. The third aircraft was used by Wernher Voss, who began to score with it on 30 August 1917. The JG.I "circus" of Manfred von Richthofen was the first complete unit to be "Tripehound" equipped and Richthofen himself was flying his scarlet Dr.I when he was killed on 21 April 1918. The Dr.I was a formidable adversary, but gained a temporary bad name in November 1917 when, after a series of crashes, the type was grounded.

**Fokker Dr.I (aircraft of
Manfred von Richthofen)**

The cause was not inherent weakness but faulty workmanship by the supplier of the wings. Full service was restored in late November, but in May 1918 surviving Dr.Is were transferred away from the Western Front to home-defence squadrons.

Fokker D.VII

D.I to D.VIII

Type: single-seat fighting scout.

Engine: (D.VII) one 160 hp Mercedes D.III six-cylinder water-cooled; (D.VIIF) 185 hp BMW IIIa; earlier designs, see text.

Dimensions: (D.VII) span 29 ft 2 in (8·9 m); (earlier models, 29 ft to 31 ft 10 in); length (D.VII) 22 ft 9¾ in (6·95 m); (earlier models, 18 ft 8 in to 20 ft 11 in); height (D.VII) 9 ft 0¼ in (2·75 m); (earlier models, 7 ft 4 in to 8 ft 2 in).

Weights: empty (D.VII) 1,477 lb (670 kg); (earlier models, lighter) loaded (D.VII) 1,984 lb (900 kg); (earlier models, 1,245–1,850 lb).

Performance: maximum speed (D.VII) 117½ mph (189 km/h); (D.I) 94 mph; (D.II) 94 mph; (D.III) 100 mph; (D.IV) 100 mph; (D.V) 106 mph; (D.VI) 122 mph; service ceiling (D.VII) 19,685 ft (6000 m); (D.I) 13,120 ft; (D.II) 13,120 ft; (D.III) 15,500 ft; (D.IV) 16,400 ft; (D.V) 13,120 ft; (D.VI) 19,685 ft); endurance (all) about 1 hr 30 min.

Armament: twin 7·92 mm Spandau machine guns on all models, except D.I, II and V had one gun only; several local modifications to type or arrangement of gun(s).

History: first flight (D.I) August 1915; (D.II) believed January 1916; (D.III) late 1916; (D.IV) late 1916; (D.V) October 1916; (D.VI) late 1917; (D.VII) January 1918.

Designed by Platz's team in a great hurry at the end of

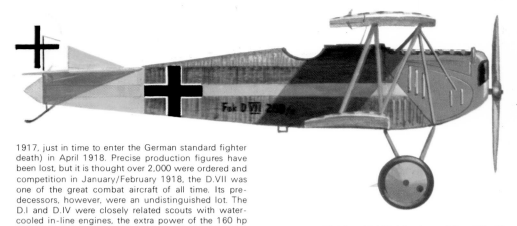

1917, just in time to enter the German standard fighter death) in April 1918. Precise production figures have been lost, but it is thought over 2,000 were ordered and competition in January/February 1918, the D.VII was one of the great combat aircraft of all time. Its predecessors, however, were an undistinguished lot. The D.I and D.IV were closely related scouts with water-cooled in-line engines, the extra power of the 160 hp D.IV being outweighed by its second gun. Likewise the 100 hp Oberursel rotary of the D.II was matched with one gun, while the 160 hp two-row Oberursel of the D.III had to fly two guns and gave only modest extra speed. The D.V was a lighter, cleaned-up design with circular cowl and spinner, while the much later D.VI was a mixture of parts borrowed from the Triplane Dr.I and scaled down from the D.VII. All were rendered obsolete by the D.VII, which walked away with the competition. After being given a longer fuselage and fixed fin it was put into widespread production, the first examples being sent to von Richthofen's JG I

Fokker D.VII (Jasta unidentified)

(commanded by Hermann Goering after Richthofen's about 1,000 completed by the Armistice. So formidable was the D.VII that it was specifically named by type in the list of items to be handed over to the victorious Allies. The D.VII's successor, the D.VIII, or E.V, did not get into full service but it was in many ways even better. Fokker and his staff managed to hide components of some 120 D.VIIs and perhaps 50 D.VIIIs and smuggle them over the border into Holland to serve as the nucleus of his post-war business.

Fokker C.V

C.V-A, -B, -C, -D and -E

Type: two-seat light bomber and reconnaissance.

Engine: various, from 350 to 730 hp; included 350, 400 and 450 hp Hispano-Suiza, 400 hp Lorraine and 525 hp Rolls-Royce Kestrel vee-12 water-cooled and 450 hp Armstrong Siddeley Jaguar, 490 hp Bristol Jupiter (built by overseas licensees) and 730 hp Bristol Pegasus air-cooled radials.

Dimensions: span (C.V-C) 47 ft 10 in; (C.V-D) 41 ft (12·5 m); (C.V-E) 50 ft 2½ in; length, depending on engine, 30 ft 4 in to 31 ft 4 in (9·58 m); height (C.V-C) 12 ft 3 in; (C.V-D) 10 ft 9¾ in (3·3 m); (C.V-E) 11 ft 1 in.

Weights: empty, all close to 3,000 lb (1814 kg); loaded (C.V-C) 5,368 lb (2450 kg); (C.V-D) 4,222 lb (1920 kg); (C.V-E) 4,894 lb (2220 kg).

Performance: maximum speed (C.V-C, typical) 146 mph (235 km/h); (C.V-D, typical) 158 mph (255 km/h); (C.V-E, Hispano) 143 mph; (C.V-E, Pegasus) 177 mph (285 km/h); service ceiling, all close to 22,970 ft (7000 m); range, no data available.

Armament: invariably one fixed machine gun (two in fighter versions) in forward fuselage and one manually aimed from rear cockpit, but more than 30 variations on gun type and arrangement; light series bomb carriers for underwing load of up to 500 lb (227 kg).

Fokker C.V-D (Norwegian Army Flying Service, Fornebu)

History: first flight 1922; (C.V-C) 1923; (C.V-D) 1924; (C.V-E) probably 1927; final deliveries from new, 1936.

There is some justification for claiming that the Fokker C.V series of military biplanes were the most successful of the period between the two World Wars. During the period 1919–22 Fokker's new factory at Amsterdam was a hive of activity, with not only excellent new military aircraft being produced but also the first models in what became the dominant families of civil airliners throughout the world in the period 1920–37. The C.V was a straightforward military biplane, larger than the single-seat fighters previously constructed and robustly

built in typical Platz tradition with welded steel tube body and wooden wings. With the C.V-C large overseas orders began to come in, some of them for float-seaplane versions. The -D model introduced a neater tapering wing plan and more streamlined fuselage. Most of these were fighter or army co-operation versions, whereas the -E had a longer span and was primarily a bomber. More than 400 of all versions were built by Fokker over a period of 13 years, while further examples were built under licence in Denmark, Norway, Finland, Italy and Switzerland. Total production probably exceeded 1,000, and several standard types in other countries were based on this classic aircraft.

Fokker C.X

C.X

Type: two-seat bomber and reconnaissance.

Engine: (Dutch) one 650 hp Rolls-Royce Kestrel V vee-12 liquid-cooled; (Finnish) one licence-built 835 hp Bristol Pegasus XXI nine-cylinder radial.

Dimensions: span, 39 ft 4 in (12 m); length (Kestrel) 30 ft 2 in (9·2 m); (Pegasus) 29 ft 9 in (9·1 m); height, 10 ft 10 in (3·3 m).

Weights: empty (both), about 3,086 lb (1400 kg); loaded (Kestrel) 4,960 lb (2250 kg); (Pegasus) 5,512 lb (2500 kg).

Performance: maximum speed (Kestrel) 199 mph (320 km/h); (Pegasus) 211 mph (340 km/h); service ceiling (Kestrel) 27,230 ft (8300 m); (Pegasus) 27,560 ft (8400 m); range (Kestrel) 516 miles (830 km); (Pegasus) 522 miles (840 km).

Armament: two 7·9 mm machine guns fixed in top of front fuselage and third manually aimed from rear cockpit; underwing racks for two 385 lb (175 kg) or four 221 lb (100 kg) bombs.

History: first flight 1934; service delivery (Dutch) 1937; (Finnish) 1938.

Derived from the C.V-E and planned as a successor, the C.X was a notably clean machine typical of good military design of the mid-1930s. By this time world-wide competition was very severe and Fokker could not achieve such widespread export success. The first orders were for ten for the Royal Netherlands East Indies Army, followed by 20 for the RNethAF (then Luchtvaartafdeling, LVA), the last 15 having enclosed cockpits and tailwheels. Further small numbers were made in Holland, at least one having a 925 hp

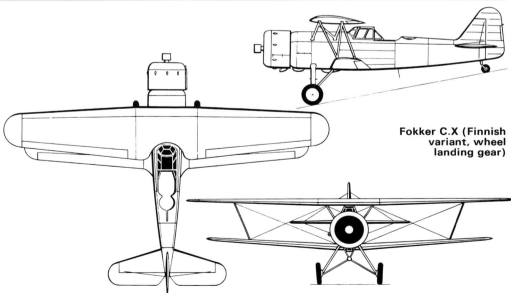

Fokker C.X (Finnish variant, wheel landing gear)

Hispano-Suiza 12Y engine with 20 mm cannon firing through the propeller hub. Fokker also developed a considerably more capable C.X for Finland, with the Pegasus radial. The Finnish Valtion Lentokonetehdas (State Aircraft Factory) at Tampere went into licence-production with this version in 1938, the engine being made at Tammerfors. The Finnish C.X had an enclosed heated cockpit, rapid cold-weather starting and either

wheel or ski landing gear. All available Dutch and Finnish C.X aircraft participated in World War II. None of the LVA machines survived the "Five Day War" of 10–15 May 1940, but the Finnish aircraft continued until at least 1944 under severe conditions and finally went into action not against the Russians but in helping them drive the Germans from Finnish territory in 1944–45.

Fokker D.XXI

D.XXI (D.21)
Type: single-seat fighter.
Engine: (Dutch) one 830 hp Bristol Mercury VIII nine-cylinder radial; (Danish) 645 hp Mercury VIS; (Finnish) 825 hp Pratt & Whitney R-1535-SB4-G Twin Wasp Junior 14-cylinder two-row radial.
Dimensions: span 36 ft 1 in (11 m); length (Mercury) 26 ft 11 in (8·22 m); (R-1535) 26 ft 3 in (8 m); height 9 ft 8 in (2·94 m).
Weights: empty (Mercury) 3,180 lb (1442 kg); (R-1535) 3,380 lb (1534 kg); loaded (Mercury) 4,519 lb (2050 kg); (R-1535) 4,820 lb (2186 kg).
Performance: maximum speed (Mercury VIII) 286 mph (460 km/h); (R-1535) 272 mph (439 km/h); climb to 9,842 ft (3000 m) 3·5 min (Mercury); 4·5 min (R-1535); service ceiling (Mercury) 36,090 ft (11,000 m); (R-1535) 32,000 ft (9750 m); range (Mercury) 590 miles (950 km); (R-1535) 559 miles (900 km).
Armament: (Dutch) four 7·9 mm FN-Brownings, two in fuselage and two in wings; (Danish) two Madsen 7·9 mm in wings and two Madsen 20 mm cannon in underwing blisters; (Finnish) four 7·7 mm machine guns in outer wings.
History: first flight, 27 March 1936; service delivery (Dutch) January 1938, (Finnish production) June 1938, (Danish production) 1939.

In the second half of the 1930s any sound warplane that was generally available could be sure of attracting widespread interest. The Fokker D.XXI came from a company with a great reputation all over the world, and though it was designed – by Ir. E. Schatzki, in 1935 – purely to meet the requirements of the Netherlands East Indies Army Air Service, it became the leading fighter of three major European nations and was planned as a standard type by a fourth. This was as well for Fokker, because the plans of the original customer were changed and a contract was never signed. Yet the little fighter was all one would expect: neat, tough and highly manoeuvrable, with good performance and heavy armament. It marked the transition between the fabric-covered biplane and the stressed-skin monoplane. The wing was wood, with bakelite/ply skin. The fuselage was welded steel tube, with detachable metal panels back to the cockpit and fabric on the rear fuselage and tail. Landing gear was fixed. The prototype flew at Welschap on a Mercury VIS engine, and in May 1937 the home government ordered 36 with a more powerful Mercury, supplied from Bristol. There were many Fokker projects for developed D.XXIs with retractable landing gear and other engines, but the production aircraft was generally similar to the prototype. In the seventh (No 217) test pilot H. Leegstra set a Dutch height record at 37,250 ft. Meanwhile production of a modified version w(s getting under way for Finland, which bought seven with a manufacturing licence. Denmark followed with an order for three and a manufacturing licence, and the fourth to adopt the D.XXI was Republican Spain. The latter set up a new plant and was about to start accepting deliveries when the area

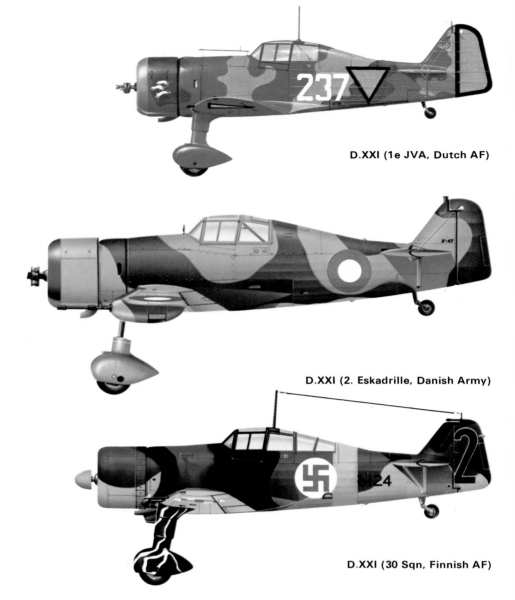

D.XXI (1e JVA, Dutch AF)

D.XXI (2. Eskadrille, Danish Army)

D.XXI (30 Sqn, Finnish AF)

was overrun by Nationalist forces. The VL (Finnish state factory) delivered 38 in 1938–39 and all of them participated very successfully in air battles against the Soviet forces from the start of the Soviet invasion on 30 November 1939. The D.XXI was put into accelerated production, but as all the Finnish-built Mercuries were needed for Blenheims the Finnish D.XXI was redesigned to take the heavier but less powerful Twin Wasp

Junior, 55 of this type being built (one having retractable landing gear). The Danish Royal Army Aircraft Factory gradually delivered ten with low-rated Mercury and two cannon, eight fighting furiously during the German invasion in March 1940. Finally, on 10 May 1940 the 29 combat-ready aircraft in Holland fought round the clock until their ammunition ran out on the third day.

Fokker G.I

Fokker G.Ib (4e JVA, Dutch AF)

G.Ia and G.Ib
Type: three-seat (G.Ib, two-seat) heavy fighter and close-support.
Engines: (G.Ia) two 830 hp Bristol Mercury VIII nine-cylinder radials; (G.Ib) two 750 hp Pratt & Whitney R-1535-SB4-G Twin Wasp Junior 14-cylinder radials.
Dimensions: span (G.Ia) 56 ft 3¼ in (17·2 m); (G.Ib) 54 ft 1½ in (16·5 m); length, (G.Ia) 37 ft 8¾ in (11·5 m); (G.Ib) 33 ft 9½ in (10·3 m); height 11 ft 1¾ in (3·4 m).
Weights: empty (G.Ia) 7,326 lb (3323 kg); (G.Ib) 6,930 lb (3143 kg); loaded, (G.Ia) 10,560 lb (4790 kg); (G.Ib) 10,520 lb (4772 kg).
Performance: maximum speed (G.Ia) 295 mph (475 km/h); (G.Ib) 268 mph (430 km/h); time to climb to 19,680 ft (6000 m), (G.Ia) 8·9 min; (G.Ib) 12·1 min; service ceiling, (G.Ia) 30,500 ft (9300 m);

(G.Ib) 28,535 ft (8695 m); range, (G.Ia) 945 miles (1520 km); (G.Ib) 913 miles (1469 km).
Armament: (G.Ia) row of eight 7·9 mm FN-Browning machine guns fixed in nose, one similar gun manually aimed in tailcone; internal bomb bay for load of 880 lb (400 kg). (G.Ib) two 23 mm Madsen cannon and two 7·9 mm FN-Brownings in nose, otherwise same.
History: first flight, 16 March 1937; service delivery, May 1938.

Appearance of the prototype G.I at the 1936 Paris Salon caused a sensation. The concept of a large twin-engined fighter was novel, and the devastating armament of the G.I caused it to be called "Le Faucheur" (the Grim Reaper). Nations practically queued to test-fly the Hispano-engined prototype and the first sale was 12 to Republican Spain in June 1937. Meanwhile

the home LVA eventually signed for 36 of a much altered version with a third crew-member (radio operator) and Mercury engines in a larger airframe. Finland sought a licence, Sweden bought 18 and Denmark bought nine plus a licence. The Dutch placed an embargo on export of the Spanish aircraft, called G.Ib, and when Germany swept into Holland on 10 May 1940 these were still lined up at Schiphol. Guns were hastily taken from crashed or damaged aircraft and fitted to the Spanish machines which were thrown into the fight. The 23 combat-ready G.Ia fighters likewise fought until all were destroyed save one (in which, in 1941, two senior Fokker pilots escaped to England). There were several non-standard G.Is, including one with a ventral observation cupola. All surviving or unfinished aircraft were impressed into the Luftwaffe and used as combat trainers and tugs.

Fokker T series

T.IV, T.5 and T.8W

Type: (T.IV) torpedo-bomber reconnaissance seaplane; (T.5) medium bomber; (T.8W) torpedo-bomber reconnaissance seaplane.

Engines: (T.IV) two 450 hp Lorraine-Dietrich W vee-12 water-cooled; (T.IVa) two 875 hp Wright GR-1820-G52 Cyclone nine-cylinder radials; (T.5) two 925 hp Bristol Pegasus XXVI nine-cylinder radials; (T.8W, T.8W/G and T.8W/M) two 450 hp Wright R-975-E3 nine-cylinder radials; (T.8W/C) two 890 hp Bristol Mercury XI nine-cylinder radials.

Dimensions: span (T.IV) 84 ft 7½ in; (T.IVa) 85 ft 11½ in (26·2 m), (T.5) 68 ft 10 in (21 m); (T.8W/G and /M) 59 ft 1 in (18 m); (T.8W/C) 65 ft 7½ in (20 m); length, (T.IV, IVa) 58 ft (17·68 m); (T.5) 52 ft 6 in (16 m); (T.8W/G and /M) 42 ft 7¾ in (13 m); (T.8W/C) 49 ft 3 in (15 m); height, (T.IV, IVa) 19 ft 8¾ in (6 m); (T.5) 16 ft 5 in (5 m); (T.8W/G and /M) 16 ft 4½ in (4·95 m); (T.8W/C) 17 ft 8½ in (5·4 m).

Weights: empty (T.IVa) 10,250 lb (4650 kg); (T.5) 9,921 lb (4500 kg); (T.8W/G) 7,055 lb (3200 kg); (T.8W/C) 9,700 lb (4400 kg); loaded (T.IVa) 15,873 lb (7200 kg); (T.5) 15,983 lb (7250 kg); (T.8W/G) 11,030 lb (5003 kg); (T.8W/C) 15,432 lb (7000 kg).

Performance: maximum speed (T.IVa) 161 mph (260 km/h); (T.5) 261 mph (420 km/h); (T.8W/G) 177 mph (285 km/h); (T.8W/C) 224 mph (360 km/h); service ceiling (T.IVa) 19,685 ft (6000 m); (T.5) 26,575 ft (8100 m); (T.8W/G) 22,310 ft (6800 m); (T.8W/C) 19,030 ft (5800 m); range (T.IVa) 970 miles (1560 km); (T.5) 1,025 miles (1650 km); (T.8W/G) 1,305 miles (2100 km); (T.8W/C) 1,056 miles (1700 km).

Armament: (T.IVa) three manually aimed 7·9 mm FN-Brownings in nose, dorsal and ventral positions; one torpedo externally or bomb load of up to 1,984 lb (900 kg) internally. (T.5) five manually aimed 7·9 mm FN-Brownings, two in nose and one each in dorsal, ventral rand tail; internal bomb load of 2,200 lb (1000 kg). (T.8W/G and /M) three manually aimed 7·9 mm FN-Brownings in nose, dorsal and ventral positions; one torpedo externally or bomb load ot 1,323 lb (600 kg).

History: first flight (T.IV) 7 June 1927; (T.IVa) 1936; (T.5) 16 October 1937; (T.8W) 1938; (T.8W/C) late 1939.

The T.4 twin-float seaplane looked ungainly but was a tough, seaworthy combat aircraft which operated gallantly and with great effect against the Japanese in the Dutch East Indies. The T.5 was a fine modern bomber, roughly in the class of the Hampden, the dozen serviceable examples of which fought to the last in May 1940 (two were shot down by Dutch AA fire). The much more formidable Hercules-powered T.9 did not get into production. The T.8W seaplane was in service as the /G and as the /M with metal skinned rear fuselage, while the bigger /C was in production for Finland. In late May 1940 eight survivors of the frantic battle over Holland escaped to Britain, forming 320 Sqn of RAF Coastal Command until they ran out of spares in late 1940. Unfinished T.8Ws were completed for the Luftwaffe.

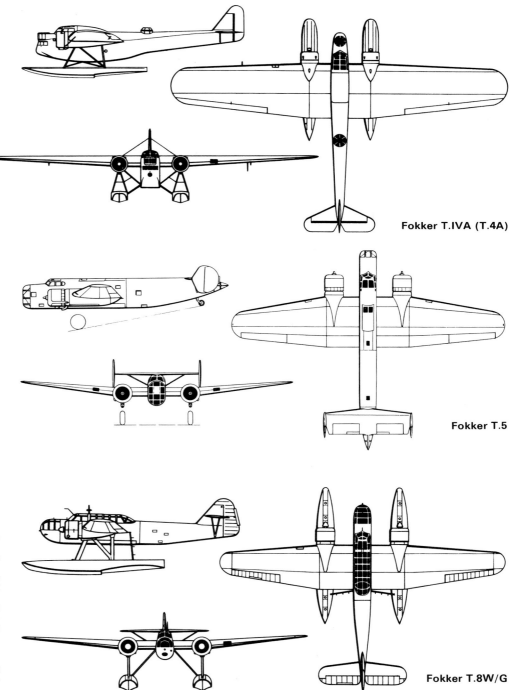

Fokker T.IVA (T.4A)

Fokker T.5

Fokker T.8W/G

Folland (Hawker Siddeley) Gnat

Fo 141 Gnat F.1, HAL Gnat and Ajit, Hawker Siddeley Gnat T.1

Type: (Gnat 1 and Ajit) single-seat fighter; (Gnat T.1) advanced trainer.

Engine: (Gnat 1) 4,520 lb (2050 kg) thrust Rolls-Royce (previously Bristol, then Bristol Siddeley) Orpheus 701 single-shaft turbojet; (Gnat II/Ajit) 4,670 lb (2118 kg) HAL-built Orpheus 701E; Gnat T.1, 4,230 lb (1920 kg) Orpheus 101.

Dimensions: span (1) 22 ft 2 in (6·75 m); (Ajit) 22 ft 1 in (6·73 m), (T.1) 24 ft (7·32 m); length (1) 29 ft 9 in (9·06 m), (Ajit) 29 ft 8 in (9·04 m), (T.1) 31 ft 9 in (9·65 m); height (1, Ajit) 8 ft 10 in (2·69 m), (T.1) 10 ft 6 in (3·2 m).

Weights: empty, (1, Ajit) typically 4,850 lb (2200 kg); (T.1) 5,613 lb (2546 kg); loaded (1, Ajit, clean) 6,650 lb (3016 kg); (1, Ajit, with external stores) 8,885 lb (4030 kg); (T.1, clean) 8,250 lb (3742 kg); (T.1, maximum) 9,350 lb (4240 kg).

Performance: maximum speed, (F.1) 714 mph (1150 km/h); (T.1) 636 mph (1026 km/h); initial climb, (F.1) 20,000 ft (6096 m)/min; (T.1) 9,850 ft (3000 m)/min; service ceiling, (F.1) over 50,000 ft (15,250 m); (T.1) 48,000 ft (14,600 m); range, all versions, maximum fuel, 1,180 miles (1900 km).

Armament: (F.1, Ajit) two 30 mm Aden cannon, each with 115 rounds; four underwing hardpoints for 1,000 lb (454 kg) total load. (T.1) no guns, but same underwing load.

History: first flight (Fo 139 Midge) 11 August 1954; (Fo 141 Gnat) 18 July 1955; (T.1) 31 August 1959; (HAL Gnat) 18 November 1959; final delivery (HAL) early 1973; Ajit, continuing.

British designer Teddy Petter planned the Gnat to reverse the trend towards larger and more complex combat aircraft, considering a simple lightweight fighter would offer equal performance at much lower cost. Folland Aircraft built the low-powered (1,640 lb Viper) Midge as a private venture and eventually gained an order for a development batch of six, the first of which flew in May 1956. India signed a licence agreement in September 1956 and by early 1973 had built 213 at Hindustan Aircraft Ltd (HAL) at Bangalore, as well as receiving 25 Mk 1 Gnats and 25 sets of parts from Folland. HAL also built the Orpheus engine. Finland bought 12, three having a three-camera nose for FR duties, and two were supplied to Yugoslavia. The Gnat was modified into a trainer for the RAF, with

Gnat 1 (FR) (11 Sqn, Finnish AF)

tandem cockpits, larger wing and many other changes and 105 were supplied by Hawker Siddeley (into which Folland was absorbed) in 1962–65. Smoke-making Gnat T.1s equip the Red Arrows aerobatic team. In 1969 HAL began to study an improved Gnat which was finally agreed in 1974. Named Gnat II or Ajit (Unconquerable), it has integral-tank wings housing the same quantity of fuel as was formerly carried in underwing tanks, thus allowing full weapon load to be carried for undiminished range; it also has improved avionics and many minor changes. HAL Gnats are progressively being brought up to this standard. In prolonged combat duty the HAL Gnats have qcquitted themselves well and proved most effective in close combat.

General Dynamics (Convair) B-36

B-36A to B-36J
Type: heavy bomber, reconnaissance and weapon platform.
Engines: B-36B, six 3,500 hp Pratt & Whitney R-4360-41 Wasp Major 28-cylinder four-row radials driving pusher propellers; B-36D, six R-4360-41 and four 5,200 lb (2360 kg) thrust General Electric J47-19 single-shaft turbojets; B-36F, H and J, six 3,800 hp R-4360-53 and four J47-19.
Dimensions: span 230 ft (70·14 m); length 162 ft (49·4 m); height 46 ft 9 in (14·26 m).
Weights: empty (B-36B) 150,000 lb (68,040 kg), (B-36D, J) 179,000 lb (81,200 kg); maximum loaded (B-36B) 278,000 lb (126,000 kg), (B-36D) 357,500 lb (162,200 kg), (B-36J) 410,000 lb (185,970 kg).
Performance: maximum speed (B-36B) 381 mph (613 km/h), (B-36D) 439 mph (707 km/h), (B-36J) 411 mph (662 km/h); service ceiling (B-36B) 42,500 ft (12,955 m), (B-36D 45,200 ft (13,780 m), (B-36J) 39,900 ft (12,162 m); typical range with bomb load (B-36B) 8,175 miles (13,160 km), (B-36D) 7,500 miles (12,070 km), (B-36J) 6,800 miles (10,945 km).
Armament: normally, sixteen 20 mm cannon in eight remotely controlled turrets, in nose and tail and in six retractable installations along the fuselage, covered by sliding doors except when extended for use; internal bomb load up to 84,000 lb (38,140 kg).
History: first flight (XB-36) 8 August 1946; (production B-36A) 28 August 1947; (YB-36) 4 December 1947; (B-36B) 8 July 1948; (B-36D) 10 March 1949; delivery of last B-36J, 14 August 1954; withdrawal from service, February 1959.

To meet the possible need to continue World War II after the collapse of Britain the B-36 was planned to operate against Nazi-held Europe from bases in the United States or Canada. The specification called for a bomb load of 10,000 lb delivered to a target 5,000 miles from its 5,000 ft runway. This was challenge enough, but the prototype programme was crippled by shortages due to its low priority and need to devote all effort to wartime production. Only at the end of World War II did the work gather momentum, and when the XB-36 flew it was the largest and most powerful aircraft to take the air anywhere in the world. The unarmed B-36A was used for training crews of the newly formed USAF Strategic Air Command (SAC), which included the controversial monster as its central item of equipment. Production aircraft had bogie main gears, pressurised front and rear crew compartments linked by an 80 ft trolley tunnel, comprehensive radar bombing and navigation system and automatically controlled defensive guns with five sighting stations. The RB-36 models had 14 cameras in place of two of the four weapon bays and a crew increased from 15 to 22. To increase over-target height and speed the B-36D was boosted by two twin-jet pods with inlet shutters which were closed in cruising flight. Main propulsion remained six Wasp Majors inside the vast

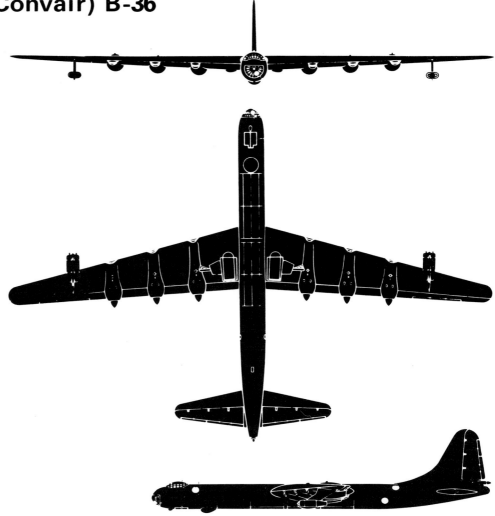

B-36D (as originally delivered)

wing, driving 19 ft pusher Curtiss Electric propellers, each engine having two exhaust turbos. Technical problems were severe and until 1951 reliability was poor. In 1944—49 it was planned to carry the tiny egg-shaped McDonnell F-85 Goblin jet fighter inside the forward bomb bay for added defence. In 1953 FICON trials were held with GRB-36Fs being used to carry and launch GRF-84F manned reconnaissance fighters.

Some of the final examples of the 385 B-36s built were stripped of most armament and used for very long range high-altitude reconnaissance carrying large quantities of ECM and other special sensing systems. The reverberating snarl of these high-flying monsters pervaded much of the globe during the Cold War of the 1950s.

General Dynamics (Convair) B-58 Hustler

General Dynamics B-58A (43rd BW, Strategic Air Command)

Model 4, B-58A and TB-58A
Type: three-seat supersonic bomber.
Engines: four 15,600 lb (7076 kg) thrust General Electric J79-5B or -5C single-shaft afterburning turbojets.
Dimensions: span 56 ft 10 in (17·31 m); length 96 ft 9 in (29·5 m); height 31 ft 5 in (9·6 m).
Weights: empty (without pod) 55,560 lb (25,200 kg); maximum (take-off) 163,000 lb (73,930 kg); maximum (after air refuelling) 177,000 lb (80,485 kg).
Performance: maximum speed 1,385 mph (2125 km/h, Mach 2); initial climb at gross weight, 17,400 ft (5310 m)/min; service ceiling 64,000 ft (19,500 m); range on internal fuel 5,125 miles (8248 km).
Armament: one 20 mm T-171 multi-barrel gun in tail with remote aiming; droppable pods of various kinds, some having their own propulsion, containing thermonuclear bomb; additionally, underwing racks for four smaller nuclear or conventional bombs to total of 7,000 lb (3175 kg). Normal payload drop weight, 19,450 lb (8820 kg).

History: first flight 11 November 1956; (production B-58A) September 1959; (TB-58) 10 May 1960; withdrawal from inventory, January 1970.
The B-58 was an historic aircraft on many counts. It was the first supersonic bomber in history and the first to reach Mach 2. It was the first aircraft constructed mainly from stainless-steel honeycomb sandwich, the first to have a slim body and fat payload pod so that, after dropping the payload (bomb plus empty fuel tank) it became a significantly smaller aircraft, the first to have stellar-inertial navigation, and the first weapon system to be procured as a single package from a prime contractor responsible for every part of the system (of which the air vehicle was only a portion). Technical difficulties were gigantic, yet the B-58 was developed with amazing speed and success. A tailless delta configuration was adopted, with very stalky landing gear with main bogies on gatefold legs all

folding into thicker boxes in the very thin wings. Pilot, navigator and defence-systems operator sat in tandem in encapsulated cockpits each capable of being ejected in emergency; the TB-58 crew trainer had stepped dual pilot cockpits, and no bomb/nav or ECM systems. In the tailcone was a 20 mm Gatling gun. Only 116 B-58s were built and in their decade in the inventory they set more world records than any other type of combat aircraft. The 43rd and 305th Bomb Wings frequently flew air-refuelled missions lasting 12 to 20 hours and set highly supersonic timings on such routes as New York to Paris and Tokyo to London. Despite its lack of high-lift devices the B-58 was pleasant to fly and straightforward to land. It was also exceptionally good in the low-level role. There were many proposals for improved B-58s, for fighter versions and for ECM, special-mission and missile-launch versions.

General Dynamics (Convair) F-102 Delta Dart

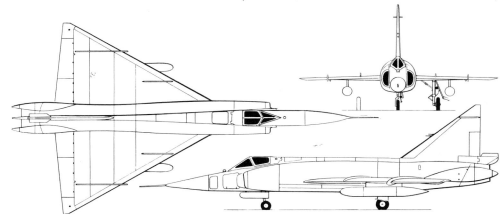

Convair F-102A (526th FIS, 86th Air Divis'on, USAFE Ramstein)

F-102A, TF-102A, QF-102A and PQM-102A

Type: (F) single-seat all-weather interceptor; (TF) trainer; (QF) manned RPV (remotely piloted vehicle); (PQM) drone target.

Engine: one 17,200 lb (7802 kg) thrust Pratt & Whitney J57-23 two-shaft afterburning turbojet.

Dimensions: span 38 ft $1\frac{1}{2}$ in (11·6 m); length, (F-102A) 68 ft 5 in (20·83 m); (TF-102A) 63 ft $4\frac{1}{2}$ in (19·3 m); height (F-102A) 21 ft $2\frac{1}{2}$ in (6·45 m); (TF-102A) 20 ft 7 in (6·27 m).

Weights: empty (F-102A) 19,050 lb (8630 kg); loaded (F-102A, clean) 27,700 lb (12,564 kg), (maximum) 31,500 lb (14,288 kg).

Performance: maximum speed (F-102A) 825 mph (1328 km/h, Mach 1·25), (TF-102A) 646 mph (1040 km/h); initial climb (F-102A) 13,000 ft (3962 m)/min; service ceiling 54,000 ft (16,460 m); range 1,350 miles (2172 km).

Armament: air-to-air guided missiles carried in internal bay, typical full load comprising three Hughes AIM-4E Falcon beam-riders with semi-active homing and three AIM-4F with infrared homing. No armament in TF, QF or PQM.

History: first flight (YF-102) 24 October 1953; (YF-102A) 20 December 1954; (TF) 8 November 1955; (QF) mid-1974; (PQM) early 1975.

In 1948 Convair flew the world's first delta-wing aircraft, the XF-92A, which was part of a programme intended to lead to a supersonic fighter. This was terminated, but the US Air Force later issued a specification for an extremely advanced all-weather interceptor to carry the Hughes MX-1179 system which included radar, computer and guided missiles. For the first time the carrier aircraft became subordinate to its avionics, as a mere portion of a weapon system. The whole weapon system represented a major challenge in 1951–52 and it did not help when early flight trials showed that the specified supersonic speed could not be reached. The whole aircraft had to be redesigned to a modified shape complying with the lately discovered Area Rule, making it much longer, and fatter at the back. One the design had been got right, 875 were delivered in 21 months, together with 63 of the subsonic side-by-side TF version. The Delta Dagger was big and impressive, painted a glossy pale grey, and had a small but comfortable cockpit where the pilot flew with two control columns, that on the left being used to adjust the sweep angle and range gate of the MG-10 radar. In the search mode the pilot flew with one hand on each stick and his eyes pressed into the viewing hood of the radar display screen. In the semi-automatic mode missiles could be extended automatically at the correct moment; as delivered, the F-102 also carried FFARs (Folding-Fin Aircraft Rockets) in the missile bay doors. By 1974 surviving F-102s – called "Deuces" – had been assigned to the US Air National Guard and to the air forces of Greece and Turkey. Sperry converted 24 into remotely piloted QF and unmanned PQM versions for use in threat evaluation, F-15 combat and other aerial research.

F-102A (with IR seeker and drop tanks)

General Dynamics (Convair) F-106 Delta Dagger

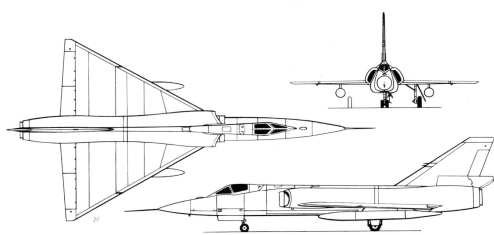

General Dynamics F-106A (94th FIS, Selfridge AFB, Michigan)

F-106A and F-106B

Type: (F-106A) single-seat all-weather interceptor; (F-106B) operational trainer.

Engine: one 24,500 lb (11,130 kg) thrust Pratt & Whitney J75-17 two-shaft afterburning turbojet.

Dimensions: span 38 ft $3\frac{1}{2}$ in (11·67 m); length (both) 70 ft $8\frac{3}{4}$ in (21·55 m); height 20 ft $3\frac{1}{4}$ in (6·15 m).

Weights: (A) empty 23,646 lb (10,725 kg); maximum loaded 38,250 lb (17,350 kg).

Performance: (both) maximum speed 1,525 mph (2455 km/h, Mach 2·31); initial climb about 30,000 ft (9144 m)/min; service ceiling 57,000 ft (17,375 m); range with drop tanks (A) 1,700 miles (2735 km); combat radius, about 600 miles (966 km).

Armament: one internal 20 mm M-61 multi-barrel cannon; internal weapon bay for air-to-air guided missiles, with typical load comprising one AIR-2A and one AIR-2G Genie rockets and two each of AIM-4E, -4F or 4G Falcons.

History: first flight (aerodynamic prototype) 26 December 1956; (F-106B) 9 April 1958; production delivery July 1959 to July 1960.

Originally designated F-102B, the 106 was a natural development of the F-102A with new engine and avionics. By redesigning from scratch to the supersonic Area Rule the fuselage was made much neater and more efficient than that of the earlier aircraft and the more powerful engine resulted in a peak speed approximately twice as fast. The Hughes MA-1 fire control, though no bulkier or heavier than that of the 102, was far more capable and integrated with the SAGE (Semi-Automatic Ground Environment) defence system covering the continental United States in an automatic manner, the pilot acting as a supervisory manager. Though bought in modest numbers, the 106 has had an exceptionally long life-span in the USAF Aerospace Defense Command front-line inventory. At several times the Improved Manned Interceptor program (IMI) has pointed the need for a replacement with longer-range look-down radar and long-range missiles, and much research has been done with the Lockheed YF-12 (p. 134). At present, however, no replacement, other than the multi-role F-15, is in sight and the F-106 and tandem-seat F-106B force (respectively numbering originally 277 and 63) will continue until at least 1980. They have been repeatedly updated, with improved avionics, infra-red sensors, drop tanks, flight refuelling and a Gatling gun.

F-106A (with drop tanks)

General Dynamics F-111

"TFX", F-111A to F-111F and FB-111A

Type: two-seat all-weather attack bomber; (FB) strategic bomber.

Engines: two Pratt & Whitney TF30 two-shaft afterburning turbofans, at following ratings: (F-111A, C) TF30-3 at 18,500 lb (8390 kg); (D, E) TF30-9 at 19,600 lb (8891 kg); (F) TF30-100 at 25,100 lb (11,385 kg); (FB) TF30-7 at 20,350 lb (9230 kg).

Dimensions: span, 72·5° sweep (A,D,E,F) 31 ft 11½ in (9·74 m); (C,FB) 33 ft 11 in (10·34 m); span, 16° sweep (A,D,E,F) 63 ft (19·2 m); (C,FB) 70 ft (21·34 m); length 73 ft 6 in (22·4 m); height 17 ft 1½ in (5·22 m).

Weights: empty (A,C) 46,172 lb (20,943 kg); (D,E,F) about 49,000 lb (22,226 kg); (FB) about 50,000 lb (22,680 kg); maximum loaded (A,C) 91,500 lb (41,500 kg); (D,E,F) 99,000 lb (44,906 kg); (FB) 119,000 lb (54,000 kg).

Performance: maximum speed (clean), Mach 2·2 at 35,000 ft or above, or about 1,450 mph (2335 km/h); maximum speed at low level (clean) Mach 1·2 or 800 mph (1287 km/h); maximum speed at maximum weight, subsonic at low level; service ceiling (clean) (A) 51,000 ft (15,500 m); (F) 60,000 ft (18,290 m); range on internal fuel (A,C) 3,165 miles (5093 km).

Armament: internal bay for two 750 lb (341 kg) bombs or 20 mm M-61 multi-barrel gun; eight underwing pylons for total of 31,500 lb (14,290 kg) of stores, inner pylons swivelling with wing sweep and outer four being fixed and loaded only with wing at 16°.

History: first flight 21 December 1964; service delivery June 1967; first F-111F with -100 engine, May 1973; EF-111A (Grumman ECM conversion 1976–7.

Developed to meet a bold Department of Defense edict that a common type of "fighter" called TFX should be developed to meet all future tactical needs of all US services, the F-111A proved both a world-beater and a great disappointment. Thrown into the public eye by acrimonious disagreement over which bidder should get the production contract, it then stayed in the news through being grossly overweight, up in drag and suffering from severe problems with propulsion, structure and systems. Eventually almost superhuman efforts cleared the F-111A for service, overcoming part of the range deficiency by a considerable increase in internal fuel. The RAAF bought 24 F-111C with long-span wings and stronger landing gear and took delivery after they had been nine years in storage. The RAF ordered 50 similar to the C but with updated avionics, but this deal was cancelled. Only 141 low-powered A-models were built, the US Navy F-111B fighter was cancelled, and the next batch was 94 of the E type with improved intakes and engines (20th Tac Ftr Wing at Upper Heyford, England). Then came the 96 F-111D with improved avionics (27th TFW in New Mexico) and finally the superb F-111F with redesigned P-100 engine of greatly increased thrust and cheaper avionics (366 TFW, in Idaho). The heavier FB-111A, with the ability to carry six AGM-69A SRAM missiles externally, was bought to replace the B-58 and early B-52 models in Strategic Air Command. Cost-inflation cut the FB order from 210 back to 76. With several RF and ECM conversions the total programme amounted to 539 plus 23 development prototypes. To keep the line open a further 12 were authorised in 1974 to be built at a low rate until 1976. No aircraft has ever had worse luck or a worse press, and in combat in South East Asia the sudden loss of three of the first six aircraft was eventually found to be due to a faulty weld in the tailplane power unit. In fact all models of the F-111 are valuable machines with great range and endurance, excellent reliability and great ability to hit a point target in a first-pass strike, even in blind conditions. These aircraft are bombers, with much greater power and weight than four-engined bombers of World War II. It was unfortunate they were loosely launched as "fighters".

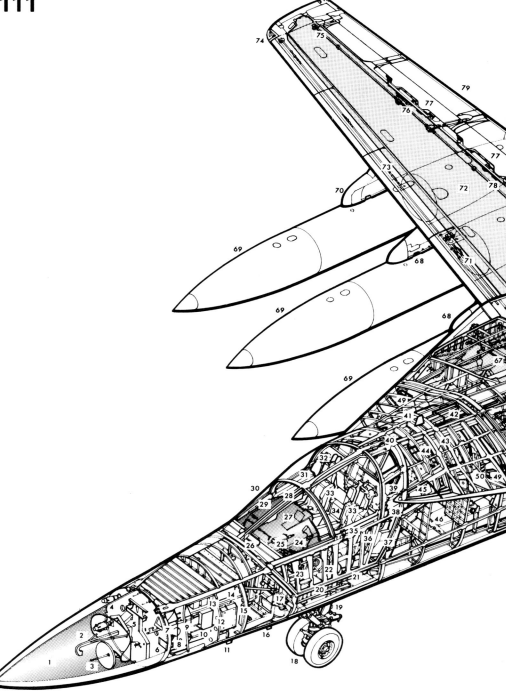

General Dynamics F-111D cutaway drawing key:

1 Hinged radome
2 General Electric APQ-113 attack radar
3 Texas Instruments APQ-110 terrain-following radar
4 Radome hinges (2)
5 Radar mounting
6 Nose lock
7 Angle-of-sideslip probe
8 Homing aerial (high)
9 Forward warning aerial
10 Homing aerial (low and mid)
11 ALR-41 aerial
12 Flight control computers
13 Feel and trim assembly
14 Forward avionics bay
14 Forward avionics bay Mk II digital computer)
15 Angle-of-attack probe
16 UHF Comm/TACAN No 2

17 Module forward bulkhead and stabilization flaps (2)
18 Twin nosewheels
19 Shock strut
20 Underfloor impact attenuation bag stowage (4)
21 Nosewheel well
22 Lox converter
23 Rudder pedals
24 Control column
25 Lox heat exchanger
26 Auxiliary flotation bag pressure bottle
27 Weapons sight
28 Forward parachute bridle line
29 De-fog nozzle
30 Windscreen
31 Starboard console
32 Emergency oxygen bottles
33 Crew seats
34 Bulkhead console
35 Wing sweep control handle
36 Recovery chute catapult

37 Provision/survival pack
38 Attenuation bags pressure bottle
39 Recovery chute
40 Aft parachute bridle line
41 UHF data link/AG IFF No 1 (see 123)
42 Stabilization-brake chute
43 Self-righting bag
44 UHF recovery
45 ECM aerials (port and starboard)
46 Forward fuselage fuel bay
47 Ground refuelling receptacle
48 Weapons bay
49 Module pitch flaps (port and starboard)
50 Aft flotation bag stowage
51 Flight refuelling receptacle
52 Primary heat-exchanger (air-to-water)
53 Ram air inlet
54 Rate gyros
55 Rotating glove

Right, General Dynamics F-111C (1 and 6 Sqns, RAAF, Amberley, Queensland)

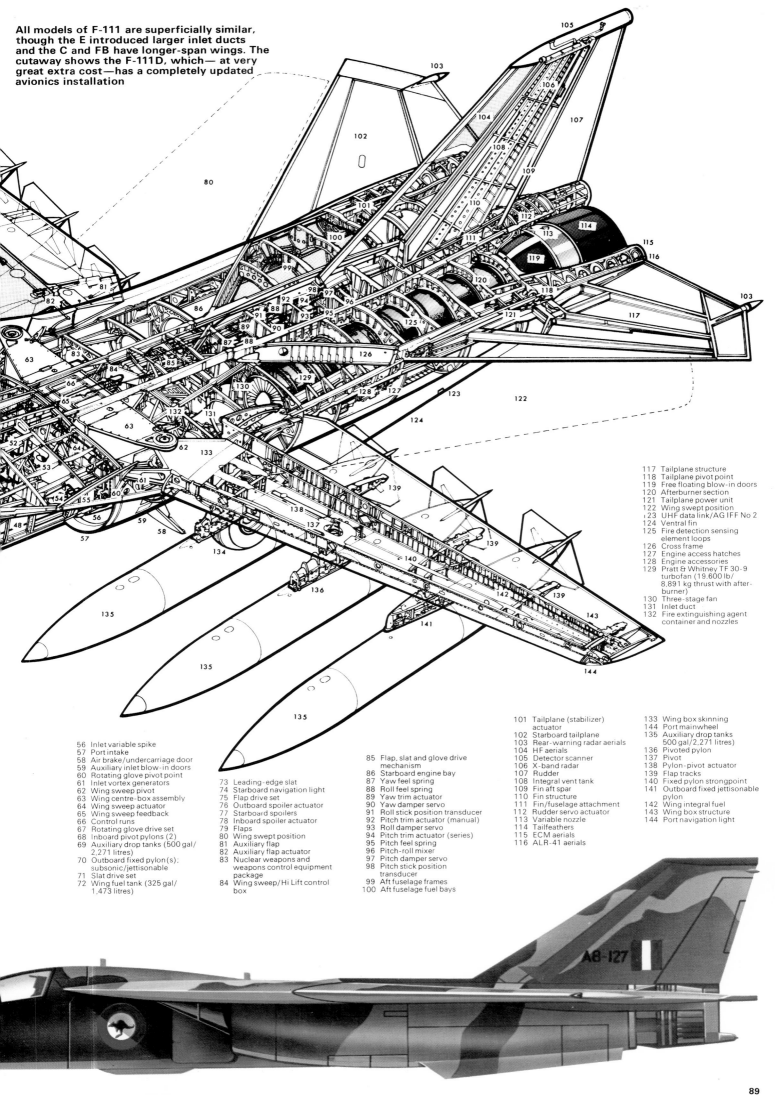

All models of F-111 are superficially similar, though the E introduced larger inlet ducts and the C and FB have longer-span wings. The cutaway shows the F-111D, which— at very great extra cost—has a completely updated avionics installation

117 Tailplane structure
118 Tailplane pivot point
119 Free floating blow-in doors
120 Afterburner section
121 Tailplane power unit
122 Wing swept position
123 UHF data link/AG IFF No 2
124 Ventral fin
125 Fire detection sensing element loops
126 Cross frame
127 Engine access hatches
128 Engine accessories
129 Pratt & Whitney TF 30-9 turbofan (19.600 lb/ 8,891 kg thrust with after-burner)
130 Three-stage fan
131 Inlet duct
132 Fire extinguishing agent container and nozzles

56 Inlet variable spike
57 Port intake
58 Air brake/undercarriage door
59 Auxiliary inlet blow-in doors
60 Rotating glove pivot point
61 Inlet vortex generators
62 Wing sweep pivot
63 Wing centre-box assembly
64 Wing sweep actuator
65 Wing sweep feedback
66 Control runs
67 Rotating glove drive set
68 Inboard pivot pylons (2)
69 Auxiliary drop tanks (500 gal/ 2,271 litres)
70 Outboard fixed pylon(s); subsonic/jettisonable
71 Slat drive set
72 Wing fuel tank (325 gal/ 1,473 litres)

73 Leading-edge slat
74 Starboard navigation light
75 Flap drive set
76 Outboard spoiler actuator
77 Starboard spoilers
78 Inboard spoiler actuator
79 Flaps
80 Wing swept position
81 Auxiliary flap
82 Auxiliary flap actuator
83 Nuclear weapons and weapons control equipment package
84 Wing sweep/Hi Lift control box

85 Flap, slat and glove drive mechanism
86 Starboard engine bay
87 Yaw feel spring
88 Roll feel spring
89 Yaw trim actuator
90 Yaw damper servo
91 Roll stick position transducer
92 Pitch trim actuator (manual)
93 Roll damper servo
94 Pitch trim actuator (series)
95 Pitch feel spring
96 Pitch-roll mixer
97 Pitch damper servo
98 Pitch stick position transducer
99 Aft fuselage frames
100 Aft fuselage fuel bays

101 Tailplane (stabilizer) actuator
102 Starboard tailplane
103 Rear-warning radar aerials
104 HF aerials
105 Detector scanner
106 X-band radar
107 Rudder
108 Integral vent tank
109 Fin aft spar
110 Fin structure
111 Fin/fuselage attachment
112 Rudder servo actuator
113 Variable nozzle
114 Tailfeathers
115 ECM aerials
116 ALR-41 aerials

133 Wing box skinning
144 Port mainwheel
135 Auxiliary drop tanks 500 gal/2,271 litres)
136 Pivoted pylon
137 Pivot
138 Pylon-pivot actuator
139 Flap tracks
140 Fixed pylon strongpoint
141 Outboard fixed jettisonable pylon
142 Wing integral fuel
143 Wing box structure
144 Port navigation light

General Dynamics F-16

Model 401, YF-16, F-16A, TF-16A

Type: single-seat fighter bomber; (TF) operational trainer.

Engine: one 24,000 lb (10,885 kg) thrust Pratt & Whitney F100-PW-100 two-shaft afterburning turbofan.

Dimensions: span over tip missile rails (YF-16) 30 ft (9·14 m); length (YF-16) 47 ft (14·32 m); (F-16A) 47 ft 7 in (14·5 m); height 16 ft 3 in (4·95 m).

Weights: empty (YF) about 12,000 lb (5443 kg); (F) about 14,800 lb (6733 kg); maximum gross (YF) 27,000 lb (12,245 kg); (F) 33,000 lb (14,969 kg).

Performance: maximum speed, Mach 1·95, equivalent to about 1,300 mph (2090 km/h); initial climb (YF) 40,000 ft (12,200 m)/min; service ceiling about 60,000 ft (18,300 m); range on internal fuel in interception mission, about 1,300 miles (2100 km); attack radius at low level with maximum weapon load, 120 miles (193 km); attack radius with six Mk 82 bombs, 339 miles (546 km).

Armament: one 20 mm M61 multi-barrel cannon on left side of fuselage; nine pylons for total external load of up to 15,200 lb (6895 kg) (YF, seven pylons for total of 11,500 lb, 5217 kg).

History: first flight (YF) 20 January 1974; service delivery, scheduled for mid-1978.

One of the most important combat aircraft of the rest of the century was started merely as a technology demonstrator to see to what degree it would be possible to build a useful fighter that was significantly smaller and cheaper than the F-15. The US Air Force Lightweight Fighter (LWF) programme was not intended to lead to a production aircraft but merely to establish what was possible, at what cost. Contracts for two prototypes of each of the two best submissions were awarded in April 1972, the aircraft being the General Dynamics 401 and a simplified Northrop P.530. As the YF-16 and YF-17 these aircraft completed a programme of competitive evaluation, as planned, in 1974. By this time the wish of four European members of NATO — Belgium, Holland, Denmark and Norway — to replace their F-104Gs with an aircraft in this class had spurred a total revision of the LWF programme. In April 1974 it was changed into the Air Combat Fighter (ACF) programme and the Defense Secretary, James Schlesinger, announced that 650 of the winning design would be bought for the USAF, with a vast support depot in Europe. In December 1974 the YF-16 was chosen as the future ACF (announced the following month) and in June 1975, after protracted and tortuous discussions, it was chosen by the four European countries. As an aircraft the F-16 is exciting. It has a flashing performance on the power of the single fully developed engine (the same as the F-15) fed by a simple fixed-geometry inlet. Structure and systems are modern, with control-configured vehicle (CCV) flight dynamics, quad-redundant electrically signalled controls (fly-by-wire), graphite-epoxy structures and a flared wing/body shape. Pilot view is outstanding and he lies back in a reclining Escapac seat and flies the aircraft through a sidestick controller. In the nose is an advanced pulse-doppler radar suitable for attack or interception missions and armament can be carried for both roles. In 1975–76 construction of 15 F-16 development aircraft was in hand at Fort Worth, four being TF-16s. Total European buy is planned to be 306, with considerable local participation in manufacture. Further sales, and new variants, are virtually certain.

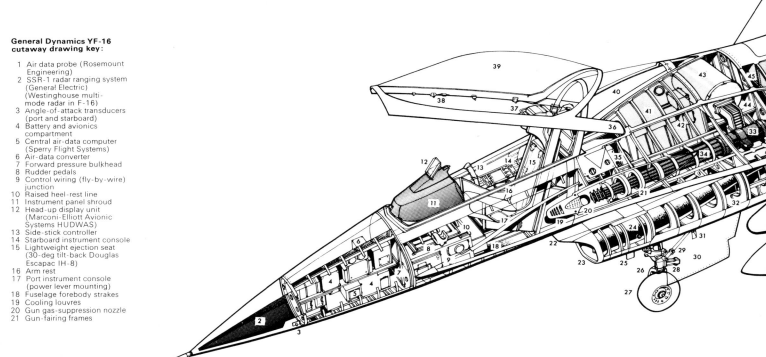

General Dynamics YF-16 cutaway drawing key:

1 Air data probe (Rosemount Engineering)
2 SSR-1 radar ranging system (General Electric) (Westinghouse multi-mode radar in F-16)
3 Angle-of-attack transducers (port and starboard)
4 Battery and avionics compartment
5 Central air-data computer (Sperry Flight Systems)
6 Air-data converter
7 Forward pressure bulkhead
8 Rudder pedals
9 Control wiring (fly-by-wire) junction
10 Raised heel-rest line
11 Instrument panel shroud
12 Head-up display unit (Marconi-Elliott Avionic Systems HUDWAS)
13 Side-stick controller
14 Starboard instrument console
15 Lightweight ejection seat (30-deg tilt-back Douglas Escapac IH-8)
16 Arm rest
17 Port instrument console (power lever mounting)
18 Fuselage forebody strakes
19 Cooling louvres
20 Gun gas-suppression nozzle
21 Gun-fairing frames

22 Boundary-layer splitter plate
23 Fixed-geometry air intake
24 Inlet duct
25 Aerial
26 Nosewheel leg (Menasco Manufacturing)
27 Aft-retracting nose gear (Goodyear Tire & Rubber)
28 Shock-absorber scissors
29 Retraction strut
30 Nosewheel door
31 Door hinge
32 Nosewheel well (below duct)
33 General Electric M61 20mm gun
34 Cannon barrels
35 Emergency power-unit pack (Sundstrand Avionics)
36 Canopy hinge
37 Headrest
38 Canopy lock
39 Frameless bubble canopy (Sierracin Corp)
40 Aft glazing
41 Forward fuselage fuel tank

42 Accelerometers (General Electric)
43 Ammunition drum
44 Ammunition feed and link return chutes (General Electric)
45 Forward/centre fuselage joint bulkhead
46 Inlet duct
47 Hydraulic equipment bay
48 Main (forward) fuselage fuel tank
49 Flight-refuelling receptacle
50 Multi-spar wing structure
51 Leading-edge flap hinge-line
52 Leading-edge manœuvre flap
53 Wing-tip missile adaptor shoe
54 AIM-9 Sidewinder missile
55 Static dischargers
56 Fixed trailing-edge section
57 Starboard flaperon
58 Aerial
59 Forward support link
60 Glass-fibre root fairing
61 Fin/fuselage attachments

62 Aluminium multi-spar fin structure
63 Aluminium-honeycomb leading-edge
64 Steel leading-edge strip
65 Graphite-epoxy skin
66 Identification/navigation light
67 Static dischargers
68 Graphite-epoxy rudder skin
69 Aluminium-honeycomb rudder
70 Empennage flight controls
71 Fully variable articulated nozzle
72 Split trailing-edge airbrake (upper and lower surfaces)
73 Static dischargers
74 Aluminium-honeycomb tailplane
75 Graphite-epoxy skin
76 Titanium spar
77 Steel leading-edge strip
78 Titanium pivot fitting
79 Tailplane actuator (Bendix Corp)
80 Fueldraulic nozzle actuators
81 Rear fuselage structure (afterburner mounting)
82 Main (aft) fuselage fuel tank
83 Main engine mounting (port)

84 Fuel tank
85 Arrester hook housing
86 Runway arrester hook
87 Ventral fins (port and starboard)
88 Flaperon actuator
89 Arrester hook pivot
90 Machined main frames
91 Pratt & Whitney F100-PW-100 turbofan (23,500 lb/10,650 kg with maximum afterburner)
92 Pitch, roll and yaw gyros (General Electric)
93 Wing attachment fittings
94 Flared wing/fuselage intersections
95 Aluminium multi-spar wing structure
96 Flaperon hinges
97 Aluminium-honeycomb flaperon
98 Outboard angled wing ribs
99 Fixed trailing-edge section
100 Static dischargers
101 Port AIM-9 Sidewinder missile
102 Wing-tip missile adapter shoe
103 Leading-edge rotary actuators
104 Aluminium-honeycomb leading-edge
105 Port leading-edge manœuvre flap

106 Port mainwheel (Goodyear Tire & Rubber)
107 Mainwheel leg (Menasco Manufacturing)
108 Retraction jack
109 Drop tank (308 gal/1,400 litres)
110 Underwing stores pylon
111 Mainwheel door
112 Fuselage-centreline pylon
113 Drop tank (125 gal/568 litres)

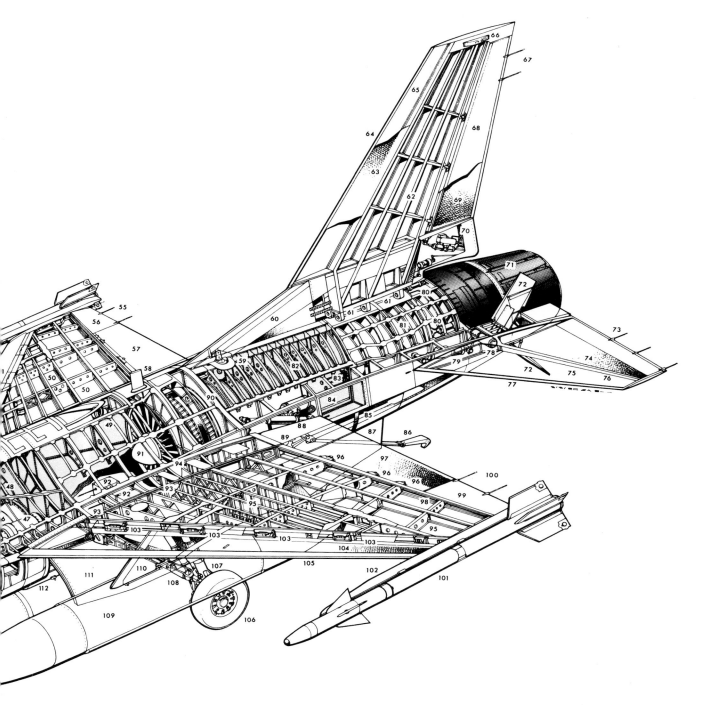

This cutaway drawing gives a clear indication of the structure, systems and weapons of the two YF-16 prototypes. Production aircraft will have a multi-mode radar by Westinghouse and many additional equipment items.

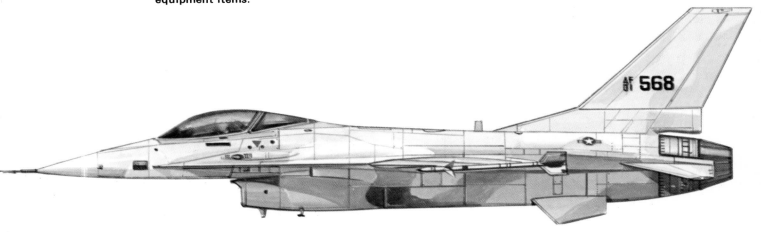

General Dynamics YF-16 (second prototype, with preliminary evaluation equipment fit and lacking the Westinghouse radar, ECM installation and definitive armament).

Gloster Grebe/Gamecock

Gloucestershire (Gloster) Grebe and Gamecock I to III
Type: single-seat fighter.
Engine: (Grebe II) one 400 hp Armstrong Siddeley Jaguar IV 14-cylinder two-row radial; (Gamecock I, II, III) one 425 hp Bristol Jupiter VI nine-cylinder radial.
Dimensions: span (Grebe) 29 ft 4 in; (Gamecock) 29 ft 9½ in (9·1 m); length (Grebe) 20 ft 3 in; (Gamecock) 19 ft 8 in (6 m); height (Grebe) 9 ft 3 in; (Gamecock) 9 ft 8 in (2·95 m).
Weights: empty (Grebe) 1,720 lb; (Gamecock) 1,930 lb (875 kg); loaded (Grebe) 2,614 lb; (Gamecock) 2,863 lb (1298 kg).
Performance: maximum speed (Grebe) 152 mph (244 km/h); (Gamecock) 155 mph (250 km/h); initial climb (Grebe) 1,320 ft (400 m)/min; (Gamecock) 1,500 ft (460 m)/min; service ceiling (Grebe) 23,000 ft (7010 m); (Gamecock) 22,000 ft (6705 m); endurance (both) about 2 hr 45 min, equivalent to about 380 miles (612 km).
Armament: (Grebe) two 0·303 in Vickers on top of fuselage, each with 600 rounds; light series carriers under lower wing for four 20 lb bombs; (Gamecock) same, but with guns firing through channels in sides of fuselage, between engine cylinders.
History: first flight (Grebe) May 1923; (Gamecock) February 1925; final delivery (Finland) 1931.

Gloster Gamecock I (23 Sqn)

Showing courage in the face of highly uncertain prospects, the Gloucestershire Aircraft Co determined to stay in the business of building combat aircraft after World War I, and had the luck to secure the former British Nieuport designer Harry Folland. From his drawing board emerged a long succession of first-class biplane fighters. The family began with the Grouse, with Folland's HLB wing formula in which efficiency was improved by increasing lift coefficient on the upper plane and reducing it on the lower. From this stemmed the nimble Grebe, of which 129 were supplied to the RAF; the first deliveries were Mk IIs,

to distinguish them from the lower-powered prototypes, at least nine were dual trainers and the Mk III incorporated minor changes. The Gamecock, to Specification 37/23, had the excellent new Jupiter engine, conferring higher performance and even greater manoeuvrability. Though still of wood and fabric construction the Gamecock was virtually unbreakable and survived 22 turns of a spin and a vertical dive at 275 mph. Colourfully painted with squadron markings, the delightful Gamecock was popular and exhilarating and 82 served in the RAF until 1932. In 1926 the company changed its name to Gloster, moving from near Cheltenham to a new factory near Gloucester, and Gamecocks were later built in Finland with Mk II upper wing, increased tankage for the Gnome Rhône Jupiter engine and optional ski landing gear.

Gloster Gauntlet

S.S.18, 19 and Gauntlet I and II
Type: single-seat fighter.
Engine: Gauntlet I, one 645 hp Bristol Mercury VIS-2 nine-cylinder radial.
Dimensions: span 32 ft 9½ in (10 m); length 26 ft 2in (7·97 m); height 10 ft 4 in (3·18 m).
Weights: empty 2,775 lb (1260 kg); loaded 3,970 lb (1801 kg).
Performance: maximum speed 230 mph (370 km/h); initial climb 2,300 ft (701 m)/min; service ceiling 33,500 ft (10,200 m); range 460 miles (740 km).
Armament: as Gauntlet, two Vickers 0·303 in in sides of fuselage, each with 600 rounds.
History: first flight (S.S.18) January 1929; (S.S.19B) August 1933; Gauntlet I, October 1934.

The Gloster S.S.18 (S.S. = single-seat) was a two-bay metal/fabric biplane, with RAF service number J9125. It was built to Specification F.9/26 and had two Vickers guns and an early 480 hp Mercury IIA engine. In 1932 it reappeared with a ring-cowled Jupiter and was then modified to meet specification F.10/27 with four added Lewis guns, each with a 97-

Gloster Gauntlet II (11 Sqn)

round drum of ammunition, arranged in each of the four mainplanes outside the propeller disc. This S.S.19 with six guns was obviously formidable, giving a cone of fire to a point 300—900 feet ahead just as several Air Ministry armament experts were soon to suggest. But eventually Specification 24/33 was published calling for a day/night fighter to replace the Bulldog and the aircraft was again modified to S.S.19B standard with

only two Vickers guns. An order for 24 followed, named Gauntlet I, two having wheel spats. Then came two orders totalling 204 of the Gauntlet II, with modified structure resulting from rationalization of techniques within the newly formed Hawker Siddeley Group. The final batches, delivered in 1937, had a Fairey-Reed three-blade metal propeller in place of the two-blade Watts of laminated wood. By this time Gauntlets equipped 14 Fighter Command squadrons (they served with 22 altogether, until July 1940 in the Middle East). In November 1937 a Gauntlet II of 32 Sqn made the world's first radar-vectored interception, on to an Imperial Airways transport flying over the Thames estuary.

Gloster Gladiator

S.S.37 Gladiator I and II and Sea Gladiator
Type: single-seat fighter; (Sea Gladiator) carrier-based fighter.
Engine: one 840 hp Bristol Mercury IX or IXS nine-cylinder radial; (Gladiator II) usually Mercury VIIIA of similar power.
Dimensions: span 32 ft 3 in (9·85 m); length 27 ft 5 in (8·38 m); height 10 ft 4 in (3·17 m).
Weights: empty 3,450 lb (1565 kg) (Sea Gladiator) 3,745 lb; loaded 4,750 lb (2155 kg) (Sea Gladiator) 5,420 lb.
Performance: maximum speed 253 mph (407 km/h); (Sea Gladiator) 245 mph; initial climb 2,300 ft (700 m)/min; service ceiling 33,000 ft (10,060 m); range 440 miles (708 km); (Sea Gladiator) 425 miles.
Armament: first 71 aircraft, two 0·303 in Vickers in fuselage, one 0·303 in Lewis under each lower wing; subsequent, four 0·303 in Brownings in same locations, fuselage guns with 600 rounds and wing guns with 400.
History: first flight (S.S.37) September 1934; (Gladiator I) June 1936; (Sea Gladiator) 1938; final delivery April 1940.

Air Ministry Specification F.7/30 recognised that future fighters would have to be faster and better armed, but the delay in placing an order extended to a disgraceful 4½ years, by which time war clouds were distantly gathering and the fabric-covered biplane was swiftly

to be judged obsolete. Folland's S.S.37 was built as a very late entrant, long after the competition to F.7/30 ought to have been settled. Though less radical than most contenders it was eventually judged best and, as the Gladiator, was at last ordered in July 1935. Features included neat single-bay wings, each of the four fuselage planes having small hydraulically depressed drag flaps; cantilever landing gear with Dowty internally sprung wheels; four guns; and, in the production aircraft, a sliding cockpit canopy. Most early production had the Watts wooden propeller, though performance was better with the three-blade metal Fairey-Reed type. The Mk II aircraft introduced desert filters, auto mixture control and electric starter from internal battery. The Sea Gladiator had full carrier equipment and a dinghy. Total production amounted to at least 767, including 480 for the RAF, 60 Sea Gladiators and 216

Gloster Gladiator I (73 Sqn)

exported to 12 foreign countries. Gladiators of the Auxiliary Air Force intercepted the first bombing raid on Britain, over the Firth of Forth in September 1939, and these highly manoeuvrable biplanes were constantly in heroic action for the next three years. Aircraft from the torpedoed *Glorious* operated from a frozen lake in Norway and three Sea Gladiators defended Malta against the Regia Aeronautica from 11 June 1940.

Gotha bombers

G.I to G.V

Type: heavy bomber.
Engines: (G.I) two 160 hp Mercedes D.III six-cylinder water-cooled; (G II) two 220 hp D.IV; (G.III, IV and V) two 260 hp D.IVa.
Dimensions: span (G.III) 77 ft 10 in; (G.IV, V) 77 ft 9¼ in (23·7 m); length (G.III) 38 ft 8¼ in; (G.IV, V) 40 ft 6¼ in (12·35 m); height (G.III) 12 ft 8 in; (G.IV, V) 12 ft 11½ in (3·95 m).
Weights: empty (G.III) 4,190 lb (1900 kg); (G.IV, V) 5,290 lb (2400 kg); loaded (G.III) 7,022 lb (3185 kg); (G.IV) 8,763 lb (3975 kg); (G.V) 8,745 lb (3966 kg).
Performance: maximum speed (G.III) 92 mph (148 km/h); (G.IV, V) 87 mph (140 km/h); service ceiling (G.III) 22,966 ft (7000 m); (G.IV, V) 21,325 ft (6500 m); range (G.III) 404 miles (650 km); (G.IV, V) 522 miles (840 km).
Armament: two 7·92 mm Parabellum machine guns manually aimed from nose and rear upper cockpits; racks under lower wing for bomb load of 881 lb (400 kg) in G.III, 1,102 lb (500 kg) in G.IV, G.V.
History: first flight (G.I) January 1915; (G.II) March 1916); (G.III) August 1916); (G.IV) December 1916); (G.V) spring 1917.

Though undistinguished aircraft, the series of G (Grossflugzeug, large aeroplane) designs from the Gothaer Wagonfabrik played a major role in German strategic bombing in World War I and from the spring of 1917 their name was on the lips of everyone in southern England. The G.I was not a Gotha design but stemmed from a prototype built under the direction of Oskar Ursinus and a German army major. Gotha built a small number under licence and they were used as tactical bomber and reconnaissance aircraft on both Eastern and Western fronts. The Gotha team under Hans Burkhard then produced the G.II, with body mounted not on the upper but the lower wing, in the usual way, and with nosewheels to prevent nosing over when landing in soft ground. About 15 had been delivered to Macedonia and other Balkan areas when it was withdrawn because of the notorious frequency of crankshaft failure of the D.IV engine (which also hit AEG bombers as described on p.8). The G.III followed with the direct-drive D.IVa engine, and a few introduced the novel tunnel extending down to the rear from the rear gunner's cockpit so that his gun could

Gotha G.Vb (irregular patch camouflage)

cover the previous "blind spot" below the tail. This tunnel was standard on the D.IV, which went into bulk production not only by Gotha but also by LVG and Siemens-Schuckert, many of the subcontracted examples having 180 hp Argus, 185 hp NAG or 230 hp Hiero engines and being used either as trainers or by Austria–Hungary on the Italian front. It was the G.IV that bore the brunt of missions against London and south east England, which by January 1918 were suffering severe casualties from fast-climbing Camel and SE.5a defenders. Only small numbers of G.V and biplane-tail G.Va and Vb were used, and in April 1918 British fighters forced night bombing over Britain to be abandoned.

Grumman GE-23

GE-23, FF-1 and -2, SF-1 and -2, Goblin I

Type: two-seat fighter.
Engine: One Wright R-1820 Cyclone nine-cylinder radial, of following sub-types: (XFF-1) 575 hp R-1820E; (FF-1 and FF-2) 750 hp R-1820-78; (SF-1) 775 hp R-1820-84; (Goblin I) 750 hp R-1820F.
Dimensions: span 34 ft 6 in (10·51 m); length 24 ft 6 in (7·47 m); height 11 ft 1 in (3·4 m).
Weights: empty (typical) 3,300 lb (1500 kg); loaded 4,828 lb (2190 kg).
Performance: maximum speed (typical) 207 mph (333 km/h); initial climb 1,600 ft (488 m)/min; service ceiling 21,100 ft (6430 m); range 920 miles (1480 km).
Armament: originally, standard armament was two 0·30 in machine guns in top of forward fuselage; some aircraft unarmed, and later there were several variations.
History: first flight (XFF-1) December 1931.

The Grumman Aircraft Engineering Corporation was incorporated in December 1929 and began operations at Bethpage, Long Island, where it has been centred ever since. One of its first contracts was with the US Navy to build seaplane floats incorporating retracting land wheels and out of this stemmed a contract, placed on 2 April 1931, for a prototype of the XFF-1.

This was the first fighter to be designed around Wright's powerful Cyclone engine and also the first in the US Navy to have retractable landing gear and all-light-alloy structure. The deep-bellied fuselage contained wheel-size depressions into which the main gears could be retracted by manually operating long jackscrews. This was one of the tasks of the observer, because the XFF-1 had tandem seats, with both cockpits covered by sliding canopies. Despite the penalty of the second man, the prototype outpaced every aircraft in the Navy at 195 mph and it exceeded 200 mph with a more powerful Cyclone engine. The Navy bought a second

Grumman GE-23 (Republican Spain)

example, designated XSF-1, equipped for scouting (reconnaissance) duties; later an XSF-2 was ordered with R-1340 Wasp engine. In 1933 came an order for 27 FF-1 fighters for use from Navy carriers, some being converted to FF-2 trainers by fitting dual pilot controls. Grumman also built 34 SF-1 scout fighters, with the rear-seat man occupied with overwater navigation and photography. In 1934 Canadian Car & Foundry decided to enter aircraft manufacture, and acquired a licence for the basic GE-23 design. In 1935–37 a total of 57 were built, 15 going to the RCAF as Goblin Is and one each to Japan and Nicaragua. The rest were bought by the Spanish Republican forces, via an agent in Turkey, and in 1936–39 these 40 two-seat fighters played a significant role against generally superior Nationalist opponents.

Grumman Wildcat

G-36, Martlet, F4F-1 to -4 and Eastern Motors FM-1 and -2

Type: single-seat naval fighter.
Engine: (XF4F-2) one 1,050 hp Pratt & Whitney R-1830-66 Twin Wasp 14-cylinder two-row radial; (G-36A, Martlet I (Wildcat I)) one 1,200 hp Wright R-1820-G205A Cyclone nine-cylinder radial; (F4F-3) 1,200 hp R-1830-76; (F4F-4 and FM-1 (Wildcat V)) R-1830-86; (FM-2 (Wildcat VI)) 1,350 hp R-1820-56.
Dimensions: span 38 ft (11·6 m); length 28 ft 9 in to 28 ft 11 in (FM-2, 28 ft 10 in, 8·5 m); height 11 ft 11 in (3·6 m).
Weights: empty (F4F-3) 4,425 lb; (F4F-4) 4,649 lb; (FM-2) 4,900 lb (2226 kg); loaded (F4F-3) 5,876 lb; (F4F-4) 6,100 lb rising to 7,952 lb (3607 kg) with final FM-1s; (FM-2) 7,412 lb.
Performance: maximum speed (F4F-3) 325 mph (523 km/h); (F4F-4, FM-1) 318 mph (509 km/h); (FM-2) 332 mph (534 km/h); initial climb, typically 2,000 ft (610 m)/min (3,300 ft/min in early versions, 1,920 main production and over 2,000 for FM-2); service ceiling, typically 35,000 ft (10,670 m); (more in light early versions); range, typically 900 miles (1448 km).
Armament: (XF4F-2) two 0·5 in Colt-Brownings in fuselage; (F4F-3) four 0·5 in outer wings; (F4F-4 and subsequent) six 0·5 in outer wings; (F4F-4, FM-1 and FM-2) underwing racks for two 250 lb (113 kg) bombs.
History: first flight (XF4F-2) 2 September 1937; (XF4F-3) 12 February 1939; production (G-36 and F4F-3) February 1940; (FM-2) March 1943; final delivery August 1945.

Designed as a biplane to continue Grumman's very successful F3F series of single-seat carrier fighters, the XF4F-1 was replanned on the drawing board in the summer of 1936 as a mid-wing monoplane. Though this lost out to the Brewster F2A Buffalo, Grumman continued with the XF4F-3 with a more powerful engine and in early 1939 received a French Aéronavale order for 100, the US Navy following with 54 in August. The French aircraft were diverted to Britain and named Martlet I. Production built up with both Twin Wasp and Cyclone engines, folding wings being introduced with the F4F-4, of which Grumman delivered 1,169 plus 220 Martlet IVs for the Fleet Air Arm. Eastern Aircraft Division of General Motors very quickly tooled up and delivered 839 FM-1s and 311 Martlet Vs, the British name then being changed to the US name of Wildcat. Grumman switched to the Avenger, Hellcat and other types, but made F4F-7 reconnaissance versions, weighing 10,328 lb and having a 24-hour endurance, as well as a floatplane version. Eastern took over the final mark, the powerful and effective FM-2, delivering 4,777 of this type (including 340 Wildcat VI) in 13 months. A Martlet I shot down a Ju 88 on Christmas Day 1940, and an F4F-3 of VMF-211 destroyed a Japanese bomber at Wake Island on 9 December 1941. Each event was the first in thousands of furious actions from which this quite old fighter emerged with a splendid reputation. Wildcats were especially valuable for their ability to operate from small escort carriers,

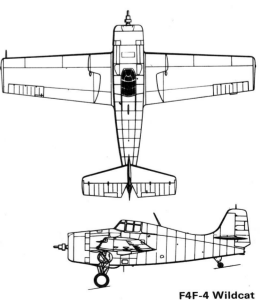

F4F-4 Wildcat

the pioneer work having been done with British Martlets based in November 1940 on the 5,000 ton captured German vessel *Audacity* on which a flat deck had been built. Noted for their strength and manoeuvrability, Wildcats even sank Japanese submarines and a cruiser.

Grumman Avenger

TBF and Eastern Aircraft TBM series
Type: originally, three-seat torpedo bomber; later ASW (anti-submarine warfare) aircraft and AEW (airborne early warning) aircraft.
Engine: one 1,700 hp Wright R-2600-8 or -20 Double Cyclone 14-cylinder two-row radial.
Dimensions: span 54 ft 2 in (16·5 m); length (to TBM-3) 40 ft (12·2 m); (TBM-3E) 40 ft 11½ in (12·48 m); height 16 ft 5 in (5 m).
Weights: empty (TBF-1) 10,100 lb (4580 kg); (TBM-3) 10,545 lb (4787 kg); loaded (TBF-1) 15,905 lb (7214 kg); (TBM-3) 18,250 lb (8278 kg); (TBM-3E) 17,895 lb (8117 kg).
Performance: maximum speed (TBF-1) 278 mph (445 km/h); (TBM-3) 267 mph (430 km/h); initial climb (TBF-1) 1,075 ft (376 m)/min; service ceiling (TBF, TBM-1 to -3) about 23,400 ft (7132 m); (TBM-3E) 30,100 ft; range with full weapon load, 1,010–1,215 miles (1600–1950 km); ferry range, 2,530 miles (4072 km).
Armament: (TBF-1, TBM-1) one 0·30 in Browning in upper forward fuselage, one 0·5 in dorsal power turret and one 0·30 in manually aimed in rear ventral position; internal bay for one 22 in torpedo or 2,000 lb (907 kg) of bombs; (TBF-1C, TBM-1C, TBM-3) as above plus one 0·5 in in each outer wing and underwing racks for eight 60 lb (27 kg) rockets. Most subsequent versions unarmed, or fitted for ASW weapons only.

History: first flight (XTBF-1) 1 August 1941; service delivery 30 January 1942; final delivery from new production, September 1945; final delivery of rebuild, August 1954.

Grumman's outstanding design and engineering staff, staff, under W. T. (Bill) Schwendler, designed and developed this big and extremely useful torpedo bomber very quickly and it became one of the key aircraft in the Pacific war. Two prototypes were ordered on 8 April 1940 and large numbers were in action at the Battle of Midway just over two years later. From the start the TBF was robust and well equipped and one could not help comparing it with the British Barracuda which lacked power, self-defence and a weapon bay. Fortunately a proportion of deliveries went to the Fleet Air Arm, which originally considered the name Tarpon before adopting the US Navy name. Of 2,293 Grumman-built aircraft delivered by December 1943, 402 went to the RN and 63 to the RNZAF. Eastern Aircraft, the second source, delivered 2,882 of the TBM-1 and -1C type, before switching to the slightly modified -3 in April 1944. Many -3s had no turret, all had strengthened wings for rockets or a radar pod, and no fewer than 4,664 were delivered by Eastern in 14 months. After 1945 development suddenly blossomed out into new versions, produced as conversions. The TBM-3E was packed with ASW search and attack equipment, the TBM-3W and -3W2 were grotesque "guppy" type early-warners with huge belly radar, the -3U was a tug and the -3R a COD (carrier on-board delivery) transport with seven passenger seats. The Fleet Air Arm put 100 TBM-3E

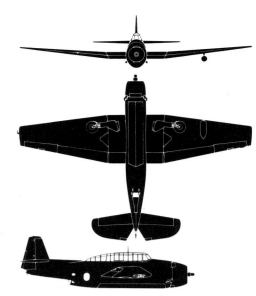

Grumman (Eastern Aircraft TBM-3)

anti-submarine versions into use as the Avenger AS.4 in 1953 and about 500 more post-war variants served with the USN, RCN, Aéronavale, Japan and Netherlands.

Grumman Hellcat

F6F-1 to -5 Hellcat
Type: single-seat naval fighter; later versions, fighter-bombers and night fighters.
Engine: early production, one 2,000 hp Pratt & Whitney R-2800-10 Double Wasp 18-cylinder two-row radial; from January 1944 (final F6F-3 batch) two-thirds equipped with 2,200 hp (water-injection rating) R-2800-10W.
Dimensions: span 42 ft 10 in (13·05 m); length 33 ft 7 in (10·2 m); height 13 ft 1 in (3·99 m).
Weights: empty (F6F-3) 9,042 lb (4101 kg); loaded (F6F-3) 12,186 lb (5528 kg) clean, 13,228 lb (6000 kg) maximum, (F6F-5N) 14,250 lb (6443 kg).
Performance: maximum speed (F6F-3, -5, clean) 376 mph (605 km/h); (-5N) 366 mph (590 km/h); initial climb (typical) 3,240 ft (990 m)/min; service ceiling (-3) 37,500 ft (11,430 m); (-5NO) 36,700 ft (11,185 m); range on internal fuel (typical) 1,090 miles (1755 km).
Armament: standard, six 0·5 in Brownings in outer wings, with 400 rounds each; a few -5N and -5 Hellcats had two 20 mm and four 0·5 in. Underwing attachments for six rockets, and centre-section pylons for 2,000 lb of bombs.
History: first flight (R-2600) 26 June 1942; (same aircraft, R-2800) 30 July 1942; (production F6F-3) 4 October 1942; production delivery (F6F-3) 16 January 1943; final delivery November 1945.

Though pugnacious rather than elegant, the Hellcat was a truly war-winning aircraft. It was designed and developed with great speed, mass-produced at a rate never equalled by any other single aircraft factory and used to such good effect that, from the very day of its appearance, the Allies were winning the air war in the Pacific. It began as the XF6F-1, a natural development of the F4F Wildcat with R-2600 Double Cyclone engine. Within a month the more powerful Double

Grumman F6F-3 (VF-9, USS Yorktown)

Grumman F6F-5 (Uruguayan Navy)

Wasp had been substituted and in the autumn of 1942 the production line took shape inside a completely new plant that was less advanced in construction than the Hellcats inside it! This line flowed at an extraordinary rate, helped by the essential rightness of the Hellcat and lack of major engineering changes during subsequent sub-types. Deliveries in the years 1942–45 inclusive were 10, 2,545, 6,139 and 3,578, a total of 12,272 (excluding two prototypes) of which 11,000 were delivered in exactly two years. These swarms of big, beefy fighters absolutely mastered the Japanese, destroying more than 6,000 hostile aircraft (4,947 by

USN carrier squadrons, 209 by land-based USMC units and the rest by Allied Hellcat squadrons). The Fleet Air Arm, which originally chose the name Gannet, used Hellcats in Europe as well as throughout the Far East. Unusual features of the F6F were its 334 sq ft of square-tipped wing, with a distinct kink, and backward-retracting landing gear. The F6F-3N and -5N were night fighters with APS-6 radar on a wing pod; the -5K was a drone and the -5P a photographic reconnaissance version. After VJ-day hundreds were sold to many nations.

Grumman Tigercat

F7F-1 to -4N Tigercat
Type: single-seat or two-seat fighter bomber or night fighter (-4N for carrier operation).
Engines: two Pratt & Whitney R-2800-22W or -34W Double Wasp 18-cylinder two-row radials each rated at 2,100 hp (dry) or 2,400 hp (water injection).
Dimensions: span 51 ft 6 in (15·7 m); length (most) 45 ft 4 in or 45 ft 4½ in (13·8 m); (-3N, -4N) 46 ft 10 in (14·32 m); height (-1, -2) 15 ft 2 in (4·6 m); (-3, -4) 16 ft 7 in (5·06 m).
Weights: empty (-1) 13,100 lb (5943 kg); (-3N, -4N) 16,270 lb (7379 kg); loaded (-1) 22,560 lb (10,235 kg); (-2N) 26,194 lb (11,880 kg); (-3) 25,720 lb; (-4N) 26,167 lb.
Performance: maximum speed (-1) 427 mph (689 km/h); (-2N) 421 mph; (-3) 435 mph; (-4N) 430 mph; initial climb (-1) 4,530 ft (1380 m)/min; service ceiling (-1) 36,200 ft; (-2N) 39,800 ft (12,131 m); (-3) 40,700 ft; (-4N) 40,450 ft; range on internal fuel (-1) 1,170 miles (1885 km); (-2N)

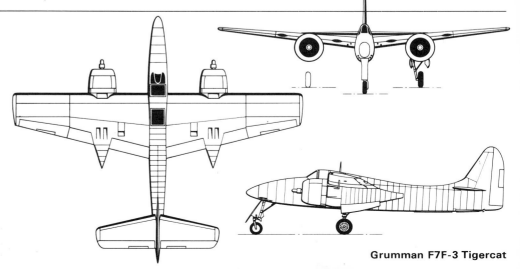

Grumman F7F-3 Tigercat

960 miles; (-3) 1,200 miles; (-4N) 810 miles.
Armament: basic (-1) four 0·5 in Browning each with 300 rounds in the nose and four 20 mm M-2 cannon each with 200 rounds in the wing roots; outer-wing pylons for six rockets or two 1,000 lb (454 kg) bombs; alternatively, one 21 in torpedo on fuselage centreline. (-3), nose guns only; (-2N, -3N, -4N) wing guns only.
History: first flight (XF7F-1) December 1943; first service delivery October 1944; final delivery, December 1946.

Ordered on the same day as the F6F Hellcat prototypes in June 1941 the F7F was one of the boldest designs in the history of combat aircraft. During the preceding

two years the US Navy had keenly studied air war in Europe and noted that the things that appeared to count were the obvious ones: engine power, armament and protective armour and self-sealing tanks. At a time when the average US Navy fighter had 1,000 hp and two machine guns the Bureau of Aeronautics asked Grumman to build a fighter with more than 4,000 hp and a weight of fire more than 200 times as great. The company had embarked on a venture along these lines in 1938 with the XF5F, which remained a one-off prototype that was judged not worth the cost and incompatible with Navy carriers. In contrast the F7F was planned on a basis of knowledge and though dramatically heavier and faster than any previous

carrier aircraft it was matched with the deck of the large Midway class carriers then under construction. Most, however, were ordered for the Marine Corps for use from land. The F7F-1, of which 34 were built, were single seaters with APS-6 radar in a wing pod. The 66 F7F-2Ns followed, with nose radar in place of guns and the observer in place of the rear fuel tank. The -3 introduced the -34W engine and so had a larger tail; most of the 250 built were -3N night fighters or -3P photographic aircraft. The final models were strengthened -4s, cleared for carrier use, the whole batch being -4Ns. Tigercats did not see action in World War II and arrived at a time when emphasis was rapidly switching to the jet.

Grumman Bearcat

F8F-1 and -2 Bearcat
Type: single-seat carrier-based fighter-bomber or night fighter.
Engine: one Pratt & Whitney R-2800-34W rated at 2,400 hp (wet) for take-off, with emergency combat rating of 2,800 hp.
Dimensions: span (-1) 35 ft 10 in; (-2) 35 ft 6 in (10·7 m); length (-1) 28 ft 3 in; (-2) 27 ft 8 in (8·43 m); height 13 ft 10 in (4·2 m).
Weights: empty (-1) 7,070 lb (3206 kg); loaded (-1) 12,947 lb; (-2) 13,494 lb (6120 kg).
Performance: maximum speed (-1) 421 mph (680 km/h); (-2) 447 mph (720 km/h); initial climb 5,000 ft (1520 m)/min; service ceiling 40,000 ft (12,190 m); range on internal fuel (-1) 1,105 miles (1775 km); (-2) 865 miles (1400 km).
Armament: (-1) four 0·5 in Brownings in inboard wings beyond propeller disc; pylons under inboard wing for two 1,000 lb (454 kg) bombs, drop tanks or rockets; (-1B, -2) four 20 mm M-2 cannon and same stores load. (-2P) only two 20 mm.
History: first flight (XF8F-1) 21 August 1944;

production F8F-1, November 1944; final delivery May 1949.

As a contrast to the big Hellcat and Corsair the Navy decided in 1943 to buy a lightweight fighter designed to the smallest size that would accommodate the R-2800 engine and specified fuel. The philosophy ran in parallel with that which produced the XP-51F and H Mustangs, except that the Navy bought a completely fresh design. Prototypes were ordered on 27 November 1943 and it took Grumman ten months to fly the first. In October 1944 Grumman were awarded a contract for 2,023, with Eastern Aircraft receiving an order for 1,876 designated F3M-1. Deliveries began on 1 December 1944 and VP-19 was almost combat-ready when the war ended. The F3M contract was cancelled, but Grumman retained a considerable order that was

Grumman F8F-1 Bearcat (2 F/B Wing, Royal Thai AF)

modified to introduce new versions. After delivering 765 F8F-1s Grumman built 100 -1Bs and 36 -1Ns with APS-6 radar, followed by 293 -2s with tall fin and 60 -2P photographic aircraft. US Navy front-line service petered out in 1951–52, but the Bearcat was one of the fastest and most manoeuvrable piston-engined aircraft ever built and attracted the interest of many air forces. More than 250 rebuilt versions, most of them F8F-1Ds with revised fuel system, served with the Armée de l'Air in Indo-China, the survivors being taken over by the Vietnamese Air Force (both North and South). Another big operator was Thailand, which received 29 -1Bs and 100 -1Ds. Several were modified for civilian racing in the United States, the hotted-up aircraft of Darryl Greenamyer setting the world speed record for non-jet aircraft at 482·5 mph in August 1969 (nowbeaten by a Sea Fury).

Grumman G-79 Panther and G-93 Cougar

F9F-1 to -5 Panther and -6 to -8 Cougar
Type: single-seat carrier-based fighter bomber; -P sub-types, photo reconnaissance; -8T, trainer.

Grumman F9F-4 Panther (VMF-334, US Marine Corps)

Engine: one single-shaft centrifugal turbojet of following types: (F9F-2) Pratt & Whitney J42-2 or -6 of 5,000 lb (2270 kg) or J42-8 of 5,750 lb; (-5) Pratt & Whitney J48-2, -6 or -8 of 7,000 lb (3175 kg) wet; (-6 and -8) J48-8 later uprated to 7,200 lb (3266 kg) wet; (-7) Allison J33-16A of 7,000 lb (3175 kg) wet.
Dimensions: span (-2, -5 excluding tip tanks) 38 ft (11·58 m); (-6, -8) 36 ft 4 in (11·1 m); length (-2) 37 ft 3 in; (-5) 38 ft 10 in (11·8 m); (-6, -8) 42 ft 7 in (13 m); (-8T) 45 ft 5 in (13·95 m); height (-2) 11 ft 4 in; (-5) 12 ft 3 in (3·72 m); (-8) 15 ft (4·57 m).
Weights: empty (-2) about 11,000 lb (4990 kg); (-5) 10,147 lb (4607 kg); (-8) about 13,000 lb (4897 kg); loaded (-2) 19,494 lb (8840 kg); (-5) 18,721 lb (8490 kg); (-8) 20,000 lb (9072 kg).
Performance: maximum speed (-2) 526 mph (849 km/h); (-5) 579 mph (931 km/h); (-8) 690 mph (1110 km/h); initial climb (-2) 5,000 ft (1524 m)/min; (-8) 6,100 ft (1860 m)/min; service ceiling (-2) 44,600 ft (13,600 m); (-5) 42,800 ft (13,060 m); (-8) 50,000 ft (15,240 m); range with external fuel (-2) 1,353 miles. (-5) 1,300 miles (2092 km); (-8) 1,000 miles (1610 km).
Armament: all versions except -P photo and -8T trainer, four 20 mm M-2 cannon; underwing pylons for up to 2,000 lb (907 kg) external load (-8, 4,000 lb).
History: first flight (XF9F-2) 24 November 1947; production (-2), 24 November 1948; (XF9F-6 Cougar) 20 September 1951; (-8T) 4 April 1956; final delivery from new, October 1959.

Grumman's first venture into jet propulsion was the G-70 anti-submarine aircraft with a 1,600 lb Westing-

Grumman F9F-6 Cougar

house 19XB (J30) in the tail helping the Double Wasp in the nose. A few months later, in January 1945, work began on the G-79 night fighter, powered by four of the same small axial engines buried in the inner wing. The design was well advanced when it was ordered on 22 April 1946 as the XF9F-1 Panther. But the US Navy had noticed the promise of the British 5,000 lb Rolls-Royce Nene and imported two for testing at the Naval Air Materiel Center at Philadelphia. So well did the British engine perform that it was quickly adopted for many American aircraft and in May 1947 Pratt & Whitney took a licence and tooled up to make an Americanised version designated J42. This was substituted for the four J30s in the Grumman F9F-2, which first flew with one of the imported Nenes. Performance, manoeuvrability, handling and pilot view were excellent, and service entry with VF-51 in May 1949 was painless. Grumman built 567 of the -2, as well as 54 more converted from the -3, which was ordered with

the Allison J33 as insurance against failure of the J42. The J33 was also to have powered the -4, but these were completed as J48-powered -5s with longer fuselage and taller fin. About 100 of the 761 -5s were -5P reconnaissance machines. Panthers were the first Navy jets in action in Korea, on 6 August 1950, thereafter flying nearly half the Navy combat missions mainly in the ground attack role. The -6 Cougar introduced a swept wing of quite different profile, deliveries beginning in December 1951. The -6 and -6P had the J48 but the -7 finally used the J33 engine. The -8 had a broader cambered wing, longer fuselage and greater fuel capacity and many were -8P photo and -8T dual trainer versions. Total Cougar production was 1,985, bringing total Panther/Cougar numbers up to 3,367. After 1955 an increasing number of these fine fighters were converted as drones and for research, and in 1962 all surviving examples were given new designations in the F-9F to TF-9J series.

Grumman G-98 Tiger

F-11 (F11F) Tiger
Type: single-seat carrier-based fighter-bomber.
Engine: (F-11A) one 11,000 lb (4990 kg) thrust Wright J65-4 single-shaft turbojet with afterburner; (F11F-1F) one 15,000 lb (6804 kg) thrust General Electric J79-3A single-shaft turbojet with afterburner.
Dimensions: span 31 ft 7½ in (9·63 m); length 44 ft 11 in (13·7 m); height 13 ft 3 in (4·05 m).
Weights: empty (F-11A) 13,428 lb (6092 kg); loaded (F-11A) 22,160 lb (10,052 kg).
Performance: maximum speed (F-11A) 890 mph (1432 km/h); (F11F-1F) about 1,350 mph (2170 km/h, Mach 2·05); initial climb (F-11A) 18,000 ft (5500 m)/min; (F11F-1F) over 25,000 ft/min; service ceiling (F-11A) 50,500 ft (15,400 m); range (F-11A) 700 miles (1130 km).
Armament: four 20 mm cannon and four AIM-9C or similar Sidewinder air-to-air missiles.
History: first flight 30 July 1954; service delivery March 1957; final delivery December 1958.

Originally designated F9F-9 the Tiger was intended to be a further development of the Panther/Cougar family, but with the agreement of the Navy Bureau of Aeronautics the attempt was changed into a totally new

Grumman F-11A Tiger (VF-21)

design. One of the insistent cries heard during the Korean War was for fighters having higher combat performance to beat the MiG-15 and this exerted a major influence on American designers. Ed Heinemann produced the A-4 Skyhawk, Kelly Johnson the F-104 Starfighter and the Grumman fighter team the G-98. It was an outstandingly attractive little design and it took shape very fast. The Navy contract for six development aircraft was placed on 27 April 1953 and first flight followed 15 months later. The timing was exactly right for the Tiger to incorporate the NACA Area Rule for minimum transonic and supersonic drag and as a result the body was waisted to allow for the volume of the wing. The latter was only 6½% thick, with full-span slats and flaps, long spoilers and skins

made from single slabs of light-alloy machined to shape. With the thrust of the J65 engine – the British Armstrong Siddeley Sapphire in an Americanised version – the Tiger was easily supersonic. It was also a delight to fly and altogether 201 production examples were delivered including 12 of the tandem dual trainer version. The superseded F9F-9 Navy designation was changed to F11F-1, the trainer being F11F-1T. In 1962 the designation was changed again to F-11A and F-11T. Tigers served in fighter/attack squadrons and also equipped the Navy Blue Angels aerobatic team. The much more powerful F11F-1F Super Tiger did not go into production, but one of the two built achieved fame by colliding from behind with 20 mm shells it had fired about a minute previously.

Grumman G-89 Tracker family

Grumman S-2E Tracker (VS-26, USS Randolph)

S-2A to -2E Tracker, DHC CS2F, C-1A Trader and E-1B Tracer
Type: (S-2) carrier ASW aircraft; (C-1) COD transport; (E-1) AEW aircraft.
Engines: two 1,525 hp Wright R-1820-82WA (early versions, -82) Cyclone nine-cylinder radials.
Dimensions: span (S-2A to -2C, C-1 and E-1) 69 ft 8 in (21·23 m); (S-2D to -2G) 72 ft 7 in (22·13 m); length (S-2A to -2C) 42 ft 3 in (12·88 m); (S-2D to -2G) 43 ft 6 in (13·26 m); height (S-2A to -2C) 16 ft 3½ in (4·96 m); (S-2D to -2G) 16 ft 7 in (5·06 m).
Weights: empty (S-2A) 17,357 lb (7873 kg); (S-2E) 18,750 lb (8505 kg); loaded (S-2A) 26,300 lb (11,929 kg); (S-2E) 29,150 lb (13,222 kg); (C-1A, E-1B) 27,000 lb (12,247 kg).
Performance: maximum speed (S-2A) 287 mph (462 km/h); (S-2E) 267 mph (430 km/h); (C-1A) 290 mph (467 km/h); initial climb (S-2A) 1,920 ft (586 m)/min; (S-2E) 1,390 ft (425 m)/min; service ceiling (S-2A) 23,000 ft (7010 m); (S-2E) 21,000 ft (6400 m); range (S-2A) 900 miles (1448 km); (S-2E) 1,300 miles (2095 km).
Armament: weapon bay accommodates two electric acoustic-homing torpedoes, two Mk 101 depth bombs (some versions, one) or four 385 lb (175 kg) depth charges; six underwing pylons for 5 in rockets, Zuni rockets or 250 lb (113 kg) bombs, or for ferrying torpedoes (two on each wing); (S-2E) as above, with provision for Betty nuclear depth charge, AS.12 or other guided missiles and 7·62 mm Miniguns; (C-1 and E-1) no armament.
History: first flight (XS2F-1) 4 December 1952; production S2F-1 (S-2A) 30 April 1953; combat service February 1954; final delivery February 1968.

This very ordinary-looking piston aircraft entered a world of advanced gas-turbine machines and has outlasted nearly all of them. It stemmed from the belief that an aircraft compatible with carrier operation could be made to combine the two roles of anti-submarine warfare (ASW) search and strike, previously accomplished by one aircraft equipped with sensors and another equipped with weapons. Grumman developed the Tracker extremely rapidly, despite the need to package an extraordinary diversity of equipment into a small space. Its low-speed handling stemmed from the long span, with almost full-span slotted flaps and fixed slots on the outer folding wings. In the nose were seats for pilot, co-pilot/navigator and two radar plotters. In the S-2A (formerly S2F-1) the radar was the APS-38, in a retractable ventral bin. A magnetic anomaly detector (MAD) boom extended behind the tail, an upper search radar had its scanner above the cockpit, a 70 million candlepower searchlight was hung under the right wing and the engine nacelles were full of sonobuoys ejected through tubes to the rear. The TS-2A was an ASW trainer and the CS2F-1 and -2 were built by de Havilland Canada. The S-2B was equipped with the Julie acoustic (explosive) echo-ranger and associated Jezebel passive acoustic sensor. The S-2C had a bulged asymmetric weapon bay and larger tail, most being converted into US-2C utility or RS 2C photo aircraft. The S-2D, ordered in 1958, was physically larger, with improved accommodation and equipment. The S-2E incorporated further new equipment. The total of these versions was 1,281, including 100 Canadian-built, and several hundred have been modified to the S-2F and G versions for service until

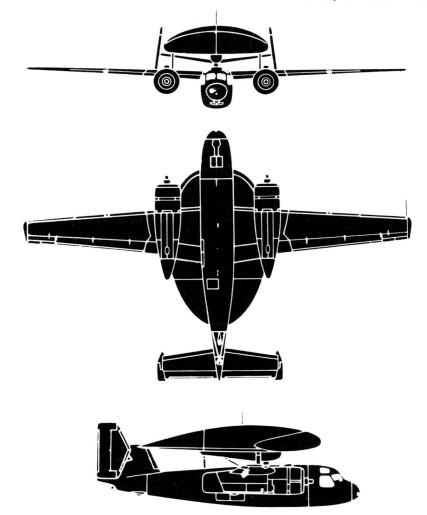

Grumman E-1B Tracer

late 1976 with many of the 12 countries that have used Trackers. The C-1A is a nine-passenger carrier onboard delivery transport, and the E-1B is an airborne

early warning machine with a huge teardrop-shaped radome above a C-1 size fuselage, with a three-finned tail.

Grumman G-134 Mohawk

OV-1A to -1D Mohawk
Type: multi-sensor tactical observation and reconnaissance.
Engines: two 1,005 shp Lycoming T53-7 or -15 free-turbine turboprops; (OV-1D) two 1,160 shp T53-701.
Dimensions: span (-1A, -C) 42 ft (12·8 m); (-1B, -D) 48 ft (14·63 m); length 41 ft (12·5 m); (-1D with SLAR, 44 ft 11 in); height 12 ft 8 in (3·86 m).
Weights: empty (-1A) 9,937 lb (4507 kg); (-1B) 11,067 lb (5020 kg); (-1C) 10,400 lb (4717 kg); (-1D) 12,054 lb (5467 kg); maximum loaded (-1A) 15,031 lb (6818 kg); (-1B, C) 19,230 lb (8722 kg); (-1D) 18,109 lb (8214 kg).
Performance: maximum speed (all) 297–310 mph (480–500 km/h); initial climb (-1A) 2,950 ft (900 m)/min; (-1B) 2,250 ft (716 m)/min; (-1C) 2,670 ft (814 m)/min; (-1D) 3,618 ft (1103 m)/min; service ceiling (all) 28,000–31,000 ft (8534–9449 m); range with external fuel (-1A) 1,410 miles (2270 km); (-1B) 1,230 miles (1980 km); (-1C) 1,330 miles (2140 km); (-1D) 1,011 miles (1627 km).
Armament: not normally fitted, but in South East Asia the 1A, -1B and -1C all operated with a wide variety of air-to-ground weapons including grenade launchers, Minigun pods and small guided missiles.
History: first flight (YOV-1A) 14 April 1959; service delivery, February 1961; final delivery December 1970.

Representing a unique class of military aircraft, the OV-1 Mohawk is a specially designed battlefield surveillance machine with characteristics roughly mid-

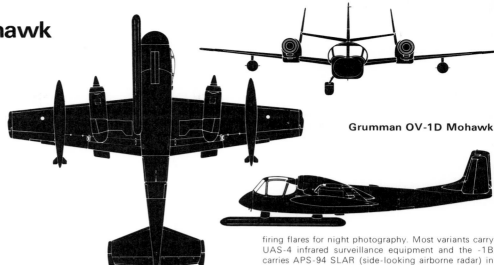

Grumman OV-1D Mohawk

way between lightplanes and jet fighters. One of its requirements was to operate from rough forward airstrips and it has exceptional STOL (short takeoff and landing) qualities and good low-speed control with full-span slats and triple fins and rudders. Pilot and observer sit in side-by-side Martin-Baker J5 seats and all versions have extremely good all-round view and very comprehensive navigation and communications equipment. All versions carry cameras and upward-firing flares for night photography. Most variants carry UAS-4 infrared surveillance equipment and the -1B carries APS-94 SLAR (side-looking airborne radar) in a long pod under the right side of the fuselage, with automatic film processing giving, within seconds of exposure, a permanent film record of radar image on either side of the flight path. The -1D combined the functions of the two previous versions in being quickly convertible to either IR or SLAR missions. Underwing pylons can carry 150 US gal drop tanks, ECM (electronic countermeasures) pods, flare/chaff dispensers, or a wide range of tactical weapons. More than 375 Mohawks were delivered, all to the US Army.

Grumman Hawkeye

E-2A, B and C Hawkeye and C-2A Greyhound
Type: E-2 series, AEW aircraft; C-2, COD transport.
Engines: two 4,050 ehp Allison T56-8/8A single-shaft turboprops.
Dimensions: span 80 ft 7 in (24·56 m); length 57 ft 7 in (17·55 m); (C-2A) 56 ft 8 in; height (E-2) 18 ft 4 in (5·59 m); (C-2) 15 ft 11 in (4·85 m).
Weights: empty (E-2C) 37,616 lb (17,062 kg); (C-2A) 31,154 lb (14,131 kg); loaded (E-2C) 51,569 lb (23,391 kg); (C-2A) 54,830 lb (24,870 kg).
Performance: maximum speed (E-2C) 374 mph (602 km/h); (C-2A) 352 mph (567 km/h); initial climb (C-2A) 2,330 ft (710 m)/min; service ceiling (both) about 28,500 ft (8650 m); range (both) about 1,700 miles (2736 km).
Armament: none.
History: first flight (W2F-1) 21 October 1960; (production E-2A) 19 April 1961; (E-2B) 20 February 1969; (E-2C) 20 January 1971; (C-2A) 18 November 1964; final delivery, early 1976.

Originally designated W2F-1, the E-2A Hawkeye was the first aircraft designed from scratch as an airborne early-warning surveillance platform (all previous AEW machines being modifications of existing types). Equipped with an APS-96 long-range radar with scanner rotating six times per minute inside a 24 ft-diameter radome, the E-2A has a flight crew of two and

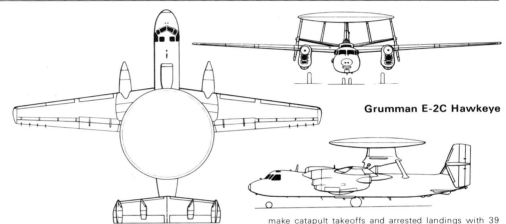

Grumman E-2C Hawkeye

three controllers seated aft in the Airborne Tactical Data System (ATDS) compartment, which is constantly linked with the Naval Tactical Data System (NTDS) in Fleet HQ or the appropriate land base. The E-2A can handle an entire air situation and direct all friendly air operations in attacking or defensive missions. From the E-2A were derived the E-2B, with microelectronic computer, and the C-2A Greyhound COD (carrier on-board delivery) transport, able to make catapult takeoffs and arrested landings with 39 passengers or bulky freight. The final version was the dramatically new E-2C, with APS-120 radar and APA-171 aerial system, with OL-93 radar data processor serving a Combat Information Center (CIC) staff with complete knowledge of all airborne targets even in a land-clutter environment. Though it has an advanced and costly airframe, more than three-quarters of the price of an E-2C is accounted for by electronics. This version entered service with squadron VAW-123 at NAS Norfolk, Virginia, in November 1973.

Grumman Intruder and Prowler

A-6A to A-6E Intruder and EA-6B Prowler
Type: (A-6A, B, C, E) two-seat carrier-based all-weather attack; (EA-6A) two-seat ECM/attack; (EA-6B) four-seat ECM; (KA-6D) two-seat air-refuelling tanker.
Engines: (except EA-6B) two 9,300 lb (4218 kg) thrust Pratt & Whitney J52-8A two-shaft turbojets; (EA-6B) two 11,200 lb (5080 kg) J52-408.
Dimensions: span 53 ft (16·15 m); length (except EA-6B) 54 ft 7 in (16·64 m); (EA-6B) 59 ft 5 in (18·11 m); height (A-6A, A-6C, KA-6D) 15 ft 7 in (4·75 m); (A-6E, EA-6A and B) 16 ft 3 in (4·95 m).
Weights: empty (A-6A) 25,684 lb (11,650 kg); (EA-6A) 27,769 lb (12,596 kg); (EA-6B) 34,581 lb (15,686 kg); (A-6E) 25,630 lb (11,625 kg); maximum loaded (A-6A and E) 60,626 lb (27,500 kg); (EA-6A) 56,500 lb (25,628 kg); (EA-6B) 58,500 lb (26,535 kg).
Performance: maximum speed (clean A-6A) 685 mph (1102 km/h) at sea level or 625 mph (1006 km/h, Mach 0·94) at height; (EA-6A) over 630 mph; (EA-6B) 599 mph at sea level; (A-6E) 648 mph (1043 km/h) at sea level; initial climb (A-6E, clean) 8,600 ft (2621 m)/min; service ceiling (A-6A) 41,660 ft (12,700 m); (A-6E) 44,600 ft (13,595 m); (EA-6B) 39,000 ft (11,582 m); range with full combat load (A-6A) 1,077 miles (1733 km); ferry range with external fuel (all) about 3,100 miles (4890 km).
Armament: all attack versions, including EA-6A, five stores locations each rated at 3,600 lb (1633 kg) with maximum total load of 15,000 lb (6804 kg); typical load 30 500 lb (227 kg) bombs; (EA-6B, KA-6D) none.

Grumman A-6A Intruder (VA-42)

History: first flight (YA2F-1) 19 April 1960; service acceptance of A-6A 1 February 1963; first flight (EA-6A) 1963; (KA-6D) 23 May 1966; (EA-6B) 25 May 1968; (A-6E) 27 February 1970; final delivery 1975.

Selected from 11 competing designs in December 1957, the Intruder was specifically planned for first-pass blind attack on point surface targets at night or in any weather. Though area ruled, the aircraft (originally designated A2F) was designed to be subsonic and is powered by two straight turbojets which in the original design were arranged with tilting jetpipes to help give lift for STOL (short takeoff and landing). Despite its considerable gross weight – much more than twice the empty weight and heavier than most of the heavy World War II four-engine bombers – the Intruder has excellent slow-flying qualities with full-span slats and flaps. The crew sit side-by-side under a broad sliding canopy giving a marvellous view in all directions, the navigator having control of the extremely comprehensive navigation, radar and attack systems which are integrated into DIANE (Digital Integrated Attack Navigation Equipment). In Vietnam the A-6A worked round the clock making pinpoint attacks which could not be accurately bombed by any other aircraft until the arrival of the F-111. The A-6E introduced a new multi-mode radar and computer and supplanted earlier versions in Navy and Marine Corps squadrons. The EA-6B introduced a valuable group of ECM (electronic countermeasures), while retaining partial attack capability, but the extraordinary EA-6B is a totally redesigned four-seat aircraft where the entire payload comprises the most advanced and comprehensive ECM equipment ever fitted to a tactical aircraft, part of it being carried in four external pods with windmill generators to supply electric power. The latest addition to attack versions was TRAM (Target Recognition Attack Multisensor), a turreted electro-optical/infrared system matched with laser-guided weapons.

Gruman Tomcat

F-14A, B and C
Type: two-seat carrier-based multi-role fighter.
Engines: (F-14A) two 20,900 lb (9480 kg) thrust
Pratt & Whitney TF30-412A two-shaft afterburning
turbofans; (B and C) two 28,090 lb (12,741 kg) thrust
Pratt & Whitney F401-400 two-shaft afterburning
turbofans.
Dimensions: span (68° sweep) 38 ft 2 in (11·63 m),
(20° sweep) 64 ft 1½ in (19·54 m); length 61 ft 2 in
(18·89 m); height 16 ft (4·88 m).
Weights: empty 37,500 lb (17,010 kg); loaded
(fighter mission) 55,000 lb (24,948 kg), (maximum)
72,000 lb (32,658 kg).
Performance: maximum speed, 1,564 mph (2517 km/
h, Mach 2·34) at height, 910 mph (1470 km/h, Mach
1·2) at sea level; initial climb at normal gross weight,
over 30,000 ft (9144 m)/min; service ceiling over
56,000 ft (17,070 m); range (fighter with external
fuel) about 2,000 miles (3200 km).
Armament: one 20 mm M61-A1 multi-barrel cannon
in fuselage; four AIM-7 Sparrow and four or eight
AIM-9 Sidewinder air-to-air missiles, or up to six
AIM-54 Phoenix and two AIM-9; maximum external
weapon load in surface attack role 14,500 lb (6577 kg).

History: first flight 21 December 1970; initial deployment with US Navy carriers October 1972; first
flight of F-14B 12 September 1973.

When Congress finally halted development of the
compromised F-111B version of the TFX in mid-1968
Gruman was already well advanced with the project
design of a replacement. After a competition for the
VFX requirement Gruman was awarded a contract
for the F-14 in January 1969. The company had to
produce a detailed mock-up by May and build 12
development aircraft. Despite sudden loss of the first
aircraft on its second flight, due to total hydraulic
failure, the programme has been a complete technical
success and produced one of the world's outstanding
combat aircraft. Basic features include use of a variable-
sweep wing, to match the aircraft to the conflicting
needs of carrier compatibility, dogfighting and attack
on surface targets at low level; pilot and naval flight
officer (observer) in tandem; an extremely advanced
airframe, with tailplane skins of boron-epoxy composite
and similar novel constructional methods, and one
canted vertical tail above each engine; and the
extremely powerful Hughes AWG-9 radar which, used

in conjunction with the Phoenix missile (carried by no
other combat aircraft) can pick out and destroy a
chosen aircraft from a formation at a distance of over
100 miles. For close-in fighting the gun is used in
conjunction with snap-shoot missiles, with the
tremendous advantage that, as a launch platform, the
Tomcat is unsurpassed (Gruman claim it to be unrivalled, and to be able — by automatic variation of
wing sweep — to outmanoeuvre all previous combat
aircraft). Introduction to the US Navy has been
smooth and enthusiastic, with VF-1 and -2 serving
aboard *Enterprise* in 1974. The export appeal of the
F-14 is obvious and Iran is introducing 80 from 1976.
But costs have run well beyond prediction, Gruman
refusing at one time to continue the programme and
claiming its existing contracts would result in a loss
of $105 million. For the same reason the re-engined
F-14B has been held to a single aircraft, while the
F-14C, with new avionics and weapons, remains a
paper programme. In 1975 all production was of the
F-14A, with total orders (including Iran) amounting to
414 aircraft. It is expected small further batches will
be bought for the US Navy annually.

For Halberstadt see p. 102.

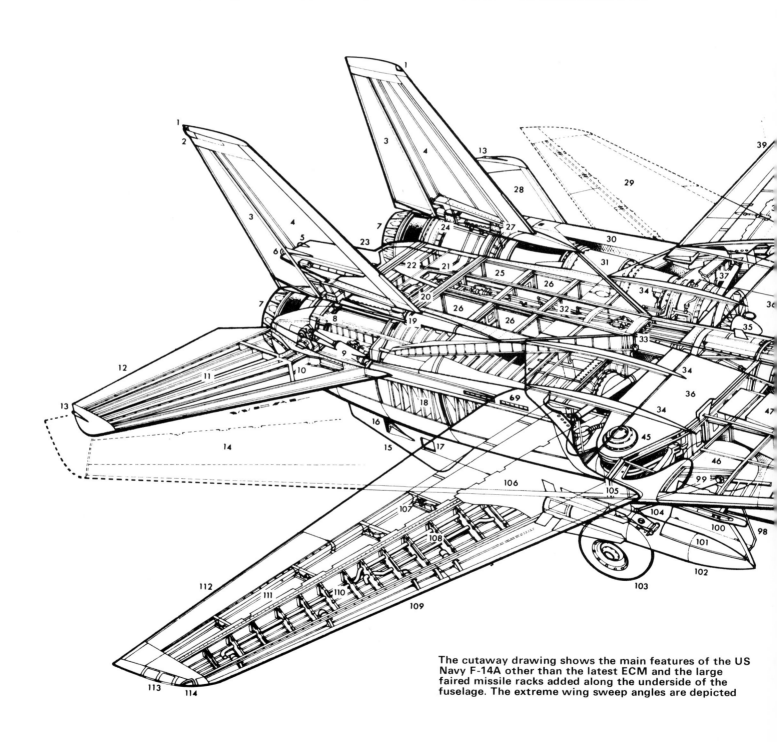

The cutaway drawing shows the main features of the US
Navy F-14A other than the latest ECM and the large
faired missile racks added along the underside of the
fuselage. The extreme wing sweep angles are depicted

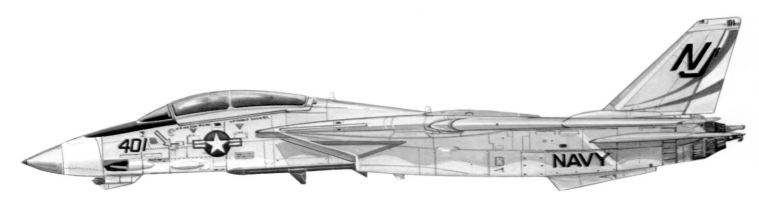

Grumman F-14A Tomcat (as originally delivered to VF-124 training and conversion squadron in 1972)

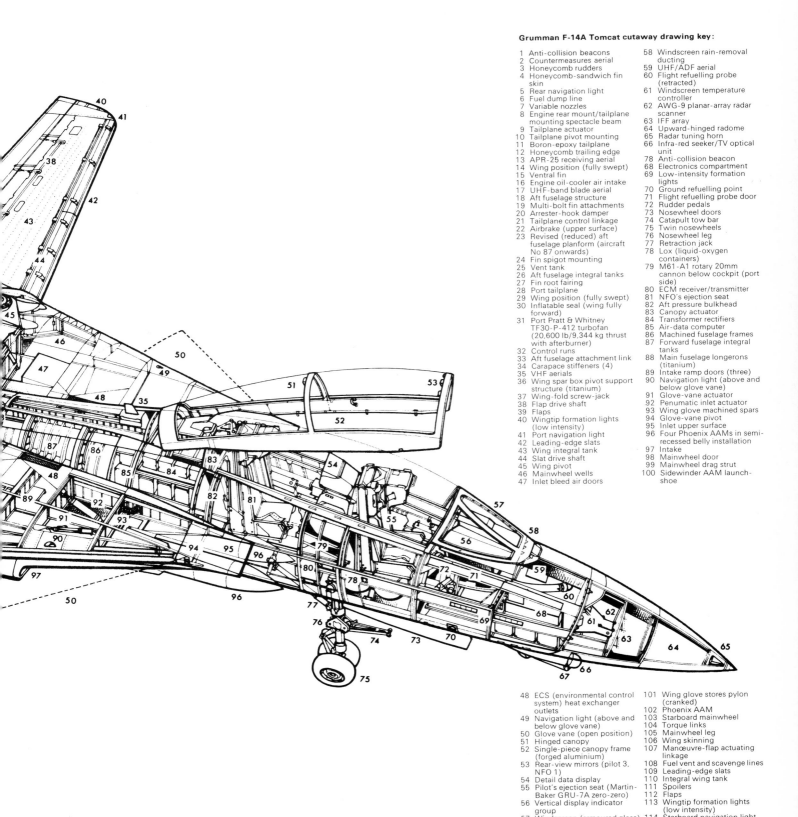

Grumman F-14A Tomcat cutaway drawing key:

1 Anti-collision beacons
2 Countermeasures aerial
3 Honeycomb rudders
4 Honeycomb-sandwich fin skin
5 Rear navigation light
6 Fuel dump line
7 Variable nozzles
8 Engine rear mount/tailplane mounting spectacle beam
9 Tailplane actuator
10 Tailplane pivot mounting
11 Boron-epoxy tailplane
12 Honeycomb trailing edge
13 APR-25 receiving aerial
14 Wing position (fully swept)
15 Ventral fin
16 Engine oil-cooler air intake
17 UHF-band blade aerial
18 Aft fuselage structure
19 Multi-bolt fin attachments
20 Arrester-hook damper
21 Tailplane control linkage
22 Airbrake (upper surface)
23 Revised (reduced) aft fuselage planform (aircraft No 87 onwards)
24 Fin spigot mounting
25 Vent tank
26 Aft fuselage integral tanks
27 Fin root fairing
28 Port tailplane
29 Wing position (fully swept)
30 Inflatable seal (wing fully forward)
31 Port Pratt & Whitney TF30-P-412 turbofan (20,600 lb/9,344 kg thrust with afterburner)
32 Control runs
33 Aft fuselage attachment link
34 Carapace stiffeners (4)
35 VHF aerials
36 Wing spar box pivot support structure (titanium)
37 Wing-fold screw-jack
38 Flap drive shaft
39 Flaps
40 Wingtip formation lights (low intensity)
41 Port navigation light
42 Leading-edge slats
43 Wing integral tank
44 Slat drive shaft
45 Wing pivot
46 Mainwheel wells
47 Inlet bleed air doors

58 Windscreen rain-removal ducting
59 UHF/ADF aerial
60 Flight refuelling probe (retracted)
61 Windscreen temperature controller
62 AWG-9 planar-array radar scanner
63 IFF array
64 Upward-hinged radome
65 Radar tuning horn
66 Infra-red seeker/TV optical unit
78 Anti-collision beacon
68 Electronics compartment
69 Low-intensity formation lights
70 Ground refuelling point
71 Flight refuelling probe door
72 Rudder pedals
73 Nosewheel doors
74 Catapult tow bar
75 Twin nosewheels
76 Nosewheel leg
77 Retraction jack
78 Lox (liquid-oxygen containers)
79 M61-A1 rotary 20mm cannon below cockpit (port side)
80 ECM receiver/transmitter
81 NFO's ejection seat
82 Aft pressure bulkhead
83 Canopy actuator
84 Transformer rectifiers
85 Air-data computer
86 Machined fuselage frames
87 Forward fuselage integral tanks
88 Main fuselage longerons (titanium)
89 Intake ramp doors (three)
90 Navigation light (above and below glove vane)
91 Glove-vane actuator
92 Penumatic inlet actuator
93 Wing glove machined spars
94 Glove-vane pivot
95 Inlet upper surface
96 Four Phoenix AAMs in semi-recessed belly installation
97 Intake
98 Mainwheel door
99 Mainwheel drag strut
100 Sidewinder AAM launch-shoe

48 ECS (environmental control system) heat exchanger outlets
49 Navigation light (above and below glove vane)
50 Glove vane (open position)
51 Hinged canopy
52 Single-piece canopy frame (forged aluminium)
53 Rear-view mirrors (pilot 3, NFO 1)
54 Detail data display
55 Pilot's ejection seat (Martin-Baker GRU-7A zero-zero)
56 Vertical display indicator group
57 Windscreen (armoured glass)

101 Wing glove stores pylon (cranked)
102 Phoenix AAM
103 Starboard mainwheel
104 Torque links
105 Mainwheel leg
106 Wing skinning
107 Manœuvre-flap actuating linkage
108 Fuel vent and scavenge lines
109 Leading-edge slats
110 Integral wing tank
111 Spoilers
112 Flaps
113 Wingtip formation lights (low intensity)
114 Starboard navigation light

Handley Page night bombers

H.P.11 O/100, H.P.12 O/400 and H.P.15 V/1500
Type: heavy night bomber, with normal crew of three.
Engines: (O/100) two 250 hp Rolls-Royce Eagle II vee-12 water-cooled (last six had 320 hp Sunbeam Cossack); (O/400) normally two 360 hp Rolls-Royce Eagle VIII, but alternatively two 350 hp Liberty 12-N, 260 hp Fiat A-12bis, 320 hp Sunbeam Cossack or 275 hp Sunbeam Maori; (V/1500) normally four 375 hp Rolls-Royce Eagle VIII, but alternatively four 450 hp Napier Lion or 500 hp Galloway Adriatic.
Dimensions: span (O/100, 400) 100 ft (30·48 m); (V/1500) 126 ft (38·4 m); length (O/100, 400) 62 ft 10¼ in (19·16 m); (V/1500) 62 ft (18·89 m); height (O/100, 400) 22 ft (6·7 m); (V/1500) 23 ft (7·01 m).
Weights: empty (O/100) 8,000 lb (3629 kg); (O/400) 8,502 lb (3857 kg); (V/1500) 16,210 lb (7352 kg); loaded (O/100) 14,000 lb (6350 kg); (O/400) 13,360 lb (6060 kg); (V/1500) 24,700 lb (11,200 kg).
Performance: maximum speed (O/100) 76 mph (122 km/h); (O/400, V/1500) 97 mph (156 km/h); service ceiling (O/100, 400) 8,500 ft (2590 m); (V/1500) 10,000 ft (3048 m); range with bomb load

Handley Page O/400 cutaway drawing key:

1 Twin 0·303in Lewis guns
2 Rotatable Scarff ring
3 Gunner's cockpit (plywood construction)
4 Folding seat
5 Slat flooring
6 Entry hatch to gunner's cockpit
7 ASI pitot tube
8 Negative lens
9 Rudder pedals
10 Control wheel
11 Clear Pyralin windshield
12 Padded cockpit coaming
13 Pilot's seat
14 Observer's seat
15 Slat flooring
16 Light-bomb rack (manual)
17 Batteries
18 Trap-type forward entry door
19 Fabric lacing
20 Transparent panel
21 Plywood turtle-deck
22 Aluminium fairing
23 Steel propeller hub
24 Brass tip sheathing
25 Four-blade walnut propeller
26 Radiator filler cap
27 Radiator
28 360 hp Rolls-Royce Eagle VIII twelve-cylinder engine
29 Exhaust manifold
30 Nacelle bracing strut/control spar
31 Oil tank (15 gal/68 litres) in each nacelle
32 Rigging lines
33 Streamlined steel struts
34 Double flying cable braces
35 Spruce/plywood inner strut
36 Double flying cable braces
37 Single landing cable brace
38 Single stagger cables
39 Spruce/plywood outer strut
40 Double flying braces
41 Outer aileron control horn
42 Cabane braces (four point)
43 Steel cabane
44 Inner aileron control horn
45 Solid end ribs
46 Wing dihedral break-line
47 Gravity-feed fuel tanks in leading edge (two, each 12 gal/54·5 litres)
48 Centre-section streamlined forward cabane strut
49 Centre-section streamlined aft cabane strut
50 Forward cylindrical fuel tank held by web straps (130 gal/591 litres)
51 Filler cap
52 Cross member
53 Engine control pulley cluster
54 Centre-section main bomb-bay
55 6V wind-driven generator (port and starboard on side of fuselage)
56 Perforated baffle plate
57 Air-driven fuel pumps
58 Aft fuel tank (130 gal/591 litres)
59 Solid rib at dihedral break-line
60 Upper gunner's seat
61 Transparent panels
62 Ammunition racks
63 Ventral gunner's hatch
64 Clear Pyralin panels
65 Gunner's slatted flooring
66 Plywood bulkheads

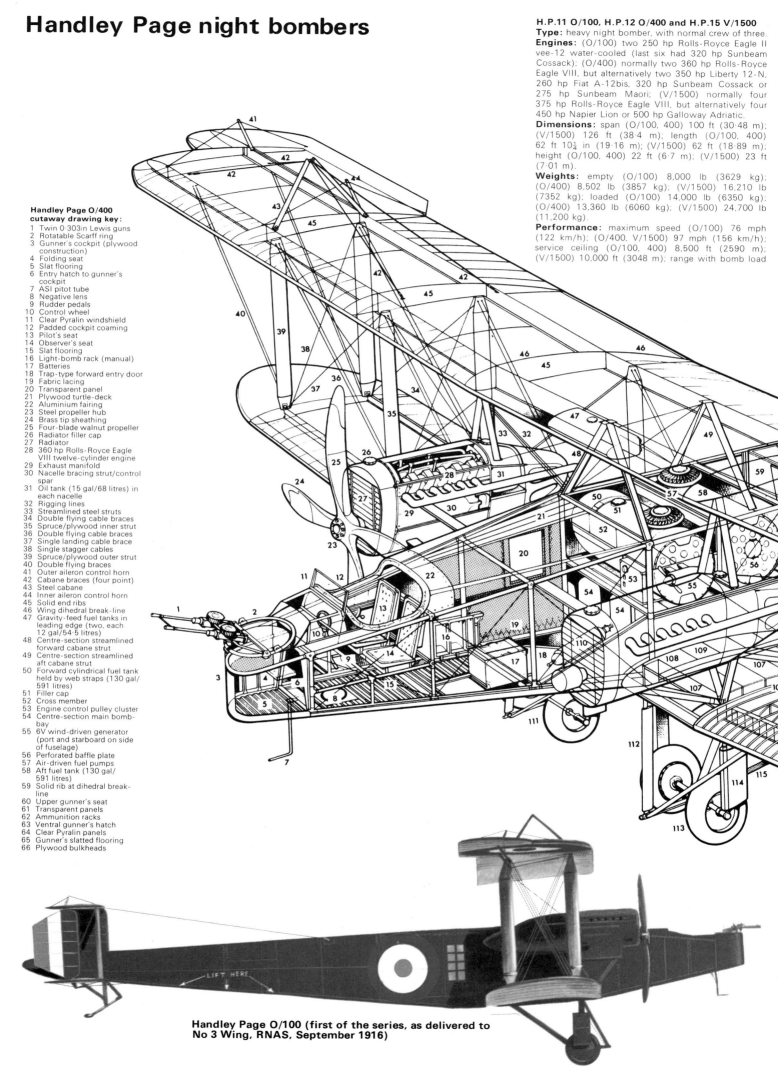

Handley Page O/100 (first of the series, as delivered to No 3 Wing, RNAS, September 1916)

(O/100) 450 miles (724 km); (O/400) 650 miles (1046 km); (V/1500) 1,200 miles (1931 km).

Armament: (O/100, 400) twin 0·303 in Lewis guns manually aimed in front cockpit and dorsal position, single Lewis aimed from rear ventral trap; internal bomb load of eight 250 lb (113 kg) or 16 112 lb bombs; V/1500, as before, with sixth Lewis aimed by gunner in extreme tail; internal bomb load of two 3,300 lb (1497 kg) or 30 250 lb bombs.

History: first flight (O/100) 18 December 1915; (production O/100) June 1916; (O/400) late 1916; (V/1500) May 1918.

In 1909 Frederick Handley Page opened at Barking the first factory in the world devoted exclusively to aircraft production (Short Brothers had started earlier but with balloons). He took up the challenge of the bold Admiralty O/100 specification of December 1914 to build a large bombing aircraft (at that time an unheard-of thing). He proposed to use two 120 hp Beardmore engines, but the dynamic head of the Air Department, Commodore Murray Sueter, communicated to "HP" his brimming enthusiasm for what he called "a bloody paralyser of an aeroplane", at which the constructor boldly scaled up his design and chose the more powerful new Rolls-Royce engine. The O/100 easily exceeded the specification and 46 were delivered to various Royal Naval Air Service squadrons on the Western Front, becoming operational in September 1916. A few caused a sensation when they began operations in Palestine and the Aegean Sea. In 1916 designer George Volkert modified the O/100 into the O/400, by moving the fuel tanks from the nacelles into the fuselage and fitting better engines. About 550 of these bombers — by far the best of World War I — were built in Britain, and 100 Liberty-engined examples were built in the USA out of 1,500 ordered in that country. Both types of Handley Page ended up as night bombers, the O/400 dropping one or two 1,650 lb (748 kg) bombs before the Armistice. The much bigger V/1500 was the first four-engined British production aircraft and the first truly strategic bomber in history. Designed to bomb Berlin from British bases, it had two push/pull double engine nacelles and, like its predecessors, folding wings to fit Bessonneau field hangars. Three were standing-by bombed-up when the Armistice was signed; contracts were then slashed, but about 33 were delivered and saw action on the North West frontier in 1919, remaining a standard RAF bomber until 1921.

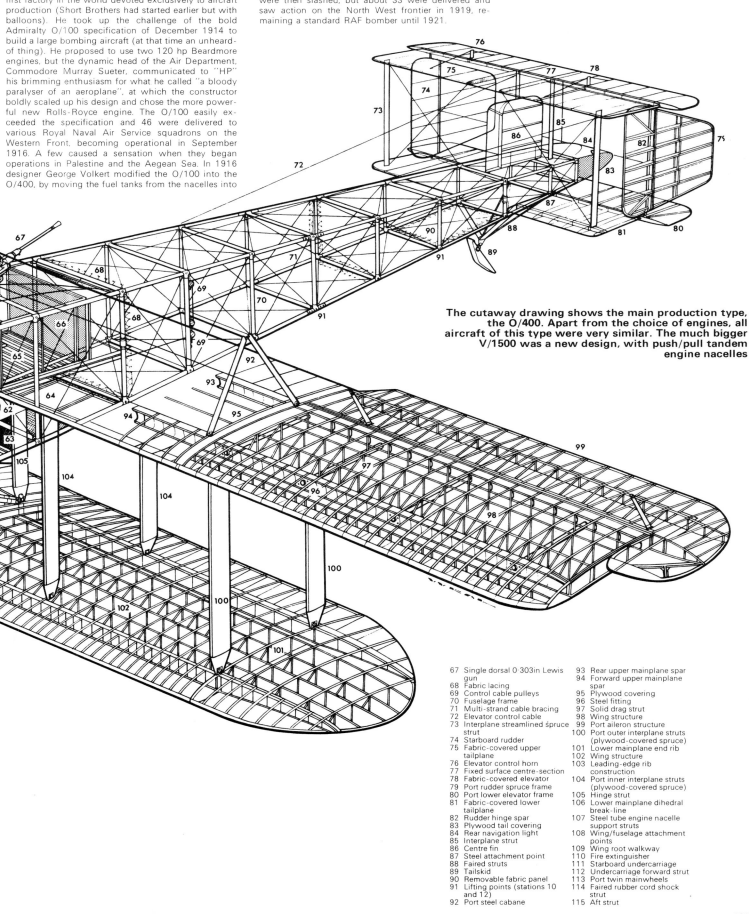

The cutaway drawing shows the main production type, the O/400. Apart from the choice of engines, all aircraft of this type were very similar. The much bigger V/1500 was a new design, with push/pull tandem engine nacelles

67 Single dorsal 0·303in Lewis gun
68 Fabric lacing
69 Control cable pulleys
70 Fuselage frame
71 Multi-strand cable bracing
72 Elevator control cable
73 Interplane streamlined spruce strut
74 Starboard rudder
75 Fabric-covered upper tailplane
76 Elevator control horn
77 Fixed surface centre-section
78 Fabric-covered elevator
79 Port rudder spruce frame
80 Port lower elevator frame
81 Fabric-covered lower tailplane
82 Rudder hinge spar
83 Plywood tail covering
84 Rear navigation light
85 Interplane strut
86 Centre fin
87 Steel attachment point
88 Faired struts
89 Tailskid
90 Removable fabric panel
91 Lifting points (stations 10 and 12)
92 Port steel cabane
93 Rear upper mainplane spar
94 Forward upper mainplane spar
95 Plywood covering
96 Steel fitting
97 Solid drag strut
98 Wing structure
99 Port aileron structure
100 Port outer interplane struts (plywood-covered spruce)
101 Lower mainplane end rib
102 Wing structure
103 Leading-edge rib construction
104 Port inner interplane struts (plywood-covered spruce)
105 Hinge strut
106 Lower mainplane dihedral break-line
107 Steel tube engine nacelle support struts
108 Wing/fuselage attachment points
109 Wing root walkway
110 Fire extinguisher
111 Starboard undercarriage
112 Undercarriage forward strut
113 Port twin mainwheels
114 Faired rubber cord shock strut
115 Aft strut

Halberstadt C, CL and D series

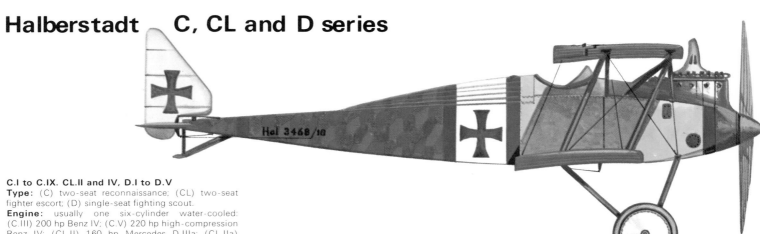

C.I to C.IX. CL.II and IV, D.I to D.V

Type: (C) two-seat reconnaissance; (CL) two-seat fighter escort; (D) single-seat fighting scout.

Engine: usually one six-cylinder water-cooled: (C.III) 200 hp Benz IV; (C.V) 220 hp high-compression Benz IV; (CL.II) 160 hp Mercedes D.IIIa; (CL.IIa) 185 hp BMW IIIa; (CL.IV, D.IIIa, D.I) 100 hp Mercedes D.I; (D.Ia, D.III) 120 hp Argus II; (D.IV) 150 hp Benz III; (D.V) Argus II; (D.II) 120 hp Mercedes D.II.

Dimensions: span (C.V) 44 ft 8½ in (13·62 m); (CL.II) 35 ft 4 in (10·77 m); (D.II) 28 ft 10½ in (8·8 m); length (C.V) 22 ft 8½ in (6·92 m); (CL.II, D.II) 23 ft 11½ in (7·3 m); height (C.V) 11 ft (3·35 m); (CL.II) 9 ft 0¼ in (2·75 m); (D.II) 8 ft 9 in (2·67 m).

Weights: empty (C.V) 2,205 lb (1000 kg); (CL.II) 2,100 lb (953 kg); (D.II) 1,213 lb (550 kg); loaded (C.V) 3,009 lb (1365 kg); (CL.II) 2,498 lb (1133 kg); (D.II) 1,609 lb (730 kg).

Performance: maximum speed (C V) 106 mph (170 km/h); (CL.II) 102½ mph (165 km/h); (D.II) 90 mph (145 km/h); service ceiling (D.V) 16,400 ft (5000 m); (CL.II) 16,732 ft (5100 m); (D.II) 13,123 ft (4000 m); range (C.V) 311 miles (500 km); (CL.II) 279 miles (450 km); (D.II) 124 miles (200 km).

Armament: (C.V) normally one 7·92 mm Spandau fixed in front fuselage, one 7·92 mm Parabellum manually aimed from rear cockpit; (CL.II) same, sometimes with twin fixed Spandaus, plus group of 22 lb (10 kg) mortar bombs or grenades in rear cockpit; (D.II) single fixed Spandau.

History: first flight (C.I) May 1916; (C.III) late 1917; (C.V) February 1918; (CL.II) about February 1917; (CL.IV) early 1918; (D.I) February 1916; (D.II) late 1916; (D.V) early 1917.

None of the products of the Halberstädter Flugzeugwerke was a world-beater, but together they made a significant contribution to the strength of the Central Powers. They also reveal the results of German design policy. The C family of reconnaissance machines were generally uninspired but serviceable machines, built in large numbers by several companies. The CL class of light two-seat escorts were quite modest aircraft,

Halberstadt D.II (of Jasta on Western Front)

which really found their niche when, during the grim Somme and Cambrai fighting of autumn 1917, they gave up escorting reconnaissance aircraft and took to ground strafing and close support. The little D series of scouts looked extremely frail but in fact were strong and manoeuvrable. Their poor speed, however, soon made them inferior to Allied fighters on the Western Front and by the spring of 1917 they were being transferred to Macedonia and Palestine.

Handley Page night bombers see pp. 100–101.

Handley Page Heyford

H.P.38 Heyford I and IA; H.P. 50 II and III

Type: four-seat heavy bomber.

Engines: two Rolls-Royce Kestrel vee-12 water-cooled; (I) 550 hp Kestrel II; (IA) 525 hp Kestrel IIIS; (II, III) 640 hp Kestrel VI.

Dimensions: span 75 ft (22·86 m); length 58 ft (17·68 m); height 17 ft 6 in (5·35 m).

Weights: empty 9,200 lb (4173 kg); loaded 16,900 lb (7665 kg).

Performance: maximum speed 142 mph (230 km/h); initial climb 700 ft (213 m)/min; service ceiling 21,000 ft (6400 m); range with half bomb load 920 miles (1481 km).

Armament: three 0·303 in Lewis manually aimed from nose, dorsal cockpit and retractable ventral bin; bomb load up to 3,500 lb (1588 kg) carried in thick centre section of lower wing.

History: first flight (prototype H.P.38) June 1930; (production H.P.38 Mk I) June 1933; final delivery July 1936; withdrawal from Bomber Command, mid-1939.

Throughout the 1920s Handley Page provided the RAF with a series of excellent biplane bomber and transport aircraft which followed naturally from the pioneer giants of World War I. The Heyford, the last RAF biplane attack aircraft, marked a complete break. It was smaller, had streamlined liquid-cooled engines, spatted wheels and was intended to go almost 50 per cent faster. Most oddly, the slim body was attached to the upper wing and there was a large gap between it and the thick portion of lower wing between the wheels in which were the bomb cells. Designed

Handley Page Heyford IA (99 Sqn, Upper Heyford)

to Specification B.19/27, the same as the Fairey Hendon, the more conservative biplane was at first preferred and 124 were eventually delivered to revised Specifications 23/32 and 27/35. Differences between marks were small apart from the changed sub-type of engine, the final batch of Mk IIIs having four-blade propellers (all propellers in the RAF at this time being fixed-pitch). All Heyfords had their fabric doped in "night bomber green", and they were pleasant to fly and popular with the crews of the 11 squadrons which were equipped with the type. From 1937 this very characteristic aircraft began to be withdrawn from operational use to serve as a trainer and in early experiments with radar and other research programmes.

Handley Page Hampden

H.P.52 Hampden I and H.P.53 Hereford I

Type: four-seat bomber (Hampden, later torpedo bomber and minelayer).

Engines: (Hampden) two (1,000 hp Bristol Pegasus XVIII nine-cylinder radials; (Hereford) two 1,000 hp Napier Dagger VIII 24-cylinder H-type air-cooled.

Dimensions: span 69 ft 2 in (21·98 m); length 53 ft 7 in (16·33 m); height 14 ft 4 in (4·37 m).

Weights: empty (Hampden) 11,780 lb (5344 kg); (Hereford) 11,700 lb (5308 kg); loaded (Hampden) 18,756 lb (8508 kg); (Hereford) 16,000 lb (7257 kg).

Performance: maximum speed 254 mph (410 km/h); initial climb 980 ft (300 m)/min; service ceiling 19,000 ft (5790 m); range with maximum bomb load 1,095 miles (1762 km).

Armament: originally, one offensive 0·303 in Vickers fixed firing ahead, one 0·303 in Lewis manually aimed from nose by nav/bomb aimer, one Lewis manually aimed by wireless operator from upper rear position and one Lewis manually aimed by rear gunner; bomb load of 4,000 lb (1814 kg). By January 1940 both rear positions had twin 0·303 in Vickers K with increased field of fire. Hard points for two 500 lb bombs added below outer wings, provision for carrying mines or one 18 in torpedo internally.

History: first flight (H.P.52 prototype) 21 June 1936; (production Hampden I) May 1938; (Hereford I) December 1939; termination of production March 1942.

Handley Page Hampden I (44 Sqn, Waddington)

On paper the Hampden, the last of the monoplane bombers to enter RAF service during the Expansion Scheme of 1936–38, was a truly outstanding aircraft. The makers considered it so fast and manoeuvrable they called it "a fighting bomber" and gave the pilot a fixed gun. They judged the three movable guns gave complete all-round defence without the penalties of heavy turrets, and while the Hampden was almost the equal of the big Whitley and Wellington in range with heavy bomb load, it was much faster than either; it was almost as fast as the Blenheim, but carried twice the load twice as far (on only fractionally greater power). Thanks to its well flapped and slatted wing it could land as slowly as 73 mph. Designed to B.9/32, the prototype was angular but the production machine, to 30/36, looked very attractive and large orders were placed, eight squadrons being operational at the start

of World War II. Hampdens were busy in September 1939 raiding German naval installations and ships (bombing German land was forbidden), until the daylight formations encountered enemy fighters. Then casualties were so heavy the Hampden was taken off operations and re-equipped with much better armament and armour – and, more to the point, used only at night. Despite cramp and near-impossibility of getting from one crew position to another, the "Flying Suitcase" had a successful career bombing invasion barges in the summer of 1940, bombing German heartlands, minelaying and, finally, as a long-range torpedo bomber over the North Sea and northern Russia. Handley Page built 500, English Electric built 770 and Canadian Associated Aircraft 160. Short Brothers built 100 Herefords which never became operational; many were converted to Hampdens.

Handley Page Halifax

Handley Page Halifax III Srs.II (640 Sqn, Leconfield)

H.P.57 Halifax I, H.P.59 Mk II Series 1A, III, H.P.61 Mk V, B.VI and VII, C.VIII and A.IX

Type: seven-seat heavy bomber; later ECM platform, special transport and glider tug, cargo transport and paratroop carrier.

Engines: four Rolls-Royce Merlin vee-12 liquid-cooled or Bristol Hercules 14-cylinder two-row sleeve-valve radial (see text).

Dimensions: span (I to early III) 98 ft 10 in (30·12 m); (from later III) 104 ft 2 in (31·75 m); length (I, II, II Srs 1) 70 ft 1 in (21·36 m); (II Srs 1A onwards) 71 ft 7 in (21·82 m); height 20 ft 9 in (6·32 m).

Weights: empty (I Srs 1) 33,860 lb (15,359 kg); (II Srs 1A) 35,270 lb (16,000 kg); (VI) 39,000 lb (17,690 kg); loaded (I) 55,000 lb (24,948 kg); (I Srs 1) 58,000 lb (26,308 kg); (I Srs 2) 60,000 lb (27,216 kg); (II) 60,000 lb; (II Srs 1A) 63,000 lb (28,576 kg); (III) 65,000 lb (29,484 kg); (V) 60,000 lb; (VI) 68,000 lb (30,844 kg); (VII, VIII, IX) 65,000 lb.

Performance: maximum speed (I) 265 mph (426 km/h); (II) 270 mph (435 km/h); (III, VI) 312 mph (501 km/h); (V, VII, VIII, IX) 285 mph (460 km/h); initial climb (typical) 750 ft (229 m)/min; service ceiling, typically (Merlin) 22,800 ft (6950 m); (Hercules) 24,000 ft (7315 m); range with maximum load (I) 980 miles (1577 km); (II) 1,100 miles (1770 km); (III, VI) 1,260 miles (2030 km).

Armament: see text.

History: first flight (prototype) 25 October 1939; (production Mk I) 11 October 1940; squadron delivery 23 November 1940; first flight (production III) July 1943; final delivery 20 November 1946.

Though it never attained the limelight and glamour of its partner, the Lancaster, the "Halibag" made almost as great a contribution to Allied victory in World War II, and it did so in a far greater diversity of roles. Planned as a twin-Vulture bomber to Specification P.13/36 with a gross weight of 26,300 lb it grew to weigh 68,000 lb as a formidable weapon platform and transport that suffered from no vices once it had progressed through a succession of early changes. By far the biggest change, in the summer of 1937, was to switch from two Vultures to four Merlins (a godsend, as it turned out) and the first 100 H.P.57s were ordered on 3 September 1937. This version, the Mk I, had a 22 ft bomb bay and six bomb cells in the wing centre-section. Engines were 1,280 hp Merlin X and defensive armament comprised two 0·303 in Brownings in the nose turret, four in the tail turret and, usually, two in manual beam positions. The first squadron was No 35 at Linton on Ouse and the first mission Le Havre on the night of 11/12 March 1942. The I Srs 2 was stressed to 60,000 lb and the Srs 3 had more fuel. The Mk II had 1,390 hp Merlin XX and Hudson-type twin-0·303 in dorsal turret instead of beam guns. On the II Srs 1 Special the front and dorsal turrets and engine flame dampers were all removed to improve performance. The II Srs 1A introduced what became the standard nose, a clear Perspex moulding with manually aimed 0·303 in Vickers K, as well as the Defiant-type 4×0·303 in dorsal turret and 1,390 hp Merlin XXII. Later Srs 1A introduced larger fins which improved

bombing accuracy; one of these, with radome under the rear fuselage, was the first aircraft to use H S ground-mapping radar on active service. In November 1942 the GR.II Srs 1A entered service with Coastal Command, with 0·5 in nose gun, marine equipment and often four-blade propellers. The III overcame all the performance problems with 1,650 hp Hercules and DH Hydromatic propellers, later IIIs having the wings extended to rounded tips giving better field length, climb, ceiling and range. The IV (turbocharged Hercules) was not built. The V was a II Srs 2A with Dowty landing gear and hydraulics (Messier on other marks), used as a bomber, Coastal GR, ASW and meteorological aircraft. The VI was the definitive bomber, with 1,800 hp Hercules 100 and extra tankage and full tropical equipment. The VII was a VI using old Hercules XVI. The C.VIII was an unarmed transport with large quick-change 8,000 lb cargo pannier in place of the bomb bay and 11 passenger seats; it led to the post-war Halton civil transport. The A.IX carried 16 paratroops and associated cargo. The III, V, VII and IX served throughout Europe towing gliders and in other special operations, including air-dropping agents and arms to Resistance groups and carrying electronic countermeasures (ECM) with 100 Group. Total production amounted to 6,176, by H.P., English Electric, the London Aircraft Production Group, Fairey and Rootes. Final mission was by a GR.VI from Gibraltar in March 1952, the Armée de l'Air phasing out its B.VI at about the same time.

Handley Page Victor

H.P.80 Victor 1, 1A and 2

Type: (B.1, 1A and 2) five-seat strategic bomber; (K.1A and 2) four-seat air-refuelling tanker; (SR.2) strategic reconnaissance.

Engines: (1, 1A) four 11,000 lb (4990 kg) thrust Rolls-Royce (previously Armstrong Siddeley and then Bristol Siddeley) Sapphire 202 single-shaft turbojets; (2) four 17,500 lb (7938 kg) thrust Rolls-Royce Conway 103 two-shaft turbofans; (B.2R, SR.2, K.2) 20,600 lb (9344 kg) thrust Conway 201.

Dimensions: span (1) 110 ft (33·53 m); (2) 120 ft (36·58 m); length 114 ft 11 in (35·05 m); height (1) 28 ft 1½ in (8·59 m); (2) 30 ft 1½ in (9·2 m).

Weights: empty (1) 79,000 lb (35,834 kg); (2) 91,000 lb (41,277 kg); loaded (1) 180,000 lb (81,650 kg); (2) 233,000 lb (101,150 kg).

Performance: maximum speed (both) about 640 mph (1030 km/h, Mach 0·92) above 36,000 ft; service ceiling (1) 55,000 ft (16,764 m); (2) 60,000 ft (18,290 m); range (1) 2,700 miles (4345 km); (2) 4,600 miles (7400 km).

Armament: no defensive armament except ECM; internal weapon bay for various nuclear or conventional weapons, including 35 1,000 lb (454 kg) bombs; (B.2 and 2R) provision for launching one Blue Steel Mk 1 air-to-surface missile carried semi-externally beneath fuselage.

History: first flight (1) 24 December 1952; (production B.1) 1 February 1956; (2) 20 February 1959; (K.1A conversion) 28 April 1965; (K.2 conversion) 1 March 1972; final delivery of new aircraft 2 May 1963.

Designed to Specification B.35/46, the same as the Vulcan, the Handley Page H.P.80 was expected to fly so fast and high as to be virtually immune to interception. To achieve the highest cruising Mach number the wing was designed to what was called a "crescent" shape, with a sharply swept but thick inner section housing the buried engines and progressively less swept but thinner outer panels, the structure being largely of light-alloy double-skin sandwich with

Handley Page Victor B.2 (139 Sqn, with Blue Steel)

Victor B(SR).2 (with underwing tanks)

corrugated or honeycomb filling. As a technical achievement the aircraft was superb. Named Victor it was the third and last of the V-bombers to go into service with RAF Bomber Command in 1955-58, but it took so long to develop that, by the time it entered service, it could be intercepted by fighters or shot down by missiles and the number ordered was so small the cost was high. To offer better protection the B.1 was brought up to B.1A standard with much enhanced ECM and survivors of the 50 built were in 1965-67 converted as K.1A tankers. The much more

powerful B.2, with completely redesigned airframe and systems, offered a great increase in all-round performance, but at height was no less vulnerable in penetrating hostile airspace and by 1964 was consigned to the low-level role, carrying the big Blue Steel missile. Several of the 30 built were converted as SR.2 strategic reconnaissance photographic aircraft and in 1973-75 the final 20 were converted as three-point K.2 tankers. This work was done by Hawker Siddeley at Woodford, the old Handley Page firm having gone into liquidation in 1970.

Hannover CL.IIIa

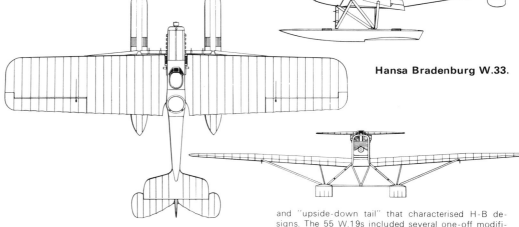

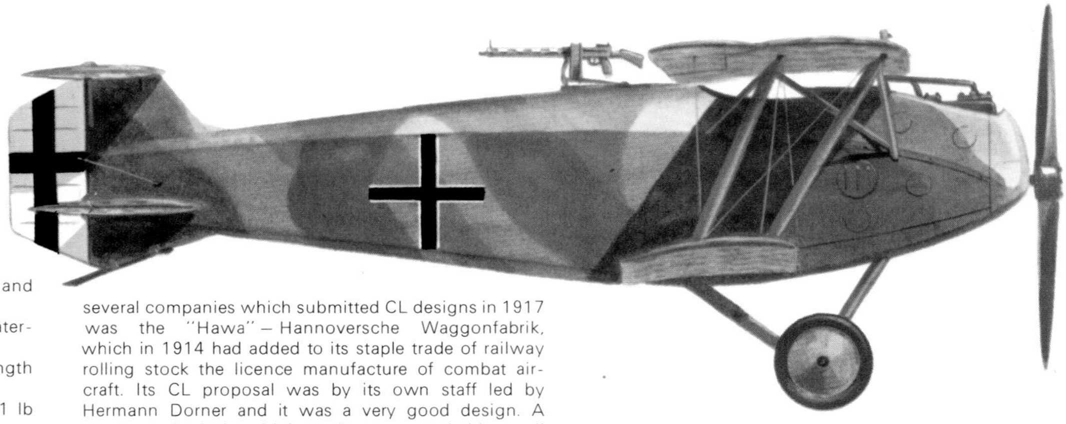

CL.II to V

Type: CL category of light two-seat fighter, escort and ground attack.

Engine: one 180 hp Argus As.III six-cylinder water-cooled; later models had other engines (see text).

Dimensions: span 38 ft 4¾ in (11·7 m); length 24 ft 10½ in (7·58 m); height 9 ft 2¼ in (2·8 m).

Weights: empty 1,764 lb (800 kg); loaded 2,381 lb (1080 kg).

Performance: maximum speed 103 mph (165 km/h); initial climb 460 ft (140 m)/min; service ceiling 24,610 ft (7500 m); endurance 3 hr, equivalent to about 270 miles (435 km).

Armament: one 7·92 mm Spandau fixed on upper centreline firing ahead, one 7·92 mm Parabellum manually aimed from rear cockpit; stick grenades or light bombs carried in rear cockpit.

History: first flight (CL.II) summer 1917; (CL.III) December 1917; (CL.IIIa) early 1918.

The CL category was originally intended to define two-seat fighters weighing not more than 750 kg (1,653 lb) empty, suitable for escort and ground attack. One of

several companies which submitted CL designs in 1917 was the "Hawa" – Hannoversche Waggonfabrik, which in 1914 had added to its staple trade of railway rolling stock the licence manufacture of combat aircraft. Its CL proposal was by its own staff led by Hermann Dorner and it was a very good design. A compact single-bay biplane, it was remarkably small (so that Allied pilots later mistook "Hannoveranas", as they were called, for single-seaters, until the observer opened fire on them) Designated CL.II, the first model was tough and manoeuvrable and at least 439 were delivered, entering service late in 1917. A unique feature was the biplane tail, which reduced the size of each tailplane and improved the observer's field of fire. The CL.II was succeeded by the CL.III, with 160 hp Mercedes, but because of demands for this engine for single-seaters, production was switched back to the As.III after 80 IIIs had been built, the only other obvious change in the III being extended overhung ailerons. The resulting IIIa was the main pro-

Hannover CL.IIIa (Imperial Military Aviation Service, three-colour irregular camouflage).

duction model, at least 537 being delivered. Many (possibly an additional quantity) were licence-built by L.F.G. (Roland) as CL.IIas. Small numbers were also made of the C.IV (not CL.IV), with bigger airframe and 245 hp Maybach IV, the CL.V with 185 hp BMW IIIa and several experimental III versions with different engines and/or extended wings.

Hansa-Brandenburg seaplanes

KDW, W.12, W.19, W.29 and W.33

Type: two-seat reconnaissance seaplane (KDW, single-seat).

Engine: (W.12, W.29) one 150 hp Benz III six-cylinder water-cooled (rarely, 160 hp Mercedes D.III); (W.19, W.33) one 245/260 hp Maybach Mb IV six-cylinder water-cooled.

Dimensions: span (KDW) 30 ft 4¼ in (9·23 m); (W.12) 36 ft 9 in (11.3 m); (W.19) 45 ft 3½ in (13·8 m); (W.29) 44 ft 3½ in (13·5 m); (W.33) 52 ft (15·85 m); length (KDW) 26 ft 3 in (8 m); (W.12) 31 ft 8 in (9·65 m); (W. 19) 35 ft (10·67 m); (W.29) 30 ft 9 in (9·4 m); (W.33) 36 ft 4 in (11·1 m); height (KDW, W.12) 10 ft 11 in (3·33 m); (W.19) 13 ft 5½ in (4·1 m); (W.29) 9 ft 10 in (3 m); (W.33) 11 ft 1 in (3·39 m).

Weights: empty (KDW) 1,763 lb (800 kg); (W.12, W.29) about 2,425 lb (1100 kg); (W.19, W.33) about 3,300 lb (1500 kg); loaded (KDW) 2,293 lb (1040 kg); (W.12) 3,230 lb (1465 kg); (W.19) 4,411 lb (2000 kg); (W.29) 3,243 lb (1471 kg); (W.33) 4,510 lb (2045 kg).

Performance: maximum speed (KDW) 106 mph (170 km/h); (W.12) 100 mph (161 km/h); (W.19) 94 mph (151 km/h); (W.29, W.33) 109 mph (175 km/h); service ceiling (KDW) 13,120 (4000 m); (W.12, W.19, W.29, W.33) all about 16,404 ft (5000 m); endurance 2 hr 30 min; (W.12) 3 hr 30 min, (W.19, W.33) 5 hr; (W.29) 4 hr 30 min.

Armament: (KDW) one (last 20 aircraft, two) 7·92 mm Spandau fixed firing ahead; (W.12, W.19, W.29, W.33) one or two fixed Spandaus and one 7·92 mm Parabellum manually aimed from rear cockpit (also see text).

History: first flight (KDW) summer 1916; (W.12) January 1917; (W.19) September 1917; (W.29) late 1917; (W.33) 1918.

Hansa Bradenburg W.33.

The Hansa und Brandenburgische Flugzeugwerke – whose chief designer was none other than Ernst Heinkel – was responsible for the most important family of German float seaplanes of World War I. The KDW (kampf doppeldecker, wasser or fighting biplane, water) was a small single-seater developed from the company's D.I landplane to fly coastal patrol missions along the Baltic, North Sea and Mediterranean shore. Only 58 were built, with Benz III, Mercedes or Maybach Mb III engines. The 146 W.12s were very active along the Flanders coast, one shooting down British airship C.27. Designed as a floatplane from the start, it introduced the upswept rear fuselage

and "upside-down tail" that characterised H-B designs. The 55 W.19s included several one-off modifications with different engines, one having a 20 mm Becker cannon in the rear cockpit. The monoplane W.29 was a classic design which set the pattern for the later Heinkel designs. Essentially a W.12 with new monoplane wing, the 78 delivered by the Armistice did well in combat from April 1918 and outperformed Allied aircraft (though, on one remarkable occasion, a large formation were beaten off by RAF Felixstowe boats, as described on p.77). The big W.33, of which only 26 were delivered before the Armistice, was likewise basically a monoplane W.19. After the war the W.29 was used by Denmark and the W.33 was built as the A-22 in Finland and also by Norway, until about 1926.

Hawker Hart family

Hart, and many variants

Type: Hart, two-seat day bomber; others, see text.

Engine: Hart, one 525 hp Rolls-Royce Kestrel IB; other types, see text.

Dimensions: span 37 ft 3 in (11·35 m); length 29 ft 4 in (8·93 m); height 10 ft 5 in (3·2 m).

Weights: (Hart) empty 2,530 lb (1148 kg); loaded 4,554 lb (2066 kg).

Performance: (Hart) maximum speed 184 mph (298 km/h); initial climb 1,200 ft (366 m)/min; service ceiling 21,320 ft (6500 m); range 470 miles (756 km).

Armament: one 0·303 in Vickers fixed in fuselage, one 0·303 in Lewis manually aimed from rear cockpit; bomb load up to 500 lb (227 kg) under lower wings.

History: first flight June 1928; other variants, see text.

Few aircraft have spawned so prolific a family as the prototype Hart, designed at Kingston by Sydney Camm in 1927 to meet RAF Specification 12/26. Beating the Fairey Fox and Avro Antelope, 15 development examples were followed by about 460 built by Hawker, Vickers, Gloster and Armstrong Whitworth, many being specially equipped for tropical or other specialised duties. About 90 more were exported, including four with Pegasus radial engine for Sweden where 42 more were built under licence. The Demon

was a two-seat fighter with fully supercharged 485 or 584 hp Kestrel, to Specification 15/30. Of 308 built, 234 were for the RAF, one having a "lobster back" hydraulic turret to shield the rear-seat gunner. The 71 Osprey two-seat fighters for the Fleet Air Arm had twin-float or wheel landing gear. The 47 Hardy general-purpose machines were specially equipped for remote regions, the 624 Audax army co-operation aircraft had special equipment, including a message pick-up hook, 65 of the 69 Hartbees for South Africa were built at Pretoria, and the final major model was the

Hawker Hart (aircraft of initial batch for 33 Sqn, shown after transfer to 57 Sqn).

Hind bomber of 1934. The RAF had 527 Hinds and over 130 were exported, some having Mercury, Pegasus or Gnome-Rhône radials. The RAF received 507 Hart Trainers, including 32 converted by Gloster from bombers, as well as 164 Hind Trainers including 139 conversions by General Aircraft. So different as to be really a new type, the 178 Hectors had straight wings and an 805 hp Napier Dagger engine; designed for army co-operation, most ended up towing gliders until late 1942. Total Hart-family production was 2,897 in Britain and about 270 overseas.

Hawker Fury (biplane)

Fury I and II
Type: single-seat interceptor.
Engine: (I) one 525 hp Rolls-Royce Kestrel IIS vee-12 water-cooled; (II) one 640 hp Kestrel VI.
Dimensions: span 30 ft (9·14 m); length 26 ft 8¾ in (4·3 m); height 10 ft 2 in (3·1 m).
Weights: empty (I) 2,623 lb (1190 kg); (II) 2,743 lb (1245 kg); loaded (I) 3,490 lb (1582 kg); (II) 3,609 lb (1637 kg).
Performance: maximum speed (I) 207 mph (333 km/h); (II) 223 mph (360 km/h); initial climb (I) 2,380 ft (727 m)/min; (II) 3,200 ft (975 m)/min; service ceiling (I) 28,000 ft (8534 m); (II) 29,500 ft (9000 m); range (I) 305 miles (490 km); (II) 260 miles (418 km).
Armament: two 0·303 in Vickers fixed above fuselage (Yugoslav Fury II, four guns, two in underwing fairings, each with 600 rounds).
History: first flight (I) 25 March 1931; (II) 3 December 1936.

The Fury epitomised the small biplane interceptor, sacrificing range and all-weather equipment for outstanding flight performance. Camm built a Mercury-engined interceptor to Specification F.20/27, followed with the Hornet with the new Rolls engine and saw the latter win over the Firefly IIM and go into production as the Fury for the RAF. It was a delight to fly, 30 mph faster than contemporary larger fighters and had outstanding climb. RAF production amounted to 117, completed in 1935; 30 were exported including 20 for Persia (Iran) with either Mercury or Hornet radial

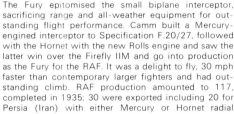

Hawker Fury I (1 Sqn, Tangmere).

The naval counterpart of the Fury was the Nimrod, designed for carrier service with the Fleet Air Arm (Nimrod of 2 Luftflotille, Royal Danish Naval Air Service)

engine. The more powerful Mk II of 1936 had spatted wheels and at low altitudes could outfly the Gauntlet (which was superior above about 7,000 ft). The RAF had 98, the last 75 built by General Aircraft. Export

versions for South Africa were similar, but Spanish Fury IIs had the Hispano 700 hp engine and the Yugoslav version had four guns, both variants having cantilever landing gear with Dowty sprung wheels like the Gladiator. Hawker also built an experimental High Speed Fury, with tapered wing, to explore fighter technology and test new engines and cooling systems (reaching just over 300 mph in one form).

Hurricane see p. 106.

Hawker Typhoon

Hawker Typhoon IB (198 Sqn, Martragny, France, July 1944).

Typhoon IA and IB
Type: single-seat fighter bomber.
Engine: (production IB) one 2,180 hp Napier Sabre II, 24-cylinder flat-H sleeve-valve liquid-cooled.
Dimensions: span 41 ft 7 in (12·67 m); length 31 ft 11 in (9·73 m); height 15 ft 3½ in (4·66 m).
Weights: empty 8,800 lb (3992 kg); loaded 13,250 lb (6010 kg).
Performance: maximum speed 412 mph (664 km/h); initial climb 3,000 ft (914 m)/min; service ceiling 35,200 ft (10,730 m); range (with bombs) 510 miles (821 km), (with drop tanks) 980 miles (1577 km).
Armament: (IA) 12 0·303 in Brownings (none delivered); (IB) four 20 mm Hispano cannon in outer wings, and racks for eight rockets or two 500 lb (227 kg) bombs.
History: first flight (Tornado) October 1939; (Typhoon) 24 February 1940; (production Typhoon) 27 May 1941; final delivery November 1945.

The Typhoon's early life was almost total disaster. Though the concept of so big and powerful a combat aircraft was bold and significant, expressed in Specification F.18/37, the Griffon and Centaurus engines were ignored and reliance was placed on the complex and untried Vulture and Sabre. The former powered the R-type fighter, later named Tornado, which ground to a halt with abandonment of the Vulture in early 1941. The N-type (Napier), named Typhoon, was held back six months by the desperate need for Hurricanes. Eventually, after most painful development, production began at Gloster Aircraft in 1941 and Nos 56 and 609 Sqns at Duxford began to re-equip with the big bluff-looking machine in September of that year. But the Sabre was unreliable, rate of climb and performance at height were disappointing and the rear fuselage persisted in coming apart. There was much talk of scrapping the programme, but, fortunately for

the Allies, the snags were gradually overcome. In November 1942 the Typhoon suddenly sprang to favour by demonstrating it could catch and destroy the fastest fighter-bombers in the Luftwaffe which were making low-level hit-and-run raids. In 1943 "Tiffy" squadrons shot-up and blasted everything that moved in northern France and the Low Countries, and in the summer of 1944 the hundreds of Typhoons — by now thoroughly proven and capable of round-the-clock operation from rough forward strips — formed the backbone of 2nd Tactical Air Force attack strength, sending millions of cannon shells, rockets and heavy bombs into German ground forces and in a single day knocking out 175 tanks in the Falaise gap. Gloster built 3,315 of the 3,330 Typhoons, the final 3,000-odd having a clear bubble hood instead of a heavy framed cockpit with a car-type door on each side.

Hawker Tempest

Tempest 2, 5 and 6
Type: single-seat fighter bomber.
Engine: (2) one 2,526 hp Bristol Centaurus 5 or 6 18-cylinder sleeve-valve two-row radial; (5) one 2,180 hp Napier Sabre II 24-cylinder flat-H sleeve-valve liquid-cooled; (6) one 2,340 hp Sabre V.
Dimensions: span 41 ft (12·5 m); length (2) 34 ft 5 in (10·5 m); (5, 6) 33 ft 8 in (10·26 m); height (2) 15 ft 10 in (4·8 m); (5, 6) 16 ft 1 in (4·9 m).
Weights: empty (2) 8,900 lb (4037 kg); (5, 6) 9,100 lb (4128 kg); loaded (2) 13,250 lb (6010 kg); (5, 6) 13,500 lb (6130 kg).
Performance: maximum speed (2) 440 mph (708 km/h); (5) 427 mph (688 km/h); (6) 438 mph (704 km/h); initial climb (2) 3,600 ft (1097 m)/min; (5, 6) 3,000 ft (914 m)/min; service ceiling, all about 37,000 ft (11,280 m); range (bombs, not tanks) (2) 820 miles (1319 km); (5, 6) 740 miles (1191 km).
Armament: four 20 mm Hispano cannon in outer wings; underwing racks for eight rockets or up to 2,000 lb (907 kg) bombs.
History: first flight (prototype Mk V) 2 September 1942; (Mk I) 24 February 1943; (production V) 21 June 1943; (Mk II) 28 June 1943; (prototype VI) 9 May 1944; (production II) 4 October 1944.

Hawker Tempest II (8 Sqn, Indian Air Force).

The Typhoon was noted for its thick wing — occasional erratic flight behaviour at high speeds was traced to compressibility (local airflow exceeding the speed of sound), which had never before been encountered. In 1940 Hawker schemed a new laminar-flow wing with a root thickness five inches less and an elliptic planform rather like a Spitfire. This was used on the Typhoon II, ordered in November 1941 to Specification F.10/41, but there were so many changes the fighter was renamed Tempest. Fuel had to be moved from the thinner wing to the fuselage, making the latter longer, and a dorsal fin was added. The short-barrel Mk V guns were buried in the wing. Though the new airframe could take the promising Centaurus engine it was the Sabre-engined Mk V that was produced first, reaching

the Newchurch Wing in time to destroy 638 out of the RAF's total of 1,771 flying bombs shot down in the summer of 1944. After building 800 Mk Vs Hawker turned out 142 of the more powerful Mk VI type with bigger radiator and oil coolers in the leading edge. After much delay, with production assigned first to Gloster and then to Bristol, the outstanding Mk II — much quieter and nicer to fly — entered service in November 1945. By this time production had returned to Hawker, who built 422 out of 472. Redesignated F.2 they survived until 1953, 89 being passed on to India and 24 being built new for Pakistan. A few Mks 5 and 6 (post-war designations) were converted as target tugs.

Hawker Hurricane

Hurricane I to XII, Sea Hurricane IA to XIIA

Type: single-seat fighter; later, fighter-bomber, tank buster and ship-based fighter.

Engine: one Rolls-Royce Merlin vee-12 liquid-cooled (see text for sub-types).

Dimensions: span 40 ft (12·19 m); length 32 ft (9·75 m); (Mk I) 31 ft 5 in; (Sea Hurricanes) 32 ft 3 in; height 13 ft 1 in (4 m).

Weights: empty (I) 4,670 lb (2118 kg); (IIA) 5,150 lb (2335 kg); (IIC) 5,640 lb (2558 kg); (IID) 5,800 lb (2631 ·kg); (IV) 5,550 lb (2515 kg); (Sea H.IIC) 5,788 lb (2625 kg); loaded (I) 6,600 lb (2994 kg); (IIA) 8,050 lb (3650 kg); (IIC) 8,250 lb (3742 kg); (IID) 8,200 lb (3719 kg); (IV) 8,450 lb (3832 kg); (Sea H. IIC) 8,100 lb (3674 kg).

Performance: maximum speed (I) 318 mph (511 km/h); (IIA, B, C) 345–335 mph (560–540 km/h); (IID) 286 mph (460 km/h); (IV) 330 mph (531 km/h); (Sea H. IIC) 342 mph (550 km/h); initial climb (I) 2,520 ft (770 m)/min; (IIA) 3,150 ft (960 m)/min; (rest, typical) 2,700 ft (825 m)/min; service ceiling (I) 36,000 ft (10,973 m); (IIA) 41,000 ft (12,500 m); (rest, typical) 34,000 ft (10,365 m); range (all, typical) 460 miles (740 km), or with two 44 Imp gal drop tanks 950 miles (1530 km).

Armament: (I) eight 0·303 in Brownings, each with 333 rounds; (IIA) same, with provision for 12 guns and two 250 lb bombs; (IIB) 12 Brownings and two 250 or 500 lb bombs; (IIC) four 20 mm Hispano cannon and bombs; (IID) two 40 mm Vickers S guns and two 0·303 in Brownings; (IV) universal wing with two Brownings and two Vickers S, two 500 lb bombs, eight rockets, smoke installation or other stores.

History: first flight (prototype) 6 November 1935; (production Mk I) 12 October 1937; (II) 11 June 1940; (Canadian Mk X) January 1940; final delivery September 1944.

Until well into 1941 the Hurricane was by far the most numerous of the RAF's combat aircraft and it bore the brunt of all the early combats with the Luftwaffe over France and Britain. Designed by Camm as a Fury Monoplane, with Goshawk engine and spatted landing gear, it was altered on the drawing board to have the more powerful PV.12 (Merlin) and inwards-retracting gear and, later, to have not four machine guns but the unprecedented total of eight. The Air Ministry wrote Specification F.36/34 around it and after tests with the prototype ordered the then-fantastic total of 600 in June 1936. In September 1939 the 497 delivered equipped 18 squadrons and by 7 August 1940 no fewer than 2,309 had been delivered, compared with 1,383 Spitfires, equipping 32 squadrons, compared with 18½ Spitfire squadrons. By this time the Hurricane I was in service with new metal-skinned wings, instead of fabric, and three-blade variable-pitch (later constant-speed) propeller instead of the wooden Watts two-blader. In the hectic days of 1940 the Hurricane was found to be an ideal bomber destroyer, with steady sighting and devastating cone of fire; turn radius was better than that of any other monoplane fighter, but the all-round performance of the Bf 109E was considerably higher. The more powerful Mk II replaced the 1,030 hp Merlin II by the 1,280 hp Merlin XX and introduced new armament and drop tanks. In North West Europe it became a ground-attack aircraft, and in North Africa a tank-buster with 40 mm guns. While operating from merchant-ship catapults and carriers it took part in countless fleet-defence actions, the greatest being the defence of the August 1942 Malta convoy, when 70 Sea Hurricanes fought off more than 600 Axis attackers, destroying 39 for the loss of seven fighters. The Hurricane was increasingly transferred to the Far East, Africa and other theatres, and 2,952 were dispatched to the Soviet Union, some receiving skis. Hurricanes were used for many special trials of armament and novel flight techniques (one having a jettisonable biplane upper wing). Total production amounted to 12,780 in Britain and 1,451 in Canada and many hundreds were exported both before and after World War II.

Typhoon and Tempest see page 105.

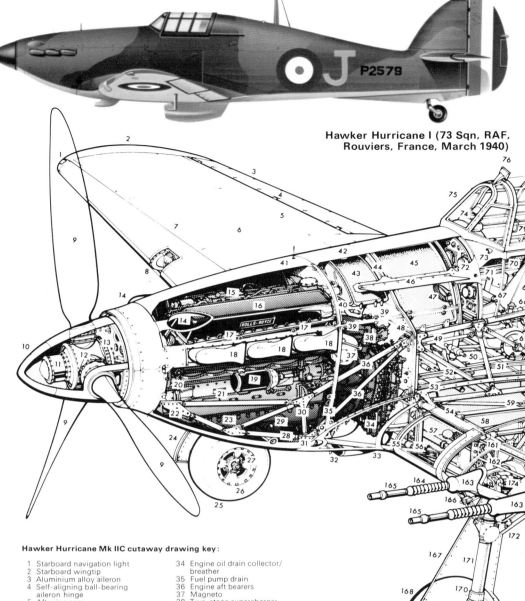

Hawker Hurricane I (73 Sqn, RAF, Rouviers, France, March 1940)

Hawker Hurricane Mk IIC cutaway drawing key:

1 Starboard navigation light
2 Starboard wingtip
3 Aluminium alloy aileron
4 Self-aligning ball-bearing aileron hinge
5 Aft wing spar
6 Aluminium alloy wing skinning (early Hurricanes, fabric)
7 Forward wing spar
8 Starboard landing light
9 Rotol or DH three-blade constant-speed propeller
10 Spinner
11 Propeller hub
12 Pitch-control mechanism
13 Spinner back plate
14 Cowling fairings
15 Coolant pipes
16 Rolls-Royce Merlin XX 12-cylinder engine, 1,185 hp
17 Cowling panel fasteners
18 'Fishtail' exhaust pipes
19 Electric generator
20 Engine forward mounting feet
21 Engine upper bearer tube
22 Engine forward mount
23 Engine lower bearer tubes
24 Starboard mainwheel fairing
25 Starboard mainwheel
26 Low pressure tyre
27 Brake drum (pneumatic brakes)
28 Hand-cranked inertia starter
29 Hydraulic system
30 Bearer joint
31 Auxiliary intake
32 Carburettor air intake
33 Wing root fillet
34 Engine oil drain collector/breather
35 Fuel pump drain
36 Engine aft bearers
37 Magneto
38 Two-stage supercharger
39 Cowling panel attachments
40 Engine tachometer
41 External bead sight
42 Removable aluminium alloy cowling panels
43 Engine coolant header tank
44 Engine firewall (armour-plated backing)
45 Fuselage (reserve) fuel tank (28 gal/127 litres)
46 Exhaust glare shield
47 Control column
48 Engine bearer attachment
49 Rudder pedals
50 Control linkage
51 Centre-section fuel tank (optional)
52 Oil system piping
53 Pneumatic system air cylinder
54 Wing centre-section/front spar girder construction
55 Engine bearer support strut
56 Oil tank (port wing root leading-edge)
57 Dowty undercarriage ram
58 Port undercarriage well
59 Wing centre-section girder frame
60 Pilot's oxygen cylinder
61 Elevator trim-tab control wheel
62 Radiator flap control lever
63 Entry footstep
64 Fuselage tubular framework
65 Landing lamp control lever
66 Oxygen supply cock
67 Throttle lever
68 Safety harness
69 Pilot's seat
70 Pilot's break-out exit panel
71 Map case
72 Instrument panel
73 Cockpit ventilation inlet
74 Reflector gunsight
75 Bullet-proof windscreen
76 Rear-view mirror
77 Rearward-sliding canopy
78 Canopy frames
79 Canopy handgrip
80 Perspex canopy panels
81 Head/back armour plate
82 Harness attachment
83 Aluminium alloy decking
84 Turnover reinforcement
85 Canopy track
86 Fuselage framework cross-bracing

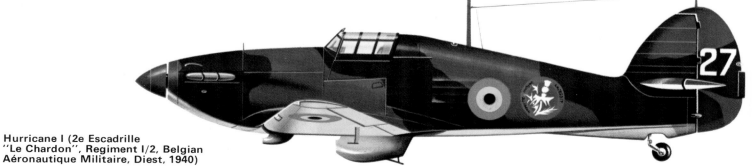

Hurricane I (2e Escadrille "Le Chardon", Regiment I/2, Belgian Aéronautique Militaire, Diest, 1940)

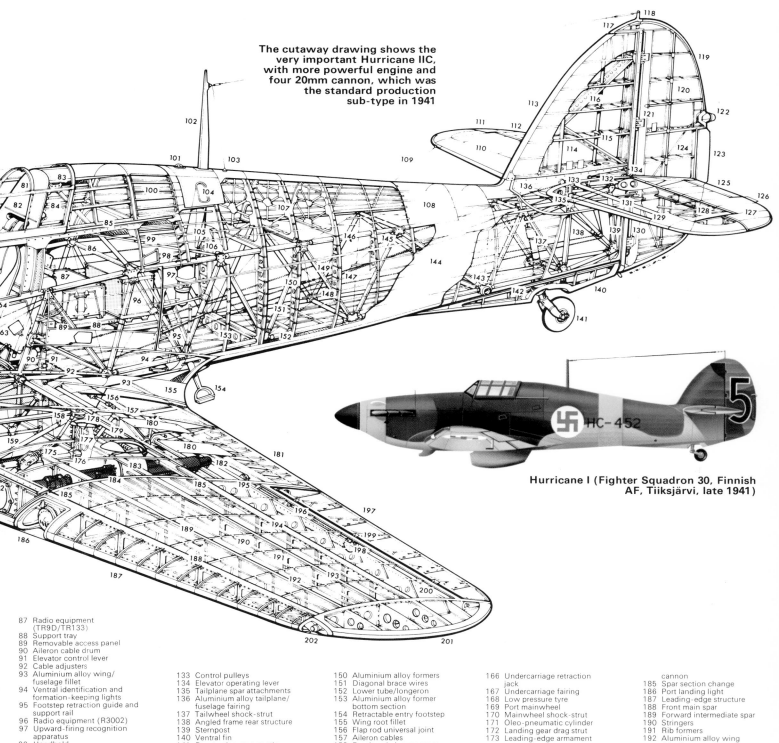

The cutaway drawing shows the very important Hurricane IIC, with more powerful engine and four 20mm cannon, which was the standard production sub-type in 1941

Hurricane I (Fighter Squadron 30, Finnish AF, Tiiksjärvi, late 1941)

87 Radio equipment (TR9D/TR133)
88 Support tray
89 Removable access panel
90 Aileron cable drum
91 Elevator control lever
92 Cable adjusters
93 Aluminium alloy wing/ fuselage fillet
94 Ventral identification and formation-keeping lights
95 Footstep retraction guide and support rail
96 Radio equipment (R3002)
97 Upward-firing recognition apparatus
98 Handhold
99 Diagonal support
100 Fuselage fairing
101 Dorsal identification light
102 Aerial mast
103 Aerial lead-in
104 Recognition apparatus cover panel
105 Mast support
106 Wire-braced upper truss
107 Wooden fuselage fairing formers
108 Fabric covering
109 Radio antenna
110 All-metal tailplane structure
111 Static and dynamic elevator balance
112 Starboard elevator
113 Light-alloy leading-edge
114 Fabric covering
115 Fin structure
116 Diagonal bracing struts
117 Built-in static balance
118 Aerial stub
119 Fabric-covered rudder
120 Rudder structure
121 Rudder post
122 Rear navigation light
123 Balanced rudder trim tab
124 Wiring
125 Elevator trim tab
126 Fixed balance tab
127 Fabric-covered elevator
128 Tailplane rear spar
129 Tailplane front spar
130 Rudder lower hinge
131 Rudder operating lever
132 Connecting rod

133 Control pulleys
134 Elevator operating lever
135 Tailplane spar attachments
136 Aluminium alloy tailplane/ fuselage fairing
137 Tailwheel shock-strut
138 Angled frame rear structure
139 Sternpost
140 Ventral fin
141 Dowty oleo-pneumatic fixed self-centering tailwheel
142 Fin framework
143 Handling-bar socket
144 Fabric covering
145 Swaged tube and steel gusset fitting and through-bolts
146 Upper tube/longeron
147 Rudder cables
148 Wooden stringers
149 Elevator cables

150 Aluminium alloy formers
151 Diagonal brace wires
152 Lower tube/longeron
153 Aluminium alloy former bottom section
154 Retractable entry footstep
155 Wing root fillet
156 Flap rod universal joint
157 Aileron cables
158 Fuselage/wing rear spar girder attachment
159 Main wing fuel tank (port and starboard: 33 gal/ 150 litres each)
160 Ventral Glycol radiator and oil cooler
161 Front spar wing fixings
162 Cannon forward mounting bracket
163 Cannon fairing
164 Recoil spring
165 Cannon barrels

166 Undercarriage retraction jack
167 Undercarriage fairing
168 Low pressure tyre
169 Port mainwheel
170 Mainwheel shock-strut
171 Oleo-pneumatic cylinder
172 Landing gear drag strut
173 Leading-edge armament access doors
174 Landing gear pivot point
175 Undercarriage sliding joint
176 Upper wing surface armament access plates
177 Rear spar wing fixing
178 Magazine blister fairings
179 Gun heating manifold
180 Breech-block access plates
181 Metal flaps
182 Cannon breech-blocks
183 Ammunition magazine drum
184 Port outer 20mm Hispano cannon
185 Spar section change
186 Port landing light
187 Leading-edge structure
188 Front main spar
189 Forward intermediate spar
190 Stringers
191 Rib formers
192 Aluminium alloy wing skinning
193 Rear intermediate spar
194 Rear spar
195 Aileron control pulley
196 Aileron inboard hinge
197 Aluminium alloy aileron
198 Aileron control gear main pulley
199 Self-aligning ball-bearing hinge
200 Aileron outboard hinge
201 Detachable wingtip
202 Port navigation light

Hawker Hurricane II C (with tropical filter, drop tanks and provision for surface attack, 3 Sqn, Indian AF, Assam 1943)

Hawker Fury (monoplane)

Fury I, FB.60, T.61 and Trainer, and Sea Fury FB.10,11, 51 and T.20

Type: single-seat fighter-bomber, naval fighter-bomber or two-seat trainer.

Engine: one 2,470 hp Bristol Centaurus 15 or 2,550 hp Centaurus 18 18-cylinder two-row sleeve-valve radial.

Dimensions: span 38 ft 4¾ in (11·69 m); length 34 ft 8 in (10·56 m); height 15 ft 10 in (4·81 m).

Weights: empty (Fury 1) 8,879 lb (4020 kg); (Sea Fury 11) 8,977 lb (4090 kg); loaded (I) 12,114 lb (5505 kg); (11) 12,500 lb (5669 kg).

Performance: maximum speed 460 mph (740 km/h) (trainers, 445 mph); initial climb 4,320 ft (1320 m)/min; service ceiling 36,000 ft (11,000 m); range on internal fuel (typical) 760 miles (1223 km).

Armament: four (T.20, two) 20 mm Hispano Mk V cannon in outer wings; in most marks, provision for underwing load up to 2,000 lb (907 kg), including 12 rockets, four Triplex rockets, bombs or tanks.

History: first flight 1 September 1944; (Griffon) 27 November 1944) (Sea Fury X, navalised prototype) 21 February 1945.

Hawker Sea Fury FB.10

Hawker Fury FB.60 (Royal Pakistan AF)

Probably the ultimate British combat aircraft to have a single piston engine, the Fury looked very like a Tempest II but in fact was a completely new design. It was triggered by the capture in June 1942 of an Fw 190, which was a revelation in compact design and the proper use of an air-cooled radial engine (which had previously been misjudged in Britain as inferior to liquid-cooled installations). As a result Specification F.6/42 for a "Light Tempest" was written, and Camm designed the Fury around Tempest wings without the centre section, joined under a new fuselage which escaped from steel-tube construction in favour of modern monocoque structure. Prototypes flew with Centaurus, Griffon and Sabre engines, while Boulton Paul developed the navalised Sea Fury through Specifications N.7/43, F.2/43 and N.22/43. At the

end of World War II RAF orders were cancelled, but 65 Furies were built for Iraq, Egypt and Pakistan, some being trainers with two bubble canopies (Egyptian Fury Trainer) or one long canopy (Pakistan T.61). The Sea Fury went into production as a standard Fleet Air Arm fighter-bomber and was also sold to Canada, the Netherlands, Australia, West Germany, Burma, Cuba and other countries. Total production amounted to 860, of which the Royal Navy received 615. The

Sea Fury was a standard combat aircraft of the RN, RAN and RCN in Korea (1950–53) and flew many thousands of sorties from light carriers in support of Allied ground forces and even succeeded in destroying a number of MiG-15s in close combat. Pakistan Furies remained in active service during all fighting with India until 1973. An American-owned Fury holds the world piston-engine speed record.

Hawker Siddeley (Gloster) Meteor

G.41 Meteor fighters, G.43 trainer, and Armstrong Whitworth Meteor night fighters

Type: originally, single-seat fighter; variants, see text.

Engines: two Rolls-Royce centrifugal turbojets (sub-types, see text).

Dimensions: span (4, 7, 8, 9 and derivatives) 37 ft 2 in (11·3 m); (1–3, 10–14) 43 ft (13·1 m); length (1–4) 41 ft 4 in (12·6 m); (7, 9) 43 ft 6 in (13·25 m); (8) 44 ft 7 in (13·59 m); (10) 44 ft 3 in; (11–13) 48 ft 6 in (14·78 m); (14) 49 ft 11½ in (15·23 m); height (1–7, 10) 13 ft (3·96 m); (8, 9, 11–14) 13 ft 10 in (4·22 m).

Weights: empty (1) 8,140 lb (3693 kg); (4) 9,980 lb (4526 kg); (7) 10,540 lb (4780 kg); (8) 10,626 lb (4820 kg); (9) 10,790 lb (4895 kg); (11–14) about 11,900 lb (5400 kg); loaded (1) 13,800 lb (6260 kg); (4) 15,175 lb (6885 kg); (7) 17,600 lb (7984 kg); (8) 19,100 lb (8664 kg); (9,10) 15,660 and 15,330 lb; (11) 22,000 lb (9979 kg); (12–14) about 20,500 lb (9300 kg).

Performance: maximum speed (1) 410 mph (660 km/h); (4, 8, 9) 585–595 mph (940–958 km/h); (7, 10–14) 579–585 mph (931–940 km/h); initial climb (1) 2,155 ft (657 m)/min; (4–10) 7,000–7,600 ft (2130–2315 m)/min; (11–14) 6,000 ft (1830 m)/min; service ceiling 40,000–44,000 ft (12,192–13,410 m), except (F.8), 50,000 ft (15,240 m); range on internal fuel (all) about 1,000 miles at altitude (1610 km).

Armament: (1–4, 8, 9) four 20 mm Hispano cannon on sides of nose; (11–14) four 20 mm Hispano in outer wings; (other marks) normally, none. Most Meteors could be modified to carry two 1,000 lb bombs, eight rockets or other offensive stores, but few actually did so apart from F.8s in non-British service.

History: first flight (prototype) 5 March 1943; squadron delivery (F.1) 12 July 1944; first flight (NF 11) 31 May 1950; final delivery (T.7) July 1954.

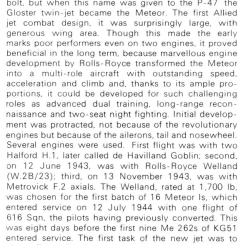

Gloster Meteor F.8 (724 Sqn, Royal Danish AF)

Designed to Specification F.9/40 by George Carter, the Gloster G.41 was to have been named Thunderbolt, but when this name was given to the P-47 the Gloster twin-jet became the Meteor. The first Allied jet combat design, it was surprisingly large, with generous wing area. Though this made the early marks poor performers even on two engines, it proved beneficial in the long term, because marvellous engine development by Rolls-Royce transformed the Meteor into a multi-role aircraft with outstanding speed, acceleration and climb and, thanks to its ample proportions, it could be developed for such challenging roles as advanced dual training, long-range reconnaissance and two-seat night fighting. Initial development was protracted, not because of the revolutionary engines but because of the ailerons, tail and nosewheel. Several engines were used. First flight was with two Halford H.1, later called de Havilland Goblin; second, on 12 June 1943, was with Rolls-Royce Welland (W.2B/23); third, on 13 November 1943, was with Metrovick F.2 axials. The Welland, rated at 1,700 lb, was chosen for the first batch of 16 Meteor Is, which entered service on 12 July 1944 with one flight of 616 Sqn, the pilots having previously converted. This was eight days before the first nine Me 262s of KG51 entered service. The first task of the new jet was to chase flying bombs, and even the Meteor 1 soon

showed that it was formidable (though the guns jammed on the first encounter and F/O Dean finally succeeded by daringly tipping the missile over with his wing tip). The first major production version was the F.3, with 2,000 lb Derwent 1s, extra tankage, sliding canopy and, on the last 15, longer nacelles. The Mk 4 introduced the redesigned Derwent 5 of 3,500 lb thrust, with bigger nacelles on a wing whose tips were clipped to improve speed and rate of roll. In 1945 a Mk 4 set a world speed record of 606 mph, raised the following year to 616 mph. The T.7 was a tandem trainer with framed canopy hinged to the right. The PR.10 was an unarmed reconnaissance variant. The F.8 introduced a redesigned tail, 3,600 lb Derwent 8s, greater tankage and improved cockpit and Martin-Baker seat; later 8s also had bigger engine inlets, spring-tab ailerons and further improved canopy. This was the most numerous "Meatbox", produced in the Benelux countries as well as Britain and widely exported. The NF.11–14 were tandem-seat night fighters, with AI. 10 or US APS-57 radar and the guns moved to the long-span wings. They were designed and built by Armstrong Whitworth, who delivered the last on 31 May 1954. Total Meteor production amounted to 3,947, of which 480 were licence-built F.8s and 547 were AWA night fighters. Major conversions included the NF(T).14 navigation trainer and the remotely piloted U.15, U.16 and U.21 and target-tug TT.20.

Hawker Siddeley Sea Hawk

Hawker P.1040, Armstrong Whitworth Sea Hawk 1–6, 50 and 100–1

Type: single-seat carrier-based fighter-bomber (F.1, 2, fighter).

Engine: one Rolls-Royce Nene single-shaft centrifugal turbojet; (Mks 1–4) 5,000 lb (2268 kg) Nene 101; (Mk 5 onwards) 5,400 lb (2450 kg) Nene 103.

Dimensions: span 39 ft (11·89 m); length 39 ft 8 in (12·08 m); height 8 ft 8 in (2·79 m); (Mks 100–1) 9 ft 9½ in (3 m).

Weights: empty 9,200–9,720 lb (4173–4410 kg);

loaded (clean) 13,220 lb (6000 kg), maximum 16,200 lb (7355 kg).

Performance: maximum speed 599 mph (958 km/h) at sea level, 587 mph (939 km/h, Mach 0·83) at height; initial climb 5,700 ft (1737 m)/min; service ceiling 44,500 ft (13,560 m); range on internal fuel 740 miles (1191 km), with drop tanks 1,400 miles (2253 km).

Armament: four 20 mm Hispano cannon each with 200 rounds beneath cockpit floor; (Mks 3, 5) underwing racks for two 500 lb (227 kg) bombs; (Mks 4, 6 and later) racks for four 500 lb bombs or equivalent.

History: first flight (P.1040) 2 September 1947; (N.7/46) 3 September 1948; (production F.1) 14 November 1951; squadron service, March 1953; final delivery, (Mk 101) December 1956, (India) 1961.

Sir Sydney Camm's first jet fighter was conventional in having a Nene engine with wing-root inlets and unswept wings and tail, but most unusual (possibly unique) in that the jet pipe was split to serve two propelling nozzles, one on each side at the trailing edge.

This gave the P.1040 a neat and graceful appearance, compared with the closely similar Grumman F9F, and also enabled a substantial fuel tank to be accommodated in the rear fuselage. RAF interest waned but naval specification N.7/46 was used for a second aircraft with carrier equipment and the span increased by 2 ft 6 in. The Royal Navy ordered 151, but Hawker Aircraft built only 35 F.1s, all subsequent design and production being handled by Armstrong Whitworth. The Coventry firm built a further 60 F.1s before delivering 40 F.2 with powered ailerons and 116 FB.3 with racks for two bombs. There followed 90 FGA.4, with four pylons, and then 86 FGA.6 with more powerful engine. Many FB.3 were converted to FB.5s by changing to the Nene 103, and many FGA.4 were brought up to Mk 6 standard. The 22 Mk 50s were Mk 6s supplied to the Royal Netherlands Navy in 1956–7 for the carrier *Karel Doorman*. The final batches comprised 34 Mk 100 similar to the FGA.6 for the West German Kriegsmarine and 34 Mk 101 night fighters with Ekco 34 radar in a pod on the right wing. Three years after production had ceased the Indian Navy ordered 24, half new and half ex-RN; eventually the Indians bought 74, serving aboard *Vikrant* and ashore until 1977.

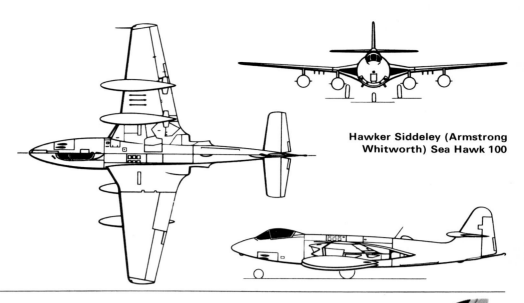

Hawker Siddeley (Armstrong Whitworth) Sea Hawk 100

Hawker Siddeley Hunter

Hawker P.1067 and Hunter 1 to 79
Type: single-seat fighter, fighter-bomber and fighter-reconnaissance; two-seat dual trainer.
Engine: one Rolls-Royce Avon single-shaft turbojet (see text).
Dimensions: span 33 ft 8 in (10·26 m); length (single-seat, typical) 45 ft 10½ in (13·98 m), (two-seat) 48 ft 10½ in (14·9 m); height 13 ft 2 in (4·26 m).
Weights: empty (1) 12,128 lb (5501 kg); (9) 13,270 lb (6020 kg); loaded (1) 16,200 lb (7347 kg); (9, clean) 17,750 lb (8051 kg); (9, maximum) 24,000 lb (10,885 kg).
Performance: maximum speed (typical of all) 710 mph (1144 km/h) at sea level, 620 mph (978 km/h, Mach 0·94) at height; initial climb (Avon 100-series) about 5,500 ft (1676 m)/min; (Avon 200-series) 8,000 ft (2438 m)/min; service ceiling 50,000 ft (15,240 m); range on internal fuel 490 miles (689 km), with maximum fuel 1,840 miles (2965 km).
Armament: four (two-seaters, usually one, sometimes two) 30 mm Aden cannon beneath cockpit floor, each with 150 rounds; single-seaters normally have underwing pylons for two 1,000 lb (454 kg) bombs and 24 3 in rockets, later or refurbished aircraft carrying two 230 Imp gal drop tanks in addition.
History: first flight (P.1067) 20 June 1951; (production F.1) 16 May 1953; (two-seater) 8 July 1955; final delivery from new, 1966.

Undoubtedly the most successful British post-war fighter, the Hunter epitomised the grace of a thoroughbred and has always delighted its pilots. The prototype, with 6,500 lb thrust Avon 100, was built to Specification F.3/48. It was easily supersonic in a shallow

Hawker Siddeley Hunter F.56 (Indian AF)

Hawker Siddeley Hunter F.51 (Royal Danish AF)

dive and packed the devastating four Aden cannon in a quick-release pack winched up as a unit. After being fitted with bulged cartridge boxes and a stuck-on airbrake under the rear fuselage it became a standard fighter, with Armstrong Whitworth building the F.2 with 8,000 lb Sapphire 101, which, unlike the early Avon, stayed going when the guns were fired. The one-off Mk 3 gained a world speed record at 727·6 mph, the F.4 had fuel capacity raised from 334 to 414 gal and carried underwing stores, and the F.5 was a Sapphire-engined 4. The F.6 introduced the 10,000 lb Avon 203 and extended-chord dog-tooth wing. The T.7 had the 8,000 lb Avon 122 and side-by-side dual controls, the

T.8 was a naval trainer, and the most important mark of all was the FGA.9 with 10,150 lb Avon 207 and heavier underwing load. The FR.10 was a camera-equipped fighter and the GA.11 was a ground-attack naval trainer. Total Hunter production was 1,985, including 445 made in Belgium and Holland. While 429 were exported as new aircraft, well over 700 additional Hunters have been refurbished or completely remanufactured for more than 17 air forces, with mark numbers up to 79. A superb all-round combat aircraft, it is gradually being recognised that, had a further 1,000 been constructed (or fewer scrapped in Britain) all would have found ready buyers today.

Hawker Siddeley Javelin

Gloster G.A.5, Javelin 1-9
Type: two-seat all-weather fighter and trainer.
Engines: two Bristol Siddeley (previously Armstrong Siddeley) Sapphire single-shaft turbojets; see text for details.
Dimensions: span 52 ft (15·85 m); length (2,6 and 8) 56 ft 3¼ in (17·15 m); (others) 56 ft 9 in (17·29 m); height 16 ft 3 in (4·98 m).
Weights: empty (1) 24,000 lb (10,886 kg); (9) 27,800 lb (12,610 kg); loaded (1) 34,000 lb (15,422 kg); (9) clean 38,400 lb, with drop tanks 42,930 lb (19,473 kg).
Performance: maximum speed (clean, all marks) 680 mph at sea level, 630 mph (1014 km/h, Mach 0·9) at height; initial climb (clean, 8 and 9) 12,000 ft (3660 m)/min; service ceiling 49,500 ft (15,100 m); range (with drop tanks) about 950 miles (1530 km).
Armament: (1–6) four 30 mm Aden cannon in outer wings, each with 200 rounds; (7–9) two 30 mm Aden and four Firestreak air-to-air missiles on underwing pylons.
History: first flight (G.A.5) 26 November 1951; (production FAW.1) 22 July 1954; (T.3) 20 August 1956; (7) 9 November 1956; (8) 9 May 1958; (9) 6 May 1959.

Designed by a team led by R. W. Walker to Specification F.4/48, the Javelin was the first aircraft designed in Britain explicitly as a night and all-weather fighter. It was on a most generous scale, with a vast delta wing

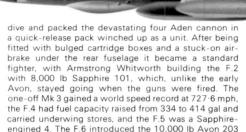

Hawker Siddeley Javelin FAW.9 (64 Sqn)

with a thickness ratio of no less than 10 per cent. This prohibited any suggestion of supersonic performance, which in any case was not dreamed of in 1948. Other features were an extremely broad and flattened fuselage, with the two engines fed by round-lipped inlets and discharging through long jetpipes, and a gigantic swept vertical tail carrying a delta tailplane with elevators on top – thus allowing the wing to have flaps and land without an excessively nose-high attitude. The whole aircraft was very conservative and it is unfortunate three of the five prototypes should have been written off in accidents. Eventually, after much alteration, Gloster embarked on a production programme which delivered 381 for inventory, though as soon as one mark had become established it was superseded by another. The FAW.1, delivered to 46 Sqn at Odiham in February 1956, was powered by 8,150 lb Sapphire 102s and had AI.10 radar, the radome being pointed half-way through the run of 40. The Mk 2 had 8,300 lb Sapphire 102s and Westinghouse APQ-43 radar. Air Service Training developed the new fuselage

for the dual T.3, which had guns but no radar. The 50 Mk 4s were much easier to fly because of their all-moving tailplane, while the 64 Mk 5s had internal tankage increased from 665 to 915 gal; the 33 Mk 6 were 5s with the US radar. The largely re-engineered FAW.7 introduced the 11,000 lb Sapphire 203 and the long-awaited missile armament, two guns being deleted. Other changes included a longer rear fuselage, blunt trailing edges on the ailerons and wing vortex generators and provision for two 250 gal slipper drop tanks under the fuselage. After building 96 attention turned to 50 Mk 8 with afterburners raising engine thrust to 13,390 lb; other changes included Sperry autopilot, drooped leading edges, extra vortex generators and yaw/pitch dampers. The last rolled out in June 1960, but the plant finished by turning 46 Mk 7s into Mk 9s by adding the Mk 8 changes plus a huge flight-refuelling probe (which four from 23 Sqn used in flying non-stop to Singapore in 1960). Javelins were finally withdrawn in 1968.

Hawker Siddeley Vulcan

Avro 698, Vulcan B.1, 1A, 2 and SR.2
Type: five-seat bomber (SR.2, strategic recon-
naissance).
Engines: four Rolls-Royce (originally Bristol, then
Bristol Siddeley) Olympus two-shaft turbojets; for
details see text.
Dimensions: span (1) 99 ft (30·18 m); (2) 111 ft
(33·83 m); length (1) 97 ft 1 in (29·6 m); (2) 105 ft 6 in
(32·15 m); (99 ft 11 in with probe removed); height
(1) 26 ft 1 in (7·94 m); (2) 27 ft 2 in (8·26 m).
Weights: not disclosed; loaded weights probably
about 170,000 lb for B.1A and 250,000 lb for B.2 and
SR.2.
Performance: maximum speed (1) about 620 mph;
(2) about 640 mph (1030 km/h) at height (Mach
0·97); service ceiling (1) about 55,000 ft; (2) about
65,000 ft (19,810 m); range with bomb load (1) about
3,000 miles; (2) about 4,600 miles (7400 km).
Armament: internal weapon bay for conventional

(21 1,000 lb bombs) or nuclear bombs; (SR.2) none.
History: first flight (Avro 698) 30 August 1952;
(production B.1) 4 February 1955; (prototype B.2)
31 August 1957; (production B.2) 30 August 1958;
final delivery 14 January 1965.

Few aircraft have ever created such an impression as
did the prototype Avro 698. This almost perfect
triangle, painted white, demonstrated fighter-like
manoeuvrability at very low levels within ten hours of
first flight, despite its great size and low-powered
engines (6,500 lb Avons). In 1953 the second prototype was repeatedly rolled at low level. From the start
the Vulcan was a winner and with a modified wing
with kinked and cambered leading edge the B.1 went
into service with the RAF in February 1957, powered
by the 11,000 lb Olympus 101. Altogether 45 Mk 1s

Hawker Siddeley Vulcan B.2 (101 Sqn, Coningsby)

and 1As were built, re-engined by the 12,000 lb
Olympus 102 and 13,500 lb Olympus 104 and, in the
1A, having an extended and bulged rear fuselage full
of countermeasures. Some B.1As carried refuelling
probes fixed above the huge bombing radar in the
nose; all were painted in anti-radiation white. The B.2
was designed to have much better performance at
great heights and matched the 17,000 lb Olympus 201
with a new thinner wing of greater span and area with
elevon controls. Most were equipped to carry the Blue
Steel stand-off missile, but by 1966 the force of about
50 had been painted in green/grey camouflage, re-
engined with the 20,000 lb Olympus 301 and deployed
in the tactical low-level role using gravity bombs, with
terrain-following radar. No 27 Sqn is equipped with
the SR.2 multi-sensor strategic reconnaissance
conversion.

Hawker Siddeley Sea Vixen

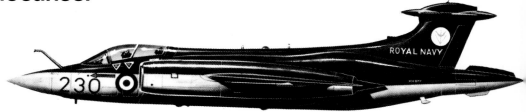

**Hawker Siddeley Sea Vixen FAW 2
(766 Sqn, Naval Air Fighter School,
Yeovilton)**

de Havilland D.H.110, Sea Vixen FAW.1 and 2
Type: two-seat carrier-based all-weather fighter.
Engines: two 11,250 lb (5102 kg) thrust Rolls-Royce
Avon 208 single-shaft turbojets.
Dimensions: span 50 ft (15·24 m); length 55 ft 7 in
(17 m); height 10 ft 9 in (3·3 m).
Weights: not disclosed, but empty weight about
22,000 lb and loaded weight about 31,000 lb (FAW.1)
and 36,000 lb (2).
Performance: maximum speed about 650 mph up to
20,000 ft (1050 km/h, Mach 0·94); initial climb (1)
8,000 ft (2440 m)/min; service ceiling 48,000 ft
(14,630 m); range on internal fuel, not disclosed, but
about 600 miles (1) and 800 miles (2).
Armament: on four inboard wing pylons, four Firestreak air-to-air missiles (FAW.1) or four Red Top
air-to-air missiles (FAW.2); on outer pylons, 150 gal
drop tanks but, alternatively, 1,000 lb bombs, Bullpup
air-to-surface missiles or equivalent stores; as built,
but not used, provision for 28 folding-fin aircraft

rockets in two flip-out boxes beneath cockpit floor.
History: first flight (D.H.110) 26 September 1951;
(second prototype) 25 July 1952; (second aircraft
semi-navalised) 20 June 1955; (pre-production FAW.1)
20 March 1957; service delivery November 1958;
(FAW.2) October 1962; final delivery 1965.

In 1946 the Air Ministry issued Specification F.44/46
for an advanced night fighter, the Admiralty issuing
N.40/46 for the same purpose. Two years of studies
followed and when the Specifications had reached
F.4/48 and N.14/49 two prototypes were ordered of
the D.H.110. When John Cunningham flew the first,
painted silver, at Hatfield in the autumn of 1951 it was
one of the few British combat aircraft of its day that
appeared to be a world-beater. Though it adhered to
the Vampire-type configuration it was totally modern,
with a highly swept wing, all-metal structure and
powered controls, and the horizontal tail carried at the
top of sharply raked fins. The pilot sat on the left of

the central nacelle and the navigator lower down on
the right under a roof window. Very soon the 110 was
making splendid double bangs, proving its supersonic
capability; then, owing to an unforeseen combination
of extreme acceleration and sharp roll at low level, it
broke up in the air over the crowd at a Farnborough
show. The officials then dithered over this outstanding
design. Six years were wasted before it finally entered
service as the Sea Vixen with the Royal Navy. By this
time it was no longer a world-beater, but it was an
advanced and well-equipped machine which at last
gave the Fleet Air Arm a formidable all-weather interception capability as well as a tremendous addition to
its surface-attack strength (because the Vixen fulfilled both roles). The 92nd FAW.1 was turned into the
first FAW.2, with substantially greater tankage in the
tail booms and a completely new armament system
for any-aspect collision-course interception. A total
of 146 Vixens were built, many Mk 1s being converted
to Mk 2s before they were withdrawn in 1971.

Hawker Siddeley Buccaneer

**Blackburn B.103, NA.39, Buccaneer S.1, 2, 2A,
2B, 2C, 2D and 50**
Type: two-seat carrier-based attack (S.50, land-
based).
Engines: (S.1) two 7,100 lb (3220 kg) thrust Bristol
Siddeley (previously de Havilland) Gyron Junior 101
single-shaft turbojets; (all later marks) two 11,030 lb
(5003 kg) Rolls-Royce Spey 101 two-shaft turbofans.
Dimensions: span (1) 42 ft 4 in (12·9 m); (2 and
subsequent) 44 ft (13·41 m); length 63 ft 5 in
(19·33 m); height 16 ft 3 in (4·95 m).
Weights: empty (1) 26,000 lb; (2) about 30,000 lb
(13,610 kg); maximum loaded (1) 46,000 lb
(20,865 kg); (2) 62,000 lb (28,123 kg).
Performance: maximum speed (all) 645 mph
(1038 km/h, Mach 0·85) at sea level; initial climb
(2, at 46,000 lb) 7,000 ft (2134 m)/min; service
ceiling not disclosed but over 40,000 ft (9144 m);
range on typical hi-lo-hi strike mission with weapon
load (2) 2,300 miles (3700 km).
Armament: rotating bomb door carries four 1,000 lb
(454 kg) bombs or multi-sensor reconnaissance pack
or 440 gal tank; (S.2 and later) four wing pylons each
stressed to 3,000 lb (1361 kg), compatible with very
wide range of guided and/or free-fall missiles. Total
internal and external stores load 16,000 lb (7257 kg).
History: first flight (NA.39) 30 April 1958; (production S.1) 23 January 1962; (prototype S.2) 17 May
1963; (production S.2) 5 June 1964; final delivery
late 1975.

After the notorious "Defence White Paper" of April
1957, which proclaimed manned combat aircraft
obsolete, the Blackburn B.103, built to meet the naval
attack specification NA.39, was the only new British
military aircraft that was not cancelled. Development
was grudgingly permitted, and this modest-sized
subsonic machine was gradually recognised as a
world-beater. Designed for carrier operation, its wing
and tail were dramatically reduced in size as a result
of very powerful tip-to-tip supercirculation (BLC,
boundary-layer control) achieved by blasting hot
compressed air bled from the engines from narrow
slits. The S.1 (strike Mk 1) was marginal in power, but
the greatly improved S.2 was a reliable and formidable
aircraft. The first 84 were ordered by the Royal Navy

Hawker Siddeley Buccaneer S.2 (801 Sqn, HMS Victorious)

and most of these have been transferred to RAF
Strike Command, designated S.2B when converted
to launch Martel missiles. Those remaining with the
Navy are S.2Ds (2C if they are not Martel-compatible).
In January 1963 the South African Air Force bought
16 S.50s with BS.605 boost rocket built into a retractable pack in the rear fuselage to facilitate use
from hot and high airstrips. Finally — perhaps rather
surprisingly, considering the scorn vented on Buccaneer during the TSR.2 era — the RAF signed in 1968
for 43 new S.2Bs with adequate equipment, including
a refuelling probe which is never used in front-line
service in Germany. Strong and unbreakable, this is
one of the most cost/effective aircraft ever designed
for tactical use.

Hawker Siddeley Harrier

Hawker P.1127, Kestrel, Harrier GR.3 and T.4, AV-8A, TAV-8A and Sea Harrier FRS.1
Type: single-seat tactical attack and reconnaissance; two-seat trainer; single-seat naval multi-role.
Engine: one 21,500 lb (9752 kg) thrust Rolls-Royce Pegasus 103 two-shaft vectored-thrust turbofan (US designation F402).
Dimensions: span 25 ft 3 in (7·7 m), (with bolt-on tips, 29 ft 8 in); length 45 ft 6 in (13·87 m), (laser nose, 47 ft 2 in; two-seat trainers, 55 ft 9½ in; Sea Harrier, 48 ft); height 11 ft 3 in (3·43 m) (two-seat, 13 ft 8 in).
Weights: empty (GR.1) 12,200 lb (5533 kg); (Sea H) 13,000 lb (5897 kg); (T) 13,600 lb (6168 kg); maximum (non-VTOL) 26,000 lb (11,793 kg).
Performance: maximum speed 737 mph (1186 km/h, Mach 0·972) at low level; maximum dive Mach number, 1·3; initial climb (VTOL weight) 50,000 ft (15,240 m)/min; service ceiling, over 50,000 ft (15,240 m); tactical radius on strike mission without drop tanks (hi-lo-hi) 260 miles (418 km); ferry range 2,070 miles (3330 km).
Armament: all external, with many options. Under-fuselage strakes both replaceable by pod containing one 30 mm Aden or similar gun, with 150 rounds. Five or seven stores pylons, centre and two inboard each rated at 2,000 lb (907 kg), outers at 650 lb (295 kg) and tips (if used) at 220 lb (100 kg) for Sidewinder or similar. Normal load 5,300 lb (2400 kg), but 8,000 lb (3630 kg) has been flown.
History: first hover (P.1127) 21 October 1960; first flight (P.1127) 13 March 1961; first flight (Kestrel) 13 February 1964; (development Harrier) 31 August 1966; (Harrier GR.1) 28 December 1967; (T.2) 24 April 1969; squadron service (GR.1) 1 April 1969.

In the 1950s the realisation that the thrust/weight ratio of the gas turbine made possible a new class of high-speed jets having VTOL (vertical takeoff and landing) capability led to a rash of unconventional prototypes and research machines. Only one has led to a useful combat aircraft. It was the P.1127, designed by Camm's team in 1957–9 around a unique engine, planned at Bristol by Stanley Hooker, in which the fan and core flows are discharged through four nozzles which, by means of chain drives from a single pneumatic motor, can be swivelled to point downwards, to lift the aircraft, or point to the rear, for propulsion. Gradually the P.1127 was transformed into the Kestrel, which equipped a UK/USA/German evaluation squadron in 1965. This was further developed into the Harrier (the much bigger, Mach 2, P.1154 for the RAF and RN having been cancelled in 1965). Powered by a Pegasus 101 at 19,000 lb, the GR.1 was capable of flying useful combinations of fuel and stores out of any hastily prepared site and did more than any other aircraft to explore the advantages and problems of operational deployment of combat aircraft well away from any airfield. Numerous flights were made from a

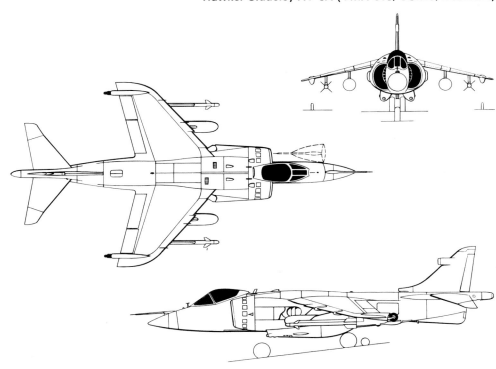

Hawker Siddeley AV-8A (VMA-513, USMC, Beaufort)

Hawker Siddeley Sea Harrier FRS. 1

wide variety of naval vessels and record flights were made from the centre of London to the centre of New York and vice versa. The GR.1A had the 20,000 lb Mk 102 engine and at this thrust the Harrier was adopted as the AV-8A by the US Marine Corps in both beach assault and defensive roles. All RAF and USMC aircraft have been re-engined with the Pegasus 103:92 GR.3, 13 T.4 112 AV-8A (plus six for Spain) and eight TAV-8A (plus two for Spain). Using VIFF (vectoring in forward flight) the Harrier

has proved an extremely effective dogfight aircraft and since 1971 Hawker Siddeley, McDonnell Douglas, Rolls-Royce and Pratt & Whitney have been investigating developments with supercritical wing and the improved Pegasus, the US Marine Corps and N(vy project number being—V-8B. The Sea Harrier FRS.1 was ordered in 1975 to equip the three RN through-deck cruisers in fighter, anti-submarine and surface-attack roles, with Blue Fox radar and different weapons.

Hawker Siddeley Hawk

P.1182 Hawk T.1
Type: two-seat trainer and tactical multi-role.
Engine: one 5,340 lb (2422 kg) Rolls-Royce/Turboméca Adour 151 two-shaft turbofan.
Dimensions: span 30 ft 10 in (9·4 m); length (over probe) 39 ft 2½ in (11·95 m); height 13 ft 5 in (4·09 m).
Weights: empty 7,450 lb (3379 kg); loaded (trainer, clean) 12,000 lb (5443 kg), (attack mission) 16,260 lb (7375 kg).
Performance: maximum speed 630 mph (1014 km/h) at low level; Mach number in shallow dive, 1·1; initial climb 6,000 ft (1830 m)/min; service ceiling 50,000 ft (15,240 m); range on internal fuel 750 miles (1207 km).
Armament: three or five hard-points (two outboard being optional) each rated at 1,000 lb (454 kg); centreline point normally equipped with 30 mm gun pod and ammunition.
History: first flight 21 August 1974; service delivery 1976.

The only entirely new all-British military aircraft for 15 years, the Hawk serves as a model of the speed and success that can be achieved when an experienced team is allowed to get on with the job. To some degree it owes its existence to the escalation of the Jaguar to a power and weight category well above that economic for use as a pure trainer. Britain never participated in the Franco-German Alpha Jet programme and instead played off the two British airframe builders, finally making a choice between the Adour without after-

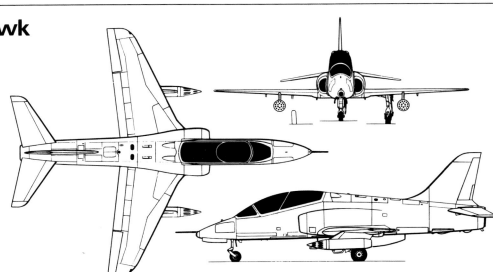

Hawker Siddeley Hawk (with gun and rocket pods)

burner and the less powerful Viper 632. With the Adour, the Hawk had a chance to be a world-beater, and backed by an immediate RAF order for 175 the Hawker Siddeley plants rapidly completed design, tooled for fast manufacture with assembly at Dunsfold and will in all probability have the Hawk close to if not actually in operational service by 1976. Owing to its very large optional weapons payload,

great structural strength over a 6,000 hour lifetime and price of under £1 million the Hawk is certain to sell in very large numbers, especially as its fast development has overtaken that of its chief rival the Alpha Jet. The first export deal may involve the supply of aircraft to Egypt and the establishment there of completely new factories to build the Hawk and Adour under licence. A single-seat close-support version is on offer.

Hawker Siddeley Nimrod

HS.801 Nimrod MR.1 and 2 and R.1

Type: (MR) maritime reconnaissance and anti-submarine aircraft, with operating crew of 12, with several secondary roles; (R) electronic reconnaissance and countermeasures.

Engines: four 11,995 lb (5441 kg) thrust Rolls-Royce Spey 250 two-shaft turbofans.

Dimensions: span 114 ft 10 in (35 m); length 126 ft 9 in (38·63 m); (R.1) 118 ft; height 29 ft 8½ in (9·08 m).

Weights: empty (MR, typical) 92,000 lb (41,730 kg); loaded 192,000 lb (87,090 kg).

Performance: maximum speed 575 mph (926 km/h); economical transit speed 490 mph (787 km/h); climb and ceiling, not disclosed; mission endurance 12 hours; ferry range, typically 5,755 miles (9265 km).

Armament: 50 ft (15 m) weapon bay capable of carrying very wide range of stores, including AS torpedoes, mines, depth bombs, nuclear weapons, conventional bombs and fuel tanks; two (optionally four) underwing pylons for air-to-surface missiles such as Martel or AS.12.

History: first flight (aerodynamic prototype) 23 May 1967; (production MR.1) 28 June 1968; service delivery 2 October 1969.

Though it is derived from the Comet civil transport the Nimrod has proved an outstandingly successful aircraft. The original MR.1 was tailored to an equipment standard which, for budgetary reasons, fell short of the ideal but still combined very complete ASW (anti-submarine warfare) sensing systems with digital and analog computers, advanced tactical displays and comprehensive inertial, doppler and three other navigation systems. The best thing about the MR.1 is the aircraft itself, which surpasses all other aircraft in use for ocean patrol in speed, quietness, flight performance, reliability and all-round mission efficiency. In emergency it can be fitted with 45 passenger seats in the rear compartment without significantly disturbing operational equipment. The RAF force of 46, which have operated around the clock in often extremely severe conditions, are being completely modernised at their half-life point, in 1977–78, with new Searchwater radar, greatly increased computer capacity and a new acoustic processing system matched with the Barra sonobuoy. The R.1 force of three aircraft are specially equipped for sensing, recording and emitting electromagnetic and other data.

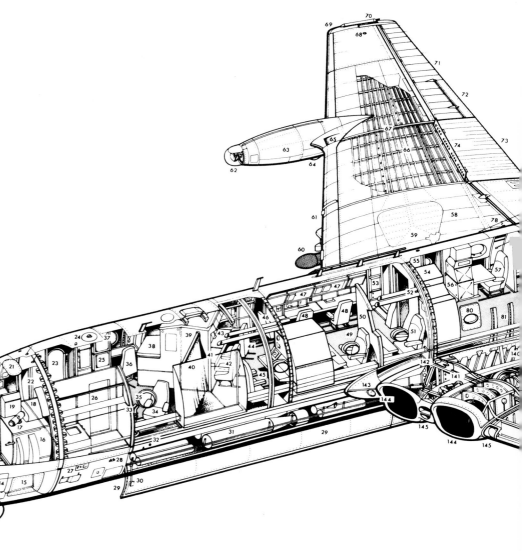

**Hawker Siddeley Nimrod
MR.1 cutaway drawing
key:**

1 Dielectric radome
2 Taxi lamp
3 ASV-21D search and weather radar (MR.2, Searchwater)
4 Radome hoist point
5 Front pressure bulkhead
6 Windscreen for all-weather use
7 Four wipers
8 Instrument panel coaming
9 Co-pilot's seat
10 Eyebrow window
11 Pilot's seat
12 Pitot head
13 Twin nosewheels
14 Sonics homing aerial
15 Doppler bay
16 Forward radio pack
17 Autolycus diesel sniffer
18 Autolycus equipment rack
19 Port D.C. electrics crate
20 Engineer's station
21 Emergency escape hatch
22 Starboard D.C. electrics crate
23 Crew entry door
24 Periscopic sextant

25 Equipment systems crate
26 Toilet
27 Ground supply socket
28 Weapons-pannier door ground control
29 Weapons-pannier door
30 Door strut
31 Mixed ASW weapons load
32 Tank blow-off
33 'On-top' sight
34 Port beam lookout's seat
35 Domed observation window (hinged, pressure-bearing, with sight linked to computer)
36 Starboard beam lookout's seat
37 Domed observation window (fixed)
38 Analog computer rack
39 Digital computer rack
40 Blackout curtain
41 Map projector station
42 Routine navigator
43 Plot display
44 Tactical navigator

45 Radio operator
46 Tactical commander
47 Sonics station (2)
48 Sonics operators (2)
49 ASV operator
50 Partition
51 Space provision for extra sensor operator's station
52 Radio trough
53 Sonics cupboard
54 Port AC electrics crate
55 Starboard AC electrics crate
56 Aft radio rack
57 ESM/MAD operator
58 Machined inner-wing skin
59 Undercarriage bay upper panel
60 Starboard weapons pylon
61 Flow spoiler
62 Searchlight, 70 million candle power
63 External fuel tank
64 Wing bumper
65 Fixed slot
66 Integral fuel tanks
67 Skin butt-joint rib

68 Over-wing filler
69 Starboard navigation light
70 Wingtip fuel vent
71 Starboard aileron
72 Aileron tab
74 Flap outer section
74 Airbrake (upper and lower surfaces)
75 Fuel dump pipes
76 Fuel vent
77 Flap inner section
78 Inboard airbrake (upper surface only)
79 Blackout curtain
80 Emergency escape panels
81 Fuselage frames
82 Electrics trough
83 Dinette
84 Fixed galley
85 Partition with folding door
86 Size A sonobuoy stowage
87 Underfloor bag-type keel tanks
88 Port lookout and stores-loader
89 Starboard lookout and stores-loader
90 Observation ports (port and starboard)
91 Pressurized launchers
92 Rotary launchers
93 Ready-use oxygen stowage
94 Intercom panel
95 Stores control panel

96 Emergency door
97 Hand extinguisher
98 Underfloor parachute stowage
99 First-aid kit
100 Escape rope stowage
101 Camera magazine stowage
102 Retro-launcher (cancels airspeed)
103 F.135 camera hatch
104 Hat-rack
105 ESM amplifier
106 Equipment cooling fans
107 Rear pressure bulkhead
108 Dorsal fin
109 HF aerial
110 Starboard tailplane
111 VOR aerial
112 Dielectric fairing
113 ESM aerial
114 Dummy ESM (test) aerial
115 Rudder
116 Fin structure
117 Dielectric tailcone
118 MAD aerial
119 Elevator tab
120 Port elevator
121 VOR aerial
122 Tailplane structure
123 Tail bumper/fuselage vent
124 Fin/fuselage frame
125 De-icing conduit
126 Rudder and elevator linkage
127 APU

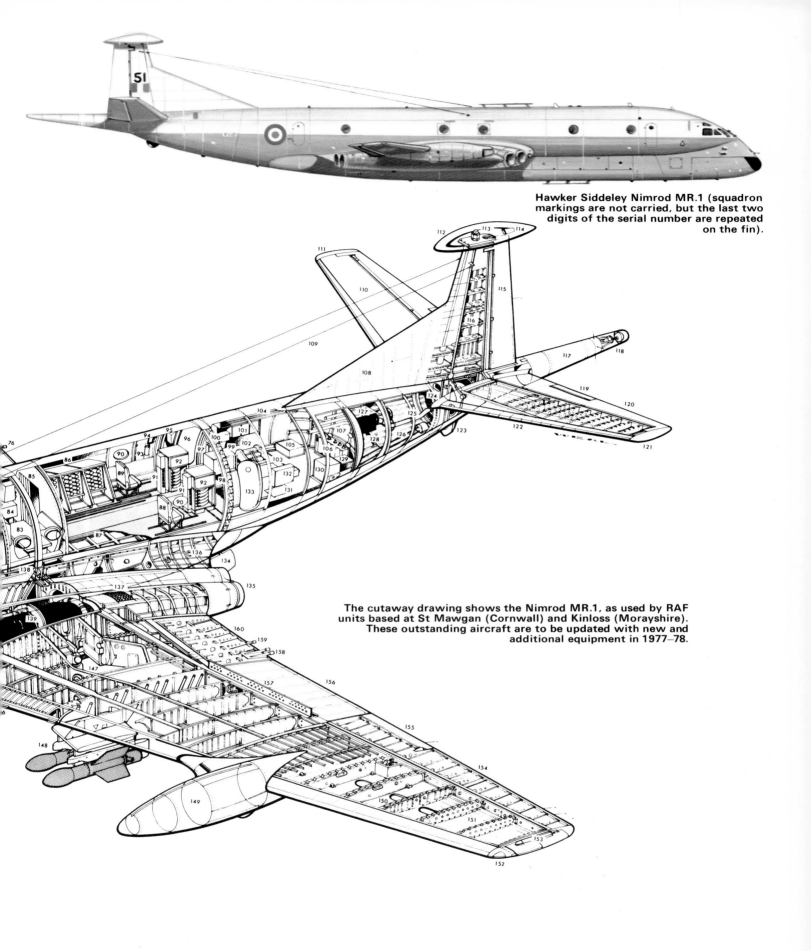

Hawker Siddeley Nimrod MR.1 (squadron markings are not carried, but the last two digits of the serial number are repeated on the fin).

The cutaway drawing shows the Nimrod MR.1, as used by RAF units based at St Mawgan (Cornwall) and Kinloss (Morayshire). These outstanding aircraft are to be updated with new and additional equipment in 1977–78.

128 APU and aft fuselage
   access hatch
129 Safe
130 Liquid oxygen pack
131 F.126 camera access hatch
132 Intercom panel
133 Main door
134 Ground-operated doors
   (rear loading of stores)
135 Tailpipes
136 Dinghy stowage
137 Thrust reverser (outboard
   only)
138 Rear spar/fuselage
   attachment point

139 Rolls-Royce Spey 250
   turbofan (12,140 lb/
   5,506 kg thrust)
140 Inboard engine bay (engine
   not shown)
141 Heat exchanger
142 Front spar/fuselage
   attachment point
143 Landing/taxi light
144 Anti-iced intakes
145 Ram air to heat exchanger
146 Flow spoiler
147 Undercarriage well
148 Weapon pylon (two
   Aérospatiale AS.12 missiles)

149 External fuel tank
150 Access panels
151 Wing structure
152 Port navigation light
153 Wingtip vent
154 Port aileron
155 Aileron tab
156 Flap outer section
157 Airbrake (upper and lower
   surfaces)
158 Dump pipes
159 Vent
160 Flap structure

Heinkel seaplanes

He 4, 5 and variants, 8
Type: three-seat (He 8, usually two-seat) reconaissance seaplane.
Engine: (4) usually one 360 hp Rolls-Royce Eagle VIII or IX vee-12 water-cooled; (5) one 450 hp Napier Lion II broad-arrow 12-cylinder water-cooled; (5a, 5b and 5c) one 480 hp Bristol Jupiter VIII or 660 hp Bristol Pegasus IIM3 nine-cylinder radial; (8) one 420 hp Armstrong Siddeley Jaguar IV 14-cylinder two-row radial.
Dimensions: span (4) 59 ft 0½ in; (others) 55 ft 1 in (16·8 m); length (4) 41 ft; (5, typical) 40 ft (12·19 m); (8) 37 ft 9 in (11·5 m); height (4) 12 ft; (5) 13 ft 11 in (4·23 m); (8) 12 ft 8 in (3·9 m).
Weights: empty (4) 3,859 lb; (5, 5a) 3,605 lb (1634 kg); (8) 3,307 lb (1500 kg); loaded (4) 5,512 lb (2500 kg); (5, 5a) 6,393 lb (2900 kg); (8) 5,126 lb (2325 kg).
Performance: maximum speed (4) 112 mph; (5) 143 mph (230 km/h); (5c) 174 mph (280 km/h); (8) 130 mph (210 km/h); service ceiling (4) 12,470 ft (3800 m); (5) 19,685 ft (6000 m); (5c) 22,970 ft (7000 m); (8) 19,685 ft (6000 m); range (all) about 500 miles (800 km).
Armament: various customer options, Swedish He 5, 5a and 5c usually having one 7·9 mm machine gun in the outer right wing and often a manually aimed gun in rearmost cockpit; Danish He 8s usually had one synchronised machine gun (probably 7·7 mm Madsen) in top of front fuselage.

Heinkel He 8 (Royal Danish Naval Flying Corps).

History: first flight (4) late 1925; (5) 1926; (8) December 1927.

When Hansa Brandenburg went into liquidation in 1919 Dr Ernst Heinkel worked for the Caspar Flugzeugwerke for a year but then left to set up his own company, registered on 1 December 1922 at Warnemünde on the Baltic shore. Forbidden by the Versailles Treaty to build military aircraft, he did what the other German designers did: form partnerships and subsidiaries in other countries. Heinkel's "cover" was a firm in Sweden and throughout the 1920s his fine seaplanes — unmistakeably descendents of the W.29 and 33 — were a familiar sight throughout Scandinavia. The first, the He 1 of May 1923, was powered by a

240 hp Siddeley Puma and led to the important He 2 which was made in quantity for the Swedish Air Force. It retained the characteristic upswept tail and extended ailerons, but was powered by a Rolls-Royce Eagle of 360 hp. The same engine powered a slightly different He 2 for Finland, a few of which actually served in the 1939 war, as well as the almost identical He 4. The most important family of all were the He 5 series, of which about 100 were made in Sweden and at Warnemünde. The initial batches had an uncowled Siemens or Swedish Jupiter but the final S.5c of 1931 had a Pegasus cowled by a Townend ring which enabled the three Swedish squadrons to handle these big machines like fighters. The slightly smaller He 8 was bought by Denmark, and later (1933–38) made under licence. Examples used to map Greenland were sprayed scarlet over their original silver, to stand out if forced down, while those used by the Royal Danish Navy were camouflaged in 1938 and were still in use in April 1940, finally being destroyed by local saboteurs in 1943.

Heinkel He 51

He 51A-1, B-2 and C-1
Type: single-seat fighter (B-2) reconnaissance seaplane; (C-1) land ground attack.
Engine: one 750 hp BMW VI 7·3Z vee-12 water-cooled.
Dimensions: span 36 ft 1 in (11 m); length 27 ft 6¾ in (8·4 m); (B-2) about 31 ft; height 10 ft 6 in (3·2 m); (B-2 m); (B-2) about 11 ft.
Weights: (A-1), empty 3,223 lb (1462 kg); loaded 4,189 lb (1900 kg).
Performance: maximum speed (A-1) 205 mph (330 km/h); initial climb 1,969 ft (600 m)/min; service ceiling 24,610 ft (7500 m); range 242 miles (390 km).
Armament: standard, two 7·92 mm Rheinmetall MG 17 synchronised above fuselage; (B-2) same plus underwing racks for up to six 22 lb (10 kg) bombs; (C-1) same plus underwing racks for four 110 lb (50 kg) bombs.
History: first flight (He 49a) November 1932; (He 49b) February 1933; (He 51A-Ø) May 1933; service delivery of A-1, July 1934.
Gradually, as the likelihood of Allied legal action receded, Heinkel dared to build aircraft that openly contravened the Versailles Treaty. The most startling was the He 37, obviously a prototype fighter, which in 1928 achieved 194 mph, or 20 mph faster than the RAF

Heinkel He 51C-1 (4/JG 88, Legion Kondor).

Bulldog which was still a year away from service. Land and seaplane versions led to a succession of He 49 fighter prototypes in the 1930s and these in turn provided the basis for the refined and formidable He 51. This was the first fighter ordered into production by the Reichsluftfahrtministerium for the reborn Luftwaffe. Though the initial order for He 51A-1s was only 75, Heinkel was unused to such an order and many were

built under licence by Ago, Erla, Arado and Fieseler — which were also fast tooling for their own designs. In March 1935 the Luftwaffe was publicly announced, and JG1 "Richthofen" fighter squadron was combat-ready at Döberitz with its new Heinkels. In November 1936, 36 He 51A-1s went to Spain with the Legion Kondor, giving a sufficiently good showing for the Nationalists to buy at least 30 from Heinkel. There followed a total of 50 of various He 51B seaplane versions, the 38 B-2s being for service aboard cruisers. The final batch comprised 79 C-1 ground attack fighters, of which 28 served in Spain. The He 51 was still in active service in September 1939, operating in the close-support role in Poland, and remained as an advanced trainer until 1943.

Heinkel He 70

He 70E-1, F-1 and F-2
Type: (E) day bomber; (F) long-range reconnaissance.
Engine: one 750 hp BMW VI 7·3 Z vee-12 water-cooled.

Heinkel He 70F-1 (3 Auflärungsgruppe F/123).

Dimensions: span 48 ft 6¾ in (14·8 m); length 38 ft 4½ in (11·7 m); height 10 ft 2 in (3·1 m).
Weights: (F-1) empty 5,732 lb (2600 kg); loaded 7,716 lb (3500 kg).
Performance: maximum speed 220 mph (355 km/h); initial climb 1,476 ft (450 m)/min; service ceiling 19,685 ft (6000 m); range 500 miles (800 km).
Armament: one MG 15 7·92 mm machine gun, with 12 magazines, manually aimed from rear cockpit; provision for up to 661 lb (300 kg) of bombs in internal bays (usually occupied by cameras).
History: first flight (He 70 prototype) 1 December 1932; (E-1) December 1933; (F-1) probably early 1935.
Until the tenth anniversary of Heinkel's company his designs had not been especially distinguished, but on that day his chief test pilot made the maiden flight of

the He 70, an aeroplane that astonished the aviation world. Designed by Siegfried and Walter Günther, who were responsible for most of Heinkel's subsequent machines, the He 70 was planned to meet the need of Deutsche Lufthansa for a fast passenger and mail transport that would beat Swissair's Lockheed Orions. As a result the He 70 was by far the most advanced aerodynamic design ever seen in Europe and, probably, in the world. So streamlined and smooth-skinned was it that it outpaced the He 51 fighter which had a more powerful engine and weighed not much more than half as much! The prototype had a 637 hp engine but more powerful BMW VI engines were used in the longer and heavier production models for Lufthansa and various other customers (one of which was Rolls-Royce, which tested Merlins and other engines on

their He 70 until 1944). The first He 70 for combat duty was the one-off E-1 bomber, but the He 70F-1 reconnaissance version went into production for the Luftwaffe and 18 were used by the Legion Kondor in Spain, together with 12 He 70F-2s with a different mark of engine. Though almost unarmed their speed saved them from frequent interception and at the end of the war only one had been lost in action. All remained with the Spanish Air Force, many surviving until after 1950. The He 170 was a Hungarian version powered by Hungarian Gnome Rhône 14K radial engine, dating from 1937. Altogether 296 military He 70 and 170 reconnaissance bombers were built, the last in 1938.

He 111 see page 116.

Heinkel He 112

He 112B-0, B-1 and He 100

Type: single-seat fighter and light ground attack.
Engine: one 680 hp Junkers Jumo 210Ea inverted-vee-12 liquid-cooled; (He 100) one 1,020 hp Daimler-Benz DB 601M of same layout.
Dimensions: (He 112) span 29 ft 10¼ in (9·1 m); length 30 ft 6 in (9·3 m); height 12 ft 7½ in (3·85 m).
Weights: empty 3,571 lb (1620 kg); loaded 4,960 lb (2250 kg).
Performance: maximum speed 317 mph (510 km/h); initial climb 2,300 ft (700 m)/min; service ceiling 27,890 ft (8500 m); range 684 miles (1100 km).
Armament: two 20 mm Oerlikon MG FF cannon in outer wings and two 7·92 mm Rheinmetall MG 17 machine guns in sides of fuselage; underwing racks for six 22 lb (10 kg) fragmentation bombs.
History: first flight (He 112V-1) September 1935; (B-series production prototype) May 1937; final delivery (Rumania) September 1939; (He 100V-1) 22 January 1938.

One of the first requirements issued by the rapidly expanded RLM under the Nazis was a specification for a completely new monoplane fighter to replace the Ar 68 and He 51. Heinkel's team under the Günthers used He 70 experience to create the shapely He 112, which was much smaller and of wholly light-alloy stressed-skin construction. Powered by a British Kestrel, it was matched at Travemünde against the similarly powered Bf 109 prototype, as well as the "also rans", the Ar 80 and Fw 159. Though Heinkel's fighter was marginally slower, it had better field performance, much better pilot view (especially on the ground), a wide-track landing gear and considerably better manoeuvrability. Many, especially Heinkel, were amazed when the Messerschmitt design was chosen for the Luftwaffe, though the He 112 was continued as an insurance. Nothing Heinkel could do with improved versions could shake the RLM's re-

jection, despite the delight of the RLM test pilots in flying them. Thirty He 112B-0 fighters were supplied to the Luftwaffe for evaluation, but 17 were promptly shipped to Spain (not as part of the Legion Kondor but flown by volunteer civilians). There they were judged superior to the Bf 109C, and 15 continued in Spanish service until after World War II. All but one of the other Luftwaffe machines were sold to the Japanese Navy, which disliked them intensely because of their high wing loading. Rumania bought 13 B-0 and 11 B-1 fighters in 1939 and used them in the 1941 invasion of the Soviet Union. The He 100 was an extremely small and good-looking fighter produced as a series of prototype and development batches, one of which gained a world speed record (464 mph, March 1939). Twelve He 100D-1s were used for fake propaganda photographs which fooled Britain into believing a new fighter called the He 113 was in large-scale service.

Heinkel He 162 Salamander

He 162A-2

Type: single-seat interceptor.
Engine: one 1760 lb (800 kg) thrust BMW 003E-1 or E-2 Orkan single-shaft turbojet.
Dimensions: span 23 ft 7¾ in (7·2 m); length 29 ft 8½ in (9 m); height 6 ft 6½ in (2·6 m).
Weights: empty 4,796 lb (2180 kg); loaded 5940 lb (2695 kg).
Performance: maximum speed 490 mph (784 km/h) at sea level, 522 mph (835 km/h) at 19,700 ft (6000 m); initial climb 4200 ft (1280 m)/min; service ceiling 39,500 ft (12,040 m); range at full throttle 434 miles (695 km) at altitude.
Armament: early versions, two 30 mm Rheinmetall MK 108 cannon with 50 rounds each; later production, two 20 mm Mauser MG 151/20 with 120 rounds each.
History: first flight 6 December 1944; first delivery January 1945.
Popularly called "Volksjäger" (People's Fighter), this incredible aircraft left behind so many conflicting

impressions it is hard to believe the whole programme was started and finished in little more than six months. To appreciate the almost impossible nature of the programme, Germany was being pounded to rubble by fleets of Allied bombers that darkened the sky, and the aircraft industry and the Luftwaffe's fuel supplies were inexorably running down. Experienced aircrew had nearly all been killed, materials were in critically short supply and time had to be measured not in months but in days. So on 8 September 1944 the RLM issued a specification calling for a 750 km/h jet fighter to be regarded as a piece of consumer goods and to be ready by 1 January 1945. Huge numbers of workers were organised to build it even before it was designed and Hitler Youth were hastily trained in primary gliders before being strapped into the new jet. Heinkel, which

had built the world's first turbojet aircraft (He 178, flown 27 August 1939) and the first jet fighter (He 280 twin-jet, flown on its jet engines 2 April 1941) won a hasty competition with a tiny wooden machine with its engine perched on top and blasting between twin fins. Drawings were ready on 30 October 1944. The prototype flew in 37 days and plans were made for production to rise rapidly to 4,000 per month. Despite extreme difficulties, 300 of various sub-types had been completed by VE-day, with 800 more on the assembly lines. I/JG1 was operational at Leck, though without fuel. Despite many bad characteristics the 162 was a fighter of a futuristic kind, created in quantity far quicker than modern aircraft are even drawn on paper.

Heinkel He 177 Greif

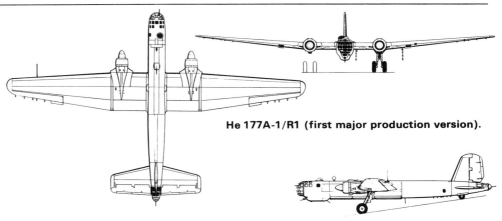

He 177A-1/R1 (first major production version).

He 177A-0 to A-5, He 277 and He 274

Type: He 177, six-seat heavy bomber and missile carrier.
Engines: two 2,950 hp Daimler-Benz DB 610A-1/B-1, each comprising two inverted-vee-12 liquid-cooled engines geared to one propeller.
Dimensions: span 103 ft 1¾ in (31·44 m); length 72 ft 2 in (22 m); height 21 ft (6·4 m).
Weights: empty 37,038 lb (16,800 kg); loaded (A-5) 68,343 lb (31,000 kg).
Performance: maximum speed (at 41 000 lb 18,615 kg) 295 mph (472 km/hr); initial climb 853 ft (260 m)/min; service ceiling 26,500 ft (7080 m); range with FX or Hs 293 missiles (no bombs) about 3,107 miles (5000 km).
Armament: (A-5/R2) one 7·92 mm MG 81J manually aimed in nose, one 20 mm MG 151 manually aimed at front of ventral gondola, one or two 13 mm MG 131 in forward dorsal turret, one MG 131 in rear dorsal turret, one MG 151 manually aimed in tail and two MG 81 or one MG 131 manually aimed at rear of gondola; maximum internal bomb load 13,200 lb (6000 kg), seldom carried; external load, two Hs 293 guided missiles, FX 1400 guided bombs, mines or torpedoes (more if internal bay blanked off and racks added below it).
History: first flight (He 177V-1) 19 November 1939; (pre-production He 177A-0) November 1941; service delivery (A-1) March 1942; (A-5) February 1943; first flight (He 277V-1) December 1943; (He 274, alias AAS 01A) December 1945.

The Heinkel 177, Germany's biggest bomber programme in World War II, is remembered as possibly the most troublesome and unsatisfactory aircraft in military history, and it was only though dogged courage and persistence that large numbers were put into service. Much of the fault lay in the stupid 1938 requirement that the proposed heavy bomber and anti-ship aircraft should be capable of dive bombing. Certainly the wish to reduce drag by using coupled pairs of engines was mistaken, because no engines in bomber history have caught fire so often in normal cruising flight. Six of the eight prototypes crashed and many of the 35 pre-production A-0s (built mainly by Arado) were written off in take-off swings or in-flight fires. Arado built 130 A-1s, followed by 170 Heinkel-built A-3s and

826 A-5s with repositioned engines and longer fuselages. About 700 served on the Eastern Front, many having 50 mm and 75 mm guns for tank-busting; a few nervously bombed Britain in 400 mph shallow dives, without any proper aiming of their bombs. So bothersome were these beasts that Goering forbade Heinkel to pester him any more with plans to use four separate engines, but Heinkel secretly flew the He 277, with four 1,750 hp DB 603A, at Vienna, as the first of a major programme. The almost completely redesigned He 274 was a high-altitude bomber developed at the Farman factory at Suresnes, with four 1,850 hp engines, a 145 ft wing and twin fins. After the liberation it was readied for flight and flown at Orléans-Bricy.

Heinkel He 111

He 111 B series, E series, H series and P series
Type: four-seat or five-seat medium bomber (later, torpedo bomber, glider tug and missile launcher).
Engines: (He 111H-3) two 1200 hp Junkers Jumo 211D-2 12-cylinder inverted-vee liquid-cooled; (He 111P-2) two 1100 hp Daimler-Benz DB 601A-1 12-cylinder inverted-vee liquid-cooled.
Dimensions: span 74 ft 1¾ in (22·6 m); length 53 ft 9½ in (16·4 m); height 13 ft 1½ in (4 m).
Weights: empty (H-3) 17,000 lb (7720 kg); (P-2) 17,640 lb (8000 kg); maximum loaded (H-3) 30,865 lb (14,000 kg); (P-2) 29,762 lb (13,500 kg).
Performance: maximum speed (H-3) 258 mph (415 km/h); (P-2) 242 mph (390 km/h) at 16,400 ft (5000 m) (at maximum weight, neither version could exceed 205 mph (330 km/h); climb to 14,765 ft (4500 m) 30–35 min at normal gross weight, 50 min at maximum; service ceiling (both) around 25,590 ft (7800m) at normal gross weight, under 16,400 ft (5000 m) at maximum; range with maximum bomb load (both) about 745 miles (1200 km).

A natural twin-engined outgrowth of the He 70, the first He 111 was a graceful machine with elliptical wings and tail, secretly flown as a bomber but revealed to the world a year later as a civil airliner. Powered by 660 hp BMW VI engines, it had typical armament of three manually aimed machine guns but the useful bomb load of 2,200 lb (1000 kg) stowed nose-up in eight cells in the centre fuselage. In 1937 a number of generally similar machines secretly flew photo-reconnaissance missions over Britain, France and the Soviet Union, in the guise of airliners of Deutsche Luft Hansa. In the same year the He 111B-1 came into Luftwaffe service, with two 880 hp Daimler-Benz DB 600C engines, while a vast new factory was built at Oranienburg solely to make later versions. In February 1937 operations began with the Legion Kondor in Spain, with considerable success, flight performance being improved in the B-2 by 950 hp DB 600CG engines which were retained in the C series. The D was faster, with the 1,000 hp Jumo 211A-1, also used in the He 111 F in which a new straight-edged wing was introduced. To a considerable degree the success of the early elliptical-winged He 111 bombers in Spain misled the Luftwaffe into considering that nothing could withstand the onslaught of their huge fleets of medium bombers. These aircraft – the trim Do 17, the broad-winged He 111 and the high-performance Ju 88 – were all extremely advanced by the standards of the mid-1930s when they were de-

signed. They were faster than the single-seat fighters of that era and, so the argument went, therefore did not need much defensive armament. So the three machine guns carried by the first He 111 bombers in 1936 stayed unchanged until, in the Battle of Britain, the He 111 was hacked down with ease, its only defence being its toughness and ability to come back after being shot to pieces. The inevitable result was that more and more defensive guns were added, needing a fifth or even a sixth crew-member. Coupled with incessant growth in equipment and armour the result was deteriorating performance, so that the record-breaker of 1936–38 became the lumbering sitting duck of 1942–45. Yet the He 111 was built in ever-greater numbers, virtually all the later sub-types being members of the prolific H-series. Variations were legion, including versions with large barrage-balloon deflectors, several kinds of missiles (including a V-1 tucked under the left wing root), while a few were completed as saboteur transports. The most numerous version was the H-6, and the extraordinary He 111Z (Zwilling) glider tug of 1942 consisted of two H-6s joined by a common centre wing carrying a fifth engine. Right to the end of the war the RLM and German industry failed to find a replacement for the old "Spaten" (spade), and the total produced in Germany and Romania was at least 6,086 and possibly more than 7,000. Merlin-engined C.2111 versions continued in production in Spain until 1956.

He 112, He 162, He 177 see page 115.

Heinkel He 111H-3 cutaway drawing key:

1 Starboard navigation light
2 Starboard aileron
3 Lattice ribs
4 Front spar
5 Rear spar
6 Aileron tab
7 Starboard flap
8 Outboard fuel tank (220 gal/1,000 litres capacity)
9 Wing centre section/outer panel break line
10 Inboard fuel tank (154 gal/700 litres capacity) inboard of nacelle
11 Oil tank cooling louvres
12 Oil cooler air intake
13 Supercharger air intake
14 Three-blade VDM propeller
15 Airscrew pitch-change mechanism
16 Junkers Jumo 211D-1 12-cylinder inverted-vee liquid-cooled engine
17 Exhaust manifold
18 Nose-mounted 7·92mm MG 15 machine gun
19 Ikaria ball-and-socket gun mounting (offset to starboard)
20 Bomb sight housing (offset to starboard)
21 Starboard mainwheel
22 Rudder pedals
23 Bomb aimer's prone pad
24 Additional 7·92mm MG 15 machine gun (fitted by forward maintenance units)
25 Repeater compass
26 Bomb aimer's folding seat

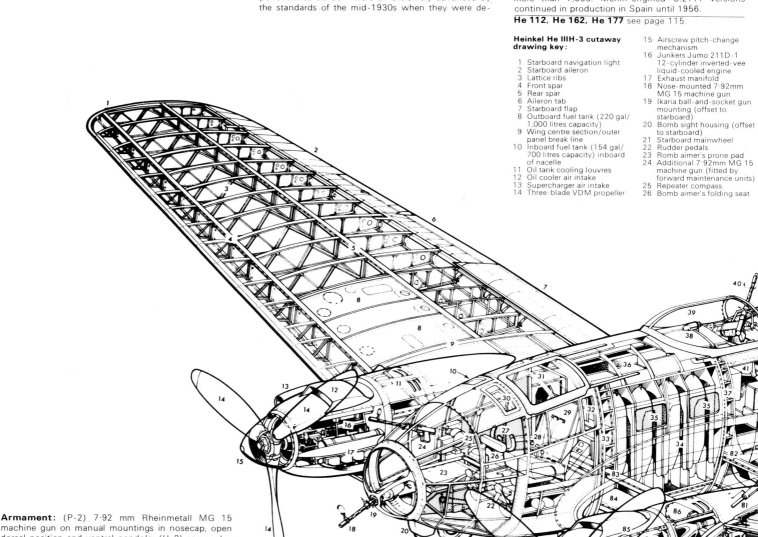

Armament: (P-2) 7·92 mm Rheinmetall MG 15 machine gun on manual mountings in nosecap, open dorsal position and ventral gondola; (H-3) same, plus fixed forward-firing MG 15 or 17; two MG 15s in waist windows and (usually) 20 mm MG FF cannon in front of ventral gondola and (sometimes) fixed rear-firing MG 17 in extreme tail; internal bomb load up to 4410 lb (2000 kg) in vertical cells, stored nose-up; external bomb load (at expense of internal) one 4410 lb (2000 kg) on H-3, one or two 1102 lb (500 kg) on others; later marks carried one or two 1686 lb (765 kg) torpedoes, Bv 246 glide missiles, Hs 293 rocket missiles, Fritz X radio-controlled glide bombs or one FZG-76 ("V-1") cruise missile.
History: first flight (He 111V1 prototype) 24 February 1935; (pre-production He 111B-0) August 1936; (production He 111B-1) 30 October 1936; (first He 111E series) January 1938; (first production He 111P-1) December 1938; (He 111H-1) January or February 1939; final delivery (He 111H-23) October 1944; (Spanish C.2111) late 1956.

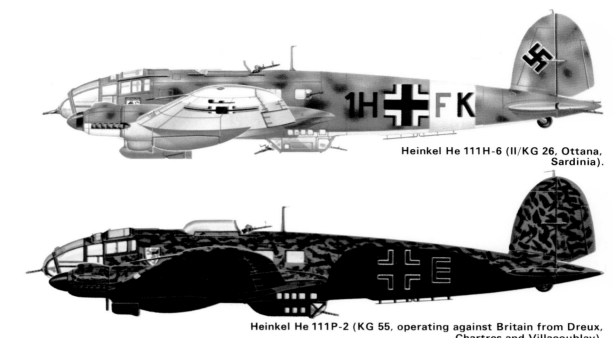

Heinkel He 111H-6 (II/KG 26, Ottana, Sardinia).

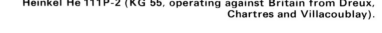

Heinkel He 111P-2 (KG 55, operating against Britain from Dreux, Chartres and Villacoublay).

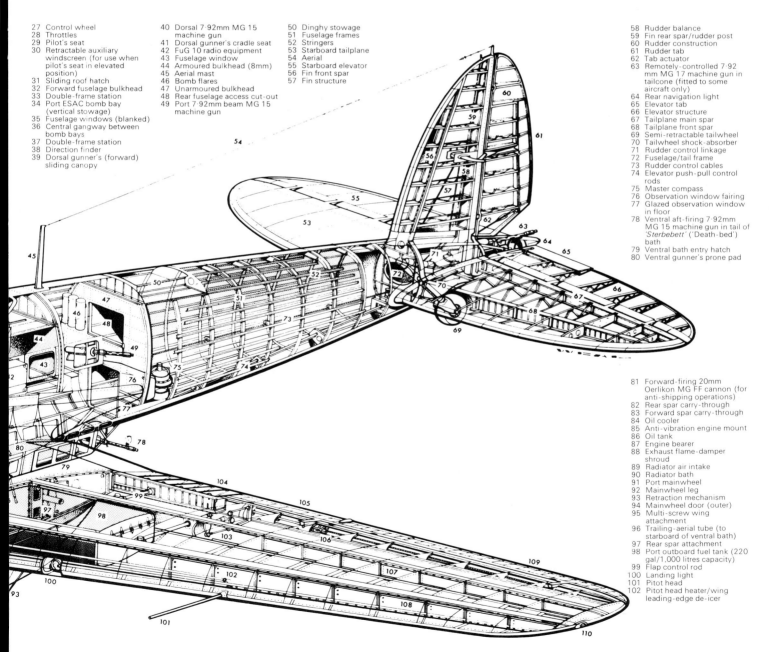

27 Control wheel
28 Throttles
29 Pilot's seat
30 Retractable auxiliary windscreen (for use when pilot's seat in elevated position)
31 Sliding roof hatch
32 Forward fuselage bulkhead
33 Double-frame station
34 Port ESAC bomb bay (vertical stowage)
35 Fuselage windows (blanked)
36 Central gangway between bomb bays
37 Double-frame station
38 Direction finder
39 Dorsal gunner's (forward) sliding canopy

40 Dorsal 7·92mm MG 15 machine gun
41 Dorsal gunner's cradle seat
42 FuG 10 radio equipment
43 Fuselage window
44 Armoured bulkhead (8mm)
45 Aerial mast
46 Bomb flares
47 Unarmoured bulkhead
48 Rear fuselage access cut-out
49 Port 7·92mm beam MG 15 machine gun

50 Dinghy stowage
51 Fuselage frames
52 Stringers
53 Starboard tailplane
54 Aerial
55 Starboard elevator
56 Fin front spar
57 Fin structure

58 Rudder balance
59 Fin rear spar/rudder post
60 Rudder construction
61 Rudder tab
62 Tab actuator
63 Remotely-controlled 7·92 mm MG 17 machine gun in tailcone (fitted to some aircraft only)
64 Rear navigation light
65 Elevator tab
66 Elevator structure
67 Tailplane main spar
68 Tailplane front spar
69 Semi-retractable tailwheel
70 Tailwheel shock-absorber
71 Rudder control linkage
72 Fuselage/tail frame
73 Rudder control cables
74 Elevator push-pull control rods
75 Master compass
76 Observation window fairing
77 Glazed observation window in floor
78 Ventral aft-firing 7·92mm MG 15 machine gun in tail of 'Sterbebett' ('Death-bed') bath
79 Ventral bath entry hatch
80 Ventral gunner's prone pad

81 Forward-firing 20mm Oerlikon MG FF cannon (for anti-shipping operations)
82 Rear spar carry-through
83 Forward spar carry-through
84 Oil cooler
85 Anti-vibration engine mount
86 Oil tank
87 Engine bearer
88 Exhaust flame-damper shroud
89 Radiator air intake
90 Radiator bath
91 Port mainwheel
92 Mainwheel leg
93 Retraction mechanism
94 Mainwheel door (outer)
95 Multi-screw wing attachment
96 Trailing-aerial tube (to starboard of ventral bath)
97 Rear spar attachment
98 Port outboard fuel tank (220 gal/1,000 litres capacity)
99 Flap control rod
100 Landing light
101 Pitot head
102 Pitot head heater/wing leading-edge de-icer

103 Flap and aileron coupling
104 Flap structure
105 Aileron tab
106 Tab actuator
107 Rear spar
108 Forward spar
109 Port aileron
110 Port navigation light

The cutaway shows the He 111H-3, one of the first of the "definitive" Jumo-powered series which remained in production until 1945, long after these once-formidable aircraft had become obsolescent.

Heinkel He 219 Uhu

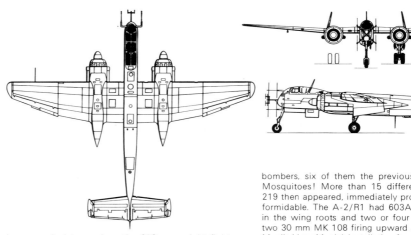

He 219A-5/R1

He 219A-0 to A-7, B and C series
Type: A series, two-seat night fighter.
Engines: usually two 1,900 hp Daimler-Benz DB 603G inverted-vee-12 liquid-cooled; other engines, see text.
Dimensions: (A-series) span 60 ft 2 in or 60 ft 8 in (18·5 m); length (with aerials) 50 ft 11¾ in (15·54 m); height 13 ft 5½ in (4·1 m).
Weights: (A-7) empty 24,692 lb (11,200 kg); loaded 33,730 kg (15,200 kg).
Performance: (A-7) maximum speed 416 mph (670 km/h); initial climb 1,804 ft (550 m)/min; service ceiling 41,660 ft (12,700 m); range 1,243 miles (2000 km).
Armament: varied, see text.
History: first flight (219V-1) 15 November 1942; service delivery (prototypes) May 1943; (production 219A-1) November 1943.

Ernst Heinkel was the pioneer of gas-turbine jet aircraft, flying the He 178 on 27 August 1939 and the He 280 twin-jet fighter as a glider on 22 September 1940 and with its engines on 2 April 1941 (before the purely experimental Gloster E.28/39). But Heinkel was unable to build the extremely promising He 280 in quantity, which was fortunate for the Allies. He had no spare capacity for the He 219 either, which had excited little official interest when submitted as the P.1060 project in August 1940 as a high-speed fighter, bomber and torpedo carrier. It was only when RAF night attacks began to hurt, at the end of 1941, that

he was asked to produce the 219 as a night fighter (Uhu meaning Owl). The He 219V-1, with 1,750 hp DB 603As and two MG 151/20 cannon, plus an MG 131 in the rear cockpit, was fast and extremely manoeuvrable and the test pilots at Rechlin were thrilled by it. Successive prototypes had much heavier armament and radar and 100 were ordered from five factories in Germany, Poland and Austria. The order was soon trebled and Luftwaffe enthusiasm was such that even the early prototypes were sent to Venlo, Holland, to form a special trials unit. The first six night sorties resulted in the claimed destruction of 20 RAF

bombers, six of them the previously almost immune Mosquitoes! More than 15 different versions of the 219 then appeared, immediately proving outstandingly formidable. The A-2/R1 had 603As, two MG 151/20 in the wing roots and two or four in a belly tray and two 30 mm MK 108 firing upward at 65° in a Schräge Musik (Jazz Music) installation for destroying bombers by formating below them. The A-7/R1 had MK 108s in the wing roots and two of these big guns and two MG 151/20 in the tray, plus the Schräge Musik with 100 rounds per gun (the most lethal of all). Some versions had three seats, long-span wing and DB 603L turbocharged engines, or Jumo 213s or even the 2,500 hp Jumo 222 with six banks of four cylinders. The B and C families would have been enlarged multi-role versions with rear turrets. Total A-type production was only 268, the officials at one time ignoring Luftwaffe enthusiasm by ordering production to be stopped!

Henschel Hs 123

Hs 123A-1
Type: single-seat dive bomber and close-support.
Engine: one 880 hp BMW 132 Dc nine-cylinder radial.
Dimensions: span 34 ft 5½ in (10·5 m); length 27 ft 4 in (8·3 m); height 10 ft 6½ in (3·2 m).
Weights: empty 3,316 lb (1504 kg); loaded 4,888 lb (2217 kg).
Performance: maximum speed 214 mph (345 km/h); initial climb 2,950 ft (900 m)/min; service ceiling 29,530 ft (9000 m); range 530 miles (850 km).
Armament: two 7·92 mm Rheinmetall MG 17 machine guns ahead of pilot; underwing racks for four 110 lb (50 kg) bombs, or clusters of antipersonnel bombs or two 20 mm MG FF cannon.
History: first flight, spring 1935 (public display given 8 May); first delivery (Spain) December 1936; final delivery, October 1938.

Though representing a class of aircraft generally considered obsolete by the start of World War II, this trim little biplane was kept hard at work until 1942, achieving results which in retrospect seem almost unbelievable. The prototype needed extensive modification to produce the A-1 production version, which was tested in the Spanish Civil War. Contrary to the staff-college theories then adhered to by the newly formed Luftwaffe, the Henschels were able to give

Henschel Hs 123A-1 (V Schlacht/LG2)

close support to ground troops of a most real and immediate kind, strafing and bombing with great accuracy despite the lack of any radio link or even an established system of operation. Eventually the Luftwaffe realised that the concept of a close-support aircraft was valid, and a few Henschels were allowed to operate in this role, but all the effort and money was put into the Ju 87, and the Hs 123 was phased out of

production before World War II. Yet in the Polish campaign these aircraft proved unbelievably useful, having the ability to make pinpoint attacks with guns and bombs and, by virtue of careful setting of the propeller speed, to make a demoralising noise. Moreover, it established an extraordinary reputation for returning to base even after direct hits by AA shells. As a result, though the whole force was incessantly threatened with disbandment or replacement by later types, the Hs 123 close-support unit II (Schlacht)/LG2 was sent intact to the Balkans in April 1941 and thence to the USSR. Here the old biplanes fought around the clock, proving far better adapted to the conditions than more modern types and continuing in front-line operations until, by the end of 1944, there were no more left.

Henschel Hs 129

Hs 129A and B series
Type: single-seat close support and ground attack.
Engines: (B-series) two 690 hp Gnome-Rhône 14M 04/05 14-cylinder two-row radials.
Dimensions: span 46 ft 7 in (14·2 m); length 31 ft 11¾ in (9·75 m); height 10 ft 8 in (3·25 m).
Weights: (typical B-1) empty 8,940 lb (4060 kg); loaded 11,265 lb (5110 kg).
Performance: (typical B-1) maximum speed 253 mph (408 km/h); initial climb 1,390 ft (425 m)/min; service ceiling 29,530 ft (9000 m); range 547 miles (880 km).
Armament: see text.

Henschel Hs 129B-2 (4/Pz Schlachtgeschwader 1)

History: first flight (Hs 129V-1) early 1939; service delivery (129A-0) early 1941; first flight (129B) October 1941; service delivery (129B) late 1942.

Though there were numerous types of specialised close support and ground attack aircraft in World War I, this category was virtually ignored until the Spanish Civil War showed, again, that it is one of the most important of all. In 1938 the RLM issued a specification for such an aircraft – the whole purpose of the Luftwaffe being to support the Wehrmacht in Blitz-krieg-type battles – to back up the purpose-designed Ju 87 dive bomber. Henschel's Dipl-Ing F. Nicholaus designed a trim machine somewhat resembling the twin-engined fighters of the period but with more

armour and less-powerful engines (two 495 hp Argus As 410A-1 air-cooled inverted-vee-12s). The solo pilot sat in the extreme nose behind a windscreen 3 in thick, with armour surrounding the cockpit. The triangular-section fuselage housed self-sealing tanks, guns in the sloping sides and a hardpoint for a bomb underneath. Test pilots at Rechlin damned the A-0 pre-production batch as grossly underpowered, but these aircraft were used on the Eastern Front by the Rumanian Air Force. The redesigned B-series used the vast numbers of French 14M engines that were available and in production by the Vichy government for the Me 323. Altogether 841 B-series were built, and used with considerable effect on the Eastern Front but with less success, in North Africa. The B-1/R1 had

two 7·92 mm MG 17 and two 20 mm MG 151/20, plus two 110 lb or 48 fragmentation bombs. The R2 had a 30 mm MK 101 clipped underneath and was the first aircraft ever to use a 30 mm gun in action. The R3 had a ventral box of four MG 17. The R4 carried up to 551 lb of bombs. The R5 had a camera for vertical photography. The B-2 series changed the inbuilt MG 17s for MG 131s and other subtypes had many kinds of armament including the 37 mm BK 3·7 and 75 mm BK 7·5 with muzzle about eight feet ahead of the nose. The most novel armament, used against Russian armour with results that were often devastating, was a battery of six smooth-bore 75 mm tubes firing recoilless shells down and to the rear with automatic triggering as the aircraft flew over metal objects.

HF-24 Marut

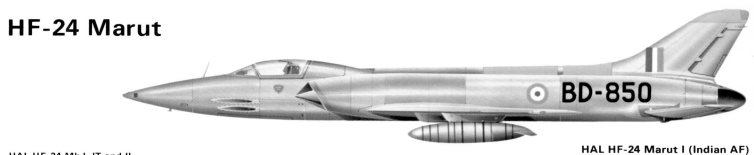

HAL HF-24 Marut I (Indian AF)

HAL HF-24 Mk I, IT and II
Type: single-seat fighter and ground attack (IT, two-seat trainer).
Engines: two 4,850 lb (2200 kg) thrust Rolls-Royce (originally Bristol, then Bristol Siddeley) Orpheus 703 single-shaft turbojets, licence-made by HAL.
Dimensions: span 26 ft 6¼ in (9 m); length 52 ft 0¾ in (15·87 m); height 11 ft 9¾ in (3·6 m).
Weights: (Mk I) empty 13,658 lb (6195 kg); loaded (clean) 19,734 lb (8951 kg); loaded (maximum) 24,085 lb (10.925 kg).
Performance: maximum speed, 691 mph (1112 km/h, Mach 0·91) at sea level, about 675 mph (1086 km/h, Mach 1·02) at altitude; time to climb to 40,000 ft (12,200 m) 9 min 20 sec; range on internal fuel about 620 miles (1000 km).
Armament: four 30 mm Aden Mk 2 cannon each with 120 rounds, retractable Matra pack of 50 SNEB 68 mm rockets, and four wing pylons each rated at 1,000 lb (454 kg).

History: first flight 17 June 1961; (pre-production) March 1963; (series production) 15 November 1967; (Mk IT) 30 April 1970.

After 1950 the Indian government decided to authorise development of an Indian combat aircraft, and the services of Dipl-Ing Kurt Tank, the renowned Focke-Wulf designer, were secured to lead a new team formed by Hindustan Aircraft at Banglore. Detail design began in 1956, the objective being to create a multi-role aircraft potentially capable of reaching Mach 2 with minimal technical risk. The prototype, powered by two of the same engines already being produced for the Gnat, proved generally successful, and two of the 18 pre-production Maruts ("Wind Spirit") were officially handed over (though as a token delivery) to the IAF in May 1964, the year the company reorganised and expanded into its present form as Hindustan Aeronautics. By the end of 1975 about 100 production

Mk Is had been delivered, many of them being used (without loss) in the December 1971 war against Pakistan. The Mk IT has a second Martin-Baker seat in place of the rocket pack and has since 1974 also been produced in small numbers as a dual conversion and weapon trainer. In 1967 the German staff left and an Indian design team has since continued the 20-year search for a more powerful engine. HAL has tested afterburning engines and flew the Marut IBX with one Orpheus replaced by an Egyptian Brandner E-300, but the most likely solution will be the HSS-73 (Marut III) with two Turbo-Union RB.199 engines in a considerably improved airframe. Despite obvious handicaps HAL has already created a useful multi-role platform which could carry radar, cameras or other equipment and has reached a satisfactory state of operational development. The Mk III could continue the same basic design to the end of the century.

IAI Kfir

IAI Kfir
Type: single-seat fighter bomber.
Engine: one 17,900 lb (8120 kg) thrust General Electric J79-17 single-shaft turbojet with afterburner.
Dimensions: span 26 ft 11½ in (8·22 m); length approximately 54 ft (16·5 m); height 13 ft 11½ in (4·25 m).
Weights: empty, about 15,000 lb (6800 kg); maximum, about 32,000 lb (14,515 kg).
Performance: maximum speed about 850 mph (1370 km/h, Mach 1·12) at sea level, 1,460 mph (2350 km/h, Mach 2·2) at altitude; initial climb about 40,000 ft (12,200 m)/min; service ceiling higher than 55,000 ft (16,765 m); range on internal fuel about 700 miles (1125 km).
Armament: not disclosed but includes 30 mm cannon and considerable external weapon load.
History: first flight, prior to 1974; service delivery, prior to 1975.

In the 1950s the beleaguered state of Israel looked principally to France for its combat aircraft and it was mainly with Israeli partnership that Dassault was able to develop the original Mirage IIIC as a combat type. In the fantastic Six-Day War of 5–10 June 1967 the Israeli Mirage IIICJ starred as the most brilliantly flown combat aircraft of modern times; but Dassault was angrily told by Gen de Gaulle not to deliver the improved Mirage 5 attack aircraft which had been developed for Israel and already paid for. With this history it was a foregone conclusion that Israel Aircraft Industries (IAI) at Lod Airport should be directed to

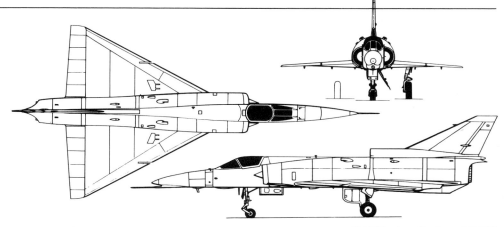

IAI Kfir (as disclosed 1975)

apply their great technical expertise to making Israel more self-sufficient in combat aircraft and, in particular, to devising an improved IAI development of the Mirage which could be built in Israel. By 1971 there were reports of a Mirage powered by the J79 engine, supposedly named Barak (Lightning), and such aircraft were even said to have participated in quantity in the 1973 Yom Kippur war. On 14 April 1975 the truth (some of it) escaped when tight Israeli security relented briefly at the public unveiling of the Kfir (Lion Cub). Described as one the cheapest modern combat aircraft, at about $4 million, the Kfir is not a remanufactured IIICJ — though doubtless the proto-

types were — but a new multi-role fighter bomber marking a significant advance over previous delta Mirages. The engine is considerably more powerful and necessitated redesign of the fuselage and addition of a ram-cooling inlet ahead of the fin. The shorter engine results in a shorter rear fuselage, but the nose is much lengthened and equipped with comprehensive avionics. The entire flight-control and weapon delivery system is by IAI companies and a generation later than that even of the Mirage F1. Though the Kfir did not participate in the 1973 war it was in full service in 1975, and available for export.

I.A.R. 80

I.A.R.80, 80A to D, 81 and 81A to C
Type: single-seat fighter (80D onwards, fighter bomber).
Engine: (80A onwards) one 1,025 hp Gnome-Rhône 14K 115 Mistral Major 14-cylinder two-row radial licence-built by I.A.R.
Dimensions: span 32 ft 10 in (10 m); length 26 ft 9½ in (8·16 m); height 11 ft 10 in (1·9 m).
Weights: (80A) empty 3,930 lb (1782 kg); loaded 5,480 lb (2485 kg).
Performance: maximum speed 342 mph (550 km/h); initial climb 2,790 ft (850 m)/min; service ceiling 34,450 ft (10,500 m); range 590 miles (950 km).
Armament: two 20 mm cannon (early, Oerlikon MG FF, later MG 151/20) in wing roots, four 7·7 mm machine guns in outer wings; wing racks for two bombs each up to 220 lb (100 kg).
History: first flight (I.A.R.80 prototype) at end of 1938; (production 80) late 1941; final delivery (81) 1943; withdrawal from service, about 1949.

Though the Industria Aeronautica Romana, at Brasov, had designed many successful military and civil aircraft by 1939 it had never seen a Romanian combat aircraft in production. Fighters had been of Polish origin, I.A.R. having prepared in 1937 for licence-production

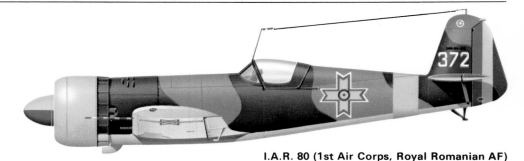

I.A.R. 80 (1st Air Corps, Royal Romanian AF)

of the P.Z.L. P-24 (p.184), which was later to form the backbone of the Romanian Air Force. At the beginning of 1938 the company's design staff under Eng Mircea Grossu-Viziru began to plan a more modern fighter derived from the Polish design and the I.A.R.80 was the result. Though almost unknown to the Allies it was an extremely neat and tough little machine which had a surprisingly troublefree development and outperformed the P-24 by a useful margin. The front and rear were virtually the same as those of the Polish machine, but the long forward fuselage was new and sat on a low cantilever wing which housed the wide-track retracting landing gear. An especially good feature was the bubble-type sliding canopy, which was as good as

that on the Fw 190. The prototypes, made with parts of P-24s, had 940 hp 14N7 engines, but the production machine built under German authority had the more powerful 14K and served on the Eastern Front from about May 1942. The heavy armament was improved in the 80C by changing to the new German Mauser cannon. The 80B had better radio and the 80D more armour and wing bomb racks. Late in 1942 the strengthened 81 supplanted the 80, with twice the bomb load and various equipment and armour standards (hence the different sub-types). About 250 of all versions were built and roughtly half survived the war remaining in Romanian Service, under Soviet domination, until replaced by Russian fighters after 1949.

Ilyushin Il-4

TsKB-26, TsKB-30, DB-3 and DB-3F (Il-4)
Type: four-seat bomber and torpedo carrier.
Engines: final standard, two 1,100 hp M-88B 14-cylinder two-row radials.
Dimensions: span 70 ft 4¼ in (21·44 m); length 48 ft 6½ in (14·8 m); height approximately 13 ft 9 in (4·2 m).
Weights: about 13,230 lb (6000 kg); loaded 22,046 lb (10,000 kg).
Performance: maximum speed 255 mph (410 km/h); initial climb 886 ft (270 m)/min; service ceiling 32,808 ft (10,000 m); range with 2,205 lb of bombs 1,616 miles (2600 km).
Armament: three manually aimed machine guns, in nose, dorsal turret and periscopic ventral position, originally all 7·62 mm ShKAS and from 1942 all 12·7 mm BS; internal bomb bay for ten 220 lb (100 kg) bombs or equivalent, with alternative (or, for short ranges, additional) racks for up to three 1,102 lb (500 kg) or one 2,072 lb (940 kg) torpedo or one 2,205 lb (1000 kg) bomb, all under fuselage.
History: first flight (TsKB-26) 1935; (production DB-3) 1937; (DB-3F) 1939; final delivery 1944.

Though much less well-known around the world than such Western bombers as the B-17 and Lancaster, the Il-4 was one of the great bombers of World War II and saw service in enormous numbers in all roles from close support to strategic bombing of Berlin and low-level torpedo attacks. Originally known by its design bureau designation of TsKB-26 (often reported in the West as CKB-26), it was officially designated DB-3 (DB for·Dalni Bombardirovshchik, long-range bomber) and went into production in early 1937. Powered by two 765 hp M-85 engines, soon replaced by 960 hp M-86, it was roughly in the class of the Hampden, with excellent speed, range, load and manoeuvrability but poor defensive armament (which was never changed, apart from increasing the calibre of the three guns). In 1939 production switched to the DB-3F with blunt nose turret replaced by a long pointed nose. In 1940, when over 2,000 were delivered, the designation was changed to Il-4, conforming with the new scheme in which aircraft were named for their designers (in this case Sergei Ilyushin). After the German invasion desperate materials shortage nearly halted production but by 1942 new plants in Siberia were building huge numbers of Il-4s with a redesigned airframe incorporating the maximum amount of wood. More than

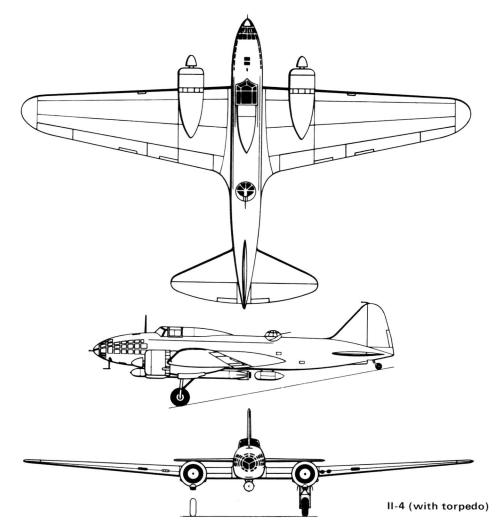

10,000 had been delivered when production was stopped in 1944. Il-4s bombed Berlin many times, the first time by a force of VVS-VMF (Soviet Navy) Il-4s

on 8 August 1941. By 1943 reconnaissance and glider towing were additional duties for these hard-worked aircraft.

Il-4 (with torpedo)

Ilyushin Il-2 Stormovik

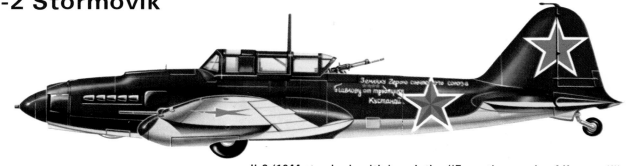

Il-2 (1944 standard, with inscription "From the people of Kustenai")

BSh-2, TsKB-57, Il-2, Il-2M3 and Il-10
Type: single-seat or two-seat close support and attack.
Engine: (Il-2) one 1,300 hp M-38 or (from 1942) 1,750 hp AM-38F; (Il-10) one 2,000 hp AM-42; all engines vee-12 liquid-cooled.
Dimensions: span (Il-2) 47 ft 11 in (14·6 m); (Il-10) 45 ft 7 in (13·9 m); length (Il-2) originally 38 ft 2¾ in, then 39 ft 4½ in (12 m); (Il-10) 40 ft 0¼ in (12·2 m); height (Il-2) 11 ft 1¾ in (3·4 m); (Il-10) 11 ft 5¾ in (3·5 m).
Weights: empty (Il-2, typical) 7,165 lb (3250 kg); (Il-10) 7,495 lb (3400 kg); loaded (Il-2M3) 12,947 lb (5872 kg); (Il-10) 13,968 lb (6336 kg).
Performance: maximum speed (Il-2) from 281 mph clean to 231 mph with 1,323 lb bomb load; (Il-10) 311 mph clean (500 km/h); initial climb (Il-2, maximum bomb load) 490 ft (150 m)/min; service ceiling (all, with bomb load, typical) 21,325 ft (6500 m); range with bomb load (all, typical) 373 miles (600 km).
Armament: (original Il-2) two 20 mm ShVAK and two 7·62 mm ShKAS fixed in wing, underwing racks for eight 82 mm rockets and four 220 lb bombs; (Il-2M3) two 20 mm VYa and/or two 37 mm in wings, one manually aimed 12·7 mm BS in added rear cockpit, bomb load of 1,323 lb (600 kg) including rockets and PTAB anti-armour bombs; (Il-10) two or

four 20 mm VYa or two or four 23 mm NS 23, often with two 7·62 mm ShKAS, dorsal turret with 20 mm VYa, racks for up to 2,205 lb (1000 kg) of weapons.
History: first flight (BSh-2) 30 December 1939; (TsKB-57) 12 October 1940; (production Il-2) March 1941; (two-seat) September 1942; (Il-10) early 1944.

Especially when a second crew-member was added, the Stormovik (more accurately BSh, Bronirovanni Shtoormovik, armoured attacker) had a lot in common with the Fairey Battle. They were similar in shape, size, weight and general performance. But, while the underpowered and underarmed Battle was a death-trap, hastily forgotten, the Soviet machine sustained what is believed to have been the biggest production run of any aircraft in history. Throughout World War II production from three large plants averaged about 1,200 per month and it is thought total Il-2 output exceeded 35,000. When the Il-10 is included the total may well surpass 40,000 (a Polish estimate is 41,400). In fact, resemblance to the Battle was only skin-deep. The skin of even the prototype BSh-2 was steel armour in all vital areas, the armour forming part of the structure and weighing over 1,540 lb (15 per cent of gross weight). Vladimir Kokkinaki flew the

prototype, finding it underpowered. With the AM-38 engine subsequent TsKB-57 prototypes did better and production began on a large scale in time for squadrons to have formed at the start of the German invasion. The single-seat Il-2 had a considerable fuel load and heavy armament which, for the first time, included effective ground-attack rockets. Produced in vast numbers in 1942, changes were called for which resulted in the M3 version with AM-38F engine, rear gun and heavier anti-tank armament. Operating in pairs at nought feet, or in sections of ten with escort at 1,000 ft the Il-2s operated day and night along the Eastern Front and often shot down Bf 109s, besides (with new guns and special bombs) managing to defeat the thick armour of PzKW 5 Panther and PzKW 6 Tiger tanks. In the opinion of the Soviet Union, no other aircraft played so decisive a role in modern land warfare. By 1943 Ilyushin's bureau was designing the more streamlined Il-10, with wheels which turned to lie flush in the revised wing, all-stressed-skin structure, more power and improved armour and armament. Chosen over the rival Su-6, it went into production following the last Il-2s in June 1944 and was in service in large numbers by VE-day. Many remained in service in Communist forces until after the Korean war (1953).

Ilyushin Il-28

Il-28, 28R, 28T and 28U

Type: three-seat bomber and ground attack; (28R) reconnaissance; (28T) torpedo carrier; (28U) dual trainer.

Engines: two 5,952 lb (2700 kg) thrust Klimov VK-1 single-shaft centrifugal turbojets.

Dimensions: span (without tip tanks) 70 ft 4¾ in (21·45 m); length 57 ft 10¾ in (17·65 m); height 22 ft (6·7 m).

Weights: empty 28,417 lb (12,890 kg); maximum loaded 46,297 lb (21,000 kg).

Performance: maximum speed 559 mph (900 km/h); initial climb 2,953 ft (900 m)/min; service ceiling 40,355 ft (12,300 m); range with bomb load 684 miles (1100 km).

Armament: (Il-28, typical) two 23 mm NR-23 cannon fixed in nose and two NR-23 in powered tail turret; internal bomb capacity of 2,205 lb (1000 kg), with option of carrying double this load or external load (such as two 400 mm light torpedoes).

History: first flight (prototype) 8 August 1948; (production Il-28) early 1950; service delivery 1950; final delivery (USSR) about 1960, (China) after 1968.

After World War II the popular media in the West published a succession of indistinct photographs, drawings and other pictures purporting to show Soviet jet aircraft. Apart from the MiG-9 and Yak-15 (and, after 1951, MiG-15) all were fictitious and by chance none happened to bear much resemblance to aircraft that actually existed. Thus, whereas the 1950 *Jane's* published a drawing and "details" of an Ilyushin four-jet bomber, it knew nothing of the extremely important Il-28 programme then coming to the production stage. Roughly in the class of the Canberra, the Il-28 prototype flew on two RD-10 (Jumo 004 development) turbojets, but the much superior British Nene was quickly substituted and, in VK-1 form, remained

Il-28 (Soviet-built, Chinese AF)

standard in the 10,000 or more subsequent examples. Unusual features are the sharply swept tail surfaces, the single-wheel main gears retracting in bulges under the jetpipes, the fixed nose cannon and the rear turret manned by the radio operator. Known to NATO as "Beagle", it equipped all the Warsaw Pact light bomber units in 1955–70 and was also adopted by the AV-MF as the Il-28T torpedo bomber (that service having originally chosen the rival Tu-14T). The Il-28U dual trainer has distinctive stepped cockpits, and the 28R reconnaissance versions (many probably converted bombers) carry a wide range of electronics and sensors. No longer a front-line type in the Soviet Union, the Il-28 remains in service with some 15 air forces outside Europe, the most important being that of China where some hundreds were built under a licence granted before 1960.

Ilyushin Il-38

Il-38

Type: maritime patrol and anti-submarine.

Engines: four Ivchenko AI-20 single-shaft turboprops, probably rated at about 5,000 shp each.

Dimensions: span 122 ft 8½ in (37·4 m); length 129 ft 10 in (39·6 m); height about 35 ft (10·7 m).

Weights: empty, approximately 90,000 lb (40,820 kg); maximum loaded, approximately 180,000 lb (81,650 kg).

Performance: maximum speed, about 450 mph (724 km/h); maximum cruising speed, about 400 mph (644 km/h); range with typical mission load, about 4,500 miles (7240 km); endurance, about 15 hr.

Armament: internal weapon bay ahead of and behind wing accommodating full range of anti-submarine torpedoes, bombs, mines and other stores; possibly external racks for stores such as guided missiles between weapon-bay doors under wing and beneath outer wings.

History: first flight (Il-18 transport) July 1957; first disclosure of Il-38, 1974, by which time it was well established in operational service.

Following the example of the US Navy and Lockheed with the Electra/P-3 transformation (p. 131), the Soviet Naval Air Arm (AV-MF) used the Il-18 transport as the basis for the considerably changed Il-38, known to NATO by the code-name of "May". Compared with the transport it has a wing moved forward and a considerably longer rear fuselage, showing the

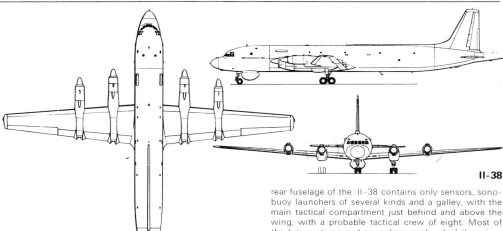

Il-38

gross shift in centre of gravity resulting from the changed role. Whereas in the transport the payload is distributed evenly ahead of and behind the wing, the

rear fuselage of the Il-38 contains only sensors, sono-buoy launchers of several kinds and a galley, with the main tactical compartment just behind and above the wing, with a probable tactical crew of eight. Most of the heavy stores and consoles are ahead of the wing, together with the search radar. The only added item at the rear is the MAD (magnetic anomaly detector) stinger, not a heavy item. So far little is known of the Il-38 and photographs show few of the items one would expect to see. There is no weapon bay below the wing and pressurised fuselage, as in the Nimrod and P-3, no major sensor outlets and aerials and no apparent external stores pylons. On the other hand the Il-38 is undeniably a major new operational type, used not only by the Soviet AV-MF but also by the Egyptian Air Force and probably other countries.

Ilyushin Il-76

Il-76

Type: heavy freight transport.

Engines: four 26,455 lb (12,000 kg) thrust Soloviev D-30KP two-shaft turbofans.

Dimensions: span 165 ft 8 in (50·5 m); length 152 ft 10½ in (46·59 m); height 48 ft 5 in (14·76 m).

Weights: empty, about 159,000 lb (72,000 kg); maximum loaded 346,125 lb (157,000 kg).

Performance: maximum speed, about 560 mph (900 km/h); maximum cruising speed 528 mph (850 km/h); normal long-range cruising height 42,650 ft (13,000 m); range with maximum payload of 88,185 lb (40,000 kg) 3,100 miles (5000 km).

Armament: normally none..

History: first flight 25 March 1971; production deliveries 1973.

First seen in the West at the 1971 Paris Salon, the Il-76 created a most favourable impression. Though superficially seeming to be another Ilyushin copy of a Lockheed design, in this case the C-141 (p. 134), in fact the resemblance is coincidental. The design was prepared to meet a basic need in the Soviet Union for a really capable freighter which, while carrying large indivisible loads, with a high cruising speed and intercontinental range, could operate from relatively poor airstrips. The result is a very useful aircraft which,

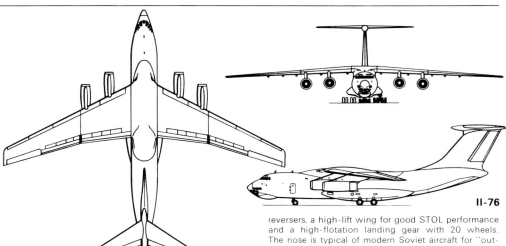

Il-76

though initially being used by Aeroflot in the 1971–5 and 1976–80 plans for opening up Siberia, the far north and far east of the Soviet Union, is obviously a first-class strategic and tactical transport for military use. It has very powerful engines, all fitted with

reversers, a high-lift wing for good STOL performance and a high-flotation landing gear with 20 wheels. The nose is typical of modern Soviet aircraft for "outback" operation, and closely resembles that of the An-22. The big fuselage, usefully larger in cross-section than that of the C-141, is fully pressurised and incorporates a powerful auxiliary power unit and freight handling systems. There seems no reason why the rear clamshell doors should not be opened in flight to permit heavy dropping. The Il-76 has the NATO code name of "Candid".

Junkers J.4-10

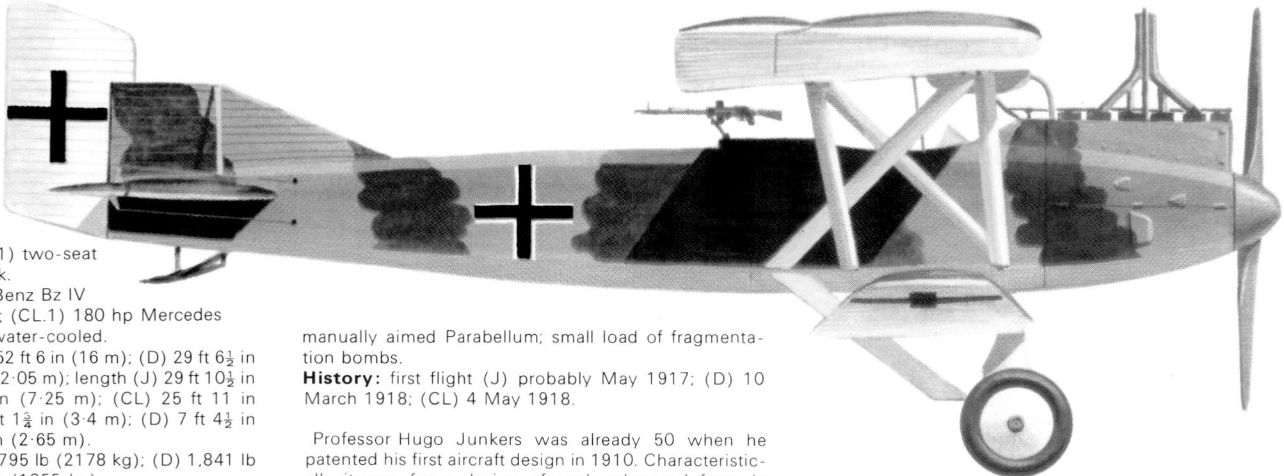

J.1 (J.4), D.1 (J.9) and CL.1 (J.10)
Type: (J.1) close support and battlefield reconnaissance; (D.1) single-seat fighter; (CL.1) two-seat escort and ground attack.
Engine: (J.1) 200 hp Benz Bz IV (D.1) 185 hp BMW IIIa; (CL.1) 180 hp Mercedes D.IIIa, all six-cylinder water-cooled.
Dimensions: span (J) 52 ft 6 in (16 m); (D) 29 ft 6½ in (9 m); (CL) 39 ft 6½ in (12·05 m); length (J) 29 ft 10½ in (9·1 m); (D) 23 ft 9½ in (7·25 m); (CL) 25 ft 11 in (7·9 m); height (J) 11 ft 1¾ in (3·4 m); (D) 7 ft 4½ in (2·25 m); (CL) 8 ft 8¼ in (2·65 m).
Weights: loaded (J) 4,795 lb (2178 kg); (D) 1,841 lb (835 kg); (CL) 2,326 lb (1055 kg).
Performance: maximum speed (J) 97 mph (155 km/h); (D) 116 mph (186 km/h); (CL) 105 mph (169 km/h); service ceiling (J) 13,100 ft (4000 m); (D, CL) 19,700 ft (6000 m); range (J) 193 miles (310 km); (D) 155 miles (250 km); (CL) 186 miles (300 km).
Armament: (J) one 7·92 mm Parabellum manually aimed from rear cockpit, and usually two (sometimes one) similar guns firing obliquely down on left side of observer's cockpit (small number of aircraft had instead one or two 7·92 mm Spandau firing ahead controlled by pilot); also small load of fragmentation bombs, grenades or smoke canisters; (D) two 7·92 mm Spandau fixed above fuselage; (CL) two fixed Spandau and one

manually aimed Parabellum; small load of fragmentation bombs.
History: first flight (J) probably May 1917; (D) 10 March 1918; (CL) 4 May 1918.

Professor Hugo Junkers was already 50 when he patented his first aircraft design in 1910. Characteristically it was for a design of such advanced form (a flying-wing transport) that nobody took it seriously; but, had he not been preoccupied with his factories and university research, he might have built it. In 1915 he proposed an aircraft built entirely of the new light alloy, Duralumin; nobody would sanction scarce metal for such a foolish idea, so he built the J 1 out of steel, with sheet iron covering! Faced with this success the officials gradually accepted that all-metal aircraft were no more impossible than metal ships and when he built the big J 4 biplane it was put into production as the J 1, more than 200 being delivered by the Armistice. Engine, crew and fuel tank were protected by a "bath" of 5 mm steel armour weighing 1,034 lb, so that this

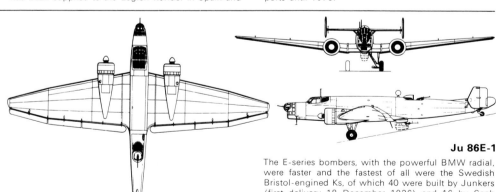

Junkers J.1 (J.4)
(October 1918 camouflage)

tough machine could reconnoitre directly over the heads of enemy troops. The next design built was the J 7, leading to the J 9 single-seat fighter, of which 41 were delivered by the Armistice as the D.1. Potentially an outstanding fighter, the J 9 continued in action with anti-Bolshevik volunteers in the Baltic states in 1919–21. The larger J 10, of which 43 were delivered as the CL.1, also served in the Baltic after the Armistice. They were bluff, squarish machines with the characteristic corrugated skin that Junkers was to see adopted in almost every civilised country before 1935.

Junkers Ju 52

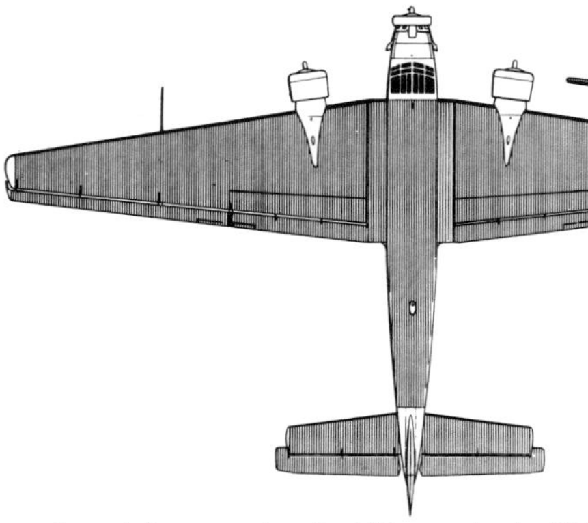

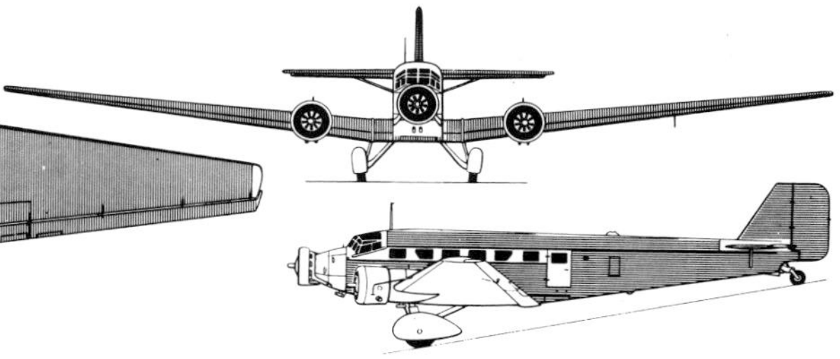

Ju 52/3m in many versions; data for 3mg5e to 3mg14e
Type: passenger and freight transport (also bomber, reconnaissance, mine countermeasures, cas-evac and glider tug).
Engines: three (one in Ju 52) of following types: 600 hp BMW Hornet, 725 hp BMW 132A, 830 hp BMW 132T (standard on nearly all wartime versions), 925 hp Bristol or PZL Pegasus, 750 hp ENMASA Beta E-9C or 710 hp Wright Cyclone (all nine-cylinder radials) or Jumo 5 diesel, Jumo 206 or BMW VI inlines.
Dimensions: span 95 ft 11½ in (29·25 m); length 62 ft (18·9 m); height (landplane) 14 ft 9 in (4·5 m).
Weights: empty 12,346 lb (5600 kg); loaded 24,317 lb (11,030 kg).
Performance: maximum speed 190 mph (305 km/h); initial climb 689 ft (210 m)/min; service ceiling 18,045 ft (5500 m); range 808 miles (1300 km).
Armament: usually none; in combat zones it was usual to mount one 13 mm MG 131 manually aimed from open dorsal cockpit and two 7·92 mm MG 15s manually aimed from beam windows.
History: first flight (Ju 52) 13 October 1930; (Ju 52/3m) May 1932; (Ju 52/3mg3e bomber) October 1934; final delivery (AAC.1) August 1947; (CASA 352-L) 1952.

One of the great aircraft of history, the Ju 52/3m was briefly preceded by the single-engined Ju 52 which had no military history. Most early Ju 52/3m versions were 15/17-passenger airliners which sold all over the world and also made up 75 per cent of the giant fleet of Lufthansa (reducing that airline's forced landings per million kilometres from 7 to only 1·5). In 1935 the 3mg3e bomber, with manually aimed MG 15s in a dorsal cockpit and ventral dustbin and bomb load of 3,307 lb (1500 kg) equipped the first bomber squadrons of the Luftwaffe. By 1936 about half the 450 built had been supplied to the Legion Kondor in Spain and

Ju 52/3m (pre-war transport)

to the Nationalist air force, but nearly all were equipped as troop transports, freighters and casualty-evacuation ambulances. These were the roles of most military versions, which were by far the most common transports on every front on which Nazi Germany fought. It is typical of the Nazi regime that, despite a wealth of later and more capable aircraft, the old "Auntie Ju" or "Iron Annie" was kept in full production throughout the war. Good STOL performance, with patented "double wing" flaps, robust construction, interchangeable wheel/ski/float landing gear and great reliability were the Ju 52's attributes. Total German output was 4,845. Many were built in France, where 400 were completed as AAC.1s in 1947. The final 170 were built in Spain as CASA 352-Ls for the Spanish Air Force, which used them as T.2B multi-role transports until 1975.

Junkers Ju 86

Ju 86D, E, G, K, P and R
Type: (D, E, G and K) bomber; (P) bomber/reconnaissance; (R) reconnaissance.
Engines: (D) two 600 hp Junkers Jumo 205C six opposed-piston cylinder diesels; (E) two 800 or 880 hp BMW 132 nine-cylinder radials; (K) two 905 hp Bristol Mercury XIX nine-cylinder radials; (P, R) two 1,000 hp Jumo 207A-1 or 207B-3/V turbocharged opposed-piston diesels.
Dimensions: span 73 ft 10 in (22·6 m); (P) 84 ft (25·6 m); (R) 105 ft (32 m); length (typical) 58 ft 8½ in (17·9 m); (G) 56 ft 5 in; (P, R) 54 ft; height (all) 15 ft 5 in (4·7 m).
Weights: empty (E-1) 11,464 lb (5200 kg); (R-1) 14,771 lb (6700 kg); loaded (E-1) 18,080 lb (8200 kg); (R-1) 25,420 lb (11,530 kg).
Performance: maximum speed (E-1) 202 mph (325 km/h); (R-1) 261 mph (420 km/h); initial climb (E) 918 ft (280 m)/min; service ceiling (E-1) 22,310 ft (6800 m); (R-1) 42,650 ft (13,000 m); range (E) 746 miles (1200 km); (R-1) 980 miles (1577 km).
Armament: (D, E, G, K) three 7·92 mm MG 15 manually aimed from nose, dorsal and retractable ventral positions; internal bomb load of four 551 lb (250 kg) or 16 110 lb (50 kg) bombs; (P) single 7·92 mm fixed MG 17, same bomb load; (R) usually none.
History: first flight (Ju 86V-1) 4 November 1934; (V-5 bomber prototype) January 1936; (production D-1) late 1936; (P-series prototype) February 1940.

Ju 86E-1

The E-series bombers, with the powerful BMW radial, were faster and the fastest of all were the Swedish Bristol-engined Ks, of which 40 were built by Junkers (first delivery 18 December 1936) and 16 by Saab (last delivery 3 January 1941). Many D and E bombers were used against Poland, but that was their swansong. By 1939 Junkers was working on a high-altitude version with turbocharged engines and a pressure cabin and this emerged as the P-1 bomber and P-2 bomber/reconnaissance which was operational over the Soviet Union gathering pictures before the German invasion of June 1941. The R series had a span increased even beyond that of the P and frequently operated over southern England in 1941–2 until – with extreme difficulty – solitary Spitfires managed to reach their altitude and effect an interception. Total military Ju 86 production was between 810 and 1,000. Junkers schemed many developed versions, some having four or six engines.

Planned like the He 111 as both a civil airliner and a bomber, the Ju 86 was in 1934 one of the most advanced aircraft in Europe. The design team under Dipl-Ing Zindel finally abandoned corrugated skin and created a smooth and efficient machine with prominent double-wing flaps and outward-retracting main gears. The diesel-engined D-1 was quickly put into Luftwaffe service to replace the Do 23 and Ju 52 as the standard heavy bomber, but in Spain the various D-versions proved vulnerable even to biplane fighters.

Junkers Ju 87

Ju 87A, B and D series
Type: two-seat dive bomber and ground attack.
Engine: (Ju 87B-1) one 1,100 hp Junkers
Jumo 211Da 12-cylinder inverted-vee
liquid-cooled; (Ju 87D-1, D-5)
1,300 hp Jumo 211J.
Dimensions: span (Ju 87B-1, D-1)
45 ft 3¼ in (13·8 m); (D-5) 50 ft 0½ in
(15·25 m); length 36 ft 5 in (11·1 m);
height 12 ft 9 in (3·9 m).
Weights: empty (B-1, D-1) about 6,080 lb (2750 kg);
loaded (B-1) 9,371 lb (4250 kg); (D-1) 12,600 lb
(5720 kg); (D-5) 14,500 lb (6585 kg).
Performance: maximum speed (B-1) 242 mph
(390 km/h); (D-1) 255 mph (408 km/h); (D-5)
250 mph (402 km/h); service ceiling (B-1) 26,250 ft
(8000 m); (D-1, D-5) 24,000 ft (7320 m); range with
maximum bomb load (B-1) 373 miles (600 km);
(D-1, D-5) 620 miles (1000 km).
Armament: (Ju 87B-1) two 7·92 mm Rheinmetall
MG 17 machine guns in wings, one 7·92 mm
MG 15 manually aimed in rear cockpit,
one 1,102 lb (500 kg) bomb on
centreline and four 110 lb (50 kg)
on wing racks; (D-1, D-5) two MG 17
in wings, twin 7·92 mm MG 81
machine guns manually aimed in rear cockpit,
one bomb of 3,968 lb (1800 kg) on centreline;
(D-7) two 20 mm MG 151/20 cannon in wings;
(Ju 87G-1) two 37 mm BK (Flak 18, or
Flak 36) cannon in underwing pods; (D-4)
two underwing WB81 weapon containers
each housing six MG 81 guns.
History: first flight (Ju 87V1) late 1935; (pre-production Ju 87A-0) November 1936; (Ju 87B-1)
August 1938; (Ju 87D-1) 1940; termination of
production 1944.

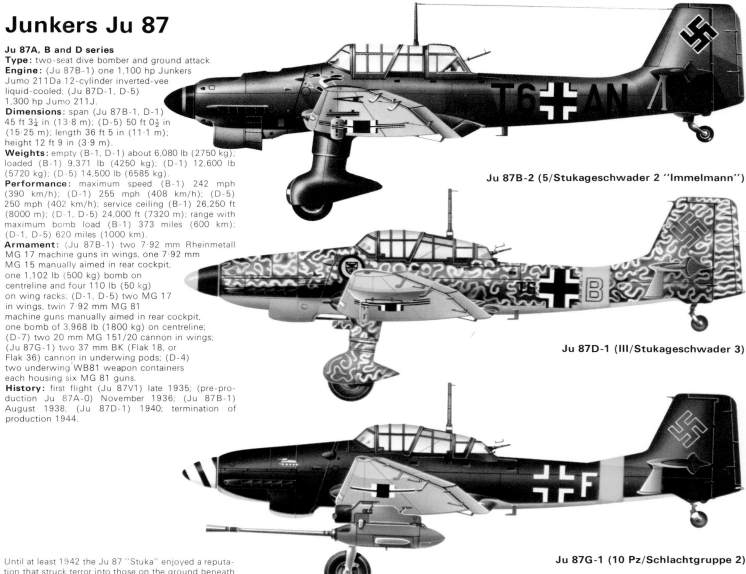

Ju 87B-2 (5/Stukageschwader 2 "Immelmann")

Ju 87D-1 (III/Stukageschwader 3)

Ju 87G-1 (10 Pz/Schlachtgruppe 2)

Until at least 1942 the Ju 87 "Stuka" enjoyed a reputation that struck terror into those on the ground beneath
it. First flown with a British R-R Kestrel engine and
twin fins in 1935, it entered production in 1937 as the
Ju 87A with large trousered landing gear and full
equipment for dive bombing, including a heavy bomb
crutch that swung the missile well clear of the fuselage
before release. The spatted Ju 87B was the first aircraft
in production with the Jumo 211 engine, almost twice
as powerful as the Jumo 210 of the Ju 87A, and it had
an automatic device (almost an autopilot) to ensure
proper pull-out from the steep dive, as well as red
lines at 60°, 75° and 80° painted on the pilot's side

window. Experience in Spain had shown that pilots
could black-out and lose control in the pull-out. Later
a whole formation of Ju 87Bs in Spain was late pulling
out over misty ground and many hit the ground. In
Poland and the Low Countries the Ju 87 was terribly
effective and it repeated its success in Greece, Crete

and parts of the Russian front. But in the Battle of
Britain its casualty rate was such that it was soon withdrawn, thereafter to attack ships and troops in areas
where the Axis still enjoyed some air superiority. In
1942–45 its main work was close support on the
Eastern front, attacking armour with big guns (Ju
87G-1) and even being used as a transport and glider
tug. Total production, all by Junkers, is believed to
have been 5,709.

Ju 88 see page 124.

Junkers Ju 188

Ju 188A, D and E series,
and Ju 388 J, K and L
Type:
five-seat bomber (D-2, reconnaissance).
Engins:
(Ju 188A) two 1,776 hp Junkers Jumo
213A 12-cylinder inverted-vee liquid-cooled;
(Ju 188D) same as A; (Ju 188E) two
1,700 hp BMW 801G-2 18-cylinder two-row radials.
Dimensions: span 72 ft 2 in (22 m); length 49 ft 1 in
(14·96 m); height 16 ft 1 in (4·9 m).
Weights: empty (188E-1) 21,825 lb (9900 kg);
loaded (188A and D) 33,730 lb (15,300 kg); (188E-1)
31,967 lb (14,500 kg).
Performance: maximum speed (188A) 325 mph
(420 km/h) at 20,500 ft (6250 m); (188D) 350 mph
(560 km/h) at 27,000 ft (8235 m); (188E) 315 mph
(494 km/h) at 19,685 ft (6000 m); service ceiling
(188A) 33,000 ft (10,060 m); (188D) 36,090 ft
(11,000 m); (188E) 31,170 ft (9500 m); range with
3,300 lb (1500 kg) bomb load (188A and E) 1,550
miles (2480 km).
Armament: (A, D-1 and E-1) one 20 mm MG 151/
20 cannon in nose, one MG 151/20 in dorsal turret,
one 13 mm MG 131 manually aimed at rear dorsal

Ju 188D-2 (F)/124, Kirkenes, Norway

position and one MG 131 or twin 7·92 mm MG 81
manually aimed at rear ventral position; 6,614 lb
(3000 kg) bombs internally or two 2,200 lb (1000 kg)
torpedoes under inner wings.
History: first flight (Ju 88B-0) early 1940; (Ju
88V27) September 1941; (Ju 188V1) December
1941; (Ju 188E-1) March 1942; (Ju 388L) May 1944.

In 1939 Junkers had the Jumo 213 engine in advanced development and, to go with it, the aircraft side
of the company prepared an improved Ju 88 with a
larger yet more streamlined crew compartment, more
efficient pointed wings and large squarish tail. After
protracted development this went into production as
the Ju 188E-1, fitted with BMW 801s because the
powerful Jumo was still not ready. The plant at Bern-
burg delivered 120 E-1s and a few radar-equipped
turretless E-2s and reconnaissance F versions before,
in mid-1943, finally getting into production with the

A-1 version. Leipzig/Mockau built the A-2 with flame-
damped exhaust for night operations and the A-3
torpedo bomber. The D was a fast reconnaissance aircraft, and the Ju 188S was a family of high-speed
machines, for various duties, capable of up to 435 mph
(696 km/h). Numerous other versions, some with a
remotely controlled twin-MG 131 tail turret, led to the
even faster and higher-flying Ju 388 family of night
fighters (J), reconnaissance (L) and bomber aircraft
(K). Altogether about 1,100 Ju 188 and about 120
388s were delivered, while at the war's end the much
larger and markedly different Ju 288 had been shelved
and the Ju 488, a much enlarged four-engined 388, was
about to fly at Toulouse. All these aircraft, and the
even greater number of stillborn projects, were evidence
of the increasingly urgent need to make up for the
absence of properly conceived new designs by wring-
ing the utmost development out of the obsolescent
types with which the Luftwaffe had started the war.

Junkers Ju 88

Many versions: data for Ju 88A-4, C-6, G-7, S-1
Type: military aircraft designed as dive bomber but developed for level bombing, close support, night fighting, reconnaissance and as pilotless missile. Crew: two to six.
Engines: (A-4) two 1,340 hp Junkers Jumo 211J 12-cylinder inverted-vee liquid-cooled; (C-6) same as A-4; (G-7) two 1,880 hp Junkers Jumo 213E 12-cylinder inverted-vee liquid-cooled; (S-1) two 1,700 hp BMW 801G 18-cylinder two-row radials.
Dimensions: span 65 ft 10½ in (20·13 m) (early versions 59 ft 10¾ in); length 47 ft 2¼ in (14·4 m); (G-7, 54 ft 1½ in); height 15 ft 11 in (4·85 m); (C-6) 16 ft 7½ in (5 m).
Weights: empty (A-4) 17,637 lb (8000 kg); (C-6b) 19,090 lb (8660 kg); (G-7b) 20,062 lb (9100 kg); (S-1) 18,300 lb (8300 kg); maximum loaded (A-4) 30,865 lb (14,000 kg); (C-6b) 27,500 lb (12,485 kg); (G-7b) 32,350 lb (14,690 kg); (S-1) 23,100 lb (10,490 kg).
Performance: maximum speed (A-4) 269 mph (433 km/h); (C-6b) 300 mph (480 km/h); (G-7b) (no drop tank or flame-dampers) 402 mph (643 km/h); (S-1) 373 mph (600 km/h); initial climb (A-4) 1,312 ft (400 m)/min; (C-6b) about 985 ft (300 m)/min; (G-7b) 1,640 ft (500 m)/min; (S-1) 1,804 ft (550 m)/min; service ceiling (A-4) 26,900 ft (8200 m); (C-6b) 32,480 ft (9900 m); (G-7b) 28,870 ft (8800 m); (S-1) 36,090 ft (11,000 m); range (A-4) 1,112 miles (1790 km); (C-6b) 1,243 miles (2000 km); (G-7b) 1,430 miles (2300 km); (S-1) 1,243 miles (2000 km).
Armament: (A-4) two 7·92 mm MG 81 (or one MG 81 and one 13 mm MG 131) firing forward, twin MG 81 or one MG 131 upper rear, one or two MG 81 at rear of ventral gondola and (later aircraft) two MG 81 at front of gondola; (C-6b) three 20 mm MG FF and three MG 17 in nose and two 20 mm MG 151/20 firing obliquely upward in Schräge Musik installation;

(G-7b) four MG 151/20 (200 rounds each) firing forward from ventral fairing, two MG 151/20 in Schrage Musik installat:on (200 rounds each) and defensive MG 131 (500 rounds) swivelling in rear roof; (S-1) one MG 131 (500 rounds) swivelling in rear roof; bomb loads (A-4) 1,100 lb (500 kg) internal and four external racks rated at 2,200 lb (1000 kg) (inners) and 1,100 lb (500 kg) (outers) to maximum total bomb load of 6,614 lb (3000 kg); (C-6b and G-7b, nil); (S-1) up to 4,410 lb (2000 kg) on external racks.
History: first flight (Ju 88V1) 21 December 1936; (first Ju 88A-1) 7 September 1939; (first fighter, Ju 88C-0) July 1939; (Ju 88C-6) mid-1942; (first G-series) early 1944; (S series) late 1943; final deliveries, only as factories were overrun by Allies.

Probably no other aircraft in history has been developed in so many quite different forms for so many purposes — except, perhaps, for the Mosquito. Flown long before World War II as a civil prototype, after a frantic design process led by two temporarily hired Americans well-versed in modern stressed-skin construction, the first 88s were transformed into the heavier, slower and more capacious A-1 bombers which were just entering service as World War II began. The formidable bomb load and generally good performance were offset by inadequate defensive armament, and in the A-4 the span was increased, the bomb load and gun power substantially augmented and a basis laid for diverse further development. Though it would be fair to describe practically all the subsequent versions as a hodge-podge of lash-ups, the Ju 88 was structurally excellent, combined large internal fuel capacity with great load-carrying capability, and yet was never so degraded in performance as to become seriously vulnerable as were the Dornier and Heinkel bombers. Indeed, with the BMW radial and the Jumo

213 engines the later versions were almost as fast as the best contemporary fighters at all altitudes and could be aerobatted violently into the bargin. A basic design feature was that all the crew were huddled together, to improve combat morale; but in the Battle of Britain it was found this merely made it difficult to add proper defensive armament and in the later Ju 188 a much large crew compartment was provided. Another distinctive feature was the large single struts of the main landing gear, sprung with stacks of chamfered rings of springy steel, and arranged to turn the big, soft-field wheels through 90° to lie flat in the rear of the nacelles. In 1940 to 1943 about 2,000 Ju 88 bombers were built each year, nearly all A-5 or A-4 versions. After splitting off completely new branches which led to the Ju 188 and 388, bomber development was directed to the streamlined S series of much higher performance, it having become accepted that the traditional Luftwaffe species of bomber was doomed if intercepted, no matter how many extra guns and crew it might carry. Indeed even the bomb and fuel loads were cut in most S sub-types, though the S-2 had fuel in the original bomb bay and large bulged bomb stowage (which defeated the objective of reducing drag). Final bomber versions included the P series of big-gun anti-armour and close-support machines, the Nbwe with flame-throwers and recoilless rocket projectors, and a large family of Mistel composite-aircraft combinations, in which the Ju 88 lower portion was a pilotless missile steered by the fighter originally mounted on top. Altogether bomber, reconnaissance and related 88s totalled 10,774, while frantic construction of night fighter versions in 1944–45 brought the total to at least 14,980. The Ju 88 night fighters (especially the properly designed G-series) were extremely formidable, bristling with radar and weapons and being responsible for destroying more Allied night bombers than all other fighters combined.
Ju 188 and Ju 388 see page 123.

Junkers Ju 88G-1 cutaway drawing key:

1. Starboard navigation light
2. Wingtip profile
3. FuG 227 Flensburg homing receiver aerial
4. Starboard aileron
5. Aileron control lines
6. Starboard flap
7. Flap-fairing strip
8. Wing ribs
9. Starboard outer fuel tank (91 gal/414 litres)
10. Fuel filler cap
11. Leading-edge structure
12. Annular exhaust slot
13. Cylinder head fairings
14. Adjustable nacelle nose ring
15. Twelve-blade cooling fan
16. Propeller boss
17. Three-blade variable-pitch VS 111 propeller
18. Leading-edge radar array
19. Lichtenstein SN-2 radar array
20. SN-2 radar
21. Bulkhead
22. Gyro compass
23. Instrument panel
24. Armoured-glass windscreen sections
25. Folding seat
26. Control column
27. Rudder pedal/brake cylinder
28. Control lines
29. Pilot's seat
30. Sliding window section
31. Headrest
32. Jettisonable canopy roof section
33. Gun restraint
34. Radio operator/gunner's seat
35. 13mm MG 131 gun
36. Radio equipment
37. Ammunition box (500 rounds)
38. Lichtenstein SN-2 indicator box
39. FuG 227 Flensburg indicator box
40. Control linkage
41. Bulkhead
42. Armoured gun mounting
43. Aerial post/traverse check
44. Fuel filler cap
45. Whip aerial
46. Forward fuselage fuel tank (105 gal/480 litres)
47. Fuselage horizontal construction joint
48. Bulkhead
49. Fuel filler cap
50. Aft fuselage fuel tank (230 gal/1,046 litres)
51. Access hatch
52. Bulkhead
53. Control linkage access plate
54. Fuselage stringers
55. Upper longeron
56. Maintenance walkway
57. Control linkage

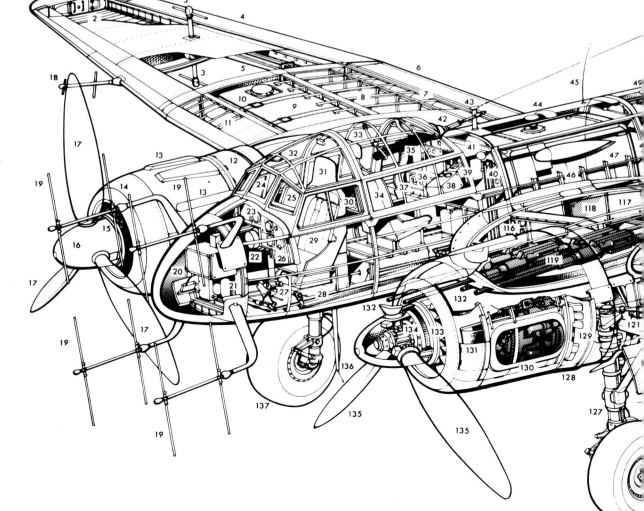

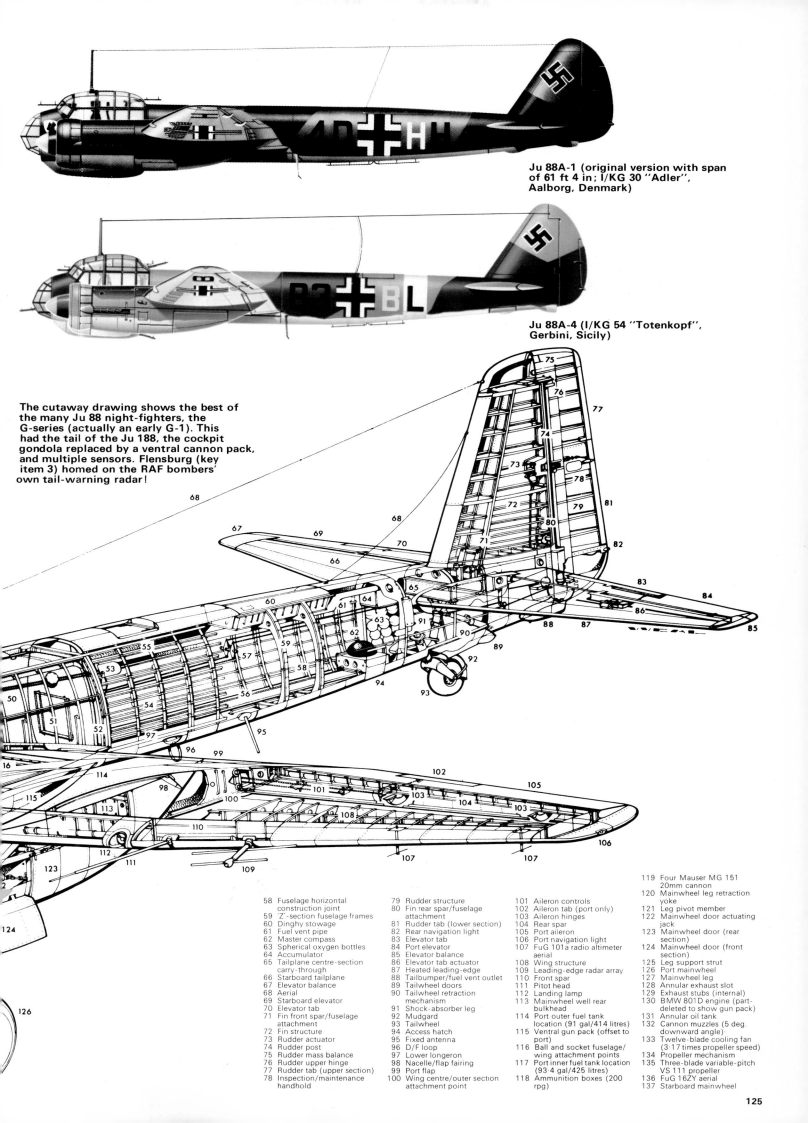

Ju 88A-1 (original version with span of 61 ft 4 in; I/KG 30 "Adler", Aalborg, Denmark)

Ju 88A-4 (I/KG 54 "Totenkopf", Gerbini, Sicily)

The cutaway drawing shows the best of the many Ju 88 night-fighters, the G-series (actually an early G-1). This had the tail of the Ju 188, the cockpit gondola replaced by a ventral cannon pack, and multiple sensors. Flensburg (key item 3) homed on the RAF bombers' own tail-warning radar!

58 Fuselage horizontal construction joint	79 Rudder structure	101 Aileron controls
59 'Z'-section fuselage frames	80 Fin rear spar/fuselage attachment	102 Aileron tab (port only)
60 Dinghy stowage	81 Rudder tab (lower section)	103 Aileron hinges
61 Fuel vent pipe	82 Rear navigation light	104 Rear spar
62 Master compass	83 Elevator tab	105 Port aileron
63 Spherical oxygen bottles	84 Port elevator	106 Port navigation light
64 Accumulator	85 Elevator balance	107 FuG 101a radio altimeter aerial
65 Tailplane centre-section carry-through	86 Elevator tab actuator	108 Wing structure
66 Starboard tailplane	87 Heated leading-edge	109 Leading-edge radar array
67 Elevator balance	88 Tailbumper/fuel vent outlet	110 Front spar
68 Aerial	89 Tailwheel doors	111 Pitot head
69 Starboard elevator	90 Tailwheel retraction mechanism	112 Landing lamp
70 Elevator tab	91 Shock-absorber leg	113 Mainwheel well rear bulkhead
71 Fin front spar/fuselage attachment	92 Mudguard	114 Port outer fuel tank location (91 gal/414 litres)
72 Fin structure	93 Tailwheel	115 Ventral gun pack (offset to port)
73 Rudder actuator	94 Access hatch	116 Ball and socket fuselage/wing attachment points
74 Rudder post	95 Fixed antenna	117 Port inner fuel tank location (93·4 gal/425 litres)
75 Rudder mass balance	96 D/F loop	118 Ammunition boxes (200 rpg)
76 Rudder upper hinge	97 Lower longeron	119 Four Mauser MG 151 20mm cannon
77 Rudder tab (upper section)	98 Nacelle/flap fairing	120 Mainwheel leg retraction yoke
78 Inspection/maintenance handhold	99 Port flap	121 Leg pivot member
	100 Wing centre/outer section attachment point	122 Mainwheel door actuating jack

123 Mainwheel door (rear section)
124 Mainwheel door (front section)
125 Leg support strut
126 Port mainwheel
127 Mainwheel leg
128 Annular exhaust slot
129 Exhaust stubs (internal)
130 BMW 801D engine (part-deleted to show gun pack)
131 Annular oil tank
132 Cannon muzzles (5 deg. downward angle)
133 Twelve-blade cooling fan (3·17 times propeller speed)
134 Propeller mechanism
135 Three-blade variable-pitch VS 111 propeller
136 FuG 16ZY aerial
137 Starboard mainwheel

Kaman Seasprite

UH-2, HH-2 and SH-2 in many versions (data for SH-2D)
Type: ship-based multi-role helicopter (ASW, anti-missile defence, observation, search/rescue and utility).
Engine(s): original versions, one 1,050 or 1,250 hp General Electric T58 free-turbine turboshaft; all current versions, two 1,350 hp T58-8F.
Dimensions: main rotor diameter 44 ft (13·41 m); overall length (blades turning) 52 ft 7 in (16 m); fuselage length 40 ft 6 in (12·3 m); height 13 ft 7 in (4·14 m).
Weights: empty 6,953 lb (3153 kg); maximum loaded 13,300 lb (6033 kg).
Performance: maximum speed 168 mph (270 km/h); maximum rate of climb (not vertical) 2,440 ft (744 m)/min; service ceiling 22,500 ft (6858 m); range 422 miles (679 km).
Armament: see text.
History: first flight (XHU2K-1) 2 July 1959; service delivery (HU2K-1, later called UH-2A) 18 December 1962; final delivery (new) 1972, (conversion) 1975.

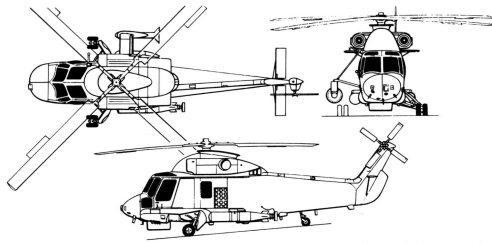

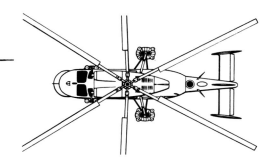

Kaman SH-2D Seasprite

Originally designated HU2K-1 and named Seasprite, this exceptionally neat helicopter was at first powered by a single turbine engine mounted close under the rotor hub and was able to carry a wide range of loads, including nine passengers, in its unobstructed central cabin, with two crew in the nose. The main units of the tailwheel-type landing gear retracted fully. About 190 were delivered and all were later converted to have two T58 engines in nacelles on each side. Some

are HH-2C rescue/utility with armour and various armament including chin Minigun turret and waist-mounted machine guns or cannon; others are un-armed HH-2D. One has been used in missile-firing (Sparrow III and Sidewinder) trials in the missile-defence role. All Seasprites have since 1970 been drastically converted to serve in the LAMPS (light airborne multi-purpose system) for anti-submarine and anti-missile defence. The SH-2D has more than

two tons of special equipment including powerful chin radar, sonobuoys, MAD gear, ECM, new navigation and communications systems and Mk 44 and/or Mk 46 torpedoes. All will eventually be brought up to SH-2F standard with improved rotor, higher gross weight and improved sensors and weapons. The same basic design is one of the contenders for the future competition for a purpose-designed LAMPS helicopter of greater size and power.

Kamov Ka-25

Ka-25 (several versions, designations unknown)
Type: ship-based ASW, search/rescue and utility helicopter.
Engines: two 900 hp Glushenkov GTD-3 free-turbine turboshaft.
Dimensions: main rotor diameter (both) 51 ft 8 in (15·75 m); fuselage length, about 34 ft (10·36 m); height 17 ft 8 in (5·4 m).
Weights: empty, about 11,023 lb (5000 kg); maximum loaded 16,535 lb (7500 kg).
Performance: maximum speed 120 mph (193 km/h); service ceiling, about 11,000 ft (3350 m); range, about 400 miles (650 km).
Armament: one or two 400 mm AS torpedoes, nuclear or conventional depth charges or other stores, carried in internal weapon bay.
History: first flight (Ka-20) probably 1960; service delivery of initial production version, probably 1965.

Nikolai Kamov, who died in 1973, was one of the leaders of rotorcraft in the Soviet Union, a characteristic of nearly all his designs being the use of superimposed co-axial rotors to give greater lift in a vehicle of smaller overall size. Large numbers of Ka-15 and -18 piston-engined machines were used by Soviet armed forces, but in 1961 the Aviation Day fly-past at Tushino included a completely new machine designated Ka-20 and carrying a guided missile on each side. It was allotted the NATO code-name of "Harp". Clearly powered by gas turbines, it looked formidable. Later

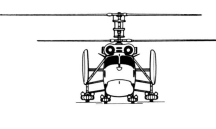

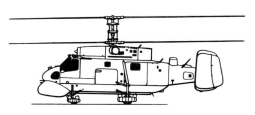

in the 1960s it became clear that from this helicopter Kamov's bureau, under chief engineer Barshevsky, had developed the standard ship-based machine of the Soviet fleets, replacing the Mi-4. Designated Ka-25 and allotted the new Western code name of "Hormone", it is in service in at least five major versions, with numerous sub-types. Whereas the "missiles" displayed in 1961 have never been seen since, and are thought to have been dummies, the Ka-25 is extremely fully equipped with all-weather anti-submarine sensing and attack equipment. The four landing wheels are each surrounded by a buoyancy bag ring which can be swiftly inflated by the gas bottles just above it. Ka-25s are used aboard the carriers *Moskva* and *Leningrad*, *Kresta* and *Kara* class cruisers and from shore bases.

Ka-25 (ship-based ASW version)

Kawanishi H8K

H8K1, H8K2; Type 2
Type: reconnaissance and attack flying boat.
Engines: four Mitsubishi Kasei 14-cylinder two-row radials, (H8K1, Model 11) 1,530 hp Kasei 12; (H8K2, Model 12) 1,850 hp Kasei 22.
Dimensions: span 124 ft 8 in (38 m); length 92 ft 3½ in (28·1 m); height 30 ft 0¼ in (9·15 m).
Weights: empty (H8K1) 34,000 lb (15,440 kg); (H8K2) 40,500 lb (18,380 kg); loaded (H8K1) 68,343 lb (31,000 kg); (H8K2) 71,650 lb (32,500 kg).
Performance: maximum speed (H8K1) 270 mph (433 km/h); (H8K2) 282 mph (454 km/h); initial climb 1,575 ft (480 m)/min; service ceiling 28,800 ft (8770 m); range, usually 3,000 miles (4800 km), but overload reconnaissance range 4,474 miles (7200 km).
Armament: normally, five 20 mm in power-driven nose, dorsal and tail turrets and three 7·7 mm manually aimed from beam and ventral rear windows; weapon load slung beneath inner wing, comprising two torpedoes or bombs to total weight of 4,410 lb (2000 kg); (H8K2-L) one 20 mm and one 12·7 mm, both manually aimed.
History: first flight late 1940; (production H8K1) August 1941.

H8K2 (Yokohama Air Corps, Imperial Navy)

Throughout the early part of the Pacific War the standard ocean patrol flying boat of the Imperial Japanese Navy was the Kawanishi H6K family (known to the Allies as "Mavis"). Though Kawanishi had a technical agreement with Short Brothers, the H6K looked like a Sikorsky S.42. It was an excellent aircraft, 217 being delivered including 36 transport versions. The question of a replacement was a challenge and the JNAF published a specification in 1938 calling for 30 per cent higher speed and 50 per cent greater range. In the H8K, Kawanishi's design team, under Dr Kikuhara, created a flying boat which has served as the biggest single jump in the technology of such aircraft in all history. It was beyond dispute the best and most advanced flying boat in the world until many years after

World War II. Its early trials were disastrous, because the great weight and narrow-beamed hull resulted in uncontrollable porpoising. The cure was found in adding a second step in the planing bottom, adjusting the powerful double-slotted Fowler flaps and adding a horizon mark on the large pitot post above the bows. Altogether the Kohnan plant built 17 H8K1, 114 H8K2 and 36 of the H8K2-L transport version (Allied name: "Emily"). They ranged alone on daring 24-hour missions and proved formidable. Their first sortie, in March 1942, was to have been a bombing raid on Oahu, Hawaii, with an intermediate refuelling from a submarine, but the target lay under dense low cloud. Later H8K2 versions carried radar and two had re-tractable stabilizing floats.

Kawanishi Shiden

N1K1-J and N1K2-J and variants
Type: single-seat fighter.
Engine: one 1,990 hp Nakajima Homare 21 18-cylinder two-row radial.
Dimensions: span 39 ft $3\frac{1}{4}$ in (11·97 m); length 29 ft $1\frac{3}{4}$ in (8·885 m); (N1K2-J) 30 ft $8\frac{1}{4}$ in (9·35 m); height 13 ft $3\frac{3}{4}$ in (4·058 m); (N1K2-J) 13 ft (3·96 m).
Weights: empty 6,387 lb (2897 kg); (N1K2-J) 6,299 lb (2657 kg); maximum loaded 9,526 lb (4321 kg); (N1K2-J) 10,714 lb (4860 kg).
Performance: maximum speed 362 mph (583 km/h); (N1K2-J) 369 mph (594 km/h); initial climb (both) 3,300 ft (1000 m)/min; service ceiling 39,698 ft (12,100 m); (N1K2-J) 35,400 ft (10,760 m); range 989 miles (1430 km); (N1K2-J) 1,069 miles (1720 km).
Armament: originally two 20 mm in wings and two 7·7 mm above fuselage; after 20 aircraft, two extra 20 mm added in underwing blisters; (N1K1-Ja) as before without 7·7 mm; N1K2-J, four 20 mm in pairs inside wing, with more ammunition, plus two 550 lb (250 kg) bombs underwing or six rockets under fuselage; later prototypes, heavier armament.
History: first flight 24 July 1943; first flight (N1K2-J) 3 April 1944.

In September 1940 the JNAF issued a requirement for a high-speed seaplane naval fighter that did not need land airfields but could maintain air superiority during island invasions. The result was the formidable N1K1 Kyofu (mighty wind), produced by Kawanishi's Naruo plant and code-named "Rex" by the Allies. It

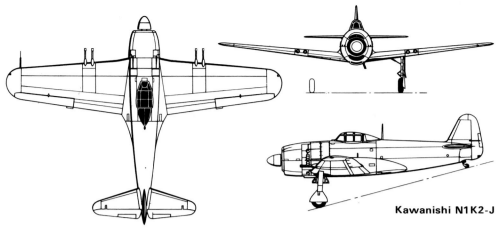

Kawanishi N1K2-J

was from this central-float seaplane that Kikuhara's team very quickly devised the N1K1-J landplane (Allied name: "George"). Though a hasty lash-up it was potentially one of the best of all Japanese fighters. Its manoeuvrability, boosted by automatic combat flaps worked by a manometer (mercury U-tube) that measured angle of attack, was almost unbelievable. Drawbacks were the engine, plagued with snags, the poor view with the mid wing and the complex and weak landing gear (legacy from the mid-wing float-plane and big four-blade propeller). Naruo therefore produced the N1K2-J with low wing, new tail and

drastically simpler airframe that could be built in half the man-hours. The unreliable engine still kept Shidens (the name meant violet lightning) mostly unserviceable, but they were potent and respected adversaries, encountered on all fronts from May 1944. Total production was 1,440. Huge production was planned from four companies and four Navy arsenals, but none produced more than ten aircraft, other than Kawanishi which delivered 543 1-Js and 362 2-Js from Naruo and 468 1-Js and 44 2-Js from Himeji. At Okinawa both versions were used in the Kamikaze role.

Kawasaki Ki-45 Toryu

Ki-45 and 45A, Heavy Fighter Type 2, Kai B, C and D
Type: originally long-range escort; later night fighter and attack.
Engines: two 1,080 hp Mitsubishi Ha-102 (Type 1 14-cylinder two-row radials.
Dimensions: span 49 ft $3\frac{1}{2}$ in (15·02 m); length (Kai C) 36 ft 1 in (11 m); height 12 ft $1\frac{1}{2}$ in (3·7 m).
Weights: empty (Kai A) 8,340 lb (3790 kg); (Kai C) 8,820 lb (4000 kg); loaded (all) 12,125 lb (5500 kg).
Performance: maximum speed (all) 336 mph (540 km/h); initial climb 2,300 ft (700 m)/min; service ceiling 32,800 ft (10,000 m); range, widely conflicting reports, but best Japanese sources suggest 1,243 miles (2000 km) with combat load for all versions.
Armament: (Ki-45-I and Kai-A) two 12·7 mm fixed in nose and two 7·7 mm manually aimed from rear cockpit; (Kai-B) same plus 37 mm cannon in lower right forward fuselage (often with only one 12·7 mm); (Kai-C) adapted for night fighting in May 1944, two 12·7 mm installed at 30° between cockpits, with two 12·7 mm and one 20 mm or 37 mm in nose; antiship versions, said to have carried 50 mm or 75 mm gun under nose, plus two 551 lb (250 kg) bombs under wings.

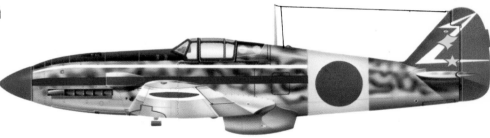

Ki-45 Kai C (Shinten-Seiku unit, 53rd Sentai, Imperial Army)

History: first flight (Ha-20 engine) January 1939; (Ha-25 engine) July 1940; (production Ki-45) September 1941.

The first twin-engined fighter of the Imperial Japanese Army, the Ki-45 Toryu (dragon-slayer) was a long time in gestation. It was designed at Kawasaki's Gifu factory to meet a 1936 requirement issued in March 1937. Kawasaki had never used twin air-cooled engines and the Nakajima Ha-20B was an undeveloped engine which misbehaved; pilots disliked the hand-cranked landing gear. After trying contraprops, the choice fell on the Navy Ha-25 Sakae engine, but this in turn was replaced by the Ha-102 soon after production began in 1941. The Akashi plant began to build the Ki-45

as a second source in late 1942, but combined output was only 1,698. Despite this modest total, and the fact that these aircraft were continually being modified, they were met on every Pacific front and known as "Nick". They were fairly fast and manoeuvrable but not really formidable until, on 27 May 1944, four Kai-B (modification B) made the first-ever suicide attack (on the north coast of New Guinea). By mid-1944 most Ki-45s had been modified to Kai-C configuration as night fighters, claiming seven victories over B-29s on the night of 15 June 1944. The two main Ki-45 bases at the close of the war were Hanoi and Anshan (Manchuria), from which aircraft made night interceptions and day Kamikaze attacks. The Ki-45 never operated in its design role of long-range escort.

Kawasaki Ki-61 Hien

Ki-61-I, II and III (Type 3 fighter) and Ki-100 (Type 5)
Type: single-seat fighter.
Engine: (Ki-61-I) one 1,175 hp Kawasaki Ha-40 inverted-vee-12 liquid-cooled; (Ki-61-II) one 1,450 hp Kawasaki Ha-140 of same layout; (Ki-100) one 1,500 hp Mitsubishi Ha-112-II 14-cylinder two-row radial.
Dimensions: span 39 ft $4\frac{1}{2}$ in (12 m); length (-I) 29 ft 4 in (8·94 m); (-II) 30 ft $0\frac{1}{2}$ in (9·16 m); (Ki-100) 28 ft $11\frac{1}{4}$ in (8·82 m); height (all) 12 ft 2 in (3·7 m).
Weights: empty (-I) 5,798 lb (2630 kg); (-II) 6,294 lb (2855 kg); (Ki-100) 5,567 lb (2525 kg); loaded (-I) 7,650 lb (3470 kg); (-II) 8,433 lb (3825 kg); (Ki-100) 7,705 lb (3495 kg).
Performance: maximum speed (-I) 348 mph (560 km/h); (-II) 379 mph (610 km/h); (Ki-100) 367 mph (590 km/h); initial climb (-I, -II) 2,200 ft (675 m)/min; (Ki-100) 3,280 ft (1000 m)/min; service ceiling (-I) 32,800 ft (10,000 m); (-II) 36,089 ft (11,000 m); (Ki-100) 37,729 ft (11,500 m); range (-I, -II) 990–1,100 miles (-I, 1800 km, -II, 1600 km); (Ki-100) 1,243 miles (2000 km).
Armament: (Ki-61-Ia) two 20 mm MG 151/20 in wings, two 7·7 mm above engine; (-Id) same but wing guns 30 mm; (-IIb) four 20 mm Ho-5 in wings; (Ki-100) two Ho-5 in wings and two 12·7 mm in fuselage, plus underwing racks for two 551 lb (250 kg) bombs.
History: first flight (Ki-60) March 1941; (Ki-61) December 1941; service delivery (Ki-61-I) August 1942; first flight (-II) August 1943; (Ki-100) 1 February 1945.

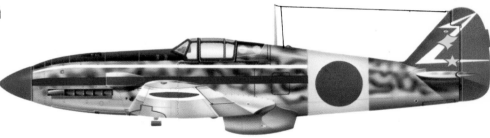

Ki-61-IIb (2nd Chutai, 244th Sentai, Imperial Army)

Kawasaki purchased a licence to build the German DB 601 engine in 1937 and the resulting revised and lightened engine emerged in 1940 as the Ha-40. Around this engine Kawasaki planned the Ki-60 and a lighter fighter designated Ki-61. Hien (the Japanese name meaning flying swallow). The latter was completed in December 1941 and flew well, reaching a speed of 368 mph. During the first half of 1942 the prototype was extensively tested, performing very well against a captured P-40E and a Bf 109E sent to Japan by submarine. The submarine also brought 800 Mauser MG 151 cannon, and these were fitted to most early Ki-61s despite the unreliability of the supply of electrically fused ammunition. The Gifu plant delivered 2,654 (according to one authority, 2,750) Ki-61-I and -Ia, the latter being redesigned for easier servicing and increased manoeuvrability. They went into action around New Guinea in April 1943, were called "Tony"

by the Allies, and were the only Japanese fighters with a liquid-cooled engine. They were constantly in air combat, later moving to the Philippines and finally back to Japan. By 1944 the Ki-61-II was trickling off the assembly line with an unreliable engine that could not meet production demands. The II had a bigger wing and new canopy, but was soon replaced by the IIa with the old, proven, wing. Only 374 of all -II versions were built, and in early 1945 one of 275 engine-less airframes was fitted with the Ha-112 radial. Despite the sudden lash-up conversion the result was a staggeringly fine fighter, easily the best ever produced in Japan. With desperate haste this conversion went into production as the Ki-100. One of the first Ki-100 units destroyed 14 Hellcats without loss to themselves in their first major battle over Okinawa and this easily flown and serviced machine fought supremely well against B-29s and Allied fighters to the end.

Lavochkin LaGG-3

I-22, LaGG-1; I-301, LaGG-3
Type: single-seat fighter.
Engine: (-1) one 1,050 hp Klimov M-105P (VK-105P) vee-12 liquid-cooled; (-3) one 1,240 hp M-105PF with improved propeller.
Dimensions: span 32 ft 2 in (9·8 m); length 29 ft 1¼ in (8·9 m); height 8 ft 10 in (3·22 m).
Weights: empty (-1) 5,952 lb (2700 kg); (-3) 5,764 lb (2620 kg); maximum loaded (-1) 6,834 lb (3100 kg); (-3) 7,275 lb (3300 kg).
Performance: maximum speed (-1) 373 mph (600 km/h); (-3) 348 mph (560 km/h); initial climb (both) 2,953 ft (900 m)/min; service ceiling (-1) 31,496 ft (9600 m); (-3) 29,527 ft (9000 m); range (both) 404 miles (650 km).
Armament: very varied; typically, one 20 mm ShVAK firing through propeller hub, with 120 rounds, two 12·7 mm BS above engine, each with 220 rounds, and underwing racks for six RS-82 rockets or various light bombs; LaGGs on Il-2 escort had three 12·7 mm and two 7·62 mm; some had a 23 mm VIa cannon and various combinations of machine guns.
History: first flight (I-22) 30 March 1939; (production LaGG-1) late 1940; (production LaGG-3) 1941; final delivery June 1942.

LaGG-3
(Ukraine front, mid-1942)

Semyon Alekseyevich Lavochkin headed a design committee which included V. P. Gorbunov and M. I. Gudkov in creating the very unusual I-22 fighter prototype of 1938–39. Though outwardly conventional, it was the only one of the world's new crop of streamlined monoplane fighters not to have metal stressed-skin construction; instead it was built of wood, except for the control surfaces, which were light alloy with fabric covering, and the flaps which, to avoid damage, were all-metal. The ply skinning was both impregnated and bonded on with phenol-formaldehyde resin, which at the time seemed quaint but today is very widely used for this purpose. The result was a neat, clean and manoeuvrable fighter, which later showed outstanding robustness and resistance to combat damage. On the other hand it was inferior to other Russian fighters in all-round performance. Several hundred had been delivered, as the LaGG-1, when production was switched to the LaGG-3. This had a better engine, leading-edge slats, and improved armament options. By 1942 all LaGG fighters had internally balanced rudder, retractable tailwheel and wing fuel system for two 22 gal drop tanks. Further development led to the switch to an air-cooled radial, from which stemmed all Lavochkin's later piston-engined fighters.

Lavochkin La-5 and La-7

La-5, -5FN, -7 and -7U
Type: single-seat fighter (-7U, dual-control trainer).
Engine: (original La-5) one 1,330 hp Shvetsov M-82A or M-82F 14-cylinder two-row radial; (all other versions) one 1,700 hp M-82FN.
Dimensions: span 32 ft 2 in (9·8 m); length 27 ft 10¾ in (8·46 m); height 9 ft 3 in (2·84 m).
Weights: empty, no data; loaded (La-5) no data; (La-5FN) 7,406 lb (3359 kg); (La-7) 7,495 lb (3400 kg).
Performance: maximum speed (La-5) 389 mph (626 km/h); (La-5FN) 403 mph (650 km/h); (La-7) 423 mph (680 km/h); initial climb (La-5FN) about 3,600 ft (1100 m)/min; (La-7) about 3,940 ft (1200 m)/min; service ceiling (La-5FN) 32,800 ft (10,000 m); (La-7) 34,448 ft (10,500 m); range (La-5) 398 miles (640 km); (La-5FN) 475 miles (765 km); (La-7) 392 miles (630 km).
Armament: (La-5, -5FN) two 20 mm ShVAK cannon, each with 200 rounds, above engine; optional underwing racks for light bombs up to total of 330 lb (150 kg); (La-7) three faster-firing ShVAK (one on right, two on left); underwing racks for six RS-82 rockets or two 220 lb (100 kg) bombs.
History: first flight (re-engined LaGG-3) January 1942; (production La-5) June 1942; (La-5FN) late 1942; (La-7) about June 1943.

La-7
(18th Guards Fighter Regiment)

Though the LaGG-3 was a serviceable fighter that used wood rather than scarce light alloys, it was the poorest performer of the new crop of combat aircraft with which the VVS-RKKA (Soviet Military Aviation Defence Forces) sought to halt the German invader. It was natural that urgent consideration should be given to ways of improving it and during 1941 Lavochkin's team converted one LaGG-3 to have an M-82 radial engine. Despite its fractionally greater installed drag (a matter of 1%) it offered speed increased from 353 to 373 mph and, in particular, improved all-round performance at height. The liquid-cooled fighter was cancelled in May 1942, all production switching to the new machine, designated LaG-5. But within a matter of weeks this in turn was replaced on the assembly line by a further improvement, tested as a prototype early in 1942, with a new fuselage containing two 20 mm guns and having a lower rear profile behind a canopy giving all-round vision. This was the La-5 which proved to be 28 mph faster than a Bf 109G-2 at below 20,000 ft. But the German fighter could outclimb it and efforts were made to reduce weight. The resulting La-5FN had an FN (boosted) engine, lighter wing with metal spars and overall weight 379 lb (presumably on both empty and gross weight) less. Thousands of -5FNs participated in the huge battles around Kursk and throughout the Eastern front in 1943, demonstrating that Soviet fighters could be more than a match for their opponents. The La-5UTI was a dual trainer. Further refinement led to the harder-hitting La-7, with reduced weight (partly by reducing fuel capacity) and much reduced drag. The -7 and -7U trainer retained the slats and big ailerons that made the Lavochkin fighters such beautiful dog-fighters and were the choice of most of the Soviet aces (Ivan Kozhedub's aircraft is in the Central Soviet Air Force Museum).

Lavochkin La-11

La-11 (Fighter Regiment occupying East Germany)

La-9, La-11
Type: single-seat fighter.
Engine: one 1,870 hp Shvetsov ASh-82FNV 14-cylinder two-row radial.
Dimensions: span (-9) 34 ft 9½ in (10·62 m); (-11) 32 ft 7½ in (9·95 m); length (-9) 29 ft 6½ in (9·0 m); (-11) 28 ft 3½ in (8·6 m); height (both) 9 ft 8 in (2·95 m).
Weights: no data available, but gross weights were probably approximately (-9) 8,820 lb (4000 kg) and (-11) 9,040 lb (4100 kg).
Performance: maximum speed (-9) 429 mph (690 km/h); (-11) 460 mph (740 km/h); initial climb (-9) 3,840 ft (1170 m)/min; (-11) 4,265 ft (1300 m)/min; service ceiling (both) 36,100 ft (11,000 m); range (-9) 373 miles (600 km); (-11) 466 miles (750 km).
Armament: (-9) four 20 mm ShVAK symmetrically arranged around top decking; (-9bis) four 23 mm

NS23 in same positions; (-11) three NS23, two on left, one on right. No wing pylons normally fitted.
History: first flight (-9) early 1944; (-11) late 1944 or early 1945; service delivery (-11) summer of 1945.

These two excellent fighters were the result of natural development and refinement, taking advantage of the wealth of combat information that came to Lavochkin's bureau from the Eastern front in 1943–44. By this time the LaGG committee had broken up, and Lavochkin himself had become a Lt-General in the Aviation Engineering Corps, a Hero of Socialist Labour (for the La-5) and won a Stalin Prize of 100,000 roubles (for the La-7). He had the satisfaction of seeing production of the -7 outstrip that of all other aircraft except the Yak-3 in 1944 (13,300 in the year), despite the fact that by December it had been supplanted by the refined La-9. This had a revised structure incorporating much more metal stressed-skin than wood, with a taller fin and rudder and stubby wings strongly reminiscent of a Fw 190 or Bearcat. The cockpit was redesigned, and firing the guns caused quite a commotion with four large cannon all blasting ahead between the propeller blades. The switch to 23 mm guns caused bulges to appear around the breeches of all four. Hundreds of La-9s were supplied to the Soviet Union's allies and friends and some were used for experiments with liquid rockets in the tail and /or pulsating athodyd engines (V-1 derived) under the wings. The final Lavochkin piston-engined fighter, the La-11, was a refined escort fighter with all-stressed-skin structure and much greater fuel capacity. It could be distinguished from the -9 by the oil cooler being moved from under the trailing edge to inside the cowling, under the engine. Many 11s were used by the Northern Air Force during the Korean War and they were important in Communist forces until 1960.

Lioré et Olivier 20

LeO 122, 20, 203, 206 and 25 series (data for LeO 20)
Type: heavy bomber
(see text for variations).
Engines: two 420 hp
Gnome-Rhône GR9 Ady (Jupiter)
nine-cylinder radials.
Dimensions: span 72 ft (21·95 m); length 45 ft 3¾ in
(13·82 m); height 13 ft 11¾ in (4·25 m).
Weights: empty 7,716 lb (3500 kg); loaded 12,037 lb
(5460 kg).
Performance: maximum speed 123 mph (198 km/h);
initial climb 330 ft (100 m)/min; service ceiling
18,860 ft (5750 m); range with bomb load, 620 miles
(1000 km).
Armament: twin 7·7 mm Lewis or MAC 1934
manually aimed from nose cockpit, two more in dorsal
cockpit and one in retractable ventral bin; external
bomb load of 1,100 lb (500 kg).
History: first flight (LeO 12) 1924; (LeO 122)
1926; (LeO 20) 1928; (LeO 203) 1931; (LeO 206)
1933; (LeO 25) November 1928; final delivery (LeO
257bis) January 1939.

Lioré et Olivier was established as an aircraft manufacturer at Levallois-Perret in March 1912. From it

came probably the greatest series of large French
military aircraft ever to be produced by a single source.
Each design stemmed from its predecessors – until
there came a dramatic break with the splendid LeO 45
of World War II, which in 1939 was unquestionably
one of the most efficient and most modern bombers in
the world. Prior to this outstanding machine LeO had
conjured up visions of lumbering biplanes, all having
perfectly rectangular wings that looked as if they were
cut from continuous strip. The LeO 12 was a two-seat
night bomber, a rival of the Farman Goliath, powered
by 400 hp Lorraine water-cooled engines. With the
much superior Jupiter engine, licence-produced by
Gnome-Rhône, it became the LeO 122, and from this
stemmed the LeO 20, the standard French heavy night

LeO 20 (GB III/7)

bomber that equipped GB regiments from 1928 until
1939. No fewer than 320 of these four-seat stalwarts
were delivered to the Armée de l'Air and dozens were
used for special trials with various modifications. The
LeO 203 and 206 were four-engined developments,
with many variants, and the LeO 25 family were even
bigger but reverted to two powerful engines (usually
the 870 hp GR14 Kirs/Kjrs), and were all twin-float
seaplanes or amphibians. Capable of being used for
bombing, torpedo attacks or reconnaissance, they
remained in production right up to World War II,
despite their antiquated appearance.

Letov S 328

S 328 and 528
Type: two-seat reconnaissance bomber and utility.
Engine: (S 328) one 635 hp Walter (Bristol licence)
Pegasus II M2 nine-cylinder radial; (S 528) one
800 hp Gnome-Rhône Mistral Major 14Krsd 14-
cylinder two-row radial.
Dimensions: span 44 ft 11¼ in (13·7 m); length
33 ft 11¾ in (10·35 m); (528) 34 ft 1½ in; height
10 ft 11 in (3·3 m); (528) 11 ft 2 in.
Weights: (328) empty 3,704 lb (1680 kg); loaded
5,820 lb (2640 kg).
Performance: maximum speed 174 mph (280 km/h);
(528) about 205 mph (330 km/h); initial climb 984 ft
(300 m)/min; service ceiling 23,600 ft (7200 m); range
435 miles (700 km), (328 with overload tank, about
795 miles, 1280 km).
Armament: four 7·92 mm Ceska-Zbrojovka Mk 30
machine guns, two fixed in upper wing and two
manually aimed from rear cockpit, with provision for
two more Mk 30 fixed in lower wings; underwing
bomb load of two 265 lb (120 kg) or six 110 lb (50 kg).
History: first flight (S 328F) February 1933; (S 528)
1935; final S 328 delivery, after March 1940.

The S 328 saw an amazing amount of active service
in various hands, and its similarity to the Swordfish
shows what it might have accomplished had it carried
a torpedo. It was designed by a team led by Alois
Smolik, who had been chief designer ever since the
Letov company evolved from the Czech Military Air
Arsenal in 1918. The basic design was the S 28 of

Letov S 328

1929, from which Smolik derived the S 228 supplied
to Estonia. In 1933 Finland ordered the S 328F. None
were delivered to that customer, but the Czech
government ordered the 328 for its own Army Air
Force reconnaissance squadrons. Though there were
small batches of 328N night fighters and 328V twin-
float seaplanes, nearly all were reconnaissance
bombers. They continued to come off the line long
after flight testing of the 528, the intended successor,
had shown superior performance. Only five 528s were

built, but when German troops occupied Bohemia-
Moravia in March 1939 more than 445 of the earlier
type had been delivered. All were impressed into the
Luftwaffe or the new Slovak Air Force, while production at Prague-Letnany continued, the final 30
being for the Bulgarian Air Force. More than 200
served in the Polish campaign and, from 1941, on the
Russian Front, tracking partisans, night-fighting against
Po-2 biplanes and even in close-support of ground
forces. Many Slovak Letovs defected and in August
1944 surviving 328s in Czechoslovakia donned Red
Stars as part of the Insurgent Combined Squadron
which fought bitterly against the occupying German
forces.

Lockheed Model 414 Hudson

**Hudson I to VI, A-28, A-29, AT-18, C-63 and
PBO-1**
Type: reconnaissance bomber and utility.
Engines: (Hudson I, II) two 1,100 hp
Wright GR-1820-G102A nine-cylinder radials;
(Hudson III, A-29, PBO-1) two 1,200 hp
GR-1820-G205A, (Hudson IV, V, VI
and A-28) two 1,200 hp Pratt &
Whitney R-1830-S3C3-G, S3C4-G
or -67 14-cylinder two-row radials.
Dimensions: span 65 ft 6 in (19·96 m);
length 44 ft 4 in (13·51 m); height 11 ft 10½ in (3·62 m).
Weights: empty (I) 12,000 lb (5443 kg); (VI)
12,929 lb (5864 kg); maximum loaded (I) 18,500 lb
(8393 kg); (VI) 22,360 lb (10,142 kg).
Performance: maximum speed (I) 246 mph (397 km/
h); (VI) 261 mph (420 km/h); initial climb 1,200 ft
(366 m)/min; service ceiling 24,500 ft (7468 m);
range (I) 1,960 miles (3150 km); (VI) 2,160 miles
(3475 km).
Armament: (typical RAF Hudson in GR role) seven
0·303 in Brownings in nose (two, fixed), dorsal turret
(two), beam windows and ventral hatch; internal
bomb/depth charge load up to 750 lb (341 kg).
History: first flight (civil Model 14) 29 July 1937;
(Hudson I) 10 December 1938; squadron delivery
February 1939; USAAC and USN delivery, October
1941.

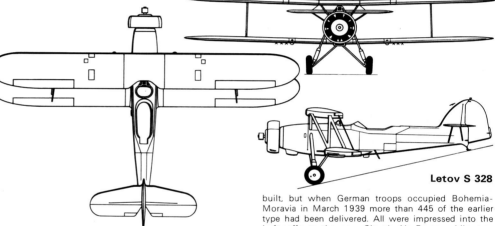

**Lockheed Hudson GR.V
(48 Sqn, Coastal Command)**

In 1938 the British Purchasing Commission was
established in Washington to seek out US aircraft that
could serve with the RAF and Royal Navy and help
bolster British strength beyond the then-small capacity
of the British aircraft industry. One of the urgent needs
was for a modern long-range reconnaissance and
navigation trainer aircraft and Lockheed Aircraft, at
Burbank – just climbing out of the Depression –
hastily built a mock-up of their Model 14 airliner to
meet the requirement. An order for 200 aircraft, many
times bigger than any previous order ever received by
Lockheed, was fulfilled swiftly and efficiently. The
order was many times multiplied and the versatile
Hudson served with several RAF commands in many
theatres of war. On 8 October 1939 a Hudson over

Jutland shot down the first German aircraft claimed
by the RAF in World War II. In February 1940 another
discovered the prison ship *Altmark* in a Norwegian
fjord and directed naval forces to the rescue. Over
Dunkirk Hudsons acted as dogfighters, in August 1941
one accepted the surrender of U-boat *U-570*, and from
1942 many made secret landings in France to deliver
or collect agents or supplies. Hudsons of later marks
carried ASV radar, rocket launchers and lifeboats.
Total deliveries were 2,584 including about 490 armed
versions for the US Army, 20 PBOs for the Navy and
300 AT-18 crew trainers. From this fine basic design
stemmed the more powerful Vega Ventura bomber and
ocean patrol aircraft and the PV-2 Harpoon at almost
twice the weight of the Hudson I.

Lockheed P-38 Lightning

XP-38 to P-38M, F-4 and F-5, RP and TP conversions
Type: single-seat long-range fighter (see text for variations).
Engines: two Allison V-1710 vee-12 liquid-cooled; (YP-38) 1,150 hp V-1710-27/29 (all P-38 engines handed with opposite propeller rotation, hence pairs of engine sub-type numbers); (P-38E to G) 1,325 hp V-1710-49/52 or 51/55; (P-38H and J) 1,425 hp V-1710-89/91; (P-38L and M) 1,600 hp V-1710-111/113.
Dimensions: span 52 ft (15·86 m); length 37 ft 10 in (11·53 m); (F-5G, P-38M and certain "droop-snoot" conversions fractionally longer); height 12 ft 10 in (3·9 m).
Weights: empty, varied from 11,000 lb (4990 kg) in YP to average of 12,700 lb (5766 kg), with heaviest subtypes close to 14,000 lb (6350 kg); maximum loaded, (YP) 14,348 lb (6508 kg); (D) 15,500 lb; (E) 15,482 lb; (F) 18,000 lb; (G) 19,800 lb; (H) 20,300 lb; (L, M) 21,600 lb (9798 kg).
Performance: maximum speed (all) 391–414 mph (630–666 km/h); initial climb (all) about 2,850 ft (870 m)/min; service ceiling (up to G) 38,000–40,000 ft; (H, J, L) 44,000 ft (13,410 m); range on internal fuel 350–460 miles (563–740 km); range at 30,000 ft with maximum fuel (late models) 2,260 miles (3650 km).
Armament: see text.
History: first flight (XP-38) 27 January 1939; (YP-38) 16 September 1940; service delivery (USAAC P-38) 8 June 1941; (F-4) March 1942; (P-38F) September 1942; final delivery September 1945.

Lockheed P-38F-5 (347th FG detached to 13th AAF, Guadalcanal)

Lockheed P-38H-5 (38th FS, 55th FG, 8th AAF)

Lockheed P-38J Lightning

In February 1937 the US Army Air Corps issued a specification for a long-range interceptor (pursuit) and escort fighter, calling for a speed of 360 mph at 20,000 ft and endurance at this speed of one hour. Lockheed, which had never built a purely military design, jumped in with both feet and created a revolutionary fighter bristling with innovations and posing considerable technical risks. Powered by two untried Allison engines, with GEC turbochargers recessed into the tops of the tail booms, it had a tricycle landing gear, small central nacelle mounting a 23 mm Madsen cannon and four 0·5 in Brownings firing parallel directly ahead of the pilot, twin fins, Fowler flaps, cooling radiators on the flanks of the booms and induction intercoolers in the wing leading edges. This box of tricks ran into a ditch on its first taxi test, and two weeks after first flight undershot at Mitchell Field, NY, and was demolished. What made headlines, however, was that it had flown to New York in 7 hr 2 min, with two refuelling stops, demonstrating a performance which in 1939 seemed beyond belief. The enthusiasm of the Air Corps overcame the doubts and high cost and by 1941 the first YP-38 was being tested, with a 37 mm Oldsmobile cannon, two 0·5s and two Colt 0·3s. Thirteen YPs were followed on the Burbank line by 20 P-38s, with one 37 mm and four 0·5, plus armour and, in the 36 D models, self-sealing tanks. In March 1940 the British Purchasing Commission had ordered 143 of this type, with the 37 mm

replaced by a 20 mm Hispano and far greater ammunition capacity. The State Department prohibited export of the F2 Allison engine and RAF aircraft, called Lightning I, had early C15 engines without turbochargers, both having right-hand rotation (P-38s had propellers turning outward). The result was poor and the RAF rejected these machines, which were later brought up to US standard. The E model adopted the British name Lightning and the RAF Hispano gun. Within minutes of the US declaration of war, on 7 December 1941, an E shot down an Fw 200C near Iceland, and the P-38 was subsequently in the thick of fighting in North Africa, North West Europe and the Pacific. The F was the first to have inner-wing pylons for 1,000 lb bombs, torpedoes, tanks or other stores. By late 1943 new G models were being flown to Europe across the North Atlantic, while in the Pacific 16 aircraft of the 339th Fighter Squadron destroyed

Admiral Yamamoto's aircraft 550 miles from their base at Guadalcanal. The J had the intercoolers moved under the engines, changing the appearance, providing room for 55 extra gallons of fuel in the outer wings. Later J models had hydraulically boosted ailerons, but retained the wheel-type lateral control instead of a stick. The L, with higher war emergency power, could carry 4,000 lb of bombs or ten rockets, and often formations would bomb under the direction of a lead-ship converted to droop-snoot configuration with a bombardier in the nose. Hundreds were built as F-4 or F-5 photographic aircraft, and the M was a two-seat night fighter with ASH radar pod under the nose. Lightnings towed gliders, operated on skis, acted as fast ambulances (carrying two stretcher cases) and were used for many special ECM missions. Total production was 9,942 and the P-38 made up for slightly inferior manoeuvrability in its range, reliability and multi-role effectiveness.

Lockheed Model 26 Neptune

P2V-1 to -7 (P-2A to H) and Kawasaki P-2J
Type: Maritime patrol and ASW aircraft.
Engines: (P2V-1) two 2,300 hp Wright R-3350-8 Cyclone 18-cylinder two-row radials; (-2) 2,800 hp R-3350-24W; (-3) 3,080 hp R-3350-26W; (later batches of -4) 3,250 hp R-3350-30W Turbo-Compound; (-5F, P-2E) same plus two 3,400 lb (1540 kg) thrust Westinghouse J34-36 turbojets; (-7, P-2H) same jets but 3,700 hp R-3350-32W Turbo-Compound; (P-2J) two 2,850 ehp GE (Ishikawajima-built) T64-IHI-10 turboprops plus two 3,085 lb (1400 kg) thrust Ishikawajima J3-7C turbojets.
Dimensions: span (early versions) 100 ft (30·48 m); (H) 103 ft 10 in (31·65 m); (J) 97 ft 8½ in (29·78 m); length (-1) 75 ft 4 in; (-2 to -4/D) 77 ft 10 in (23·7 m); (E) 81 ft 7 in; (H) 91 ft 8 in (27·94 m); (J) 95 ft 10¾ in (29·23 m); height 28 ft 1 in (8·58 m); (H, J, 29 ft 4 in, 8·94 m).
Weights: empty (-1) 31,000 lb (14,061 kg); (-3) 34,875 lb (15,833 kg); (H) 49,935 lb (22,650 kg); (J) 42,500 lb (19,277 kg); maximum loaded (-1) 61,153 lb (27,740 kg); (-3) 64,100 lb (29,075 kg); (H) 79,895 lb (36,240 kg); (J) 75,000 lb (34,019 kg).
Performance: maximum speed (-1) 303 mph (489 km/h); (H) 356 mph (403 mph, 648 km/h, with jets); (J) about 380 mph (612 km/h); initial climb (all) about 1,200 ft (366 m)/min; (H and J, 1,800 ft/min

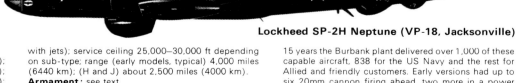

Lockheed SP-2H Neptune (VP-18, Jacksonville)

with jets); service ceiling 25,000–30,000 ft depending on sub-type; range (early models, typical) 4,000 miles (6440 km); (H and J) about 2,500 miles (4000 km).
Armament: see text.
History: first flight (XP2V-1) 17 May 1945; service delivery (-1) March 1947; (-7, H) 26 April 1954; (J) first flight of converted H, 21 July 1966, (production J) 8 August 1969.

On 1 October 1946 the P2V leapt into prominence. Three days earlier the third production P2V-1 had taken off from Perth, Western Australia, at 85,000 lb, with fuel weighing 1½ times its empty weight. By flying non-stop 11,235 miles to Columbus, Ohio, it set a world distance record for piston-engined aircraft that has never been broken. In the course of the next

15 years the Burbank plant delivered over 1,000 of these capable aircraft, 838 for the US Navy and the rest for Allied and friendly customers. Early versions had up to six 20mm cannon firing ahead, two more in a power tail turret and two 0·5 in in the dorsal turret. Gradually defensive or offensive gun armament was removed, later models having instead many tons of extra anti-submarine sensing systems, as well as retaining the 8,000 lb (3629 kg) weapon bay. The final models, no longer in first-line use, were the anti-submarine SP-2H and Antarctic ski-equipped LP-2H. The Japanese P-2J is a major redesign with longer fuselage housing a tactical team of ten seated at sensor and tactical consoles based on those of early P-3A Orions. Use of turboprop main engines saved enough weight for fuel capacity also to be increased.

Lockheed Model 80 family

P-80 (F-80) Shooting Star series, F-94 Starfire, T-33 series and T-1A Sea Star

Type: (F-80) single-seat fighter bomber; (F-94) two-seat night and all-weather fighter; (T-33) dual-control trainer.

Engine: (P-80A and B) one 4,600 lb (2087 kg) thrust Allison J33-9 or -19 single-shaft centrifugal turbojet; (P-80C or F-80C) one 5,400 lb (2450 kg) thrust J33-23; (F-94A and B) one 6,000 lb (2722 kg) thrust J33-33 with Solar afterburner; (F-94C) one 8,750 lb (3970 kg) thrust Pratt & Whitney J48-5 Turbo-Wasp (R-R Tay derived) centrifugal turbojet with afterburner; (T-33A) one 5,200 lb (2360 kg) Allison J33-35; (CL-30) one 5,100 lb (2313 kg) Rolls-Royce Nene 10 centrifugal turbojet; (T2V-1, T-1A) one 6,100 lb (2767 kg) J33-24.

Dimensions: span (basic) 38 ft 10½ in (11·85 m); (F-94C) 42 ft 5 in (12·9 m); length (F-80) 34 ft 6 in (10·51 m); (F-94A) 40 ft 1 in (12·2 m); (F-94C) 44 ft 6 in (13·57 m); (T-33) 37 ft 9 in (11·48 m); height (F-80, T-33) 11 ft 8 in (3·55 m); (F-94A) 12 ft 8 in (3·89 m); (F-94C) 14 ft 11 in (4·56 m).

Weights: empty (F-80C) 8,240 lb (3741 kg); (F-94A) 11,090 lb (5030 kg); (F-94C) 13,450 lb (6100 kg); (T-33A) 8,084 lb (3667 kg); (T-1A) 11,965 lb (5428 kg); maximum loaded (F-80C) 15,336 lb (6963 kg); (F-94A) 15,710 lb (7125 kg); (F-94C) 24,200 lb (10,980 kg); (T-33A) 14,442 lb (6551 kg); (T-1A) 15,800 lb (7167 kg).

Performance: maximum speed (all) 590–606 mph (950–975 km/h); initial climb (all) about 5,000 ft (1524 m)/min; service ceiling (all) about 48,000 ft (14,630 m); range (all) 1,100–1,250 miles (1770–2000 km).

Armament: see text.

History: first flight (XP-80) 8 January 1944; service delivery (YP-80A) October 1944; first flight (TF-80C) 22 March 1948; (F-94A) 1 July 1949; final delivery (Lockheed) August 1959, (Canada) 1958, (Japan) 1959.

Lockheed F-80C Shooting Star (Korean campaign)

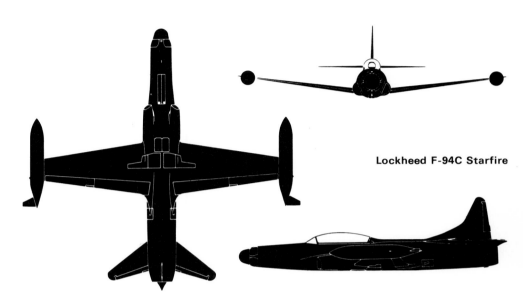

Lockheed F-94C Starfire

Lockheed sketched a jet fighter in 1941, but dropped it for lack of a suitable engine. In June 1943 Wright Field, excited by the imported Whittle engine but depressed by the obvious unsuitability of the P-59 Airacomet for combat duty, sent Col M. S. Roth to talk over the prospect of a Lockheed jet fighter with chief engineer Clarence L. "Kelly" Johnson. The latter decided to go ahead within a time limit of 180 days and fly a fighter designed around the British Halford H.1 (Goblin). The schedule was beaten easily and ground running began in December 1943. Unfortunately Lockheed had not heeded the warning of a resident British engineer that the skin of the inlet ducts was too thin and these collapsed and were sucked into the engine at full throttle. Generously, de Havilland sent Lockheed the engine that was being installed in the second prototype Vampire. With this installed behind stronger inlets test pilot Milo Burcham took off on a maiden flight which was such sheer joy he turned it into a breathtaking

display of low-level aerobatics! By January 1945 two Shooting Stars were serving under combat conditions in Italy and more soon came to Britain, but the type did not reach squadrons until after VJ-day. In the Korean War the F-80C bore the brunt of the initial fighting, flying 15,000 sorties in the first four months and shooting down the first MiG-15 on 8 November 1950 in what is thought to have been the first jet-v-jet combat. Total Shooting Star production was 1,718, many being converted into FP-80 (later called RF-80) reconnaissance and QF-80 drone versions. The tandem-seat F-94 required an afterburner to lift off with 940 lb of added radar even though the nose armament was cut from six 0·5 in to four. The interim F-94B had much bigger Fletcher tanks centred on the wing tips instead of hung beneath and improved all-weather instruments. The redesigned F-94C Starfire had much more thrust, a thinner wing, swept tailplane and much longer fuselage with new AI radar. Surrounding the

radar were arranged 24 Mighty Mouse rockets and a further 24 were salvoed from pods projecting ahead of the wing. Altogether 853 F-94s were delivered, the A and B models being used in Korea on various very difficult night missions. The T-33 has for 20 years been the world's most widely used jet trainer, the whole programme stemming from an F-80C taken from the production line and given an extra section of fuselage with a second seat, covered by a long clamshell canopy. Normal "T-bird" armament is two 0·5 in guns. Lockheed delivered approximately 5,820, including 217 of an improved T2V (T-1A) SeaStar model for the Navy with a new airframe having a raised instructor seat and slatted wing. Canadair built 656 CL-30 Silver Stars with Nene engine and Kawasaki built 210 in Japan. More than 2,000 T-33s were converted into RT (photo), WT (weather), DT (drone director), QT (drone or RPV) or AT (close-support attack) versions.

Lockheed Model 185 Orion

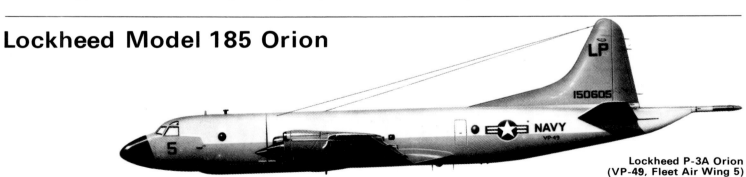

Lockheed P-3A Orion (VP-49, Fleet Air Wing 5)

P-3A, -3B and -3C with derivatives

Type: maritime reconnaissance and anti-submarine, normally with flight crew of five and tactical crew of five; variants, see text.

Engines: four Allison T56 single-shaft turboprops; (P-3A) T56-10W, 4,500 ehp with water injection; (remainder) T56-14, 4,910 ehp.

Dimensions: span 99 ft 8 in (30·37 m); length 116 ft 10 in (35·61 m); height 33 ft 8½ in (10·29 m).

Weights: empty (typical B, C) 61,491 lb (27,890 kg); maximum loaded 142,000 lb (64,410 kg).

Performance: maximum speed 473 mph (761 km/h); initial climb 1,950 ft (594 m)/min; service ceiling 28,300 ft (8625 m); range 4,800 miles (7725 km).

Armament: very varied load in bulged unpressurised weapon bay ahead of wing and on ten wing pylons; maximum internal load 7,252 lb (3290 kg) can include two depth bombs, four Mk 44 torpedoes, 87 sonobuoys

and many other sensing and marking devices; underwing load can include six 2,000 lb (907 kg) mines or various mixes of torpedoes, bombs, rockets or missiles. Maximum expendable load 20,000 lb (9071 kg).

History: first flight (aerodynamic prototype) 19 August 1958; (YP-3A) 25 November 1959; (production P-3A) 15 April 1961; (P-3C) 18 September 1968.

In August 1957 the US Navy issued a requirement for an "off the shelf" anti-submarine patrol aircraft derived from an established type, and this was met in April 1958 by Lockheed's proposal for a conversion of the Electra turboprop airliner. The third Electra was quickly modified as an aerodynamic prototype and deliveries of production P-3As began in August 1962. From the 110th aircraft the Deltic system was fitted with more sensitive sensors and improved displays. Four early A models were converted as WP-3A weather

reconnaissance aircraft, while others became EP-3A flying special electronic missions. Three As were supplied ex-USN to Spain. The B model introduced more powerful engines without water/alcohol injection and many were sold to Australia, New Zealand and Norway or modified, as EP-3B electronic reconnaissance and countermeasures, with huge "canoe radars" above and below and a radome under the forward fuselage. The completely different P-3C packages into the same airframe a new and more modern tactical system with sensors and weapons controlled by a digital computer. Derivatives include the P-3F for Iran and a variant for Australia. Other versions include the RP-3D for mapping the Earth's magnetic field and special reconnaissance and transport conversions. Deliveries by 1976 exceeded 500 aircraft.

Lockheed Model 382 Hercules

C-130 variants, see text (data for C-130H)

Type: basic aircraft, multi-role transport; for variants see text.

Engines: four Allison T56 single-shaft turboprops; (C-130A) 3,750 ehp T56-1A; (B and E families) 4,050 ehp T56-7; (F and H families) 4,910 ehp T56-15 or -16 flat-rated at 4,508 ehp.

Dimensions: span 132 ft 7 in (40·41 m); length 97 ft 9 in (29·78 m); (HC-130H and AC-130H and certain others are longer, owing to projecting devices); height 38 ft 3 in (11·66 m).

Weights: empty 65,621 lb (34,300 kg); maximum loaded 175,000 lb (79,380 kg; YC-130, 108,000 lb).

Performance: maximum speed 384 mph (618 km/h); initial climb 1,900 ft (579 m)/min; service ceiling 33,000 ft (10,060 m); range (maximum payload) 2,487 miles (4,002 km); (maximum fuel) 5,135 miles (8,264 km).

Armament: normally none; (AC-130H) one 105 mm howitzer, one 40 mm cannon, two 20 mm cannon or T-171 "Gatlings", two 7·62 mm "Gatling" Miniguns; optional grenade dispenser, rockets, missiles, bombs and various night or day sensors and target designators.

History: first flight (YC-130) 23 August 1954; (production C-130A) 7 April 1955; service delivery December 1956.

Though actually conventional and logical and a synthesis of known techniques, the YC-130 appeared radical and bold in 1954. Among its features were a pressurized fuselage with full-section rear doors which could be opened in flight, very neat turboprop engines and rough-field landing gear retracting into bulges outside the pressure hull. Lockheed-Georgia delivered 461 A and more powerful B models, following in 1962 with 503 heavier E series with more internal fuel. The H introduced more powerful engines and gave rise to numerous other sub-types. Special role versions related to the E or H include DC RPV-directors, EC electronics, communications and countermeasures, HC search/rescue, helicopter fueller and spacecraft retrieval, KC assault transport and probe/drogue tanker, LC wheel/ski and WC weather (the RAF uses the W.2 meteorological conversion of the British C-130K). The colour profile shows the AC-130H gunship, with formidable armament for night interdiction and equipped with forward-looking infra-red (FLIR), low-light-level TV (LLLTV), laser target designator and other fire control devices. Known and respected all over the world as the "Herky bird", the C-130 has remained in production for more than 20 years and no end to new orders can yet be seen. Constant product-improvement has steadily improved payload, range, fatigue life and reliability and in the mid-1970s the C-130 remained the standard transport and special-equipment platform for a growing list of users. Though the later fan-engined C-141 and C-5A were completed programmes, demand for the C-130 has actually increased as more and more military and civil customers find it meets their needs. Total deliveries by 1976 exceeded 1,500 (including civil L 100 series) and Hercules were in use with 30 military customers. Finding a replacement has proved extremely difficult but the Advanced Medium STOL Transport (AMST) programme aims to do this, choosing either the McDonnell Douglas YC-15 or Boeing YC-14 (p. 29).

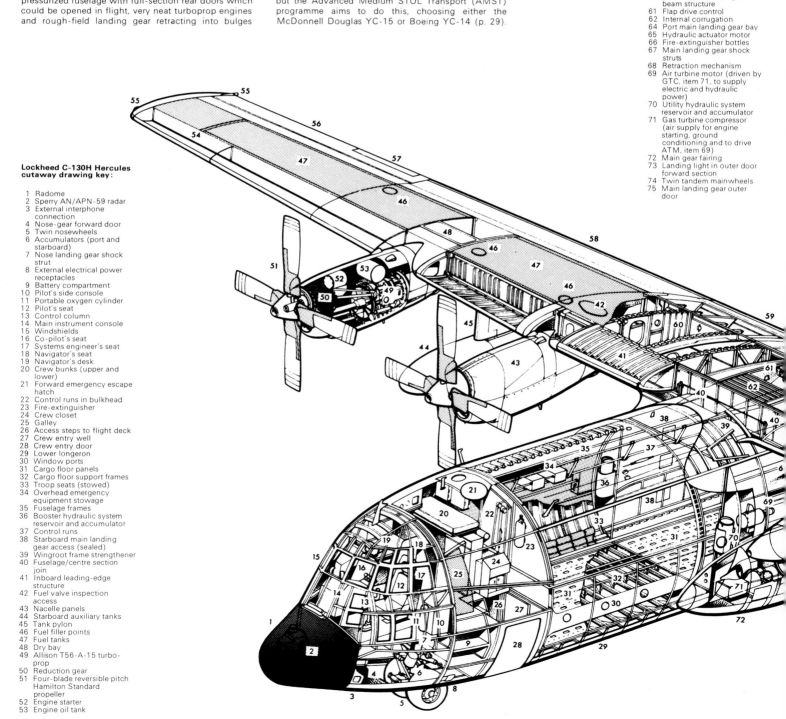

Lockheed C-130H Hercules cutaway drawing key:

1 Radome
2 Sperry AN/APN-59 radar
3 External interphone connection
4 Nose-gear forward door
5 Twin nosewheels
6 Accumulators (port and starboard)
7 Nose landing gear shock strut
8 External electrical power receptacles
9 Battery compartment
10 Pilot's side console
11 Portable oxygen cylinder
12 Pilot's seat
13 Control column
14 Main instrument console
15 Windshields
16 Co-pilot's seat
17 Systems engineer's seat
18 Navigator's seat
19 Navigator's desk
20 Crew bunks (upper and lower)
21 Forward emergency escape hatch
22 Control runs in bulkhead
23 Fire-extinguisher
24 Crew closet
25 Galley
26 Access steps to flight deck
27 Crew entry well
28 Crew entry door
29 Lower longeron
30 Window ports
31 Cargo floor panels
32 Cargo floor support frames
33 Troop seats (stowed)
34 Overhead emergency equipment stowage
35 Fuselage frames
36 Booster hydraulic system reservoir and accumulator
37 Control runs
38 Starboard main landing gear access (sealed)
39 Wingroot frame strengthener
40 Fuselage/centre section join
41 Inboard leading-edge structure
42 Fuel valve inspection access
43 Nacelle panels
44 Starboard auxiliary tanks
45 Tank pylon
46 Fuel filler points
47 Fuel tanks
48 Dry bay
49 Allison T56-A-15 turbo-prop
50 Reduction gear
51 Four-blade reversible pitch Hamilton Standard propeller
52 Engine starter
53 Engine oil tank
54 Limit of wing walkway
55 Starboard navigation lights
56 Starboard aileron
57 Aileron tab
58 Outer wing flap
59 Centre-section flap
60 Centre-section wing box beam structure
61 Flap drive control
62 Internal corrugation
64 Port main landing gear bay
65 Hydraulic actuator motor
66 Fire-extinguisher bottles
67 Main landing gear shock struts
68 Retraction mechanism
69 Air turbine motor (driven by GTC, item 71, to supply electric and hydraulic power)
70 Utility hydraulic system reservoir and accumulator
71 Gas turbine compressor (air supply for engine starting, ground conditioning and to drive ATM, item 69)
72 Main gear fairing
73 Landing light in outer door forward section
74 Twin tandem mainwheels
75 Main landing gear outer door

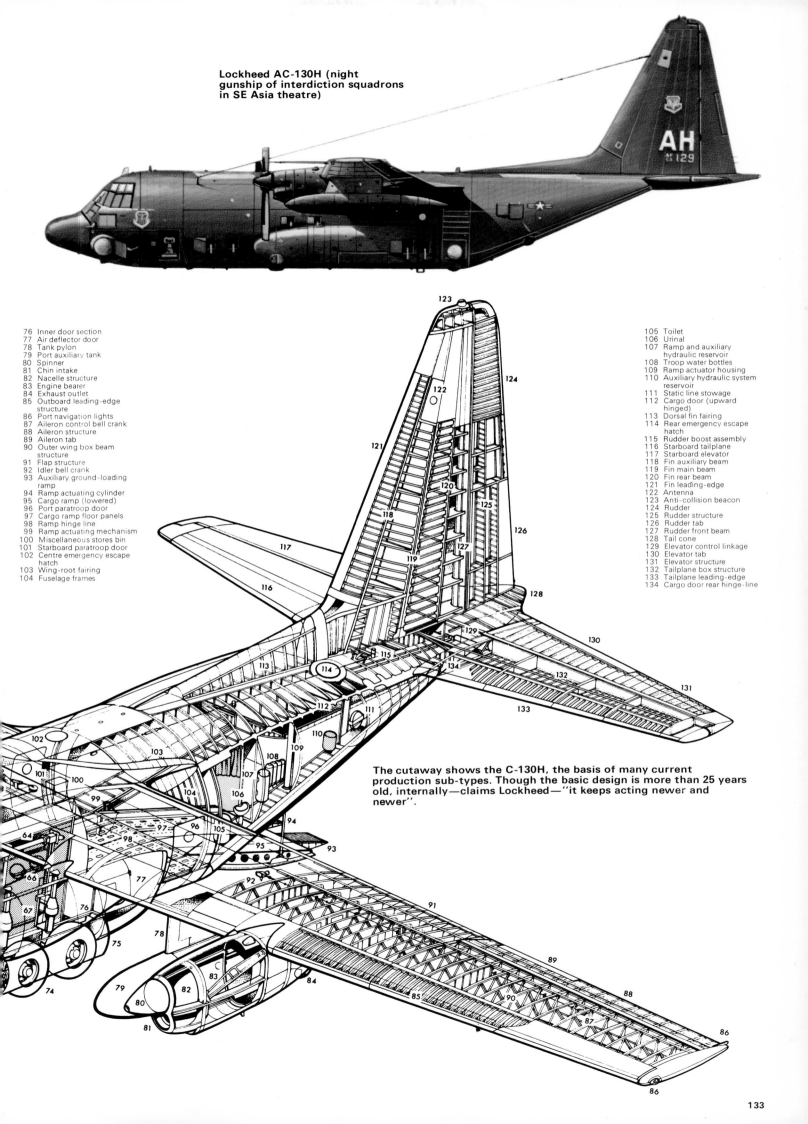

Lockheed AC-130H (night gunship of interdiction squadrons in SE Asia theatre)

76 Inner door section
77 Air deflector door
78 Tank pylon
79 Port auxiliary tank
80 Spinner
81 Chin intake
82 Nacelle structure
83 Engine bearer
84 Exhaust outlet
85 Outboard leading-edge structure
86 Port navigation lights
87 Aileron control bell crank
88 Aileron structure
89 Aileron tab
90 Outer wing box beam structure
91 Flap structure
92 Idler bell crank
93 Auxiliary ground-loading ramp
94 Ramp actuating cylinder
95 Cargo ramp (lowered)
96 Port paratroop door
97 Cargo ramp floor panels
98 Ramp hinge line
99 Ramp actuating mechanism
100 Miscellaneous stores bin
101 Starboard paratroop door
102 Centre emergency escape hatch
103 Wing-root fairing
104 Fuselage frames

105 Toilet
106 Urinal
107 Ramp and auxiliary hydraulic reservoir
108 Troop water bottles
109 Ramp actuator housing
110 Auxiliary hydraulic system reservoir
111 Static line stowage
112 Cargo door (upward hinged)
113 Dorsal fin fairing
114 Rear emergency escape hatch
115 Rudder boost assembly
116 Starboard tailplane
117 Starboard elevator
118 Fin auxiliary beam
119 Fin main beam
120 Fin rear beam
121 Fin leading-edge
122 Antenna
123 Anti-collision beacon
124 Rudder
125 Rudder structure
126 Rudder tab
127 Rudder front beam
128 Tail cone
129 Elevator control linkage
130 Elevator tab
131 Elevator structure
132 Tailplane box structure
133 Tailplane leading-edge
134 Cargo door rear hinge-line

The cutaway shows the C-130H, the basis of many current production sub-types. Though the basic design is more than 25 years old, internally—claims Lockheed—"it keeps acting newer and newer".

Lockheed U-2

U-2A, B, C, D and WU-2

Type: high-altitude photo-reconnaissance, multi-sensor and electronic reconnaissance and upper-air sampling (WU).
Engine: (U-2A) one 11,200 lb (5080 kg) Pratt & Whitney J57-13A or 37A two-shaft turbojet; (U-2B, C, D) one 17,000 lb (7711 kg) Pratt & Whitney J75-13 two-shaft turbojet.
Dimensions: span 80 ft (24·38 m); length 49 ft 7 in (15·1 m); height 13 ft (3·96 m).
Weights: empty (A) 9,920 lb (4500 kg); (others, typical) 11,700 lb (5305 kg); maximum loaded (A) 17,270 lb (7833 kg); (others) about 19,850 lb (9005 kg).
Performance: maximum speed (A) 494 mph (795 km/h); (others) 528 mph (850 km/h); service ceiling (A) 70,000 ft (21,340 m); (others) 85,000 ft (25,910 m); maximum range (A) 2,600 miles (4185 km); (others) 4,000 miles (6437 km).
Armament: none.
History: first flight 1 August 1955; service delivery, early 1956; final delivery of new aircraft, July 1958.

No aircraft in history has a record resembling the U-2. It was in operational use from Lakenheath (England) and Wiesbaden (Germany) in 1956, attracting the attention of spotters and amateur photographers who commented on its graceful glider-like appearance and on the odd fact that at take-off it jettisoned the small outrigger wheels under the outer wings, returning to land on small centreline wheels and the downturned

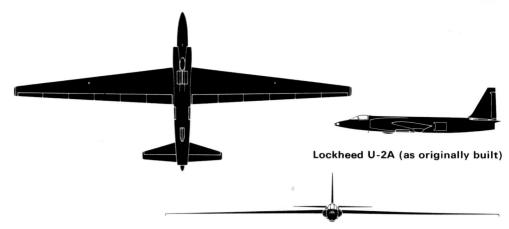

Lockheed U-2A (as originally built)

wingtips. When interest had reached fever-pitch the government blandly announced that the U-2, as it was called (a Utility designation) was used by the NACA (the National Advisory Committee for Aeronautics) for atmospheric research at heights up to 55,000 ft. When one force-landed in Japan the public were frantically kept away at gun-point and it was clear the incident was regarded as serious. In fact the U-2 had been designed for clandestine reconnaissance over the territory of any nation. Aircraft were delivered to Watertown Strip, a remote airfield in Nevada, where CIA pilots converted and prepared for operational missions over Communist territory. Their aircraft bore no markings and operated – immune to interception,

and often undetected – at far above the announced 55,000 ft. Other U-2s were assigned to the 4080th Strategic Wing and carried USAF markings. Most were of the more powerful U-2B type with much greater height and range. On 1 May 1960 a U-2B flown by a CIA pilot took off from Peshawar (Pakistan) to fly across the Soviet Union to Bodo (Norway), but was shot down over Sverdlovsk, presenting the Russians with unprecedented material for a diplomatic incident. Later U-2s were shot down over China and Cuba, and the survivors were assigned to lawful missions involving many kinds of surveillance and sampling. The C and two-seat D make up the bulk of the fleet used by the USAF and NASA; total production was 53.

Lockheed C-141 StarLifter

C-141A

Type: Strategic transport.
Engines: four 21,000 lb (9525 kg) thrust Pratt & Whitney TF33-7 two-shaft turbofans.
Dimensions: span 159 ft 11 in (48·74 m); length 145 ft (44·2 m); height 39 ft 3 in (11·96 m).
Weights: empty 133,773 lb (60,678 kg); loaded 316,600 lb (143,600 kg).
Performance: maximum speed 571 mph (919 km/h); initial climb 3,100 ft (945 m)/min; service ceiling 41,600 ft (12,680 m); range with maximum (70,847 lb, 32,136 kg) payload 4,080 miles (6565 km).
Armament: none.
History: first flight 17 December 1963; service delivery October 1964; final delivery July 1968.

Designed to meet a requirement of USAF Military Airlift Command, the StarLifter has since been the most common of MAC's transports and has a very useful combination of range and payload. Compared with civil jet transports in the same weight category it has a less-swept wing and thus lower cruising speed (typically 495 mph, 797 km/h), but can lift heavier loads out of shorter airstrips. The body cross-section is the same 10 ft by 9 ft as the C-130, and this has proved the only real shortcoming in prohibiting carriage of many bulky items (though it is said the C-141 can carry "90 per cent of all air-portable items in the Army or Air Force"). The largest item normally carried is the

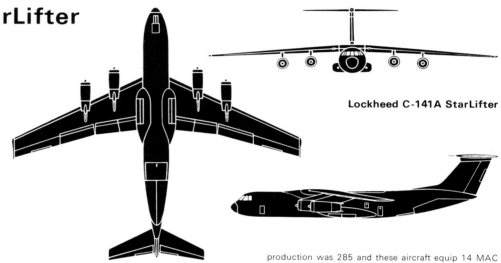

Lockheed C-141A StarLifter

packaged Minuteman ICBM, for which purpose several StarLifters have had the cargo floor slightly reinforced to bear the box skids of this 86,207 lb load. Alternative loads are 154 troops, 123 paratroops or 80 stretchers (litters) and 16 attendants. A C-141 holds the world record for air-dropping, with a load of 70,195 lb. Total

production was 285 and these aircraft equip 14 MAC squadrons. During the Vietnam war they bore the main burden of airlifting supplies westwards and casualties eastwards. All are fitted with an all-weather landing system. In 1975 Lockheed-Georgia was expecting to rebuild the surviving 274 aircraft with a fuselage extended by 23 ft, boom-type air refuelling and a new wing/body fairing to reduce drag.

Lockheed Model 83 Starfighter

F-104A to G, J and S, CF-104, QF-104, RF and RTF-104, TF-104 (data for F-104G)

Type: (A, C) single-seat day interceptor; (G) multi-mission strike fighter; (CF) strike-reconnaissance; (TF) dual trainer; (QF) drone RPV; (F-104S) all-weather interceptor; (RF and RTF) reconnaissance.
Engine: one General Electric J79 single-shaft turbojet with afterburner; (A) 14,800 lb (6713 kg) J79-3B; (C, D, F, J) 15,800 lb (7165 kg) J79-7A; (G, RF/RFT, CF) 15,800 lb (7165 kg) J79-11A; (S) 17,900 lb (8120 kg) J79-19 or J1Q.
Dimensions: span (without tip tanks) 21 ft 11 in (6·68 m); length 54 ft 9 in (16·69 m); height 13 ft 6 in (4·11 m).
Weights: empty 14,082 lb (6387 kg); maximum loaded 28,779 lb (13,054 kg).
Performance: maximum speed 1,450 mph (2330 km/h, Mach 2·2); initial climb 50,000 ft (15,250 m)/min; service ceiling 58,000 ft (17,680 m) (zoom ceiling over 90,000 ft, 27,400 m); range with maximum weapons, about 300 miles (483 km); range with four drop tanks (high altitude, subsonic) 1,380 miles (2220 km).
Armament: in most versions, centreline rack rated at 2,000 lb (907 kg) and two underwing pylons each rated at 1,000 lb (454 kg); additional racks for small missiles (eg Sidewinder) on fuselage, under wings or on tips; certain versions have reduced fuel and one

20 mm M61 Vulcan multi-barrel gun in fuselage.
History: first flight (XF-104) 7 February 1954; (F-104A) 17 February 1956; (F-104G) 5 October 1960; (F-104S) 30 December 1968; final delivery from United States 1964; final delivery from Aeritalia (F-104S) 1975.

Clarence L. ("Kelly") Johnson planned the Model 83 after talking with fighter pilots in Korea in 1951. The apparent need was for superior flight performance, even at the expense of reduced equipment and other penalties. When the XF-104 flew, powered by a 10,500 lb J65 Sapphire with afterburner, it appeared

to have hardly any wing; another odd feature was the downward-ejecting seat. The production F-104A had a more powerful engine and blown flaps and after lengthy development entered limited service with Air Defense Command in 1958. Only 153 were built and, after a spell with the Air National Guard, survivors are back in ADC service with the powerful GE-19 engine. Three were modified as Astronaut trainers with rocket boost, one gaining a world height record at nearly 119,000 ft in 1963. The B was a dual tandem trainer, the C a fighter-bomber for Tactical Air Command with

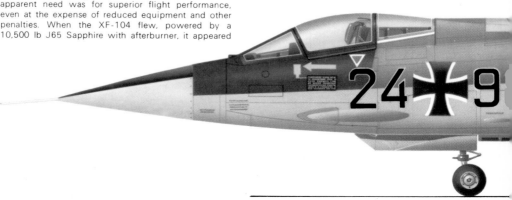

Lockheed Model 500 Galaxy

C-5A
Type: strategic transport.
Engines: four 41,100 lb (18,642 kg) thrust General Electric TF39-1 two-shaft turbofans.
Dimensions: span 222 ft 8½ in (67·88 m); length 247 ft 10 in (75·54 m); height 65 ft 1½ in (19·85 m).
Weights: empty 325,244 lb (147,528 kg); loaded 769,000 lb (348,810 kg).
Performance: maximum speed 571 mph (919 km/h); initial climb 1,800 ft (549 m)/min; service ceiling at 615,000 lb, 34,000 ft (10,360 m); range with maximum (220,967 lb, 100,228 kg) payload 3,749 miles (6033 km); ferry range 7,991 miles (12,860 km).
History: first flight 30 June 1968; service delivery 17 December 1969; final delivery May 1973.

On some counts the C-5A is the world's largest aircraft, though it is surpassed in power and weight by late models of B.747. Compared with the civil 747 it has less sweep and is considerably slower, because part of the Military Airlift Command requirement was that it should lift very heavy loads out of rough short airstrips. To this end it has a "high flotation" landing gear with 28 wheels capable of operating at maximum weight from unpaved surfaces. During development extremely difficult aerodynamic and structural problems had to be solved and there were severe difficulties concerned

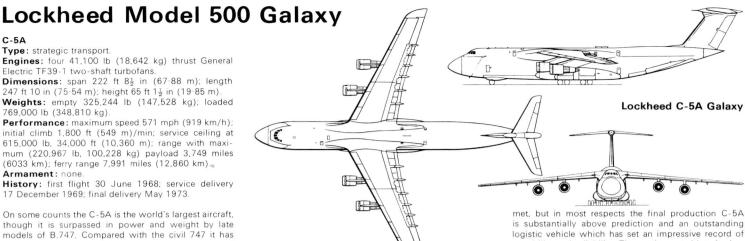

Lockheed C-5A Galaxy

with fatigue and structure weight. As a result of these problems, combined with inflation, the price escalated and eventually the production had to be cut to a total of 81, equipping four squadrons. The original requirement of carrying 125,000 lb for 8,000 miles was not

met, but in most respects the final production C-5A is substantially above prediction and an outstanding logistic vehicle which has set an impressive record of capability and reliability. The unobstructed interior has a section 19 ft wide and 13 ft 6 in high, not including the upper deck. Freight is normally carried in containers or on 36 standard Type 463L pallets; two M-60 battle tanks can be driven on board and there is room for three packaged CH-47 Chinook heavy helicopters. Equipment includes a refuelling boom receptacle in the roof and a Norden multi-mode radar in the nose.

Lockheed A-11 family

A-11, YF-12A and C, SR-71A, B and C (data for SR-71A)
Type: YF-12, research interceptor; SR-71, strategic reconnaissance.
Engines: two 32,500 lb (14,740 kg) thrust Pratt & Whitney J58 (JT11D-20B) single-shaft by-pass turbojets with afterburner.
Dimensions: span 55 ft 7 in (16·95 m); length 107 ft 5 in (32·74 m); height 18 ft 6 in (5·64 m).
Weights: empty (typical) 60,000 lb (27,215 kg); loaded 170,000 lb (77,110 kg).
Performance: maximum speed, in excess of 2,000 mph (3220 km/h, Mach 3); service ceiling, higher than 80,000 ft (24,400 m); range at Mach 3 at 78,740 ft (24,000 m), 2,982 miles (4800 km). Performance limit, about 2,200 mph and altitude of 84,000 ft sustained.
Armament: SR-71 series, none; YF-12, see text.
History: first flight 26 April 1962; (production SR-71A) 22 December 1964; final delivery, about 1968.

Despite their great size and intense noise these amazing aircraft were designed, built, test flown and put into use without a word leaking out into public until disclosed by President Johnson in February 1964. The A-11 was originally designed as a follow-on to the U-2, capable of flying even higher and many times faster in penetrating hostile airspace on clandestine overflights. Early in their career the three A-11s, with serial numbers 60-6934 to 6936, did overfly Communist territories in several parts of the world. Later they were completed as YF-12A research aircraft in the Improved

Lockheed SR-71A

Manned Interceptor programme, carrying Hughes ASG-18 pulse-doppler radar, infra-red sensors and eight Hughes AIM-47A large long-range air-to-air missiles in an internal bay. Made largely of a specially developed alloy of titanium, the YF-12A was the most advanced aircraft of its day and the only one to sustain a speed of Mach 3. One set a world speed record at 2,070 mph on 1 May 1965, and the type holds many other speed and height records. Later the two surviving YF-12s were used for extensive supersonic transport research, without armament, operated by NASA. The SR-71 strategic reconnaissance aircraft is longer and heavier, with a fuel capacity of over 80,000 lb. Known

as "Blackbirds" (though officially their external areas are painted indigo blue), they equip the 9th Strategic Reconnaissance Wing, from which detachments have operated over Vietnam, the Middle East and many other trouble-spots. Total production is at least 30, including SR-71B and C dual trainer versions. In September 1974 a standard A model set a transatlantic record at almost Mach 3 with a time from passing New York to passsing London of 1 hr 55 min. Most SR-71s in the active inventory (some are stored) use special JP-7 high-temperature fuel, air-refuelled by specially equipped KC-135Q tankers.

refuelling probe, the D a trainer version of the C and the DJ and F respectively Japanese and German versions of the D. The G was a complete redesign to meet the needs of the Luftwaffe for a tactical nuclear strike and reconnaissance aircraft. Structurally different, it introduced Nasarr multi-mode radar, inertial navigation system, manoeuvring flaps and other new items. Altogether 1,266 were built, including 970 by a NATO European consortium and 110 by Canadair. Canadair also built 200 basically similar CF-104s, while Japan built 207 J models closely resembling the earlier

C. The German RF and RTF are multi-role multi-sensor reconnaissance and trainer versions, while increasing numbers of all versions are being turned into various QF-104 RPVs. The only model built as new since 1967 has been the Italian F-104S interceptor, with improved air-to-air radar and carrying two Sparrow missiles in its armament; it has nine stores pylons and a slightly improved flight performance. Total production by Aeritalia was 241, including 36 for Turkey.

Lockheed RF-104G Starfighter (Aufklärungsgeschwader 52)

Lockheed S-3 Viking

S-3A
Type: four-seat carrier-based anti-submarine aircraft.
Engines: two 9,275 lb (4207 kg) General Electric TF34-2 or TF34-400 two-shaft turbofans.
Dimensions: span 68 ft 8 in (20·93 m); length 53 ft 4 in (16·26 m); height 22 ft 9 in (6·93 m).
Weights: empty 26,600 lb (12,065 kg); normal loaded for carrier operation 42,500 lb (19,277 kg); maximum loaded 47,000 lb (21,319 kg).
Performance: maximum speed 506 mph (814 km/h); initial climb, over 4,200 ft (1280 m)/min; service ceiling, above 35,000 ft (10,670 m); combat range, more than 2,303 miles (3705 km); ferry range, more than 3,454 miles (5558 km).
Armament: split internal weapon bays can house four Mk 46 torpedoes, four Mk 82 bombs, four various depth bombs or four mines; two wing pylons can carry single or triple ejectors for bombs, rocket pods, missiles, tanks or other stores.
History: first flight 21 January 1972; service delivery October 1973; operational use (VS-41) 20 February 1974; final delivery after 1980.

Designed to replace the evergreen Grumman S-2, the S-3 is perhaps the most remarkable exercise in packaging in the history of aviation. It is also an example of an aircraft in which the operational equipment costs considerably more than the aircraft itself. Lockheed-California won the Navy competition in partnership with LTV (Vought) which makes the wing, engine pods, tail and F-8-type landing gear. To increase transit

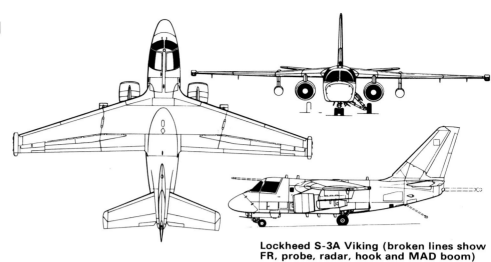

Lockheed S-3A Viking (broken lines show FR, probe, radar, hook and MAD boom)

speed the refuelling probe, MAD tail boom, FLIR (forward-looking infra-red) and certain other sensors all retract, while the extremely modern specially designed APS-116 radar is within the nose. Equipment includes CAINS (carrier aircraft inertial navigation system), comprehensive sonobuoy dispensing and control systems, doppler, very extensive radio navaid and altitude systems, radar warning and ECM systems, extensive communications, and a Univac digital pro-

cessor to manage all tactical and navigation information. By the end of 1975 more than 100 of the first buy of 186 Vikings were in service and foreign orders (beginning with Federal Germany) were being discussed. Developed versions, including a COD transport version, were in the design stage. Tanker, ECM and AEW versions are also possible, for both carrier and land operation.

Macchi M.C.200 Saetta

M.C.200 (Serie I-XXI) and M.C.201
Type: single-seat day fighter.
Engine: one 870 hp Fiat A74RC38 14-cylinder two-row radial.
Dimensions: span 34 ft 8½ in (10·58 m); length 26 ft 10½ in (8·2 m); height 11 ft 6 in (3·38 m).
Weights: (typical) empty 4,188 lb (1900 kg); (prototype) 3,902 lb; (final production Serie XXI) 4,451 lb; loaded 5,182 lb (2350 kg); (prototype) 4,850 lb; (Series XXI) 5,598 lb.
Performance: maximum speed 312 mph (501 km/h); initial climb 3,215 ft (980 m)/min; service ceiling 29,200 ft (8900 m); range 354 miles (570 km).
Armament: two 12·7 mm Breda-SAFAT machine guns firing above engine cowling; late-Serie aircraft also had two 7·7 mm in the wings; M.C.200 C.B. (caccia bombardiere) had underwing racks for two bombs of up to 352 lb (160 kg) each, or two 33 gal drop tanks.
History: first flight 24 December 1937; service delivery October 1939; final delivery, about December 1944.

Mario Castoldi's design team at Aeronautica Macchi, at Varese in the north Italian lakeland, was the source

Macchi M.C. 200 (90o Squadriglia, 10o Gruppo)

of the best fighters used by the Regia Aeronautica in World War II. Castoldi's staff had earlier gained great experience with high-speed aircraft with their record-breaking Schneider seaplanes, but their first monoplane fighter, the C.200, bore little evidence of this. Though a reasonably attractive stressed-skin monoplane, it had an engine of low power and the performance was correspondingly modest. Moreover it never had anything that other countries would have regarded as proper armament, though the pilot did have the advantage of cockpit indicators showing the number of rounds of ammunition unfired. Italian fighter pilots were by nature conservative; their protests caused the

main production aircraft to have an open cockpit and fixed tailwheel, unlike the first batches, and combat equipment was simple in the extreme. Yet in combat with the lumbering Hurricane it proved effective, with outstanding dogfight performance and no vices. From late 1940 until Italy's surrender in September 1943 the C.200 saw more combat than any other Italian type, both around North Africa and Sicily and on the Eastern Front with the Corpo di Spedizione Italiano which claimed 88 Russian aircraft for the loss of 15 Saettas. The name Saetta, meaning lightning, refers to the lightning-bolts held by Jupiter, and is sometimes rendered as Arrow or Thunderbolt.

Macchi (Aermacchi) M.B.326

M.B.326 and 326 GB and GC (AT-26 Xavante), 326K (Atlas Impala), 326L and M.B.339
Type: two-seat basic trainer and light attack aircraft; (326K) single-seat trainer/attack; (339) two-seat all-through trainer.
Engine: one-Rolls-Royce Viper single-shaft turbojet; (original production versions) 2,500 lb (1134 kg) thrust Viper 11; (GB, GC, H and M) 3,410 lb (1547 kg) Viper 20 Mk 540; (K, L and 339) 4,000 lb (1814 kg) R-R/Fiat Viper 632-43.
Dimensions: span (over tip tanks) 35 ft 7 in (10·85 m); length 34 ft 11 in (10·64 m); height 12 ft 2½ in (3·72 m).
Weights: empty (G trainer) 5,920 lb (2685 kg); (G attack) 5,640 lb (2558 kg); (K) 6,240 lb (2830 kg); maximum loaded (G trainer) 10,090 lb (4577 kg); (G attack) 11,500 lb (521 kg); (K and 339) 12,500 lb (5670 kg).
Performance: maximum speed (G clean) 539 mph (867 km/h); (K clean) 553 mph (890 km/h); (339) 560 mph (901 km/h); initial climb (G clean) 6,050 ft (1844 m)/min; (G attack at max wt) 3,100 ft (945 m)/min; (K clean and 339) 6,500 ft (1980 m)/min; service ceiling (G trainer clean) 47,000 ft (14,325 m); (G attack, max wt) 35,000 ft (10,700 m); range on internal fuel (G trainer) 1,150 miles (1850 km); (K with max weapons) about 160 miles (260 km).
Armament: six underwing pylons for load of up to 4,000 lb (1814 kg) including bombs, rockets, tanks, missiles, reconnaissance pods or gun pods; some versions, including 339, have single 7·62 mm or similar gun (or Minigun) in fuselage; 326K (Impala) has two

M.B. 326G
(stores pylons and wing gun pods)

30 mm DEFA 553 cannon in fuselage, each with 125 rounds.
History: first flight 10 December 1957; (production 326) 5 October 1960; (K prototype) 22 August 1970; (339) during 1976.

The most successful Italian military aircraft programme in history, the 326 was designed by a team led by Ermanno Bazzocchi and was put into production

as a trainer for the Regia Aeronautica, which received 90. In addition the South African AF has over 150 K models, built by Atlas Aircraft with locally built engines, and expects to build over 200, while other big customers include Australia (114, 85 built by CAC in Melbourne), Brazil (112 locally built Xavantes) and many emergent nations. The latest sub-types are the 326K with the most powerful Viper, the 326L with two seats but K attack capability, the M uncompromised dual trainer and the M.B.339 with redesigned airframe for all-through training, with raised instructor seat under a sloping canopy.

McDonnell F-2 Banshee

F-2A (F2D, then F2H-1) to F-2D (F2H-4)
Type: carrier-based fighter, later all-weather fighter-bomber.
Engines: two Westinghouse J34 single-shaft axial turbojets; (F2H-1) 3,000 lb (1361 kg) thrust J34-22; (F-2B (F2H-2 family) and F-2C (F2H-3)) 3,250 lb (1474 kg) J34-34; (F-2D (F2H-4)) 3,600 lb (1633 kg) J34-38.
Dimensions: span (F2H-1) 41 ft 6 in, (F2H-2, -3) 44 ft 10 in (13·67 m); (F-2D) 44 ft 11 in; length (-1) 39 ft, (-2) 40 ft 2 in (12·24 m), (F-2C and D) 47 ft 6 in (14·48 m); height (-1) 14 ft 2 in, (others) 14 ft 6 in (4·4 m).
Weights: empty (-1) 10,600 lb; (F-2C, D) 12,790 lb (5800 kg); maximum loaded (-1) 17,000 lb; (-2) 22,312 lb (10,270 kg); (F-2C, D, clean) 19,000 lb (8618 kg).
Performance: maximum speed (-1) 587 mph; (-2, maximum weapons) 532 mph; (F-2C, D) 610 mph (982 km/h); initial climb (all, clean) 9,000 ft (2743 m)/min; service ceiling (-1) 48,500 ft; (-2, maximum weapons) 44,800 ft; (F-2C, D, clean) 56,000 ft (17,000 m); range (-1, -2) 1,400 miles (2250 km); (F-2C, D) 2,000 miles (3220 km).
Armament: four 20 mm M-2 cannon, each with 160 rounds; F2H-2 had four underwing racks for total load of 3,000 lb (1361 kg) and F-2C and D had eight pylons for total load of 4,000 lb (1814 kg); many C and D were wired for two or four Sidewinder air-to-air missiles.

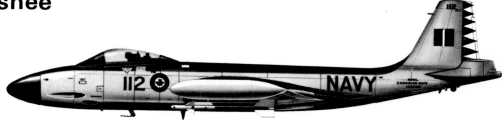

McDonnell F-2C (VF-870, Royal Canadian Navy)

History: first flight 11 January 1947; service delivery March 1949; final delivery (F2H-4) October 1953.

While the Royal Navy decided jets were too dangerous for aircraft carriers (having experimented in 1945 with a Vampire) the US Navy kept an open mind and in March 1945 contracted with the infant McDonnell Company for a purpose-designed carrier jet. This machine, the FD-1 (later FH-1) Phantom, proved entirely satisfactory and 60 were used as fighter-trainers. From this was derived the outstanding Banshee, originally designated F2D, later F2H and finally F-2. The design team under vice-president G. C. Covington kept to the unswept formula with two Westinghouse axial engines inside the fattened wing roots, but with the Banshee engine thrust was adequate

for a formidable multi-role machine. An order for 56 F2H-1 fighters was placed in May 1947, followed by one for 188 F2H-2s, with longer fuselage for extra fuel and 200 US gal tip tanks. A further 146 -2s followed, many of them -2N radar night fighter or -2P photo versions. Almost all were hard-worked in Korea in carrier attack missions, as vividly portrayed in the best-selling novel "The Bridges of Toko-Ri". The F2H-3 (F-2C) was longer still, with increased fuel capacity and Westinghouse APQ-41 radar, plus a flight refuelling probe. The F2H-4 (F-2D) had more powerful engines. All Banshees had laminar wings, high-gloss finish, and electric flaps, gear and wing folding. Altogether 800 were built, 60 F-2Cs being passed in 1955 to what was then the Royal Canadian Navy.

McDonnell F3H Demon

F3H-1, F3H-2, -2M and -2N (F-3 series)
Type: carrier-based interceptor, later all-weather fighter.
Engine: originally one 11,600 lb (5262 kg) thrust Westinghouse J40-22 single-shaft turbojet with afterburner; finally one 14,250 lb (6463 kg) Allison J71-2 of same layout.
Dimensions: span 35 ft 4 in (10·76 m); length (F3H-1) 58 ft 4 in; (others) 58 ft 11 in (17·95 m); height (F3H-1) 13 ft 11 in; (others) 14 ft 7 in (4·45 m).
Weights: empty (F3H-1) 14,990 lb; (others, typical) 22,300 lb (10,115 kg); maximum loaded (F3H-1) 23,400 lb; (others, typical) 33,900 lb (15,376 kg).
Performance: maximum speed (F3H-1, intended) 758 mph, (production F-3, typical) 647 mph (1040 km/h); initial climb 12,000 ft (3660 m)/min; service ceiling (F-3) 42,650 ft (13,000 m); maximum combat range 1,370 miles (2200 km).
Armament: four 20 mm M-2 cannon; (F-3 versions) four underwing pylons for various ordnance, see text.
History: first flight (XF3H-1) 7 August 1951; (F3H-2) 23 April 1955; service delivery (-2N) 7 March 1956; final delivery November 1959.

"Mr Mac's" prowess as a producer of extremely advanced jet combat aircraft was unsurpassed from the very first XFD-1 Phantom, and the severe challenge of

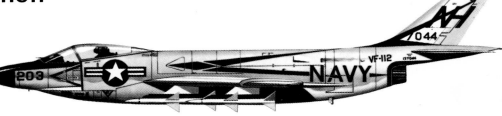

McDonnell MF-3B Demon (VF-112)

the XF3H Demon found the company equal to it. Ordered in September 1949, the Demon was to equal in performance the fastest land-based fighters and a completely new all-swept layout was chosen with a single powerful afterburning engine and an exceedingly advanced airframe. Unfortunately the J40 engine proved totally unacceptable, with poor reliability and inadequate thrust, while ever-greater demands caused aircraft weight to grow. After catastrophic failures the J40 was abandoned and in June 1953 the J71 was adopted instead. Orders for 529 F3H-1Ns were cut, Temco's second-source line was cancelled and of the

60 completed -1s, 21 were used as ground trainers and 29 converted to J71-powered -2s. McDonnell's hard work rescued the Demon as a fine fighter which joined the Navy carrier squadrons and served hard operations in many theatres. The basic F-3B was a strike fighter with 6,600 lb weapon load; the F-3C had Hughes APG-51A radar, four Sidewinder missiles and limited all-weather capability; and the MF-3B had APG-51A and four AIM-7C Sparrow III missiles, the first aircraft ever to carry these formidable all-weather air-to-air weapons. Total Demon production was 519.

McDonnell F-101 Voodoo

McDonnell F-101B-100 (2nd FIS, ADC, Suffolk County AFB)

F-101A, B and C and RF-101A to H
Type: (A, C) day fighter-bomber; (B) all-weather interceptor; (RF) all-weather reconnaissance.
Engines: two Pratt & Whitney J57 two-shaft turbojets with afterburner; (F-101B) 14,990 lb (6800 kg) J57-53 or -55; (others) 14,880 lb (6750 kg) J57-13.
Dimensions: span 39 ft 8 in (12·09 m); length 67 ft 4¾ in (20·55 m); (RF) 69 ft 3 in; height 18 ft (5·49 m).
Weights: empty (typical of all) 28,000 lb (12,700 kg); maximum loaded (B) 46,700 lb (21,180 kg); (all versions, overload 51,000 lb, 23,133 kg).
Performance: maximum speed (B) 1,220 mph (1963 km/h, Mach 1·85); (others, typical) 1,100 mph; initial climb (B) 17,000 ft (5180 m)/min; service ceiling 52,000 ft (15,850 m); range on internal fuel (B) 1,550 miles (2500 km); (others) 1,700 miles (2736 km).

Armament: (B) three Falcon (usually AIM-4D) air-to-air missiles semi-submerged in underside, sometimes supplemented by two AIR-2A Genie nuclear rockets on fuselage pylons; (C) three 20 mm M-39 cannon (provision for four, with Tacan removed) in fuselage; (RF) none. As built, all A and C and derivatives fitted with centreline crutch for 1 MT tactical nuclear store and wing pylons for two 2,000 lb (907 kg) bombs, four 680 lb (310 kg) mines or other ordnance.
History: first flight 29 September 1954; service delivery (A) May 1957; final delivery (B) March 1961.

By far the most powerful fighter of its day, the Voodoo was based on the XF-88 Voodoo prototype flown on 20 October 1948. Originally a long-range escort for Strategic Air Command, the F-101A became a tactical

attack machine; 50 were followed by 47 improved C models, all of which set records for accident-free operation and were converted to unarmed RF-101G and H for the Air National Guard, augmenting 35 RF-101A and 166 RF-101C built earlier and used intensively at all levels in Vietnam. The B interceptor sacrificed fuel for a radar operator to work the MG-13 radar fire-control; 478 were built and converted to F-101F or dual-control TF-101F for Air Defense Command (now Air National Guard). In 1961 66 ex-ADC aircraft were transferred to the RCAF as CF-101s; in 1970 the CAF exchanged the 58 survivors for 66 improved F and TF and these still serve as the only CAF all-weather fighters.

F-4 Phantom see page 142.

McDonnell Douglas A-4 Skyhawk

A-4A to A-4S and TA-4 series

Type: single-seat attack bomber; TA, dual-control trainer.

Engine: (B, C, L, P, Q, S) one 7,700 lb (3493 kg) thrust Wright J65-16A single-shaft turbojet (US Sapphire); (E, J) 8,500 lb (3856 kg) Pratt & Whitney J52-6 two-shaft turbojet; (F, G, H, K) 9,300 lb (4218 kg) J52-8A; (M, N) 11,200 lb (5080 kg) J52-408A.

Dimensions: span 27 ft 6 in (8·38 m); length (A) 39 ft 1 in; (B) 39 ft 6 in (42 ft 10¾ in over FR probe); (E, F, G, H, K, L, P, Q, S) 40 ft 1½ in (12·22 m); (M, N) 40 ft 3¼ in (12·27 m); (TA series, excluding probe) 42 ft 7¼ in (12·98 m); height 15 ft (4·57 m); (early single-seaters 15 ft 2 in, TA series 15 ft 3 in).

Weights: empty (A) 7,700 lb; (E) 9,284 lb; (typical modern single-seat, eg M) 10,465 lb (4747 kg); (TA-4F) 10,602 lb (4809 kg); maximum loaded (A) 17,000 lb; (B) 22,000 lb; (all others, shipboard) 24,500 lb (11,113 kg); (land-based) 27,420 lb (12,437 kg).

Performance: maximum speed (clean) (B) 676 mph; (E) 685 mph; (M) 670 mph (1078 km/h); (TA-4F) 675 mph; maximum speed (4,000 lb, 1814 kg bomb load (F) 593 mph; (M) 645 mph; initial climb (F) 5,620 ft (1713 m)/min; (M) 8,440 ft (2572 m)/min; service ceiling (all, clean) about 49,000 ft (14,935 m); range (clean, or with 4,000 lb weapons and max fuel, all late versions) about 920 miles (1480 km); maximum range (M) 2,055 miles (3307 km).

Armament: standard on most versions, two 20 mm Mk 12 cannon, each with 200 rounds; (H, N and optional on other export versions) two 30 mm DEFA 553, each with 150 rounds. Pylons under fuselage and wings for total ordnance load of (A, B, C) 5,000 lb (2268 kg); (E, F, G, H, K, L, P, Q, S) 8,200 lb (3720 kg); (M, N) 9,155 lb (4153 kg).

History: first flight (XA4D-1) 22 June 1954; (A-4A) 14 August 1954; squadron delivery October 1956; (A-4C) August 1959; (A-4E) July 1961; (A-4F) August 1966; (A-4M) April 1970; (A-4N) June 1972; first of TA series (TA-4E) June 1965.

Most expert opinion in the US Navy refused to believe the claim of Ed Heinemann, chief engineer of what was then Douglas El Segundo, that he could build a jet attack bomber weighing half the 30,000 lb specified by the Navy. The first Skyhawk, nicknamed "Heinemann's Hot Rod", not only flew but gained a world record by flying a 500 km circuit at over 695 mph. Today, more than 20 years later, greatly developed versions are still in production, setting an unrivalled record for sustained manufacture. These late versions do weigh close to 30,000 lb, but only because the basic design has been improved with more powerful engines, increased fuel capacity and much heavier weapon load. The wing was made in a single unit, forming an integral fuel tank and so small it did not need to fold. Hundreds of Skyhawks have served aboard carriers, but many serve with the US Marine Corps and with Argentina, Australia, Israel, New Zealand and Singapore. In early versions the emphasis was on improving range and load and the addition of all-weather avionics. The F model introduced the dorsal hump containing additional avionics, and the M, the so-called Skyhawk II, marked a major increase in mission effectiveness. Most of the TA-4 trainers closely resemble the corresponding single-seater, but the mass-produced TA-4J of the US Navy (and used in South East Asia by the Marines as a high-speed Forward Air Control aircraft) is a simplified version and the TA-4S has two cockpit humps. In late 1975 total deliveries exceeded 3,100.

McDonnell Douglas A-4M Skyhawk cutaway key

1 Fixed flight refuelling probe
2 Dielectric nose
3 APG-53A radar scanner
4 Pitot head
5 Electronics pack
6 Avionics pack
7 Cockpit forward bulkhead
8 Control column
9 Rudder pedal
10 Internal armour plate
11 Single nosewheel door
12 Oleo leg
13 Steering cylinder
14 Nosewheel
15 Shortening link
16 Retraction jack
17 Integral armour area
18 Port instrument console
19 Throttle control lever
20 Instrument panel shroud
21 Fixed or lead-computing gunsight
22 Bullet-resistant rectangular windscreen
23 Cockpit canopy
24 Headrest
25 Zero-zero ejection seat
26 Leading-edge slat (open position)
27 Starboard flow fences
28 Leading-edge slat
29 Starboard navigation lamp
30 Aerials
31 Vortex generators
32 Aerodynamically-balanced aileron
33 Wing inspection panels
34 Split flap
35 Aerial
36 Dorsal avionics pack
37 Self-sealing fuel cell (200 gal/909 litres)
38 Engine intake
39 Intake trunk
40 11,200 lb (5,443 kg) thrust Pratt & Whitney J52–408 two-shaft turbojet
41 Inspection panel
42 Power-supply amplifier
43 Compass adapter
44 Engine firewall
45 Upper anti-collision lamp
46 Combustion chamber
47 Turbine section
48 Aft fuselage frame
49 Oxygen converter
50 Rudder cables
51 Fin construction
52 Tip of fin containing antenna
53 Externally-braced rudder construction
54 Rudder hinge post
55 Rudder control power unit
56 Trim tab
57 Rear navigation lamp
58 Tailplane incidence control power unit
59 Elevator actuator
60 Elevator
61 Tailplane
62 Submerged tailpipe outlet
63 Drag 'chute housing
64 Tailpipe
65 Port air brake
66 Arrester hook
67 Arrester-hook actuating

The subject of the cutaway drawing, the A-4M, was the first sub-type to be dubbed "Skyhawk II". Since being designed in 1952 the A-4 family has been improved by several thousand engineering changes, yet the basic airframe remains amazingly close to the original—even to the hastily schemed single—surface rudder with half-ribs on each side, introduced as a temporary measure in 1954!

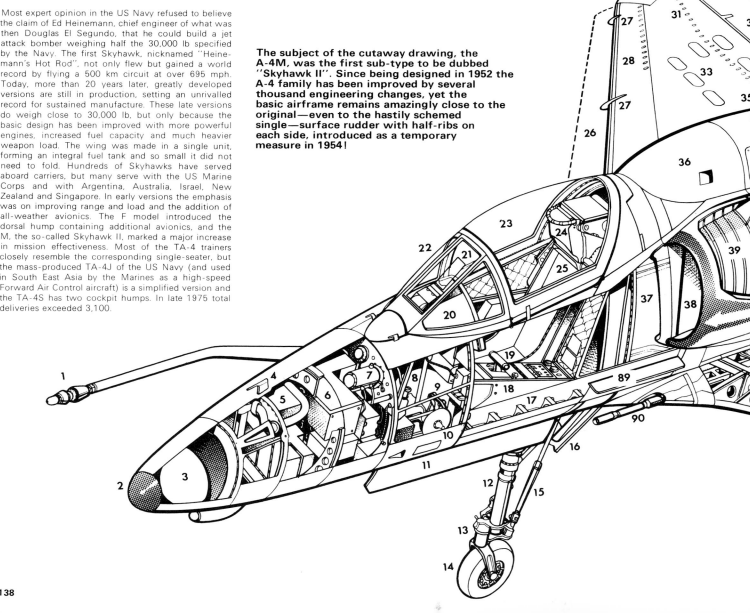

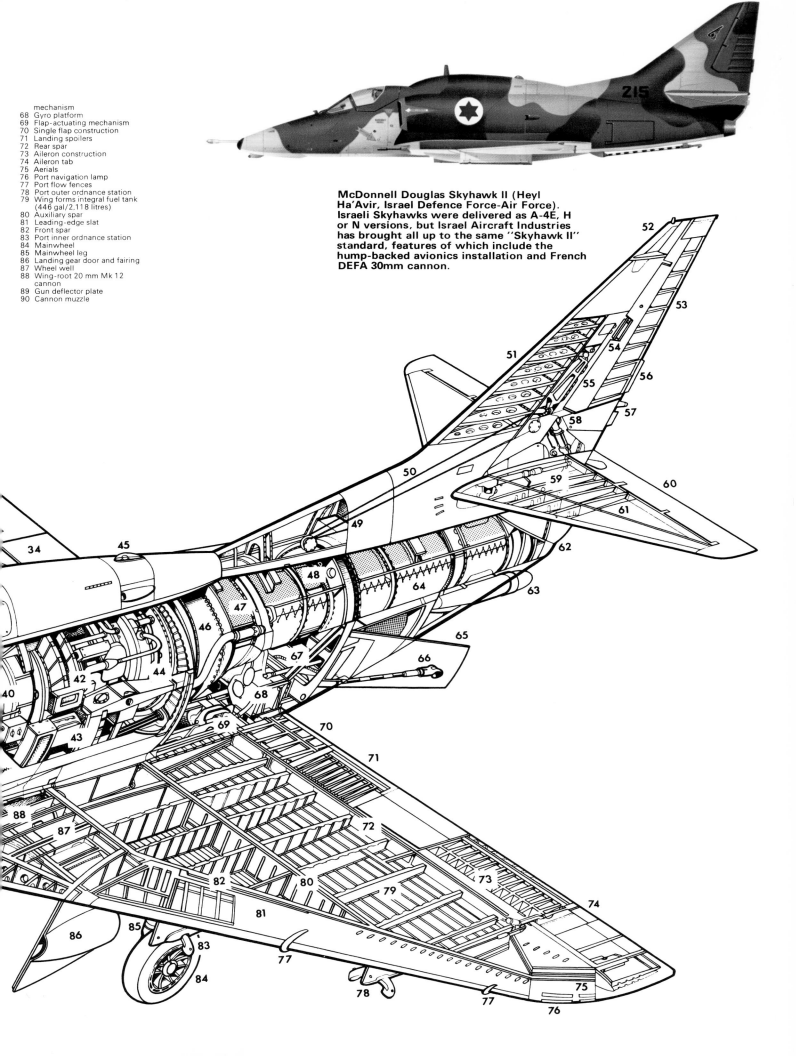

mechanism
68 Gyro platform
69 Flap-actuating mechanism
70 Single flap construction
71 Landing spoilers
72 Rear spar
73 Aileron construction
74 Aileron tab
75 Aerials
76 Port navigation lamp
77 Port flow fences
78 Port outer ordnance station
79 Wing forms integral fuel tank
   (446 gal/2,118 litres)
80 Auxiliary spar
81 Leading-edge slat
82 Front spar
83 Port inner ordnance station
84 Mainwheel
85 Mainwheel leg
86 Landing gear door and fairing
87 Wheel well
88 Wing-root 20 mm Mk 12
   cannon
89 Gun deflector plate
90 Cannon muzzle

McDonnell Douglas Skyhawk II (Heyl Ha'Avir, Israel Defence Force-Air Force). Israeli Skyhawks were delivered as A-4E, H or N versions, but Israel Aircraft Industries has brought all up to the same "Skyhawk II" standard, features of which include the hump-backed avionics installation and French DEFA 30mm cannon.

McDonnell Douglas F-15 Eagle

F-15A, TF-15A
Type: single-seat all-weather air-superiority fighter; (TF) dual-control trainer.
Engines: two Pratt & Whitney F100-100 two-shaft augmented turbofans, each rated at 14,871 lb (6744 kg) thrust dry and 23,810 lb (10,800 kg) with maximum augmentation.
Dimensions: span 42 ft 9¾ in (13.05 m); length 63 ft 9¾ in (19.45 m); height 18 ft 7½ in (5.68 m).
Weights: empty, about 28,000 lb (12,700 kg); loaded (F or TF, clean) 39,500 lb; (F with four Sparrows) about 40,500 lb, (three 600 gal drop tanks) 54,000 lb, (three tanks and two FAST packs) 66,000 lb (29,937 kg).
Performance: maximum speed (low) over 921 mph (1482 km/h, Mach 1.22), (high) over 1,650 mph (2660 km/h, Mach 2.5); initial climb, over 50,000 ft (15,240 m)/min; service ceiling, over 70,000 ft (21,000 m); range on internal fuel, about 1,200 miles (1930 km); ferry range with maximum fuel, over 3,700 miles (5955 km).
Armament: one 20 mm M-61 multi-barrel gun with 960 rounds; four AIM-7 Sparrow air-to-air missiles on

corners of fuselage and four AIM-9 Sidewinder air-to-air missiles on lateral rails at upper level of wing pylons; centreline pylon stressed for 4,500 lb (2041 kg) for 600 gal tanks, reconnaissance pod or any tactical weapon; inner wing pylons stressed for 5,100 lb (2313 kg) for any tanks or weapon; outer wing pylons stressed for 1,000 lb (454 kg) for ECM pods or equivalent ordnance load. Normal external load limit, with or without FAST packs, 12,000 lb (5443 kg).
History: first flight 27 July 1972; (TF) 7 July 1973; service delivery March 1974 (Cat. II test), November 1974 (inventory).

Emergence of the MiG-23 and -25 in 1967 accentuated the belief of the US Air Force that it was falling behind in true fighter aircraft. Studies for an FX (a new air-superiority fighter) were hastened and, after a major competition, McDonnell's team at St Louis was selected to build the new aircraft. The Air Force funded a new engine, won by Pratt & Whitney, and a new 25 mm gun using caseless ammunition (abandoned after difficult development). The Eagle has emerged

as probably the best fighter in the world, with thrust at low levels considerably greater than clean gross weight, a fixed wing of no less than 530 sq ft area, a single seat and an advanced Hughes X-band pulse-doppler radar. Though planned as an uncompromised machine for interception and air combat the Eagle also has formidable attack capability over intercontinental ranges. Undoubtedly its chief attributes are its combat manoeuvrability (it can outfly almost any other US machine without using afterburner) and the advanced automaticity of its radar, head-up display, weapon selectors and quick-fire capability. Internal fuel capacity of 11,200 lb can be almost trebled by adding a FAST (fuel and sensor, tactical) pack on each side, a "conformal pallet" housing 10,000 lb of fuel and target designators or weapons. Very extensive electronic systems for attack and defence, far beyond any standard previously seen in a fighter, are carried. A USAF buy of 729 is planned and these are being delivered at the rate of nine per month at $7.5 million each. Several countries are likely to purchase this outstanding fighter.

McDonnell Douglas F-15A Eagle cutaway drawing key:'

1. Nose radome
2. Planar-array radar scanner
3. Hughes APG-63 multi-mode radar
4. Forward bulkhead
5. Instrument panel shroud
6. Head-up display sight
7. Curved windscreen (polycarbonate with cast acrylic surfaces)
8. Polycarbonate one-piece canopy
9. Pilot's headrest
10. Ejection seat (Douglas Escapac)
11. Port control console
12. Nosewheel door
13. Retraction strut
14. Landing/taxi lights
15. Forward-retracting nosewheel
16. Nosewheel fairing door
17. Port intake
18. Variable inlet ramps
19. Inlet pivot line
20. Port missile station (Sidewinder, Sparrow or advanced missile)
21. Avionics stowage
22. Wing-intake fairing
23. Flight refuelling receptacle
24. Auxiliary intake (and grille)
25. Canopy hinges
26. Provision for second crew member (TF-15)
27. Starboard inlet
28. General Electric M61 20mm gun
29. Ammunition drum, 1,000 rounds
30. Ammunition feed
31. Dorsal speed-brake (shaded, shown retracted)
32. Centre-section fuel tanks (4)
33. Starboard wing tank
34. Vent tank
35. Aluminium wing skinning
36. Honeycomb outboard leading-edge
37. Starboard wingtip aerials
38. Fuel vent pipe
39. Starboard aileron
40. Aileron actuator
41. Flap actuator
42. Starboard flap
43. Starboard Pratt & Whitney F100-PW-100 turbofan (23,810 lb/10,885 kg with maximum afterburner)
44. Aluminium vertical tail surface leading and trailing edges (honeycomb)
45. Advanced composite construction
46. Starboard stabilator (tailplane)
47. ECM aerials
48. Tail navigation and formation-keeping lights
49. Starboard rudder section (advanced composite construction)
50. Engine nozzle actuators
51. Multi-flap articulated nozzle
52. Airfield arrester hook fairing
53. Titanium fin spars
54. Stabilator (tailplane) spindle (titanium)
55. Aluminium stabilator leading and trailing edges (honeycomb)
56. Stabilator torque box (boron epoxy skin)
57. Leading-edge dog-tooth
58. Titanium centre-fuselage bulkheads
59. Intermediate frames
60. Wing/fuselage attachment (seven lugs)
61. Port mainwheel
62. Aluminium front spar
63. Titanium wing spars (3)
64. Port flap
65. Port aileron
66. Wingtip
67. Wingtip aerials
68. Port navigation light

The cutaway depicts the basic F-15A, without FAST packs, ECM or offensive ordnance. Though the bare price charged to the USAF is the figure given in the text, a truer measure of "total cost of ownership" is the 1976 Israeli contract for 25, priced at $600 million.

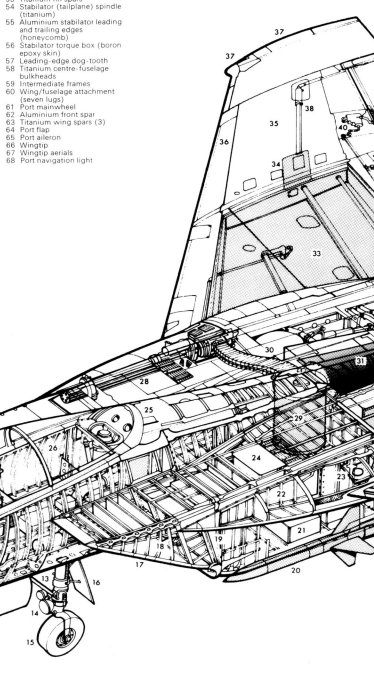

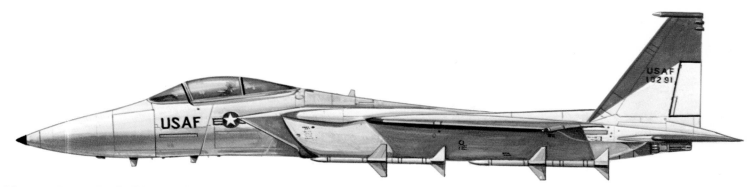

McDonnell Douglas F-15A Eagle (YF-15 evaluation and test aircraft, 1972)

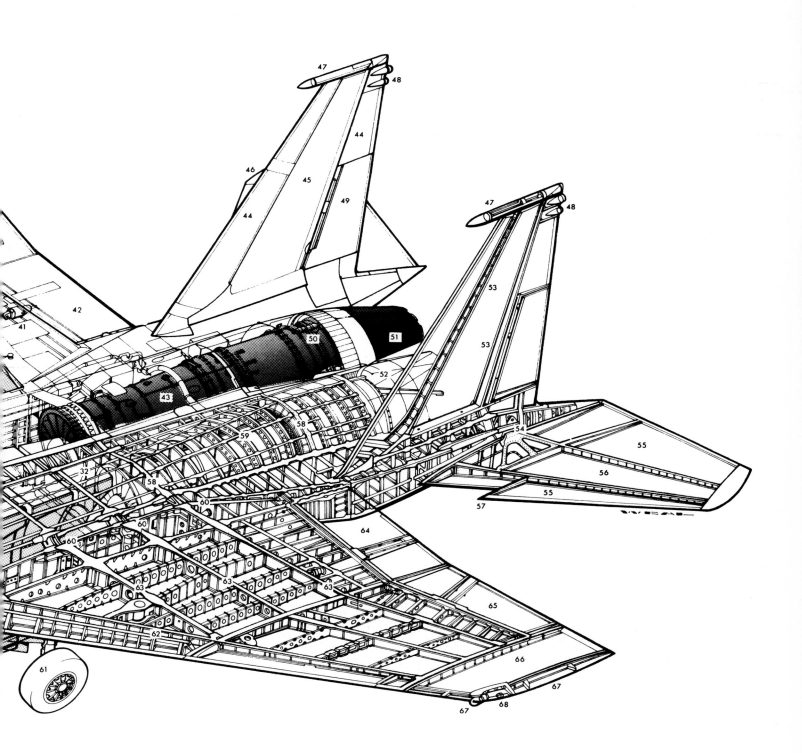

McDonnell Douglas F-4 Phantom

F-4A to F-4N, RF-4, QF-4
Type: originally carrier-based all-weather interceptor; now all-weather multi-role fighter for ship or land operation; (RF) all-weather multisensor reconnaissance; (QF) RPV.
Engines: (B, G) two 17,000 lb (7711 kg) thrust General Electric J79-8 single-shaft turbojets with afterburner; (C, D) 17,000 lb J79-15; (E, EJ, F) 17,900 lb (8120 kg) J79-17; (J, N) 17,900 lb J79-10; (K, M) 20,515 lb (9305 kg) Rolls-Royce Spey 202/203 two-shaft augmented turbofans.
Dimensions: span 38 ft 5 in (11·7 m); length (B, C, D, G, J, N) 58 ft 3 in (17·76 m); (E, EJ, F and all RF versions) 62 ft 11 in or 63 ft (19·2 m); (K, M) 57 ft 7 in (17·55 m); height (all) 16 ft 3 in (4·96 m).
Weights: empty (B, C, D, G, J, N) 28,000 lb (12,700 kg); (E, EJ, F and RF) 29,000 lb (13,150 kg); (K, M) 31,000 lb (14,060 kg); maximum loaded (B) 54,600 lb; (C, D, G, J, K, M, N, RF) 58,000 lb (26,308 kg); (E, EJ, F) 60,630 lb (27,502 kg).
Performance: maximum speed with Sparrow missiles only (low) 910 mph (1464 km/h, Mach 1·19) with J79 engines, 920 mph with Spey, (high) 1,500 mph (2414 km/h, Mach 2·27) with J79 engines, 1,386 mph with Spey; initial climb, typically 28,000 ft (8534 m)/min with J79 engines, 32,000 ft/min with Spey; service ceiling, over 60,000 ft (19,685 m) with J79 engines, 60,000 ft with Spey; range on internal fuel (no weapons) about 1,750 miles (2817 km); ferry range with external fuel, typically 2,300 miles (3700 km) (E and variants, 2,600 miles (4184 km).
Armament: (all versions except RF, QF which have no armament) four AIM-7 Sparrow air-to-air missiles recessed under fuselage; inner wing pylons can carry two more AIM-7 or four AIM-9 Sidewinder missiles; in addition all E versions except RF have internal 20 mm M-61 multi-barrel gun, and virtually all versions can carry the same gun in external centreline pod; all except RF, QF have centreline and four wing pylons for tanks, bombs or other stores to total weight of 16,000 lb (7257 kg).
History: first flight (XF4H-1) 27 May 1958; service delivery (F-4A) February 1960 (carrier trials), February 1961 (inventory); first flight (Air Force F-4C) 27 May 1963; (YF-4K) 27 June 1966; (F-4E) 30 June 1967.

McDonnell designed the greatest fighter of the post-war era as a company venture to meet anticipated future needs. Planned as an attack aircraft with four 20 mm guns, it was changed into a very advanced gunless all-weather interceptor with advanced radar and missile armament. In this form it entered service as the F-4A, soon followed by the F-4B used in large

**McDonnell Douglas F-4B
(VF-84, USS Independence)**

**McDonnell Douglas F-4E
(Heyl Ha'Avir, Israel)**

numbers (635) by the US Navy and Marine Corps, with Westinghouse APQ-72 radar, IR detector in a small fairing under the nose, and many weapon options. Pilot and radar intercept officer sit in tandem and the aircraft has blown flaps and extremely comprehensive combat equipment. A level Mach number of 2·6 was achieved and many world records were set for speed, altitude and rate of climb. Not replaced by the abandoned F-111B, the carrier-based Phantom continued in production for 17 years through the F-4G with digital communications, F-4J with AWG-10 pulse-doppler radar, drooping ailerons, slatted tail and increased power, and the N (rebuilt B). In 1961 the F-4B was formally compared with all US Air Force fighters and found to outperform all by a wide margin, especially in weapon load and radar performance. As a result it was ordered in modified form as the F-110, soon redesignated F-4C, for 16 of the 23 Tactical Air Command Wings. The camera/radar/IR linescan RF-4C followed in 1965. In 1964 the Royal Navy adopted the Anglicised F-4K, with wider fuselage housing Spey

fan engines and, of 48 delivered to Britain as Phantom FG.1, 28 served with the Royal Navy. The other 20 went to RAF Strike Command, which has also received 120 F-4M (UK designation Phantom FGR.2) which combine the British features with those of the F-4C plus the option of a multi-sensor centreline reconnaissance pod whilst retaining full weapons capability. In the US Air Force the C was followed by the much-improved D with APQ-100 radar replaced by APQ-109, inertial navigation added and many added or improved equipment items. This in turn was followed by the dramatically improved F-4E with slatted wing, internal gun and increased power, the EJ being the version built in Japan and the F being a Luftwaffe version. The Luftwaffe also operate the multi-sensor RF-4E. Other big users of the Phantom include Iran, Israel, Greece, Turkey, Spain, Australia and South Korea. By the end of 1975, when production was at last showing signs of running down, total deliveries were approaching 6,000.

A-4 Skyhawk and F-15 Eagle see pages 138–141.

McDonnell Douglas/Northrop F-18

F-18 and TF-18
Type: single-seat carrier-based multi-role fighter (TF, dual trainer).
Engines: two 16,000 lb (7257 kg) thrust General Electric F404-400 two-shaft augmented turbofans.
Dimensions: span (with missiles) 40 ft 8½ in (12·41 m), (without missiles) 37 ft 6 in (11·42 m); length 56 ft (17·07 m); height 14 ft 9½ in (4·50 m).
Weights: (provisional) empty 20,583 lb (9336 kg); loaded (clean) 33,642 lb (15,260 kg); maximum loaded (catapult limit) 50,064 lb (22,710 kg).
Performance: maximum speed (clean, at altitude) 1,320 mph (2125 km/h, Mach 2·0), (maximum weight, sea level) subsonic; sustained combat manoeuvre ceiling, over 49,000 ft (14,935 m); absolute ceiling, over 60,000 ft (18,290 m); combat radius (air-to-air mission, high, no external fuel) 461 miles (741 km); ferry range, about 3,000 miles (4830 km).
Armament: one 20 mm M61 Gatling in upper part of forward fuselage; nine external weapon stations for maximum load (catapult launch) of 13,400 lb (6080 kg), including bombs, sensor pods, ECM, missiles (including Sparrow) and other stores, with tip-mounted Sidewinders.
History: first flight (YF-17) 9 June 1974; (first of 11 test YF-18) 1978; service delivery, not before 1979.

In 1971 the US Navy became concerned at the cost of the F-14 and the resulting reduced rate of procurement and total number that could be afforded. In 1973 it studied low-cost versions and compared them with

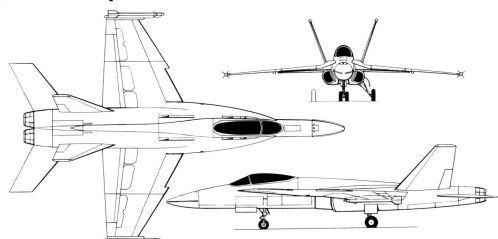

McDonnell Douglas/Northrop YF-18

navalised F-15 versions and improved F-4s. In 1974 the VFX specification emerged for a wholly new and smaller fighter somewhat along the lines of the Air Force Air Combat Fighter. In May 1975 the Navy and Marine Corps announced their choice of the F-18, developed from the existing land-based Northrop F-17 by McDonnell Douglas and Northrop. In fact the F-18 will be almost twice as heavy as the original F-17 proposal but, with more powerful engines, is expected to have adequate dogfight performance through the 1980s. Features include an unswept wing with large

dogteeth and forebody strakes at the roots, twin canted vertical tails, simple fixed engine inlets and extensive graphite/epoxy structure. Search radar will be used in the interception and surface-attack roles, and a very wide range of weapons will be carried. In 1975–76 the F-18 programme was still vulnerable on grounds of cost/effectiveness, but it is hoped to show savings in cost and manpower over a max of F-14 and A-7E. The plan is to buy 811 by 1989 at a price of $5,924 million without spares.

Martin Bomber

Model 123, 139 and 166, B-10, -12 and -14
Type: 4/5-seat medium bomber.
Engines: (YB-10) two 775 hp Wright R-1820-25 Cyclone nine-cylinder radials; (YB-12) two 665 hp Pratt & Whitney R-1690-11 Hornet nine-cylinder radials; (XB-14) two 850 hp P&W R-1830-9 Twin Wasp 14-cylinder two-row radials; (most export 139) 750 hp Cyclone SGR-1820-F3S; (export 166) usually 850 hp Cyclone R-1820-G2, but some 900 hp Twin Wasp R-1830-SC3-G.
Dimensions: span 70 ft 6 in (21·48 m); length 44 ft 8¾ in (13·63 m); (XB-10) 45 ft; (B-12A) 45 ft 3 in; (export 166) 44 ft 2 in; height 11 ft (3·35 m); (XB-10) 10 ft 4 in; (B-10B) 15 ft 5 in; (export 166) 11 ft 7 in.
Weights: empty (typical B-10, 139) 8,870–9,000 lb; (166) 10,900 lb (4944 kg); maximum loaded (XB-10) 12,560 lb; (B-10B) 14,600 lb (6622 kg); (B-12A) 14,200 lb; (139) 14,192 lb; (166) 15,624 lb (Cyclone) or 16,100 lb (Twin Wasp).
Performance: maximum speed (all B-10, 139, B-12) 207–213 mph (340 km/h); (166) 255 mph (W) or 268 mph (P&W); initial climb (all) 1,290–1,455 ft (about 410 m)/min; service ceiling (all) 24,200–25,200 ft (about 7500 m); range with bomb load (typical) 700 miles (1125 km); maximum range with extra fuel (early models) 1,240 miles, (166) 2,080 miles.
Armament: (all) three rifle-calibre (usually 0·3 in) machine guns manually aimed from nose turret, rear cockpit and rear ventral hatch; bomb load of 1,000 lb (454 kg) in internal bay beneath centre section in fuselage.
History: first flight (Model 123) January 1932; service delivery (123) 20 March 1932; (YB-10) June 1934; (export 139) late 1935; (166) January 1938.

The Glenn L. Martin Company, of Baltimore, was one of the earliest important suppliers of US Army and Navy

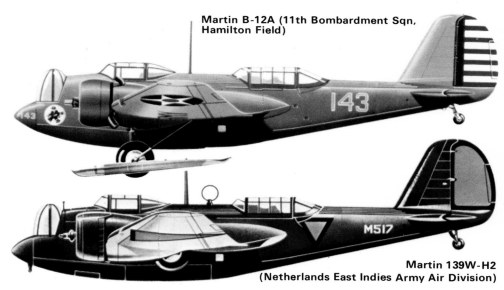

Martin B-12A (11th Bombardment Sqn, Hamilton Field)

Martin 139W-H2 (Netherlands East Indies Army Air Division)

aircraft, and "Billy" Mitchell used Martin MB-2 bombers to demonstrate, in 1922, that battleships could be sunk from the air. After many historic heavy bombers, torpedo bombers, dive bombers and flying boats, Martin built the Model 123 as a company venture. Several recent observers have judged "the Martin Bomber" one of the most significant single advances in the history of military aircraft. For the first time it introduced cantilever monoplane wings, flaps, stressed-skin construction, retractable landing gear, advanced engine cowls, variable-pitch propellers and an internal bomb bay with power-driven doors. Despite only 600 hp Cyclone engines the prototype walked away from every pursuit (fighter) in the US Army and the Model 139 went into production as the YB-10, followed by the 12 and 14, total delivery being 152 by 1936. Export sales were inevitable and once these were permitted, in 1935, a further 189 were built. By far the largest user was the Dutch East Indies, which bought 120 Martin 139W and 18 of the improved 166 with single "glasshouse" canopy. All the Netherlands Indies machines were in constant action from December 1941 as the only bombers available until late January 1942, fighting fiercely and with much success against Japanese sea and land forces. Other major users were Argentina (25) and Turkey (20).

Martin Maryland

Model 167 Maryland I and II
Type: three-seat reconnaissance bomber.
Engines: two Pratt & Whitney Twin Wasp 14-cylinder two-row radials; (Maryland I) 1,050 hp R-1830-S1C3-G; (II) 1,200 hp R-1830-S3C4-G.
Dimensions: span 61 ft 4 in (18·69 m); length 46 ft 8 in (14·22 m); height 10 ft 1 in (3·07 m).
Weights: empty 11,213 lb (RAF Mk II); maximum loaded (I) 15,297 lb; (II) 16,809 lb (7694 kg).
Performance: maximum speed (prototype) 316 mph; (I) 304 mph; (II) 280 mph (451 km/h); initial climb 1,790 ft (545 m)/min; service ceiling (I) 29,500 ft (8992 m); (II) 26,000 ft (7925 m); range with bomb load 1,080 miles (1738 km).
Armament: four 0·303 in Browning (France, 7·5 mm MAC 1934) fixed in outer wings; two 0·303 in Vickers K (France, MAC 1934) manually aimed from dorsal turret and rear ventral position; internal bomb load of 2,000 lb (907 kg) (France 1,874 lb, 850 kg; Maryland I, 1,250 lb, 567 kg).

History: first flight 14 March 1939; (production 167F) 7 August 1939; service delivery (France) October 1939; final delivery 1941.
Designed as the US Army XA-22 attack bomber, the Martin 167 was not adopted but immediately attracted a big French order for the Armée de l'Air as the 167F, with Armée de l'Air designation 167A-3. Of 215 purchased, about 75 reached France before the June 1940 capitulation, squadrons GB I/62 and I/63 completing conversion and, despite being chosen for dangerous missions, suffering only 8 per cent casualties (the lowest of any French bomber type). Some survivors and undelivered aircraft went to the RAF, while

Martin 167A-3 (GB I/63, Armée de l'Air)

most surviving French aircraft served the Vichy Air Force and operated against the Allies over Gibraltar, North Africa and Syria. The RAF accepted 75 ex-French machines and bought a further 150 with two-stage supercharged engines as the Maryland II, using all 225 as reconnaissance bombers in Cyrenaica, Malta and other Middle East areas. A few went to the Fleet Air Arm (one gave first warning of the departure of *Bismarck*) and four squadrons served with the South African AF. In basic arrangement rather like Luftwaffe bombers, the Maryland was quite fast, nice to fly, but cramped and inadequately armed.

Martin Baltimore

Model 187, Baltimore I to V (US Army A-30)
Type: four-seat light bomber.
Engines: two Wright Cyclone 14-cylinder two-row radials; (I, II) 1,600 hp R-2600-A5B; (III, IV) 1,660 hp R-2600-19; (V) 1,700 hp R-2600-29.
Dimensions: span 61 ft 4 in (18·69 m); length 48 ft 6 in (14·78 m); height 17 ft 9 in (5·41 m).
Weights: empty (III) 15,200 lb (6895 kg); maximum loaded (I) 22,958 lb; (III) 23,000 lb (10,433 kg); (V) 27,850 lb (12,632 kg).
Performance: maximum speed (I) 308 mph; (III, IV) 302 mph; (V) 320 mph (515 km/h); initial climb 1,500 ft (457 m)/min; service ceiling (typical) 24,000 ft (7315 m); range with 1,000 lb bomb load (typical) 1,060 miles (1700 km).
Armament: four 0·303 in Brownings fixed in outer wings; mid-upper position with manually aimed 0·303 in Vickers K (I), twin Vickers (II), Boulton Paul turret with two or four 0·303 in Browning (III), Martin turret with two 0·5 in Browning (IV, V); rear ventral position with two 0·303 in Vickers K; optional four or six fixed 0·303 in guns firing directly to rear or obliquely downward. Internal bomb load up to 2,000 lb (907 kg).
History: first flight 14 June 1941; service delivery October 1941; final delivery May 1944.

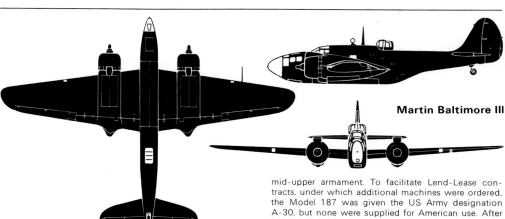

Martin Baltimore III

Martin received an RAF order in May 1940 for 400 improved Maryland bombers with deeper fuselages to allow intercommunication between crew members. In the course of design the more powerful R-2600 engine was adopted and the final aircraft marked an appreciable all-round improvement. The 400 were made up of 50 Mk I, 100 Mk II and 250 Mk III differing mainly in

mid-upper armament. To facilitate Lend-Lease contracts, under which additional machines were ordered, the Model 187 was given the US Army designation A-30, but none were supplied for American use. After 281 Mk IIIA, identical to the III but on US Lend-Lease account, and 294 Mk IV, production completed with 600 Mk V (A-30A), the total being 1,575 all for the RAF. Many were passed on to the South African AF, and a few to the Royal Navy, all being worked very hard in Cyrenaica, Tunisia, Sicily and Italy in bombing and close-support missions. In 1944 units of the co-belligerent Italian forces received ex-RAF machines and formed the Stormo Baltimore which was active over Yugoslavia and the Balkans.

Martin B-26 Marauder

Model 179, B-26A to G, Marauder I to III
Type: five- to seven-seat medium bomber.
Engines: two Pratt & Whitney Double Wasp 18-cylinder two-row radials; (B-26) 1,850 hp R-2800-5; (A) 2,000 hp R-2800-39; (B, C, D, E, F, G) 2,000 hp R-2800-43.
Dimensions: span (B-26, A and first 641 B-26B) 65 ft (19·8 m); (remainder) 71 ft (21·64 m); length (B-26) 56 ft, (A, B) 58 ft 3 in (17·75 m); (F, G) 56 ft 6 in (17·23 m); height (up to E) 19 ft 10 in (6·04 m); (remainder) 21 ft 6 in (6·55 m).
Weights: empty (early, typical) 23,000 lb (10,433 kg); (F, G) 25,300 lb (11,490 kg); maximum loaded (B-26) 32,000 lb; (A) 33,022 lb; (first 641 B) 34,000 lb, then 37,000 lb (16,783 kg); (F) 38,000 lb; (G) 38,200 lb (17,340 kg).
Performance: maximum speed (up to E, typical) 310 mph (500 km/h); (F, G) 280 mph (451 km/h); initial climb 1,000 ft (305 m)/min; service ceiling (up to E) 23,000 ft (7000 m); (F, G) 19,800 ft (6040 m); range with 3,000 lb (1361 kg) bomb load (typical) 1,150 miles (1850 km).
Armament: (B-26, A) five 0·30 in or 0·50 in Browning in nose (1 or 2), power dorsal turret (2), tail (1, manual) and optional manual ventral hatch; (B to E) one 0·5 in manually aimed in nose, twin-gun turret, two manually aimed 0·5 in waist guns, one "tunnel gun" (usually 0·5 in), two 0·5 in in power tail turret and four 0·5 in fixed as "package guns" on sides of forward fuselage; (F, G) same but without tunnel gun; some variations and trainer and Navy versions unarmed. Internal bomb load of 5,200 lb (2359 kg) up to 641st B,

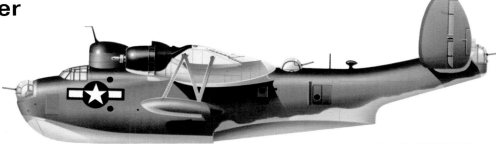

Martin B-26B-55 Marauder (397th BG, 9th AAF)

after which rear bay was disused (eliminated in F, G) to give maximum load of 4,000 lb (1814 kg). Early versions could carry two torpedoes.
History: first flight 25 November 1940; service delivery 25 February 1941; final delivery March 1945.

With its background of leadership in bomber design Martin pulled out all the stops to win the 1939 Medium Bomber competition of the US Army, and boldly chose a wing optimised for high-speed cruise efficiency rather than for landing. Though the Model 179 won the competition – 201 being ordered "off the drawing board" on 5 July 1939 – the actual hardware proved too much for inexperienced pilots to handle, with unprecedented wing loading. In fact there were no real problems, but the newness of the first B-26 versions, coupled with their reputation of being a "widow maker", created a vicious circle of high casualties. Production B-26A models, with torpedo shackles between the bomb doors, were deployed to Australia the day after Pearl Harbor (8 December 1941), and later B models saw extensive South West Pacific service with the rear bomb bay used as a fuel tank (maximum bomb load 2,000 lb). From the 641st B the wing and vertical tail were extended and on 14 May 1943 the Marauder began its career as the chief medium bomber of the 9th AF in the ETO (European Theatre of Operations). By VE-day the B-26 had set a record for the lowest loss-rate of any US Army bomber in Europe. About 522 also served with the RAF and South African AF in Italy. Total production amounted to 5,157 for the US Army (including Allied forces) plus a few dozen JM-1 and -2 target tug, reconnaissance and utility versions for the US Navy and about 200 AT-23 (later called TB-26) trainers. In 1948 the Marauder was withdrawn, and the B-26 designation passed to the Douglas Invader.

Martin PBM Mariner

Model 162, PBM-1 to 5A, Mariner GR.I
Type: maritime patrol and anti-submarine flying boat with typical crew of nine.
Engines: (PBM-1) two 1,600 hp Wright R-2600-6 Double Cyclone 14-cylinder two-row radials; (3C, 3S, 3R) 1,700 hp R-2600-12; (3D) 1,900 hp R-2600-22; (5, 5A) 2,100 hp Pratt & Whitney R-2800-34 Double Wasp 18-cylinder two-row radials.
Dimensions: span 118 ft (36 m); length (-1, 3S) 77 ft 2 in (23·5 m); (3C) 80 ft (24·38 m); (5, 5A) 79 ft 10 in; height (-1) 24 ft 6 in; (remainder) 27 ft 6 in (8·4 m).
Weights: empty (-1) 26,600 lb; (-3, typical) 32,328 lb (14,690 kg); (-5A) 34,000 lb (15,422 kg); maximum loaded (-1) 41,139 lb; (3S) 56,000 lb (25,400 kg); (5) 60,000 lb (27,216 kg).
Performance: maximum speed (all) about 205 mph (330 km/h); initial climb (typical) 800 ft (244 m)/min; service ceiling (-1) 22,400 ft; (3S) 16,900 ft; (5) 20,200 ft (6160 m); maximum range with military load (-1) 3,450 miles; (3C) 2,137 miles; (3S) 3,000 miles (4828 km); (5) 2,700 miles (4345 km).
Armament: (-1) one 0·5 in Browning in nose turret, two in dorsal turret and two manually aimed from waist windows, one 0·30 in in extreme tail (manually aimed over small cone of fire); (3B, 3C) twin-0·5 in dorsal, nose and tail turrets; (3S) four manually aimed 0·5 in in nose, tail and two waist windows; (5)

Martin PBM-5 Mariner

eight 0·5 in in three power turrets and two waist windows; weapon bays in engine nacelles with capacity of 2,000 lb (907 kg) in (-1) 4,000 lb (1814 kg) in all later versions (with provision for two externally hung torpedoes).
History: first flight (XPBM-1) 18 February 1939; service delivery (-1) September 1940; first flight (-5) May 1943; final delivery (5A) April 1949.

Had it not been for the Catalina the PBM would have been by far the most important Allied patrol flying boat of World War II. It was designed in 1936 and proved by flying a quarter-scale model (Martin 162A). The full-size prototype was ordered on 3 June 1937, followed by 20 production -1 in December 1937. These were advanced and challenging boats, with high wing and power loading and stabilizing floats which retracted inwards into the wing. Only one XPBM-2 was built, with long-range tanks and stressed for catapulting. Hundreds followed of the -3, -3C (which sank the U-boat which sank *Ark Royal*), -3R transport and -3S long-range anti-submarine versions, followed by the turreted -3D used throughout the South West Pacific. A small number of -3B served with RAF Coastal Command in 1943. The more powerful -5 had improved dorsal ASV radar (usually APS-15), the -5A was an amphibian and the post-war 5E had later equipment. Total deliveries were 1,235, and over 500 were in front-line service in the Korean war in 1950–53.

Martin P-5 Marlin

P-5A and B, SP-5 and TP-5 series
Type: maritime patrol and anti-submarine flying boat with normal crew of eight, with sub-types described in text.
Engines: (P-5A family) two 3,250 hp Wright R-3350-30WA Turbo-Compound 18-cylinder two-row compound radials; (B) 3,700 hp (wet rating) R-3350-32W.
Dimensions: span 118 ft (36 m); (B family) 118 ft 2 in; length (A, typical) 90 ft 8 in (27·69 m); (B, typical) 101 ft 1 in (30·9 m); height (A) 37 ft 3 in (11·35 m); (B) 32 ft 8 in (9·95 m).
Weights: empty (A, typical) 47,200 lb (21,400 kg); (B, typical) 50,485 lb (22,900 kg); maximum loaded (A) 72,837 lb (33,040 kg); (B) 85,000 lb (38,555 kg).
Performance: maximum speed (A) 262 mph (421 km/h); (B) 251 mph (403 km/h); initial climb 1,200 ft (366 m)/min; service ceiling (A) 22,400 ft, (B) 24,000 ft (7315 m); range with full combat ordnance load (A) 3,600 miles (5800 km); (SP-5B) 2,050 miles (3300 km).
Armament: (A) two 20 mm M-2 cannon in radar-directed tail turret; four 2,000 lb bombs or two torpedoes in nacelles or eight 1,000 lb bombs on underwing racks, with wide range of other stores; (B) no guns, but same offensive weapon load.
History: first flight (XP5M-1) 30 April 1948; (pro-

Martin SP-5B Marlin
(VP-40, Sangley Point, Philippines)

duction P5M-1) 22 June 1951; service delivery December 1951; first flight (P-5B) 29 April 1954; final delivery 20 December 1960.

Designed as a logical successor to the PBM, the Marlin turned out to be both the final type of Martin aircraft to go into service and the final operational flying boat outside the Soviet Union and Japan. Its main advances were much more powerful and efficient engines and a new hull of greater length/beam ratio and improved hydrodynamic form. Another major advance was replacing the bow turret with the search radar, the large and powerful APS-80 occupying a huge radome and giving outstanding power and discrimination. The US Navy received 114 P5M-1 by 1954, most seeing active service at Iwakuni and other bases in support of the Korean war. Under the 1962 designation system these boats became the P-5A, the specialised anti-submarine version with Julie/Jezebel underwater detection system being SP-5A. In 1951 the Marlin was revised with T-tail and lowered bow chine and 82 of the new P5M-2 model were delivered by 1957, followed by ten for the French Aéronavale. Redesignated SP-5B these continued in first-line service until 1968, the last squadron being VP-47. Sub-types included the P5M-1G rescue aircraft of the Coast Guard and the TP-5A anti-submarine trainers.

Martin and General Dynamics B-57 Canberra

Martin B-57B (31 Bomber Wing, Royal Pakistan AF)

B-57A to B-57G, RB-57A, D and F

Type: two-seat tactical attack and reconnaissance (RB versions, strategic reconnaissance at extreme altitude).

Engines: (A, B, C, E, G) two 7,220 lb (3275 kg) thrust Wright J65-5 (US Sapphire) single-shaft turbojets; (D) two 11,000 lb (4990 kg) Pratt & Whitney J57-37A two-shaft turbojets; (F) two 18,000 lb (8165 kg) Pratt & Whitney TF33-11A two-shaft turbofans and two 3,300 lb (1500 kg) Pratt & Whitney J60-9 single-shaft turbojets.

Dimensions: span (A, B, C, E, G) 64 ft (19·5 m); (D) 106 ft (32·3 m); (F) 122 ft 5 in (37·32 m); length (A, B, C, D, E) 65 ft 6 in (19·96 m); (G) 67 ft (20·42 m); (F) 69 ft (21·03 m); height (A, B, C, E, G) 15 ft 7 in (4·75 m); (D) 14 ft 10 in (4·52 m); (F) 19 ft (5·79 m).

Weights: empty (A, B, C, E, typical) 26,800 lb (12,200 kg); (G) about 28,000 lb (12,700 kg); (D) 33,000 lb (14,970 kg); (F) about 36,000 lb (16,330 kg); maximum loaded (A) 51,000 lb; (B, C, E, G) 55,000 lb (24,950 kg); (D) not disclosed, (F) 63,000 lb (28,576 kg).

Performance: maximum speed (A, B, C, E, G) 582 mph (937 km/h); (D, F) over 500 mph (800 km/h); initial climb (A, B, C, E, G) 3,500 ft (1070 m)/min; (D, F) about 4,000 ft (1220 m)/min; service ceiling (A, B, C, E, D) 48,000 ft (14,630 m); (D) 65,000 ft (19,800 m); (F) 75,000 ft (22,860 m); maximum range with combat load (high altitude) (A, B, C, E, G) 2,100 miles (3380 km); (D) about 3,000 miles (4828 km); (F) about 3,700 miles (5955 km).

Armament: (A and all RB versions) none; (B, C, E, G) provision for four 20 mm or eight 0·5 in guns fixed in outer wings (very rarely, other guns fixed in forward fuselage); internal bomb load of 5,000 lb (2268 kg) on rotary bomb door plus eight rockets, two 500 lb bombs or other stores on underwing pylons (while retaining tip tanks).

History: first flight (Canberra in UK) 13 May 1949; (production B-57A) 20 July 1953; (B) 28 June 1954.

In October 1949 Martin flew the extremely advanced XB-51 trijet attack bomber; but this proved to be inflexible and operationally unattractive. The much less advanced British Canberra, on the other hand, proved to have precisely the qualities the US Air Force was seeking, with near-perfect operational flexibility, versatility, outstanding manoeuvrability, long range and endurance and a good weapon load. The decision to adopt this foreign combat aircraft – a step unprecedented in the US since 1918 – was swiftly followed by choice of Martin and development of the B-57A as a version built to US standards with many small modifications. The main batch comprised B-57B tandemseaters, with dual C trainers and multi-role (tactical bomber/recce/trainer/tug) E models. Martin also made 20 grossly redesigned RB-57D reconnaissance aircraft with J57 engines on greatly extended wings. Though incapable of Canberra-style manoeuvres, nor of high speeds at low levels, the D flew many valuable multi-sensor missions over a great deal of Communist territory with the USAF and Nationalist Chinese. There were at least three D sub-types, some having countermeasures and sensing pods on the wing tips and/or

tail and one version having large radomes at each end of the fuselage for strategic electronic reconnaissance. Another B-57D task was to work with U-2Ds in upperatmospheric sampling, but all of this type were grounded in 1963 as a result of structural fatigue. It was partly because of the interim nature of the D that, in 1960, General Dynamics was entrusted with the task of designing and building an even more dramatic highaltitude B-57 version, the F. Though the 21 of this type were not new aircraft, little of the old is evident. The wing is entirely new, with more than double the area of the original Canberra wing and a new fatigueresistant multi-spar structure. Most of the fuselage is new, as is the vertical tail. There are four underwing hard points for pylons, two of which are often occupied by the J60 boost engine pods supplementing the large turbofans. The nose is packed with electronics, and multi-sensor equipment can be seen all over the fuselage. Various F models have operated from the United States, Europe and Middle East, Japan, Alaska, Panama, Argentina and possibly other countries. Meanwhile many of the B, C and E models have been updated by the fitment of modern night and allweather sensing, target designation and weaponaiming systems, the rebuilt aircraft being B-57G. Major new items are low-light TV, infra-red detector and laser ranging. About half the 403 B-57s served in the night attack role in Vietnam, the G being developed just too late for that conflict. Though 10 to 15 years old, the B-57 established an outstanding record in accurate weapon delivery under the most difficult conditions.

Martinsyde F.4 Buzzard

Martinsyde F.4 Buzzard (RAF Communications Wing)

F.3, F.4 Mk I

Type: single-seat fighter.

Engine: (F.3) one 275 hp Rolls-Royce Falcon vee-12 water-cooled; (F.4) one 300 hp Hispano-Suiza of same layout.

Dimensions: span 32 ft 9¾ in (9·99 m); length 25 ft 6 in (7·77 m); height (F.3) 8 ft 8 in; (F.4) 10 ft 4 in (3·15 m).

Weights: empty (both) about 1,760 lb (800 kg); loaded (F.3) 2,446 lb; (F.4) 2,398 lb (1088 kg).

Performance: maximum speed (F.3) 130 mph; (F.4) 145 mph (233 km/h); initial climb 1,000 ft (305 m)/min; service ceiling 24,000 ft (7320 m); range, probably about 400 miles (650 km).

Armament: two 0·303 in Vickers synchronised to fire ahead through propeller disc.

History: first flight (F.3) November 1917; (F.4) May 1918; final delivery, probably March 1919.

The Martin and Handasyde company supplied the Royal Flying Corps with a succession of extremely fine fighting scouts throughout World War I. With the F.3 designer G. H. Handasyde created an outstanding machine, considerably more potent than most of its contemporaries and possibly the first aircraft that could truly be called a fighter, as distinct from a mere scout. Only six were built, four being used by RFC Home Defence squadrons, because the Air Board kept on insisting on engineering changes. A further snag was that virtually all Falcon engines were needed for Bristol F.2B Fighters, so eventually the 300 hp Hispano was selected. After many further modifications the F.3 had been altered so much it was given a new designation, F.4. Officially named Buzzard Mk I, the F.4 was officially measured at 145 mph, faster than

any other British combat aircraft, and judged "superior to any other contemporary single-seat fighter". Large orders were placed, including 700 with Martinsyde, 500 with Boulton Paul, 300 with Standard Motor and 200 from Hooper & Co. Production got into its stride in the autumn of 1918, and by the Armistice 52 had been delivered and the first two squadrons were about to convert. Unfortunately for Martinsyde the Sopwith Snipe was chosen for the post-war RAF and Buzzard contracts were cancelled, though the parent firm went on to build about 200 in all. As the fastest machines available, two were used as couriers between London and Paris during the 1919 Peace Conference. Many of these superb fighters were sold to foreign powers, including Portugal, Finland, Ireland, Latvia, Spain and Japan.

Messerschmitt Bf 109

Bf 109B, C, D, E, F, G, H and K series, S-99 and 199, Ha-1109-1112.

Type: single-seat fighter (many, fighter bomber).

Engine: (B, C) one 635 hp Junkers Jumo 210D inverted-vee-12 liquid-cooled; (D) 1,000 hp Daimler-Benz DB 600Aa, same layout; (E) 1,100 hp DB 601A, 1,200 hp DB 601N or 1,300 hp DB 601E; (F) DB 601E; (G) 1,475 hp DB 605A-1, or other sub-type up to DB 605D rated 1,800 hp with MW50 boost; (H-1) DB 601E; (K) usually 1,550 hp DB 605ASCM/DCM rated 2,000 hp with MW50 boost; (S-199) 1,350 hp Jumo 211F; (HA-1109) 1,300 hp Hispano-Suiza 12Z-89 upright vee-12 or (M1L) 1,400 hp R-R Merlin 500-45.

Dimensions: span (A to E) 32 ft 4½ in (9.87 m); (others) 32 ft 6½ in (9.92 m); length (B, C) 27 ft 11 in; (D, E, typical) 28 ft 4 in (8.64 m); (F) 29 ft 0½ in; (G) 29 ft 8 in (9.04 m); (K) 29 ft 4 in; (HA-1109-M1L) 29 ft 11 in; height (E) 7 ft 5½ in (2.28 m); (others) 8 ft 6 in (2.59 m).

Weights: empty (B-1) 3,483 lb; (E) 4,189 lb (1900 kg) to 4,421 lb; (F) around 4,330 lb; (G) 5,880 lb (2667 kg) to 6,180 lb (2800 kg); (K, typical) 6,000 lb; maximum loaded (B-1) 4,850 lb; (E) 5,523 lb (2505 kg) to 5,875 lb (2665 kg); (F-3) 6,054 lb; (G) usually 7,496 lb (3400 kg); (K) usually 7,439 lb (3375 kg).

Performance: maximum speed (B-1) 292 mph; (D) 323 mph; (E) 348–354 mph (560–570 km/h); (F-3) 390 mph; (G) 353 to 428 mph (569–690 km/h); (K-4) 452 mph (729 km/h); initial climb (B-1) 2,200 ft/min; (E) 3,100 to 3,280 ft (1000 m)/min; (G) 2,700 to 4,000 ft/min; (K-4) 4,823 ft (1470 m)/min; service ceiling (B-1) 26,575 ft; (E) 34,450 ft (10,500 m) to 36,090 ft (11,000 m); (F, G) around 38,000 ft (11,600 m); (K-4) 41,000 ft (12,500 m); range on internal fuel (all) 365–460 miles (typically, 700 km).

Armament: (B) three 7.92 mm Rheinmetall-Borsig MG 17 machine guns above engine and firing through propeller hub; (C) four MG 17, two above engine and two in wings, with fifth through propeller hub in C-2; (early E-1) four MG 17, plus four 50 kg or one 250 kg (551 lb) bomb; (later E-1 and most other E) two MG 17 above engine, each with 1,000 rounds (or two MG 17 with 500 rounds, plus 20 mm MG FF firing through propeller hub) and two MG FF in wings, each with 60-round drum; (F-1) two MG 17 and one MG FF; (F-2) two 15 mm MG 151 and one MG FF; (F-4) two MG 151, one MG FF and one 20 mm MG 151 in fairing under each wing; (G-1) two MG 17 or 13 mm MG 131 over engine and one MG 151; (G-6) one 30 mm MK 108, two MG 131 above engine and two MG 151 under wings; (K-4) two MG 151 above engine and one MK 108 or 103; (K-6) two MG 131 above engine, one MK 103 or 108 and two MK 108 under wings; (S-199) two MG 131 above engine and two MG 151 under wings; (HA-1109 series) two wing machine guns or 20 mm Hispano 404. Many German G and K carried two 210 mm rocket tubes under wings or various bomb loads.

History: first flight (Bf 109 V-1) early September 1935 (date is unrecorded); (production B-1) May 1937; (Bf 109E) January 1939; (Bf 109F prototype) July 1940; replacement in production by Bf 109G, May 1942.

During World War II the general public in the Allied nations at first regarded the Messerschmitt as an inferior weapon compared with the Spitfire and other Allied fighters. Only in the fullness of time was it possible to appreciate that the Bf 109 was one of the greatest combat aircraft in history. First flown in 1935, it was a major participant in the Spanish Civil War and a thoroughly proven combat aircraft by the time of Munich (September 1938). Early versions were the Bf 109B, C and D, all of lower power than the definitive 109E. The E was in service in great quantity by the end of August 1939 when the invasion of Poland began. From then until 1941 it was by far the most important fighter in the Luftwaffe, and it was also supplied in quantity to Bulgaria, Hungary, Romania, Slovakia, Yugoslavia, Switzerland (which made the 109 under licence), Japan and the Soviet Union. During the first year of World War II the "Emil", as the various E sub-types were called, made mincemeat of

continued on page 148

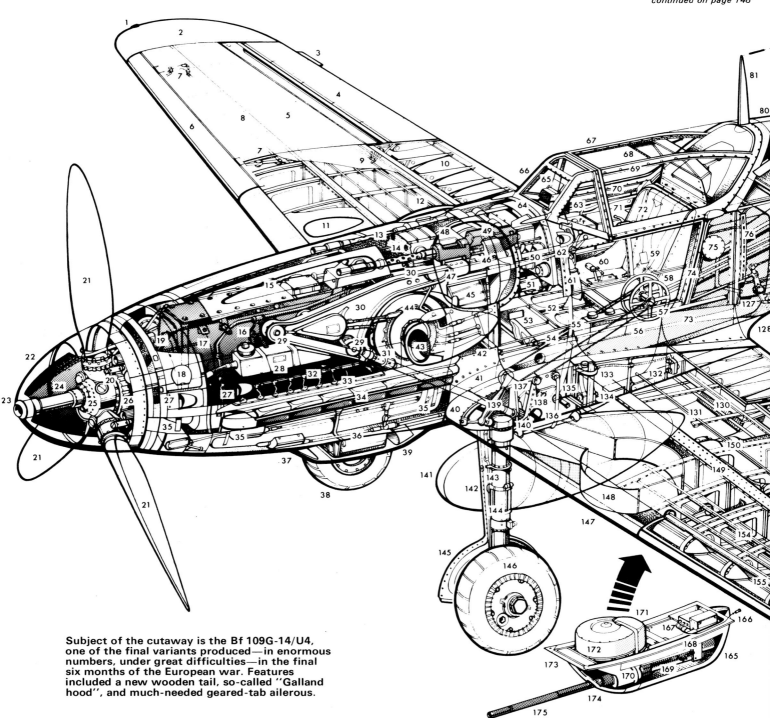

Subject of the cutaway is the Bf 109G-14/U4, one of the final variants produced—in enormous numbers, under great difficulties—in the final six months of the European war. Features included a new wooden tail, so-called "Galland hood", and much-needed geared-tab ailerons.

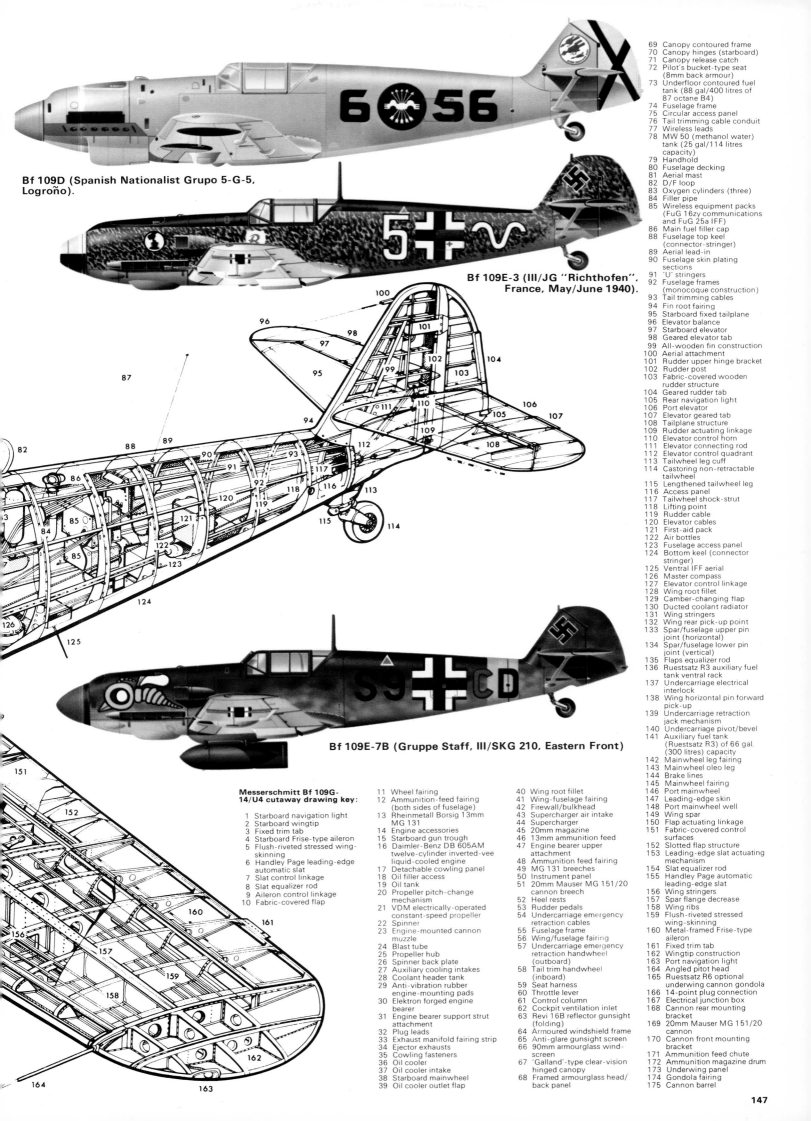

Bf 109D (Spanish Nationalist Grupo 5-G-5, Logroño).

Bf 109E-3 (III/JG "Richthofen", France, May/June 1940).

Bf 109E-7B (Gruppe Staff, III/SKG 210, Eastern Front)

Messerschmitt Bf 109G-14/U4 cutaway drawing key:

1 Starboard navigation light
2 Starboard wingtip
3 Fixed trim tab
4 Starboard Frise-type aileron
5 Flush-riveted stressed wing-skinning
6 Handley Page leading-edge automatic slat
7 Slat control linkage
8 Slat equalizer rod
9 Aileron control linkage
10 Fabric-covered flap
11 Wheel fairing
12 Ammunition-feed fairing (both sides of fuselage)
13 Rheinmetall Borsig 13mm MG 131
14 Engine accessories
15 Starboard gun trough
16 Daimler-Benz DB 605AM twelve-cylinder inverted-vee liquid-cooled engine
17 Detachable cowling panel
18 Oil filler access
19 Oil tank
20 Propeller pitch-change mechanism
21 VDM electrically-operated constant-speed propeller
22 Spinner
23 Engine-mounted cannon muzzle
24 Blast tube
25 Propeller hub
26 Spinner back plate
27 Auxiliary cooling intakes
28 Coolant header tank
29 Anti-vibration rubber engine-mounting pads
30 Elektron forged engine bearer
31 Engine bearer support strut attachment
32 Plug leads
33 Exhaust manifold fairing strip
34 Ejector exhausts
35 Cowling fasteners
36 Oil cooler
37 Oil cooler intake
38 Starboard mainwheel
39 Oil cooler outlet flap
40 Wing root fillet
41 Wing-fuselage fairing
42 Firewall/bulkhead
43 Supercharger air intake
44 Supercharger
45 20mm magazine
46 13mm ammunition feed
47 Engine bearer upper attachment
48 Ammunition feed fairing
49 MG 131 breeches
50 Instrument panel
51 20mm Mauser MG 151/20 cannon breech
52 Heel rests
53 Rudder pedals
54 Undercarriage emergency retraction cables
55 Fuselage frame
56 Wing/fuselage fairing
57 Undercarriage emergency retraction handwheel (outboard)
58 Tail trim handwheel (inboard)
59 Seat harness
60 Throttle lever
61 Control column
62 Cockpit ventilation inlet
63 Revi 16B reflector gunsight (folding)
64 Armoured windshield frame
65 Anti-glare gunsight screen
66 90mm armourglass windscreen
67 'Galland'-type clear-vision hinged canopy
68 Framed armourglass head/back panel
69 Canopy contoured frame
70 Canopy hinges (starboard)
71 Canopy release catch
72 Pilot's bucket-type seat (8mm back armour)
73 Underfloor contoured fuel tank (88 gal/400 litres of 87 octane B4)
74 Fuselage frame
75 Circular access panel
76 Tail trimming cable conduit
77 Wireless leads
78 MW 50 (methanol water) tank (25 gal/114 litres capacity)
79 Handhold
80 Fuselage decking
81 Aerial mast
82 D/F loop
83 Oxygen cylinders (three)
84 Filler pipe
85 Wireless equipment packs (FuG 16zy communications and FuG 25a IFF)
86 Main fuel filler cap
88 Fuselage top keel (connector-stringer)
89 Aerial lead-in
90 Fuselage skin plating sections
91 'U' stringers
92 Fuselage frames (monocoque construction)
93 Tail trimming cables
94 Fin root fairing
95 Starboard fixed tailplane
96 Elevator balance
97 Starboard elevator
98 Geared elevator tab
99 All-wooden fin construction
100 Aerial attachment
101 Rudder upper hinge bracket
102 Rudder post
103 Fabric-covered wooden rudder structure
104 Geared rudder tab
105 Rear navigation light
106 Port elevator
107 Elevator geared tab
108 Tailplane structure
109 Rudder actuating linkage
110 Elevator control horn
111 Elevator connecting rod
112 Elevator control quadrant
113 Tailwheel leg cuff
114 Castoring non-retractable tailwheel
115 Lengthened tailwheel leg
116 Access panel
117 Tailwheel shock-strut
118 Lifting point
119 Rudder cable
120 Elevator cables
121 First-aid pack
122 Air bottles
123 Fuselage access panel
124 Bottom keel (connector stringer)
125 Ventral IFF aerial
126 Master compass
127 Elevator control linkage
128 Wing root fillet
129 Camber-changing flap
130 Ducted coolant radiator
131 Wing stringers
132 Wing rear pick-up point
133 Spar/fuselage upper pin joint (horizontal)
134 Spar/fuselage lower pin joint (vertical)
135 Flaps equalizer rod
136 Ruestsatz R3 auxiliary fuel tank ventral rack
137 Undercarriage electrical interlock
138 Wing horizontal pin forward pick-up
139 Undercarriage retraction jack mechanism
140 Undercarriage pivot/bevel
141 Auxiliary fuel tank (Ruestsatz R3) of 66 gal. (300 litres) capacity
142 Mainwheel leg fairing
143 Mainwheel oleo leg
144 Brake lines
145 Mainwheel fairing
146 Port mainwheel
147 Leading-edge skin
148 Port mainwheel well
149 Wing spar
150 Flap actuating linkage
151 Fabric-covered control surfaces
152 Slotted flap structure
153 Leading-edge slat actuating mechanism
154 Slat equalizer rod
155 Handley Page automatic leading-edge slat
156 Wing stringers
157 Spar flange decrease
158 Wing ribs
159 Flush-riveted stressed wing-skinning
160 Metal-framed Frise-type aileron
161 Fixed trim tab
162 Wingtip construction
163 Port navigation light
164 Angled pitot head
165 Ruestsatz R6 optional underwing cannon gondola
166 14-point plug connection
167 Electrical junction box
168 Cannon rear mounting bracket
169 20mm Mauser MG 151/20 cannon
170 Cannon front mounting bracket
171 Ammunition feed chute
172 Ammunition magazine drum
173 Underwing panel
174 Gondola fairing
175 Cannon barrel

Messerschmitt Bf 109 (continued)

Bf 109F-2 (III/JG 54 "Grünherz", Leningrad front 1941-2)

Bf 109G-5/U2 (31 Fighter Sqn, Finnish AF, Utti).

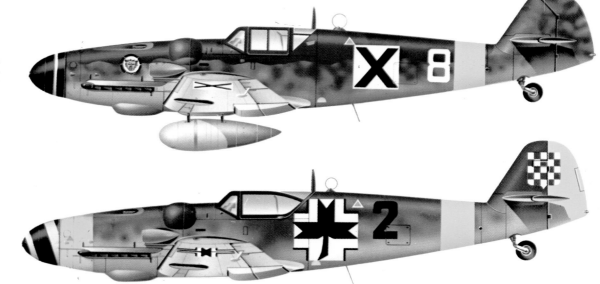

Bf 109G-6 (Royal Bulgarian 6th Fighter Regiment, Wrasdebna)

Bf 109G-10/U4 (Groatian Jagdstaffel, Eichwalde)

S199 (101 Sqn, the first Israeli fighter unit, Ekron)

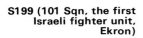

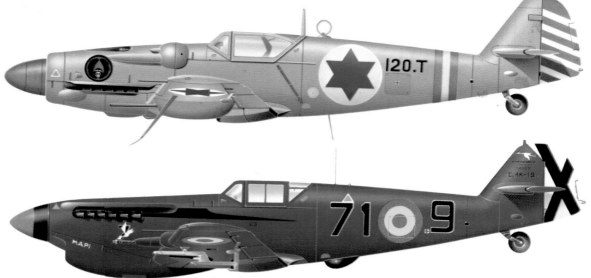

Hispano HA-1112-M1L (71 Escuadron, Ala núm 7 de Cazabombardes)

the many and varied types of fighter against which it was opposed, with the single exception of the Spitfire (which it greatly outnumbered). Its good points were small size, fast and cheap production, high acceleration, fast climb and dive, and good power of manoeuvre. Nearly all 109Es were also fitted with two or three 20 mm cannon, with range and striking power greater than a battery of eight rifle-calibre guns. Drawbacks were the narrow landing gear, severe swing on take-off or landing, extremely poor lateral control at high speeds, and the fact that in combat the slats on the wings often opened in tight turns; while this prevented a stall, it snatched at the ailerons and threw the pilot

off his aim.

After 1942 the dominant version was the 109G ("Gustav") cohich made up over 70 per cent of the total received by the Luftwaffe. Though formidably armed and equipped, the vast swarms of "Gustavs" were nothing like such good machines as the lighter E and F, demanding constant pilot attention, constant high power settings, and having landing characteristics described as "malicious". Only a few of the extended-span high-altitude H-series were built, but from October 1944 the standard production series was the K with clear-view "Galland hood", revised wooden tail and minor structural changes. After World War II the Czech Avia firm found

their Bf 109 plant intact and began building the S-99; running out of DB 605 engines they installed the slow-revving Jumo, producing the S-199 with even worse torque and swing than the German versions (pilots called it "Mezek" meaning mule), but in 1948 managed to sell some to Israel. The Spanish Hispano Aviación flew its first licence-built 1109 in March 1945 and in 1953 switched to the Merlin engine to produce the 1109-M1L Buchón (Pigeon). Several Hispano and Merlin versions were built in Spain, some being tandem-seat trainers. When the last HA-1112 flew out of Seville in late 1956 it closed out 21 years of manufacture of this classic fighter, during which total output probably exceeded 35,000.

Messerschmitt Bf 110

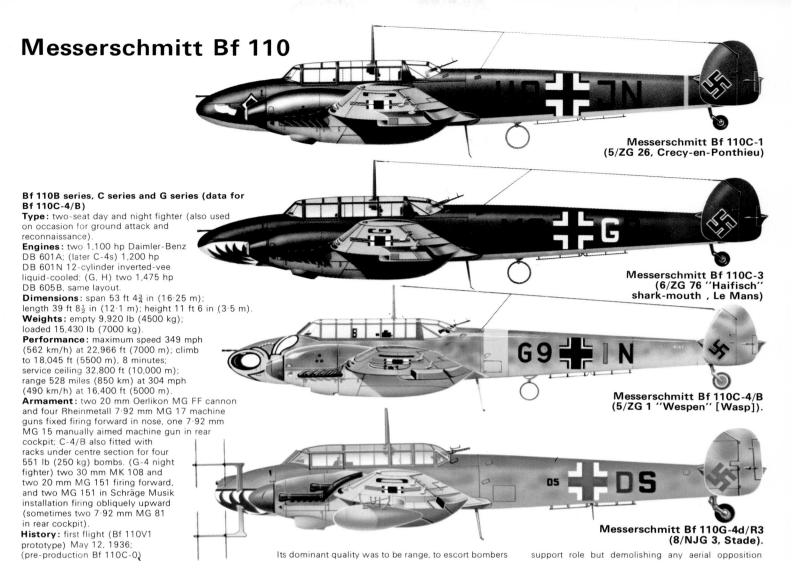

Messerschmitt Bf 110C-1
(5/ZG 26, Crecy-en-Ponthieu)

Messerschmitt Bf 110C-3
(6/ZG 76 "Haifisch"
shark-mouth , Le Mans)

Messerschmitt Bf 110C-4/B
(5/ZG 1 "Wespen" [Wasp]).

Messerschmitt Bf 110G-4d/R3
(8/NJG 3, Stade).

Bf 110B series, C series and G series (data for Bf 110C-4/B)
Type: two-seat day and night fighter (also used on occasion for ground attack and reconnaissance).
Engines: two 1,100 hp Daimler-Benz DB 601A; (later C-4s) 1,200 hp DB 601N 12-cylinder inverted-vee liquid-cooled; (G, H) two 1,475 hp DB 605B, same layout.
Dimensions: span 53 ft 4¾ in (16·25 m); length 39 ft 8½ in (12·1 m); height 11 ft 6 in (3·5 m).
Weights: empty 9,920 lb (4500 kg); loaded 15,430 lb (7000 kg).
Performance: maximum speed 349 mph (562 km/h) at 22,966 ft (7000 m); climb to 18,045 ft (5500 m), 8 minutes; service ceiling 32,800 ft (10,000 m); range 528 miles (850 km) at 304 mph (490 km/h) at 16,400 ft (5000 m).
Armament: two 20 mm Oerlikon MG FF cannon and four Rheinmetall 7·92 mm MG 17 machine guns fixed firing forward in nose, one 7·92 mm MG 15 manually aimed machine gun in rear cockpit; C-4/B also fitted with racks under centre section for four 551 lb (250 kg) bombs. (G-4 night fighter) two 30 mm MK 108 and two 20 mm MG 151 firing forward, and two MG 151 in Schräge Musik installation firing obliquely upward (sometimes two 7·92 mm MG 81 in rear cockpit).
History: first flight (Bf 110V1 prototype) May 12, 1936; (pre-production Bf 110C-0) February 1939; operational service with Bf 110C-1, April 1939; final run-down of production (Bf 110H-2 and H-4) February 1945.

As in five other countries at about the same time, the Reichsluftfahrtministerium decided in 1934 to issue a requirement for a new kind of fighter having two engines and exceptional range. Called a Zerstörer (destroyer), it was to be capable of fighting other aircraft as well as small single-seaters, possibly making up in firepower for any lack in manoeuvrability.

Its dominant quality was to be range, to escort bombers on raids penetrating deep into enemy heartlands. Powered by two of the new DB 600 engines, the prototype reached 316 mph, considered an excellent speed, but it was heavy on the controls and unimpressive in power of manoeuvre. Too late to be tested in the Spanish Civil War, the production Bf 110B-1, which was the first to carry the two cannon, was itself supplanted by the C-series with the later DB 601 engine with direct fuel injection and greater power at all heights. By the start of World War II the Luftwaffe had 195 Bf 110C fighters, and in the Polish campaign these were impressive, operating mainly in the close-

support role but demolishing any aerial opposition they encountered. It was the same story in the Blitzkrieg war through the Low Countries and France, when 350 of the big twins were used. Only when faced with RAF Fighter Command in the Battle of Britain did the Bf 110 suddenly prove a disaster. It was simply no match for the Spitfire or even the Hurricane, and soon the Bf 109 was having to escort the escort fighters! But production of DB 605-powered versions, packed with radar and night-fighting equipment, was actually trebled in 1943 and sustained in 1944, these G and H models playing a major part in the night battles over the Reich in 1943–45.

Messerschmitt Me 210 and 410 Hornisse

Me 210A, B and C series, Me 410A and B series
Type: two-seat tactical aircraft for fighter, attack and reconnaissance duties with specialised variants.
Engines: (Me 210, usual for production versions) two 1,395 hp Daimler-Benz DB 601F inverted-vee-12 liquid-cooled; (Me 410A series, usual for production versions) two 1,750 hp DB 603A of same layout; (Me 410B series) two 1,900 hp DB 603G.
Dimensions: span (210) 53 ft 7¼ in, later 53 ft 7¾ in (16·4 m); (410) 53 ft 7¾ in; length (without 50 mm gun, radar or other long fitment) (210) 40 ft 3 in (12·22 m); (410) 40 ft 10 in or 40 ft 11½ in (12·45 m); height (both) 14 ft 0½ in (4·3 m).
Weights: empty (210A) about 12,000 lb (5440 kg); (410A-1) 13,560 lb (6150 kg); maximum loaded (210A-1) 17,857 lb (8100 kg); (410A-1) 23,483 lb (10,650 kg).
Performance: maximum speed (both, clean) 385 mph (620 km/h); initial climb (both) 2,133 ft (650 m)/min; service ceiling (210A-1) 22,967 ft (7000 m); (410A-1) 32,800 ft (10,000 m); range with full bomb load (210A-1) 1,491 miles (2400 km); (410A-1) 1,447 miles (2330 km).
Armament: varied, but basic aircraft invariably defended by two remotely-controlled powered barbettes on sides of fuselage each housing one 13 mm MG 131 and, if bomber version, provided with internal weapon bay housing two 1,102 lb (500 kg) bombs; external racks on nearly all (210 and 410) for two 1,102 lb stores (exceptionally, two 2,204 lb). Normal fixed forward-firing armament of two 20 mm MG 151/20 and two 7·92 mm MG 17. Me 410 versions had many kinds of bomber-destroyer armament, as described in the text.

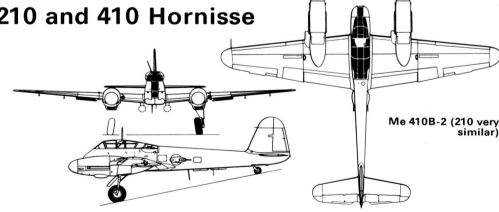

Me 410B-2 (210 very similar)

History: first flight (Me 210V-1) 2 September 1939; (pre-production 210A-0) April 1941; final delivery (210) April 1942; first flight (310) 11 September 1943; (410V-1) probably December 1942.

Planned in 1937 as a valuable and more versatile successor to the Bf 110 twin-engined escort fighter, the Me 210 was little more than a flop and made hardly any contribution to the German war effort. After severe flight instability and landing-gear problems some progress was made in 1941 towards producing an acceptable machine which could be put into production against the order for 1,000 placed "off the drawing board" in June 1939. Accidents were nevertheless frequent and manufacture was terminated at the 352nd aircraft. This major blow to the Luftwaffe and the company, which was reflected in an official demand for Willi Messerschmitt's resignation from the board,

was partly salvaged by a further redesign and change to the DB 603 engine. The Me 310 was a high-altitude fighter-bomber with 58 ft 9 in wing and pressure cabin, but this was abandoned in favour of a less radical change designated 410. As with the 210, the reconnaissance 410s usually had cameras in the bomb bay and no MG 17s, while some attack or destroyer versions had four forward-firing MG 151 cannon, or two MG 151 and a 50 mm BK 5 gun with 21 rounds. The Me 410A-2/U-2 was an important night fighter with SN-2 Lichtenstein radar and two MG 151 and two 30 mm MK 108. Many of the 1,121 Me 410s carried Rüstsatz external packs housing two more MG 151, MK 108 or MK 103, and occasionally experienced pilots fitted as many as eight MG 151 all firing ahead. The 210 mm rocket tube was a common fitment by 1944, some aircraft having the pack of six rotating tubes in the bomb bay.

Messerschmitt Me 163 Komet

Me 163B-1

Type: single-seat interceptor.

Engine: one 3,750 lb (1700 kg) thrust Walter HWK 509A-2 bi-propellant rocket burning concentrated hydrogen peroxide (T-stoff) and hydrazine/methanol (C-stoff).

Dimensions: span 30 ft 7 in (9·3 m); length 18 ft 8 in (5·69 m); height 9 ft (2·74 m).

Weights: empty 4,191 lb (1905 kg); loaded 9,042 lb (4110 kg).

Performance: maximum speed 596 mph (960 km/h) at 32,800 ft (10,000 m); initial climb 16,400 ft (5000 m)/min; service ceiling 54,000 ft (16,500 m); range depended greatly on flight profile but under 100 km (62 miles); endurance 2½ min from top of climb or eight min total.

Armament: two 30 mm MK 108 cannon in wing roots, each with 60 rounds.

History: first flight (Me 163V1) spring 1941 as glider, August 1941 under power; (Me 163B) August 1943; first operational unit (I/JG400) May 1944.

Of all aircraft engaged in World War II the Me 163 Komet (Comet) was the most radical and, indeed, futuristic. The concept of the short-endurance local-defence interceptor powered by a rocket engine was certainly valid and might have been more of a thorn in the Allies' side than it was. Even the dramatically unconventional form of the Me 163, with no horizontal tail and an incredibly short fuselage, did not lead to great difficulty; in fact, the production fighter was

Messerschmitt Me163B-1a (II/JG.400, Brandis)

Lippisch, who liked tailless designs. Choice of two rocket propellants that reacted violently when they came into contact solved the problem of ignition in the combustion chamber but added an extremely large element of danger. Moreover, the 163 had no landing gear, taking off from a jettisoned trolley and landing on a sprung skid, and the landing impact often sloshed residual propellants together causing a violent explosion. Many aircraft were lost this way, and the original test pilot, glider champion Heini Dittmar, was badly injured when the skid failed to extend. Nevertheless by 1944 these bat-like specks were swooping on US bomber formations with devastating effect. Numerous improved versions were flying at VE day, but only 370 Komets had seen service and these had suffered high attrition through accidents.

widely held to have the best and safest flight characteristics of any aircraft in the Luftwaffe. But the swift strides into uncharted technology were bold in the extreme. It was partly to save weight and drag that the tailless configuration was adopted, and partly because the moving spirit behind the project was at first Dr Alex

---

Messerschmitt Me 262

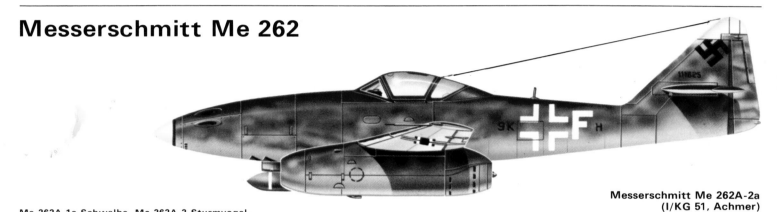

Messerschmitt Me 262A-2a (I/KG 51, Achmer)

Me 262A-1a Schwalbe, Me 262A-2 Sturmvogel, Me 262B-1a

Type: (A-1a) single-seat fighter, (A-2a) single-seat bomber, (262B-1a) two-seat night fighter.

Engines: two 1,980 lb (900 kg) thrust Junkers Jumo 004B single-shaft axial turbojets.

Dimensions: span 40 ft 11½ in (12·5 m); length 34 ft 9½ in (10·6 m), (262B-1a, excluding radar aerials) 38 ft 9 in (11·8 m); height 12 ft 7 in (3·8 m).

Weights: empty (A-1a, A-2a) 8,820 lb (4000 kg); (B-1a) 9,700 lb (4400 kg); loaded (A-1a, A-2a) 15,500 lb (7045 kg); (B-1a) 14,110 lb (6400 kg).

Performance: maximum speed (A-1a) 540 mph (870 km/h); (A-2a, laden) 470 mph (755 km/h); (B-1a) 497 mph (800 km/h); initial climb (all) about 3,940 ft (1200 m)/min; service ceiling 37,565 ft (11,500 m); range on internal fuel, at altitude, about 650 miles (1050 km).

Armament: (A-1a) four 30 mm MK 108 cannon in nose, two with 100 rounds each, two with 80; (A-1a/U1) two 30 mm MK 103, two MK 108 and two 20 mm MG 151/20; (A-1b) as A-1a plus 24 spin-stabilised R4/M 50 mm rockets; (B-1a) as A-1a; (B-2a) as A-1a plus two inclined MK 108 behind cockpit in Schräge Musik installation; (D) SG 500 Jagdfaust with 12 rifled mortar barrels inclined in nose; (E) 50 mm MK 114 gun or 48 R4/M rockets; bomb load of two 1,100 lb (500 kg) bombs carried by A-2a.

History: first flight (262V1 on Jumo 210 piston engine) 4 April 1941; (262V3 on two Jumo 004A-0 turbojets) 18 July 1942; (Me 262A-1a) 7 June 1944; first delivery (A-0 to Rechlin) May 1944; first experimental combat unit (EK 262) 30 June 1944; first regular squadron (8/ZG26) September 1944.

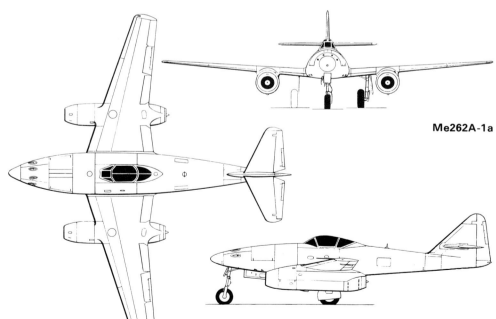

Me262A-1a

In the Me 262 the German aircraft industry created a potentially war-winning aircraft which could have restored to the Luftwaffe command of the skies over Germany. Compared with Allied fighters of its day, including the RAF Meteor I, which entered service at the same time, it was much faster and packed a much heavier punch. Radar-equipped night fighter versions and sub-types designed to stand off from large bomber formations and blast them out of the sky were also developments against which the Allies had no answer. Yet for years the programme was held back by official disinterest, and by the personal insistence of Hitler

that the world-beating jet should be used only as a bomber!

It was in the autumn of 1938 that Messerschmitt was asked to study the design of a jet fighter, and the resulting Me 262 was remarkably unerring. First flown on a piston engine in the nose, it then flew on its twin turbojets and finally, in July 1943, the fifth development aircraft flew with a nosewheel. Despite numerous snags, production aircraft were being delivered in

July 1944 and the rate of production was many times that of the British Meteor. On the other hand the German axial engines were unreliable and casualties due to engine failure, fires or break-up were heavy. The MK 108 gun was also prone to jam, and the landing gear to collapse. Yet the 262 was a beautiful machine to handle and, while Allied jets either never reached squadrons or never engaged enemy aircraft, the 100 or so Me 262s that flew on operations and had fuel available destroyed far more than 100 Allied bombers and fighters. Even more remarkably, by VE-day total deliveries of this formidable aircraft reached 1,433.

Messerschmitt Me 323 Gigant

Me 321A and B, Me 323D and E
Type: (321) heavy cargo glider; (323) heavy cargo transport.
Engines: (321) none; (323 production variants) six 1,140 hp Gnome-Rhône 14N 48/49 14-cylinder two-row radials.
Dimensions: span 180 ft 5½ in (55 m); length 92 ft 4¼ in (28·15 m); height (321B-1) 33 ft 3½ in (10·15 m); (323) 31 ft 6 in (9·6 m).
Weights: empty (321B-1) 27,432 lb (12,400 kg); (323D-6) 60.260 lb (27,330 kg); (323E-1) 61,700 lb (28,010 kg); maximum loaded (321B-1) 75,852 lb (34,400 kg); (323D-6) 94,815 lb (43,000 kg); (323E-1) 99,208 lb (45,000 kg).
Performance: maximum speed (321 on tow) 99 mph (160 km/h); (323D series) 177 mph (285 km/h); initial climb (321 towed by three Bf 110) 492 ft (150 m)/min; (323D series) 710 ft (216 m)/min; service ceiling (323D) about 13,100 ft (4000 m); range with "normal" payload (presumably not maximum) 684 miles (1100 km).
Armament: see text.
History: first flight (321V-1) 7 March 1941; service delivery (321) about June 1941; final delivery (321) April 1942; first flight (323V-1) some reports claim April 1941 but others, much more plausible, state "autumn 1941"; service delivery (323D-1) May 1942; final delivery March 1944.

Following the dramatic vindication of the previously untried Blitzkrieg concept of airborne forces in May 1940 the Reichsluftfahrtministerium (RLM) asked Junkers and Heinkel to design huge transport gliders far bigger than the little DFS 230 used in the invasion of the Benelux countries. Junkers' Ju 322 Mammut

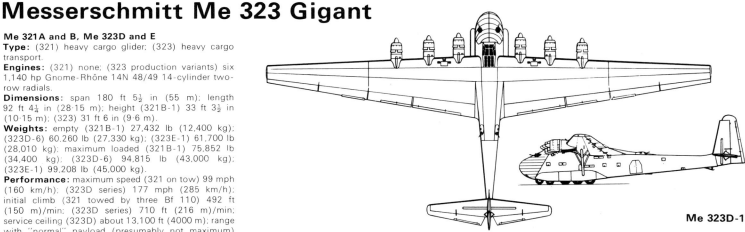

Me 323D-1

was an expensive failure, but the Me 323 Gigant went into production, despite the fact it was extremely tiring to fly on account of the very high control forces needed. Made chiefly of welded steel tube, with ply-wood or fabric covering, it carried the large payload of 48,500 lb (22 tonnes), or a company of infantry. The 321A-1 had a single pilot but most of the 175 built were 321B-1 with a pair of crew who served as navigator and radio operator and manned two twin 7·92 mm MG 15 machine guns in beam windows. Usual towing scheme was three Bf 110 in formation, but the specially built He 111Z was preferable and many units used various arrangements of take-off

boost rockets. Dipl-Ing Degel then studied the powered 321C and D and eventually these became the 323V-1 with four engines (complete nacelles already in production at SNCASO for the Bloch 175) and 323V-2 with six. The six-engined Gigant went into production, the D-1 having three-blade metal propellers and the D-2 two-blade wooden, each having five MG 15 in the nose and mounts for six MG 34 infantry m.g. in beam windows. Most later had five 13 mm MG 131 added, but this did not stop Beaufighters shooting 14 into the sea as they ferried petrol to Rommel. Final versions in the run of 210 were the E-series with 1,340 hp Jumo 211F, the E-1 having an MG 151 20 mm turret above each centre-engine nacelle, and the 323G with 1,320 hp Gnome-Rhône 14R.

Mikoyan MiG-3

MiG-1 (I-61), MiG-3, MiG-5 and MiG-7
Type: single-seat fighter.
Engine:
(-1) one 1,200 hp Mikulin AM-35 vee-12 liquid-cooled; (-3) one 1,350 hp AM-35A; (-5) one 1,600 hp ASh-82A 14-cylinder radial; (-7) one 1,700 hp VK-107A vee-12.
Dimensions: span (all) 33 ft 9½ in (10·3 m); length (-1, -3) 26 ft 9 in (8·15 m); (-5) about 26 ft; (-7) not known; height (-1; -3) reported as 8 ft 7 in (2·61 m).
Weights: empty (-1) 5,721 lb (2595 kg); (others) not known; maximum loaded (-1) given as 6,770 lb and as 7,290 lb; (-3) given as 7,390 lb and 7,695 lb (3490 kg); (-5) normal loaded 7,055 lb (3200 kg); (-7) not known.
Performance: maximum speed (-1) 390 mph (628 km/h); (-3) 398 mph (640 km/h), (also given as 407 mph); (-5) over 400 mph; (-7) probably over 440 mph; initial climb (-1) 3,280 ft (1000 m)/min; (-3) 3,937 ft (1200 m)/min; (-5, -7) not known; service ceiling (-1, -3) 39,370 ft (12,000 m); (-5) not known; (-7) 42,650 ft (13,000 m); range (-1) 454 miles (730 km); (-3) 776 miles (1250 km); (-5, -7) not known.
Armament: (-1, -3) one 12·7 mm BS and two 7·62 mm ShKAS all in nose, later supplemented as field modification by underwing pods for two further

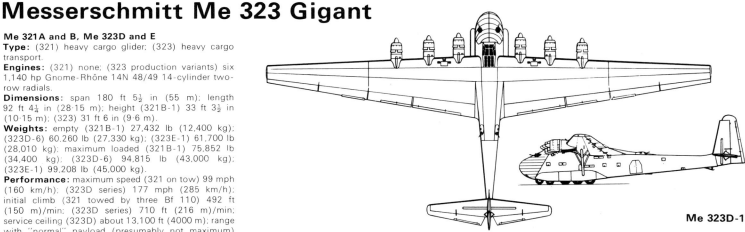

MiG-3 (34th Fighter Aviation Regiment, IA-PVO, Vnukovo)

unsynchronised BS; underwing rails for six RS-82 rockets or two bombs up to 220 lb (100 kg) each or two chemical containers; (-5) as above except four 7·62 mm ShKAS disposed around cowling, no BS guns; (-7) not known but probably included 20 mm ShVAK firing through propeller hub.
History: first flight (I-16) 5 April (also reported as March) 1940; (production MiG-1) September 1940; (MiG-3) about May 1941; final delivery (MiG-3) late 1941; first flight (-5) 1942; (MiG-7) 1943.
There were probably several new Soviet fighter prototypes in 1938–40, but apart from the Yak-1 information is available on only one other, the I-16 designed by the new partnership of Artem I. Mikoyan and Mikhail I. Gurevich. Though handicapped by its long

and heavy engine, which held the armament to a poor level, the mixed wood/metal fighter was a fair performer and went into production as the MiG-1, its only serious vice being an extreme tendency to swing on take-off and landing. In view of the amazing rapidity of its development this was an acceptable penalty and 2,100 are said to have been delivered before it was replaced in production by the refined MiG-3 with more powerful engine, new propeller, additional fuel tank, increased dihedral and sliding canopy. "Several thousand" are said to have been delivered, but despite adding extra guns they were no match for Luftwaffe fighters and by 1942 were being used for armed reconnaissance and close support. The MiG-5 was used in only small numbers, and few details are available of the all-metal high-altitude MiG-7 with pressurised cockpit.

Mikoyan MiG-9

I-300, MiG-9
Type: single-seat fighter.
Engines: two 1,764 lb (800 kg) thrust RD-20 single-shaft axial turbojets.
Dimensions: span 32 ft 9¾ in (10 m); length 32 ft (9·75 m); height, not known.
Weights: empty, not known but about 7,000 lb (3175 kg); loaded 11,177 lb (5070 kg).
Performance: maximum speed 559 mph (900 km/h); initial climb 4,265 ft (1300 m)/min; service ceiling 42,650 ft (13,000 m); range, not known.
Armament: one 37 mm Nudelmann cannon with 90 rounds between inlet ducts; two 23 mm Nudelmann-Suranov cannon, each with 150 rounds, in underside of nose.
History: first flight (I-300) 24 April 1946; (production MiG-9) late 1946; final delivery, February 1949.
Though the Soviet Union was naturally aware of gas-turbine development by Britain and Germany during World War II, virtually no such work is known to have been done in the Soviet Union until near the end of that conflict, and then it was based on German designs. In February 1945 a specification was issued for a single-

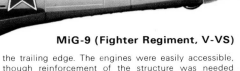

MiG-9 (Fighter Regiment, V-VS)

seat jet fighter, and most of the large design bureaux — certainly including Mikoyan-Gurevich, Ilyushin and Yakovlev, and probably Lavochkin — all made proposals. Mikoyan-Gurevich's project was by far the best, being very close to the optimum design that could be achieved in the circumstances, with only ex-German engines to choose from and a dearth of really advanced structures and systems. The I-300 prototype was a clean and efficient machine, with two engines hung side-by-side under the 9 per cent laminar-flow wing, fed by nose inlets and exhausting without any added jetpipes directly under the fuselage in line with

the trailing edge. The engines were easily accessible, though reinforcement of the structure was needed above the nozzles. Ample fuel capacity was available behind the pressurised cockpit and in the wing. For the first time in a Soviet production aircraft a nosewheel landing fear was adopted, the neat main legs being hinged at the wing roots and retracting outwards. Many problems were encountered and solved and the MiG-9 delivered to VVS squadrons. Given the NATO code-name "Fargo", it was an extremely refined and well developed fighter. Its heavy guns packed a big punch and their blast did not appear to affect engine operation. In 1948 MiG-9s began to carry drop tanks just inboard of the wing tips. There was probably a trainer MiG-9U, but this has never been disclosed.

Mikoyan MiG-15

MiG-15 and -15bis (Lim-2, S-103), MiG-15UTI (SBLim-1, CS-102, F-2)

Type: (-15) single-seat fighter; (-15UTI) dual-control trainer.

Engine: (-15) one 5,005 lb (2270 kg) thrust RD-45F single-shaft centrifugal turbojet; (-15bis and most -15UTI) one 5,952 lb (2700 kg) VK-1 of same layout; (later -15bis) 6,990 lb (wet rating) VK-1A.

Dimensions: span 33 ft 0¾ in (10·08 m); length (-15, -15bis) 36 ft 3¼ in (11·05 m); (-15UTI) 32 ft 11¼ in (10·04 m); height (-15, -15bis) 11 ft 1⅜ in (3·4 m); (-15UTI) 12 ft 1½ in (3·7 m).

Weights: empty (all) close to 8,820 lb (4000 kg); maximum loaded (-15) 12,566 lb (5700 kg), (11,270 lb clean); (-15UTI) 11,905 lb (5400 kg), (10,692 lb clean).

Performance: maximum speed (-15) 668 mph (1075 km/h); (-15bis) 684 mph (1100 km/h); (-15UTI) 630 mph (1015 km/h); initial climb (-15, -15UTI) 10,500 ft (3200 m)/min; (-15bis) 11,480 ft (3500 m)/min; service ceiling (-15, -15bis) 51,000 ft (15,545 m); (-15UTI) 47,980 ft (14,625 m); range (at height, with slipper tanks) 885 miles (1424 km).

Armament: (-15, as first issued) one 37 mm N cannon under right side of nose and one 23 mm NS under left side; (-15, -15bis and variants) one 37 mm with 40 rounds under right and two 23 mm each with 80 rounds under left, with two underwing hardpoints for slipper tanks or stores of up to 1,102 lb (500 kg); (-15UTI) single 23 mm with 80 rounds or 12·7 mm UBK-E with 150 rounds under left side, plus same underwing options.

History: first flight 30 December 1947; (MiG-15UTI) 1948; service delivery August 1948; final delivery, probably 1953 (USSR) and about 1954 in Poland and Czechoslovakia.

No combat aircraft in history has had a bigger impact on the world scene than the MiG-15. Its existence was unsuspected in the West until American fighter pilots suddenly found themselves confronted by all-swept silver fighters which could fly faster, climb and dive faster and turn more tightly. Gradually the whole story, and the start of the world pre-eminence of the Mikoyan-Gurevich bureau, could be traced back to the decision of the British government to send to the Soviet Union the latest British turbojet, the Rolls-Royce Nene (long before the Nene was used in any British service aircraft). At one stroke this removed the very serious lack of a suitable engine for the advanced fighter the bureau were planning, and within eight months the prototype MiG-15 had flown and the Nene was frantically being put into production (without a licence) in slightly modified form as the RD-45. The original MiG-15 owed a lot to the Ta-183 and other

German designs, but the production machine had a lower tailplane, anhedral, wing fences and other changes. Notable features were the extensive use of high-quality welding and the quick-detach package housing the two (later three) heavy cannon. Production rapidly outstripped that of any other aircraft in the world, at least 8,000 being built in the Soviet Union in about five years, plus a further substantial number at Mielec, Poland, as the Lim-2, and at the newly established Vodochody works near Prague as the S-103 (S = stihac, fighter). The two satellite countries also

made the UTI trainer under an extension of their original licences, finally producing several thousand trainers by rebuilding MiG-15 fighters phased out of front-line service after 1954. In 1958 the Chinese plant at Shenyang began licence-production of the MiG-15UTI as the F-2. Most MiG-15 fighters were of the more powerful 15bis type with perforated flaps and redesigned rear-fuselage airbrakes; small numbers were made of a night fighter version with simple AI radar and of a ground-attack version with large ordnance carriers inboard of the drop tanks (the latter being

Key to MiG-15bis cutaway drawing

1. Bifurcated air intake
2. Landing light (moved to port wing root on later aircraft)
3. Combat camera fairing
4. Battery
5. Radio transmitter
6. Radio receiver
7. Armour-glass windscreen
8. Gyro gunsight
9. Starboard electrics control panel
10. Ejector seat
11. Aft-sliding canopy (open position)
12. VHF blade aerial
13. Wing fence
14. Slipper-type drop tank (54·4 gal/247·5 litres)
15. Pitot head
16. Compass unit
17. Starboard navigation light
18. Starboard aileron
19. Main fuel cell
20. Rear fuselage attachment joint
21. Engine bearers
22. Klimov VK-1 turbojet, 5,005 lb/2,270 kg thrust
23. Control rods
24. Rear fuselage frames
25. Fin main spar
26. Rudder balance weight
27. Rudder (upper section)
28. Tail navigation light
29. Elevator trim tab
30. Port elevator
31. Single-spar fixed tailplane
32. Jetpipe fairing
33. Air brake (partly extended)
34. Walkway (rubber coated)
35. Split flap
36. Trim operating mechanism
37. Aileron operating rods
38. Trim tab
39. Port aileron
40. Port rear spar
41. Port navigation light
42. Main spar
43. Rib
44. Attachment for slipper tank
45. Inward-retracting main landing gear
46. Main-spar branch
47. Twin air inlet ducts
48. Wing centre section
49. Fuel tank
50. Canopy jettison knob
51. Control column
52. Radio altimeter
53. Port air duct
54. Gun pack (shown cable-lowered for servicing)
55. Ammunition tank
56. Twin 23mm NS-23 cannon
57. Single 37mm N-37 cannon
58. Forward-retracting nosewheel
59. Nosewheel doors
60. Blast protection panel

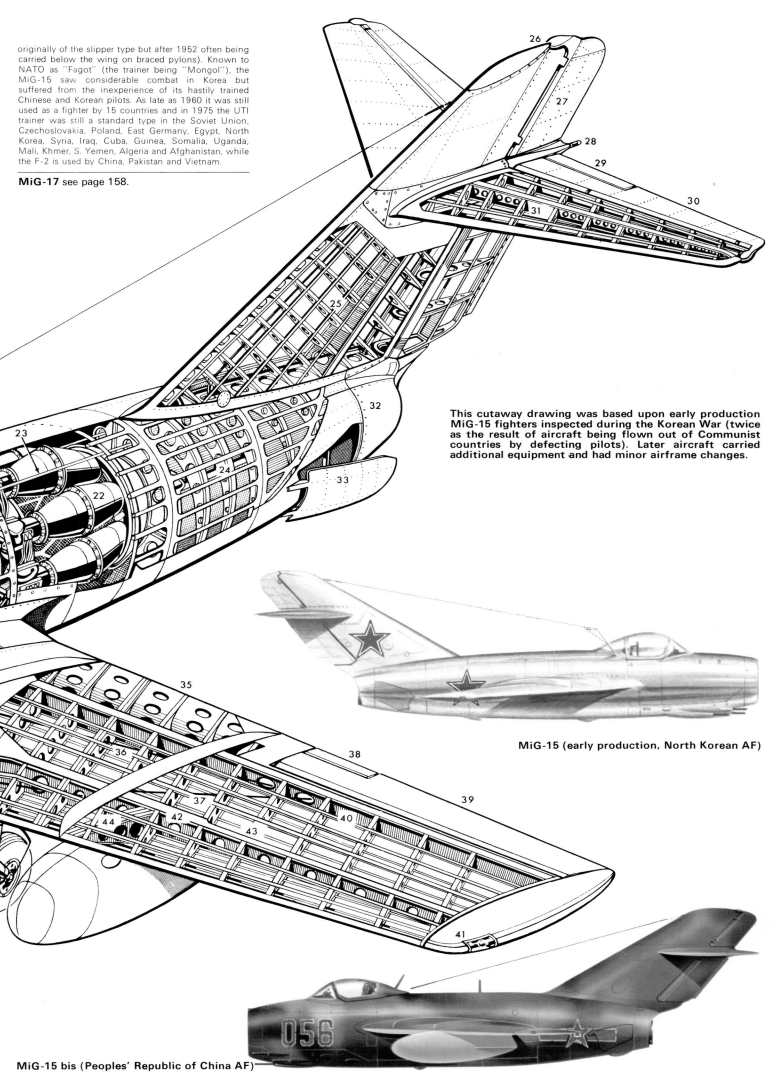

originally of the slipper type but after 1952 often being carried below the wing on braced pylons). Known to NATO as "Fagot" (the trainer being "Mongol"), the MiG-15 saw considerable combat in Korea but suffered from the inexperience of its hastily trained Chinese and Korean pilots. As late as 1960 it was still used as a fighter by 15 countries and in 1975 the UTI trainer was still a standard type in the Soviet Union, Czechoslovakia, Poland, East Germany, Egypt, North Korea, Syria, Iraq, Cuba, Guinea, Somalia, Uganda, Mali, Khmer, S. Yemen, Algeria and Afghanistan, while the F-2 is used by China, Pakistan and Vietnam.

MiG-17 see page 158.

This cutaway drawing was based upon early production MiG-15 fighters inspected during the Korean War (twice as the result of aircraft being flown out of Communist countries by defecting pilots). Later aircraft carried additional equipment and had minor airframe changes.

MiG-15 (early production, North Korean AF)

MiG-15 bis (Peoples' Republic of China AF)

Mikoyan MiG-19

MiG-19, -19S, -19SF (Lim-7, S-105, F-6), -19PF and -19PM; NATO code name "Farmer".
Type: single-seat fighter (PF, PM, all-weather interceptor).
Engines: (-19, -19S) two 6,700 lb (3,040 kg) thrust (afterburner rating) Mikulin AM-5 single-shaft afterburning turbojets; (-19SF, PF, PM) two 7,165 lb (3250 kg) thrust (afterburner) Klimov RD-9B afterburning turbojets (probably single-shaft engines).
Dimensions: span 29 ft 6½ in (9 m); length (S, SF, excluding pitot boom) 42 ft 11¼ in (13·08 m); (-19PF, PM) 44 ft 7 in; height 13 ft 2¼ in (4·02 m).
Weights: empty (SF) 12,698 lb (5760 kg); loaded (SF, clean) 16,755 lb (7600 kg); (maximum, SF) 19,180 lb (8700 kg); (PM) 20,944 lb (9500 kg).
Performance: maximum speed (typical) 920 mph at 20,000 ft (1480 km/h, Mach 1·3); initial climb (SF) 22,640 ft (6900 m)/min; service ceiling (SF) 58,725 ft (17,900 m); maximum range (high, with two drop tanks) 1,367 miles (2200 km).
Armament: see text.
History: first flight, September 1953; service delivery early 1955; first flight (F-6) December 1961.

With the MiG-19 the Mikoyan-Gurevich bureau established itself right in the front rank of the world's fighter design teams. The new fighter was on the drawing board as the I-350 before even the MiG-15 had been encountered in Korea, the five prototypes being ordered on 30 July 1951. Maj Grigori Sedov flew the first aircraft on 18 September 1953 on the power of two non-afterburning AM-5 engines giving only 4,410 lb thrust each. Nevertheless, despite the high wing loading and bold sweep angle of 55° (at 25% chord), the MiG-19 handled well, large fences and Fowler flaps giving satisfactory low-speed control. With afterburning engines the MiG-19 became the first Russian supersonic fighter and it was put into production on a very large scale, rivalling that of the MiG-15 and -17, despite a 100 per cent increase in price. After about 500 had been delivered the MiG-19S (stabilizator) supplanted the early model with the fixed tailplane and manual elevators replaced by a fully powered slab. At the same time the old armament (unchanged since MiG-15 and -17) was replaced by three of the new 30 mm NR-30 guns, one in each wing root and one under the right side of the nose. A large ventral airbrake was also added. In 1956 the AM-5 engine was replaced by the newer and more powerful RD-9, increasing peak Mach number from 1·1 to 1·3. The new fighter was designated MiG-19SF (forsirovanni, increased power), and has been built in very large numbers. Total production possibly exceeds

10,000, including licence-manufacture as the Lim-7 in Poland, S-105 in Czechoslovakia and F-6 in China. The corresponding MiG-19PF (perekhvatchik, interceptor) has an Izumrud AI radar (called "Scan Odd" by NATO) in a bullet carried on the inlet duct splitter, with the ranging unit in the upper inlet lip, changing the nose shape and adding 22 in to the aircraft length. The final production version was the MiG-19PM (modifikatsirovanni), with guns removed and pylons for four early beam-rider air-to-air missiles (called "Alkali" by NATO). All MiG-19s can carry the simple K-13A missile (the copy of Sidewinder, called "Atoll" by NATO) and underwing pylons can carry two 176 gal drop tanks plus two 551 lb weapons or dispensers. Perhaps surprisingly, there has been no evidence of a two-seat trainer version of this fine fighter, which in 1960 was judged obsolete and in 1970 was fast being reappraised as an extremely potent dogfighter. Part of the understanding of the MiG-19's qualities has resulted from its purchase in large numbers by Pakistan as the F-6 from the Chinese factory at Shenyang. The notable features of the F-6 were its superb finish, outstanding dogfight manoeuvrability and tremendous hitting power of the NR-30 guns, each projectile having more than twice the kinetic energy of those of the Aden or DEFA of similar calibre. F-6 or MiG-19 fighters remain in use with Pakistan, Tanzania, Indonesia and many Warsaw Pact countries.

This cutaway drawing shows the main features of the major production version, the MiG-19SF. This is perhaps the most basic of the world's supersonic fighters, and the F-6, Lim-7 and S-105 versions built outside the Soviet Union are almost identical.

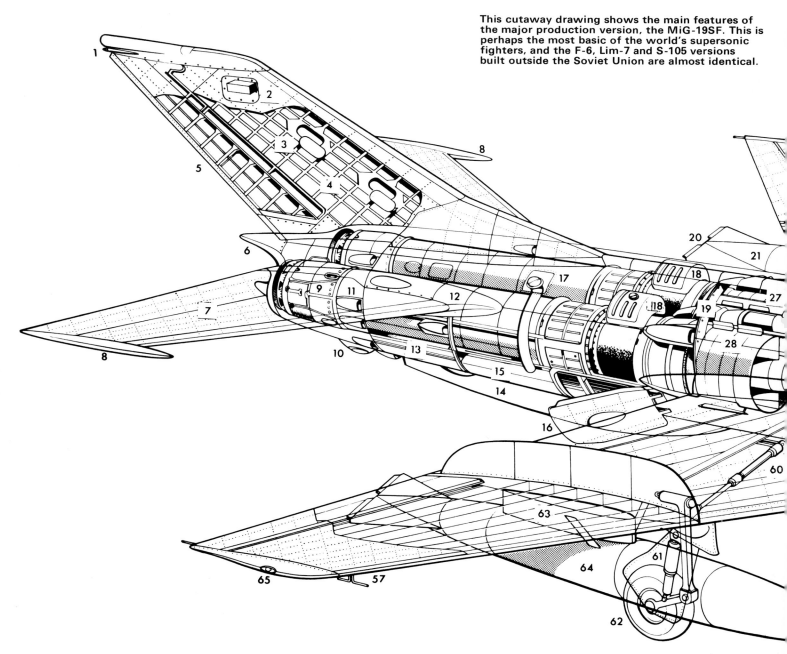

F-6, Chinese-built MiG-19SF (Peoples' Republic of China AF).

F-6 (Pakistani AF, with camouflage which became standard during 1973 war).

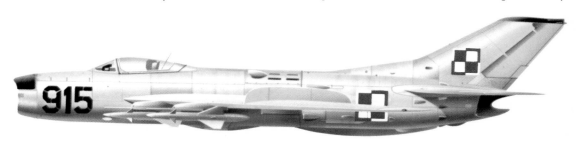

MiG-19PM (Polish AF, showing radar and four "Alkali" missiles).

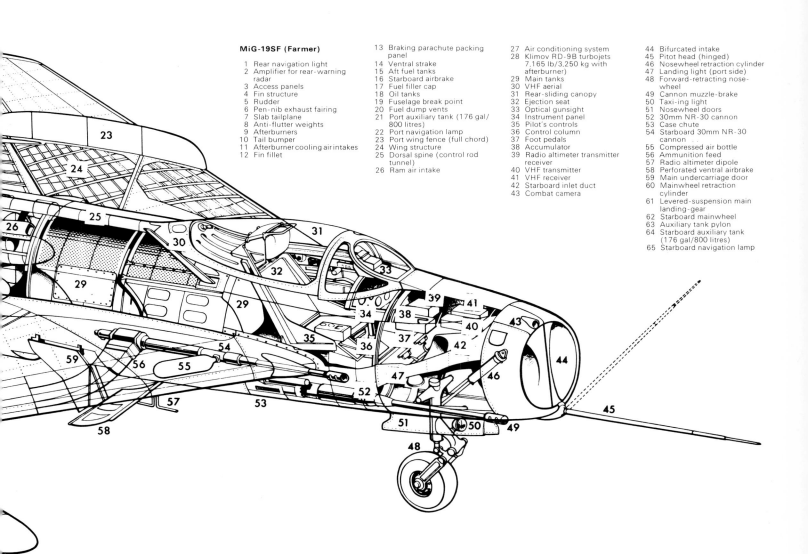

MiG-19SF (Farmer)

1. Rear navigation light
2. Amplifier for rear-warning radar
3. Access panels
4. Fin structure
5. Rudder
6. Pen-nib exhaust fairing
7. Slab tailplane
8. Anti-flutter weights
9. Afterburners
10. Tail bumper
11. Afterburner cooling air intakes
12. Fin fillet
13. Braking parachute packing panel
14. Ventral strake
15. Aft fuel tanks
16. Starboard airbrake
17. Fuel filler cap
18. Oil tanks
19. Fuselage break point
20. Fuel dump vents
21. Port auxiliary tank (176 gal/800 litres)
22. Port navigation lamp
23. Port wing fence (full chord)
24. Wing structure
25. Dorsal spine (control rod tunnel)
26. Ram air intake
27. Air conditioning system
28. Klimov RD-9B turbojets 7,165 lb/3,250 kg with afterburner)
29. Main tanks
30. VHF aerial
31. Rear-sliding canopy
32. Ejection seat
33. Optical gunsight
34. Instrument panel
35. Pilot's controls
36. Control column
37. Foot pedals
38. Accumulator
39. Radio altimeter transmitter receiver
40. VHF transmitter
41. VHF receiver
42. Starboard inlet duct
43. Combat camera
44. Bifurcated intake
45. Pitot head (hinged)
46. Nosewheel retraction cylinder
47. Landing light (port side)
48. Forward-retracting nose-wheel
49. Cannon muzzle-brake
50. Taxi-ing light
51. Nosewheel doors
52. 30mm NR-30 cannon
53. Case chute
54. Starboard 30mm NR-30 cannon
55. Compressed air bottle
56. Ammunition feed
57. Radio altimeter dipole
58. Perforated ventral airbrake
59. Main undercarriage door
60. Mainwheel retraction cylinder
61. Levered-suspension main landing-gear
62. Starboard mainwheel
63. Auxiliary tank pylon
64. Starboard auxiliary tank (176 gal/800 litres)
65. Starboard navigation lamp

Mikoyan MiG-21

MiG-21, 21F (S-107), 21FA, 21PF, 21FL, 21PFS, 21PFM, 21PFMA, 21M, 21R, 21MF, 21U, 21US and 21UM, plus countless special versions. Several versions made in China as F-8.

Type: single-seat fighter; (PFMA and MF) limited all-weather multi-role; (R) reconnaissance; (U) two-seat trainer.

Engine: in all versions, one Tumansky single-shaft turbojet with afterburner; (-21) R-11 rated at 11,240 lb (5100 kg) with afterburner; (-21F) R-11-F2-300 rated at 13,120 lb (5950 kg); (-21FL, PFS, PFM and PFMA) R-11-G2S-300 rated at 13,668 lb (6200 kg); (-21MF and derivatives) R-13-300 rated at 14,550 lb (6600 kg).

Dimensions: span 23 ft 5½ in (7·15 m); length (excluding probe) (-21) 46 ft 11 in; (-21MF) 48 ft 0½ in (14·6 m); height (little variation, but figure for MF) 14 ft 9 in (4·5 m).

Weights: empty (-21) 11,464 lb (5200 kg); (-21MF) 12,346 lb (5600 kg); maximum loaded (-21) 18,740 lb (8500 kg); (-21MF) 21,605 lb (9800 kg) (weight with three tanks and two K-13A, 20,725 lb).

Performance: maximum speed (MF, but typical of all) 1,285 mph (2070 km/h, Mach 2·1); initial climb (MF, clean) 36,090 ft (11,000 m)/min; service ceiling 59,050 ft (18,000 m); range (high, internal fuel) 683 miles (1100 km); maximum range (MF, high, three tanks) 1,118 miles (1800 km).

Armament: see text.

History: first flight (E-5 prototype) late 1955; (production -21F) late 1957; service delivery early 1958.

Undoubtedly the most widely used combat aircraft in the world in the 1970s, this trim little delta has established a superb reputation for cost effectiveness and in its later versions it also packs a formidable multi-role punch. It was designed in the 18 months following the Korean War. While Sukhoi developed large supersonic fighters to rival the American F-100, the Mikoyan-Gurevich bureau, by now led only by Col-Gen Mikoyan (who died in 1970), concentrated on a small day interceptor of the highest possible performance. Prototypes were built with both swept and delta wings, both having powered slab tailplanes, and the delta was chosen for production. At least 30 pre-production aircraft had flown by the time service delivery started and the development effort was obviously considerable. The initial MiG-21 abounded in interesting features including Fowler flaps, fully powered controls, upward ejection seat fixed to the rear of the front-hinged canopy (which incorporated the whole front of the cockpit enclosure except the bullet-proof windshield) to act as a pilot blast-shield, and internal fuel capacity of only 410 gal. Armament was two 30 mm NR-30 in long fairings under the fuselage, the left gun usually being replaced by avionics. Part of these avionics served the two K-13 ("Atol") missiles carried on wing pylons on the slightly more powerful 21F. This had radar ranging, 515 gal fuel, broader fin, upward-hinged pitot boom attached under the nose (to prevent people walking into it) and two dorsal blade aerials. Czech-built aircraft (still called 21F) did not have the rear-view windows in the front of the dorsal spine. The F was called "Fishbed C" by NATO and Type 74 by the Indian Air Force; it was also the type supplied to China in 1959 and used as the pattern for the Chinese-built F-8. As the oldest active variant it was also the first exported or seen in the West,

the Finnish AF receiving the 21F-12 in April 1963.

At Tushino in 1961 the prototype was displayed of what became the 21PF, with inlet diameter increased from 27 in to 36 in, completely changing the nose shape and providing room for a large movable centre-body housing the scanner of the R1L (NATO "Spin Scan") AI radar. Other changes included deletion of guns (allowing simpler forward airbrakes), bigger main-wheels (causing large fuselage bulges above the wing), pitot boom moved above the inlet, fatter dorsal spine (partly responsible for fuel capacity of 627 gal) and many electronic changes. All PF had an uprated engine, late models had take-off rocket latches and final batches had completely new blown flaps (SPS) which cut landing speed by 25 mph and reduced nose-up attitude for better pilot view. The FL was the export PF (L = *lokator*, denoting R2L radar) with even more powerful engine. Like the F models rebuilt in 1963–4, this can carry the GP-9 gunpack housing the excellent GSh-23 23 mm twin-barrel gun, has a still further broadened vertical tail and drag-chute repositioned above the jetpipe. The PFS was the PF with SPS blown flaps, while the PFM was a definitive improved version with another 19 in added to the fin (final fillet eliminated), a conventional seat and side-hinged canopy, and large flush aerials in the fin. One-off versions were built to prove STOL with lift jets and to fly a scaled "analogue" of the wing of the Tu-144 SST. The very important PFMA, made in huge numbers, was the first multi-role version, with straight top line from much deeper spine (housing equipment and not fuel and holding tankage to 572 gal), and four pylons for two 1,100 lb and two 551 lb bombs, four S-24 missiles and/or tanks or K-13A missiles. The 21M has an internal GSh-23 and since 1973 has been built in India as Type 88. The 21R has multi-sensor reconnaissance internally and in pods and wing-tip ECM fairings, as do late models of the 21MF, the first to have the new R-13 engine. The RF is the R-13-powered reconnaissance version.

Code-named "Mongol" and called Type 66 in India, the U is the tandem trainer; the US has SPS flaps and UM the R-13 engine and four pylons. Many other versions have been used to set world records. About 10,000 MiG-21s have been built, and among users are Afghanistan, Algeria, Bangladesh, Bulgaria, China, Cuba, Czechoslovakia, Egypt, Finland, East Germany, Hungary, India, Indonesia, Iraq, North Korea, Poland, Romania, Syria, Vietnam and Yugoslavia.

MiG-21F (Interceptor Regiment, Romanian AF)

MiG-21MF cutaway drawing key

1. Pitot-static boom
2. Pitch vanes
3. Yaw vanes
4. Conical three-position intake centrebody
5. "Spin Scan" search-and-track radar scanner
6. Boundary layer slot
7. Engine air intake
8. Radar ("Spin Scan")
9. Lower boundary layer exit
10. Aerials
11. Nosewheel doors
12. Nosewheel leg and shock absorbers
13. Castoring nosewheel
14. Anti-shimmy damper
15. Avionics bay access
16. Attitude sensor
17. Nosewheel well
18. Spill door
19. Nosewheel retraction pivot
20. Bifurcated inlet duct
21. Avionics bay
22. Electronics equipment
23. Inlet duct
24. Upper boundary layer exit
25. Dynamic pressure probe for q-feel
26. Semi-elliptical armour-glass windscreen
27. Gunsight mounting
28. Fixed quarterlight
29. Radar scope
30. Control column (with tailplane trim switch and two firing buttons)
31. Rudder pedals
32. Underfloor control runs
33. KM-1 two-position zero-level ejection seat
34. Port instrument console
35. Undercarriage handle
36. Seat harness
37. Canopy release/lock
38. Starboard wall switch panel
39. Rear-view mirror fairing
40. Starboard-hinged canopy
41. Ejection-seat headrest
42. Avionics bay
43. Control rods
44. Air-conditioning plant
45. Suction relief door
46. Inlet duct
47. Wing root attachment fairing
48. Wing/fuselage spar-lug attachments (four)
49. Fuselage ring frames
50. Intermediate frames
51. Main fuselage fuel tank
52. RSIU radio bay
53. Auxiliary intake
54. Leading-edge integral fuel tank
55. Starboard outer weapons pylon
56. Outboard wing construction
57. Starboard navigation light
58. Leading-edge suppressed aerial
59. Wing fence
60. Aileron control jack
61. Starboard aileron
62. Flap actuator fairing
63. Starboard blown flap— SPS (*sduva pogranichnovo*)

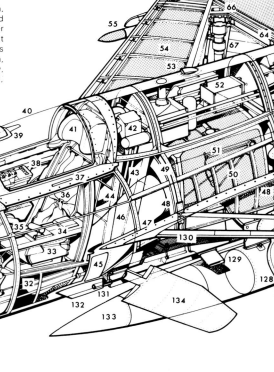

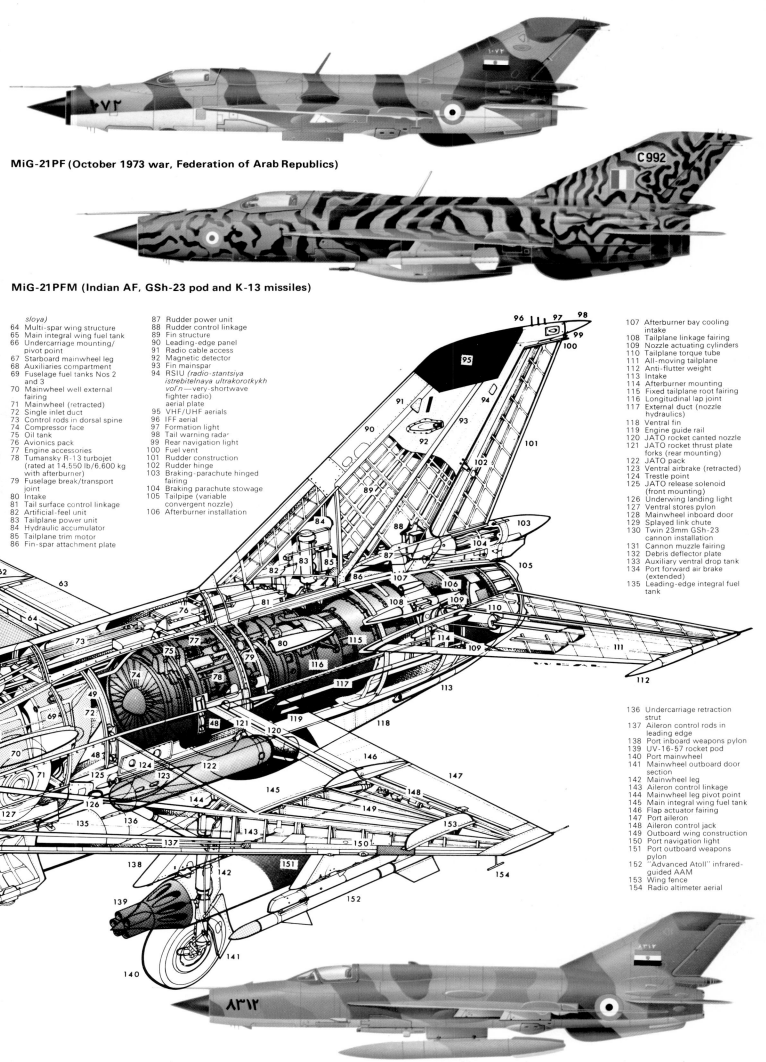

MiG-21PF (October 1973 war, Federation of Arab Republics)

MiG-21PFM (Indian AF, GSh-23 pod and K-13 missiles)

sloya)
64 Multi-spar wing structure
65 Main integral wing fuel tank
66 Undercarriage mounting/ pivot point
67 Starboard mainwheel leg
68 Auxiliaries compartment
69 Fuselage fuel tanks Nos 2 and 3
70 Mainwheel well external fairing
71 Mainwheel (retracted)
72 Single inlet duct
73 Control rods in dorsal spine
74 Compressor face
75 Oil tank
76 Avionics pack
77 Engine accessories
78 Tumansky R-13 turbojet (rated at 14,550 lb/6,600 kg with afterburner)
79 Fuselage break/transport joint
80 Intake
81 Tail surface control linkage
82 Artificial-feel unit
83 Tailplane power unit
84 Hydraulic accumulator
85 Tailplane trim motor
86 Fin-spar attachment plate

87 Rudder power unit
88 Rudder control linkage
89 Fin structure
90 Leading-edge panel
91 Radio cable access
92 Magnetic detector
93 Fin mainspar
94 RSIU *(radio-stantsiya istrebitelnaya ultrakorotkykh vol'n* —very-shortwave fighter radio) aerial plate
95 VHF/UHF aerials
96 IFF aerial
97 Formation light
98 Tail warning radar
99 Rear navigation light
100 Fuel vent
101 Rudder construction
102 Rudder hinge
103 Braking-parachute hinged fairing
104 Braking parachute stowage
105 Tailpipe (variable convergent nozzle)
106 Afterburner installation

107 Afterburner bay cooling intake
108 Tailplane linkage fairing
109 Nozzle actuating cylinders
110 Tailplane torque tube
111 All-moving tailplane
112 Anti-flutter weight
113 Intake
114 Afterburner mounting
115 Fixed tailplane root fairing
116 Longitudinal lap joint
117 External duct (nozzle hydraulics)
118 Ventral fin
119 Engine guide rail
120 JATO rocket canted nozzle
121 JATO rocket thrust plate forks (rear mounting)
122 JATO pack
123 Ventral airbrake (retracted)
124 Trestle point
125 JATO release solenoid (front mounting)
126 Underwing landing light
127 Ventral stores pylon
128 Mainwheel inboard door
129 Splayed link chute
130 Twin 23mm GSh-23 cannon installation
131 Cannon muzzle fairing
132 Debris deflector plate
133 Auxiliary ventral drop tank
134 Port forward air brake (extended)
135 Leading-edge integral fuel tank

136 Undercarriage retraction strut
137 Aileron control rods in leading edge
138 Port inboard weapons pylon
139 UV-16-57 rocket pod
140 Port mainwheel
141 Mainwheel outboard door section
142 Mainwheel leg
143 Aileron control linkage
144 Mainwheel leg pivot point
145 Main integral wing fuel tank
146 Flap actuator fairing
147 Port aileron
148 Aileron control jack
149 Outboard wing construction
150 Port navigation light
151 Port outboard weapons pylon
152 "Advanced Atoll" infrared-guided AAM
153 Wing fence
154 Radio altimeter aerial

MiG-21MF (Egyptian AF, Federation of Arab Republics insignia)

157

Mikoyan MiG-17

MiG-17, -17P, -17F (Lim-5P and -5M, S-104, F-4), -17PF and -17PFU (NATO name "Fresco")
Type: single-seat fighter; (PF, PFU) limited all-weather interceptor.
Engine: (-17, -17P) one 5,952 lb (2700 kg) thrust

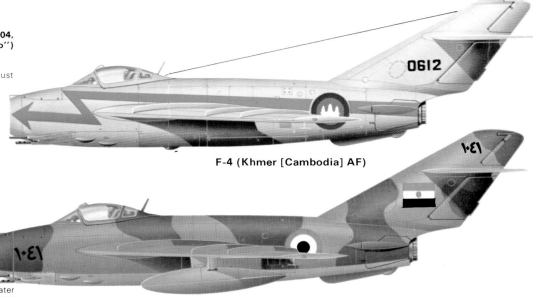

F-4 (Khmer [Cambodia] AF)

Klimov VK-1 single-shaft centrifugal turbojet; (later versions) one 4,732/7,452 lb (3380 kg) VK-1F with afterburner.
Dimensions: span 31 ft (9·45 m); length (all) 36 ft 3 in (11·05 m); height 11 ft (3·35 m).
Weights: empty (all) about 9,040 lb (4100 kg); loaded (F, clean) 11,773 lb (5340 kg); maximum (all) 14,770 lb (6700 kg).
Performance: maximum speed (F, clean at best height of 9,840 ft) 711 mph (1145 km/h); initial climb 12,795 ft (3900 m)/min; service ceiling 54,460 ft (16,600 m); range (high, two drop tanks) 913 miles (1470 km).
Armament: (-17) as MiG-15, one 37 mm and two 23 mm NS-23; (all later versions) three 23 mm Nudelmann-Rikter NR-23 cannon, one under right side of nose and two under left; four wing hardpoints for tanks, total of 1,102 lb (500 kg) of bombs, packs of eight 55 mm air-to-air rockets or various air-to-ground missiles.
History: first flight (prototype) January 1950; service delivery, 1952; service delivery (F-4) January 1956; final delivery (Soviet Union) probably 1959.
Only gradually did Western observers recognise the MiG-17 as not merely a slightly modified MiG-15 but

MiG-17F (Syrian AF, Federation of Arab Republics insignia)

a completely different aircraft. Even then it was generally believed it had been hastily designed to rectify deficiencies shown in the MiG-15's performance in Korea, but in fact the design began at the beginning of 1949, long before the Korean war. This was because from the first the MiG-15 had shown bad behaviour at high speeds, and though the earlier fighter was eventually made completely safe (partly by arranging for the air brakes to open automatically at Mach 0·92) it was still a difficult gun platform due to its tendency to snake and pitch. The MiG-17 — which was probably the last fighter in which Gurevich played a direct personal role — had a new wing with thickness reduced from 11 per cent to about 9 per cent, a different section and planform and no fewer than three fences. Without taper and with inboard sweep of 47° this made a big difference to high-Mach behaviour, and in fact there are reasons to believe the MiG-17 can be dived to make a sonic bang. With a new tail on a longer rear fuselage the transformation was completed by considerable revision of systems and equipment,

though at first the VK-1 engine was unchanged. In 1958 the first limited all-weather version, the -17P, went into modest production with longer nose housing the same Izumrud ("Scan Odd") AI radar and ranging avionics as was also in production for the MiG-19. With the introduction of an afterburning engine the airbrakes were moved aft of the wing, away from the hot back end, but this was not a good position and they were returned (in enlarged rectangular form) to the tail in the most important sub-type the -17F. This was made in Poland as the Lim-5P (the -5M being a rough-field close-support version with larger tyres and drag chute), in Czechoslovakia as the S-104 and in China as the F-4. The PF was the afterburning all-weather version, and the final model was the PFU with guns removed and wing pylons for four beam-riding "Alkali" air-to-air missiles. Total production for at least 22 air forces must have considerably exceeded 5,000, exports from China alone exceeding 1,000. Many 17F remained in use in the mid-1970s.

MiG-19 and MiG-21 see pages 154—157.

Mikoyan MiG-23

Above, MiG-23S (Soviet IA-PVO air defence force)

MiG-23, -23B, -23S and -23U ("Flogger")
Type: (-23B) single-seat tactical attack; (-23S) single-seat all-weather interceptor; (-23U) dual-control trainer.
Engine: one afterburning turbofan (possibly turbojet) of unknown type, with maximum rating of about 21,000 lb (9525 kg).
Dimensions: (estimated) span (21° sweep) 46 ft 9 in (14·25 m), (72°) 26 ft 9½ in (8·17 m); length 55 ft 1½ in (16·8 m), (-23U may be slightly longer); height 15 ft 9 in (4·8 m).
Weights: (estimated) empty 20,000 lb (9070 kg); loaded (clean) 30,000 lb (13,600 kg); maximum loaded 40,000 lb (18,145 kg).
Performance: maximum speed, clean, 840 mph (1350 km/h, Mach 1·1) at sea level, 1,520 mph (2445 km/h, Mach 2·3) at altitude; maximum speed at altitude with two air-to-air missiles, about Mach 2; service ceiling, over 60,000 ft (18,290 m); combat radius (hi-lo-hi mission) 600 miles (966 km); ferry range, 2,000 miles (3220 km).
Armament: (-23B attack version) one 23 mm GSh-23 twin-barrel gun in belly pack projecting below centre-line; two body pylons and two pylons on fixed inboard wings, each rated at about 2,000 lb (907 kg) and used for variety of weapons or tanks. (23 fighter) two or four "Anab" missiles; no gun.
History: first flight, probably 1965; (first production aircraft) believed 1970; service delivery, believed 1971.

MiG-23B (FA, frontal aviation)

Revealed at the 1967 Moscow Aviation Day, the proto-type swing-wing MiG-23 was at first thought to be a Yakovlev design, though it appeared in company with a jet-lift STOL fighter having an identical rear fuselage and tail and strong MiG-21-like features (though much bigger than a MiG-21). Over the next four years the Mikoyan bureau greatly developed this aircraft, which originally owed something to the F-111 and Mirage G. By 1971 the radically different production versions, the -23B attack and -23U trainer, were entering service in quantity, and by 1975 several hundred had been delivered to Warsaw Pact air forces and also to Egypt, Iraq, Libya, Syria and possibly other countries. Though there is no doubt its technology is older than that of MRCA, the MiG-23 is a versatile and formidable aircraft; the variable-sweep wing strongly suggests multi-role use. There are at least three versions in service: fighter, attack and trainer. The attack machine has a pointed nose (no radar), fixed inlets and simpler engine nozzle. In 1973 the then Secretary of the US Air Force stated the official view that the fighter version carried radar and missile systems comparable with the latest Phantom, and most MiG-23 versions seem well equipped with ECM (countermeasures).

Mikoyan MiG-25

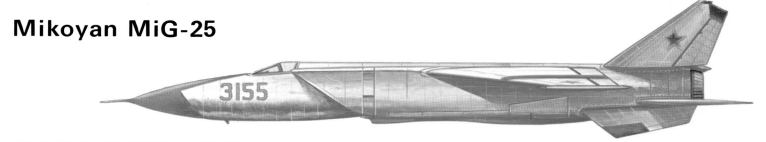

MiG-25 ("Foxbat A"), MiG-25R and MiG-25U
Type: "Foxbat A" (believed to be MiG-25S), all-weather long-range interceptor; MiG-25R, reconnaissance; MiG-25U, tandem-seat dual trainer with stepped cockpits.
Engines: two afterburning turbofans or turbojets, believed to be of Tumansky design and each rated at an estimated 31,000 lb (14,100 kg) thrust.
Dimensions: (estimated) span 41 ft (12·5 m); length 69 ft 9 in (21·2 m); height 19 ft (5·8 m).
Weights: (estimated) empty 34,000 lb (15,425 kg); maximum loaded 64,200 lb (29,120 kg).
Performance: (estimated) maximum speed at altitude 2,100 mph (3380 km/h, Mach 3·2); initial climb, about 50,000 ft (15,240 m)/min; service ceiling 80,000 ft (24,400 m); high-altitude combat radius without external fuel, 700 miles (1130 km).

Armament: ("-A") four underwing pylons each carrying one AA-6 air-to-air missile (two radar, two infra-red) or other store; no guns; ("-B") none.
History: first flight (E-266 prototype) probably 1964; (production reconnaissance version) before 1969; (production interceptor) probably 1969; service delivery (both) 1970 or earlier.

This large and powerful aircraft set a totally new level in combat-aircraft performance. The prototypes blazed a trail of world records in 1965–67 including closed-circuit speeds, payload-to-height and rate of climb records. The impact of what NATO quickly christened "Foxbat" was unprecedented. Especially in the Pentagon, Western policymakers recognised that here

MiG-25 ("Foxbat A", without 21 foot AA-6 missiles)

was a combat aircraft that outclassed everything else, and urgent studies were put in hand for a new US Air Force fighter (F-15 Eagle) to counter it. By 1971 at least two pairs of "Foxbat-B" reconnaissance aircraft were flying with impunity over Israel, too high and fast for Phantoms to catch, while others have made over-flights deep into Iran. This version is different in many respects, the nose having cameras instead of a large "Fox Fire" pulse-doppler radar, and other sensors being carried under the large body. Both versions have twin outward-sloping vertical tails, single mainwheels and a flush canopy shaped for speed rather than pilot view. In speed and altitude the MiG-25 still far out-classes all Western aircraft, and both versions appear to carry comprehensive ECM (countermeasures).

Mil Mi-6 and -10

Mi-6, Mi-10 and -10K
Type: -6, heavy transport helicopter; -10, crane helicopter for bulky loads; -10K, crane helicopter.
Engines: (-6, -10) two 5,500 shp Soloviev D-25V single-shaft free-turbine engines driving common R-7 gearbox; (-10K) two 6,500 shp D-25VF.
Dimensions: Main rotor diameter 114 ft 10 in (35 m); overall length (rotors turning) (-6) 136 ft 11½ in (41·74 m); (-10, -10K) 137 ft 5½ in (41·89 m); fuselage length (-6) 108 ft 10½ in (33·18 m); (10, -10K) 107 ft 9¾ in (32·86 m); height (-6) 32 ft 4 in (9·86 m); (-10) 32 ft 2 in (9·8 m); (-10K) 25 ft 7 in (7·8 m).

Weights: empty (-6, typical) 60,055 lb (27,240 kg); (-10) 60,185 lb (27,300 kg); (-10K) 54,410 lb (24,680 kg); maximum loaded (-6) 93,700 lb (42,500 kg); (-10) 96,340 lb (43,700 kg); (-10K) 83,776 lb (38,000 kg) with 5,500 shp engines (90,390 lb, 41,000 kg expected with D-25VF engines).
Performance: maximum speed (-6) 186 mph (300 km/h) (set 100 km circuit record at 211·36 mph, beyond flight manual limit); (-10) 124 mph (200 km/h); service ceiling (-6) 14,750 ft (4500 m); (-10, -10K, limited) 9,842 ft (3000 m); range (-6 with half payload) 404 miles (650 km); (-10 with 12,000 lb platform load) 155 miles (250 km); (-10K with 11,000 kg payload, 6,500 shp engines) over 280 miles (450 km).
Armament: normally none, but Mi-6 often seen with manually aimed nose gun of about 12·7 mm calibre.
History: first flight (-6) probably early 1957; (-10) 1960; (-10K) prior to 1965.

Development by Mikhail L. Mil's design bureau at Zaporozhye of the dynamic system (rotors and

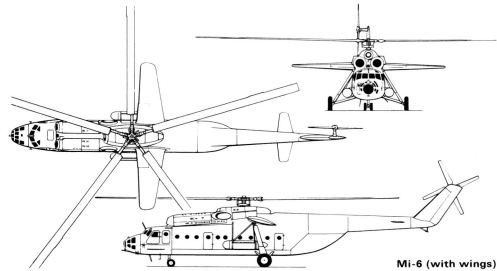

Mi-6 (with wings)

shafting) of the Mi-6 was a task matched only by Soloviev's development of the huge R-7 gearbox, which weighs 7,054 lb (much more than the pair of engines). By far the biggest rotor system yet flown, this served to lift by far the biggest helicopter, the Mi-6 (NATO code name "Hook"), which quickly set world records for speed and payload, though the normal load is limited to 26,450 lb (12,000 kg) internally, loaded via huge clamshell rear doors, or 19,840 lb (9000 kg) externally slung. About 500 have been built, possibly half being in military use with the Soviet Union, and the armed forces of Bulgaria, Egypt, Indonesia, Iraq, Syria and

Vietnam. Most have the rotor unloaded in cruising flight (typically 150 mph) by a fixed wing of 50 ft 2½ in span. These huge helicopters have played an active role in field exercises carrying troops (typically 68) and tactical missiles or vehicles in the class of the BRDM. The Mi-10 (code name "Harke") has lofty landing gears which enable it to straddle a load, such as a bus or prefabricated building, 3·75 m (12 ft 3½ in) high; heavy loads weighing 33,070 lb (15,000 kg) and up to over 65 ft in length have been flown. It uses a TV viewing system for load control, but the short-legged Mi-10K has an under-nose gondola.

Mil Mi-8

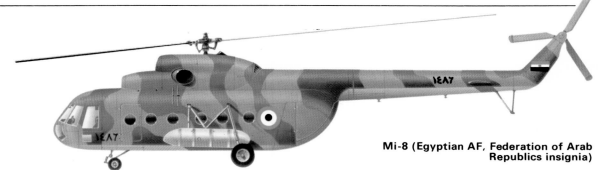

Mi-8 (Egyptian AF, Federation of Arab Republics insignia)

Mi-8, Mi-8T
Type: general utility helicopter for internal loads and externally mounted weapons.
Engines: two 1,500 shp Isotov TV2-117A single-shaft free-turbine engines driving common VR-8A gearbox.
Dimensions: main rotor diameter 69 ft 10½ in (21·29 m); overall length, rotors turning 82 ft 9¾ in (25·24 m); fuselage length 60 ft 0¾ in (18·31 m); height 18 ft 6½ in (5·65 m).
Weights: empty (-8T) 15,026 lb (6816 kg); maximum loaded (all) 26,455 lb (12,000 kg) (heavier weights for non-VTO operation).
Performance: maximum speed 161 mph (260 km/h); service ceiling 14,760 ft (4500 m); range (-8T, full payload, 5 per cent reserve at 3,280 ft) 298 miles (480 km).

Armament: optional fitting for external pylons for up to eight stores carried outboard of fuel tanks (always fitted); typical loads eight pods of 57 mm rockets, or mix of gun pods and anti-tank missiles (Mi-8 not normally used in anti-tank role).
History: first flight 1960 or earlier; service delivery of military versions, before 1967.

Originally powered by a single 2,700 shp Soloviev engine, the Mi-8 soon appeared with its present engines and in 1964 added a fifth blade to its main rotor. It has since been the chief general utility helicopter of the Warsaw Pact powers and many other nations. By mid-1974 it was announced that more

than 1,000 had been built, the majority for military use, with about 300 having been exported to Bangladesh, Bulgaria, Czechoslovakia, Egypt, Ethiopia, Finland, East Germany, Hungary, India, Iraq, Pakistan, the Sudan, Syria and Vietnam. The Mi-8 is a passenger and troop carrier normally furnished with quickly removable seats for 28 in the main cabin. The -8T is the utility version without furnishing and with circular windows, weapon pylons, cargo rings, a winch/pulley block system for loading and optional electric hoist by the front doorway. All versions have large rear clam-shell doors (the passenger version having airstairs incorporated) through which a BRDM and other small vehicles can be loaded.

Mil Mi-24

Mi-24 versions with NATO names Hind-A and -B.
Type: Tactical multi-role helicopter.
Engines: almost certainly two 1,500 shp Isotov TV2-117A free-turbine turboshaft.
Dimensions: (estimated) diameter of five-blade main rotor 55 ft 9 in (17 m); length overall (ignoring rotors) 55 ft 9 in (17 m); height overall 14 ft (4·25 m).
Weights: (estimated) empty 14,300 lb (6500 kg); maximum loaded 25,400 lb (11,500 kg).
Performance: maximum speed 170 mph (275 km/h); general performance, higher than Mi-8.
Armament: (Hind-A) usually one 12·7 mm gun aimed from nose; two stub wings providing rails for four wire-guided anti-tank missiles and four other stores (bombs, missiles, rocket or gun pods). (Hind-B) two stub wings of different type with four weapon pylons.
History: first flight, before 1972; service delivery, before 1974.

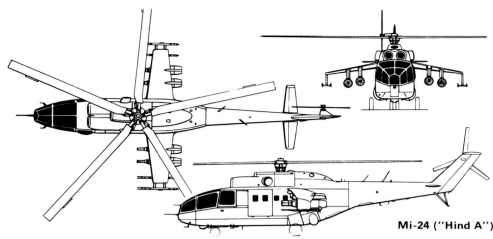

Mi-24 ("Hind A")

Few details are yet known of this attractive-looking battlefield helicopter, though in 1974 many were seen in service in East Germany and two versions were disclosed to the West in photographs. It appears to be based on the Mi-8, though the engines look smaller and the main rotor has blades of considerably shorter length but increased chord. The nosewheel-type landing gear is fully retractable, and the cabin is large enough for a crew of two and 12 to 14 troops. The exterior is well streamlined, broken only by avionic aerials and the prominent weapon stub-wings. The Mi-24 is much larger than the British Lynx, yet smaller than the Mi-8. One reason may be that it is the smallest machine capable of using the well-tried Mi-8 dynamic components, and in the anti-tank role the surplus payload could be used for spare missiles or infantry teams that could be dropped and then recovered later. Maximum slung load is estimated at 8,000 lb (3630 kg).

Mitsubishi Ki-15

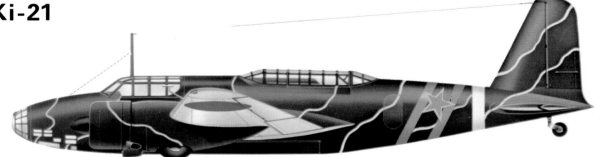

Mitsubishi Ki-15-I (1st Chutai, 15th Hikosentai, Imperial Army)

Ki-15-I, Ki-15-II, C5M, Karigane
Type: two-seat light attack bomber.
Engine: (I) one 750 hp Nakajima Ha-8 nine-cylinder radial; (II) one 800 hp Mitsubishi A.14 (later named Kinsei) 14-cylinder two-row radial.
Dimensions: span 39 ft 4¾ in (12·0 m); length (I) 27 ft 11 in (8·50 m); height 9 ft 10 in (3·0 m).
Weights: empty (I) 3,968 lb (1800 kg); maximum loaded (I) 5,070 lb (2300 kg); (II) 6,834 lb (3100 kg).
Performance: maximum speed (I) 280 mph (450 km/h); (II) about 298 mph (480 km/h); initial climb (both) about 1,640 ft (500 m)/min; service ceiling (I) 28,220 ft (8600 m); range with bomb load (both) about 1,100 miles (1800 km).
Armament: one 7·7 mm Type 89 (not always fitted) fixed in outer wing firing forward, and one manually aimed from rear cockpit; bomb load of up to 551 lb (250 kg) in (I) or 1,100 lb (500 kg) in (II) carried externally.
History: first flight (Karigane prototype) May 1936; (Ki-15-I) probably late 1936.

This trim little machine stemmed from a private venture by the giant Mitsubishi company, inspired by the emergence in the United States of modern stressed-skin monoplanes (particularly the Northrop A-17). With company funds, but sponsored by the Asahi (Rising Sun) newspaper, a prototype was built to demonstrate the ability of the fast-growing Japanese industry to build modern aircraft. It was a time of intense nationalism and the resulting machine, named Karigane (Wild Goose) by Mitsubishi, was individually christened "Kamikaze" (Divine Wind) and prepared as an instrument of national publicity. Its greatest achievement was a notably trouble-free flight of 9,900 miles from Tokyo to London in April 1937. Others were built for similar purposes (one being "Asakaze" (Morning Wind) of the Asahi Press) and as fast mailplanes, while in 1938 a small batch was built with the 550 hp Kotobuki (licence-built Bristol Jupiter) replaced by the much more powerful A.14 engine. In 1937 construction began of 437 military Ki-15 series for the Army and these were soon one of the first really modern types to go into action in the Sino-Japanese war, which had simmered for years and finally broke out in 1937. The Ki-15 was used for level bombing, close support and photo-reconnaissance, but was replaced by the Ki-30 (p. 162). In 1939 the Imperial Navy began to receive 50 of two C5M versions with different engines. Allied code name was "Babs".

Mitsubishi Ki-21

Mitsubishi Ki-21-I (2nd Chutai, 60th Hikosentai, Imperial Army)

Ki-21-I, -IIa and -IIb
Type: seven-seat heavy bomber.
Engines: (I) two 850 hp Nakajima Ha-5-Kai 14-cylinder two-row radials; (II) two 1,490 hp Mitsubishi Ha-101 of same layout.
Dimensions: span 73 ft 9¾ in (22·5 m); length 52 ft 6 in (16·0 m); height 15 ft 11 in (4·85 m).
Weights: empty (I) 10,341 lb (4691 kg); (II) 13,382 lb (6070 kg); maximum loaded (I) 16,517 lb (7492 kg); (II) 21,395 lb (9710 kg).
Performance: maximum speed (I) 268 mph (432 km/h); (II) 297 mph (478 km/h); initial climb (I) 1,150 ft (350 m)/min; (II) 1,640 ft (500 m)/min; service ceiling (I) 28,220 ft (8600 m); (II) 32,800 ft (10,000 m); range with full bomb load (I) 1,678 miles (2700 km); (II) 1,370 miles (2200 km).
Armament: see text for defensive armament; internal bomb bay in fuselage for load of (I) 1,653 lb (750 kg) or (II) 2,205 lb (1000 kg).
History: first flight November 1936; service delivery 1937; first flight (Ki-21-II) mid-1940; final delivery September 1944.

In 1936 the Imperial Japanese Army issued a challenging specification for a new heavy bomber, demanding a crew of at least four, an endurance of five hours, a bomb load of 750 kg and speed of 400 km/h. Mitsubishi won over the Nakajima Ki-19 and built five prototypes powered by the company's own A.14 (Kinsei Ha-6) engine. The fields of fire of the three manually aimed 7·7 mm machine guns were inadequate and the Army also requested a change to the Ha-5 engine. With various modifications it was accepted as the Type 97 (also called OB-97, omoshi bakudanki meaning heavy bomber) and put into production not only by Mitsubishi but also, in 1938, by Nakajima. It rapidly became the premier Japanese Army heavy bomber and served throughout the "Chinese incident", the operational results being efficiently fed back to the procurement machine and the manufacturer. This led to the defensive armament being increased to five guns, one remotely controlled in the extreme tail, the crew being increased to seven. The bomb bay was enlarged, the flaps were increased in size and crew armour was dramatically augmented. The result was the Ki-21-Ib. Increase in fuel capacity and addition of a sixth (beam) gun resulted in the -Ic variant. In 1939 work began on the much more powerful -II, with increased-span tailplane. Several hundred of both versions were in use in December 1941 and they were met on all fronts in the Pacific war (being fairly easy meat for Hurricanes in Burma). Code-named "Sally" they faded from front-line service in 1943, though the -IIb with "glasshouse" replaced by a dorsal turret (one 12·7 mm) improved defence when it entered service in 1942. Total production was 2,064 (351 by Nakajima), plus 500 transport versions (called MC-20, Ki-57 and "Topsy").

Mitsubishi A5M

A5M1 to A5M4
Type: single-seat carrier-based fighter.
Engine: one Nakajima Kotobuki (Jupiter) nine-cylinder radial; (1) 585 hp 2-Kai-I; (2) 610 hp 2-Kai-3; (4) 710 hp Kotobuki 41 or (A5M4 Model 34) 3-Kai.
Dimensions: span (2) 35 ft 6 in, (4) 36 ft 1 in (11·0 m); length (2) 25 ft 7 in; (4) 24 ft 9½ in (7·55 m); height 10 ft 6 in (3·2 m).
Weights: empty (2, typical) 2,400 lb (1090 kg); (4) 2,681 lb (1216 kg); maximum loaded (2) 3,545 lb (1608 kg); (4) 3,763 lb (1708 kg).
Performance: maximum speed (2) 265 mph (426 km/h); (4) 273 mph (440 km/h); initial climb (2) 2,215 ft (675 m)/min; (4) 2,790 ft (850 m)/min; service ceiling (typical, all) 32,800 ft (10,000 m); range (2) 460 miles (740 km); (4, auxiliary tank) 746 miles (1200 km).
Armament: (all) two 7·7 mm Type 89 machine guns firing on each side of upper cylinder of engine; racks for two 66 lb (30 kg) bombs under outer wings.
History: first flight 4 February 1935; service delivery 1936; final delivery December 1939.

One of the neatest little warplanes of its day, the A5M was the chief fighter of the Imperial Japanese Navy throughout the Sino-Japanese war and was numerically the most important at the time of Pearl Harbor. It was built to meet a 1934 specification calling for a speed of 218 mph and ability to reach 16,400 ft in 6½ minutes, and beat these figures by a wide margin. Within days of first flight at Kagamigahara the Ka-14 prototype exceeded 279 mph and reached 16,400 ft in

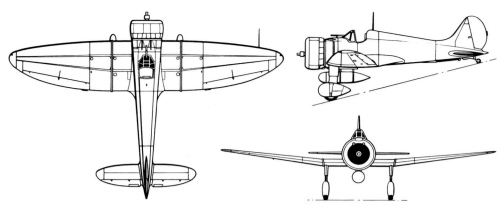

Mitsubishi A5M4

5 min 54 sec, which the Japanese considered "far above the world level at that time". It was the Navy's first monoplane fighter, and one of the first all-metal stressed-skin machines built in Japan. The production A5M1, called Type 96 or S-96 and later given the Allied code name "Claude", abandoned the prototype's inverted-gull wing, originally chosen to try to improve pilot view, and also switched to a direct-drive engine. The elliptical wing had split flaps, manoeuvrability was superb and from their first combat mission on 18 September 1937, with the 2nd Combined Air Flotilla based at Shanghai, they acquitted themselves very well. During the conflict with the Soviet Union

along the Manchukuo-Mongolian border throughout 1939 the A5M proved the biggest menace to the Russian aircraft, having earlier, on 2 December 1937, destroyed no fewer than ten I-16Bs of the Chinese in one dogfight over Nanking. Such results completely overcame the Naval pilots' earlier distrust of so speedy a monoplane and when the final A5M4 model entered service it was very popular. Mitsubishi built "about 800" (one source states 782), while Kyushu Aircraft and the Sasebo naval dockyard made 200 more. The final version was the A5M4-K dual trainer produced by conversion of fighters in 1941.

Mitsubishi A6M Zero-Sen

A6M1 to A6M8c and Nakajima A6M2-N
Type: single-seat carrier-based fighter; (A6M2-N) float seaplane.
Engine: (A6M1) one 780 hp Mitsubishi MK2 Zuisei 13 14-cylinder two-row radial; (M2) 925 hp Nakajima NK1C Sakae 12 of same layout; (M3) 1,130 hp Sakae 21; (M5) as M3 with individual exhaust stacks; (M6c) Sakae 31 with same rated power but water/methanol boost to 1,210 hp for emergency; (M8c) 1,560 hp Mitsubishi Kinsei 62 of same layout.
Dimensions: span (1, 2) 39 ft 4½ in (12·0 m); (remainder) 36 ft 1 in (11·0 m); length (all landplanes) 29 ft 9 in (9·06 m); (A6M2-N) 33 ft 2¾ in (10·13 m); height (1,2) 9 ft 7 in (2·92 m); (all later landplanes) 9 ft 8 in (2·98 m); (A6M2-N) 14 ft 1¼ in (4·3 m).
Weights: empty (2) 3,704 lb (1680 kg); (3) 3,984 lb (1807 kg); (5) typically 3,920 lb (1778 kg); (6c) 4,175 lb (1894 kg); (8c) 4,740 lb (2150 kg); (A6M2-N) 3,968 lb (1800 kg); maximum loaded (2) 5,313 lb (2410 kg); (3) 5,828 lb (2644 kg); (5) 6,050 lb (2733 kg; 2952 kg as overload); (6c) as 5c; (8c) 6,944 lb (3149 kg); (A6M2-N) 5,423 lb (2460 kg).
Performance: maximum speed (2) 316 mph (509 km/h); (3) 336 mph (541 km/h); (5c, 6c) 354 mph (570 km/h); (8c) 360 mph (580 km/h); (A6M2-N) 273 mph (440 km/h); initial climb (1, 2, 3) 4,500 ft (1370 m)/min; (5, 6c) 3,150 ft (960 m)/min; (2-N) not known; service ceiling (1, 2) 33,790 ft (10,300 m); (3) 36,250 ft (11,050 m); (5c, 6c) 37,500 ft (11,500 m); (8c) 39,370 ft (12,000 m); (A6M2-N) 32,800 ft (10,000 m); range with drop tank (2) 1,940 miles (3110 km); (5) 1,200 miles (1920 km).
Armament: (1, 2, 3 and 2-N) two 20 mm Type 99 cannon each with 60-round drum fixed in outer wings, two 7·7 mm Type 97 machine guns each with 500 rounds above front fuselage, and wing racks for two 66 lb (30 kg) bombs; (5a) two 20 mm Type 99 Mk 4 with belt of 85 rounds per gun, two 7·7 mm in fuselage and wing racks for two 132 lb (60 kg) bombs; (5b) as 5a but one 7·7 mm replaced by 12·7 mm; (5c and all later versions) two 20 mm Type 99 Mk 4 and two 13·2 mm in wings, one 13·2 mm (optional) in fuselage, plus wing racks for two 60 kg.
History: first flight 1 April 1939; service delivery (A6M1) late July 1940; first flight (A6M2-N) December 1941; (A6M5) August 1943; (A6M2-K) January 1942.

The most famous of all Japanese combat aircraft possessed the unique distinction of being the first carrier-based fighter ever to outperform corresponding land-based machines; it was also a singularly unpleasant shock to US and British staff which had apparently never studied the behaviour of this fighter in China or even discovered its existence. It was designed by Mitsubishi to meet the severe demands of the 1937 Navy carrier-based fighter specification, seeking a successor to the A5M. Demands included a speed of 500 km/h (311 mph) and armament of two cannon and two machine guns. Under team leader Jiro Horikoshi the new fighter took shape as a clean,

Mitsubishi A6M2 (Hiryu fighter group, Pearl Harbor)

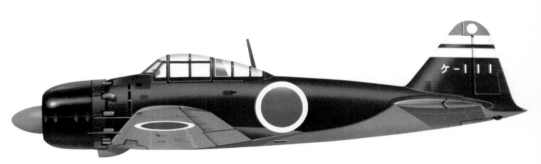

Mitsubishi A6M5 (Genzan Air Corps, Imperial Navy, at Wonsan, Korea)

efficient but lightly built aircraft with outstanding manoeuvrability. With a more powerful engine it was accepted for production as the A6M2, though as it was put into production in 1940, the Japanese year 5700, it became popularly the Zero-Sen (Type 00 fighter), and to millions of its enemies was simply the "Zero" (though the official Allied code name was "Zeke"). Before official trials were completed two squadrons with 15 aircraft were sent to China in July 1940 for trials under operational conditions. They eliminated all opposition, as forcefully reported to Washington by Gen Claire Chennault, commander of the Flying Tigers volunteer force (his warning was obviously filed before being read). More than 400 had been delivered by the time the A6M2 and clipped-wing M3 appeared at Pearl Harbor. During the subsequent year it seemed that thousands of these fighters were in use, their unrivalled manoeuvrability being matched by unparalleled range with a small engine, 156 gal internal fuel and drop tanks. So completely did the A6M sweep away Allied air power that the Japanese

nation came to believe it was invincible. After the Battle of Midway the Allies slowly gained the ascendancy, and the A6M found itself outclassed by the F4U and F6F. Mitsubishi urgently tried to devise improved versions and the A6M5 was built in quantities far greater than any other Japanese combat aircraft. Improvements were mainly small and the combat-boosted Sakae 31 engine did not appear until the end of 1944. Only a few of the much more powerful A6M8c type were produced, the main reason for this change of engine being destruction of the Nakajima factory. The final model was the A6M7 Kamikaze version, though hundreds of Zeros of many sub-types were converted for suicide attacks. Total production amounted to 10,937, of which 6,217 were built by Nakajima which also designed and built 327 of the attractive A6M2-N single-float seaplane fighter version (code name "Rufe") which operated throughout the Pacific war. The A6M2-K was one of several dual trainer versions.

Mitsubishi Ki-30

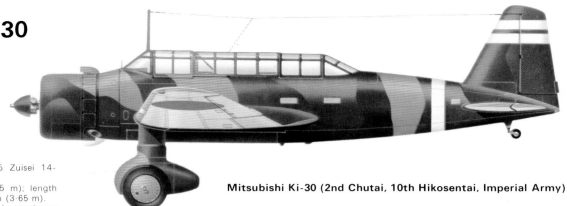

Mitsubishi Ki-30 (2nd Chutai, 10th Hikosentai, Imperial Army)

K-30

Type: two-seat light bomber.

Engine: one 950 hp Mitsubishi Ha-5 Zuisei 14-cylinder two-row radial.

Dimensions: span 47 ft 8¾ in (14·55 m); length 33 ft 11 in (10·34 m); height 11 ft 11¾ in (3·65 m).

Weights: empty 4,915 lb (2230 kg); maximum loaded 7,324 lb (3322 kg).

Performance: maximum speed 263 mph (423 km/h); initial climb 1,640 ft (500 m)/min; service ceiling 28,117 ft (8570 m); range (bomb load not stated) 1,056 miles (1700 km).

Armament: one 7·7 mm Type 89 machine gun fixed in wing (sometimes both wings) and one manually aimed from rear cockpit; internal bomb bay for three 220 lb (100 kg) or equivalent bomb load.

History: first flight February 1937; service delivery October 1938; final delivery 1941.

With the Ki-32, Ki-27 fighter and Ki-21 heavy bomber, the Ki-30 was one of the important new stressed-skin monoplanes ordered by the Imperial Army under its modernisation plan of 1935. It was the first in Japan to have a modern two-row engine, as well as internal bomb bay, flaps and constant-speed propeller. It was notably smaller than the otherwise similar Fairey Battle produced in Britain. Unlike the British bomber the bomb bay was in the fuselage, resulting in a mid wing and long landing gear (which was fixed). The pilot and observer/bomb aimer had a good view but were unable to communicate except by speaking tube. The Ki-30 was in service in numbers in time to be one of the major types in the Sino-Japanese war. In 1942 surviving aircraft played a large part in the advance to the Philippines, but then swiftly withdrew from first-line operations. Mitsubishi built 638 at Nagoya and 68 were completed at the Tachikawa Army Air Arsenal. In conformity with the Allied system of code-naming bombers after girls, the Ki-30 was dubbed "Ann". It was the ultimate development of the Karigane family of high-performance monoplanes.

Mitsubishi G4M

Mitsubishi G4M2 (763rd Air Corps, Imperial Navy)

G4M1 to G4M3c and G6M

Type: land-based naval torpedo bomber and missile carrier.

Engines: (G4M1) two 1,530 hp Mitsubishi Kasei 11 14-cylinder two-row radials; (subsequent versions) two Kasei 22 rated at 1,850 hp with water/methanol injection.

Dimensions: span 81 ft 7¾ in (24·89 m); length (1) 65 ft 6¼ in; (later versions) 64 ft 4¾ in (19·63 m); height (1) 16 ft 1 in; (later versions) 13 ft 5⅔ in (4·11 m).

Weights: empty (1) 14,860 lb (6741 kg); (2) 17,623 lb (7994 kg); (3) 18,500 lb (8391 kg); loaded (1) 20,944 lb (9500 kg); (2, 3) 27,550 lb (12,500 kg); max overload (1) 28,350 lb (12,860 kg); (2, 3) 33,070 lb (15,000 kg).

Performance: maximum speed (1) 265 mph (428 km/h); (2) 271 mph (437 km/h); (3) 283 mph (455 km/h); initial climb (1) 1,800 ft (550 m)/min; (2, 3) 1,380 ft (420 m)/min; service ceiling (all) about 30,000 ft (9144 m); range (with bombs at overload weight) (1) 3,132 miles (5040 km); (2) 2,982 miles (4800 km); (3) 2,262 miles (3640 km).

Armament: (1) three manually aimed 7·7 mm in nose, dorsal and ventral positions and 20 mm manually aimed in tail; internal bomb load of 2,205 lb (1000 kg) or 1,764 lb (800 kg) torpedo externally; (2) as before but electric dorsal turret (one 7·7 mm) and revised tail position with increased arc of fire; (2e, and, retroactively, many earlier G4M2) one 7·7 mm in nose, one 20 mm in dorsal turret and manual 20 mm in tail and two beam windows. (G4M2e) adapted to carry Oka piloted missile (p. 228).

History: first flight October 1939; service delivery April 1941; first flight (G4M2) November 1942.

Designed to an incredibly difficult 1938 Navy specification, the G4M family (Allied name, "Betty") was the Imperial Japanese Navy's premier heavy bomber in World War II; yet the insistence on the great range of 2,000 nautical miles (3706 km) with full bomb load made the saving of weight take priority over defence and the aircraft was highly vulnerable and not very popular. The wing was of the same Mitsubishi 118 section as the Zero-Sen and boldly designed as an integral fuel tank to accommodate no less than 5,000 litres (1,100 gal). The company kept recommending four engines and being overruled by the Navy, which, during the early flight-test stage, wasted more than a year, and 30 aircraft, in trying to make the design into the G6M bomber escort with crew of ten and 19 guns. Eventually the G4M1 was readied for service as a bomber and flew its first missions in South East China in May 1941. More than 250 operated in the Philippines and Malayan campaigns, but after the Solomons battle in August 1942 it began to be apparent that, once intercepted and hit, the unprotected bomber went up like a torch (hence the Allied nickname "one-shot lighter"). Total production reached the exceptional quantity of 2,479, most of them in the many sub-types of G4M2 with increased fuel capacity and power. Finally the trend of development was reversed with the G4M3 series with full protection and only 968 gal fuel.

Mitsubishi F1M

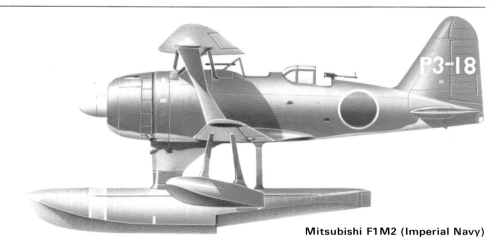

Mitsubishi F1M2 (Imperial Navy)

F1M1, F1M2

Type: design role, reconnaissance (but see text).

Engine: (1) one 820 hp Nakajima Hikari 1 nine-cylinder radial; (2) one 875 hp Mitsubishi Zuisei 13 14-cylinder two-row radial.

Dimensions: span 36 ft 1 in (11·0 m); length 31 ft 2 in (9·5 m); height 13 ft 1½ in (4·0 m).

Weights: (2) empty 4,330 lb (1964 kg); normal loaded 5,620 lb (2550 kg); maximum overload 6,296 lb (2856 kg).

Performance: maximum speed 230 mph (370 km/h); initial climb 1,969 ft (600 m)/min; service ceiling 30,970 ft (9440 m); range (normal weight) 276 miles (445 km), (overload) 670 miles (1070 km).

Armament: two 7·7 mm Type 89 fixed above engine, one manually aimed from rear cockpit; underwing racks for two 132 lb (60 kg) bombs.

History: first flight (F1M1 prototype) June 1936; (production F1M2) October 1939; service delivery 1941; final delivery March 1944.

At first glance a small observation biplane for catapulting from surface vessels might seem hardly to rank as much of a warplane, but in fact the F1M served throughout World War II in such roles as area-defence fighter, bomber, convoy escort, anti-submarine attack aircraft, ocean patrol, rescue and even transport. It was in 1934 that the Imperial Japanese Navy issued a requirement for a new shipboard reconnaissance machine to succeed the Nakajima E8N (code name "Dave"). Mitsubishi's design team, led by Eitaro Sano, won over Aichi and Kawanishi rivals (using "Dave"-type floats) and notable features of the F1M1 were extreme attention to detail cleanliness and exceptional manoeuvrability at all speeds. After protracted development to improve stability, with the elliptical wings made straight-tapered and the tail enlarged, the floats enlarged and the engine changed, the F1M2 version went into production. Altogether 524 were delivered, including about 180 made at the Navy arsenal at Sasebo. For a while the Allies, who codenamed it "Pete", thought the F1M a Sasebo design. "Petes" were active in dogfights in the Aleutians, Solomons and many other campaigns; almost the only thing they proved incapable of doing effectively was deliver 551 lb bombs.

Mitsubishi J2M Raiden

J2M1 to J2M7

Type: single-seat Navy land-based interceptor.
Engine: most versions, one 1,820 hp Mitsubishi MK4R-A Kasei 23a 14-cylinder two-row radial; (J2M5) 1,820 hp MK4U-A Kasei 26a.
Dimensions: span 35 ft 5¼ in (10.8 m); length (most) 31 ft 9¾ in (9.70 m); (J2M5) 32 ft 7¾ in (9.95 m); height (most) 12 ft 6 in (3.81 m); (J2M5) 12 ft 11¼ in (3.94 m).
Weights: empty (2) 5,572 lb (2527 kg); (3) 5,675 lb (2574 kg); (5) 6,259 lb (2839 kg); normal loaded (2) 7,275 lb (3300 kg); (3) 7,573 lb (3435 kg); (5) 7,676 lb (3482 kg); max overload (2, 3) 8,700 lb (3946 kg).
Performance: maximum speed (2) 371 mph (596 km/h); (3) 380 mph (612 km/h); (5) 382 mph (615 km/h); initial climb (2, 3) 3,610 ft (1100 m)/min; (5) 3,030 ft (925 m)/min; range (2, 3 at normal gross) 655 miles (1055 km); (2, 3 overload) 1,580 miles (2520 km); (5, normal gross with 30 min reserve) 345 miles (555 km).
Armament: see text.
History: first flight (prototype) 20 March 1942; service delivery (J2M2) December 1943; first flight (J2M5) May 1944.

Though designed by a team led by the legendary Jiro

Horikoshi, creator of the Zero-Sen, this utterly different little interceptor did little to enhance reputations, though there was nothing fundamentally faulty in its conception. It broke totally new ground, partly in being an interceptor for the Navy (previously the preserve of the Army) and partly in the reversal of design parameters. Instead of concentrating on combat manoeuvrability at all costs the J1M was designed solely for speed and fast climb. Manoeuvrability and even handling took second place. Unusual features in the basic design included a tiny laminar-flow wing fitted with combat flaps, a finely streamlined engine with propeller extension shaft and fan cooling, a very shallow enclosed canopy and a surprising number of forged parts in the stressed-skin airframe. Powered by a 1,460 hp Kasei, the prototype Mitsubishi M-20, named Raiden (Thunderbolt), gave a great deal of trouble and was almost redesigned to produce the

J2M2 with different engine, much deeper canopy, multi-stack exhaust and new four-blade propeller. Even then the Raiden suffered endless snags and crashes, but eventually 155 J2M2 were delivered with two 20 mm Type 99 and two 7.7 mm above the fuselage. Production then switched to the J2M3 with machine guns removed and the wing fitted with two Type 99 and two fast-firing Type 99-II. The J2M3a had four Type 99-II. Fitted with bulged canopy these models became the J2M6 and 6a. A few high-flying J2M4 turbocharged versions were built, with six cannon, the two added guns being in the top fuselage decking. Best of all was the J2M5 with only two (wing) cannon but a far better engine, and it proved formidable against high-flying B-29s. After VJ-day, when only 480 of all models had been built (one month's planned output!), the Allies (who called this fighter "Jack") spoke in glowing terms of its performance and handling.

Mitsubishi J2M3 (302nd Air Corps, Imperial Navy)

Mitsubishi Ki-46

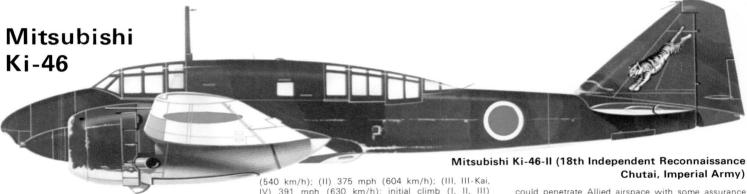

Mitsubishi Ki-46-II (18th Independent Reconnaissance Chutai, Imperial Army)

Type 100 Models 1-4 (Ki-46-I to Ki-46-IVb)

Type: strategic reconnaissance (Ki-46-III-Kai, night fighter).
Engines: (I) two 870 hp Mitsubishi Ha-26-I 14-cylinder two-row radials; (II) two 1,080 hp Mitsubishi Ha-102 of same layout; (III) two 1,500 hp Mitsubishi Ha-112-II of same layout; (IV) Ha-112-IIRu, same rated power but turbocharged.
Dimensions: span 48 ft 2¾ in (14.7 m); length (all except III-Kai) 36 ft 1in (11.0 m); (III-Kai) 37 ft 8 in (11.47 m); height 12 ft 8¾ in (3.88 m).
Weights: empty (I) 7,450 lb (3379 kg); (II) 7,193 lb (3263 kg); (III) 8,446 lb (3831 kg); (IV) 8,840 lb (4010 kg); loaded (no overload permitted) (I) 10,630 lb (4822 kg); (II) 11,133 lb (5050 kg); (III) 12,620 lb (5724 kg); (IV) 13,007 lb (5900 kg); (III-Kai) 13,730 lb (6227 kg).
Performance: maximum speed (I) 336 mph

(540 km/h); (II) 375 mph (604 km/h); (III, III-Kai, IV) 391 mph (630 km/h); initial climb (I, II, III) about 1,970 ft (600 m)/min; (IV) 2,625 ft (800 m)/min; service ceiling (I, II, III) 34,500–36,000 ft (10,500–11,000 m); (IV) 38,000 ft (11,500 m); range (I) 1,305 miles (2100 km); (II) 1,490 miles (2400 km); (III) 2,485 miles (4000 km); (III-Kai) 1,243 miles (2000 km); (IV) not known, but at least 4000 km.
Armament: (I, II) one 7.7 mm manually aimed from rear cockpit; other types, none, except III-Kai, two 20 mm Ho-5 cannon fixed in nose firing ahead and 37 mm Ho-203 firing at elevation of 30° from top of fuselage.
History: first flight November 1939; (production II) March 1941; (III) December 1942; (III-Kai conversion) about September 1944.

One of the most trouble-free and popular aircraft of the whole Pacific war, the Ki-46 "Shitei" (reconnaissance for HQ), code-named "Dinah" by the Allies, was one of only very few Japanese aircraft that

could penetrate Allied airspace with some assurance it would survive. It was also almost the only machine with the proven ability to operate at the flight levels of the B-29. In the first year of its use, which extended to every part of the Japanese war throughout the Pacific and China, much trouble was experienced from sparking-plug erosion and crew anoxia, both rectified by improved design and greater oxygen storage. Allied radar forced Ki-46 to fly even faster and higher, leading to the almost perfectly streamlined Ki-46-III. These entered service in 1943, in which year many earlier versions were converted to Ki-46-II-Kai dual conversion trainers. Total production amounted to 1,742, all made by Mitsubishi at Nagoya and Toyama. Only four prototypes were finished of the turbocharged IVa, but many III models were hastily converted by the Army Tachikawa base into III-Kai night fighters capable of intercepting B-29s. No radar was carried. At VJ-day Mitsubishi was trying to produce IIIc and IVb fighters and the IIIb ground-attack version.

Mitsubishi Ki-67 Hiryu

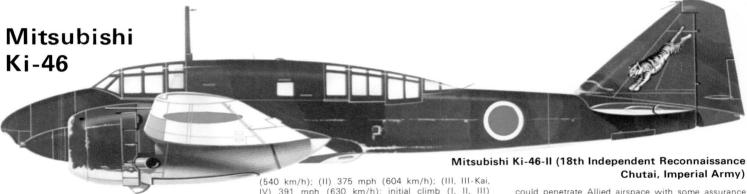

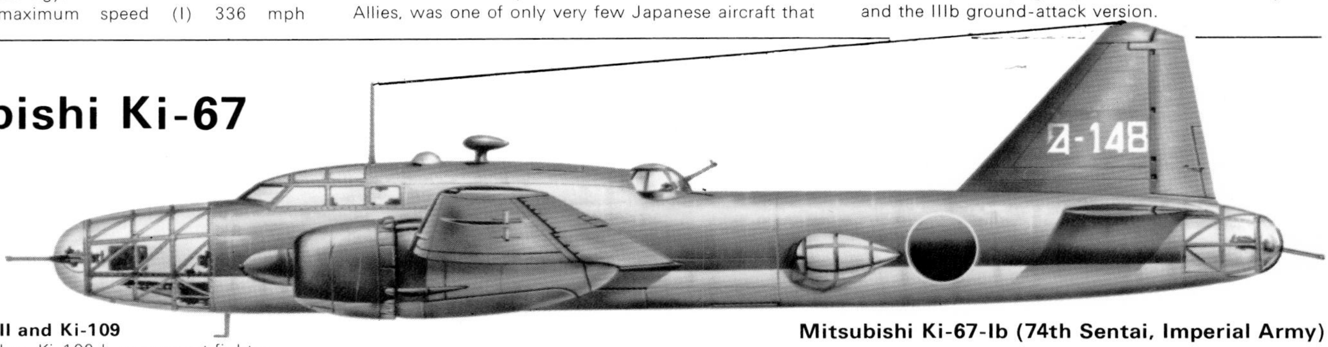

Mitsubishi Ki-67-Ib (74th Sentai, Imperial Army)

Ki-67-Ia, Ib and II and Ki-109

Type: heavy bomber; Ki-109 heavy escort fighter.
Engines: two 1,900 hp Mitsubishi Ha-104 18-cylinder two-row radials.
Dimensions: span 73 ft 9¾ in (22.5 m); length 61 ft 4¼ in (18.7 m); height 18 ft 4½ in (5.60 m).
Weights: (Ib) empty 19,068 lb (8649 kg); loaded 30,346 lb (13,765 kg).
Performance: (Ib) maximum speed 334 mph (537 km/h); initial climb 1,476 ft (450 m)/min; service ceiling 31,070 ft (9470 m); range with full bomb load 621 miles (1000 km) plus 2 hr reserve, also reported as total range 1,740 miles (2800 km).
Armament: standard on Ia, Ib, one 20 mm Ho-5 in electric dorsal turret and single 12.7 mm Type 1 manually aimed from nose, tail and two beam positions; internal bomb load 1,764 lb (800 kg).
History: first flight "beginning of 1943"; service delivery April 1944; first flight (Ki-109) August 1944.

Designed by a team led by Dr Hisanojo Ozawa to meet a February 1941 specification, this Army bomber not only met the demand for much higher speed but also proved to have the manoeuvrability of a fighter. It also lacked nothing in armour and fuel-tank protection, and was probably the best all-round bomber produced in Japan during World War II. With a crew of six/eight, it was often looped and shown to have excellent turning power, better than that of several Japanese fighters. Indeed the Ki-69 escort fighter version was developed in parallel with the bomber during 1942 but had to be shelved as delays to the bomber were becoming serious. These delays were due to inefficiency, material shortage and continual changes requested by the customer. By 1944 only 15 (all different) had been built, but production was then allowed to begin in earnest and by VJ-day the creditable total of 727 had

been delivered, 606 by Mitsubishi and the rest by Kawasaki, Nippon Hikoki and (one only) the Tachikawa arsenal. At first the Ki-67 Hiryu (Flying Dragon) was used as a torpedo bomber in the Philippine Sea battle, receiving the Allied name "Peggy". Later it operated against Iwo Jima, the Marianas and Okinawa and in the defence of Japan. There were only two versions used, the Ib having bulged waist blisters. Of many projected versions, of which the Ki-67-II with 2,500 hp Ha-214 engines marked the biggest advance, only the Ki-109 reached the service trials stage. Armed with a 75 mm gun with 15 hand-loaded rounds, plus a 12.7 mm in the tail, this was meant to have 2,000 hp turbocharged Ha-104 engines but none were available. With ordinary Ha-104s the Ki-109 could not get up to B-29 altitude!

Mitsubishi T-2

XT-2, T-2A and FST-2-Kai

Type: (T-2A) two-seat supersonic trainer; (FST-2) single-seat close-support fighter-bomber.

Engines: two Ishikawajima-Harima TF40-801A (licence-built Rolls-Royce/Turboméca Adour 102) two-shaft augmented turbofans with maximum rating of 7,140 lb (3238 kg); (FST-2) may later have more powerful version.

Dimensions: span 25 ft 10 in (7·87 m); length 58 ft 7 in (17·86 m); height (T-2) 14 ft 7 in (4·445 m), (FST-2) 14 ft 9 in.

Weights: empty (T-2) 13,668 lb (6200 kg); (FST-2) 14,330 lb (6500 kg); loaded (T-2, clean) 21,274 lb (9650 kg); (T-2 maximum) 24,750 lb (11,200 kg); (FST-2 maximum) 30,200 lb (13,700 kg).

Performance: maximum speed (at clean gross weight) 1,056 mph (1700 km/h, Mach 1·6); initial climb 19,680 ft (6000 m)/min; service ceiling 50,025 ft (15,250 m); range (T-2 with external tanks) 1,785 miles (2870 km); (FST-2 with eight 500 lb bombs) 700 miles (1126 km).

Armament: one 20 mm M-61 multi-barrel gun under left side of cockpit floor; pylon hardpoints under centre-line and inboard and outboard on wings, with light stores attachments at tips. Total weapon load (T-2) normally 2,000 lb (907 kg); (FST-2) 6,000 lb (2722 kg) comprising 12 500 lb bombs, eight 500 lb plus two tanks of 183 gal, or two 1,300 lb (590 kg) ASM-1 anti-ship missiles, and four Sidewinders.

History: first flight (XT-2) 20 July 1971; (T-2A) January 1975; (FST-2) June 1975; service delivery (T-2A) March 1975.

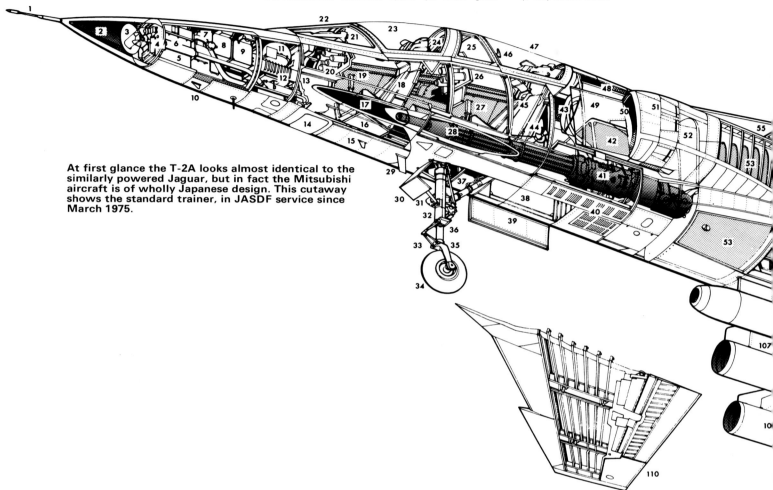

At first glance the T-2A looks almost identical to the similarly powered Jaguar, but in fact the Mitsubishi aircraft is of wholly Japanese design. This cutaway shows the standard trainer, in JASDF service since March 1975.

Mitsubishi T-2 cutaway drawing key

1 Pitot probe
2 Nose cone
3 Radar dish scanner
4 Mounting frame/bulkhead
5 Radar
6 Attitude/heading reference system
7 Toyo Communication J/APX-100 SIF/IFF
8 Nippon Electric J/ARN-53 TACAN
9 Mitsubishi Electric J/ARC-51 UHF
10 TACAN aerial
11 Liquid-oxygen converter
12 Cooling louvres
13 Rudder pedals
14 UHF/DF aerial
15 SIF/IFF aerial
16 Seat mounting frame
17 Gun trough
18 Weber ES-7J zero-zero ejection seat
19 Control column
20 Instrument panel
21 Optical sight
22 Windscreen
23 Rearward-hinged jettisonable forward canopy
24 Canopy actuating mechanism
25 Mid-section glazing
26 Instrument panel
27 Control column
28 Gun forward support
29 UHF aerial
30 Nosewheel doors
31 Door actuating member
32 Nosewheel leg
33 Torsion links
34 Nosewheel
35 Single-fork axle
36 Shock absorber
37 Retraction strut
38 Nosewheel bay
39 Pre-closing nosewheel door
40 Cooling louvres
41 M-61A-1 Vulcan multi-barrel 20mm cannon (combat training version only)
42 No 1 fuselage tank
43 Ammunition feed
44 Control quadrant
45 Weber ES-7J zero-zero ejection seat
46 Canopy release lever
47 Rearward-hinged jettisonable rear canopy
48 Ammunition drum (750 rounds)
49 Intake splitter plate
50 Fixed-geometry intake
51 Supplementary blow-in intake doors
52 Fuselage frame
53 No 2 fuselage tank
54 No 3 fuselage tank
55 Wing root fillet
56 Leading-edge flap actuator
57 Honeycomb-structure leading-edge inboard flap (electrically actuated)
58 Leading-edge dog-tooth
59 Port wingtip (AAM attachment)
60 Honeycomb trailing-edge structure
61 Electrically-actuated flap
62 Stores pylons
63 Practice rocket pods (19 x 2·75in)
64 Wing/fuselage pick-up points
65 Wing multi-spar torsion box
66 No 4 fuselage tank
67 Port mainwheel door
68 No 5 fuselage tank
69 Auxiliary intake
70 No 6 fuselage tank
71 7,070 lb (3,206 kg) thrust Ishikawajima-Harima TF40-IHI-801A (Adour) turbofans
72 No 7 fuselage tank
73 Fuel valve
74 Fin structure
75 Formation light
76 Fuel vent pipe
77 UHF aerial
78 Rear navigation light
79 Vent outlet
80 Hydraulically-operated rudder
81 Rudder actuator
82 Control runs
83 Rolling (differential) tailplane actuator
84 Tailplane pivot
85 Port tailplane
86 Upward-hinged tailcone
87 Braking parachute housing
88 Starboard tailplane
89 Arrester hook
90 Heat shield
91 Variable nozzle
92 Nozzle actuators
93 Afterburner
94 Engine starter
95 Accessories
96 Ventral fins
97 Air brakes (extended)
98 Port mainwheel
99 Shock absorbers (oleo-pneumatic)
100 Axle forks
101 Main undercarriage leg
102 Landing lights
103 Retraction struts
104 Mainwheel bay (pre-closing doors)
105 Centreline pylon
106 Weapons (reconnaissance pod
107 Stores pylons
108 Practice rocket pods (19 x 2·75in)
109 Starboard mainwheel
110 Starboard wing structure

Japan's first post-war military aircraft was the Fuji T-1 tandem-seat intermediate trainer, looking like an F-86 Sabre and powered by a licence-built Bristol Orpheus. First flown in 1958, 42 were delivered as the T-1A, followed by 22 T-1B with the Japanese J3 engine. To replace the T-1 and other trainers such as the T-33 a design team led by Dr Kenji Ikeda designed the T-2, Japan's first supersonic aircraft, using the Anglo-French Jaguar as a basis. After flight trials had shown the validity of the design a single-seat version, the FST-2-Kai, was ordered to replace the F-86 as a close-support fighter. The two aircraft are almost identical apart from replacement of the rear cockpit by equipment and addition of a tubular passive warning radar aerial (ECM) along the top of the fin. By mid-1975 orders had been placed for 46 T-2A trainers and the first 4th Air Wing unit had formed at Matsushima air base. A further 17 were expected to be bought in 1976 to complete the programme. The first 18 FST-2 fighters had also been bought, with four flown in 1975 and deliveries starting in 1976. Total FST-2 procurement is to be 68, all delivered by the end of 1979. The FST-2 has a Ferranti inertial nav/attack system which, with other equipment, replaces the raised rear instructor seat of the T-2A.

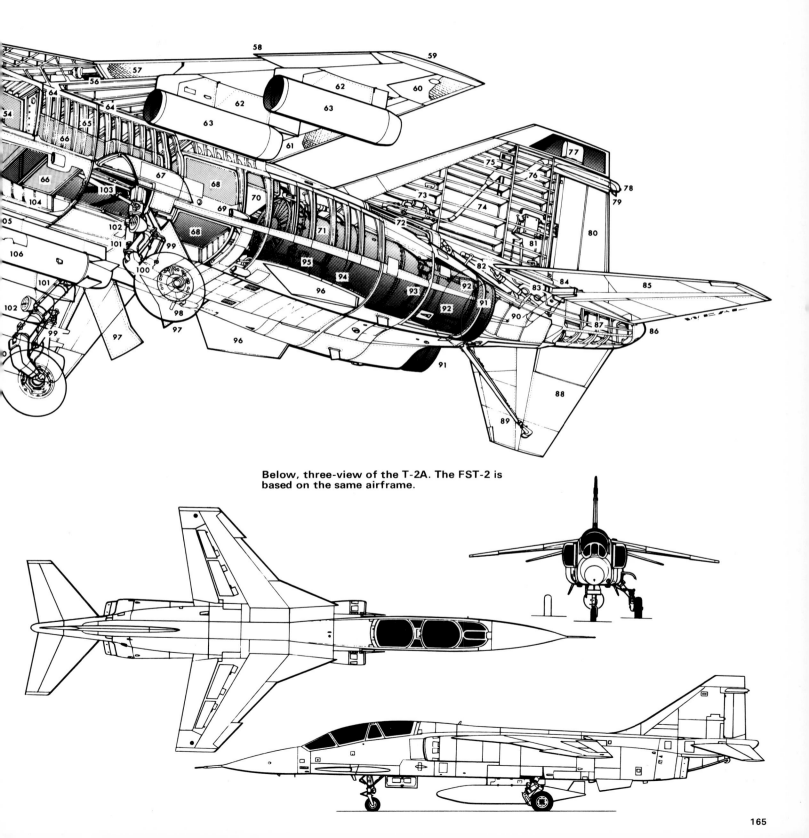

Below, three-view of the T-2A. The FST-2 is based on the same airframe.

Morane-Saulnier L

Type L (MS.3), LA (MS.4) and P (MS.21 and 26)
Type: two-seat scout (reconnaissance) with ability to fire gun and drop bombs.
Engine: one nine-cylinder rotary; (MS.3, 4) 80 hp Gnome or Le Rhône 9C; (MS.21) 110 hp Le Rhône 9J; (MS.26) 110 hp Le Rhône 9Jb.
Dimensions: span 33 ft 9½ in (10·3 m); length 20 ft 9 in (6·32 m); height 10 ft 4 in (3·15 m).
Weights: empty 1,080 lb (490 kg); maximum loaded 1,499 lb (680 kg).
Performance: maximum speed (MS.3) 71½ mph (115 km/h); initial climb 656 ft (200 m)/min; service ceiling 13,123 ft (4000 m); range 280 miles (450 km).
Armament: usually none, but see text.
History: first flight 1913; service delivery, early 1914; (Type LA) 1914; (Type P) 1916.

With the B.E.2 series from Farnborough, the Morane scouts can be regarded as the world's first military aircraft (Bleriot and other types were actually used in military operations as early as 1911, but they were merely civil flying machines flown by military pilots). The Morane Type L, called MS.3 by the Aviation Militaire, set the pattern for this company's aircraft for the next 22 years by being a parasol monoplane, the wing being mounted above the fuselage. It was a primitive two-seater, with lateral control by wing-warping in the manner pioneered by the Wright Brothers. On the other hand, despite being a two-seater, it was much faster than most German machines and pilots and observers soon began to use the Morane as an offensive weapon, using cavalry carbines or even pistols. Morane's pilot, Roland Garros — who had

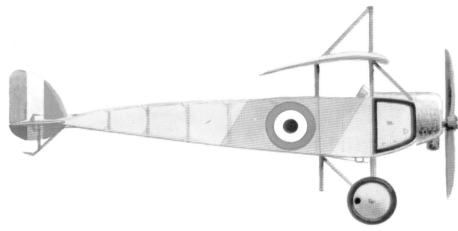

Morane-Saulnier Type L (Royal Naval Air Service, before British red/white/blue order was reversed)

become famous before the war — wished Raymond Saulnier had been able to get official support for the interrupter gear he was trying to devise to allow a machine gun to fire ahead past the rotating propeller. Instead Garros made do with steel deflector plates and in the first three weeks of 1915 shot down three enemy aircraft with an 8 mm Hotchkiss. Shot down and captured on 19 April, it was this crude lash-up (often incorrectly said to have been fitted to a Morane Type N) that inspired Fokker to produce a synchronization

gear and, hence, the terrible "Fokker Scourge". Type Ls served with the Imperial Russian Air Service and with the RNAS in the Aegean and France, Sub-Lt Warneford winning the VC for destroying the first Zeppelin by air combat, using six 25 lb (11 kg) bombs. The LA had ailerons and the P family were bigger and had proper fixed-Vickers movable-Lewis armament. Nearly 600 Type L, a few LA and 565 Type P were built.

Morane-Saulnier N

Type N (MS.5C-1) and Type AC (MS.23C-1)
Type: single-seat fighting scout.
Engine: one 80 hp Gnome or 110 hp Le Rhône 9C or 9Ja nine-cylinder rotary; Type AC, one 120 hp Le Rhône.
Dimensions: span 27 ft 2¾ in (8·30 m); (some, 27 ft 4¾ in); (AC) 32 ft 2 in; length 21 ft 11¾ in (6·70 m); (some, 22 ft 4¾ in) (AC) 22 ft 3¼ in; height 8 ft 2½ in (2·5 m); (AC) 7 ft 6½ in.
Weights: empty (typical) 816 lb (370 kg); loaded (N, typical) 1,124 lb (510 kg).
Performance: maximum speed 102½ mph (165 km/h); initial climb 820 ft (250 m)/min; service ceiling 13,123 ft (4000 m); range 140 miles (225 km).
Armament: one synchronised machine gun in top of fuselage; Aviation Militaire, 7·7 mm Vickers; RFC, 0·303 in Lewis.
History: first flight April 1914; service delivery summer 1914; (Type AC) 1916.

Popularly called "the Bullet" by the RFC, this neat little fighter was almost the only non-parasol design of Morane-Saulnier. It was built only in small numbers (49) but saw plenty of action with the RFC, Aviation Militaire and Imperial Russian Air Service. They were built without ailerons and were fast-landing machines needing plenty of skill. The big propeller spinner

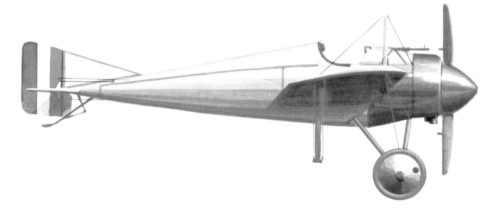

Morane-Saulnier Type N (Aviation Militaire; drawing shows bullet deflectors on propeller, as used by Garros on Type L)

sometimes caused engine overheating and by 1915 was often left off, making the "Bullet" look much less streamlined. The bigger Type AC, of which 31 were built, had rigid wing struts instead of wires. Morane-Saulnier next built the Type AI (MS.29C-1), a really

advanced parasol fighter of which 1,121 were built for many countries. They followed with a succession of parasol fighters for what had become the French Armée de l'Air.

Morane-Saulnier M.S.406

M.S.405, M.S.406C-1
Type: single-seat fighter.
Engine: one 860 hp Hispano-Suiza 12Y-31 vee-12 liquid-cooled.
Dimensions: span 34 ft 9¾ in (10·60 m); length 26 ft 9¼ in (8·16 m); height 9 ft 3¾ in (2·83 m).
Weights: (406) empty 4,189 lb (1900 kg); loaded 5,364–5,445 lb; maximum loaded 6,000 lb (2722 kg).
Performance: maximum speed 302 mph (485 km/h); initial climb 2,789 ft (850 m)/min; service ceiling 30,840 ft (9400 m); range (without external tanks) 497 miles (800 km).
Armament: one 20 mm Hispano-Suiza HS-9 or 404 cannon with drum of 60 rounds, and two 7·5 mm MAC 1934 in wings each with 300 rounds.
History: first flight (405) 8 August 1935; (production 405) 3 February 1938; (production 406) 29 January 1939; service delivery (406) 1 March 1939.

After their unbroken series of parasol monoplanes Morane-Saulnier built the M.S.405 secretly to meet a 1934 specification of the Armée de l'Air. Compared with other fighters at the start of World War II it was underpowered, lacking in performance and somewhat lacking in firepower. On the other hand its early start meant it was at least available, while other French fighters were mainly a vast collection of prototypes. Altogether 17 M.S.405 were built, most becoming

Morane-Saulnier M.S. 406C-1 (1e Escadrille, GC I/2, Nimes)

prototypes of proposed future versions and ultimately giving rise to the Swiss D-3800 series of fighters which, unlike most 405s, did not have a retractable radiator. An unusual feature was the fact that, except for the fabric-covered rear fuselage, most of the covering was Plymax (light alloy bonded to plywood). The M.S.406 was the 405 production version incorporating all the requested modifications. The production was shared out among the nationalised groups (Morane retaining only a small part of the work), with production lines at Bouguenais and Puteaux. By the time of the collapse

in June 1940 no fewer than 1,081 had been completed, despite desperate shortage of engines. In May 1940 the 406 equipped 19 of the 26 French combat-ready fighter groups. One who flew them said they were "free from vices, but too slow to catch German aircraft and too badly armed to shoot them down. Poorly protected, our own losses were high". The Vichy government fitted 32 gal drop tanks to Moranes sent to Syria to fight the RAF. Many were used by Finland, fitted with skis and often with Soviet M-105P engines of higher power (the so-called LaGG-Morane).

Myasishchev Mya-4

Mya-4 (three versions, known to West as "Bison A, B and C")

Type: (A) heavy bomber; (B) strategic reconnaissance and ECM; (C) multi-role reconnaissance bomber.

Engines: (A) four 19,180 lb (8700 kg) Mikulin AM-3D single-shaft turbojets; (B and C) four 28,660 lb (13,000 kg) D-15 engines (design bureau unknown, probably two-shaft turbojets, not turbofans).

Dimensions: (A) estimated, span 165 ft 7½ in (50·48 m); length 154 ft 10 in (47·2 m); height 46 ft (14·1 m).

Weights: estimated, empty (A) 154,000 lb (70,000 kg); (B, C) 176,400 lb (80,000 kg); maximum loaded (A) 352,740 lb (160,000 kg); (B, C) 375,000 lb (170,000 kg).

Performance: (estimated) maximum speed (all) 560 mph (900 km/h); service ceiling (A) 42,650 ft (13,000 m); (B, C) 49,200 ft (15,000 m); range (all) 6,835 miles (11,000 km) with 9,920 lb. (4500 kg) of bombs or electronic equipment.

Armament: (A) ten 23 mm NR-23 cannon in manned turret in tail and four remotely controlled turrets above and below front and rear fuselage (two guns in each turret); internal bomb bays in tandem for at least 22,050 lb (10,000 kg) stores; (B, C) six 23 mm cannon in two forward turrets and tail turret; internal bay for at least 10,000 lb (4500 kg) stores. In many versions a single 23 mm gun is fixed on the right side of the nose, firing ahead.

History: first flight, probably 1953; service delivery, probably 1955; final delivery, probably about 1958.

Mya-4 (alternatively styled M-4; version known to NATO as "Bison C")

A single example of this large aircraft took part in the 1954 May Day parade fly past over Moscow, its size being gauged from the escorting MiG fighters. It was expected to appear in large numbers, but little was heard of it for years. In fact a useful run of about 150 had been delivered, at first being used as bombers ("Bison A"). In 1959 a re-engined aircraft, called Type 201-M, set up world records by lifting a payload of 10,000 kg (22,046 lb) to 50,253 ft (15,317 m) and the formidable weight of 55,220 kg (121,480 lb) to

2000 m (6,561 ft). By this time the Mya-4 bombers were being likewise fitted with more powerful engines, and their role changed from bomber to long-range oversea reconnaissance, ECM and, in some cases, flight-refuelling tanker. All aircraft were given large fixed FR probes, the rear turrets were removed and a vast amount of special reconnaissance equipment fitted, with from five to 17 aerials visible all over the aircraft. In the "Bison C" sub-type a large search radar fills the entire nose, lengthening the nose by about 6 ft and changing its shape. Since 1967 these now obsolescent aircraft have been frequently encountered on probing missions far over the Arctic, Atlantic, Pacific and elsewhere, at both high and very low levels, the C-model having been seen most frequently.

Nakajima Ki-27

Ki-27a and -27b

Type: single-seat interceptor fighter and light attack.

Engine: prototype, one 650 hp Nakajima Ha-1a (Jupiter-derived) nine-cylinder radial; 27a and 27b, one 710 hp Ha-1b.

Dimensions: span 37 ft 0¾ in (11·3 m); length 24 ft 8½ in (7·53 m); height 9 ft 2¼ in (2·8 m).

Weights: empty 2,403 lb (1090 kg); loaded 3,638 lb (1650 kg); (27b) up to 3,946 lb.

Performance: maximum speed 286 mph (460 km/h); initial climb 2,953 ft (900 m)/min; service ceiling, not recorded but about 34,400 ft (10,500 m); range 389 miles (625 km).

Armament: two 7·7 mm Type 89 machine guns fixed in sides of fuselage, firing inside cowling; external racks for four 55 lb (25 kg) bombs.

History: first flight 15 October 1936; service delivery, early 1938; service delivery (Ki-27b) March 1939; final delivery July 1940.

The Imperial Japanese Army's first low-wing monoplane fighter, the Ki-27 was in continuous production from 1937 to 1940 and was not only built in much larger quantities than other Japanese aircraft of its day but outnumbered almost every Japanese warplane of World War II. It was designed to meet a 1935 fighter requirement and competed against designs from Kawasaki and Mitsubishi. Though not the fastest, it was

Nakajima Ki-27b, distinguished from Ki-27a by modified canopy (1st Chutai, 1st Hikosentai, Imperial Army)

easily the most manoeuvrable; in fact it was probably the most manoeuvrable military aircraft of its day and possibly in all history, with plenty of engine power and (the Army having chosen the biggest of three possible sizes of wing) the extremely low wing loading of 17·9 lb/ft². The loaded weight was roughly half that of contemporary Western fighters, and the penalty was paid in light construction and light armament. At the time Japanese pilots cared nothing for speed, firepower or armour, but sacrificed everything for good

visibility and manoeuvrability, and they resisted the introduction of later aircraft such as the Ki-43 (p. 168). Hundreds of Ki-27s fought Chinese and Soviet aircraft over Asia, scoring about 90 per cent of the claimed 1,252 Soviet aircraft shot down in 1939 after the Nomonhan Incident. Other Ki-27s served with the Manchurian air force, and at the time of Pearl Harbor they outnumbered all other Japanese fighters. Called "Nate" by the Allies, they continued in front-line use throughout the first year of the Pacific War. No fewer than 3,386 were built, 2,079 by Nakajima and 1,307 by Tachikawa and the Manchurian (Mansyu Hikoki) company.

Nakajima B5N (Type 97)

B5N1 and B5N2

Type: (B5N1) three-seat carrier-based bomber; (2) torpedo bomber.

Engine: (B5N1 Model 11) one 770 hp Nakajima Hikari 3 nine-cylinder radial; (B5N1 Model 12) 970 or 985 hp Nakajima Sakae 11 14-cylinder two-row radial; (B5N2) 1,115 hp Sakae 21.

Dimensions: span 50 ft 11 in (15·52 m); length (1) 33 ft 11 in; (2) 33 ft 9½ in (10·3 m); height 12 ft 1¾ in (3·70 m).

Weights: empty (1) 4,645 lb (2107 kg); (2) 5,024 lb (2279 kg); normal loaded (1) 8,047 lb (3650 kg); (2) 8,378 lb (3800 kg); maximum loaded (2) 9,039 lb (4100 kg).

Performance: maximum speed (1) 217 mph (350 km/h); (2) 235 mph (378 km/h); initial climb (both) 1,378 ft (420 m)/min; service ceiling (both) about 25,000 ft (7640 m); range (1) 683 miles (1100 km); (2) normal gross, 609 miles (980 km), overload (4100 kg) 1,237 miles (1990 km).

Armament: (1) one 7·7 mm Type 89 manually aimed from rear cockpit; underwing racks for two 551 lb (250 kg) or six 132 lb (60 kg) bombs. (2) two 7·7 mm manually aimed from rear cockpit, two 7·7 mm fixed above forward fuselage; centreline rack for 1,764 lb (800 kg, 18 in) torpedo or three 551 lb bombs.

History: first flight January 1937; (production B5N1) late 1937; (B5N2) December 1939; final delivery, probably 1942.

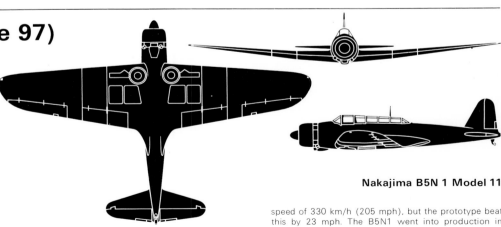

Nakajima B5N 1 Model 11

Designed to meet a 1935 requirement, the B5N was judged ordinary and obsolescent in World War II, yet in its day it was advanced and bold. The Japanese keenly studied the stressed-skin aircraft of Northrop, Douglas and Clark, and swiftly copied new features. The B5N had not only a thoroughly modern structure but also variable-pitch propeller (not on RAF Hurricanes until mid-1940!), hydraulically retracting landing gear, Fowler flaps, NACA cowling, integral wing fuel tanks and, until judged troublesome, hydraulic wing-folding. The challenging specification demanded a

speed of 330 km/h (205 mph), but the prototype beat this by 23 mph. The B5N1 went into production in time to serve in the Sino-Japanese war; a few of the rival fixed-gear Mitsubishi B5M were bought as an insurance. By 1940 some attack B5N were converted into B5N1-K trainers, but 103 bombed at Pearl Harbor. In the same attack 40 of the new B5N2 torpedo bombers attacked, at least half finding their mark. Subsequently the B5N2 played the chief role in sinking the US carriers *Yorktown, Lexington, Wasp* and *Hornet*. They soldiered on into 1944 alongside their replacement the B6N. Total production exceeded 1,200, some made by Aichi. Their Allied name was "Kate".

Nakajima Ki-43 Hayabusa

Ki-43-I to Ic, IIa and b, IIIa and b
Type: single-seat interceptor fighter (from IIa, fighter-bomber).
Engine: (Ki-43-I series) one 975 hp Nakajima Ha-25 (Ha-35/12) Sakae 14-cylinder two-row radial; (II) 1,105 hp Ha-115 Sakae; (III) 1,250 hp Ha-112 (Ha-33/42) Kasei of same layout.
Dimensions: span (I) 37 ft 10½ in (11·437 m); (IIa) 37 ft 6¼ in (10·83 m); length (I) 28 ft 11¾ in (8·82 m); (II, III) 29 ft 3¼ in (8·92 m); height (all) 10 ft 8¾ in (3·273 m).
Weights: empty (I) 4,354 lb (1975 kg); normal loaded (I) 5,824 lb (2642 kg); (II series) 5,825–5,874 lb (typically 2655 kg); (III) 6,283 lb (2850 kg).
Performance: maximum speed (I) 308 mph; (II) 320 mph (515 km/h); (III) 363 mph (585 km/h); initial climb (typical II) 3,250 ft (990 m)/min; service ceiling (I) 38,500 ft; (II, III) 36,800 ft (11,215 m); range (I) 746 miles (1200 km); (II, III) internal fuel 1,060 miles (1700 km), with two 45-gal drop tanks 1,864 miles (3000 km).
Armament: (Ia) two 7·7 mm Type 80 above engine; (Ib) one 12·7 mm, one 7·7 mm; (Ic) two 12·7 mm; (all II series) two 12·7 mm, each with 250 rounds, and wing racks for two 551 lb (250 kg) bombs; (IIIa) same; (IIIb) two 20 mm Ho-5 cannon replacing 12·7 mm in top decking, same bomb racks.

History: first flight January 1939; (production Ki-43-I) March 1941; (prototype IIa) February 1942; (prototype IIb) June 1942; (IIIa) December 1944.

Code-named "Oscar" by the Allies, the Ki-43 Hayabusa (Peregrine Falcon) was the most numerous of all Imperial Army warplanes and second only in numbers to the Zero-Sen. Compared with the famed Navy fighter it was smaller, lighter and much cheaper to produce. It was cast in the traditional Army mould in which everything was sacrificed for manoeuvrability, through the first prototype (designed by Hideo Itokawa) to meet a 1938 Army contract which was simply awarded to Nakajima, without any industrial competition) was very heavy on the controls and disappointing. One prototype was even given fixed landing gear to save weight, but after many changes, and especially after adding a "combat manoeuvre flap" under the wings, the Ki-43 was turned into a dog-

Nakajima Ki-43-IIa (1st Chutai, 50th Sentai, Imperial Army)

fighter that could outmanoeuvre every aircraft ever ranged against it. After a few had carelessly got in the way of Allied fighters the more powerful II appeared with some armour, self-sealing tanks and slightly reduced span. The mass-produced clipped-wing IIb followed, serving in every Japanese battle. To the end, this nimble fighter remained totally deficient in fire-power (except for the few examples of the IIIb at the end of the war), and owing to its very light structure often disintegrated when hit by 0·5 in fire. On the other hand, most of Japan's Army aces gained nearly all their scores on this popular little fighter. It was kept in production long after it was obsolete, 5,751 being delivered, including 2,629 by Tachikawa and 49 by the 1st Arsenal.

Nakajima Ki-44 Shoki

Nakajima Ki-44-IIb (Shinten unit, 47th Sentai, Imperial Army)

Ki-44-Ia, b and c, IIa, b and c and III
Type: single-seat interceptor fighter and (II onwards) fighter-bomber.
Engine: (Ia) one 1,260 hp Nakajima Ha-41 14-cylinder two-row radial; (Ib and all subsequent) 1,520 hp Nakajima Ha-109 of same layout.
Dimensions: span 31 ft (9·448 m); length 28 ft 8½ in (8·75 m); height 10 ft 8 in (3·248 m).
Weights: empty (Ia) 3,968 lb (1800 kg); (II, typical) 4,643 lb (2106 kg); normal loaded (no overload permitted) (Ia) 5,622 lb (2550 kg); (IIc) 6,107 lb (2770 kg); (III) 5,357 lb (2430 kg).
Performance: maximum speed (Ia) 360 mph (579 km/h); (IIc) 376 mph (605 km/h); initial climb (IIc) 3,940 ft (1200 m)/min; service ceiling (IIc) 36,745 ft (11,200 m); range on internal fuel (typical) 560 miles (900 km) (endurance, 2 hr 20 min).
Armament: (Ia) two 12·7 mm Type I in wings and two 7·7 mm Type 89 in fuselage; (Ib, IIa, IIb) four

12·7 mm Type I, two in fuselage and two in wings, with (II series) wing racks for two 220 lb (100 kg) bombs; (IIc) two 12·7 mm in fuselage, two 40 mm Ho-301 low-velocity cannon; (III) two 12·7 mm in fuselage, two 20 mm Ho-5 cannon in wings.
History: first flight (first of ten prototypes) August 1940; (production Ki-44-Ia) May 1942; (Ib, Ic) 1943; (IIb) December 1943.

Marking a complete break with the traditional emphasis on manoeuvrability, the Ki-44 (code-named "Tojo" by the Allies) contrasted with the Ki-43 as did the J2M with the Zero-Sen. Suddenly the need was for greater speed and climb, even at the expense of poorer manoeuvrability and faster landing. In late 1940 a Ki-44 was tested against a Kawasaki Ki-60 and an imported Bf 109E, outflying both; but production was delayed until mid-1942 by the priority accorded the

old Ki-43. Pilots did not like the speedy small-winged fighter, with poor view on take-off and such poor control that flick rolls and many other manoeuvres were banned. But gradually the fact that the Ki-44 could climb and dive as well as its enemies brought some measure of popularity, even though many inexperienced pilots were killed in accidents. Most Shokis (Demons) were -II series with retractable tailwheel and other changes, including a glazed teardrop canopy. The heavy cannon of the -IIc, firing caseless ammunition at 400 rounds per minute, were effective against Allied bombers. Probably the most successful mission ever flown in defending Japan was that of 19 February 1945 when a small force of Ki-44 (probably -IIc) climbed up to 120 B-29s and destroyed ten, two reportedly by suicide collisions. Total production was 1,233, including a few of the lightened -III series.

Nakajima B6N Tenzan

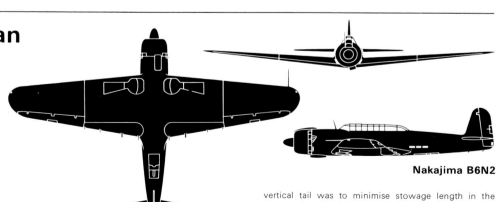

B6N1, B6N2
Type: three-seat carrier-based torpedo bomber.
Engine: (B6N1) one 1,870 hp Nakajima Mamori 11 14-cylinder two-row radial; (B6N2) 1,850 hp Mitsubishi Kasei 25 of same layout.
Dimensions: span 48 ft 10¼ in (14·894 m); length 35 ft 7½ in (10·865 m); height (1) 12 ft 1¾ in (3·7 m); (2) 12 ft 5½ in (3·8 m).
Weights: empty 6,636 lb (3010 kg) (1, 2 almost identical); normal loaded 11,464 lb (5200 kg); maximum overload 12,456 lb (5650 kg).
Performance: maximum speed (1) 289 mph (465 km/h); (2) 299 mph (482 km/h); initial climb (1) 1,720 ft (525 m)/min; (2) 1,885 ft (575 m)/min; service ceiling (1) 28,379 ft (8650 m); (2) 29,659 ft (9040 m); range (normal weight) (1) 907 miles (1460 km); (2) 1,084 miles (1745 km), (overload) (1) 2,312 miles (3720 km); (2) 1,895 miles (3050 km).
Armament: one 7·7 mm Type 89 manually aimed from rear cockpit and one manually aimed by middle crew-member from rear ventral position, with fixed 7·7 mm firing forward in left wing (often absent from B6N1); 1,764 lb (800 kg, 18 in) torpedo carried offset to right of centreline, or six 220 lb (100 kg) bombs under fuselage.
History: first flight March 1942; service delivery (B6N1) early 1943; (B6N2) December 1943.

Nakajima B6N2

Named Tenzan (Heavenly Mountain) after a worshipped mountain in China, and code-named "Jill" by the Allies, the B6N was another conventional-looking aircraft which in fact was in many respects superior to the seemingly more advanced machines of the Allies (in this case the Grumman TBF and Fairey Barracuda). Designed as a replacement for B5N, Tenzan was slim and clean, with no internal weapon bay. The torpedo was offset, and to increase clearance on torpedo release the big oil cooler was offset in the other direction (to the left). The distinctive shape of the

vertical tail was to minimise stowage length in the three-point attitude in carriers. Nakajima's big Mamori engine, driving a four-blade Hamilton-type propeller, suffered severe vibration and overheating, and though the B6N1 was kept in service it was replaced in production by the B6N2. The lower power of the proven Kasei was counteracted by the improved installation with less drag, and jet-thrust from the exhaust stubs. Tenzans went into action off Bougainville in the Marshalls campaign in June 1944. Subsequently they were heavily committed, many being later equipped with ASV radar for night attacks and ending in April–June 1945 with a hectic campaign of torpedo and suicide attacks off Okinawa and Kyushu. By this time the Imperial Navy had no operating carrier and hardly any skilled pilots.

Nakajima J1N1

J1N1-C, J1N1-F, J1N1-S Gekko and J1N1-C-Kai

Type: (C, F) three-seat reconnaissance; (S, C-Kai) two-seat night fighter.

Engines: all operational versions, two 1,130 hp Nakajima Sakae 21 14-cylinder two-row radials.

Dimensions: span 55 ft 8½ in (16·98 m); length (all, excluding nose guns or radar) 39 ft 11½ in (12·18 m); height 14 ft 11½ in (4·562 m).

Weights: empty (C, S) 10,697 lb (4852 kg); loaded (C) 15,984 lb (7250 kg); (S) 15,212 lb (6900 kg); maximum overload (both) 16,594 lb (7527 kg).

Performance: maximum speed (C, S) 315 mph (507 km/h); initial climb (C, S) 1,968 ft (600 m)/min; service ceiling 30,578 ft (9320 m); range (C, S, normal gross) 1,585 miles (2550 km), (overload) 2,330 miles (3750 km).

Armament: (J1N1-C) one 20 mm Type 99 cannon and two 7·7 mm Type 97 fixed in nose; (J1N1-S) four 20 mm Type 99 Model 2 cannon fixed in rear cockpit, two firing obliquely upwards and two firing obliquely downwards; (J1N1-F) manual dorsal turret with single 20 mm gun.

History: first flight May 1941; (production C) August 1942; service delivery (C) end of 1942; first flight (S) August 1943.

In 1938, before the Zero-Sen had flown, the Imperial Navy issued a specification for a twin-engined, long-range escort fighter, to reach a speed of 280 knots, and have a range of 1,300 nautical miles or 2,000 n.m. with

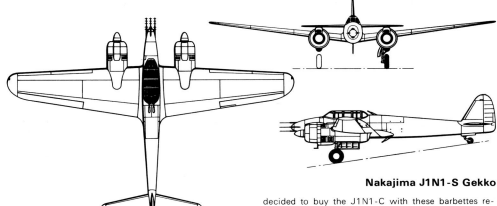

Nakajima J1N1-S Gekko

extra fuel (the n.m. was the standard naval unit in Japan). Mitsubishi abandoned this project, but Nakajima's design team under K. Nakamura succeeded in producing a large prototype which proved to have remarkable manoeuvrability. Fitted with large fabric-covered ailerons, slotted flaps (opened 15° for combat) and leading-edge slats, it could dogfight well with a Zero and the prototype was eventually developed to have no flight limitations. But the Navy doubted the practicability of the complex scheme of two dorsal barbettes, each mounting two 7·7 mm guns, remotely aimed in unison by the navigator. Eventually the Navy

decided to buy the J1N1-C with these barbettes removed to serve as a three-seat photographic aircraft. (Some reports claim the failure as a fighter was due to lateral control problems, but Nakajima test pilots insist it was simply a matter of armament.) Soon after sorties began over the Solomons in the spring of 1943 the commander of the 251st Air Corps, Yasuna Kozono, hit on a way of intercepting Allied heavy night bombers. He had several aircraft modified as C-Kai night fighters with upper and lower pairs of oblique cannon. The armament proved effective, and most of the 477 J1N aircraft were built as J1N1-S Gekko (Moonlight) fighters with nose radar and a smoother cabin outline. They were good, robust aircraft, but unable to intercept the fast, high-flying B-29. Their Allied name was "Irving".

Nakajima Ki-49 Donryu

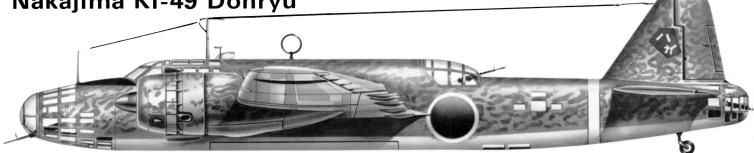

Ki-49-I, IIa, IIb, III and Ki-58

Type: eight-seat heavy bomber; Ki-58, escort fighter.

Engines: (I) two 1,250 hp Nakajima Ha-41 14-cylinder two-row radials; (II) two 1,450 hp Nakajima Ha-109-II of same layout; (III) two 2,500 hp Nakajima Ha-117 18-cylinder two-row radials.

Dimensions: span 66 ft 7¼ in (20·3 m); length 53 ft 1¾ in (16·2 m); height 13 ft 11½ in (4·25 m).

Weights: empty (II) 15,653 lb (7100 kg); normal loaded 23,545 lb (10,680 kg).

Performance: maximum speed (II) 304 mph (490 km/h); initial climb 1,312 ft (400 m)/min; service ceiling 26,772 ft (8160 m); range with bomb load, 1,491 miles (2400 km).

Armament: (I) one 20 mm cannon manually aimed in dorsal position, single 7·7 mm manually aimed at nose and tail; (IIa) as (I) plus extra 7·7 mm in ventral and two beam positions (total five); (IIb) as IIa but

with all 7·7 mm replaced by 12·7 mm, thus 20 mm dorsal and single 12·7 mm in nose, tail, ventral and two beam positions; all versions, internal bay for bomb load up to 2,205 lb (1,000 kg).

History: first flight August 1939; (production Ki-49-I) probably May 1940; (II) 1942; final delivery December 1944.

Designed to a late 1938 specification aimed at replacing the Mitsubishi Ki-21, the Ki-49 was the first Japanese bomber to mount a 20 mm cannon; but it was at first only slightly faster than the Ki-21, had a poor ceiling and never did achieve any advance in range and bomb load. The 1,160 hp Nakajima Ha-5B engines of the prototype were replaced by the Ha-41, and 129 of the -I model were built at Ohta, after whose Donryu (Dragon Swallower) shrine the type was named. The production machine was the Type 100 heavy bomber, and the Allied code name was "Helen".

Nakajima Ki-49-IIb (unknown sentai, New Guinea, 1943)

Its first mission was a raid on Port Darwin from a New Guinea base on 19 February 1942. The main model was the better-armed -II series, of which 649 were built by Nakajima, 50 by Tachikawa and a few by Mansyu in Harbin, Manchuria. Though met in all parts of the Japanese war, the Ki-49 was not very effective; many were destroyed at Leyte Gulf, and by late 1944 all were being used either for non-combatant purposes or as suicide machines or, with ASV radar or magnetic-mine detectors, for ocean patrol. As it was a poor bomber three were converted as Ki-58 fighters with five 20 mm cannon and three 12·7 mm guns, while two were rebuilt as Ki-80 leadships for attack by fighter-bomber or suicide aircraft. The much more powerful III model was not ready by August 1945, though six were built.

Nakajima Ki-84 Hayate

Ki-84-I to Ic, and many projects

Type: single-seat fighter-bomber.

Engine: in all production models, one 1,900 hp Nakajima Homare Ha-45 Model 11 18-cylinder two-row radial.

Dimensions: span 36 ft 10½ in (11·238 m); length 32 ft 6½ in (9·92 m); height 11 ft 1¼ in (3·385 m).

Weights: empty 5,864 lb (2680 kg); normal loaded 8,267 lb (3750 kg); maximum overload (seldom authorised) 9,150 lb (4150 kg).

Performance: maximum speed 388 mph (624 km/h); initial climb 3,600 ft (1100 m)/min; service ceiling 34,450 ft (10,500 m); range on internal fuel 1,025 miles (1650 km); range with two 98-gal drop tanks, 1,815 miles (2920 km).

Armament: (Ia) two 20 mm Ho-5 in wings, each with 150 rounds, and two 12·7 mm Type 103 in top of fuselage with 350 rounds; (Ib) four 20 mm, each with 150 rounds, two in wings and two in fuselage; (Ic) two 20 mm in fuselage and two 30 mm Ho-105 cannon in wings; (all operational models) two racks under outer wings for tanks or bombs up to 551 lb (250 kg) each.

History: first flight March 1943; (production Ia) August 1943; service delivery April 1944.

Code-named "Frank" by the Allies, the Ki-84 of the Imperial Army was generally regarded as the best Japanese fighter of World War II. Yet it was not without

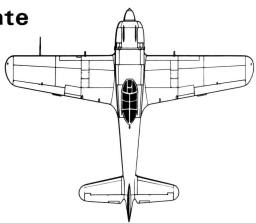

Nakajima Ki-84-Ia (-Ib very similar)

its problems. Part of its fine all-round performance stemmed from the extremely advanced direct-injection engine, the first Army version of the Navy NK9A; yet this engine gave constant trouble and needed skilled maintenance. T. Koyama designed the Ki-84 to greater strength factors than any earlier Japanese warplane, yet poor heat-treatment of the high-strength steel meant that landing gears often simply snapped. Progressive deterioration in quality control meant that

pilots never knew how particular aircraft would perform, whether the brakes would work or whether, in trying to intercept B-29s over Japan, they would even be able to climb high enough. Despite this, the Ki-84 was potentially superb, a captured -Ia out-climbing and outmanoeuvring a P-51H and P-47N! First batches went to China, where the 22nd Sentai flew rings round Gen Chennault's 14th Air Force. The unit then moved to the Philippines, where the rot set in, with accidents, shortages and extremely poor serviceability. Frequent bombing of the Musashi engine factory and extreme need to conserve raw material led to various projects and prototypes made of wood (Ki-84-II series and Ki-106) or steel (Ki-113) and advanced models with the 2,000 hp Ha-45ru turbocharged engine, Ha-45/44 with two-stage three-speed blower and 2,500 hp Ha-44/13. Total production of the Hayate (Hurricane) was 3,513 (2,686 at Ohta, 727 at Utsonomiya and 100 in Manchuria by Mansyu, which also flew the Ki-116 with smaller Ha-112 engine).

Nieuport XI

Types X and XII, XI and XVI (data for XI)
Type: single-seat fighting scout.
Engine: 80 hp Gnome or, more often, Le Rhône 9C nine-cylinder rotary.
Dimensions: span 24 ft 9¼ in (7·55 m); length 19 ft 0½ in (5·8 m); height 8 ft 0½ in (2·45 m).
Weights: empty 728 lb (330 kg); loaded 1,058 lb (480 kg).
Performance: maximum speed 97 mph (156 km/h); initial climb, not known but probably about 660 ft (200 m)/min; service ceiling 15,090 ft (4600 m); range, about 200 miles (320 km) (endurance 2 hr 30 min).
Armament: XI, one 0·303 in Lewis fixed above upper wing; XVI, one 0·303 in Vickers synchronised to fire ahead through propeller disc.
History: first flight (Bébé racer) late 1914; XI, early 1915; XVI, 1916.

In January 1914 designer Gustave Delage joined the Etablissements Nieuport and started the series of military aircraft that made both him and the company famous. They were trim, smaller than average and had sesquiplane wings (the lower much smaller than the upper) braced by V-struts. The first of Delage's war-planes was the Type X (Nieuports are sometimes written in Arabic numerals, giving, in this case, Type 10). This two-seat observation machine came in two forms, one with the observer and gun in front of the pilot and the other behind; soon most had been converted to single-seat scouts (XC-1 or Nie.10C-1). The

XII was slightly larger and had a 110 or 130 hp rotary instead of 80 hp. French and British-built examples served the RFC and RNAS. The much smaller XI single-seater was developed from the Bébé (Baby) racer of 1914 intended for the Gordon-Bennett race. Many hundreds were built, including 646 by Macchi in Italy. They were among the first real fighters of the RFC and RNAS and were used in large numbers by the French and Belgian Aviation Militaire, and Imperial Russian Air Service. The XVI had a synchronised gun in the

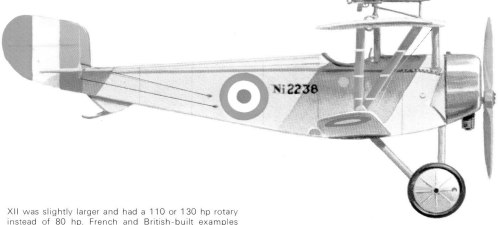

Nieuport XI (Aviation Militaire)

fuselage and the 110 hp Le Rhône engine. Many carried Le Prieur rockets on the V-struts for destroying observation balloons. These early Nieuports were the only Allied aircraft respected by the Fokker E-types.

Nieuport XVII

Types XVII, XXI (21) and 23
Type: single-seat fighting scout; (XXI) two-seat trainer.
Engine: (XVII) usually 110 hp Le Rhône 9J or 120 hp 9Jb nine-cylinder rotary; (XVIIbis) 130 hp Clerget 9B of same layout; (XXI) 80 hp Gnome; 23, Le Rhône 9J.
Dimensions: span 26 ft 11½ in (8·22 m); length 18 ft 10 in (5·74 m); height 7 ft 7¾ in (2·33 m).
Weights: empty (17C-1) 705 lb (320 kg); loaded 1,179–1,246 lb (565 kg).
Performance: maximum speed 109 mph (176 km/h); initial climb, not known, but about 820 ft (250 m)/min; service ceiling 17,388 ft (5300 m); range 186 miles (300 km).
Armament: early production, one machine gun (usually 0·303 in Lewis) on Foster mounting above upper wing; later, one machine gun (usually 0·303 in Vickers) in fuselage, synchronised to fire past propeller blades. A few aircraft carried two synchronised guns, and many had eight Le Prieur rockets on interplane struts. In Type 23 the gun was moved from upper centreline to right side.
History: first flight, probably January 1916; service delivery May 1916; (21, 23) 1917.
The Nieuport XVII, or 17C-1, meaning Type 17, chasse (fighter) one seat, was one of the greatest Allied combat aircraft of World War I. It was very similar to the XVI but slightly larger and, to avoid the wing-twist problem that afflicted the XI and XVI at high speeds,

the lower wing was considerably stiffened. Though the belated availability of synchronised guns did much to redress the balance, the "Fokker Scourge" was finally ended by the delivery of the Type XVII and, a little later, other good Allied fighters. Many hundreds served the RFC and RNAS, Aviation Militaire, Russia, Holland, Italy, Belgium, Finland and United States. The XVII was the chosen mount of the Escadrille des Cicognes, Escadrille Lafayette and of Nungesser, Guynemer, Ball, Bishop and many other famous aces. Large numbers survived the war and were bought by other air forces,

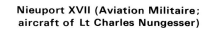

Nieuport XVII (Aviation Militaire; aircraft of Lt Charles Nungesser)

notably that of Switzerland. The 23 was an advanced development with tail like that of the N.28; the XXI trainer was used by the US Army Air Service.

Nieuport 28

Nie.28
Type: single-seat fighter.
Engine: 160/170 hp Gnome Monosoupape 9N nine-cylinder rotary.
Dimensions: span 26 ft 8¾ in (8·15 m); length 21 ft (6·4 m); height 8 ft 2½ in (2·5 m).
Weights: empty 1,047 lb (475 kg); loaded 1,625 lb (737 kg).
Performance: maximum speed 122 mph (196 km/h); initial climb 1,640 ft (500 m)/min; service ceiling 17,000 ft (5182 m); range 155 miles (250 km).
Armament: two fixed synchronised machine guns, usually either 0·303 in Vickers or, in AEF machines, 0·30 in Marlin.
History: first flight 14 June 1917; service delivery (AEF) March 1918.

With this good-looking machine Delage made the break from the famed V-strut sesquiplanes. Unfortunately it was not as good as it looked, and though put into production (almost as routine) by the French government, it went through a succession of modifications yet never satisfied the Aviation Militaire. Its worst fault was certainly the Monosoupape engine (also designated Le Rhône 9N) which was totally unreliable; a further failing was that at high speeds any violent manoeuvre tended to rip the fabric from the upper wing. Despite these known shortcomings it happened to be the only fighter readily available to the

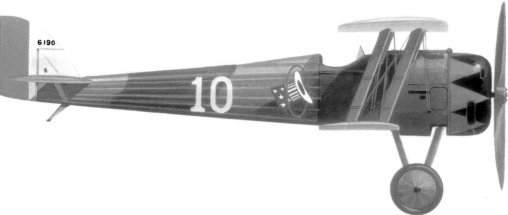

Nieuport 28 (94th Aero Sqn, AEF; aircraft of Lt Doug Campbell)

United States AEF (American Expeditionary Force), whose Pursuit Squadrons began arriving in France in early 1918. Eventually the Nie.28 equipped Nos 27, 94, 95, 103 and 147 Aero Squadrons, and was flown by the first American ace, Lt Douglas Campbell. Capt Eddie Rickenbacker flew it for a while and two other

aces, Raoul Lufbery (third highest scorer with 17 kills) and Quentin Roosevelt, were killed in this type. The AEF managed to start changing to Spads in July 1918, though many Nieuport 28s found their way back to the United States. Others were sold to Greece and Switzerland.

North American NA-16 family

BT-9 series and Yale; AT-6/BC-1/SNJ series (Texan) and Harvard; many other variants (data for post-war T-6G).

Type: two-seat (some, single-seat) basic or advanced trainer and light attack.
Engine: typically one 550 hp Pratt & Whitney R-1340-AN1 nine-cylinder radial (see text).
Dimensions: span 42 ft 0¼ in (12·8 m); length 29 ft 6 in (8·99 m); height 11 ft 8½ in (3·56 m).
Weights: empty 4,271 lb (1938 kg); loaded 5,617 lb (2546 kg).
Performance: maximum speed 212 mph (341 km/h); initial climb 1,640 ft (500 m)/min; service ceiling 24,750 ft (7338 m); range 870 miles (1400 km).
Armament: normally provision for machine gun in either or both wing roots and manually aimed in rear cockpit; light series bomb racks under wings (see text).
History: first flight (NA-16 prototype) April 1935; (production BT-9) April 1936; (NA-26) 1937; (Wirraway) 27 March 1939.

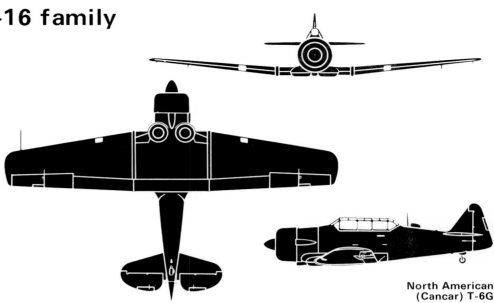

North American (Cancar) T-6G

Perhaps the most varied family of aircraft in history began as a little monoplane trainer, with fixed gear and two open cockpits, flown as a US civil machine in 1935. Its first offspring was the BT-9 basic trainer, supplied to many countries and made in many more (Yale was the RCAF name), powered by Wright R-975 Whirlwind, P&W Wasp Junior or Wasp engine. About 970 were built by North American. A second family were combat warplanes, notably the NA-44, 50, 69, A-27 attack and single-seat P-64, usually with R-1820 Cyclone engine, multiple guns and about 550 lb bomb load. Biggest family were the T-6 Harvard/Texan trainers, of which 15,109 were made by NAA in 1938–45, 755 in Australia as CAC Wirraways, 2,610 by Noorduyn in Canada, 176 by Japan (even receiving an Allied code-name: "Oak") and 136 by Saab in

Sweden. By far the most important Allied training machine in World War II, thousands were refurbished or remanufactured (2,068 by the original maker) in 1946–59 for 54 nations. The T-6G is the updated US/Canadian post-war trainer, Cancar building 555 from new in 1951–54 to bring total production to about 20,300 trainers plus several hundred purpose-designed combat machines. Even today hundreds of T-6s of

various kinds are used as counter-insurgency and paramilitary combat machines. In Spain the trainer is the E.16, while the combat version is the C.6. In Brazil armed Co-In versions are still in use, as are many in African air forces. The successor to the T-6, the tricycle-gear T-28, is also an important light attack and Co-In machine, the latest version being turboprop-powered.

North American NA-62 Mitchell

North American B-25C-10 (487th BS, 340th BG, 12th AAF, Sicily)

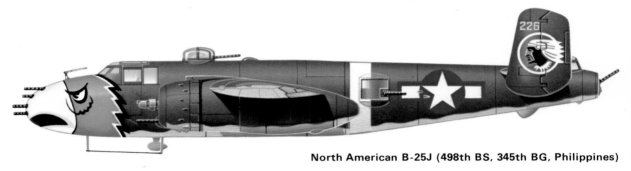

North American B-25J (498th BS, 345th BG, Philippines)

B-25 to TB-25N, PBJ series, F-10

Type: medium bomber and attack with crew from four to six (see text).
Engines: (B-25, A, B), two 1,700 hp Wright R-2600-9 Double Cyclone 14-cylinder two-row radials; (C, D, G) two 1,700 hp R-2600-13; (H, J, F-10), two 1,850 hp (emergency rating) R-2600-29.
Dimensions: span 67 ft 7 in (20·6 m); length (B-25, A) 54 ft 1 in; (B, C, J) 52 ft 11 in (16·1 m); (G, H) 51 ft (15·54 m); height (typical) 15 ft 9 in (4·80 m).
Weights: empty (J, typical) 21,100 lb (9580 kg); maximum loaded (A) 27,100 lb; (B) 28,640 lb; (C) 34,000 lb (15,422 kg); (G) 35,000 lb (15,876 kg); (H) 36,047 lb (16,350 kg); (J) normal 35,000 lb, overload 41,800 lb (18,960 kg).
Performance: maximum speed (A) 315 mph; (B) 300 mph; (C, G) 284 mph (459 km/h); (H, J) 275 mph (443 km/h); initial climb (A, typical) 1,500 ft (460 m)/min; (late models, typical) 1,100 ft (338 m)/min; service ceiling (A) 27,000 ft (8230 m); (late models, typical) 24,000 ft (7315 m); range (all, typical) 1,500 miles (2414 km).
Armament: see text.
History: first flight (NA-40 prototype) January 1939; (NA-62, the first production B-25) 19 August 1940; (B-25G) August 1942.

Named in honour of the fearless US Army Air Corps officer who was court-martialled in 1924 for his tiresome (to officialdom) belief in air power, the B-25 — designed by a company with no previous experience of twins, of bombers or of high performance warplanes — was made in larger quantities than any other American twin-engined combat aircraft and has often been described as the best aircraft in its class in World War II. Led by Lee Atwood and Ray Rice, the design team first created the Twin Wasp-powered NA-40, but had to start again and build a sleeker and more powerful machine to meet revised Army specifications demanding twice the bomb load (2,400 lb, 1089 kg). The Army ordered 184 off the drawing board, the first 24 being B-25s and the rest B-25A with armour and self-sealing tanks. The defensive armament was a 0·5 in manually aimed in the cramped tail and single 0·3 in manually aimed from waist windows and the nose; bomb load was 3,000 lb (1361 kg). The B had twin 0·5 in in an electrically driven dorsal turret and a retractable ventral turret, the tail gun being removed. On 18 April 1942 16 B-25Bs led by Lt-Col Jimmy Doolittle made the daring and morale-raising raid on Tokyo, having made free take-offs at gross weight from the carrier *Hornet* 800 miles distant. Extra fuel, external bomb racks and other additions led to the C, supplied to the RAF, China and Soviet Union, and as

PBJ-1C to the US Navy. The D was similar but built at the new plant at Kansas City. In 1942 came the G, with solid nose fitted with a 75 mm M-4 gun, loaded manually with 21 rounds. At first two 0·5 in were also fixed in the nose, for flak suppression and sighting, but in July 1943 tests against Japanese ships showed that more was needed and the answer was four 0·5 in "package guns" on the sides of the nose. Next came the B-25H with the fearsome armament of a 75 mm, 14 0·5 in guns (eight firing ahead, two in waist bulges and four in dorsal and tail turrets) and a 2,000 lb (907 kg) torpedo or 3,200 lb (1451 kg) of bombs. Biggest production of all was of the J, with glazed nose, normal bomb load of 4,000 lb (1814 kg) and 13 0·5 in guns supplied with 5,000 rounds. The corresponding attack version had a solid nose with five additional 0·5 in guns. Total J output was 4,318, and the last delivery in August 1945 brought total output to 9,816. The F-10 was an unarmed multi-camera reconnaissance version, and the CB-25 was a post-war transport model. The wartime AT-24 trainers were redesignated TB-25 and, after 1947, supplemented by more than 900 bombers rebuilt as the TB-25J, K, L and M. Many ended their days as research hacks or target tugs and one carried the cameras for the early Cinerama films.

North American NA-73 Mustang

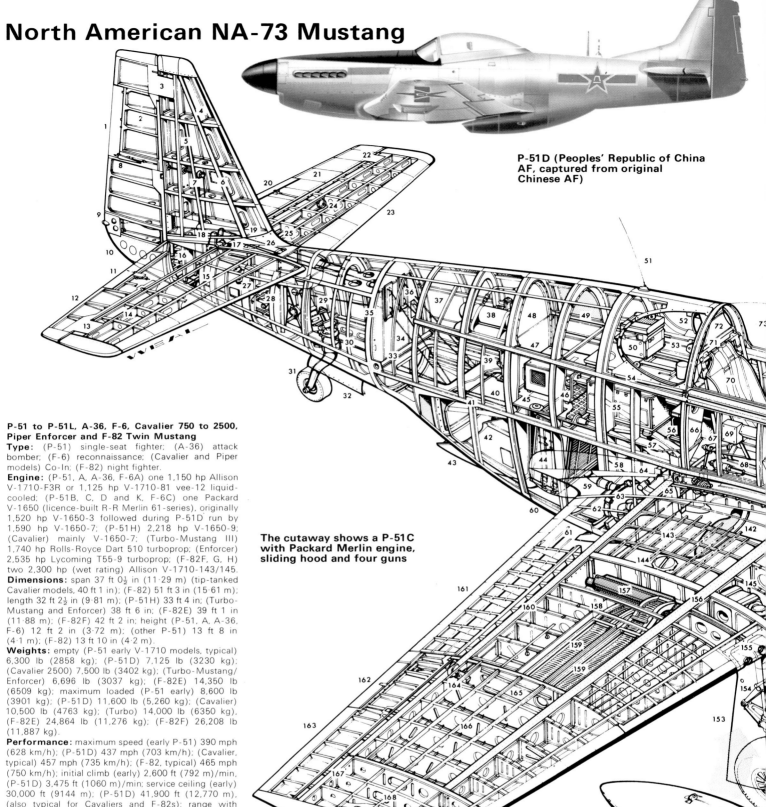

P-51D (Peoples' Republic of China AF, captured from original Chinese AF)

The cutaway shows a P-51C with Packard Merlin engine, sliding hood and four guns

P-51 to P-51L, A-36, F-6, Cavalier 750 to 2500, Piper Enforcer and F-82 Twin Mustang

Type: (P-51) single-seat fighter; (A-36) attack bomber; (F-6) reconnaissance; (Cavalier and Piper models) Co-In; (F-82) night fighter.

Engine: (P-51, A, A-36, F-6A) one 1,150 hp Allison V-1710-F3R or 1,125 hp V-1710-81 vee-12 liquid-cooled; (P-51B, C, D and K, F-6C) one Packard V-1650 (licence-built R-R Merlin 61-series), originally 1,520 hp V-1650-3 followed during P-51D run by 1,590 hp V-1650-7; (P-51H) 2,218 hp V-1650-9; (Cavalier) mainly V-1650-7; (Turbo-Mustang III) 1,740 hp Rolls-Royce Dart 510 turboprop; (Enforcer) 2,535 hp Lycoming T55-9 turboprop; (F-82F, G, H) two 2,300 hp (wet rating) Allison V-1710-143/145.

Dimensions: span 37 ft 0½ in (11·29 m) (tip-tanked Cavalier models, 40 ft 1 in); (F-82) 51 ft 3 in (15·61 m); length 32 ft 2½ in (9·81 m); (P-51H) 33 ft 4 in; (Turbo-Mustang and Enforcer) 38 ft 6 in; (F-82E) 39 ft 1 in (11·88 m); (F-82F) 42 ft 2 in; height (P-51, A, A-36, F-6) 12 ft 2 in (3·72 m); (other P-51) 13 ft 8 in (4·1 m); (F-82) 13 ft 10 in (4·2 m).

Weights: empty (P-51 early V-1710 models, typical) 6,300 lb (2858 kg); (P-51D) 7,125 lb (3230 kg); (Cavalier 2500) 7,500 lb (3402 kg); (Turbo-Mustang/Enforcer) 6,696 lb (3037 kg); (F-82E) 14,350 lb (6509 kg); maximum loaded (P-51 early) 8,600 lb (3901 kg); (P-51D) 11,600 lb (5,260 kg); (Cavalier) 10,500 lb (4763 kg); (Turbo) 14,000 lb (6350 kg); (F-82E) 24,864 lb (11,276 kg); (F-82F) 26,208 lb (11,887 kg).

Performance: maximum speed (early P-51) 390 mph (628 km/h); (P-51D) 437 mph (703 km/h); (Cavalier, typical) 457 mph (735 km/h); (F-82, typical) 465 mph (750 km/h); initial climb (early) 2,600 ft (792 m)/min, (P-51D) 3,475 ft (1060 m)/min; service ceiling (early) 30,000 ft (9144 m); (P-51D) 41,900 ft (12,770 m), (also typical for Cavaliers and F-82s); range with maximum fuel (early) 450 miles (724 km); (P-51D) combat range 950 miles, operational range 1,300 miles with drop tanks and absolute range to dry tanks of 2,080 miles; (Cavaliers) 750—2,500 miles depending on customer choice; (Turbo) 2,300 miles; (F-82E) 2,504 miles; (F-82F) 2,200 miles.

Armament: (RAF Mustang I) four 0·303 in in wings, two 0·5 in in wings and two 0·5 in in lower sides of nose; (Mustang IA) four 20 mm Hispano in wings; (P-51A and B) four 0·5 in in wings; (A-36A) six 0·5 in in wings and wing racks for two 500 lb (227 kg) bombs; (all subsequent P-51 production models) six 0·5 in Browning MG53-2 with 270 or 400 rounds each, and wing racks for tanks or two 1,000 lb (454 kg) bombs; (Cavalier or Turbo, typical) six 0·5 in with 2,000 rounds, two hardpoints each 1,000 lb and four more each 750 lb; (F-82, typical) six 0·5 in in centre wing, six or eight pylons for tanks, radars or up to 4,000 lb weapons.

History: first flight (NA-73X) 26 October 1940; (production RAF Mustang I) 1 May 1941; service delivery (RAF) October 1941; first flight (Merlin conversion) 13 October 1942; (P-51B) December 1942; final delivery (P-51H) November 1945; first flight (XP-82A) 15 April 1945; final delivery (F-82G) April 1949.

In April 1940 the British Air Purchasing Commission concluded with "Dutch" Kindelberger, chairman of North American Aviation, an agreement for the design and development of a completely new fighter for the RAF. Completed in 117 days (and then held up six weeks by failure of Allison to deliver the engine) this silver prototype was the start of the most successful fighter programme in history. The RAF received 620 Mustang I, 150 IA and 50 II, while the US Army adopted the type with 500 A-36A and 310 P-51A. In 1942 the brilliant airframe was matched with the Merlin engine, yielding the superb P-51B, bulged-hood C (Mustang III) and teardrop-canopy D (Mustang IV), later C and all D models having six 0·5 in guns and a dorsal fin. The final models were the K (different propeller) and better-shaped, lighter H, the fastest of all at 487 mph. Total production was 15,586. Mustang and P-51 variants served mainly in Europe, their prime mission being the almost incredible one of flying all the way from British bases to targets of the 8th AF deep in Germany – to Berlin or beyond – escorting heavies and gradually establishing Allied air superiority over the heart of Germany. After the war the Mustang proved popular with at least 55 nations, while in 1947–49 the US Air Force bought 272 examples of the appreciably longer Twin Mustang (two Allison-powered fuselages on a common wing), most of them radar night fighters which served in Korea. In 1945–48 Commonwealth Aircraft of Australia made under licence 200 Mustangs of four versions. In 1967 the P-51 was put back into production by Cavalier for the US Air Force and other customers, and the turboprop Turbo III and Enforcer versions were developed for the Pave Coin programme for Forward Air Control and light attack missions. Many of the new or remanufactured models of 1968–75 are two-seaters.

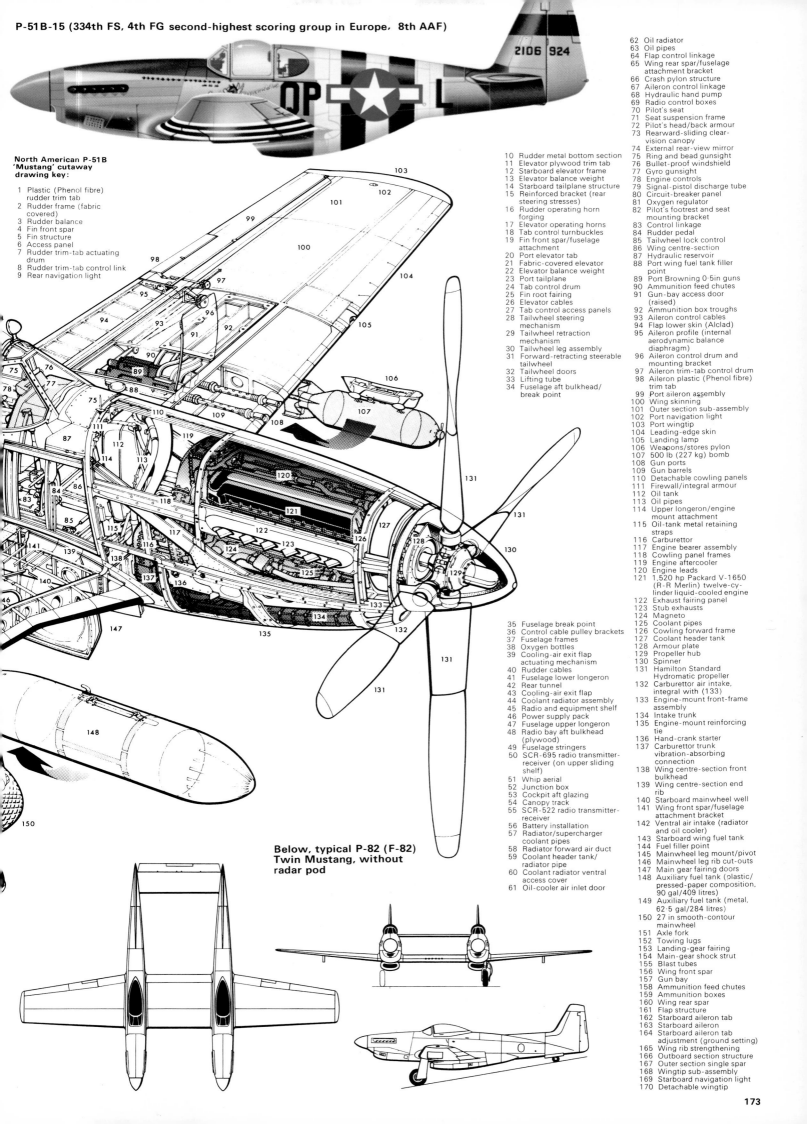

P-51B-15 (334th FS, 4th FG second-highest scoring group in Europe, 8th AAF)

2106 924

QP-L

North American P-51B 'Mustang' cutaway drawing key:

1 Plastic (Phenol fibre) rudder trim tab
2 Rudder frame (fabric covered)
3 Rudder balance
4 Fin front spar
5 Fin structure
6 Access panel
7 Rudder trim-tab actuating drum
8 Rudder trim-tab control link
9 Rear navigation light
10 Rudder metal bottom section
11 Elevator plywood trim tab
12 Starboard elevator frame
13 Elevator balance weight
14 Starboard tailplane structure
15 Reinforced bracket (rear steering stresses)
16 Rudder operating horn forging
17 Elevator operating horns
18 Tab control turnbuckles
19 Fin front spar/fuselage attachment
20 Port elevator tab
21 Fabric-covered elevator
22 Elevator balance weight
23 Port tailplane
24 Tab control drum
25 Fin root fairing
26 Elevator cables
27 Tab control access panels
28 Tailwheel steering mechanism
29 Tailwheel retraction mechanism
30 Tailwheel leg assembly
31 Forward-retracting steerable tailwheel
32 Tailwheel doors
33 Lifting tube
34 Fuselage aft bulkhead/break point
35 Fuselage break point
36 Control cable pulley brackets
37 Fuselage frames
38 Oxygen bottles
39 Cooling-air exit flap actuating mechanism
40 Rudder cables
41 Fuselage lower longeron
42 Rear tunnel
43 Cooling-air exit flap
44 Coolant radiator assembly
45 Radio and equipment shelf
46 Power supply pack
47 Fuselage upper longeron
48 Radio bay aft bulkhead (plywood)
49 Fuselage stringers
50 SCR-695 radio transmitter-receiver (on upper sliding shelf)
51 Whip aerial
52 Junction box
53 Cockpit aft glazing
54 Canopy track
55 SCR-522 radio transmitter-receiver
56 Battery installation
57 Radiator/supercharger coolant pipes
58 Radiator forward air duct
59 Coolant header tank/radiator pipe
60 Coolant radiator ventral access cover
61 Oil-cooler air inlet door
62 Oil radiator
63 Oil pipes
64 Flap control linkage
65 Wing rear spar/fuselage attachment bracket
66 Crash pylon structure
67 Aileron control linkage
68 Hydraulic hand pump
69 Radio control boxes
70 Pilot's seat
71 Seat suspension frame
72 Pilot's head/back armour
73 Rearward-sliding clear-vision canopy
74 External rear-view mirror
75 Ring and bead gunsight
76 Bullet-proof windshield
77 Gyro gunsight
78 Engine controls
79 Signal-pistol discharge tube
80 Circuit-breaker panel
81 Oxygen regulator
82 Pilot's footrest and seat mounting bracket
83 Control linkage
84 Rudder pedal
85 Tailwheel lock control
86 Wing centre-section
87 Hydraulic reservoir
88 Port wing fuel tank filler point
89 Port Browning 0·5in guns
90 Ammunition feed chutes
91 Gun-bay access door (raised)
92 Ammunition box troughs
93 Aileron control cables
94 Flap lower skin (Alclad)
95 Aileron profile (internal aerodynamic balance diaphragm)
96 Aileron control drum and mounting bracket
97 Aileron trim-tab control drum
98 Aileron plastic (Phenol fibre) trim tab
99 Port aileron assembly
100 Wing skinning
101 Outer section sub-assembly
102 Port navigation light
103 Port wingtip
104 Leading-edge skin
105 Landing lamp
106 Weapons/stores pylon
107 500 lb (227 kg) bomb
108 Gun ports
109 Gun barrels
110 Detachable cowling panels
111 Firewall/integral armour
112 Oil tank
113 Oil pipes
114 Upper longeron/engine mount attachment
115 Oil-tank metal retaining straps
116 Carburettor
117 Engine bearer assembly
118 Cowling panel frames
119 Engine aftercooler
120 Engine leads
121 1,520 hp Packard V-1650 (R-R Merlin) twelve-cylinder liquid-cooled engine
122 Exhaust fairing panel
123 Stub exhausts
124 Magneto
125 Coolant pipes
126 Cowling forward frame
127 Coolant header tank
128 Armour plate
129 Propeller hub
130 Spinner
131 Hamilton Standard Hydromatic propeller
132 Carburettor air intake, integral with (133)
133 Engine-mount front-frame assembly
134 Intake trunk
135 Engine-mount reinforcing tie
136 Hand-crank starter
137 Carburettor trunk vibration-absorbing connection
138 Wing centre-section front bulkhead
139 Wing centre-section end rib
140 Starboard mainwheel well
141 Wing front spar/fuselage attachment bracket
142 Ventral air intake (radiator and oil cooler)
143 Starboard wing fuel tank
144 Fuel filler point
145 Mainwheel leg mount/pivot
146 Mainwheel leg rib cut-outs
147 Main gear fairing doors
148 Auxiliary fuel tank (plastic/pressed-paper composition, 90 gal/409 litres)
149 Auxiliary fuel tank (metal, 62·5 gal/284 litres)
150 27 in smooth-contour mainwheel
151 Axle fork
152 Towing lugs
153 Landing-gear fairing
154 Main-gear shock strut
155 Blast tubes
156 Wing front spar
157 Gun bay
158 Ammunition feed chutes
159 Ammunition boxes
160 Wing rear spar
161 Flap structure
162 Starboard aileron tab
163 Starboard aileron
164 Starboard aileron tab adjustment (ground setting)
165 Wing rib strengthening
166 Outboard section structure
167 Outer section single spar
168 Wingtip sub-assembly
169 Starboard navigation light
170 Detachable wingtip

Below, typical P-82 (F-82) Twin Mustang, without radar pod

North American Sabre

NA-134 (XFJ-1), NA-140 (XP-86), F-86A to L, FJ-1 to 4B (F-1A to AF-1E), CL-13 (and Orenda-Sabre), CA-26 (and Avon-Sabre).

Type: basically, single-seat fighter-bomber; certain versions, all-weather interceptor or (Furies) carrier-based fighter-bomber.

Engine: (FJ-1) one 4,000 lb (1814 kg) thrust Allison J35-2 single-shaft axial turbojet; (F-86A) one 4,850 lb (2200 kg) General Electric J47-1 of same layout; (F-86D) one J47-17 or -33 rated at 7,650 lb (3470 kg with afterburner); (F-86E) one 5,200 lb (2358 kg) J47-13; (F-86F) one 5,970 lb (2710 kg) J47-27; (F-86H) one 8,920 lb (4046 kg) GE J73-3E of same layout; (F-86K) one J47-17B rated at 7,500 lb (3402 kg) with afterburner; (FJ-2) one 6,100 lb (2767 kg) J47-27A; (FJ-3, (F-1C)) one 7,200 lb (3266 kg) Wright J65-2 (Sapphire) single-shaft turbojet; (FJ-4, (F-1E)) one 7,800 lb (3538 kg) J65-4; (FJ-4B, (AF-1E)) one 7,700 lb J65-16A; (CL-13A Sabre 5) one 6,355 lb (2883 kg) Orenda 10 single-shaft turbojet; (CL-13B Sabre 6) one 7,275 lb (3300 kg) Orenda 14; (CA-27 Sabre 32) one 7,500 lb (3402 kg) CAC-built Rolls-Royce Avon 26 single-shaft turbojet.

Dimensions: span (most) 37 ft 1½ in (11·31 m); (F-86F-40 and later blocks, F-86H, K, L, CL-13 Sabre 5 (not 6), F-1E, AF-1E) all 39 ft 1 in or 39 ft 1½ in (11·9 m); length (most) 37 ft 6 in (11·43 m); (D) 40 ft 3¼ in, (H) 38 ft 10 in; (K) 40 ft 11 in; (F-1C) 37 ft 7½ in; (F-1E, AF-1E) 36 ft 4 in; height (typical) 14 ft 8¾ in (4·47 m).

Weights: empty (A) 10,606 lb; (F) 11,125 lb (5045 kg); (H) 13,836 lb; (D) 13,498 lb; (K) 13,367 lb; (AF-1E) 13,990 lb; (Sabre 32) 12,120 lb; maximum loaded (A) 16,223 lb; (F) 20,611 lb (9350 kg); (H) 24,296 lb; (D) 18,483 lb; (K) 20,171 lb; (AF-1E) 26,000 lb; (Sabre 32) 18,650 lb.

Performance: maximum speed (A) 675 mph; (F) 678 mph (1091 km/h); (H, D, K) 692 mph; (AF-1E) 680 mph; (Sabre 6, 32) both about 705 mph (peak Mach of all versions, usually 0·92); initial climb (clean) typically 8,000 ft (2440 m)/min, with D, H, K and Sabre 6 and 32 at 12,000 ft/min; service ceiling (clean) typically 50,000 ft (15,240 m); range, with external fuel, high, typically 850 miles (1368 km), except (F-1E) 2,020 miles and (AF-1E) 2,700 miles.

Armament: (A, E, F, 5, 6) six 0·5 in Colt-Browning M-3, usually with 267 rounds per gun, underwing hardpoints for two tanks or two stores of 1,000 lb (454 kg) each, plus eight rockets or two Sidewinders; (D, L) retractable pack of 24 2·75 in folding-fin aircraft rockets; (H) four 20 mm M-39 each with 150 rounds plus 1,200 lb tac-nuke or 3,000 lb of external stores or tanks; (K) four 20 mm M-24 cannon each with 132 rounds and two Sidewinders; (Sabre 32) two 30 mm Aden with 150 rounds and two Sidewinders; (FJ-2, F-1C, F-1E) four 20 mm M-24; (AF-1E) four 20 mm and four tanks, six Sidewinders, five Bullpups or 5,500 lb of other stores.

History: first flight (XFJ-1) 27 November 1946; (XP-86) 1 October 1947; service delivery (F-86A) December 1948; first flight (YF-86D) 22 December 1949; (XFJ-2) 27 December 1951; (FJ-3) 3 July 1953; (FJ-4) 28 October 1954.

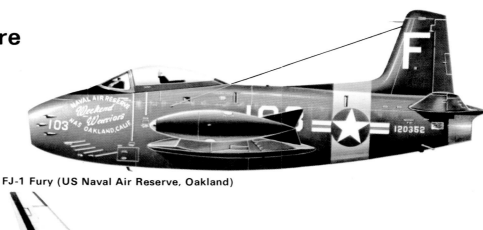

FJ-1 Fury (US Naval Air Reserve, Oakland)

F-86A Sabre (4th FIW, USAF)

Canadair CL-13 Sabre 6 (439 Sqn, RCAF, France)

Canadair Sabre 6 (17 Sqn, Royal Pakistan AF)

F-86D Sabre (726 Sqn, Royal Danish AF)

FJ-4B (AF-1E) Fury (VA-151, USN)

Certainly the most famed combat aircraft of its day, if not of the whole period since World War II, the Sabre story began with the award of Army and Navy contracts for jet fighters in 1944. The land-based programme moved fastest, with prototype contracts signed on 18 May 1944; but by 1945 the plans were boldly discarded and replaced by new ones with swept-back wings and tail. The three Navy prototypes, ordered on 1 January 1945, were continued and flown as conventional straight-wing aircraft. The order for 100 Furies was cut to 30, but VF-5A (later VF-51) operated it at sea and this otherwise undistinguished fighter was the first jet to complete an operational tour at sea. The more dramatic XP-86 set a speed of 618 mph even with its primitive 3,750 lb Chevrolet-built GE TG-180 engine and, with the 5,000 lb TG-190 (J47) in 1949, soon broke the world speed record at 671 mph (without being in any way modified from the standard fighter). Many hundreds of Sabres were soon on order, and in the Korean war the F-86E, with slatted wing and powered "flying tail", and F-86F, with extended leading edge and small fence, were brilliantly flown against the MiG-15 and established marked superiority, despite inferior climb and altitude performance. The very complex F-86D interceptor introduced the new concept of gunless collision-course interception directed by radar and autopilot; the K was a simpler stern-chase interceptor with guns which was mass-

produced by a consortium in Italy and Germany. USAF Sabres were completed by the powerful H model, but Navy counterparts soon appeared, the FJ-2 resembling a cannon-armed F and the FJ-3 and 4 (F-1C and E) having much greater power in a new airframe. The AF-1E was the pinnacle of Sabre development with toss-bombing system, FR probe, extensive new avionics and greatly increased fuel capacity. The

CL-13 series built by Canadair began as licenced E and F models (430 being supplied by Mutual Aid funds to the ailing RAF) and continued with the native Orenda engine; Australian CA-27 versions had the Avon and 30 mm guns. Total production, including 300 assembled in Japan by Mitsubishi, amounted to 9,502. This handsomely exceeds the total of any other Western military aircraft since 1945.

North American F-100 Super Sabre

F-100A to F-100F and DF-100F

Type: single-seat fighter-bomber; (F-100F) two-seat operational trainer; (DF) missile or RPV director aircraft.

Engine: one Pratt & Whitney J57 two-shaft turbojet with afterburner, (most blocks of A) 14,500 lb (6576 kg) J57-7; (late A, all C) 16,000 lb (7257 kg) J57-29; (D, F) 16,950 lb (7690 kg) J57-21A (all ratings with afterburner).

Dimensions: span (original A) 36 ft 7 in; (remainder) 38 ft 9½ in (11·81 m); length (except F, excluding pitot boom) 49 ft 6 in (15·09 m), (fuselage, 47 ft exactly); (F) 52 ft 6 in (16·0 m), (boom adds about 6 ft to all models); height (original A) 13 ft 4 in; (remainder) 16 ft 2¾ in (4·96 m).

Weights: empty (original A) 19,700 lb; (C) 20,450 lb; (D) 21,000 lb (9525 kg); (F) 22,300 lb (10,115 kg); maximum loaded (original A) 28,935 lb; (C, D) 34,832 lb (15,800 kg); (F, two tanks but no weapons) 30,700 lb (13,925 kg).

Performance: maximum speed (typical of all) 864 mph at height (1390 km/h, Mach 1·31); initial climb (clean) 16,000 ft (4900 m)/min; service ceiling (typical) 45,000 ft (13,720 m); range (high, two 375 gal tanks) 1,500 miles (2415 km).

Armament: usually four (F, only two) 20 mm M-39E cannon each with 200 rounds; (A) pylons for two 375 gal supersonic tanks and four additional hardpoints (seldom used) for 4,000 lb ordnance; (C, D)

two tanks and six pylons for 7,500 lb (3402 kg) ordnance; (F) two tanks and maximum of 6,000 lb (2722 kg) ordnance.

History: first flight (YF-100) 25 May 1953; production (A) 29 October 1953; final delivery October 1959.

The success of the Sabre made it natural to attempt a successor, and in February 1949 this was planned as a larger and much more powerful machine able to exceed the speed of sound in level flight (had it been started two years later it might have been smaller, in view of the Korean pressure for simple fighters with the highest possible climb and performance at extreme altitudes). Unusual features were the 6 per cent wing with 45° sweep, no flaps, inboard ailerons, full-span slats and a slab tailplane mounted as low as possible. Level supersonic speed was achieved, for the first time with a combat aircraft, but after very rapid development, with the first (479th) wing fully equipped, the F-100A was

grounded in November 1954. Trouble due to inertia coupling between the roll and yaw axes necessitated urgent modification, the wings and fin being lengthened. Subsequently the career of the "Hun" was wholly successful, the 203 A fighters being followed by the stronger C fighter-bomber, the D with flaps and autopilot and the tandem-seat F. Total production was lower than expected at 2,294, many being built by NAA's newly occupied factory at Columbus, Ohio. In their early years the later versions pioneered global deployment of tactical aircraft by means of probe/drogue refuelling, and in Vietnam they proved outstandingly good at both low attack and top cover, flying more missions than over 15,000 Mustangs flew in World War II. In the 1970s "Huns" flew with the Air National Guard, Armée de l'Air, Denmark, Turkey and Nationalist China.
Later North American aircraft see under Rockwell

Northrop P-61 Black Widow

P-61A, B and C and F-15 (RF-61C) Reporter

Type: (P-61) three-seat night fighter; (F-15) two-seat strategic reconnaissance.

Engines: two Pratt & Whitney R-2800 Double Wasp 18-cylinder two-row radials; (P-61A) 2,000 hp R-2800-10; (B) 2,000 hp R-2800-65; (C and F-15) 2,800 hp (wet rating) R-2800-73.

Dimensions: span 66 ft (20·12 m); length (A) 48 ft 11 in (14·92 m); (B, C) 49 ft 7 in (15·1 m); (F-15) 50 ft 3 in (15·3 m); height (typical) 14 ft 8 in (4·49 m).

Weights: empty (typical P-61) 24,000 lb (10,886 kg); (F-15) 22,000 lb (9979 kg); maximum loaded (A) 32,400 lb (14,696 kg); (B) 38,000 lb (17,237 kg); (C) 40,300 lb (18,280 kg); (F-15, clean) 28,000 lb (12,700 kg).

Performance: maximum speed (A, B) 366 mph (590 km/h); (C) 430 mph (692 km/h); (F-15)

440 mph (708 km/h); initial climb (A, B) 2,200 ft (670 m)/min; (C, F-15) 3,000 ft (914 m)/min; service ceiling (A, B) 33,000 ft (10,060 m); (C, F-15) 41,000 ft (12,500 m); range with maximum fuel (A) 500 miles; (B, C) 2,800 miles (4500 km); (F-15) 4,000 miles (6440 km).

Armament: four fixed 20 mm M-2 cannon in belly, firing ahead (plus, in first 37 A, last 250 B and all C) electric dorsal turret with four 0·5 in remotely controlled from front or rear sight station and fired by pilot; (B and C) underwing racks for 6,400 lb load; (F-15A) no armament.

History: first flight (XP-61) 21 May 1942; service delivery (A) May 1944; first flight (F-15A) 1946.

The first aircraft ever ordered to be designed explicitly as a night fighter, the XP-61 prototypes were ordered in

January 1941 on the basis of combat reports from the early radar-equipped fighters of the RAF. A very big aircraft, the P-61 had the new SCR-720 AI radar in the nose, the armament being mounted well back above and below the rather lumpy nacelle housing pilot, radar operator and gunner with front and rear sighting stations. The broad wing had almost full-span double-slotted flaps, very small ailerons and lateral-control spoilers in an arrangement years ahead of its time. Black-painted (hence the name), the P-61A entered service with the 18th Fighter Group in the South Pacific and soon gained successes there and in Europe. Buffet from the turret led to this soon being deleted, but the B and C had pylons for the very heavy load of four 250 gal tanks or 6,400 lb (2900 kg) bombs. Total production was 941, followed by 35 slim photo-reconnaissance versions.

Northrop F-89 Scorpion

F-89 to F-89J

Type: two-seat all-weather and night fighter.

Engines: two Allison J35 single-shaft axial turbojets with simple afterburners (augmented ratings given); (XF-89) 3,750 lb J35-13; (F-89A) 6,800 lb J35-21; (B) 7,000 lb J35-33; (C) 7,500 lb (3402 kg) J35-35. (D, H, J) 7,500 lb (3402 kg) J35-47.

Dimensions: span (A) 56 ft (17·07 m); (remainder, over pods) 59 ft 8 in (18·18 m); length (A) 53 ft 6 in (16·33 m); (remainder) 53 ft 10 in (16·4 m); height (typical) 17 ft 7 in (5·36 m).

Weights: empty (A) 19,800 lb; (H) 26,100 lb (11,840 kg); loaded (A) 32,500 lb (14,740 kg); (D) 41,000 lb (18,600 kg); (H, J) 46,000 lb (20,865 kg).

Performance: maximum speed (A) 570 mph; (D) 610 mph (982 km/h); (H, J) 595 mph (958 km/h); initial climb (typical) 5,250 ft (1600 m)/min; service ceiling (typical) 36,000 ft (10,980 m); range (A) 1,300 miles; (remainder, typical) 1,000 miles (1610 km).

Armament: (A, B, C) six 20 mm M-2 cannon each with 300 rounds; (D) 104 Mighty Mouse 2·75 in FFAR (folding-fin aircraft rockets) in wing-tip pods, all guns being removed; (H) six GAR-1D or -2A (later AIM-4C or -4D) Falcon semi-submerged around tip pods, plus two MB-1 (AIR-2A or -2B) Genie on wing pylons, plus 42 FFAR inside tip pods; (J) two AIR-2A or -2B Genie on wing pylons, plus four AIM-4C or -4D on wing pylons (tip pods fuel only).

History: first flight (XF-89) 16 August 1948; (YF-89A) 27 June 1950; (YF-89D, converted from B) June 1952; final delivery (from new (H)) 1956.

F-89H or F-89J (without guided missiles)

Having cut their teeth with the P-61, Northrop naturally responded to an Army Air Force request dated September 1945 for a jet night fighter. The F.189 entered production in March 1949. It was a large but slim machine, with a thin but very broad unswept wing passing below the crew but above the two rather

primitive engines. To fit inside the wing the main wheels were very thin and so were made of extraordinary diameter. All controls were powered and the large ailerons could open into upper and lower halves to serve as "decelerons" (ailerons/air brakes) to assist the pilot in getting into firing position behind his quarry. The observer in the back seat managed the SCR-720 radar, carried ahead of the six cannon. After delivering 30, production was switched to the slightly different B, followed by 164 improved C models. Then came 682 of the dramatically different F-89D with an autopilot linked to a big new radar to fly the aircraft automatically on a collision course. Final batches added up to 156 of the H model (bringing the total to 1,050) armed with guided missiles, 350 of the D-type being similarly updated and restyled F-89J. After arduous service all over the world the Scorpion passed to the Air National Guard from 1958 and out of service in 1963.

Northrop F-5

F-5A, B, E and F, CF-5A and D, NF-5A and B, RF-5A, E and G, and SF-5A and B

Type: (with suffix A, E and G) single-seat fighter-reconnaissance; (with suffix B, D and F) two-seat dual fighter/trainer.

Engines: (A, B, D, G) two 4,080 lb (1850 kg) thrust General Electric J85-13 single-shaft afterburning turbojets; (E, F) two 5,000 lb (2268 kg) J85-21.

Dimensions: span (A, B, D, G) 25 ft 3 in (7·7 m); (E, F) 26 ft 8 in (8·13 m); length (A, G) 47 ft 2 in (14·38 m); (B, D) 46 ft 4 in (14·12 m); (E) 48 ft 3¾ in (14·73 m); (F) 51 ft 9¾ in (15·80 m); height (A, G) 13 ft 2 in (4·01 m); (B, D) 13 ft 1 in (3·99 m); (E, F) 13 ft 4½ in (4·08 m).

Weights: empty (A, G) 8,085 lb (3667 kg); (B, D) 8,361 lb (3792 kg); (E) 9,588 lb (4349 kg); (F) 9,700 lb (4400 kg); maximum loaded (A, G) 20,677 lb (9379 kg); (B, D) 20,500 lb (9298 kg); (E, F) 24,080 lb (10,922 kg).

Performance: maximum speed at altitude (A, G) 925 mph (1489 km/h, Mach 1·40); (B, D) 885 mph (1424 km/h, Mach 1·34); (E) 1,060 mph (1705 km/h, Mach 1·60); initial climb (A, G) 28,700 ft (8760 m)/min; (B, D) 30,400 ft (9265 m)/min; (E) 31,600 ft (9630 m)/min; service ceiling (A, G) 50,500 ft (15,390 m); (B, D) 52,000 ft (15,850 m); (E) 54,000 ft (16,460 m); range with max fuel, with reserves, tanks retained, (A, G) 1,387 miles (2232 km); (B, D) 1,393 miles (2241 km); (E) 1,974 miles (3175 km).

Armament: two 20 mm M-39A2 cannon each with 280 rounds in nose (can be retained in RF versions); five pylons for total external load of about 4,400 lb (2000 kg) in A, G (total military load for these models, including guns and ammunition, is 5,200 lb) or 7,000 lb (3175 kg) in E; rails on wingtips for AIM-9 Sidewinder missiles.

History: first flight (XT-38) 10 April 1959, (N-156F) 30 July 1959, (F-5A) 19 May 1964, (F-5E) 11 August 1972, (F-5F) 25 September 1974.

In 1955 Northrop began the project design of a lightweight fighter, known as Tally-Ho, powered by two J85 missile engines slung in pods under a very small unswept wing. It was yet another of the many projects born in the Korean era when pilots were calling for lighter, simpler fighters with higher performance. Gradually Welko Gasich and his team refined the design, putting the engines in the fuselage and increasing the size, partly to meet the needs of the Navy. In June 1956 the Navy had pulled out, while the Air Force ordered the trainer version as the T-38 Talon. Over the next 15 years Northrop delivered 1,200 Talons, all to the USAF or NASA, as the standard supersonic trainer of those services. With this assured programme the company took the unique decision to go ahead and build a demonstration fighter in the absence of any orders — the only time this has ever been done with a supersonic aircraft. By the time it was ready for flight in 1959 the N-156F, dubbed Freedom Fighter, had received some US Defense funding, and the prototype carried US serial and stencil markings but no national markings. It was a simple little fighter, carrying about 485 gallons of fuel, two cannon and an old F-86 style sight, and having racks for two little Sidewinder missiles. Today the little prototype would have remained unsold, but in October 1962 the

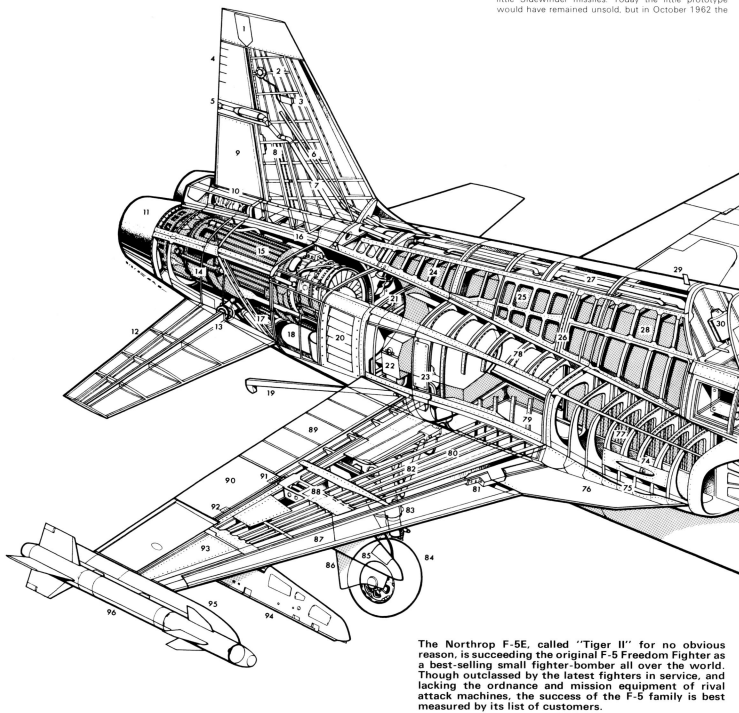

The Northrop F-5E, called "Tiger II" for no obvious reason, is succeeding the original F-5 Freedom Fighter as a best-selling small fighter-bomber all over the world. Though outclassed by the latest fighters in service, and lacking the ordnance and mission equipment of rival attack machines, the success of the F-5 family is best measured by its list of customers.

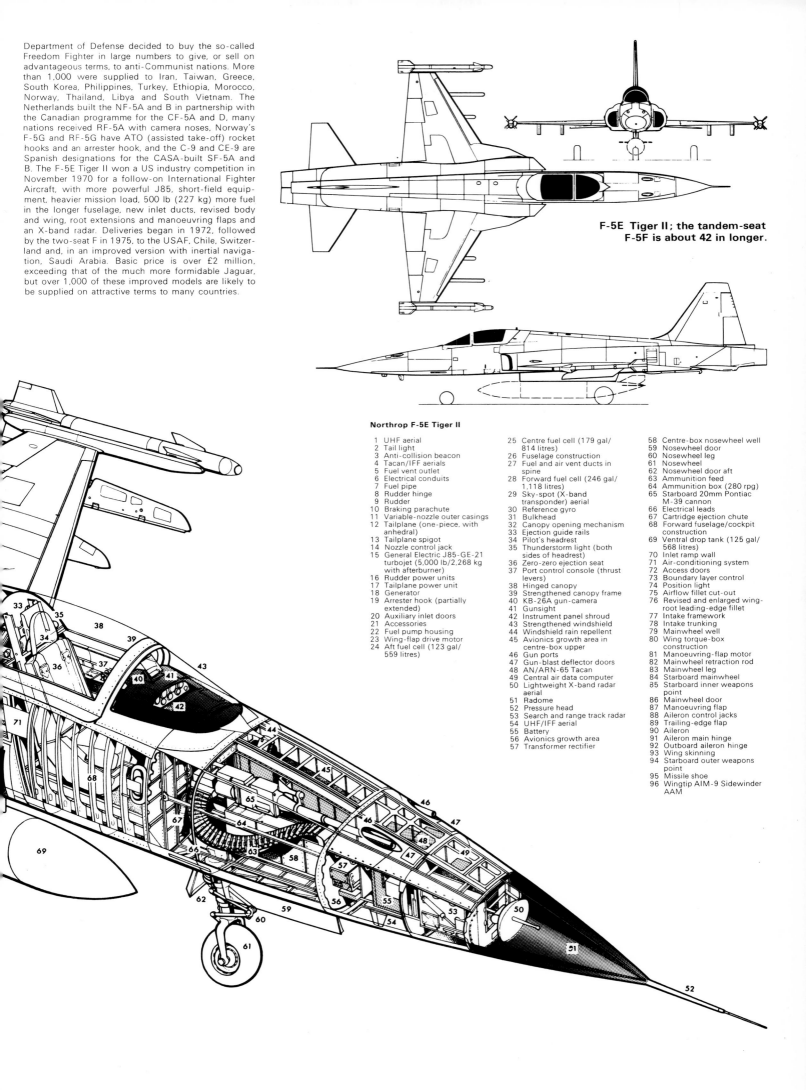

Department of Defense decided to buy the so-called Freedom Fighter in large numbers to give, or sell on advantageous terms, to anti-Communist nations. More than 1,000 were supplied to Iran, Taiwan, Greece, South Korea, Philippines, Turkey, Ethiopia, Morocco, Norway, Thailand, Libya and South Vietnam. The Netherlands built the NF-5A and B in partnership with the Canadian programme for the CF-5A and D, many nations received RF-5A with camera noses, Norway's F-5G and RF-5G have ATO (assisted take-off) rocket hooks and an arrester hook, and the C-9 and CE-9 are Spanish designations for the CASA-built SF-5A and B. The F-5E Tiger II won a US industry competition in November 1970 for a follow-on International Fighter Aircraft, with more powerful J85, short-field equipment, heavier mission load, 500 lb (227 kg) more fuel in the longer fuselage, new inlet ducts, revised body and wing, root extensions and manoeuvring flaps and an X-band radar. Deliveries began in 1972, followed by the two-seat F in 1975, to the USAF, Chile, Switzerland and, in an improved version with inertial navigation, Saudi Arabia. Basic price is over £2 million, exceeding that of the much more formidable Jaguar, but over 1,000 of these improved models are likely to be supplied on attractive terms to many countries.

F-5E Tiger II; the tandem-seat F-5F is about 42 in longer.

Northrop F-5E Tiger II

1 UHF aerial
2 Tail light
3 Anti-collision beacon
4 Tacan/IFF aerials
5 Fuel vent outlet
6 Electrical conduits
7 Fuel pipe
8 Rudder hinge
9 Rudder
10 Braking parachute
11 Variable-nozzle outer casings
12 Tailplane (one-piece, with anhedral)
13 Tailplane spigot
14 Nozzle control jack
15 General Electric J85-GE-21 turbojet (5,000 lb/2,268 kg with afterburner)
16 Rudder power units
17 Tailplane power unit
18 Generator
19 Arrester hook (partially extended)
20 Auxiliary inlet doors
21 Accessories
22 Fuel pump housing
23 Wing-flap drive motor
24 Aft fuel cell (123 gal/ 559 litres)
25 Centre fuel cell (179 gal/ 814 litres)
26 Fuselage construction
27 Fuel and air vent ducts in spine
28 Forward fuel cell (246 gal/ 1,118 litres)
29 Sky-spot (X-band transponder) aerial
30 Reference gyro
31 Bulkhead
32 Canopy opening mechanism
33 Ejection guide rails
34 Pilot's headrest
35 Thunderstorm light (both sides of headrest)
36 Zero-zero ejection seat
37 Port control console (thrust levers)
38 Hinged canopy
39 Strengthened canopy frame
40 KB-26A gun-camera
41 Gunsight
42 Instrument panel shroud
43 Strengthened windshield
44 Windshield rain repellent
45 Avionics growth area in centre-box upper
46 Gun ports
47 Gun-blast deflector doors
48 AN/ARN-65 Tacan
49 Central air data computer
50 Lightweight X-band radar aerial
51 Radome
52 Pressure head
53 Search and range track radar
54 UHF/IFF aerial
55 Battery
56 Avionics growth area
57 Transformer rectifier
58 Centre-box nosewheel well
59 Nosewheel door
60 Nosewheel leg
61 Nosewheel
62 Nosewheel door aft
63 Ammunition feed
64 Ammunition box (280 rpg)
65 Starboard 20mm Pontiac M-39 cannon
66 Electrical leads
67 Cartridge ejection chute
68 Forward fuselage/cockpit construction
69 Ventral drop tank (125 gal/ 568 litres)
70 Inlet ramp wall
71 Air-conditioning system
72 Access doors
73 Boundary layer control
74 Position light
75 Airflow fillet cut-out
76 Revised and enlarged wing-root leading-edge fillet
77 Intake framework
78 Intake trunking
79 Mainwheel well
80 Wing torque-box construction
81 Manoeuvring-flap motor
82 Mainwheel retraction rod
83 Mainwheel leg
84 Starboard mainwheel
85 Starboard inner weapons point
86 Mainwheel door
87 Manoeuvring flap
88 Aileron control jacks
89 Trailing-edge flap
90 Aileron
91 Aileron main hinge
92 Outboard aileron hinge
93 Wing skinning
94 Starboard outer weapons point
95 Missile shoe
96 Wingtip AIM-9 Sidewinder AAM

Panavia MRCA Tornado

Model 200 MRCA (S), (AD) and (T)

Type: two-seat multi-role combat aircraft, (S) optimised for strike, (AD) for air defence, (T) dual trainer.
Engines: two 14,500 lb (6577 kg) thrust Turbo-Union RB.199-34R three-shaft augmented turbofans.
Dimensions: span (25°) 45 ft 7¼ in (13·90 m), (65°) 28 ft 2½ in (8·60 m); length 54 ft 9½ in (16·70 m); height 18 ft 8½ in (5·70 m).
Weights: empty, about 24,000 lb (10,890 kg); loaded (clean) about 35,000 lb (15,880 kg); maximum loaded, about 50,000 lb (22,680 kg).

Performance: maximum speed (clean), at sea level, about 910 mph (1465 km/h, Mach 1·2), at height, over 1,320 mph (2135 km/h, Mach 2); service ceiling over 50,000 ft (15,240 m); range, about 1,000 miles (1610 km) on internal fuel (high, wings spread), or over 3,000 miles (4830 km) in ferry mode with maximum fuel.
Armament: two 27 mm Mauser cannon in lower forward fuselage; external load exceeding 15,000 lb (6804 kg) carried on three fixed body pylons and four swivelling wing pylons.
History: first flight 14 August 1974; planned service delivery 1977.

No combat aircraft in history has ever been planned with such care by so many possible customers. Studies began in 1967, after the French had abandoned the AFVG aircraft in the same class and decided not to participate in collaborative aircraft of this type. Panavia Aircraft was registered on 26 March 1969 in

ception; reconnaissance; training. At one time it was planned that the three nations should develop slightly different versions with either one or two seats and dry or wet wings, but all basic aircraft now in production are identical, with two seats and sealed integral-tank wings. From stem to stern the MRCA is totally modern — a fact which its many competitors have sought to counter by claiming it to be "complicated" or "expensive". In fact it is not possible to fly the required missions without carrying the equipment, and the fly-away price of £3·9 million (in September 1974 sterling) is by a very wide margin cheaper than any comparable aircraft. The only aircraft that bears comparison with MRCA is the larger F-14, which cannot meet the MRCA requirements in the attack and reconnaissance roles. Other combat aircraft with but one seat and a fixed (non-swinging) wing are grossly deficient in nearly all roles, though comparable in high-altitude combat.

The basic MRCA has outstandingly efficient and compact engines of extremely advanced design, with automatically scheduled inlets and nozzles. Flight control is by large tailerons, augmented at low sweep

Munich as a three-nation company to manage the MRCA (multi-role combat aircraft) programme, with shares held in the ratio BAC 42½ per cent, MBB 42½ per cent and Aeritalia 15 per cent. In September 1969, after intense competition with the United States, the RB.199 was selected as the engine and a month later Turbo-Union was formed as the engine-management company with shares held in the ratio Rolls-Royce 40 per cent, MTU 40 per cent and Fiat 20 per cent. Thanks to the careful planning the MRCA programme has since demonstrated that it is possible for several nations to work together to create a modern military aircraft which promises to exceed all possible rivals in mission effectiveness, versatility and low cost, having already demonstrated better mission capability than the latest competing types designed specifically for that mission. Its design missions are: close air support/battlefield interdiction; long-range interdiction/strike; naval strike; air superiority; air defence/inter-

Panavia Tornado MRCA

1 Fin-tip aerial
2 Passive ECM aerial fairings (MSDS/Decca/Plessey)
3 Rear navigation light
4 Plate aerial
5 Aerial housing
6 Fixed fin
7 Two-spar fin construction
8 Rudder
9 Rudder lower hinge
10 Fin/fuselage attachment
11 Fairey power unit inside rudder
12 Convergent nozzle
13 Afterburner
14 Nozzle position indication system
15 Thrust reverser
16 Runway arrester hook
17 Tailplane structure
18 Tailplane frame
19 Tailplane actuator and pivot
20 Airbrake
21 Machined fuselage frames
22 Turbo-Union RB 199-34R three-shaft turbofans (over 14,500 lb/6.577 kg with maximum afterburner)
23 Engine accessories and integral oil tank
24 Three-stage engine fan
25 Intake trunking
26 Integral fuel stowage
27 Fin/Fuselage attachment
28 Fin root fairing
29 Air outlet
30 Ram intake (conditioning air)
31 Port airbrake (extended)
32 Port elevator/taileron
33 Line of wing sweep
34 Flap position (extended)
35 Full span double-slotted flaps
36 Spoilers
37 Flap actuator linkage
38 Port navigation light
39 Wing access panels
40 Pylon swivel mechanism
41 Port outer pylon
42 Launcher pod
43 Wing torque box
44 Spoiler actuators (Fairey)
45 Integral fuel tank
46 Full-span leading-edge slats (extended)
47 Pylon pivot point
48 Port inner pylon
49 Ferry tank
50 Wing sealing glove
51 Slat actuator (Microtecnica)
52 Wing sweep actuator (Microtecnica) and equaliser rods

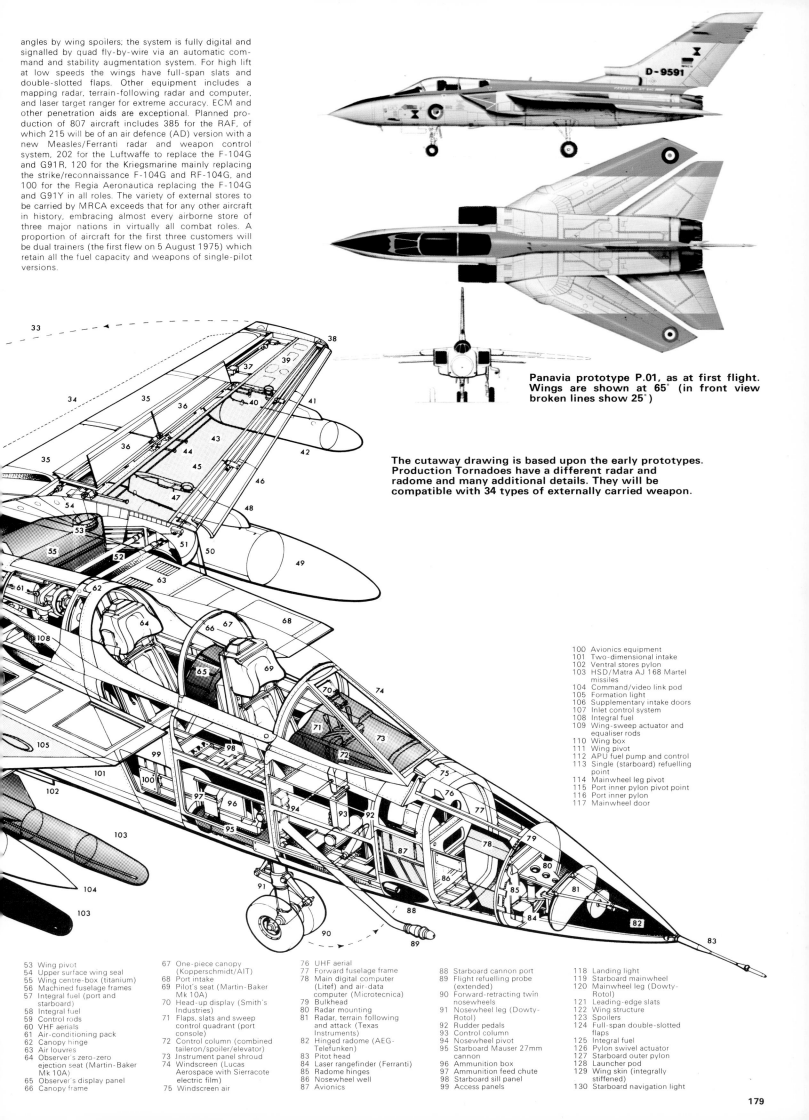

angles by wing spoilers; the system is fully digital and signalled by quad fly-by-wire via an automatic command and stability augmentation system. For high lift at low speeds the wings have full-span slats and double-slotted flaps. Other equipment includes a mapping radar, terrain-following radar and computer, and laser target ranger for extreme accuracy. ECM and other penetration aids are exceptional. Planned production of 807 aircraft includes 385 for the RAF, of which 215 will be of an air defence (AD) version with a new Measles/Ferranti radar and weapon control system, 202 for the Luftwaffe to replace the F-104G and G91R, 120 for the Kriegsmarine mainly replacing the strike/reconnaissance F-104G and RF-104G, and 100 for the Regia Aeronautica replacing the F-104G and G91Y in all roles. The variety of external stores to be carried by MRCA exceeds that for any other aircraft in history, embracing almost every airborne store of three major nations in virtually all combat roles. A proportion of aircraft for the first three customers will be dual trainers (the first flew on 5 August 1975) which retain all the fuel capacity and weapons of single-pilot versions.

Panavia prototype P.01, as at first flight. Wings are shown at 65° (in front view broken lines show 25°)

The cutaway drawing is based upon the early prototypes. Production Tornadoes have a different radar and radome and many additional details. They will be compatible with 34 types of externally carried weapon.

100 Avionics equipment
101 Two-dimensional intake
102 Ventral stores pylon
103 HSD/Matra AJ 168 Martel missiles
104 Command/video link pod
105 Formation light
106 Supplementary intake doors
107 Inlet control system
108 Integral fuel
109 Wing-sweep actuator and equaliser rods
110 Wing box
111 Wing pivot
112 APU fuel pump and control
113 Single (starboard) refuelling point
114 Mainwheel leg pivot
115 Port inner pylon pivot point
116 Port inner pylon
117 Mainwheel door

53 Wing pivot
54 Upper surface wing seal
55 Wing centre-box (titanium)
56 Machined fuselage frames
57 Integral fuel (port and starboard)
58 Integral fuel
59 Control rods
60 VHF aerials
61 Air-conditioning pack
62 Canopy hinge
63 Air louvres
64 Observer's zero-zero ejection seat (Martin-Baker Mk 10A)
65 Observer's display panel
66 Canopy frame

67 One-piece canopy (Kopperschmidt/AIT)
68 Port intake
69 Pilot's seat (Martin-Baker Mk 10A)
70 Head-up display (Smith's Industries)
71 Flaps, slats and sweep control quadrant (port console)
72 Control column (combined taileron/spoiler/elevator)
73 Instrument panel shroud
74 Windscreen (Lucas Aerospace with Sierracote electric film)
75 Windscreen air

76 UHF aerial
77 Forward fuselage frame
78 Main digital computer (Litef) and air-data computer (Microtecnica)
79 Bulkhead
80 Radar mounting
81 Radar, terrain following and attack (Texas Instruments)
82 Hinged radome (AEG-Telefunken)
83 Pitot head
84 Laser rangefinder (Ferranti)
85 Radome hinges
86 Nosewheel well
87 Avionics

88 Starboard cannon port
89 Flight refuelling probe (extended)
90 Forward-retracting twin nosewheels
91 Nosewheel leg (Dowty-Rotol)
92 Rudder pedals
93 Control column
94 Nosewheel pivot
95 Starboard Mauser 27mm cannon
96 Ammunition box
97 Ammunition feed chute
98 Starboard sill panel
99 Access panels

118 Landing light
119 Starboard mainwheel
120 Mainwheel leg (Dowty-Rotol)
121 Leading-edge slats
122 Wing structure
123 Spoilers
124 Full-span double-slotted flaps
125 Integral fuel
126 Pylon swivel actuator
127 Starboard outer pylon
128 Launcher pod
129 Wing skin (integrally stiffened)
130 Starboard navigation light

Petlyakov Pe-2

Pe-2, 2I, 2R, 2U and 3bis
Type: (2) attack bomber; (2I) interceptor fighter; (2R) reconnaissance; (2U) dual trainer; (3bis) fighter reconnaissance.
Engines: two Klimov (Hispano-Suiza basic design) vee-12 liquid-cooled; (2, pre-1943) 1,100 hp M-105R or RA; (2, 1943 onwards, 2R, 2U, 3bis) 1,260 hp M-105PF; (2I) 1,600 hp M-107A.
Dimensions: span 56 ft $3\frac{1}{2}$ in (17·2 m); length 41 ft $4\frac{1}{4}$ in to 41 ft 6 in (12·6–12·66 m); height 11 ft 6 in (3·5 m).
Weights: empty (typical) 12,900 lb (5870 kg); normal loaded 16,540–16,976 lb (7700 kg); maximum loaded (all versions) 18,780 lb (8520 kg).
Performance: maximum speed (typical, 105R) 336 mph (540 km/h); (105PF) 360 mph (580 km/h); (107A) 408 mph (655 km/h); initial climb (typical) 1,430 ft (436 m)/min; service ceiling (except 2I) 28,870 ft (8800 m); (2I) 36,100 ft (11,000 m); range with bomb load (105R) 746 miles (1200 km); (105PF) 721 miles (1160 km).
Armament: see text.
History: first flight (VI-100) 1939; (production Pe-2) June 1940; final delivery, probably January 1945.

Not until long after World War II did Western observers appreciate the importance of the Pe-2. Built throughout the war, it was one of the outstanding combat aircraft of the Allies and, by dint of continual improvement, remained in the front rank of tactical fighting along the entire Eastern front right up to the German surrender.
It was planned by Vladimir M. Petlyakov's design team in 1938 as a high-altitude fighter designated VI-100. When adapted to high-level bombing it kept the fighter's

slim fuselage and this feature, coupled with intensive aerodynamic refinement, always made it fast enough to be difficult for German fighters to intercept it. Level bombing at height proved inaccurate, so dive brakes were added under the wings and the Pe-2 went into service in August 1940 as a multi-role dive and attack bomber, with crew of three and four 7·62 mm ShKAS machine guns, two fixed firing ahead above the nose,

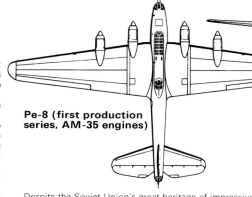

Pe-2 (basic bomber version)

one aimed from the upper rear position and one aimed from a retracting ventral mount with periscopic sight. Up to 2,205 lb (1000 kg) of bombs could be carried, either all externally or partly in the bomb bay and part in the rear of the long nacelles. The Pe-3bis fighter of 1941 had manoeuvre flaps instead of dive brakes, and additional fixed 20mm ShVAK and 12·7 mm BS guns. During 1942 a 12·7 mm power turret replaced the upper rear gun, the lower rear gun was made 12·7 mm calibre and two 7·62 mm beam guns were added. Extra armour, self-sealing tanks with cold exhaust-gas purging, detail drag-reduction and PF engines followed. The final versions had M-107 (VK-107) engines, various heavier armament and up to 6,615 lb (3000 kg) bomb load. Total production was 11,400.

Petlyakov Pe-8

ANT-42, TB-7, Pe-8 (various sub-types)
Type: heavy bomber with normal crew of nine.
Engines: (prototype) see text; (first production) four 1,300 hp Mikulin AM-35A vee-12 liquid-cooled; (second production) four 1,475 hp Charomski M-30B vee-12 diesels; (third production) four 1,630 hp Shvetsov ASh-82FNV 14-cylinder two-row radials.
Dimensions: span 131 ft $0\frac{1}{2}$ in (39·94 m); length 73 ft $8\frac{3}{4}$ in (22·47 m); height 20 ft (6·1 m).
Weights: empty (first production) 37,480 lb (17,000 kg); (typical late production) about 40,000 lb (18,000 kg); maximum loaded (early) 63,052 lb (28,600 kg); (late, M-30B) 73,469 lb (33,325 kg); (ASh-82) 68,519 lb (31,080 kg).
Performance: maximum speed (AM-35) 276 mph (444 km/h); (M-30B) 272 mph (438 km/h); (ASh-82) 280 mph (451 km/h); initial climb (typical) 853 ft (260 m)/min; service ceiling (AM-35, M-30B) about 22,966 ft (7000 m); (ASh-82) 29,035 ft (8850 m); range, see text.
Armament: (typical) one 20 mm ShVAK in dorsal and tail turrets, two 7·62 mm ShKAS in nose turret and one 12·7 mm BS manually aimed from rear of each inner nacelle; bomb load, see text.
History: first flight (ANT-42) 27 December 1936; (production TB-7) early 1939; (ASh-82 version) 1943; final delivery 1944.

Pe-8 (first production series, AM-35 engines)

Despite the Soviet Union's great heritage of impressive heavy bombers the TB-7 was the only aircraft in this category in World War II and only a few hundred were built. This stemmed from a Germanic concentration on twin-engined tactical machines rather than any shortcoming in the Pe-8 and there was at no time any serious problem with propulsion, though the type of engine kept changing. The prototype, built to a 1934 specification, had four 1,100 hp M-105 engines supercharged by a large blower driven by an M-100 engine in the rear fuselage. Another had AM-34FRN engines,

but the AM-35A was chosen for production at Kuznets in 1939, by which time the complex ACN-2 supercharging system had been abandoned. Performance at 8000 m (26,250 ft, double the maximum-speed height for earlier Soviet heavies) was outstanding and faster than the Bf 109B. In 1940, in line with the new Soviet designation system, the TB-7 was credited to Petlyakov, leader of the design team. Unfortunately he was killed in a crash two years later and most of the wartime development was managed by I. F. Nyezeval. Maximum bomb load was 8,818 lb (4000 kg), the range of 2,321 miles being raised to over 3,000 miles by the diesel engines substituted when AM-35 production ceased. The final radial-engined version could carry 11,600 lb for 2,500 miles and many long missions were made into Hungary, Romania and East Germany, the first major mission being on Berlin in mid-1941.

Pfalz D.III

D.III and IIIa (data for III)
Type: single-seat fighter.
Engine: one Mercedes six-cylinder water-cooled; (D.III) 160 hp D.III; (D.IIIa) 180 hp D.IIIa.
Dimensions: span 30 ft $10\frac{1}{4}$ in (9·4 m); length 22 ft $9\frac{3}{4}$ in (6·95 m); height 8 ft $9\frac{1}{4}$ in (2·68 m).
Weights: empty 1,653 lb (750 kg), loaded 2,056 lb (933 kg).
Performance: maximum speed 102 mph (165 km/h); initial climb 820 ft (250 m)/min; service ceiling 17,060 ft (5200 m); range, about 217 miles (350 km).
Armament: two 7·92 mm Spandau machine guns fixed in top decking (in early III, on lower sides of nose).
History: first flight (III) summer (probably June) 1917; service delivery, September 1917; (IIIa) February 1918.
The Pfalz Flugzeugwerke, at Speyer, was administered by the Bavarian government and supplied its aircraft

(at least in the early years of World War I) only to Bavarian units. At first it built Moranes and other types under licence, but the D.III was a completely fresh design into which was incorporated much experience gained in 1916–17 with the production of LFG-Roland fighters. Though fractionally inferior in performance to the best contemporary Albatros and Fokker scouts, the III and IIIa were strong and well liked. About 600 were built, the more powerful IIIa having rounded wings and tailplane. Pfalz fuselages were streamlined wooden monocoques built on Deperdussin principles. Pfalz's next design was the excellent D.XII, essentially a refined and even stronger III with radiator moved from the top wing to the front of the cylinder block. It suffered

Pfalz D.III (aircraft of, Jagdstaffel 10)

unfairly from production and propaganda priority given to the rival Fokker D.VII, but in some respects it was even superior to that better-known machine.

Polikarpov I-15

TsKB-3, I-15, I-15bis, I-153
Type: single-seat fighter (15bis, 153, fighter-bomber).
Engine: (15) one 700 hp Shvetsov M-25 (Wright Cyclone); (15bis) 750 hp M-25B; (153) 1,000 hp M-63, all nine-cylinder radials.
Dimensions: span 29 ft 11½ in (9·13 m); (bis) 33 ft 6 in; (153) 32 ft 9¾ in; length 20 ft 7½ in (6·29 m); (bis) 20 ft 9¼ in; (153) 20 ft 3 in; height 9 ft 7 in (2·92 m); (bis) 9 ft 10 in; (153) 9 ft 3 in.
Weights: empty 2,597 lb (1178 kg); (bis) 2,880 lb; (153) 3,168 lb; maximum loaded 3,027–3,135 lb (1370–1422 kg); (bis) 4,189 lb; (153) 4,431 lb.
Performance: maximum speed 224 mph (360 km/h); (bis) 230 mph; (153) 267 mph; initial climb (all) about 2,500 ft (765 m)/min; service ceiling 32,800 ft (10,000 m); (bis) 26,245 ft; (153) 35,100 ft; range 450 miles (720 km); (bis) 280 miles; (153) 298 miles.
Armament: four (sometimes two) 7·62 mm DA or ShKAS in fuselage; (bis) as 15, plus two 110 lb (50 kg) or four 55 lb bombs or six RS-82 rockets; (153) as 15bis but two 165 lb bombs.
History: first flight (TsKB-3) October 1933; service delivery 1934; service delivery (bis) 1937; (153) 1939.

One might jump to the conclusion that these Polikarpov biplanes were superseded by the I-16 monoplane (p. 182). In fact the I-16 flew before any of them, was in

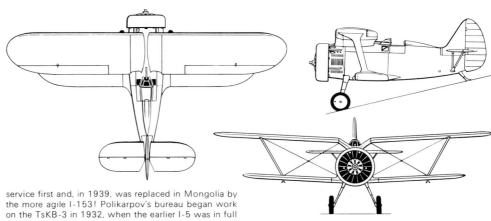

service first and, in 1939, was replaced in Mongolia by the more agile I-153! Polikarpov's bureau began work on the TsKB-3 in 1932, when the earlier I-5 was in full production. Unlike the I-5 the new fighter had a small lower wing and large upper gull wing curved down at the roots to meet the fuselage. As the I-15 the highly manoeuvrable fighter gained a world altitude record before serving in very large numbers (about 550) in Spain, where it was dubbed "Chato" (flat-nosed). It even served against the Finns and Luftwaffe, but by 1937 was being replaced by the I-15bis with continuous upper wing carried on struts. Over 300 of these served in Spain, and many were used as dive bombers

I-15 (original production configuration)

against the Germans in 1941. The ultimate development was the powerful 153, with retractable landing gear, either wheels or skis folding to the rear. Some thousands served in the Far East, Spain, Finland and on the Eastern Front. Later sub-types had variable-pitch propellers and drop tanks well outboard under the lower wings.

Polykarpov 1-16 see page 182.

Potez 63 series

630, 631, 633, 637 and 63·11
Type: (630, 631) two- (sometimes three-) seat day and night fighter; (633) two-seat light attack bomber; (63.11) three-seat army co-operation and reconnaissance.
Engines: (630) two 725 hp Hispano-Suiza 14AB 14-cylinder two-row radials; all other versions, two 700 hp Gnome-Rhône 14M of same layout.
Dimensions: span 52 ft 6 in (16 m); length 36 ft 4 in (11·07 m); (63·11 only) 36 ft 1 in; (11 m); height 11 ft 9¾ in (3·6 m).
Weights: empty (630, 631, 633) typically 5,730 lb (2600 kg); (637) 6,390 lb (2900 kg); (63·11) 6,912 lb (3205 kg); maximum loaded (631) 8,235 lb (3735 kg); (633, 637) 9,285 lb (4210 kg); (63·11) 9,987 lb (4530 kg).
Performance: maximum speed (630, 631, 633) 273 mph (440 km/h); (637) 267 mph (430 km/h); (63·11) 264 mph (425 km/h); initial climb (typical) 1,800 ft (550 m)/min; service ceiling (630, 631) 32,800 ft (10,000 m); (others, typical) 26,250 ft (8000 m).

Potez 63·11 (aircraft 831, after Allied invasion of N Africa)

Armament: see text.
History: first flight (Potez 63) 25 April 1936; production 630, February 1938; prototype 63·11, December 1938.

Winner of a 1934 competition for a C3 (three-seat fighter) for the Armée de l'Air, the Potez 63 was a clean twin-finned machine powered by two of the new Hispano slim radials. It soon branched into a host of sub-variants, including many for foreign customers. The first 80 production aircraft were 630s, but they were soon grounded due to severe engine failure after only a few hours. The 631, however, was more successful and 208 were delivered (121 in May 1940 alone), equipping five fighter squadrons, two Aéronavale squadrons and many other units and shooting down 29 German aircraft (12 by the navy squadrons)

in the Battle for France. Most had two (some only one) 20 mm Hispano 9 or 404 cannon, one or two 7·5 mm MAC in the rear cockpit and, from February 1940, six MAC faired under the outer wings. The 633 had only two machine guns, one forward-firing and the other in the rear cockpit, and the profusion of export variants had several different kinds of gun. Maximum bomb load was 1,323 lb (600 kg), including 880 lb (400 kg) internal. Many 633s had a busy war, Greek examples fighting with the Allies and Romanian examples fighting the Russians. The 637 was used in numbers in May 1940 but was only a stop-gap for the 63·11, with glazed nose and humped rear canopy, which was used in large numbers by the Luftwaffe, Vichy French, Free French and others. Over 900 were built, bringing the total for the 63 family to more than 1,300.

Potez (Aérospatiale) Magister

CM 170, CM 170-2, CM 175
Type: basic trainer and light attack.
Engines: (CM 170, 175) two 880 lb (400 kg) thrust Turboméca Marboré IIA centrifugal turbojets; (CM 170-2) two 1,058 lb (480 kg) Marboré VIC.
Dimensions: span 37 ft 5 in (11·4 m) (39 ft 10 in, 12·15 m, over tip tanks invariably fitted); length 33 ft (10·06 m); height 9 ft 2 in (2·80 m).
Weights: empty (170, 175) about 4,740 lb (2150 kg); (170-2) 5,093 lb (2310 kg); maximum loaded (all) 7,055 lb (3200 kg).
Performance: maximum speed 403 mph (650 km/h); (170-2) 440 mph (710 km/h); initial climb 2,950 ft (900 m)/min; (170-2) 3,540 ft/min; service ceiling 36,090 ft (11,000 m); (170-2) 44,300 ft; range (all) about 735 miles (1250 km).
Armament: normally two rifle-calibre (usually 7·5 mm or 7·62 mm) machine guns in nose and two underwing pylons for 110 lb (50 kg) bombs, AS.11 missiles, rocket pods or other stores.
History: first flight 23 July 1952; (production CM 170) 29 February 1956; final delivery, 1967.

The first jet basic trainer in history, the Magister has remained an active programme through a succession of upheavals in its manufacturer. The initials in its designation signify Castello and Mauboussin, who designed it at the Fouga company in 1950. Despite its novel butterfly tail, with just two surfaces inclined diagonally serving as rudders and elevators, it was a delight to fly and gave a much-needed boost to French

CM 170 (alternative designation CM 170-1)

morale as the first really useful post-war aircraft from the French industry that did not tag along behind other nations. After prolonged testing the Magister was put into production for the Armée de l'Air, while a hooked version for the Aéronavale was produced as the CM 175 Zéphyr. Total production of these, plus five for the CEV test centre, amounted to 437. Total output was brought up to 916 by the many versions built for

foreign customers, the last 130 of which were of the more powerful 170-2 type. Fouga was absorbed into Potez in 1958 and in turn Potez was absorbed into Aérospatiale in 1967. Potez built 40 for the German Luftwaffe, for which 210 more were built by Heinkel/Messerschmitt (Union-Süd); of 82 for Finland, 62 were built by Valmet Oy; of 52 for Israel, 36 were built by IAI. Israeli Magisters set the trend in the Six-Day War in June 1967 of using this nimble machine in combat roles. Subsequently Magisters were popular in local wars, especially in Africa.

Polikarpov I-16

I-16 Types 1, 4, 5, 10, 17, 18, 24, SPB and UTI
Type: single-seat fighter (except SPB dive bomber and UTI two-seat trainer).
Engine: (Type 1) one 480 hp M-22 (modified Bristol Jupiter) nine-cylinder radial; (Type 4) 725 hp M-25A (modified Wright Cyclone) of same layout; (Types 5, 10, 17) 775 hp M-25B; (Types 18 and 24) 1,000 hp Shvetsov M-62R (derived from M-25).
Dimensions: span 29 ft 6½ in (9·00 m); length (to Type 17) 19 ft 11 in (6·075 m); (18, 24 and UTI) 20 ft 1¼ in (6·125 m); height (to 17) 8 ft 1¼ in (2·45 m); (18, 24) 8 ft 5 in (2·56 m).
Weights: empty (1) 2,200 lb (998 kg); (4, 5, 10) 2,791 lb (1266 kg); (18) 3,110 lb (1410 kg); (24) 3,285 lb (1490 kg); loaded (1) 2,965 lb (1345 kg); (4) 3,135 lb (1422 kg); (5) 3,660 lb (1660 kg); (10)

3,782 lb (1715 kg); (17) 3,990 lb (1810 kg); (18) 4,034 lb (1830 kg); (24) 4,215 lb (1912 kg) (24 overload, 4,546 lb, 2062 kg).
Performance: maximum speed (1) 224 mph (360 km/h); (4–18) 280–288 mph (450–465 km/h); (24) 326 mph (525 km/h); initial climb (4–24, typical) 2,790 ft (850 m)/min; service ceiling (typical) 29,500 ft (9000 m); range (1–18) 500 miles (800 km); (24) 248 miles (400 km), (with two 22 gal drop tanks, 435 miles, 700 km).
Armament: (1, 4, 5) two 7·62 mm ShKAS machine guns in wings; (10) two ShKAS in wings, two in top decking of fuselage; (17) two ShKAS in top decking, two 20 mm ShVAK cannon in wings; (18) as 10 or 17; (24) as 17; SPB, various guns plus external bomb load of 220 lb (100 kg). Many versions were later fitted with underwing rails for two RS-82 rockets.
History: first flight (I-16-1) 31 December 1933; production delivery (1) autumn 1934; (4) autumn 1935; final delivery (24) probably early 1942.

Possibly influenced by the Gee Bee racers of the United States, the TsKB-12, or I-16, was an extremely short and simple little fighter which — perhaps because of its slightly "homebuilt" appearance — was almost ignored by the West. Nobody outside the Soviet Union appeared to notice that this odd fighter, with wooden monocoque body and metal/fabric wing, was a cantilever monoplane with retractable landing gear and v-p propeller, which in its first mass-produced form was 60–75 mph faster than contemporary fighters of other countries. It suddenly came into prominence when it was shipped to the Spanish Republicans, where its reliability, 1,800 rounds/min guns, manoeuvrability and fast climb and dive surprised its opponents, who called it the "Rata" (rat). A few old Type 10 remained in Spanish use until 1952. Hundreds of several types fought Japanese aircraft over China and Manchuria, where many I-16s were fitted with the new RS-82 rocket. The final, more powerful versions were built in far greater numbers than any others, about one in 30 being a UTI trainer with tandem open cockpits (and in some versions with fixed landing gear). Total production of this extremely important fighter is estimated at 7,000, of which probably 4,000 were engaged in combat duty against the German invader in 1941–43. Heroically flown against aircraft of much later design and often used for deliberate ramming attacks, the stumpy I-16 operated on wheels or skis long after it was obsolete yet today is recognised as one of the really significant combat aircraft of history.

For Potez aircraft see page 181.

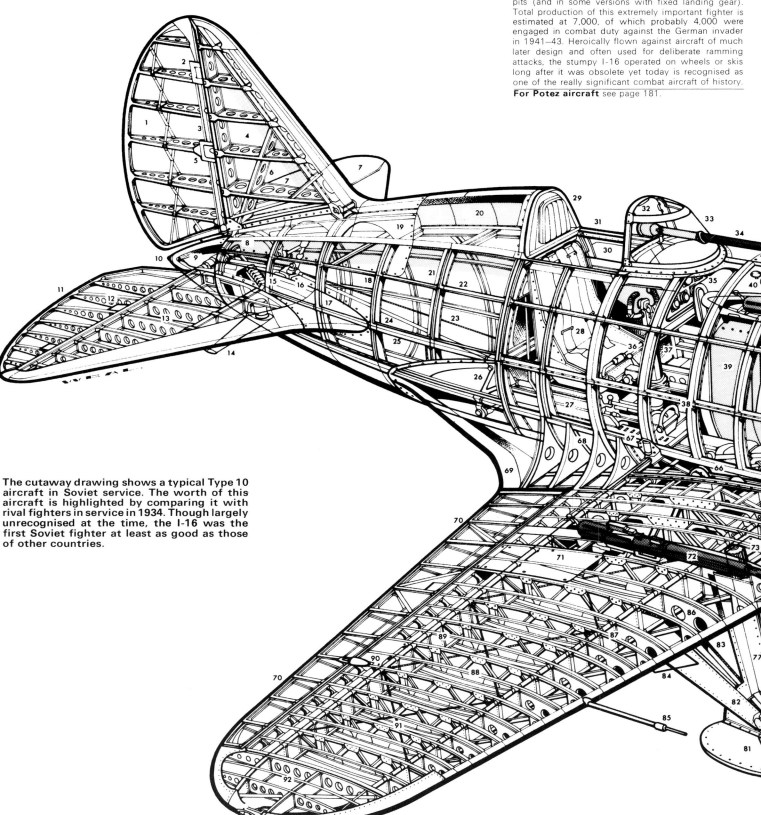

The cutaway drawing shows a typical Type 10 aircraft in Soviet service. The worth of this aircraft is highlighted by comparing it with rival fighters in service in 1934. Though largely unrecognised at the time, the I-16 was the first Soviet fighter at least as good as those of other countries.

Polikarpov I-16 Type 10

1 Rudder construction
2 Rudder upper hinge
3 Rudder post
4 Fin construction
5 Rudder lower hinge
6 Fin auxiliary spar
7 Port tailplane
8 Rudder actuating mechanism
9 Tailcone
10 Rear navigation light
11 Elevator construction
12 Elevator hinge
13 Tailplane construction
14 Tailskid
15 Tailskid damper
26 Control linkage crank
27 Seat support frame
28 Pilot's seat
29 Headrest
30 Cockpit entry flap (port)
31 Open cockpit
32 Rear-view mirror (optional)
33 Curved one-piece windshield
34 Tubular gunsight (PBP-1 reflector sight optional)
35 Instrument panel
36 Undercarriage retraction handcrank

37 Control column
38 Rudder pedal
39 Fuel tank (56 gal/255 litres)
40 Fuel filler caps
41 Ammunition magazines
42 Machine-gun fairing
43 Split-type aileron (landing flap)
44 Aileron hinge fairing
45 Fabric wing covering
46 Port navigation light
47 Aluminium alloy leading-edge skin
48 Two-blade propeller
49 Conical spinner
50 Hucks-type starter dog
51 Hinged mainwheel cover
52 Port mainwheel
53 Lip intake
54 Adjustable (shuttered) cooling apertures
55 Propeller shaft support frame
56 Machine gun muzzles
57 M-25V radial engine, 750 hp
58 Oil tank
59 Starboard synchronized 7·62mm ShKAS machine gun
60 Exhaust exit ports
61 Engine bearers
62 Firewall/bulkhead

63 Centre-section truss-type spar carry-through
64 Wheel-well
65 Fuselage/front spar attachment
66 Retraction linkage
67 Fuselage/rear spar attachment

68 Wing root frames
69 Wing root fillet
70 Aileron construction
71 Ammunition access panel
72 Starboard wing 7·62mm ShKAS machine gun
73 Undercarriage pivot point
74 Machine-gun muzzle
75 Centre/outer section break-point
76 Mainwheel leg
77 Leg cover
78 Starboard mainwheel
79 Mainwheel cover
80 Axle
81 Hinged cover flap
82 Actuating rod cover
83 Retraction actuating rod
84 Cover flap
85 Pitot head
86 Leading-edge construction
87 KhMA chrome-molybdenum steel front spar
88 Alternate dural ribs/frames
89 KhMA chrome-molybdenum steel rear spar
90 Aileron hinge fairing
91 Wire cross-bracing
92 Wingtip construction
93 Starboard navigation light
94 Wingtip edging

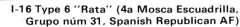

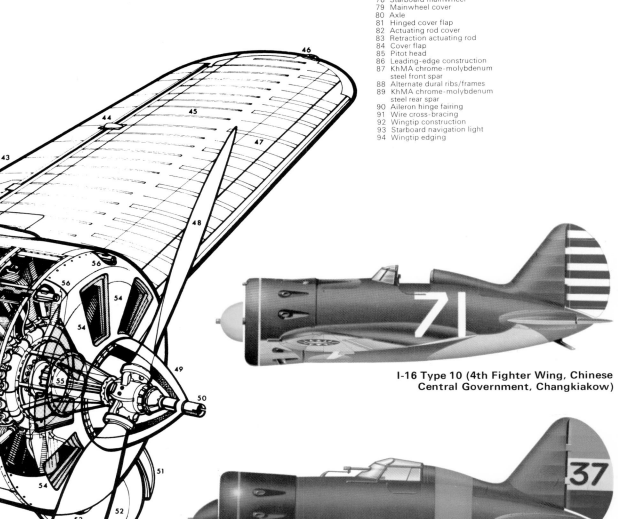

I-16 Type 6 ''Rata'' (4a Mosca Escuadrilla, Grupo núm 31, Spanish Republican AF)

I-16 Type 10 (4th Fighter Wing, Chinese Central Government, Changkiakow)

I-16 Type 10 (with enclosed cockpit; Grupo núm 21, Spanish Republican AF)

I-16 Type 24 (bearing slogan ''For Stalin!'', central sector, 1941)

PZL P.11

P.11a, 11b and 11c
Type: single-seat fighter.
Engine: one Bristol-designed nine-cylinder radial: (11a) 500 hp Skoda Mercury IVS2; (11b) 595 hp IAR Gnome-Rhône K9 (Jupiter); (11c) 645 hp PZL Mercury VIS2.
Dimensions: span 35 ft 2 in (10·72 m); length 24 ft 9 in or 24 ft 9½ in (7·55 m); height 9 ft 4 in (2·85 m).
Weights: empty (11c) 2,524 lb (1145 kg); loaded 3,960 lb (1795 kg).
Performance: maximum speed (11c) 242 mph (390 km/h); initial climb 2,625 ft (800 m)/min; service ceiling 36,090 ft (11,000 m); range (economic cruise, no combat) 503 miles (810 km).
Armament: (11a) two 7·7 mm (0·303 in) Browning, each with 700 rounds, in sides of fuselage; (11c) two 7·7 mm KM Wz 33 machine guns, each with 500 rounds, in sides of fuselage, and two more, each with 300 rounds, inside wing at junction of struts; provision for two 27 lb (12·25 kg) bombs.
History: first flight (P.11/I) August 1931; (production P.11a) June 1933.

Having hired brilliant young designer Zygmund Pulaski at its formation in 1928, the Polish PZL (National Aero Factory) set itself to building gull-winged monoplane fighters of outstanding quality. All the early production models were powered by Polish-built Jupiter engines, and large numbers of P.7a fighters formed the backbone of the young Polish Air Force. The P.11 was the natural successor, but when the

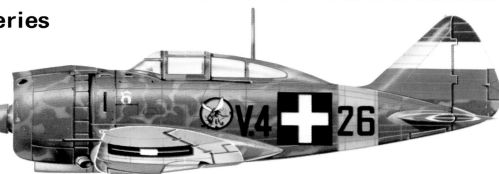

PZL P.11c (113 Sqn, 1st Air Regiment, Polish AF)

prototype was about to fly Pulaski was killed in a crash and his place was taken by W. Jakimiuk (later designer for D. H. Canada and SNCASE). The first P.11 was powered by a Gnome-Rhône Jupiter and subsequent prototypes by a Mistral and Mercury from the same source, but after prolonged trials the P.11a went into production with the Polish-built Mercury IVS. In 1934 the fuselage was redesigned to improve pilot view by lowering the engine and raising the pilot

(11c). A new tail and modified wings were introduced and provision was made for two wing guns and radio, but these were usually not available for fitting. The final production model was the export version of the 11a, the 11b, which was built in Romania as the IAR P.11f. Many further developments were planned, but the main fighter force defending Poland in September 1939 comprised 12 squadrons of P.11c, most with only two guns and operating with no warning system in chaotic conditions. They nevertheless destroyed 126 Luftwaffe aircraft for the loss of 114 of their own number. Final PZL fighter was the P.24 family, of which there were many variants produced entirely for export.

PZL P.23 and 43 Karaś

P.23A and B, P.43A and B
Type: three-seat reconnaissance bomber.
Engine: (P.23A) one 580 hp PZL (Bristol-licence) Pegasus II nine-cylinder radial; (P.23B) 680 hp PZL Pegasus VIII; P.43A, 930 hp Gnome-Rhône 14 Kfs 14-cylinder two-row radial; (P.43B) 980 hp G-R 14N1.
Dimensions: span 45 ft 9 in (13·95 m); length (23) 31 ft 9 in (9·68 m); (43) 32 ft 10 in; height 11 ft 6 in (3·5 m).
Weights: empty (23, typical) 4,250 lb (1928 kg); loaded (23) 6,918 lb (3138 kg); maximum overload 7,774 lb (3526 kg).
Performance: maximum speed (23A) 198 mph (320 km/h); (23B) 217 mph (350 km/h); (43B) 227 mph (365 km/h); initial climb (typical) 985 ft (300 m)/min; service ceiling (typical) 24,600 ft (7500 m); range with bomb load, 410 miles (660 km) (overload, 932 miles, 1500 km).
Armament: (23) one 7·7 mm Browning or KM Wz 33 firing forward, one on PZL hydraulically assisted mount in rear cockpit and third similarly mounted in rear ventral position; external bomb load of up to 1,543 lb (700 kg); (43) as 23 but with two forward-firing guns, one on each side of cowling.
History: first flight (P.23/I) August 1934; (production Karaś A) June 1936; (P.43A) 1937.

Designed by a team led by Stanisław Prauss, the P.23 was hardly beautiful yet it provided the tactical attack capability of one of Europe's largest air forces in the late 1930s. By the outbreak of World War II, 14 of the bomber regiments of the Polish Air Force had been equipped with the Karaś (Carp); its successor, the

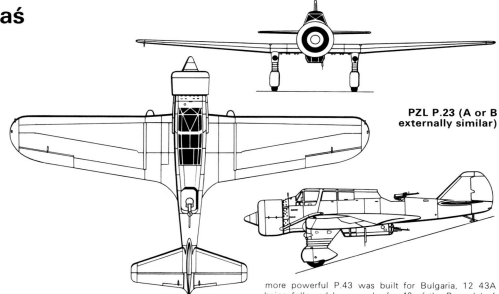

PZL P.23 (A or B externally similar)

greatly improved Sum, was about to enter service. When designed, in 1931–32, the Karaś was an outstandingly modern aircraft, one of its radical features being use of smooth skin of light-alloy/balsa sandwich construction. It carried a bomb load far heavier than any of its contemporaries and had no defence "blind spots", though its firepower was meagre. The

more powerful P.43 was built for Bulgaria, 12 43A being followed by an order for 42 of the B model of which nearly all were delivered by the start of World War II. Despite skill and heroism the Polish squadrons were soon overwhelmed, but a handful of Karaś managed to reach Romania, where they were refurbished, put into service with Romanian crews and used on the Bessarabian front in the invasion of the Soviet Union in 1941.

Reggiane Re 2000 series

Re 2000 Falco I (Falcon), 2001 Falco II, 2002 Ariete (Ram) and 2005 Sagittario (Archer).
Type: single-seat fighter.
Engine: (2000) one 1,025 hp Piaggio P.XIbis RC40 14-cylinder two-row radial; (2001) 1,175 hp Alfa Romeo RA.1000 RC41 (DB 601) inverted-vee-12; (2002) 1,175 hp Piaggio P.XIX RC45, (as P.XIbis); (2005) 1,475 hp Fiat RA.1050 RC58 Tifone (Typhoon) (DB 605, as DB 601).
Dimensions: span 36 ft 1 in (11 m); length (2000) 26 ft 2½ in (7·95 m); (2001–2) 26 ft 10 in; (2005) 28 ft 7¾ in; height (typical) 10 ft 4 in (3·15 m).
Weight: empty (2000) 4,200 lb (1905 kg); maximum loaded (2000) 5,722 lb (2595 kg); (2001) 7,231 lb; (2002) 7,143 lb; (2005) 7,848 lb.
Performance: maximum speed (2000–2) 329–337 mph (say, 535 km/h); (2005) 391 mph (630 km/h); initial climb (typical) 3,600 ft (1100 m)/min; service ceiling (2000) 36,745 ft (11,200 m); range (typical) 590 miles (950 km).
Armament: see text.
History: first flight (2000) 1938; (2001) 1940; (2002) late 1941; (2005) September 1942.

Re 2000 Héja (1./1 Fighter Sqn, Hungarian AF)

A subsidiary of Caproni, the Reggiane company copied the Seversky P-35 to produce the nimble but lightly built Re 2000. Extremely manoeuvrable, it had two 12·7 mm Breda-SAFAT on the top decking and could carry a 441 lb (200 kg) bomb. Almost all the 170 built served non-Italian forces, Sweden using 60 (as the J 20) and Hungary about 100 (as the Héja) on the

Eastern front. Production of the 2001 reached 252, in four series with two 12·7 mm either alone or augmented by two 7·7 mm or (most often) 20 mm wing guns, plus a 1,410 lb (640 kg) bomb. About 50 2002 were built and only 48 of the excellent 2005 with three 20 mm and two 12·7 mm.
Republic P-47 Thunderbolt see page 186.

Republic F-84

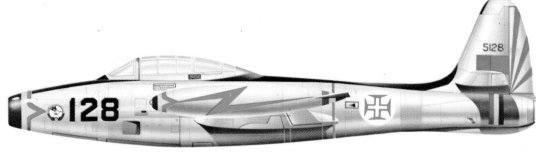

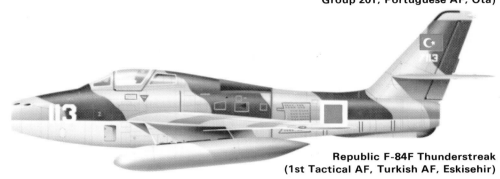

F-84A, B, C, D and G Thunderjet, F-84F Thunderstreak and RF-84F Thunderflash

Type: single-seat fighter-bomber (RF-84F, photo-reconnaissance).

Engine: one single-shaft axial turbojet: (A) 3,750 lb Allison J35-15; (B, C) 4,000 lb J35-15C or -13; (D) Allison J35-15; (B, C) 4,000 lb J35-15C or -13; (D, E) 5,000 lb (2268 kg) J35-17D; (G) 5,600 lb (2540 kg) J35-29; (F) 7,220 lb (3275 kg) Wright J65-3 (US Sapphire); (RF-84F) 7,800 lb (3538 kg) J65-7.

Dimensions: span (not including tip tanks) 36 ft 5 in (11·09 m); (F/RF-84F) 33 ft 7¼ in (10·24 m); length (B, C, D) 37 ft 5 in; (G) 38 ft 1 in (11·61 m); (F-84F) 43 ft 4¾ in (13·22 m); (RF-84F) 47 ft 7¾ in (14·51 m); height (B, C, D) 12 ft 10 in; (G) 12 ft 7 in (3·84 m); (F-84F) 14 ft 4¾ in (4·38 m); (RF-84F) 15 ft (4·57 m).

Weights: empty (B) 9,540 lb (4325 kg); (G) 11,095 lb (5030 kg); (F) 13,800 lb (6260 kg); maximum loaded (B) 15,800 lb (7167 kg); (G) 23,525 lb (10,670 kg); (F, RF) 28,000 lb (12,700 kg).

Performance: maximum speed (B) 587 mph; (G) 622 mph (1000 km/h); (F) 695 mph (1118 km/h); (RF) 679 mph (1093 km/h); initial climb (B) 5,800 ft/min; (G) 5,000 ft (1524 m)/min; (F) 8,200 ft (2500 m)/min; service ceiling (B, C, D, G) 41,000 ft (12,500 m); (F, RF) 46,000 ft (14,000 m); range (hi, clean) all models, about 870 miles (1400 km); maximum range with maximum fuel (all) 2,000–2,200 miles (3500 km).

Armament: six 0·5 in Colt-Browning M-3; four in nose and two in wing roots (RF-84F, four, in wing above inlet ducts); underwing pylons for eight rockets (B, C) or two 375 gal drop tanks (RF) or variety of tanks, nuclear and/or conventional bombs or other stores to total load of 4,000 lb (1814 kg), (D, E, G) or 6,000 lb (2722 kg), (F).

History: first flight (XP-84) 28 February 1946; (production F-84B) May 1947; (production F-84F) 22 November 1952; final delivery (G) July 1953; (F/RF) March 1958.

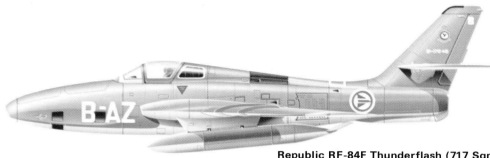

After studying derivatives of the P-47 with an axial turbojet, the P-84 was begun in November 1944 as a completely new design. It had a slender fuselage, nose intake to ducts which split each side of the nosewheel bay and cockpit, and unswept 12 per cent wing. Two prototypes and 13 YP-84A had early GE or Allison TG-180 (J35) engines, M-2 guns and no provision for bombs. The 226 F-84B had fast-firing M-3 guns, ejection seats and provision for light external load, and 191 C were similar. The 154 D had thicker wing skins and carried a heavy load, as did 843 E and 3,025 G models, of which 1,936, plus 100 E, went free to NATO allies on MAP funds. Take-off was very long at full load and often marginal on a hot day, but the 4,457 straight-wing Thunderjets did a great job in Korea and provided much-needed muscle in Western Europe in 1951–57. The F-84F eventually emerged as a completely new design with broad swept wing, different engine and transonic performance. Of 2,713 built, 450 went to the newly formed Luftwaffe and 900 others to European allies. The RF-84F likewise was important in NATO, European forces receiving 386 out of 715.

Republic F-105 Thunderchief

F-105B, D, F and G

Type: single-seat all-weather fighter-bomber; (F-105F) two-seat operational trainer; (G) two-seat ECM.

Engine: one Pratt & Whitney J75 two-shaft afterburning turbojet; (B) 23,500 lb (10,660 kg) J75-5; (D, F, G) 24,500 lb (11,113 kg) J75-19W.

Dimensions: span 34 ft 11¼ in (10·65 m); length (B, D) 64 ft 3 in (19·58 m); (F, G) 69 ft 7½ in (21·21 m); height (B, D) 19 ft 8 in (5·99 m); (F, G) 20 ft 2 in (6·15 m).

Weights: empty (D) 27,500 lb (12,474 kg); (F, G) 28,393 lb (12,879 kg); maximum loaded (B) 40,000 lb (18,144 kg); (D) 52,546 lb (23,834 kg); (F, G) 54,000 lb (24,495 kg).

Performance: maximum speed (B) 1,254 mph; (D, F, G) 1,480 mph (2382 km/h, Mach 2·25); initial climb (B, D, typical) 34,500 ft (10,500 m)/min; (F, G) 32,000 ft (9750 m)/min; service ceiling (typical) 52,000 ft (15,850 m); tactical radius with 16 750 lb bombs (D) 230 miles (370 km); ferry range with maximum fuel (typical) 2,390 miles (3846 km).

Armament: one 20 mm M-61 gun with 1,029 rounds in left side of fuselage; internal bay for ordnance load of up to 8,000 lb (3629 kg), and five external pylons for additional load of 6,000 lb (2722 kg).

History: first flight (YF-105A) 22 October 1955; (production B) 26 May 1956; (D) 9 June 1959; (F) 11 June 1963; final delivery 1965.

The AP-63 project was a private venture by Republic Aviation to follow the F-84. Its primary mission was delivery of nuclear or conventional weapons in all-weathers, with very high speed and long range. Though it had only the stop-gap J57 engine the first Thunderchief exceeded the speed of sound on its first flight, and the B model was soon in production for Tactical

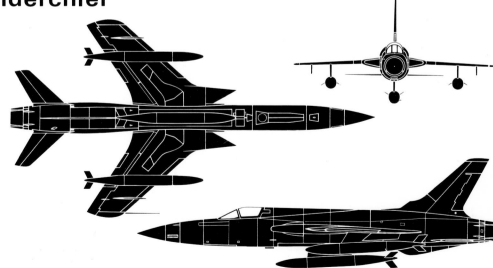

Air Command of the USAF. Apart from being the biggest single-seat, single-engine combat aircraft in history, the 105 was notable for its large bomb bay and unique swept-forward engine inlets in the wing roots. Only 75 B were delivered but 600 of the advanced D were built, with Nasarr monopulse radar and doppler navigation. Production was completed with 143 tandem-seat F with full operational equipment and dual controls. Known as "the Thud" the greatest of single-engined combat jets bore a huge burden throughout the Vietnam war. About 350 D were rebuilt during that conflict with the Thunderstick (T-stick) all-

F-105D (prior to Wild Weasel T-stick II and rebuilds)

weather blind attack system — a few also being updated to T-stick II — with a large saddleback fairing from cockpit to fin. About 30 F were converted to ECM (electronic countermeasures) attackers, with pilot and observer and Wild Weasel and other radar homing, warning and jamming systems. Westinghouse jammers and Goodyear chaff pods were carried externally.

Republic P-47 Thunderbolt

P-47B, C, D,M and N
Type: single-seat fighter; (D and N) fighter-bomber.
Engine: one Pratt & Whitney R-2800 Double Wasp 18-cylinder two-row radial; (B) 2,000 hp R-2800-21; (C, most D) 2,300 hp R-2800-59; (M, N) 2,800 hp R-2800-57 or -77 (emergency wet rating).
Dimensions: span 40 ft 9¼ in (12·4 m); length (B) 34 ft 10 in; (C, D, M, N) 36 ft 1¼ in (11·03 m); height (B) 12 ft 8 in; (C, D) 14 ft 2 in (4·3 m); (M, N) 14 ft 8 in.
Weights: empty (B) 9,010 lb (4087 kg); (D) 10,700 lb (4853 kg); maximum loaded (B) 12,700 lb (5760 kg); (C) 14,925 lb; (D) 19,400 lb (8800 kg); (M) 14,700 lb; (N) 21,200 lb (9616 kg).
Performance: maximum speed (B) 412 mph; (C) 433 mph; (D) 428 mph (690 km/h); (M) 470 mph; (N) 467 mph (751 km/h); initial climb (typical) 2,800 ft (855 m)/min; service ceiling (B) 38,000 ft; (C-N) 42,000–43,000 ft (13,000 m); range on internal fuel (B) 575 miles; (D) 1,000 miles (1600 km); ultimate range (drop tanks) (D) 1,900 miles (3060 km); (N) 2,350 miles (3800 km).

Armament: (except M) eight 0·5 in Colt-Browning M-2 in wings, each with 267, 350 or 425 rounds (M) six 0·5 in; (D and N) three to five racks for external load of tanks, bombs or rockets to maximum of 2,500 lb (1134 kg).
History: first flight (XP-47B) 6 May 1941; production delivery (B) 18 March 1942; final delivery (N) September 1945.

Before the United States entered World War II it was eagerly digesting the results of air combats in Europe and, in 1940, existing plans by Republic's chief designer, Alexander Kartveli were urgently replaced by sketches for a much bigger fighter with the new R-2800 engine. This appeared to be the only way to meet the Army Air Corps' new targets for fighter performance. Kartveli began by designing the best installation of the big engine and its turbocharger, placed under the rear fuselage. The air duct had to pass under the elliptical wing, and there were problems in achieving ground clearance for the big propeller (12 ft diameter, even though it had the unprecedented total of four blades) with landing gear able to retract inwards and still leave room in the wing for the formidable armament of eight 0·5 in guns. After severe and protracted technical

difficulties the P-47B was cleared for production in early 1942 and at the beginning of 1943 two fighter groups equipped with the giant new fighter (one the famed 56th, to become top scorers in Europe) joined the 8th AF in Britain to begin escorting B-17 and B-24 heavies. Their value was dramatically increased when they began to carry drop tanks and fly all the way to the target. The same capability turned the big and formidable fighter into a much-feared bomber and, with devastating firepower, vast numbers of P-47Ds strafed and bombed throughout the European and Pacific theatres until the end of World War II. Republic's output of D models (12,602) is the largest total of one sub-type of any fighter in history, total production of the "Jug" amounting to 15,660. The lightweight M was too late for its role of chasing flying bombs but scored successes against the Me 262 and Ar 234 jets, while the long-range P-47N matched the M fuselage with a bigger wing for the Pacific war. After World War II the "Jug" was popular with many air forces until well into the 1950s.

Republic F-84 and Republic F-105 Thunderchief see page 185.
Rockwell A-5 Vigilante and OV-10 Bronco see page 190

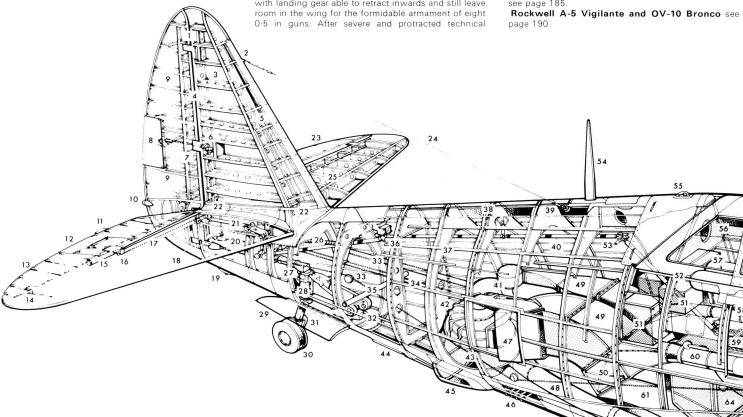

Republic P-47D-10 'Thunderbolt'

1 Rudder upper hinge
2 Aerial attachment
3 Fin flanged ribs
4 Rudder post/fin rear spar
5 Fin front spar
6 Rudder trim-tab actuating mechanism (chain-driven worm gear)
7 Rudder centre hinge
8 Rudder trim tab
9 Rudder structure
10 Tail navigation light
11 Elevator fixed tab
12 Elevator trim tab
13 Starboard elevator structure
14 Elevator outboard hinge
15 Elevator torque tube
16 Elevator trim tab actuating mechanism (worm gear)
17 Chain drive
18 Starboard tailplane (stabilizer)
19 Tail jacking point
20 Rudder control cables
21 Elevator control rod and linkage
22 Fin spar/fuselage attachment points
23 Port elevator
24 Aerial
25 Port tailplane structure (two spars, flanged ribs)
26 Tailwheel retraction worm gear
27 Tailwheel anti-shimmy damper
28 Tailwheel oleo
29 Tailwheel doors
30 Retractable and steerable tailwheel
31 Tailwheel fork
32 Tailwheel mount and pivot
33 Rudder cables
34 Rudder and elevator trim cables

35 Lifting tube
36 Elevator rod linkage
37 Semi-monocoque all-metal fuselage construction
38 Fuselage dorsal 'razorback' profile
39 Aerial lead-in
40 Fuselage stringers
41 Supercharger air filter
42 Supercharger
43 Turbine casing
44 Turbo-supercharger compartment air vent
45 Turbo-supercharger exhaust flight hood fairing (stainless steel)
46 Outlet louvres
47 Intercooler exhaust doors (port and starboard)
48 Exhaust pipes
49 Cooling air ducts
50 Intercooler unit (cooling and supercharged air)
51 Radio transmitter and receiver packs (Detrola)
52 Canopy track
53 Elevator rod linkage
54 Aerial mast
55 Formation light
56 Rearward-vision frame cut-out and glazing
57 Oxygen bottles
58 Supercharged and cooling air pipe to carburettor (port)
59 Elevator linkage
60 Supercharged and cooling air pipe to carburettor (starboard)
61 Central duct (to intercooler unit)
62 Wing root air louvres
63 Wing root fillet
64 Auxiliary fuel tank (100 gal/ 455 litres)
65 Auxiliary fuel filler point
66 Rudder cable turnbuckle
67 Cockpit floor support
68 Seat adjustment lever
69 Pilot's seat

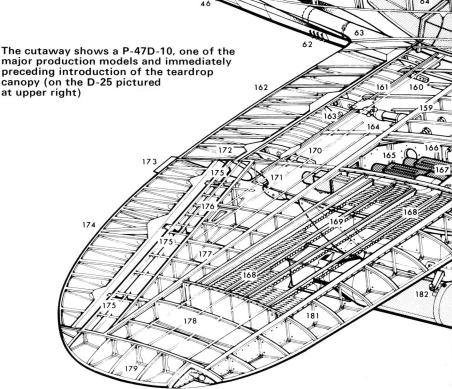

The cutaway shows a P-47D-10, one of the major production models and immediately preceding introduction of the teardrop canopy (on the D-25 pictured at upper right)

70 Canopy emergency release (port and starboard)
71 Trim-tab controls
72 Back and head armour
73 Headrest
74 Rearward-sliding canopy
75 Rear-view mirror fairing
76 Vee windshields with central pillar
77 Internal bulletproof glass screen
78 Gunsight
79 Engine control quadrant (cockpit port wall)
80 Control column
81 Rudder pedals
82 Oxygen regulator
83 Underfloor elevator control quadrant
84 Rudder cable linkage
85 Wing rear spar/fuselage attachment (tapered bolts/bushings)
86 Wing-supporting lower bulkhead section
87 Main fuel tank (205 gal/932 litres)
88 Fuselage forward structure
89 Stainless steel/Alclad firewall bulkhead
90 Cowl flap valve
91 Main fuel filler point
92 Anti-freeze fluid tank
93 Hydraulic reservoir
94 Aileron control rod
95 Aileron trim-tab control cables
96 Aileron hinge access panels
97 Aileron and tab control linkage
98 Aileron trim tab (port wing only)
99 Frise-type aileron
100 Wing rear (No 2) spar
101 Port navigation light
102 Pitot head
103 Wing front (No 1) spar
104 Wing stressed skin

105 Four-gun ammunition troughs (individual bays)
106 Staggered gun barrels
107 Removable panel
108 Inter-spar gun-bay access panel
109 Forward gunsight bead
110 Oil feed pipes
111 Oil tank (28·6 gal/130 litres)
112 Hydraulic pressure line
113 Engine upper bearers
114 Engine control correlating cam
115 Eclipse pump (anti-icing)
116 Fuel level transmitter
117 Generator
118 Battery junction box
119 Storage battery
120 Exhaust collector ring
121 Cowl flap actuating cylinder
122 Exhaust outlets to collector ring
123 Cowl flaps

124 Supercharged and cooling air ducts to carburettor (port and starboard)
125 Exhaust upper outlets
126 Cowling frame
127 2,000 hp Pratt & Whitney Double Wasp R-2800-21 eighteen-cylinder two-row engine
128 Cowling nose panel
129 Magnetos
130 Propeller governor
131 Propeller hub
132 Reduction gear casing
133 Spinner
134 Propeller cuffs
135 Curtiss constant-speed electric propeller (12 ft 2in)

136 Oil cooler intakes (port and starboard)
137 Supercharger intercooler (central) air intake
138 Ducting
139 Oil-cooler feed pipes
140 Starboard oil cooler
141 Engine lower bearers
142 Oil-cooler exhaust variable shutter
143 Fixed deflector
144 Excess exhaust gas gate
145 Belly stores/weapon shackles
146 Metal auxiliary drop tank (75 gal/341 litres)
147 Inboard mainwheel well door
148 Mainwheel well door actuating cylinder

149 Camera gun port
150 Cabin air-conditioning intake (starboard wing only)
151 Wing root fairing
152 Wing front spar/fuselage attachment (tapered bolts/bushings)
153 Wing inboard rib mainwheel well recess
154 Wing front (No 1) spar
155 Undercarriage pivot
156 Hydraulic retraction cylinder
157 Auxiliary (undercarriage mounting) wing spar
158 Gun bay warm air flexible duct
159 Wing rear (No 2) spar
160 Landing flap inboard hinge
161 Auxiliary (No 3) wing spar inboard section (flap mounting)
162 NACA slotted landing flaps
163 Landing flap centre hinge
164 Landing flap hydraulic cylinder
165 Four 0·5 in Browning guns
166 Inter-spar gun bay inboard rib
167 Ammunition feed chutes
168 Individual ammunition troughs (350 rpg)
169 Underwing stores/weapons pylon
170 Landing flap outboard hinge
171 Flap door
172 Landing flap profile
173 Aileron fixed tab (starboard wing only)
174 Frise-type aileron structure
175 Aileron hinge/steel forging spar attachments
176 Auxiliary (No 3) wing spar outboard section (aileron mounting)
177 Multi-cellular wing construction
178 Wing outboard ribs
179 Wingtip structure
180 Starboard navigation light
181 Leading-edge rib sections
182 Bomb shackles
183 500 lb (227 kg) M-43 demolition bomb
184 Undercarriage leg fairing (overlapping upper section)
185 Mainwheel fairing (lower section)
186 Wheel fork
187 Starboard mainwheel
188 Brake lines
189 Landing gear air/oil shock strut
190 Gun barrel blast tubes
191 Staggered gun barrels
192 Rocket-launcher slide bar
193 Centre strap
194 Front mount (attached below front spar between inboard pair of guns)
195 Deflector arms
196 Triple-tube 4·5in rocket-launcher (Type M10)
197 Front retaining band
198 4·5in M8 rocket projectile

Republic P-47D-25 (352nd FS, 353rd FG, 8th AAF, Raydon)

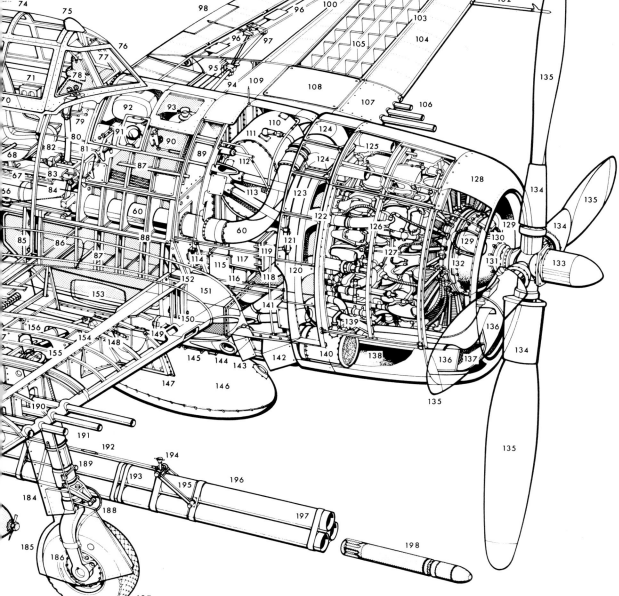

Rockwell International B-1

B-1

Type: four-seat strategic bomber and missile platform.
Engines: four 30,000 lb (13.610 kg) class General Electric F101-100 two-shaft augmented turbofans.
Dimensions: span (15°) 136 ft 8½ in (41·7 m) (67½°) 78 ft 2½ in (23·8 m); length 150 ft 2½ in (45·8 m); height 33 ft 7 in (10·24 m).
Weights: empty, about 140,000 lb (63,500 kg); maximum loaded 395,000 lb (179,170 kg), (gross weight likely to settle at about 400,000 lb).
Performance: maximum speed at sea level (std day) about 646 mph (1040 km/h, Mach 0·85); maximum speed at high altitude 1,320 mph (2135 km/h, Mach 2.0); service ceiling over 60,000 ft (18,300 m); range with maximum weapon load, 6,100 miles (9820 km).
Armament: 24 Improved SRAM (AGM-69B thermonuclear missiles) internally, with provision for eight more externally; 75,000 lb (34,020 kg) of bombs internally with provision for 40,000 lb (18,144 kg) externally.
History: first flight 23 December 1974; service delivery possible in 1979.

By far the most expensive combat aircraft in history, the B-1 has also had by far the longest, most minutely studied and most costly gestation period. When the B-52 was bought for Strategic Air Command in 1951 it was just another aircraft – albeit a large and costly one, with a unit price of around $6 million – but in the mid-1970s cost-inflation has put the much-needed B-1 almost out of reach. There are many, including Congressmen who vote on defence procurement, who cannot understand how a large manned vehicle can penetrate hostile airspace without getting shot down. This book is not the place to spell out the several compelling reasons for retaining a manned bomber in SAC's inventory, but the fact must be emphasised that the B-1 has been planned with unbelievable care and is being professionally developed with inadequate funds in an environment of extreme parsimony. Only a single prototype was carrying the entire flight test programme as this book was written, with the second

flight article due to fly in early 1976. The technology of the B-1 is of immense breadth and depth, extending to every branch of aerodynamics, structures, propulsion and weapons. Much smaller than the B-52, it uses extremely advanced and efficient engines and a high-lift variable-sweep wing to carry twice the weapon load for a much greater distance at much higher speed and with many times greater penetrative capability. Almost all B-1 missions would be flown at about tree-top height; Mach 2.0 at high altitude would be used extremely rarely. Seen from the front a B-1's radar signature is approximately one-thirtieth as great as that of a B-52, and its defensive avionics (managed by associate contractor Boeing) are the most powerful and comprehensive ever fitted into a combat aircraft. These systems guard the B-1 against defensive radars by jamming, confusing and spoofing, in ways at present highly classified. Another design feature is the ability to scramble quickly from an airfield under nuclear attack and to survive the effects of enemy thermonuclear explosions in fairly close proximity. All systems can be automatically checked and held at immediate readiness for long periods, so that on an alert being sounded the first man to reach the aircraft has only to hit a button behind the nose landing gear to energise all engines and systems for immediate take-off even before the crew are completely strapped in. Yet another design feature is low-altitude ride control (LARC) effected by gust sensors and operated by small canard surfaces on each side of the nose and the lowest section of rudder, to guide the speeding monster through turbulent air without the crew compartment suffering significant undulation. The decision on whether or not to put the B-1 into production must be taken in 1976 – at about the same time as the US Presidential election. The USAF desperately hope to be able to buy at least a small B-1 force, to form the third leg of the strategic deterrent Triad (the others being submarine-launched missiles and land-silo missiles). The SAC requirement is for 241 aircraft, at an estimated unit price of $77 million (allowing for all R&D and inflation), amounting to a total investment of $18,600,000,000.

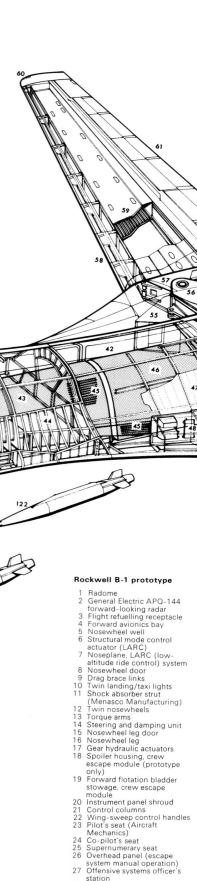

Rockwell B-1 prototype

1 Radome
2 General Electric APQ-144 forward-looking radar
3 Flight refuelling receptacle
4 Forward avionics bay
5 Nosewheel well
6 Structural mode control actuator (LARC)
7 Noseplane, LARC (low-altitude ride control) system
8 Nosewheel door
9 Drag brace links
10 Twin landing/taxi lights
11 Shock absorber strut (Menasco Manufacturing)
12 Twin nosewheels
13 Torque arms
14 Steering and damping unit
15 Nosewheel leg door
16 Nosewheel leg
17 Gear hydraulic actuators
18 Spoiler housing, crew escape module (prototype only)
19 Forward flotation bladder stowage, crew escape module
20 Instrument panel shroud
21 Control columns
22 Wing-sweep control handles
23 Pilot's seat (Aircraft Mechanics)
24 Co-pilot's seat
25 Supernumerary seat
26 Overhead panel (escape system manual operation)
27 Offensive systems officer's station
28 Systems operator instructor's fold-down seat
29 Defensive systems officer's station

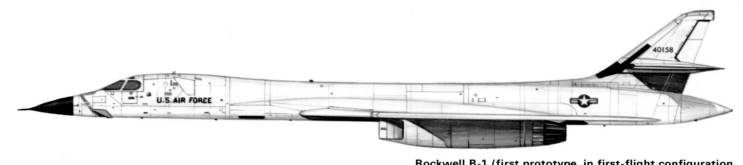

Rockwell B-1 (first prototype, in first-flight configuration but with landing gear retracted)

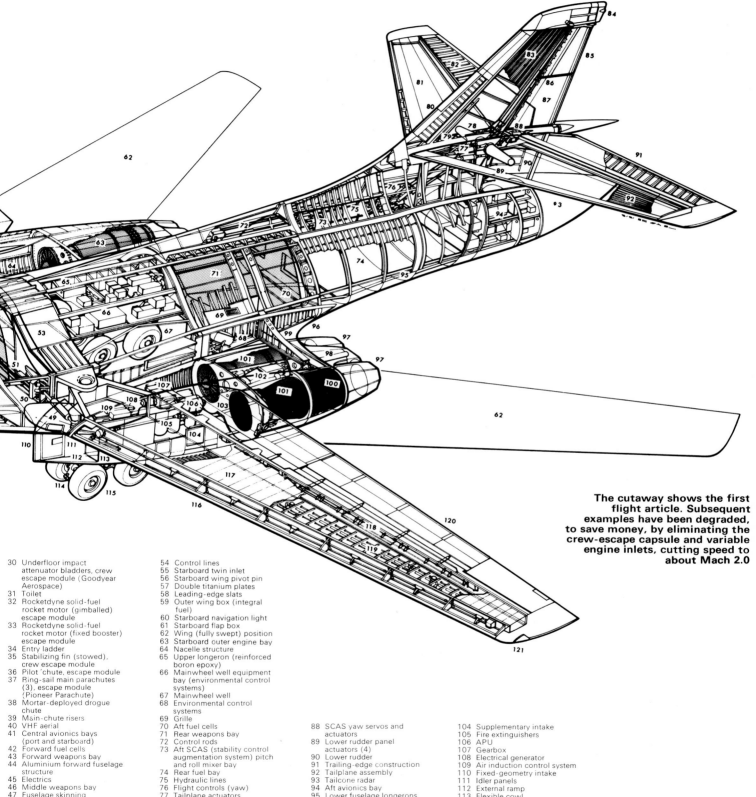

The cutaway shows the first flight article. Subsequent examples have been degraded, to save money, by eliminating the crew-escape capsule and variable engine inlets, cutting speed to about Mach 2.0

30 Underfloor impact attenuator bladders, crew escape module (Goodyear Aerospace)
31 Toilet
32 Rocketdyne solid-fuel rocket motor (gimballed) escape module
33 Rocketdyne solid-fuel rocket motor (fixed booster) escape module
34 Entry ladder
35 Stabilizing fin (stowed), crew escape module
36 Pilot 'chute, escape module
37 Ring-sail main parachutes (3), escape module (Pioneer Parachute)
38 Mortar-deployed drogue chute
39 Main-chute risers
40 VHF aerial
41 Central avionics bays (port and starboard)
42 Forward fuel cells
43 Forward weapons bay
44 Aluminium forward fuselage structure
45 Electrics
46 Middle weapons bay
47 Fuselage skinning
48 Fuselage side fairing bay (penetration aids systems)
49 Wing sweep actuator
50 Wing sweep power drive unit
51 Flap/slat power drive unit
52 Fuselage centre line
52 Fuselage centreline longeron
53 Titanium (diffusion bonded) wing carry-through assembly

54 Control lines
55 Starboard twin inlet
56 Starboard wing pivot pin
57 Double titanium plates
58 Leading-edge slats
59 Outer wing box (integral fuel)
60 Starboard navigation light
61 Starboard flap box
62 Wing (fully swept) position
63 Starboard outer engine bay
64 Nacelle structure
65 Upper longeron (reinforced boron epoxy)
66 Mainwheel well equipment bay (environmental control systems)
67 Mainwheel well
68 Environmental control systems
69 Grille
70 Aft fuel cells
71 Rear weapons bay
72 Control rods
73 Aft SCAS (stability control augmentation system) pitch and roll mixer bay
74 Rear fuel bay
75 Hydraulic lines
76 Flight controls (yaw)
77 Tailplane actuators
78 Tailplane spigot
79 Fin root rib
80 Leading-edge structure
81 Starboard tailplane (Martin Marietta)
82 Lower trailing-edge skin
83 Fin assembly
84 Rear navigation light
85 Upper rudder
86 Rudder controls
87 Intermediate rudder

88 SCAS yaw servos and actuators
89 Lower rudder panel actuators (4)
90 Lower rudder
91 Trailing-edge construction
92 Tailplane assembly
93 Tailcone radar
94 Aft avionics bay
95 Lower fuselage longerons
96 Titanium wing-root fairing
97 Exhaust nozzles
98 Ram-air overboard dump
99 Nacelle bearer
100 Engine shroud
101 General Electric F101 turbofans (over 30,000 lb/ 13,610 kg thrust)
102 Pre-cooler
103 Engine installation firewall/ frame

104 Supplementary intake
105 Fire extinguishers
106 APU
107 Gearbox
108 Electrical generator
109 Air induction control system
110 Fixed-geometry intake
111 Idler panels
112 External ramp
113 Flexible cowl
114 Four-wheel bogie assembly (Cleveland Pneumatic Tool)
115 Goodyear mainwheel brakes and tyres
116 Leading-edge slat actuators
117 Wing skinning
118 Flight controls
119 Wing structure (integral fuel)
120 Single-slotted main flaps
121 Port navigation light

Rockwell International A-5 Vigilante

A-5A, A-5B and RA-5C

Type: (A, B) carrier-based attack; (C) carrier-based reconnaissance, with crew of two.
Engines: two General Electric J79 single-shaft afterburning turbojets; (A, B) as originally built, 16,150 lb J79-2 or-4; (RA-5C, pre-1969), 17,000 lb (7710 kg) J79-8, (post-1969) 17,860 lb (8118 kg) J79-10.
Dimensions: span 53 ft (16·15 m); length 75 ft 10 in (23·11 m), (folds to 68 ft); height 19 ft 5 in (5·92 m).
Weights: empty (C) about 38,000 lb (17,240 kg); maximum loaded, 80,000 lb (36,285 kg).
Performance: maximum speed at height 1,385 mph (2230 km/h, Mach 2·1); service ceiling (C) 67,000 ft (20,400 m); range with external fuel, about 3,200 miles (5150 km).
Armament: none (A, see text).
History: first flight (YA3J-1) 31 August 1958; (A-5A) January 1960; (A-5B) 29 April 1962; (RA-5C) 30 June 1962; final delivery of new aircraft 1971.

RA-5C (drop tanks, no ECM)

No aircraft in history introduced more new technology than the first Vigilante, planned in 1956 as a carrier-based attack aircraft. Among its features were automatically scheduled engine inlets and nozzles, single-surface vertical tail, differential slab tailplanes, linear bomb bay between the engines (with two emptied fuel tanks and a nuclear weapon ejected rearwards in the form of a long tube) and a comprehensive radar-inertial navigation system. Another feature was flap-blowing, and in the A-5B full-span leading-edge droop blowing was added to allow a 15,000 lb weight increase from saddle tanks in the new hump-backed fuselage. When carriers gave up a strategic nuclear role, the 57 A-5A were followed by the RA-5C, the airborne element of an integrated intelligence system serving the whole fleet and other forces. The RA-5C is extremely comprehensively equipped with multiple sensors including a side-looking radar under the fuselage. These valuable aircraft have been hard-worked in many theatres; 63 were built in 1962–66, 53 A-5A and the 6 A-5B were converted to RA-5C standard, and in 1969–71 the production line at Columbus was reopened for 46 Phase II with GE-10 engines and improved intakes and wing/body fillets.

Rockwell International OV-10 Bronco

OV-10A to -10E

Type: (except B) two-seat multi-role counter-insurgency; (B) target tug.
Engines: (except B(Z)) two 715 ehp AiResearch T76-410/411 single-shaft centrifugal turboprops; (B(Z)) as other versions plus General Electric J85-4 turbojet of 2,950 lb (1338 kg) thrust above fuselage.
Dimensions: span 40 ft (12·19 m); length (except D) 41 ft 7 in (12·67 m); (D) 44 ft (13·4 m); height 15 ft 2 in (4·62 m).
Weights: empty (A) 6,969 lb (3161 kg); maximum loaded (A) 14,466 lb (6563 kg).
Performance: maximum speed (A, sea level, clean) 281 mph (452 km/h); initial climb 2,300 ft (700 m)/min; (B(Z)) 6,800 ft/min; service ceiling 30,000 ft (9150 m); range with maximum weapon load, about 600 miles (960 km); ferry range at 12,000 lb gross, 1,428 miles (2300 km).
Armament: four 7·62 mm M60C machine guns in sponsons; 1,200 lb (544 kg) hardpoint on centreline and four 600 lb (272 kg) points under sponsons; one Sidewinder missile rail under each wing; (OV-10D) as other versions plus three-barrel 20 mm cannon in remotely aimed ventral power turret.
History: first flight 16 July 1965; (production OV-10A) 6 August 1967; (YOV-10D) 9 June 1970.

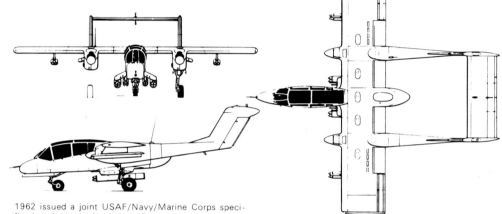

OV-1A (with partial weapon load)

Recognising that no US aircraft was tailored to the urgent task of fighting Co-In (counter-insurgency) operations, or "brush-fire wars", the US Department of Defense in 1960 began study of the problem and in 1962 issued a joint USAF/Navy/Marine Corps specification for a Light Armed Reconnaissance Aircraft (LARA). The winner, in 1964, was the Bronco. Designed to operate from short rough strips (or on floats or skis) it can carry a wide range of tactical equipment and weapons, including doppler radar, TV reconnaissance, five paratroops or two casualties. The OV-10A was ordered in October 1966 and by 1969 the Marine Corps had 114, while the USAF were using 157 for Forward Air Control (FAC) duties in Vietnam. In 1969 Pave Nail conversion of 15 aircraft fitted them with laser rangers, stabilized night sighting system, Loran and other devices for night FAC, attack or target illumination for other aircraft. Export sales include 32 OV-10C for Thailand and 16 OV-10E for Venezuela. The B and jet-boosted B(Z) are used by the Luftwaffe. The OV-10D has Night Observation Gunship (NOGS) equipment, with long-nosed IR sensor, cannon turret and, as a conversion, 1,000 ehp T76 engines.

Rockwell B-1 see page 188.

Saab 17

B17A, B17B, S17B, S17BS and B17C

Type: (B17) two-seat light bomber; (S17) reconnaissance.
Engine: (A) one 1,065 hp Swedish-built R-1830-S1C3G Twin Wasp 14-cylinder two-row radial; (B) 980 hp Swedish-built Bristol Mercury 24 nine-cylinder radial; (C) 1,000 hp imported Piaggio P.XIbis RC40 14-cylinder two-row radial.
Dimensions: span 44 ft 11 in (13·7 m); length 32 ft 6 in (9·9 m); height 12 ft (3·68 m).
Weights: empty (typical) 5,510 lb (2500 kg); loaded (A) 8,356 lb (3790 kg); (B) 7,947 lb (3605 kg); (B seaplane) 8,433 lb (3825 kg); (C) 8,532 lb (3870 kg).
Performance: maximum speed (A, C) 270 mph (435 km/h); (B) 245 mph (395 km/h); (B seaplane) 214 mph (345 km/h); service ceiling (typical) 26,250 ft (8000 m); range with bomb load (typical) 560 miles (900 km).
Armament: typically, two 13·2 mm guns in wings firing forward and one 7·9 mm manually aimed from rear cockpit; bomb load of up to 1,500 lb (680 kg) in internal bay, under fuselage and under wings.
History: first flight 18 May 1940; service delivery May 1941; final delivery (Ethiopia) 1950.

The first aircraft designed by Saab (Svenska Aeroplan Aktiebolaget), the Type 17 began as a study for a new reconnaissance machine in 1937. The infant design team at Linköping was augmented by about 40 Americans, mostly engineers skilled in stressed-skin

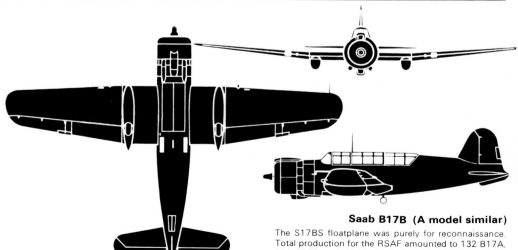

Saab B17B (A model similar)

structures, until the Swedes felt they could stand on their own feet. The first prototype had a Mercury engine and was equipped not only for reconnaissance but also for level and dive bombing. Saab made the main landing gear fold back into large underwing bulges and stressed the legs to serve as dive brakes. The ski versions had added dive brakes on the front ski struts. The S17BS floatplane was purely for reconnaissance. Total production for the RSAF amounted to 132 B17A, 114 B17B and S17B (including 38 S17BS) and 77 B17C. Swedish service was reliable and lasted until 1950. In 1944 a batch were supplied to the "free Danish air force" which formed in Sweden but which did not become operational before Denmark was liberated. In 1947–50 a total of 60 (mostly B17A) were sold to Ethiopia, remaining in service until 1969. Saab's next design was the Type 18 twin-engined bomber/reconnaissance family reminiscent of Dornier bombers.

Saab 21

J21A-1 and A-2, B21A-3 and J21RA and RB

Type: single-seat fighter; (B21) attack.
Engine: (A models) one 1,475 hp imported or SFA-built Daimler-Benz DB 605B inverted vee-12 liquid-cooled; (RA) one 3,000 lb (1360 kg) thrust DH Goblin 2 centrifugal turbojet; (RB) one 3,300 lb (1500 kg) SFA-built Goblin 3.
Dimensions: span (A) 38 ft 0¾ in (11·6 m); (R) 37 ft 4 in (11·37 m); length (all) 34 ft 3 in (10·45 m); height (A, over vertical propeller blade) 13 ft 1½ in (4 m); (R) 9 ft 8 in (2·90 m).
Weights: empty (A-1) 7,165 lb (3250 kg); (R, typical) 7,055 lb (3200 kg); maximum loaded (A-1) 9,149 lb (4150 kg); (R) 11,023 lb (5000 kg).
Performance: maximum speed (A) 398 mph (640 km/h); (RA) 497 mph (800 km/h); (RB) 522 mph (840 km/h); initial climb (A) 2,790 ft (850 m)/min; (RA) 4,600 ft (1400 m)/min; service ceiling (A-1) 36,100 ft (11,000 m); (RA) 39,400 ft (12,000 m); range (A) 466 miles (750 km); (R) 450 miles (720 km).
Armament: (A) one 20 mm Hispano cannon and two 13·2 mm M/39A in nose; in most variants, two further M/39A in fronts of tail booms; (R) one 20 mm Bofors cannon and four 13·2 mm; both versions equipped to carry pod under centreline housing eight 13·2 mm guns; (B21A, and R) underwing racks for up to ten rockets.

Saab J21RA (F7 Skaraborgs Flygflottilj)

History: first flight (A) 30 July 1943; service delivery (A-1) June 1945; final delivery (A-3) 1948; first flight (RA) 10 March 1947; service delivery (RA) February 1949; final delivery (RB) early 1951.

Noteworthy as the only design in the world to have seen front-line service with both piston and jet power, the Saab 21 was an excellent basic aircraft, being robust, manoeuvrable and a rock-steady weapon platform. The original design was sketched in two weeks in March 1941 by Frid Wänström, in response to a request from the Royal Swedish Air Board for a replacement for the miscellaneous obsolescent fighters then in use. After many problems the J21A-1 went into production in 1945, with DB 605B engine from Germany, pusher propeller, and – because of the bail-out hazard – an ejection seat. The 54 A-1 were followed by 124 A-2 with Swedish-built engines and 120 A-3, many A-3 being the attack version (B21A) with external stores. Though problems were greater than expected, the conversion to jet power was amazingly successful and 30 RA and 30 RB were built. The tailplane was carried high on altered fins, the landing gear was shortened and there were many other changes, but the J21R was a most popular machine. Production was stopped only because of the coming J29.

Saab 29

J29A, B, D, E and F, and S29C

Type: (J29) single-seat fighter bomber; (S29) reconnaissance.
Engine: one Svenska Flygmotor RM2 (de Havilland Ghost) centrifugal turbojet; (early A) 4,400 lb (2000 kg) RM2; (late A, B, C) 5,000 lb (2270 kg) RM2 (Ghost 50); (D, E, F) 6,170 lb (2800 kg) RM2B with afterburner.
Dimensions: span 36 ft 1 in (11 m); length 33 ft 2½ in (10·12 m); height 12 ft 3½ in (3·75 m).
Weights: empty (A) 9,479 lb; (F) 10,141 lb (4600 kg); maximum loaded (A) 13,360 lb; (F) 17,637 lb (8000 kg).
Performance: maximum speed (all, Mach-limited) 659 mph (1060 km/h, Mach 0·86); initial climb (A) 7,500 ft/min; (F) 11,810 ft (3600 m)/min; service ceiling (A) 45,000 ft; (F) 50,850 ft (15,500 m); range on internal fuel (A) 810 miles (1300 km); (F) 1,060 miles (1700 km); ferry range (all) about 1,678 miles (2700 km).
Armament: (S29C) none; (others) four 20 mm Swedish Hispano Mk V under forward fuselage; wing pylons or hardpoints for up to 1,100 lb (500 kg), including two 88-gal tanks or (F only) two Rb324 (Sidewinder) missiles.
History: first flight 1 September 1948; (production prototype) July 1950; service delivery April 1951; final delivery (F) April 1956.

Saab 29F (1 Jagdbomber Staffel, Austrian AF)

The first swept-wing fighter to be built in Western Europe, the Saab 29 was aptly nicknamed "Tunnan" (barrel). Availability of the British Ghost turbojet enabled Lars Brising and his design team to raise their sights and go for higher performance with a very strong, swept wing. Snags were remarkably few, rate of roll and turn radius being outstanding and pilots coping well with the narrow-track landing gear. The J29A, with outboard ailerons, fuselage airbrakes and plain flaps, entered service with F13 at Norrköping in May 1951. Eventually a total of 661 Tunnan were delivered, the J29B having extra fuel, the S29C carrying up to six cameras, the J29D testing the afterburning engine introduced in the course of the E batch with sawtooth leading edge, and the F incorporating all earlier improvements. After final delivery 308 B, D and E were rebuilt as J29Fs. Many of these fine machines served with the UN peace force in the Congo in 1961–63 and 30 ex-Flygvapnet J29F were sold to Austria in 1961–62.

Saab 32 Lansen

Saab J32B Lansen (1 Sqn, F12 Wing, Kalmar)

A32A, J32B, S32C

Type: (A) two-seat all-weather attack; (B) all-weather and night fighter; (C) reconnaissance.
Engine: one Svenska Flygmotor licence-built Rolls-Royce Avon single-shaft turbojet with afterburner; (A and C) 10,362 lb (4700 kg) thrust RM5A2; (B) 15,190 lb (6890 kg) RM6A.
Dimensions: span 42 ft 7¾ in (13 m); length (A) 49 ft 0¾ in (14·94 m); (B) 47 ft 6¾ in (C) 48 ft 0¾ in; height 15 ft 3 in (4·65 m).
Weights: empty (A) 16,398 lb (7438 kg); (B) 17,600 lb; (C) 16,520 lb; maximum loaded (A) 28,660 lb (13,600 kg); (B) 29,800 lb; (C) typically 26,500 lb.
Performance: maximum speed (all) 692 mph (1114 km/h, Mach 0·91); initial climb (A, C) 11,800 ft (3600 m)/min; (B) 19,700 ft/min; service ceiling (A, C) 49,200 ft (15,000 m); (B) 52,500 ft; range with external fuel (all, typical) 2,000 miles (3220 km).
Armament: (A) four 20 mm Swedish Hispano Mk V under nose; wing pylons for external load of up to 3,000 lb including two Rb04C air-to-surface missiles or two 1,320 lb (600 kg) bombs; (B) four 30 mm Aden M/55 cannon under nose and four Rb324 (Sidewinder) missiles or FFAR pods; (C) none.
History: first flight 3 November 1952; service delivery (A) December 1955; first flight (B) 7 January 1957; (C) 26 March 1957; final delivery (B) 2 May 1960.

Designed to replace the Saab 18, the Type 32 was a large all-swept machine of outstanding quality, designed and developed ahead of similar aircraft elsewhere in Western Europe. Owing to its size it was capable of development for three dissimilar missions, proving so valuable that many survie in front-line service well into the 1970s. Supersonic in a shallow dive, the A32A entered service with F17 and soon gained a great reputation for good handling, ease of maintenance and accurate weapon delivery. It equipped all four Swedish attack wings until the Saab AJ37 began to replace it in 1971. The more powerful J32B night fighter was fitted with S6 radar fire control for lead/pursuit interception and equipped seven squadrons in 1958–70. The S32C force was several times updated by fitting advanced new sensors and ECM, and is only now (1976) being replaced by the SF37 and SH37. Total Lansen (meaning lance) production was 450.

Saab 35 Draken see page 194.

Saab 37 Viggen

AJ37, JA37, SF37, SH37 and Sk37

Type: (AJ) single-seat all-weather attack; (JA) all-weather fighter; (SF) armed photo-reconnaissance; (SH) armed sea surveillance; (Sk) dual trainer.

Engine: one Svenska Flygmotor RM8 (licence-built Pratt & Whitney JT8D two-shaft turbofan redesigned in Sweden for Mach 2 and fitted with SFA afterburner): (AJ, SF, SH and Sk) 25,970 lb (11,790 kg) RM8A; (JA) 28,086 lb (12,750 kg) RM8B.

Dimensions: span of main wing 34 ft 9¼ in (10·6 m); length (53 ft 5¾ in) (16·3 m); JA37 with probe 53 ft 11 ins; height 18 ft 4½ in (5·6 m).

Weights: not disclosed, except AJ37 "normal armament" gross weight of 35,275 lb (16,000 kg).

Performance: maximum speed (clean) about 1,320 mph (2135 km/h, Mach II), or Mach 1·1 at sea level initial climb, about 40,000 ft (12,200 m)/min (time from start of take-off run to 32,800 ft–10,000 m = 100 sec); service ceiling, over 60,000 ft (18,300 m); tactical radius with external stores (not drop tanks), hi-lo-hi profile, over 620 miles (1000 km).

Armament: seven pylons (option: nine) for aggregate external load of 13,200 lb (6000 kg), including Rb04E or Rb05A missiles for attack, and Rb27, Rb28 and Rb324 missiles for defence. In addition the JA37 has a 30 mm Oerlikon KCA gun and will carry "new long- and short-range missiles for air-to-air interception".

History: first flight 8 February 1967; (production AJ) 23 February 1971; service delivery (AJ) June 1971.

Yet again blazing a trail ahead of other nations, the Royal Swedish Air Board planned System 37 in 1958–61 as a standardized weapon system to be integrated with the Stril 60 air-defence environment of radars, computers and displays. Included in the system is a standard platform (in this case a supersonic manned aircraft) produced in five versions each tailored to a specific task. Thanks to a unique configuration with a 400 sq ft wing preceded by a canard foreplane with trailing-edge flaps, the Viggen (Thunderbolt) has outstanding STOL (short take-off and landing) performance and excellent turn radius at all speeds. Efficient and prolonged operations are possible from narrow strips 500 m (1,640 ft) in length, such as stretches of highway. Equipment in all versions includes headup display, autothrottle/speed control on approach, no-flare landing autopilot and thrust reverser. The AJ operates camouflaged in attack wings F7, F15 and F6, with production continuing in 1976. The multi-sensor SF and SH versions are also in service, and all units have one or more Sk 37 trainers. The JA37 is considerably different, with a new engine, very powerful gun, UAP 1023 pulse-doppler radar, digital automatic flight control system and extremely advanced inertial measurement and central computer systems. The development effort for the JA37 rivals that for the complete original aircraft, but with the help of a fleet of special-purpose test aircraft the JA37 is expected to be cleared for production in 1976. Actual production of the JA began in 1974, for RSAF delivery in 1978.

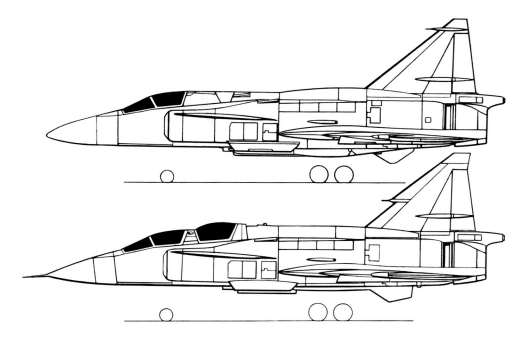

The two side elevations above depict the JA37 (top) and Sk37. The JA37 is the most advanced of all Viggen versions, with RM8B engine, new radar and completely different avionics and weapons planned primarily for the air-to-air role. The Sk37 is the tandem conversion trainer for all Viggen pilots.

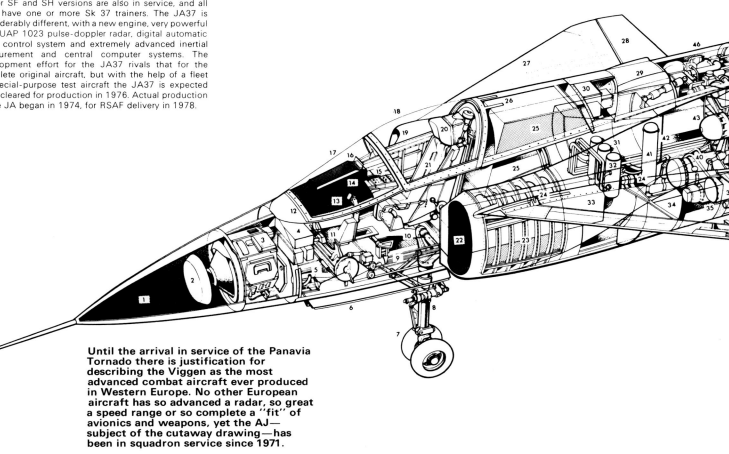

Until the arrival in service of the Panavia Tornado there is justification for describing the Viggen as the most advanced combat aircraft ever produced in Western Europe. No other European aircraft has so advanced a radar, so great a speed range or so complete a "fit" of avionics and weapons, yet the AJ—subject of the cutaway drawing—has been in squadron service since 1971.

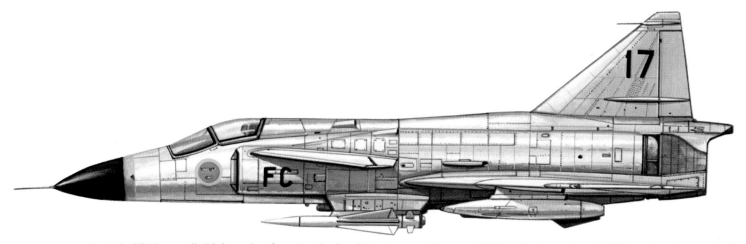

Saab AJ37 Viggen (initial production standard, without camouflage or ECM fit, but carrying Rb05A on fuselage pylon).

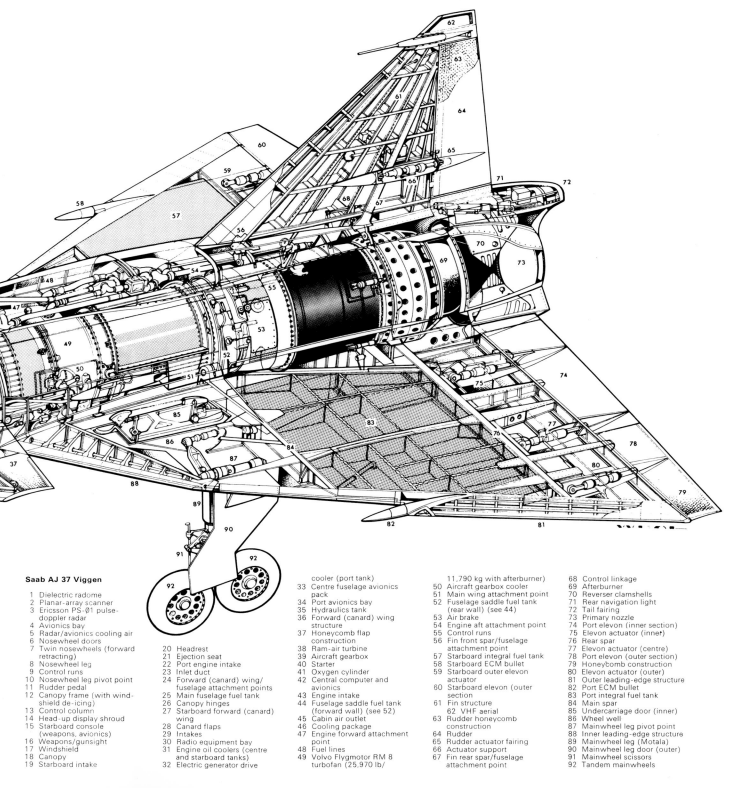

Saab AJ 37 Viggen

1 Dielectric radome
2 Planar-array scanner
3 Ericsson PS-Ø1 pulse-doppler radar
4 Avionics bay
5 Radar/avionics cooling air
6 Nosewheel doors
7 Twin nosewheels (forward retracting)
8 Nosewheel leg
9 Control runs
10 Nosewheel leg pivot point
11 Rudder pedal
12 Canopy frame (with wind-shield de-icing)
13 Control column
14 Head-up display shroud
15 Starboard console (weapons, avionics)
16 Weapons/gunsight
17 Windshield
18 Canopy
19 Starboard intake
20 Headrest
21 Ejection seat
22 Port engine intake
23 Inlet duct
24 Forward (canard) wing/fuselage attachment points
25 Main fuselage fuel tank
26 Canopy hinges
27 Starboard forward (canard) wing
28 Canard flaps
29 Intakes
30 Radio equipment bay
31 Engine oil coolers (centre and starboard tanks)
32 Electric generator drive

33 Centre fuselage avionics pack
34 Port avionics bay
35 Hydraulics tank
36 Forward (canard) wing structure
37 Honeycomb flap construction
38 Ram-air turbine
39 Aircraft gearbox
40 Starter
41 Oxygen cylinder
42 Central computer and avionics
43 Engine intake
44 Fuselage saddle fuel tank (forward wall) (see 52)
45 Cabin air outlet
46 Cooling package
47 Engine forward attachment point
48 Fuel lines
49 Volvo Flygmotor RM 8 turbofan (25,970 lb/

cooler (port tank)
11,790 kg with afterburner)
50 Aircraft gearbox cooler
51 Main wing attachment point
52 Fuselage saddle fuel tank (rear wall) (see 44)
53 Air brake
54 Engine aft attachment point
55 Control runs
56 Fin front spar/fuselage attachment point
57 Starboard integral fuel tank
58 Starboard ECM bullet
59 Starboard outer elevon actuator
60 Starboard elevon (outer section)
61 Fin structure
62 VHF aerial
63 Rudder honeycomb construction
64 Rudder
65 Rudder actuator fairing
66 Actuator support
67 Fin rear spar/fuselage attachment point

68 Control linkage
69 Afterburner
70 Reverser clamshells
71 Rear navigation light
72 Tail fairing
73 Primary nozzle
74 Port elevon (inner section)
75 Elevon actuator (inner)
76 Rear spar
77 Elevon actuator (centre)
78 Port elevon (outer section)
79 Honeycomb construction
80 Elevon actuator (outer)
81 Outer leading-edge structure
82 Port ECM bullet
83 Port integral fuel tank
84 Main spar
85 Undercarriage door (inner)
86 Wheel well
87 Mainwheel leg pivot point
88 Inner leading-edge structure
89 Mainwheel leg door (outer)
90 Mainwheel leg door (outer)
91 Mainwheel scissors
92 Tandem mainwheels

Saab 35 Draken

J35A, B, D and F, Sk35C, S35E and export versions

Type: (J35) single-seat all-weather fighter-bomber; (Sk35) dual trainer; (S35) single-seat all-weather reconnaissance.

Saab J35A Draken (F13, Royal Swedish Air Force, Norrköping)

Engine: one Svenska Flygmotor RM6 (licence-built Rolls-Royce Avon with SFA afterburner): (A, B, C) 15,000 lb (6804 kg) RM6B; (D, E, F and export) 17,110 lb (7761 kg) RM6C.

Dimensions: span 30 ft 10 in (9·4 m); length 50 ft 4 in (15·4 m) (S35E, 52 ft); height 12 ft 9 in (3·9 m).

Weights: empty (D) 16,017 lb; (F) 18,180 lb (8250 kg); maximum loaded (A) 18,200 lb; (D) 22,663 lb (6804 kg); (F) 27,050 lb (12,270 kg); (F-35) 35,275 lb (16,000 kg).

Performance: maximum speed (D onwards, clean) 1,320 mph (2125 km/h, Mach 2·0), (with two drop tanks and two 1,000 lb bombs) 924 mph (1487 km/h, Mach 1·4); initial climb (D onwards, clean) 34,450 ft (10,500 m)/min; service ceiling (D onwards, clean) about 65,000 ft (20,000 m); range (internal fuel plus external weapons, typical) 800 miles (1300 km), (maximum fuel) 2,020 miles (3250 km).

Armament: (A) two 30 mm Aden M/55 in wings, four Rb 324 (Sidewinder) missiles; (B) as A plus attack ordnance to maximum of 2,200 lb (1000 kg); (C) none; (D) as B; (E) usually none but provision as A; (F) one 30 mm Aden plus two Rb27 Falcon (radar) and two Rb28 Falcon (infra-red) missiles, plus two or four Rb324; (F-35) two 30 mm Aden plus nine stores pylons each rated at 1,000 lb (454 kg) all usable simultaneously, plus four Rb324.

History: first flight 25 October 1955; (production J35A) 15 February 1958; final delivery (TF-35) 1974, (35XS) 1975.

Again in advance of any other country in Western Europe, the Saab 35 was designed in 1949–51 as an all-weather supersonic fighter able to use small airfields. Erik Bratt and his team arrived at the unique "double delta" shape after studying different ways of packaging the fuel and equipment, the best arrangement being with items one behind the other giving a long aircraft of very small frontal area. In 1960 attack wing F13 found the A (Adam) simple to fly and maintain, sensitive in pitch and yet virtually unbreakable. B (Bertil) was more complex, with S7 collision-course fire control integrated with the Swedish Stril 60 air defence environment. Most Sk35C trainers were converted Adams. D (David) was first to reach Mach 2, despite continual increases in weight mainly due to fuel capacity raised from 493 to 680 gallons. E (Erik) carries French OMERA cameras and in 1973 was updated with external British Vinten night/low-level pods. F (Filip) is an automatic interceptor with Ericsson (Hughes basis) radar of pulse-doppler type. Production was closed at 606 with 40 multi-role F-35/RF-35/TF-35 aircraft for Denmark and 12 XS for Finland assembled by Valmet Oy.

Saab 37 Viggen see page 192.

Savoia-Marchetti S.M.79 Sparviero

Savoia-Marchetti S.M.79-JR (3rd Air Corps, Royal Air Forces of Romania)

S.M.79-I, II and III, 79B and 79-JR

Type: 4/5-seat bomber, torpedo bomber and reconnaissance.

Engines: (I) three 780 hp Alfa-Romeo 126 RC34 nine-cylinder radials; (II) three 1,000 hp Piaggio P.XI RC40 14-cylinder two-row radials (one batch, 1,030 hp Fiat A.80 RC41); (79B) two engines (many types); (79-JR) two 1,220 hp Junkers Jumo 211Da inverted-vee-12 liquid-cooled.

Dimensions: span 69 ft 6½ in (21·2 m); length (I) 51 ft 10 in; (II) 53 ft 1¾ in (16·2 m); (B, -JR) 52 ft 9 in; height (II) 13 ft 5½ in (4·1 m).

Weights: empty (I) 14,990 lb (6800 kg); (II) 16,755 lb (7600 kg); (-JR) 15,860 lb (7195 kg); maximum loaded (I) 23,100 lb (10,500 kg); (II) 24,912 lb (11,300 kg); (-JR) 23,788 lb (10,470 kg).

Performance: maximum speed (I) 267 mph; (II) 270 mph (434 km/h); (B) 255 mph; (-JR) 276 mph; initial climb (typical) 1,150 ft (350 m)/min; service ceiling (all) 21,325–23,300 ft (7000 m); range with bomb load (not torpedoes), typical, 1,243 miles (2000 km).

Armament: (typical) one 12·7 mm Breda-SAFAT fixed firing ahead from above cockpit, one 12·7 mm manually aimed from open dorsal position, one 12·7 mm manually aimed from rear of ventral gondola and one 7·7 mm Lewis manually aimed from either beam window; internal bomb bay for up to 2,200 lb (1000 kg) or two 450 mm torpedoes slung externally; (79B and -JR) no fixed gun, typically three/five 7·7 mm guns and bomb load up to 2,640 lb (1200 kg).

History: first flight (civil prototype) late 1934; service delivery (I) late 1936; (II) October 1939; final delivery (III) early 1944.

Though often derided — as were most Italian arms in World War II — the S.M.79 Sparviero (Hawk) was a fine and robust bomber that unfailingly operated in the most difficult conditions with great reliability. The prototype, fitted with various engines and painted in civil or military liveries, set various world records in 1935–36, despite its mixed structure of steel tube, light alloy, wood and fabric. Built at unprecedented rate for the Regia Aeronautica, the 79-I established an excellent reputation with the Aviación Legionaria in the Spanish civil war, while other Stormi laid the basis for great proficiency with torpedoes. Altogether about 1,200 of all versions served with the Regia Aeronautica, while just over 100 were exported. Most exports were twin-engined 79B versions, but the Romanian-built 79-JR was more powerful and served on the Russian front in 1941–44.

S.E.5a

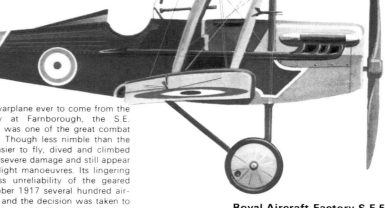

Royal Aircraft Factory S.E.5 (aircraft of Lt-Col W. A. "Billy" Bishop)

Royal Aircraft Factory S.E.5 and 5a

Type: single-seat fighting scout.

Engine: (5) one 150 hp Hispano-Suiza 8A vee-8 water-cooled; (5a) one 200, 220 or 240 hp Hispano-Suiza, or (final standard) 200 hp Wolseley W.4a Viper (same layout).

Dimensions: span 26 ft 7½ in (8·11 m); length 20 ft 11 in (6·38 m); height 9 ft 6 in (2·89 m).

Weights: empty (typical) 1,410 lb (639 kg); maximum loaded 1,890–2,048 lb; (typical 5a, Viper) 1,988 lb (902 kg).

Performance: maximum speed (5a, Viper) 120 mph (193 km/h); initial climb 770 ft (235 m)/min; service ceiling 17,000–22,000 ft; (5a, Viper) 19,500 ft (5944 m); range, typically 300 miles (483 km).

Armament: typically one 0·303 in Vickers on left of fuselage with Constantinesco synchronizing gear, and one 0·303 in Lewis on Foster mount on upper wing (both guns commonly harmonised at 150 ft ahead). Many aircraft fitted with fuselage racks for four 25 lb (11 kg) Cooper bombs.

History: first flight 22 November 1916; service delivery (5) March 1917, (5a) June 1917.

Undoubtedly the best warplane ever to come from the Royal Aircraft Factory at Farnborough, the S.E. (Scout Experimental) 5 was one of the great combat aircraft of World War I. Though less nimble than the Camel, it was much easier to fly, dived and climbed faster and could accept severe damage and still appear to be unbreakable by flight manoeuvres. Its lingering curse was the hopeless unreliability of the geared French engine; by October 1917 several hundred airframes were engineless and the decision was taken to fit them with faulty engines (this being judged better than none). Only when Wolseley developed the Hispano into the high-compression, direct-drive Viper was this problem removed. Many of the great Allied aces gained most of their victories on the 5a, among them Ball, Beauchamp-Procter, Bishop, Mannock, McCudden and McElroy. About 5,000 were built in Britain for the RFC and American Expeditionary Force and Curtiss flew the first off a US line that, had the war continued, would soon have delivered a further 1,000.

SEPECAT Jaguar see page 196

Shin Meiwa SS-2

PX-S, SS-2 (PS-1) and SS-2A (PS-1 Kai)
Type: (2) anti-submarine flying boat; (2A) air/sea rescue amphibian.
Engines: four 3,060 ehp Ishikawajima-built General Electric T64-IHI-10 single-shaft turboprops (plus one 1,400 shp or 1,250 shp T58-IHI-10 in hull for blowing flaps, rudder and elevators).
Dimensions: span 108 ft 8¾ in (33·14 m); length 109 ft 11 in (33·5 m); height (2) 31 ft 10½ in (9·715 m); (2A) 32 ft 1 in.
Weights: empty (2) 58,000 lb (26,300 kg); (2A) 56,218 lb (25,500 kg); maximum loaded (2) 94,800 lb (43,000 kg); (2A) 99,200 lb (45,000 kg).
Performance: maximum speed (2) 340 mph (547 km/h); (2A) 299 mph (481 km/h); initial climb (2) 2,264 ft (690 m)/min; service ceiling (2) 29,500 ft (9000 m); range with full weapon load (2) 1,347 miles (2168 km).
Armament: (2) weapons compartment on upper deck accommodates four 330 lb (150 kg) AS bombs (plus much heavier load of sensors); external pylons between engines carry containers each housing two homing torpedoes; launchers on wing tips for triple groups of 5 in rockets.
History: first flight (2) 5 October 1967; (production PS-1) 1972; (2A) 1974.

After seven years of study Shin Meiwa were awarded a contract for the prototype of a novel ASW (anti-sub-

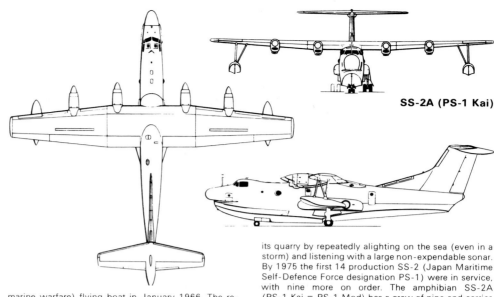

SS-2A (PS-1 Kai)

marine warfare) flying boat in January 1966. The resulting PX-S demonstrated the technique of flying not much faster than submerged nuclear submarines, using extensive blowing over flaps and tail, and of tracking

its quarry by repeatedly alighting on the sea (even in a storm) and listening with a large non-expendable sonar. By 1975 the first 14 production SS-2 (Japan Maritime Self-Defence Force designation PS-1) were in service, with nine more on order. The amphibian SS-2A (PS-1 Kai = PS-1 Mod) has a crew of nine and carries 64 passengers and cargo or 12 seated and 12 stretcher (litter) survivors. Deliveries to the JMSDF began in 1975.

Short S.25 Sunderland

Sunderland I, II, III and V (MR.5)
Type: ocean patrol and anti-submarine flying boat with typical crew of 13.
Engines: (I) four 1,010 hp Bristol Pegasus 22 nine-cylinder radials; (II, III) four 1,065 hp Pegasus XVIII; (V) four 1,200 hp Pratt & Whitney R-1830-90B Twin Wasp 14-cylinder two-row radials.
Dimensions: span 112 ft 9½ in (34·39 m); length 85 ft 4 in (26 m); height 32 ft 10½ in (10·1 m).
Weights: empty (III) 34,500 lb (15,663 kg); (V) 37,000 lb (16,783 kg); maximum loaded (III) 58,000 lb (26,308 kg); (V) 60,000 lb (27,216 kg).
Performance: maximum speed (III, V) 213 mph (343 km/h); initial climb (III) 720 ft (220 m)/min; (V) 840 ft (256 m)/min; service ceiling (typical) 17,400 ft (5300 m); maximum range (III, V) 2,900 miles (4670 km).
Armament: (I) eight 0·303 in Browning, two in nose turret, four in tail turret and two manually aimed from hatches behind each wing root; internal load of 2,000 lb (907 kg) of bombs, depth charges, mines and pyrotechnics wound out on rails under inner wing to release position inboard of inner engines; (II, III) as (I) but twin-0·303 in dorsal turret in place of manual guns; (V) as (II, III) with addition in some aircraft of four fixed 0·303 in in nose; in many aircraft, also two manually aimed 0·5 in Brownings from beam windows, usually in place of dorsal turret.
History: first flight 16 October 1937; service delivery May 1938; final delivery June 1946.

Derived from the Imperial Airways Empire flying boat to meet Specification R.2/33, the Sunderland marked a vast improvement in fighting capability over previous biplane boats. From the outbreak of World War II these

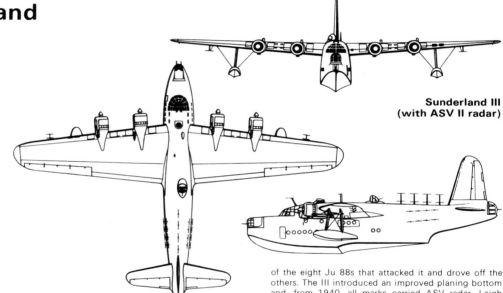

Sunderland III (with ASV II radar)

capacious, reliable and long-ranged boats were ceaselessly at work finding and sinking U-boats, rescuing seamen from sunken vessels and engaging in such fierce battles with enemy aircraft that the Sunderland became known to the Luftwaffe as "Flying Porcupine". Many times single Sunderlands fought off five or more hostile aircraft, and once a Sunderland shot down three

of the eight Ju 88s that attacked it and drove off the others. The III introduced an improved planing bottom and, from 1940, all marks carried ASV radar, Leigh lights and an increasing amount of avionics. Altogether 739 were built, 240 by Blackburn at Dumbarton, the Mk III being by far the most numerous. After the war the MR.5 was used on the Berlin Airlift, in Korea, against terrorists in Malaya, on the North Greenland Expedition and by the French Navy and RNZAF. Last sortie was on 15 May 1959 from Singapore, from where Sunderlands had begun combat duty 21 years earlier.

Short S.29 Stirling

Stirling I to V
Type: (I–III) heavy bomber with crew of 7/8; (IV) glider tug and special transport; (V) strategic transport.
Engines: (I) four 1,595 hp Bristol Hercules XI 14-cylinder sleeve-valve radials; (II) 1,600 hp Wright R-2600-A5B Cyclone; (III, IV, V) 1,650 hp Bristol Hercules XVI.
Dimensions: span 99 ft 1 in (30·2 m); length (except V) 87 ft 3 in (26·6 m); (V) 90 ft 6¾ in (27·6 m); height 22 ft 9 in (6·94 m).
Weights: empty (I) 44,000 lb (19,950 kg); (III) 46,900 lb (21,273 kg); (IV, V, except V) 43,200 lb (19,600 kg); maximum loaded (I) 59,400 lb (26,943 kg); (III, IV, V) 70,000 lb (31,750 kg).
Performance: maximum speed (I–III) 270 mph (435 km/h); (IV, V) 280 mph (451 km/h); initial climb (typical) 800 ft (244 m)/min; service ceiling (I–III) 17,000 ft (5182 m); range (III) 590 miles (950 km)

with 14,000 lb bombs or 2,010 miles (3235 km) with 3,500 lb; range (IV, V) 3,000 miles (4828 km).
Armament: (I) two 0·303 in Brownings in nose and dorsal turrets and four in tail turret, plus (early batches) two in remote control ventral turret; maximum bomb load 18,000 lb (8165 kg) in fuselage and inner wings; (II, III) as (I) but different dorsal turret; (IV) sole armament, tail turret; (V) none.
History: first flight 14 May 1939; (production Mk I) May 1940; final delivery (V) November 1945.

Though extremely impressive, with vast length, unprecedented height and even two separate tailwheels, the

Stirling was unpopular. Partly owing to short wing span it had a poor ceiling and sluggish manoeuvrability except at low level. Though it carried a heavy bomb load, it could not carry bombs bigger than 2,000 lb (the largest size when the design was completed in 1938). Operations began with daylight attacks in February 1941, soon switched to night, and by 1943 the Stirling was regarded mainly as a tug and transport and carrier of ECM jamming and spoofing devices for 100 Group. The RAF received 2,221 bomber versions, excluding the two Mk II conversions, and Short's new Belfast plant finally built 160 of the streamlined Mk V transports which carried 40 troops or heavy freight.

Short Stirling I (214 Sqn, Stradishall)

SEPECAT Jaguar

Jaguar GR.1 and T.2, Jaguar A and E, and Jaguar International

Type: (GR.1, A and International (I.)) single-seat all-weather attack; (T.2 and E) dual operational trainer.

Engines: two Rolls-Royce/Turboméca Adour two-shaft augmented turbofans: (except I.) 7,305 lb (3313 kg) Adour 102; (I.) 8,000 lb (3630 kg) Adour 804.

Dimensions: span 28 ft 6 in (8·69 m); length (except T.2, E) 50 ft 11 in (15·52 m); (T.2, E) 53 ft 11 in (16·42 m); height 16 ft 1½ in (4·92 m).

Weights: empty, classified but about 15,000 lb (6800 kg); "normal take-off" (ie, internal fuel and some external ordnance) 23,000 lb (10,430 kg); maximum loaded 34,000 lb (15,500 kg).

Performance: maximum speed (lo, some external stores) 820 mph (1320 km/h, Mach 1·1), (hi, some external stores) 1,055 mph (1700 km/h, Mach 1·6); climb and ceiling, classified; attack radius, no external fuel, hi-lo-hi with bombs, 507 miles (815 km); ferry range 2,614 miles (4210 km).

Armament: (A, E) two 30 mm DEFA 553 each with 150 rounds; five pylons for total external load of 10,000 lb (4536 kg); (GR.1) as above but guns two 30 mm Aden; (T.2) as above but single Aden. (International) wide range of options including increased external loads.

History: first flight (E) 8 September 1968; (production E) 2 November 1971; (production GR.1) 11 October 1972; squadron delivery (E, A) May 1972, (GR, T) June 1973.

Developed jointly by BAC in Britain and Dassault-Breguet in France, to meet a joint requirement of the Armée de l'Air and RAF, the Jaguar is a far more powerful and effective aircraft than originally planned and has already demonstrated unmatched capabilities in service. The original idea was a light trainer and close-support machine, with 1,300 lb weapon load, but with British pressure this was upgraded to today's outstanding aircraft whose only marketing problem is the fact that the French partner which prefers aircraft which appear to be all-French (yet, in fact, Dassault makes only the same proportion of the Mirage F1 as it does of the Jaguar, namely, about 50 per cent). Despite this unhappy political scene the sheer merit of the Jaguar, and the enthusiastic missionary work done by its operating units in the Armée de l'Air and RAF, is gradually

SEPECAT Jaguar A (in original configuration on delivery to Armée de l'Air 7e Escadre, St Dizier, 1972)

winning valuable orders, beginning with Ecuador and Oman in 1974. Further sales are likely with the more powerful International version now flying. The two basic single-seat versions share a common airframe but are totally different in equipment. The French A model has a simple twin-gyro platform, doppler, and a basic navigation computer. The RAF GR.1 has inertial navigation, head-up display, projected-map display, radar height, integrated nav/attack system and laser ranger, as well as comprehensive ECM and option of a multi-sensor reconnaissance pod. All versions can have nose radar, refuelling probe and the option of overwing pylons for light dogfight missiles. By the end of 1975 about 280 aircraft had been delivered of initial French and British orders for 400 (split 50/50), with several further orders in negotiation.

For Shin Meiwa and Short aircraft see page 195.

SEPECAT Jaguar GR.1

1 Pitot head
2 Pitot probe
3 'Chisel nose' with glass windows
4 Ferranti laser ranger and target marker
5 Air data computer
6 Waveform generator
7 Two total-pressure probes
8 Radio altimeter
9 HF/VHF power amplifier
10 Equipment bay cooling ducts

11 Intake
12 Nav/attack electronics compartments
13 External emergency canopy release
14 Ajax feel unit (pitch control)
15 Nosewheel well
16 Instrument panel
17 Projected map display (head-down)
18 Windscreen
19 Head-up display panel
20 Upward-hinged canopy
21 Martin-Baker Mk 9 zero-zero ejector seat
22 Honeycomb cockpit side panels
23 Instrument console
24 Access panels
25 Cannon barrel
26 Battery and electrics bay
27 Intake
28 Spring-loaded auxiliary inlet doors
29 30mm Aden cannon
30 Main undercarriage side door
31 Undercarriage retraction jack
32 Integrally-stiffened frame
33 Ammunition trough
34 Duct bolt-up joints
35 Inlet duct frames
36 Duct/fuselage attachment plate
37 Cold-air unit
38 Ram-air intake
39 Twin VHF homer aerials
40 Inner dorsal spine (hydraulic and cable runs)
41 Slat motor and gearbox
42 Drop tank (264 gal/1,200 litres)
43 Starboard inner pylon
44 1000 lb (454 kg) bomb
45 Starboard outer stores pylon

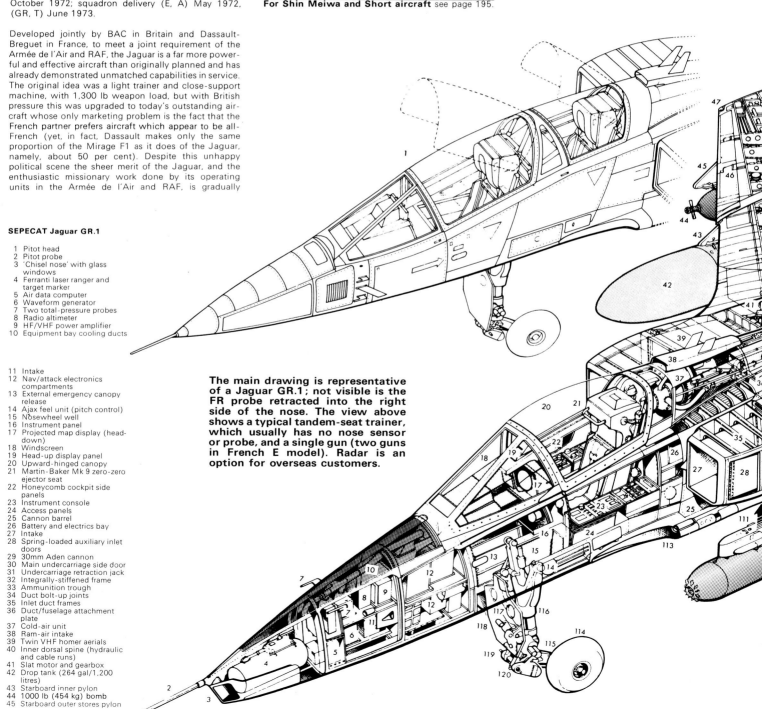

The main drawing is representative of a Jaguar GR.1; not visible is the FR probe retracted into the right side of the nose. The view above shows a typical tandem-seat trainer, which usually has no nose sensor or probe, and a single gun (two guns in French E model). Radar is an option for overseas customers.

Below, three-view of RAF Jaguar GR.1 before completion of ECM installation)

46 Leading-edge steel slat-rail
47 Starboard navigation light
48 Honeycomb-filled spoiler
49 Wing fence
50 Pylon mount
51 Fuel lines
52 Wing construction
53 Starboard wing integral fuel tank
54 Dorsal anti-collision beacon
55 Control rods
56 Wing centre-joint
57 Forward wing-fixing joint
58 Box-section centre-keel
59 Ram-air intake
60 Honeycomb-filled flap
61 Primary heat-exchanger
62 Upper fuselage access panels

63 Engine forward mounting point
64 Accumulator No 2 system
65 Hydraulic system pressure reservoir No 2
66 Air extractor duct
67 Upper fuselage access panels
68 Inward/outward vent valve
69 Starboard tailplane
70 Fin construction
71 Magnetic detector
72 Built-up leading edge
73 Passive ECM sensor fairing
74 VHF/UHF aerial
76 Rear navigation light
77 HF aerial
78 Honeycomb-filled rudder

79 Fuel dump vent
80 Braking parachute housing
81 Rudder power control unit
82 Control run linkage
83 Tailplane control units
84 Tailplane pivot point
85 Tailplane construction
86 Tailplane discontinuity (inboard rear portion higher)
87 Honeycomb-filled outer section
88 Arrester hook (extended)
89 Variable nozzle flaps
90 Afterburner
91 Aft fuselage integral fuel tanks
92 Engine aft mounting point
93 Rolls-Royce/Turbomeca

Adour 102 turbofans (7,305 lb/3,313 kg thrust with maximum afterburner)
94 Centre fuselage section
95 Air brake actuator
96 Air brake (extended)
97 Wing fence
98 Pylon mount
99 Full-span trailing-edge double-slotted flaps
100 Port navigation light
101 1,000 lb (454 kg) bomb
102 Port outer stores pylon
103 Leading-edge slat
104 Port inner stores pylon
105 Drop tank (264 gal/ 1,200 litres)
106 Low-pressure twin main-

wheel tyres
107 Shock-absorber strut
108 Mainwheel leg
109 Drag strut
110 Undercarriage flap
111 Centreline ventral stores pylon (shown lowered)
112 Tandem BL 755 cluster bombs
113 Cannon port
114 Nosewheel
115 Single (starboard) axle fork
116 Nosewheel leg
117 Two landing lights (one 450W, one 250W)
118 Nosewheel door
119 Anti-shimmy gear
120 Towing lug

Siemens-Schuckert fighters

D.I to D.IV

Type: single-seat fighting scout.
Engine: one 160 hp Siemens und Halske Sh.III 11-cylinder geared rotary or (late D.III) 200 hp Sh.IIIa.
Dimensions: span (III) 27 ft 8 in (8·43 m); (IV) 27 ft 4¾ in; length 18 ft 8½ in (5·70 m); height (III) 9 ft 2¼ in (2·80 m); (IV) 8 ft 11 in.
Weights: empty (III) 1,014 lb (460 kg); loaded (III) 1,598 lb (725 kg); (IV) 1,620 lb.
Performance: maximum speed (III) 112 mph (180 km/h); (IV) 118 mph; initial climb (III) 1,480 ft (450 m)/min; (IV) 1,640 ft/min; service ceiling (both) 26,575 ft (8100 m); range (both) about 200 miles (322 km).
Armament: two 7·92 mm synchronised Spandau machine guns.
History: first flight (D.II) June 1917; (III) October 1917; (IV) early 1918; service delivery (III) January 1918; final delivery (IV) summer 1919.

SSW, Siemens-Schuckert Werke, a subsidiary of the vast Siemens electrical firm, began building experi-

Siemens-Schuckert D.IV (unidentified Jasta, Imperial Military Aviation Service)

mental aeroplanes and airships at the turn of the century and later, in 1916, built small numbers of the D.I, a copy of the French Nie.17. In 1917 the sister firm Siemens u Halske produced the remarkable Sh.III engine and this was seized by SSW's chief engineer Dipl-Ing Harald Wolff for D.II prototypes with different spans. The engine was exceptionally promising, but imperfectly developed. The mid-span machine went into production as the D.III, and demonstrated great speed, climb and manoeuvrability. Withdrawn through engine failures, they were re-engined with the IIIa engine, with lower cowling cut away to improve cooling, and became very popular in home defence squadrons. The long-span machine eventually was refined into the D.IV, even faster and quicker-climbing but tricky to land. It appeared too late to influence the war, but in October 1918 was described officially as "superior by far to all single-seaters in use at the Front today".

Sikorsky Ilya Mourometz

IM-B, -V, -G, -D and -Ye with sub-variants

Type: heavy bomber and transport with crew numbering four to seven.
Engines: see text.
Dimensions: span, 97 ft 9¼ in to 113 ft 2¼ in; (V) 97 ft 9¼ in (29·80 m); length 55 ft 2 in to about 67 ft; (V) 56 ft 1 in (17·09 m); height (V) 15 ft 6 in (4·72 m).
Weights: empty (V) about 6,000 lb (2720 kg); maximum loaded 9,989 to 15,432 lb; (V) 10,130 lb (4595 kg).
Performance: maximum speed 59–85 mph; (V) 75 mph (121 km/h); service ceiling 6,560–10,500 ft; (V) 9,843 ft (3000 m); range 217–435 miles; (V) about 340 miles (550 km).
Armament: see text.
History: first flight May 1913; service delivery (-B) summer 1914; final deliveries 1918.

Young Igor Sikorsky collaborated with G. I. Lavrov in designing the first four-engined aeroplane in the world, officially called Russkii Vitiaz (Russian Knight) but commonly called "Le Grand" on account of its size. The second monster was planned as a bomber, named after the 10th-century hero Il'ya Muromets or Ilya Mourometz, which became a class name for an amazing series of more than 75 huge bombers which followed. Production was handled by the RBVZ (Russo-Baltic Wagon Works). Only about four unarmed IM-B were built (two 135 hp and two 200 hp Salmson), but by the time the Eskadra Vozdushnykh Korablei (squadron of flying ships) was formed in December 1914 they had three machine guns each and a 1,100 hp bomb load. The 33 IM-V then built had four 150 hp Sunbeam engines (four had other engines) and carried 1,660 lb bombs. The bigger G series had four 150 hp RBVZ-6 or two of these and two 220 hp Renault. The Ye-1 family had four 220 hp Renaults and were among the largest and fastest of all. Other

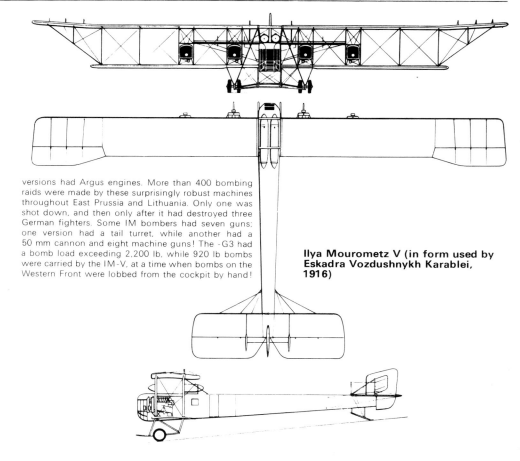

versions had Argus engines. More than 400 bombing raids were made by these surprisingly robust machines throughout East Prussia and Lithuania. Only one was shot down, and then only after it had destroyed three German fighters. Some IM bombers had seven guns; one version had a tail turret, while another had a 50 mm cannon and eight machine guns! The -G3 had a bomb load exceeding 2,200 lb, while 920 lb bombs were carried by the IM-V, at a time when bombs on the Western Front were lobbed from the cockpit by hand!

Ilya Mourometz V (in form used by Eskadra Vozdushnykh Karablei, 1916)

Sikorsky S-61

SH-3A and -3D Sea King, HH-3A, RH-3A and many other variants

Type: see text.
Engines: two General Electric T58 free-turbine turboshaft: (SH-3A and derivatives) 1,250 shp T58-8B; (SH-3D and derivatives) 1,400 shp T58-10; (S-61R versions) 1,500 hp T58-5.
Dimensions: diameter of main rotor 62 ft (18·9 m); length overall 72 ft 8 in (22·15 m); (61R) 73 ft; height overall 16 ft 10 in (5·13 m).
Weights: empty (simple transport versions, typical) 9,763 lb (4428 kg); (ASW, typical) 11,865 lb (5382 kg); (armed CH-3E) 13,255 lb (6010 kg); maximum loaded (ASW) about 18,626 lb (8449 kg); (transport) usually 21,500 lb (9750 kg); (CH-3E) 22,050 lb (10,000 kg).
Performance: maximum speed (typical, maximum weight) 166 mph (267 km/h); initial climb (not vertical but maximum) varies from 2,200 to 1,310 ft (670–400 m)/min, depending on weight; service ceiling, typically 14,700 ft (4480 m); range with maximum fuel, typically 625 miles (1005 km).
Armament: very variable.
History: first flight 11 March 1959

Right, typical S-61 in passenger transport form

Representing a quantum jump in helicopter capability, the S-61 family soon became a staple product of Sikorsky Aircraft, founded in March 1923 by Igor Sikorsky who left Russia after the Revolution and settled in the United States. He flew the first wholly practical helicopter in 1940, and his R-4 was the first helicopter in the world put into mass production (in 1942). A development, the S-51, was in 1947 licensed to the British firm Westland Aircraft, starting collaboration reviewed on later pages. The S-55 and S-58 were made in great numbers in the 1950s for many civil and military purposes, both now also flying with various turbine engines. The S-61 featured an amphibious hull, twin turbine engines located above the hull close to the drive gearbox and an advanced flight-control system. First versions carried anti-submarine warfare (ASW) sensors and weapons, but later variants were equipped for various transport duties, minesweeping, drone or spacecraft recovery (eg lifting Astronauts from the sea), electronic surveillance and (S-61R series) transport/gunship and other combat duties.

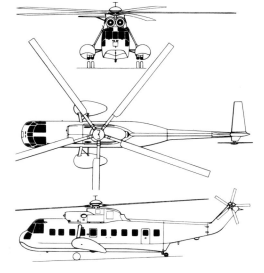

Sikorsky S-65

CH-53A Sea Stallion, HH-53, RH-53 and many variants

Type: see text.
Engines: (early versions) two 2,850 shp General Electric T64-6 free-turbine turboshaft; (CH-53D and G) 3,925 shp T64 versions; (RH-53D) 4,380 shp T64 versions; (CH-53E) three 4,380 shp T64-415.
Dimensions: diameter of main rotor (most) 72 ft 3 in (22·02 m); (CH-53E) seven-blades, 79 ft (24·08 m); length overall (typical) 88 ft 3 in (26·9 m); height overall 24 ft 11 in (7·6 m).
Weights: empty (CH-53D) 23,485 lb (10,653 kg); maximum loaded (most) 42,000 lb (19,050 kg); (RH-53D) 50,000 lb; (CH-53E) over 60,000 lb.
Performance: maximum speed (most) 196 mph (315 km/h); (CH-53E) over 200 mph; initial climb (maximum) typically 2,180 ft (664 m)/min; service ceiling, typically 20,400 ft (6220 m); range, typically 540 miles (869 km).

Armament: most, none.
History: first flight 14 October 1964; service delivery (CH-53A) May 1966.

Obviously developed from the S-61, the S-65 family includes the largest and most powerful helicopters in production outside the Soviet Union. The dynamic parts (rotors, gearboxes and control system) were originally similar to those of the S-64 Skycrane family, but using titanium and with folding main-rotor blades. Most versions served in Vietnam from January 1967, performing countless tasks including recovery of downed aircraft. In 1968 a standard CH-53A completed a prolonged series of loops and rolls, while others set records for speed and payload. Most of the 153 CH-53D for the German army were built in Germany, together with the engines. Latest versions are the RH-53D for mine countermeasures (MCM) with comprehensive tow/sweep systems and 0·5 in guns for exploding surfaced mines, and the three-engined CH-53E for carrying slung loads up to 18 tons.

Typical CH-53 in original twin engined form equipped as assault transport.

SO.4050 Vautour

Vautour IIA, IIB and II.1N

Type: (A) single-seat attack; (B) two-seat bomber; (1N) two-seat night and all-weather fighter.
Engines: two 7,716 lb (3500 kg) thrust SNECMA Atar 101E-3 single-shaft turbojets.
Dimensions: span 49 ft 6½ in (15·1 m); length (A) 51 ft 1½ in; (B, 1N) 51 ft 11¾ in (15·84 m); height 16 ft 2½ in (4·95 m).
Weights: empty (A, B, typical) 22,000 lb (9979 kg); (1N) 24,250 lb (11,000 kg); maximum loaded 45,635 lb (20,700 kg).
Performance: maximum speed (all) 684 mph (1100 km/h); initial climb 11,800 ft (3600 m)/min; service ceiling 49,200 ft (15,000 m); range (clean) about 1,990 miles (3200 km).
Armament: (B) internal bomb load up to six 750 lb (340 kg) plus external up to 4,000 lb (1814 kg) to combined total 5,300 lb (2400 kg); (A) as B plus four 30 mm DEFA 553 cannon; (1N) four 30 mm DEFA 553, each with 100 rounds, plus 2–4 Matra R.530 missiles, 2–4 Sidewinder or Magic missiles, 232 SNEB rockets.
History: first flight 16 October 1952; (production IIA) 30 April 1956; (IIB) 31 July 1957; final delivery (1N) 1959.

Perhaps the greatest achievement of the French industry in the immediate post-war period, the Vautour (Vulture) was an extremely bold design by the SNCASO (south-west) nationalised group in 1951. By chance, Yakovlev's bureau in the Soviet Union was planning an aircraft of identical layout; though initially inferior (page 226) it led to production on a far greater

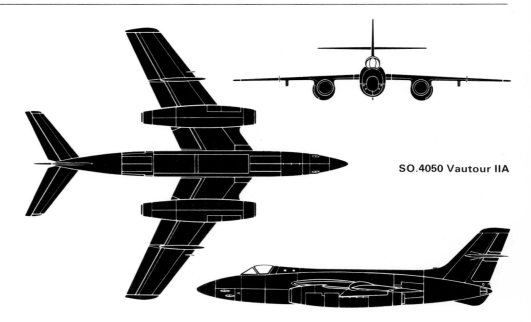

SO.4050 Vautour IIA

scale, because of the different size of market. In 1952–55 nine prototype Vautours were flown configured as fighters, bombers and reconnaissance aircraft, with contrasting equipment but all having "bicycle" landing gear, powered controls, bonded-metal structure, integral tanks and a variable-incidence tailplane. Eventually 30 IIA were built, 25 being sold

to Israel where they fought hard and well (a few survive in second-line roles). The Armée de l'Air received 70 II.1N night fighters, which served until replaced by the Mirage F1-C in 1973–76. The 40 IIB bombers formed the nucleus of the CFAS (French Strategic Air Command) and in 1960 survivors were sold to Israel.

Soko Galeb

G2-A Galeb, J-1 Jastreb

Type: (Galeb) dual armed trainer; Jastreb, single-seat attack.
Engine: one Rolls-Royce Viper single-shaft turbojet: (G) 2,500 lb (1134 kg) thrust Mk 22-6; (J) 3,000 lb (1360 kg) Mk 531.
Dimensions: span (excluding tip tanks) 34 ft 4½ in (10·47 m); (J) 34 ft 8 in; length 33 ft 11 in (10·34 m); (J) 35 ft 1½ in; height 10 ft 9 in (3·28 m); (J) 11 ft 11½ in.
Weights: empty 5,775 lb (2620 kg); (J) 6,217 lb; maximum loaded 9,210 lb (4178 kg); (G, clean, fully aerobatic) 7,438 lb; (J) 10,287 lb.
Performance: maximum speed 505 mph (812 km/h); (J) 510 mph; initial climb 4,500 ft (1370 m)/min; service ceiling 39,375 ft (12,000 m); range (hi, max fuel) 770 miles (1240 km); (J) 945 miles.
Armament: (G) two 12·7 mm guns in nose, each with 80 rounds; underwing pylons for two 220 lb (100 kg) bombs, or light loads of rockets. (J) three 12·7 mm in nose, each with 135 rounds; eight underwing hardpoints, two furthest inboard carrying stores of 551 lb (250 kg), the rest single 127 mm rockets.
History: first flight (G) May 1961; service delivery (G) 1965.

The first Yugoslav jet to go into production, the tandem-seat Galeb (Seagull) has been fully developed and built in modest numbers for the Yugoslav Air Force and Zambia. Pupil and instructor sit in Folland lightweight seats, and an air-conditioning system is

an option. The Jastreb (Hawk) uses a similar airframe, with local strengthening for the more powerful engine and heavier external stores. Again Zambia has received an export version, but without the optional

cabin pressurization and self-contained engine-start system. Jastrebs can carry cameras in the fuselage and in the nose of the tip tanks, and also tow an aerial target.

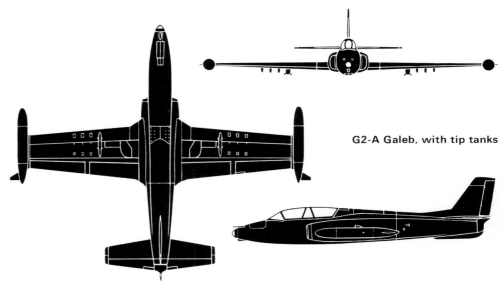

G2-A Galeb, with tip tanks

Sopwith Tabloid

Tabloid, Schneider and Baby

Type: (T) two-seat scout (reconnaissance); (S, B) single-seat maritime patrol and attack, float seaplane.
Engine: one 80 hp Gnome nine-cylinder rotary, (S) 100 hp Gnome Monosoupape, (B) 130 hp Clerget, both of same layout.
Dimensions: span 25 ft 6 in (7·77 m); length 20 ft 4 in (6·20 m); (S, B, 23 ft); height 8 ft 5 in (2·56 m); (S, B, 10 ft).
Weights: empty, about 720 lb (327 kg); (S, B, about 1,200 lb); maximum loaded 1,120 lb (508 kg); (S, B, 1,580–1,715 lb).
Performance: maximum speed 92 mph (148 km/h); (B) 100 mph; service ceiling, about 15,000 ft (4600 m); range 315 miles (510 km).
Armament: none fitted (but see text).
History: first flight autumn (fall) 1913; service delivery, probably March 1914.

In the summer of 1913 young Tommy Sopwith bought the lease on a former skating rink at Canbury Park Road, Kingston-upon-Thames and set up the Sopwith Aviation & Engineering Co. He had hired Fred Sigrist to look after his yacht and the two now bent over drawing boards and began to design aeroplanes, while Harry Hawker was taken on as pilot and manager of the growing staff. From this tiny beginning came thousands of the greatest combat aircraft of World

Sopwith Tabloid (actually the second of two Gordon Bennett Racers, externally similar, acquired by the Admiralty for the RNAS)

War I, followed by the famed Hawker aircraft of later years and the vast Hawker Siddeley Group of today. The first aircraft to be built by Sopwith was a racing biplane, so small it was called the Tabloid. Sopwith had never subscribed to the view that biplanes had to be inferior performers, and after Hawker had completed initial tests at Brooklands it was flown to Farnborough where it astonished everyone by reaching 92 mph

with a passenger, and reaching 1,200 ft in one minute after leaving the ground. About 40 were subsequently built for the RFC and RNAS. On 8 October 1914 two RNAS Tabloids set out to bomb Zeppelin hangars and F/Lt Marix's machine dropped its four 20 lb bombs squarely on the shed at Dusseldorf, destroying the new Z.IX. Many Tabloids later carried a Lewis gun, as did the Schneider and Baby seaplanes.

Sopwith 1½-Strutter

Type 9400, Type 9700

Type: multi-role combat aircraft, 9400 two-seat, 9700 single-seat.
Engine: one 110 hp Clerget 9Z nine-cylinder rotary; late models often had 130 hp Clerget 9B or 110 hp Le Rhône.
Dimensions: span 33 ft 6 in (10·21 m); length 25 ft 3 in (7·70 m); height 10 ft 3 in (3·12 m).
Weights: empty (9400) 1,260 lb (570 kg) (9700, 130 hp) 1,340 lb (608 kg); maximum loaded (9400) 2,149 lb (975 kg); (9700, 130 hp) 2,342 lb (1062 kg).
Performance: maximum speed 102–106 mph (165 km/h); service ceiling (9400) 15,500 ft (4730 m); (9700, 130 hp) 13,000 ft (3960 m); range (typical) 350 miles (565 km).
Armament: usually, one 0·303 in Vickers synchronised to fire between propeller blades, one 0·303 in Lewis manually aimed, and bomb load under fuselage of up to 130 lb (60 kg); (Type 9700) usually fixed Vickers and bomb load of up to four 65 lb (29·5 kg) bombs, internally behind pilot.
History: first flight December 1915; service delivery April 1916.

Deriving its nickname — by which it became universally known—from the "1½" sets of struts attaching the upper wing, the 1½-Strutter was one of the most significant military aircraft. It was the first aircraft ever to be designed from the start with a synchronised gun, and (apart from the Russian Sikorskys) the first to equip a

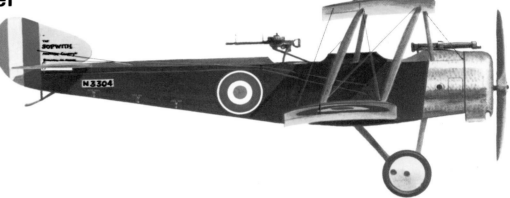

Sopwith 1½-Strutter (RNAS; this aircraft survived the war and received civil registration G-EAVB)

strategic bombing force. It included such unexpected features as a variable-incidence tailplane and airbrakes on the lower wings and it was pleasant to fly. At least 1,513 were built in Britain, most of the later versions being single-seat 9700 bombers and "Ship Strutters" for the new RN carriers; one made the first wheeled take-off

from a ship (along a platform on a gun turret). Many were made in France and Russia and both single- and two-seat versions served with at least eight Allied forces. By 1917 the "Strutter" was a pre-eminent British coastal patrol and night fighter aircraft, being equally good at fighting and bombing.

Sopwith Pup

Type 9901

Type: single-seat fighting scout.
Engine: normally one 80 hp Le Rhône 9C nine-cylinder rotary; some models, 80 hp Gnome or 100 hp Gnome Monosoupape.
Dimensions: span 26 ft 6 in (8·08 m); length 19 ft 3¾ in (5·89 m); height 9 ft 5 in (2·87 m).
Weights: empty (Le Rhône) 790 lb (358 kg); maximum loaded 1,225 lb (556 kg).
Performance: maximum speed 111½ mph (179 km/h); service ceiling 17,500 ft (5334 m); range, about 310 miles (500 km).
Armament: usually, one 0·303 in Vickers synchronised by Sopwith-Kauper gear to fire between propeller blades; alternatively, one 0·303 in Lewis aimed obliquely through cut-out in centre-section of upper wing. Anti-airship armament, usually two quartets of Le Prieur rockets launched from interplane struts.
History: first flight February 1916; service delivery, September 1916.

Officially named Type 9901 (from one of the first-batch serial numbers) by the Admiralty, the Pup got its abiding nickname from its likeness to a baby 1½-Strutter. Service trials for the RNAS in May 1916 revealed the 9901 to be as nearly perfect in flying qualities as an aeroplane can be. Pilots whose careers spanned 50 years of aviation named the Pup as the most delightful of all flying machines. It was very small, simple and reliable and its generous wing area gave it excellent

Sopwith Pup (built by Standard Motor Co. for RNAS)

performance at height. With 80 hp it soon became underpowered for combat with the best German fighters, though compared with an Albatros it could turn twice for a single turn by the enemy. It was the type which established the famous "Naval Eight" (8 Sqn, RNAS, assigned to help the RFC on the Western Front), which scored 20 confirmed victories in the last months of 1916. In 1917 Sqn Cdr Dunning made the first landing on a carrier under way at sea,

while Pups with wheels, skids and inflatable flotation bags conducted pioneer experiments in carrier arrester gear. Sopwith built 170 for the RNAS, while other firms built 1,670 for the RFC, many being assigned to Home Defence units.

Sopwith Triplane

N500 type
Type: single-seat fighting scout.
Engine: one 130 hp Clerget 9B nine-cylinder rotary (prototype, 110 hp Clerget 9Z).
Dimensions: span 26 ft 6 in (8·08 m); length 18 ft 10 in (5·74 m); height 10 ft 6 in (3·20 m)
Weights: empty 1,101 lb (500 kg); maximum loaded 1,541 lb (699 kg).
Performance: maximum speed 113 mph (182 km/h); initial climb 1,200 ft (366 m)/min; service ceiling 20,500 ft (6250 m); range 280 miles (450 km).
Armament: one (rarely, two) 0·303 in Vickers synchronised to fire between propeller blades.
History: first flight 28 May 1916; service delivery November 1916.

Aerial combat appeared to demand the highest possible rate of climb and manoeuvrability and, by fitting three slender planes, chief designer Herbert Smith sought to exceed even the Pup in these respects. He was partly successful; though the Pup could not be rivalled for sheer manoeuvrability (especially in rate of roll), the new Triplane could outclimb everything else in the sky. Anthony Fokker was very concerned as the first examples went into action and began designing his own Dr.I before the first wreckage of a shot-down Triplane reached Germany for examination. By early 1917 almost every German fighter firm was designing

a triplane, though only the Dr.I saw major service. Thanks to a deal which gave the RFC urgently needed Spads, all the Triplanes went to the RNAS, where they scored notable ascendancy over practically every Germany type. On one occasion 13 "Tripehounds" fought 15 enemy scouts and shot down five without loss. The famed "Black Flight" of RNAS 10 Sqn., with Canadian pilots, destroyed 87 German aircraft between

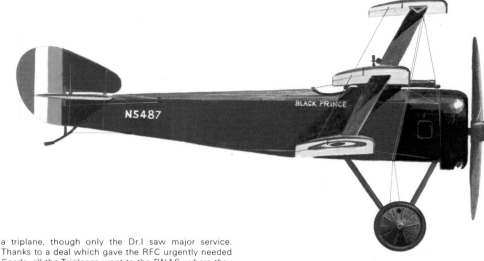

Sopwith Triplane (aircraft of Lt Alexander of "Black Flight", 10 Sqn, RNAS)

May and July 1917. By this time the Camel was beginning to replace the Triplane, but not because of any urgency to do so.

Sopwith Camel

Sopwith F.1, 2F.1
Type: single-seat fighting scout; (2F.1) carrier-based fighter.
Engine: usually, one 130 hp Clerget 9B nine-cylinder rotary; prototype and a few production, 110 hp Clerget 9Z; alternatively, 110 hp Le Rhône 9J, 100 hp Gnome Monosoupape, 150 hp Monosoupape or 150 hp Bentley B.R.1.
Dimensions: span 28 ft (8·53 m); (2F.1) 26 ft 11 in; length 18 ft 9 in (5·72 m); (other versions) 18 ft 6 in to 19 ft; height 8 ft 6 in (2·59 m), (other versions) 8 ft 9 in to 9 ft 1 in.
Weights: empty, typically 930 lb (422 kg); maximum loaded 1,453 lb (659 kg); (other versions) 1,387–1,530 lb.
Performance: maximum speed 113 mph (182 km/h), (124 mph with B.R.1); initial climb, about 1,000 ft (305 m)/min; service ceiling 19,000 ft (5790 m); range about 250 miles (400 km).
Armament: normally two 0·303 in Vickers synchronised to fire between propeller blades; optional racks under fuselage for four 25 lb (11·3 kg) bombs.
History: first flight December 1916; service delivery June 1917.

Perhaps the most famous aircraft of World War I, the hump-backed Camel destroyed at least 1,294 enemy aircraft, a greater total than that attained by any other aircraft in that conflict. It was a natural outgrowth of the Pup and Triplane, but gained its formidable combat performance at the cost of losing the earlier types'

peerless handling. Indeed the Camel was renowned for its sensitivity and need for skill and experience, and casualties among pupils were high. Once mastered the Camel was a superb dogfighter, one of its favourite tricks being its unbelievably swift right-hand turn, aided by the torque of the big rotary engine; many pilots wishing to turn left chose to turn 270° to the right! Total production is believed to have reached 5,490, though this may not include the quantity of 2F.1 shipboard Camels with detachable rear ends (for compact carrier stowage) and slim steel wing struts. Many 2F.1s had only one Vickers and a Lewis on the top wing, or even two Lewis on a Foster mount, as did most of the Le Rhône-engined Camels of night Home Defence units. Camels were launched from airship

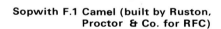

Sopwith F.1 Camel (built by Ruston, Proctor & Co. for RFC)

R.23; there was also a TF (trench fighter) attack version. Camels served with many Allied forces, and at least two RFC pilots achieved the feat of shooting down six of the enemy in a single day. The Camel's most famous victim was von Richthofen, killed by Canadian Roy Brown on 21 April 1918.

Sopwith Dolphin

Sopwith 5F.1
Type: single-seat fighter.
Engine: one 200/220 hp Hispano-Suiza 8E vee-8 water-cooled; (Mk II) 300 hp Hispano; (Mk III) 200 hp direct-drive Hispano.
Dimensions: span 32 ft 6 in (9·91 m); length 22 ft 3 in (6·78 m); height 8 ft 6 in (2·59 m).
Weights: empty (4 guns and crash pylons, typical) 1,480 lb (671 kg); maximum loaded (2 Vickers only) 1,920 lb (867 kg), (4 guns) up to 2,100 lb (953 kg).
Performance: maximum speed (2 guns) 125 mph (200 km/h); initial climb, 855 ft (260 m)/min; service ceiling 21,000 ft (6400 m); range 195 miles (315 km).
Armament: two 0·303 in Vickers synchronised to fire between propeller blades; often, additionally, one or two 0·303 in Lewis aimed by pilot obliquely upwards through centre section. External racks for four 25 lb (11·3 kg) bombs.
History: first flight late May 1917; service delivery, probably October 1917.

With the Dolphin Sopwith's now very experienced design staff tried a different formula for the best fighting scout, laying emphasis on pilot view and armament. Using a slim but heavy Hispano engine, the fuselage was so arranged that the pilot's head projected above the upper centre section, where he could see in almost all directions. The heavy armament of four guns was fitted to most aircraft on delivery and was on all the 121 that were on RFC charge at the end of 1917. Deliveries would have been faster but for the unreliability of the engine's reduction gear. Many pilots removed one or both Lewis guns and to give the pilot a chance of surviving a nose-over crash most Dolphins were fitted with crash pylons either on each side of the cockpit or on the upper wing. At the end of the war the Mks II and III came into small-scale use with better engines, but nearly all the 1,532 delivered were Mk Is.

Sopwith 5F.1 Dolphin (20th aircraft of batch of 500)

Official opinion underrated this formidable machine, which in the hands of many famed pilots – especially in 79 and 19 Sqns – established a remarkable combat record. No 141 Sqn used Dolphins as night fighters, while 85 repositioned the Lewises on the lower wings.

Sopwith Snipe

Sopwith 7F.1

Type: single-seat fighter.
Engine: one 230 hp Bentley B.R.2 nine-cylinder rotary; single aircraft, one 200 hp Clerget 11Eb 11-cylinder rotary or 268 hp (alleged 320 hp) ABC Dragonfly nine-cylinder radial.
Dimensions: span 30 ft (9·14 m), (upper plane with balanced ailerons, 31 ft 1 in); length 19 ft 2 in (5·84 m), (final rudder, 19 ft 10 in); height 9 ft 6 in (2·89 m).
Weights: empty 1,312 lb (595 kg); maximum loaded 2,020 lb (916 kg).
Performance: maximum speed 121 mph (195 km/h); initial climb 1,500 ft (460 m)/min; service ceiling 19,500 ft (5945 m); range 310 miles (500 km).
Armament: two 0·303 in Vickers synchronised to fire

between propeller blades; racks for four 25 lb (11·3 kg) Cooper bombs.

History: first flight, probably September 1917; production 7F.1, June 1918; final delivery March 1919. Designed as a successor to the Camel, the Snipe emerged into a world utterly different from that of the Tabloid four years earlier. It was a world packed with expertise, and with a horde of competitors, and the six Snipe prototypes — all different — underwent long and meticulous testing aginst such machines as the Bobolink and Nieuport B.N.1 before, in March 1918, the Air Board finally decided to order it into production. The Mk I was armed with twin Vickers, the Lewis previously fitted to the upper plane having been found too difficult to aim. Countless modifications took place during development, but the production machine proved fast, reliable, manoeuvrable and very strong, and pilot view was notably better than in the Camel.

Standard equipment for the first time included electric heating and pilot oxygen. Deliveries to France started only eight weeks before the Armistice, but one or two clashes with the enemy showed the quality of what would have been one of the leading Allied combat aircraft, with no fewer than 4,515 on order. On 27 October 1918 Maj W. G. Barker, then attached to 201 Sqn RFC, ran into 15 Fokker D. VIIs and took them on single-handed. He was awarded the VC and ended the war with 53 confirmed victories. The only major variant to see service was the Mk Ia, with an enlarged main fuel tank giving a range of about 450 miles (the rearward shift in centre of gravity being countered by slightly sweeping back the wings). These were intended to escort the heavy bombers of the Independent Air Force. Snipes served in the post-war RAF as a standard type, some being converted to dual trainers. The last survived in Egypt, Iraq and India until 1927.

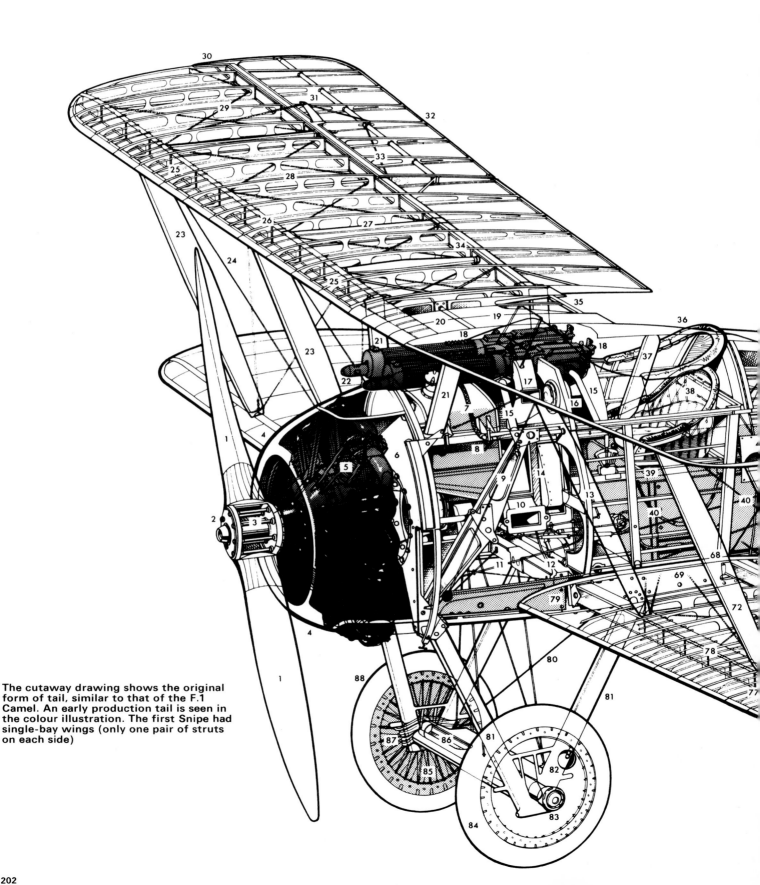

The cutaway drawing shows the original form of tail, similar to that of the F.1 Camel. An early production tail is seen in the colour illustration. The first Snipe had single-bay wings (only one pair of struts on each side)

Sopwith 7F.1 Snipe (aircraft of Maj W. G. Barker, 201 Sqn, RAF)

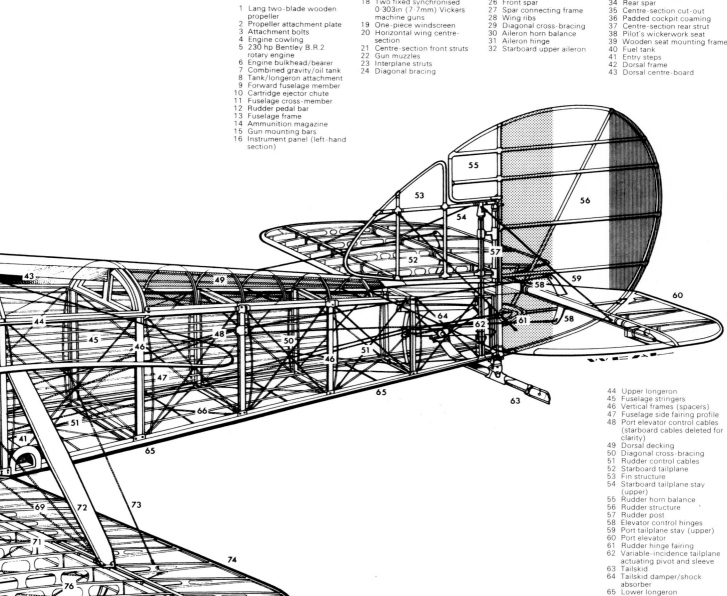

Sopwith 7F.1 Snipe

1 Lang two-blade wooden propeller
2 Propeller attachment plate
3 Attachment bolts
4 Engine cowling
5 230 hp Bentley B.R.2 rotary engine
6 Engine bulkhead/bearer
7 Combined gravity/oil tank
8 Tank/longeron attachment
9 Forward fuselage member
10 Cartridge ejector chute
11 Fuselage cross-member
12 Rudder pedal bar
13 Fuselage frame
14 Ammunition magazine
15 Gun mounting bars
16 Instrument panel (left-hand section)

17 Link ejector chute
18 Two fixed synchronised 0·303in (7·7mm) Vickers machine guns
19 One-piece windscreen
20 Horizontal wing centre-section
21 Centre-section front struts
22 Gun muzzles
23 Interplane struts
24 Diagonal bracing

25 Leading-edge stiffeners
26 Front spar
27 Spar connecting frame
28 Wing ribs
29 Diagonal cross-bracing
30 Aileron horn balance
31 Aileron hinge
32 Starboard upper aileron

33 Aileron cable (interplane)
34 Rear spar
35 Centre-section cut-out
36 Padded cockpit coaming
37 Centre-section rear strut
38 Pilot's wickerwork seat
39 Wooden seat mounting frame
40 Fuel tank
41 Entry steps
42 Dorsal frame
43 Dorsal centre-board

44 Upper longeron
45 Fuselage stringers
46 Vertical frames (spacers)
47 Fuselage side fairing profile
48 Port elevator control cables (starboard cables deleted for clarity)
49 Dorsal decking
50 Diagonal cross-bracing
51 Rudder control cables
52 Starboard tailplane
53 Fin structure
54 Starboard tailplane stay (upper)
55 Rudder horn balance
56 Rudder structure
57 Rudder post
58 Elevator control hinges
59 Port tailplane stay (upper)
60 Port elevator
61 Rudder hinge fairing
62 Variable-incidence tailplane actuating pivot and sleeve
63 Tailskid
64 Tailskid damper/shock absorber
65 Lower longeron
66 Flat undersides
67 Interplane strut (inner)
68 Rear spar/fuselage attachment
69 Interplane cross-bracing
70 Wing ribs
71 Rear spar
72 Interplane struts (outer)
73 Aileron control cable
74 Port lower aileron
75 Aileron control hinge
76 Diagonal cross-bracing
77 Leading-edge stiffeners
78 Front spar
79 Front spar/fuselage attachment
80 Undercarriage 'X'-brace
81 Undercarriage legs
82 Valve access
83 Axle support
84 Port mainwheel
85 Wheel spokes
86 Axle fairing
87 Elastic cord shock-absorber
88 Starboard mainwheel

Spad VII

VII, 72 and 62
Type: single-seat fighting scout.
Engine: one 150 hp (later 189 and 200 hp) Hispano-Suiza 8Aa vee-8 water-cooled.
Dimensions: span 25 ft 7¾ in (7·81 m) (about 26 ft 4 in with 180,200 hp engines); length 20 ft 2½ (or 3½) in (6·18 m); height 6 ft 11½ in (2·13 m).
Weights: empty, typically 1,124 lb (510 kg); maximum loaded 1632 lb (740 kg).
Performance: maximum speed 119 mph (192 km/h); initial climb 900 ft (275 m)/min; service ceiling 17,500 ft (5334 m); range, about 225 miles (360 km).
Armament: one 0·303 in (7·65 mm) Vickers offset to right ahead of pilot; some also one 0·303 in Lewis on upper wing.
History: first flight April 1916; service delivery 2 September 1916; (Types 72 and 62) 1923.

The pre-war Deperdussin company had the initials SPAD and in 1915 it was renamed Société Anonyme Pour l'Aviation et ses Dérivés, with the same initials. It produced some of the best combat aircraft of World War I and the first to gain wide acclaim was the Type VII. The key to this was the new vee-8 engine designed in 1915 by Marc Birkigt, chief designer of Hispano-Suiza (who was also rapidly perfecting the first of the famed line of 20 mm aircraft cannon). Of fabric-covered wood, the Span VII was soon bought in quantity by France for l'Aviation Militaire. The first order was for 268, but the type was so sturdy and useful that eventually about 6,000 were built, 220 of them by firms in Britain for the RFC and RNAS (the RNAS swapped theirs for Sopwith Triplanes). The vast output of Spad VIIs saw service with almost every

Spad VII
(Escadrille SPA.3, "Les Cicognes")

Allied air service, the most famous unit being France's SPA.3 Les Cicognes (Storks). The Types 72 and 62 were developed in the 1920s as a single-seat fighter and dual trainer.

Spad XIII

XIIIC-1, XIIICa-1, XIV, XVII and XXIX
Type: single-seat fighter.
Engine: one Hispano-Suiza vee-8 water-cooled; successively, 200 hp or 220 hp 8Be 235 hp 8BEc and (XVII) 300 hp 8FBc.
Dimensions: span 26 ft 6 in or 26 ft 10½ in (8·20 m); length 20 ft 4¼ in or 20 ft 8 in (6·30 m) height 7 ft 8½ in or 7 ft 11¼ in (2·42 m).
Weights: empty, typical, 1255 lb (570 kg); maximum loaded 1808–1862 lb (820-845 kg).
Performance: maximum speed 138 mph (220 km/h); initial climb 1500 ft (460 m)/min; service ceiling 21,800 ft (6650 m); range 185–220 miles (300–350 km).
Armament: two 7·65 mm Vickers ahead of the pilot.
History: first flight 4 April 1917; service delivery, late May 1917.

This superb fighter is the aircraft immediately conjured up by the name "Spad". It was built in greater numbers than any other Allied fighter and was not only extremely fast, strong and reliable but was designed, developed and put into action with amazing rapidity. It equipped no fewer than 81 French fighter squadrons and was the mount of virtually all the great French aces of the time. It was also the main type used by 16 pursuit squadrons of the American Expeditionary Force in France and was to be built in vast numbers by Curtiss in the United States. Responsive yet steady in combat, it was almost perfect for an experienced pilot, but, like its main British partner the Camel, it was tricky to a novice. The XIIICa had a 37 mm Hotchkiss cannon in the vee of the engine cylinders, but the 300 built were not very successful. The XIV was a float-seaplane version, the XVII was a more powerful version (used by Les Cicognes in

Spad XIII C-1
(aircraft of Capt E. Rickenbacker, Cdr 94th Aero Sqn, AEF)

mid-1918) and the XXIV was a variant for use aboard aircraft carriers. Total production was at least 8,472, and large numbers were dispersed after 1918 to many nations. The US Army re-engined 435 with the 180 hp Wright-Hispano E and used the resulting Spad 13E as a trainer.

Sukhoi Su-2

Su-2 (of unidentified second-line unit, Sverdlovsk 1942-43)

ANT-51, BB-1, Su-2
Type: two-seat tactical attack bomber.
Engine: (most) one 1,000 hp Shvetsov M-88B 14-cylinder, two-row radial; (late batches) 1,520 hp M-82 (ASh-82), same layout.
Dimensions: span 46 ft 11 in (14·30 m); length 33 ft 7½ in (10·25 m); height, not known accurately.
Weights: empty, typically 6,615 lb (3000 kg); maximum loaded 8,994–9,645 lb (4375 kg).
Performance: maximum speed (M-88B) 283 mph (455 km/h); service ceiling 28,870 ft (8800 m); range with 882 lb (400 kg) bombs, 746 miles (1200 km).
Armament: (typical) four 7·62 mm ShKAS machine guns fixed in wings, one in manual dorsal turret; internal bomb bay for load of 882 lb (400 kg), with underwing racks for additional bombs or RS-82 rockets (ten) to overload maximum of 1,323 lb (600 kg).
History: first flight (ANT-51) August 1937; (production BB-1) 1940; final delivery, probably 1943.

Pavel Sukhoi, a young member of the great Tupolev design bureau, designed the ANT-51 in 1936–37 as a replacement for the disappointing R-10. The prototype achieved 250 mph on its M-62 (Cyclone) engine and further prototypes with 950 hp M-87 engines (derived from the Gnome-Rhône 14K) were more promising. Eventually the BB-1 was put into large-scale production, seeming to be a fine aircraft with docile handling, good armour, fair bomb load and adequate performance for its day. In early 1941 the more powerful M-88B was fitted and the designation changed from that of function to the new Soviet scheme naming the designer (thus, Su-2). Some 1,500 or more were in service with the Frontovaya Aviatsya (tactical air forces) when Germany invaded the Soviet Union in June 1941, and production went ahead rapidly with variants with or without the turret (and possibly including a single-seater). But losses were high, and even later substitution of the powerful M-82 engine made little difference. In late 1941 an Su-2 was flown with the 2,100 hp M-90 engine, but neither this nor the completely redesigned (and much better) Su-6 was put into production.

Sukhoi Su-7/11

Su-7B, -7BM, -7U, -9, -11, -17 and -20.
Type: (-7B and BM) single-seat close-support and attack; (-7U and -9U) dual-control trainer; (-9 and -11) single-seat all-weather interceptor.
Engine: one 22,046 lb (10,000 kg) thrust Lyulka AL-7F single-shaft afterburning turbojet.
Dimensions: span (-7) 29 ft 3½ in (8·93 m); (-9, -11) 27 ft (8·23 m); length (including pitot boom) (-7) 57 ft (17·37 m); (-9, -11) about 58 ft (17·68 m); height (-7) 15 ft 5 in (4·70 m); (-9, -11) 16 ft (4·88 m).
Weights: empty (-7BM) 19,000 lb (8620 kg); (-11) about 20,000 lb (9072 kg); maximum loaded (-7BM) 29,750 lb (13,500 kg); (-11) about 30,000 lb (13,610 kg).
Performance: maximum speed at altitude, clean (-7BM) 1055 mph (1700 km/h, Mach 1·6); (-11,

Below, Su-7B (Frontal Aviation, Czech AF)

Su-7BM (Egyptian AF)

Su-7BM (Indian AF)

highly swept Su-7B became the standard Soviet bloc attack aircraft, some thousands being supplied to all Warsaw Pact nations and to Egypt, Cuba, India, Syria, Hungary, Iraq and North Vietnam. There are many sub-variants, the -7BM being a STOL rough-field version. The delta -9 fighter was used in large numbers as a standard Soviet (P-VO Strany) defensive fighter, replaced from 1968 by the Su-11 with long nose, large radar and inlet and new missiles. Code names of tandem trainers are Su-7U Moujik and Su-9U Maiden. In 1971–72 deliveries began of the Su-17 ("Fitter C") with slatted variable-sweep wings, and the Su-20 export version operated by the Polish Air Force with large drop tanks on pylons under the wing pivots.

on wing pylons; no guns.

History: first flight (-7 prototype) not later than 1955; (-9 prototype) before mid-1956; service delivery (-7B) 1959; (-9) 1959; (-11) probably 1968.

Two of the wealth of previously unknown Soviet aircraft revealed at the 1956 Aviation Day at Tushino were large Sukhoi fighters, one with a swept wing (called "Fitter" by NATO) and the other a tailed delta (called "Fishpot"). Both were refined into operational types, losing some of their commonality in the process. The

estimated) 1,190 mph (1915 km/h, Mach 1·8); initial climb (-7BM) 29,900 ft (9120 m)/min; (-11) 27,000 ft (8230 m)/min; service ceiling (-7BM) 49,700 ft (15,150 m); (-11) 55,000 ft (16,765 m); range with twin drop tanks (all) 900 miles (1450 km).

Armament: (-7) two 30 mm NR-30 cannon, each with 70 rounds, in wing roots; four wing pylons, inners rated at 1,653 lb (750 kg) and outers at 1,102 lb (500 kg), but when two tanks are carried on fuselage pylons total external weapon load is reduced to 2,205 lb (1000 kg); (-9) four "Alkali" air-to-air missiles on wing pylons; no guns. (-11) two "Anab" air-to-air missiles, one radar-homing and one infra-red,

Sukhoi Su-15

Versions known to the West are code-named "Flagon-A to -E"
Type: most versions, all-weather interceptor.
Engines: two afterburning engines, believed to be 14,550 lb (6600 kg) Tumansky RD-13-300 single-shaft turbojets.
Dimensions: (estimated) span 30 ft (9·15 m); length 68 ft (20·5 m); height 19 ft (5·79 m).
Weights: ("Flagon-A", estimated) empty 23,000 lb (10,435 kg); maximum loaded 35,275 lb (16,000 lb).
Performance: (estimated) maximum speed at altitude, with two missiles, 1,520 mph (2445 km/h, Mach 2·3); initial climb 35,000 ft (10,670 m)/min; service ceiling 65,000 ft (19,800 m); combat radius 450 miles (725 km); ferry range about 1,400 miles (2250 km).
Armament: two underwing pylons normally carry one radar "Anab" and one infra-red "Anab"; two fuselage pylons normally carry drop tanks.
History: first flight (Su-15 prototype) probably 1964; (production Su-15) probably 1967.

Following naturally on from the Su-11, and strongly resembling the earlier aircraft in wings and tail, the Su-15 has two engines which not only confer increased performance but also leave the nose free for a large AI

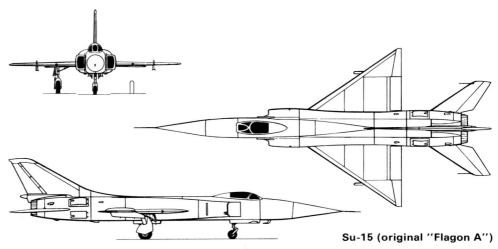

Su-15 (original "Flagon A")

radar. The initial "Flagon-A" version entered IA-PVO Strany service in 1969. "Flagon-B" is a STOL rough-field version with three lift jets in the fuselage and a revised "double delta" wing. "Flagon-C" is the Su-15U dual trainer, "-D" is basically a "-B" without lift

jets, and "-E" has completely updated electronics and more powerful engines. In 1971 a US official estimated that 400 Su-15 were in service, with production at about 15 monthly. Small batches have served overseas, notably in Egypt in 1973.

Sukhoi Su-19

Su-19 versions known to NATO as "Fencer"
Type: two-seat multi-role combat aircraft.
Engines: two afterburning turbofan or turbojet engines, each in the 21,000 lb (9525 kg) thrust class (possibly same as engine of MiG-23).
Dimensions: (estimated) span (spread, about 22°) 56 ft 3 in (17·15 m), swept (about 72°) 31 ft 3 in (9·53 m); length 69 ft 10 in (21·29 m); height 21 ft (6·4 m).
Weights: (estimated) empty 35,000 lb (15,875 kg); maximum loaded 70,000 lb (31,750 kg).
Performance: (estimated) maximum speed, clean, 950 mph (1530 km/h, Mach 1·25) at sea level, about 1,650 mph (2655 km/h, Mach 2·5) at altitude; initial climb, over 40,000 ft (12,200 m)/min; service ceiling, about 60,000 ft (18,290 m); combat radius with maximum weapons, about 500 miles (805 km); ferry range, over 2,500 miles (4025 km).
Armament: one 23 mm GS-h-23 twin-barrel cannon in lower centreline; at least six pylons on fuselage, fixed and swinging wings, for wide range of stores included guided and unguided air-to-ground or air-to-air missiles.
History: first flight, probably about 1970; service delivery, 1974 or earlier.
First identified publicly in the West by the Chairman of the US Joint Chiefs of Staff, who described the Su-19 as "the first modern Soviet fighter to be developed specifically as a fighter-bomber for the ground-attack mission", this aircraft will probably be the chief

Provisional three-view and side profile of original Su-19, the former showing the range of wing sweep.

Sukhoi Su-19 Fencer

tactical attack aircraft of the Soviet V-VS in 1980. Like the rival but much smaller MiG-23, the Su-19 is an extremely clean machine strongly reminiscent of the F-111 and Mirage G, having side-by-side seats and wing and tailplane at the same level, as in the US machine, yet following the French aircraft in general

layout. In general capability the nearest Western equivalent is the F-14 Tomcat, which shows just how formidable this aircraft is. Whereas "Foxbat" was on many Western lips in the 1960s, so is "Fencer" a big scare-word in the 1970s.

Supermarine Spitfire

Mks I to 24 and Seafire I, III, XV, XVII and 45-47
Type: single-seat fighter, fighter-bomber or reconnaissance; (Seafire) carrier-based fighter.
Engine: one Rolls-Royce Merlin or Griffon vee-12 liquid-cooled (see text).
Dimensions: span 36 ft 10 in (11·23 m), clipped, 32 ft 2 in, or, more often, 32 ft 7 in (9·93 m), extended, 40 ft 2 in (12·24 m); length 29 ft 11 in (9·12 m), later, with two-stage engine, typically 31 ft 3½ in (9·54 m), Griffon engine, typically 32 ft 8 in (9·96 m), final (eg Seafire 47) 34 ft 4 in (10·46 m); height 11 ft 5 in (3·48 m), with Griffon, typically 12 ft 9 in (3·89 m).
Weights: empty (Mk I) 4,810 lb (2182 kg); (IX) 5,610 lb (2545 kg); (XIV) 6,700 lb (3040 kg); (Sea.47) 7,625 lb (3458 kg); maximum loaded (I) 5,784 lb (2624 kg); (IX) 9,500 lb (4310 kg); (XIV) 10,280 lb (4663 kg); (Sea.47) 12,750 lb (5784 kg).
Performance: maximum speed (I) 355–362 mph (580 km/h); (IX) 408 mph (657 km/h); (XIV) 448 mph (721 km/h); (Sea.47) 451 mph (724 km/h); initial climb (I) 2,530 ft (770 m)/min; (IX) 4,100 ft (1250 m)/min; (XIV) 4,580 ft (1396 m)/min; (Sea.47) 4,800 ft (1463 m)/min; range on internal fuel (I) 395 miles (637 km); (IX) 434 miles (700 km); (XIV) 460 miles (740 km); (Sea.47) 405 miles (652 km).
Armament: see text.
History: first flight (prototype) 5 March 1936; (production Mk I) July 1938; final delivery (Mk 24) October 1947.

Possibly the most famous combat aircraft in history, the Spitfire was designed by the dying Reginald Mitchell to Specification F.37/34 using the new Rolls-Royce PV.12 engine later named Merlin. It was the first all-metal stressed-skin fighter produced in Britain. The following were main versions.
I Initial version, 450 ordered in June 1936 with 1,030 hp Merlin II, two-blade fixed-pitch propeller and four 0·303 in Browning guns. Later Mk IA with eight guns, bulged canopy and three-blade DH v-p propeller and Mk IB with two 20 mm Hispano and four 0·303. Production: 1,566.
II Mk I built at Castle Bromwich with 1,175 hp Merlin XII and Rotol propeller. Production: 750 IIA (eight 0·303), 170 IIB (two 20 mm, four 0·303).
IV Confusing because Mk IV was first Griffon-engined, one built. Then unarmed Merlin photo-reconnaissance Mk IV delivered in quantity. Production: 229
V Like PR.IV powered by 1,440 hp Merlin 45, many detail changes, main fighter version 1941–42 in three forms: VA, eight 0·303; VB, two 20 mm and four 0·303; VC, "universal" wing with either guns plus two 250 lb (113 kg) bombs. All with centreline rack for 500 lb (227 kg) bomb or tank. Many with clipped

wings and/or tropical filter under nose. Production: VA, 94; VB, 3,923; VC, 2,447.
VI High-altitude interim interceptor, 1,415 hp Merlin 47, pressurised cockpit, two 20 mm and four 0·303. Production: 100.
VII High-altitude, extended wing-tips, new 1,660 hp Merlin 61 with two-stage supercharger (and symmetrical underwing radiators); retractable tailwheel. later broad and pointed rudder. Pressurised cockpit. Production: 140.
VIII Followed interim Mk IX, virtually unpressurised Mk VII in LF (low-altitude, clipped), F (standard) and HF (high-altitude, extended) versions. Production: 1,658.
IX Urgent version to counter Fw 190, quick lash-up of V with Merlin 61; again LF, F and HF versions, plus IXE with two 20 mm and two 0·5 in. Production: 5,665.
X Pressurised photo-reconnaissance, Merlin 77, whole leading edge forming fuel tank. Production: 16.
XI As X but unpressurised, 1,760 hp Merlin 63A or 1,655 hp Merlin 70. Mainstay of Photo Reconnaissance Unit 1943–45. Production: 471.
XII Low-altitude to counter Fw 190 hit-and-run bomber, 1,735 hp Griffon III or IV, strengthened VC airframe, clipped. Production: 100.
XIII Low-level reconnaissance, low-rated 1,620 hp Merlin 32, four 0·303. Production: 16.
XIV First with two-stage Griffon, 2,050 hp Mk 65 with deep symmetric radiators and five-blade propeller, completely redesigned airframe with new fuselage, broad fin/rudder, inboard ailerons, retractable tail-

Continued on page 208

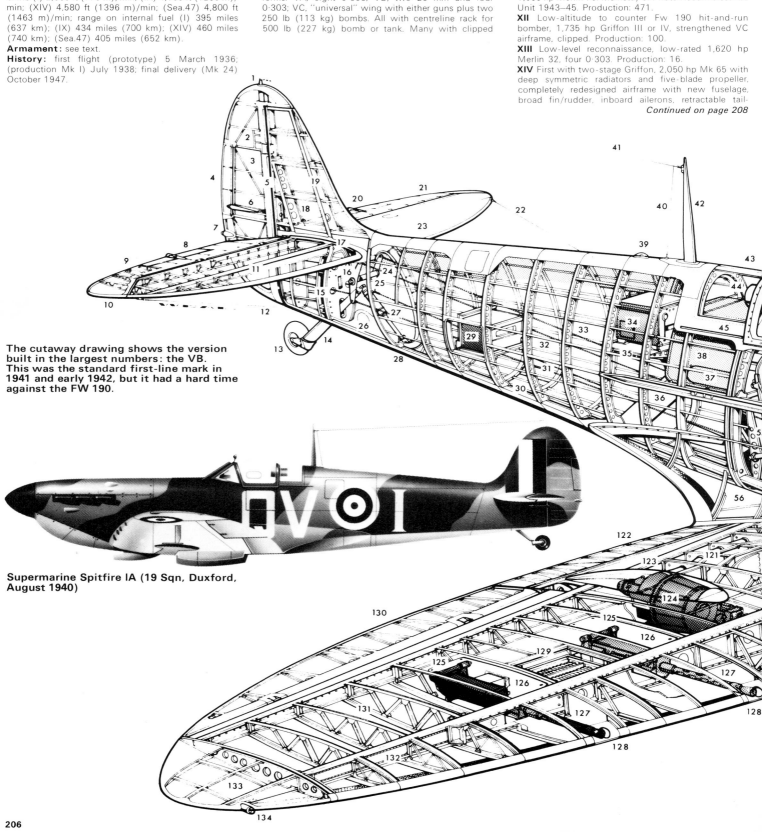

The cutaway drawing shows the version built in the largest numbers: the VB. This was the standard first-line mark in 1941 and early 1942, but it had a hard time against the FW 190.

Supermarine Spitfire IA (19 Sqn, Duxford, August 1940)

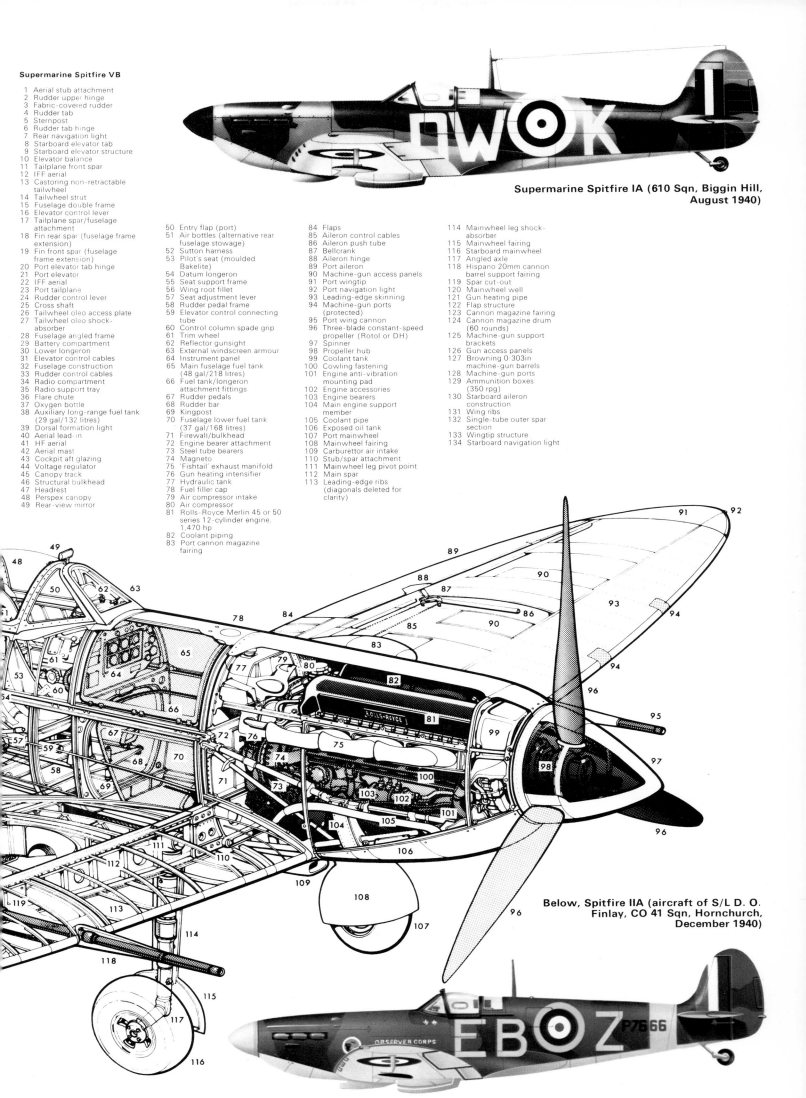

Supermarine Spitfire VB

1 Aerial stub attachment
2 Rudder upper hinge
3 Fabric-covered rudder
4 Rudder tab
5 Sternpost
6 Rudder tab hinge
7 Rear navigation light
8 Starboard elevator tab
9 Starboard elevator structure
10 Elevator balance
11 Tailplane front spar
12 IFF aerial
13 Castoring non-retractable tailwheel
14 Tailwheel strut
15 Fuselage double frame
16 Elevator control lever
17 Tailplane spar/fuselage attachment
18 Fin rear spar (fuselage frame extension)
19 Fin front spar (fuselage frame extension)
20 Port elevator tab hinge
21 Port elevator
22 IFF aerial
23 Port tailplane
24 Rudder control lever
25 Cross shaft
26 Tailwheel oleo access plate
27 Tailwheel oleo shock-absorber
28 Fuselage angled frame
29 Battery compartment
30 Lower longeron
31 Elevator control cables
32 Fuselage construction
33 Rudder control cables
34 Radio compartment
35 Radio support tray
36 Flare chute
37 Oxygen bottle
38 Auxiliary long-range fuel tank (29 gal/132 litres)
39 Dorsal formation light
40 Aerial lead-in
41 HF aerial
42 Aerial mast
43 Cockpit aft glazing
44 Voltage regulator
45 Canopy track
46 Structural bulkhead
47 Headrest
48 Perspex canopy
49 Rear-view mirror

50 Entry flap (port)
51 Air bottles (alternative rear fuselage stowage)
52 Sutton harness
53 Pilot's seat (moulded Bakelite)
54 Datum longeron
55 Seat support frame
56 Wing root fillet
57 Seat adjustment lever
58 Rudder pedal frame
59 Elevator control connecting tube
60 Control column spade grip
61 Trim wheel
62 Reflector gunsight
63 External windscreen armour
64 Instrument panel
65 Main fuselage fuel tank (48 gal/218 litres)
66 Fuel tank/longeron attachment fittings
67 Rudder pedals
68 Rudder bar
69 Kingpost
70 Fuselage lower fuel tank (37 gal/168 litres)
71 Firewall/bulkhead
72 Engine bearer attachment
73 Steel tube bearers
74 Magneto
75 'Fishtail' exhaust manifold
76 Gun heating intensifier
77 Hydraulic tank
78 Fuel filler cap
79 Air compressor intake
80 Air compressor
81 Rolls-Royce Merlin 45 or 50 series 12-cylinder engine, 1,470 hp
82 Coolant piping
83 Port cannon magazine fairing

84 Flaps
85 Aileron control cables
86 Aileron push tube
87 Bellcrank
88 Aileron hinge
89 Port aileron
90 Machine-gun access panels
91 Port wingtip
92 Port navigation light
93 Leading-edge skinning
94 Machine-gun ports (protected)
95 Port wing cannon
96 Three-blade constant-speed propeller (Rotol or DH)
97 Spinner
98 Propeller hub
99 Coolant tank
100 Cowling fastening
101 Engine anti-vibration mounting pad
102 Engine accessories
103 Engine bearers
104 Main engine support member
105 Coolant pipe
106 Exposed oil tank
107 Port mainwheel
108 Mainwheel fairing
109 Carburettor air intake
110 Stub/spar attachment
111 Mainwheel leg pivot point
112 Main spar
113 Leading-edge ribs (diagonals deleted for clarity)

114 Mainwheel leg shock-absorber
115 Mainwheel fairing
116 Starboard mainwheel
117 Angled axle
118 Hispano 20mm cannon barrel support fairing
119 Spar cut-out
120 Mainwheel well
121 Gun heating pipe
122 Flap structure
123 Cannon magazine fairing
124 Cannon magazine drum (60 rounds)
125 Machine-gun support brackets
126 Gun access panels
127 Browning 0·303in machine-gun barrels
128 Machine-gun ports
129 Ammunition boxes (350 rpg)
130 Starboard aileron construction
131 Wing ribs
132 Single-tube outer spar section
133 Wingtip structure
134 Starboard navigation light

Supermarine Spitfire IA (610 Sqn, Biggin Hill, August 1940)

Below, Spitfire IIA (aircraft of S/L D. O. Finlay, CO 41 Sqn, Hornchurch, December 1940)

Supermarine Spitfire (continued)

Supermarine Spitfire IX (725 Sqn, Royal Danish AF)

wheel. F.XIV, two 20 mm and four 0·303; F.XIVE, two 20 mm and two 0·5 in; FR.XIVE, same guns, cut-down rear fuselage and teardrop hood, clipped wings, F.24 camera and extra fuel. Active in 1944, destroyed over 300 flying bombs. Production: 957.

XVI As Mk IX but 1,705 hp Packard Merlin 266; LF.IXE, E-guns and clipped, many with teardrop hood, extra fuel. Production: 1,054.

XVIII Definitive wartime fighter derived from interim XIV, extra fuel, stronger, F and FR versions, some of latter even more fuel and tropical equipment. Production: 300.

XIX Final photo-reconnaissance, 2,050 hp Griffon 65 and unpressurised, then Griffon 66 with pressure cabin and increased wing tankage; both option of deep slipper tank for 1,800 mile (2900 km) range. Made last RAF Spitfire sortie, Malaya, 1 April 1954. Production: 225.

21 Post-war, redesigned aircraft with different structure and shape, 2,050 hp Griffon 65 or 85, four 20 mm and 1,000 lb (454 kg) bombs. Production: 122.

22 Bubble hood, 24-volt electrics, some with 2,375 hp Griffon 65 and contraprop. Production: 278.

24 Redesigned tail, short-barrel cannon, zero-length rocket launchers. Production: 54. Total Spitfire production 20,334.

Seafire IB Navalised Spitfire VB, usually 1,415 hp low-rated Merlin 46. Fixed wings but hook and slinging points. Conversions: 166.

Seafire IIC Catapult spools, strengthened landing gear, 1,645 hp Merlin 32 and four-blade propeller. Various sub-types, Universal wing. Production: 262 Supermarine, 110 Westland.

III Manual double-fold wing, 1,585 hp Merlin 55M, various versions. Production: 870 Westland, 350 Cunliffe-Owen.

XV (later F.15) 1,850 hp Griffon VI, four-blade, asymmetric radiators, cross between Seafire III and Spitfire XII. Production: 390.

XVII (F.17) Increased fuel, cut-down fuselage and bubble hood. Production (cut by war's end): 232.

45 New aircraft entirely, corresponding to Spitfire 21; Griffon 61 (five-blade) or 85 (contraprop); fixed wing, four 20 mm. Production: 50.

46 Bubble hood like Spitfire 22. Production: 24.

47 Navalised Spitfire 24, hydraulically folding wings, carb-air intake just behind propeller, increased fuel. Fought in Malaya and Korea. Production: 140. Total Seafires: 2,556.

Supermarine Attacker

Attacker F.1, FB.1 and FB.2
Type: single-seat carrier- or land-based fighter bomber.
Engine: one 5,100 lb (2313 kg) thrust Rolls-Royce Nene 3 centrifugal turbojet.

Supermarine Attacker (land-based, 11 Sqn, Royal Pakistan AF)

Dimensions: span 36 ft 11 in (11·25 m); length 37 ft 6 in (11·43 m); height 9 ft 11 in (3·02 m).
Weights: empty, typically 8,434 lb (3825 kg); maximum loaded 11,500 lb (5216 kg).
Performance: maximum speed 590 mph (950 km/h); initial climb 6,350 ft (1937 m)/min; service ceiling 45,000 ft (13,720 m); range 590 miles (949 km), 1,190 miles (1915 km) with external belly tank.
Armament: four 20 mm Hispano Mk 5 cannon; FB versions, also two 1,000 lb (454 kg) bombs or eight 60 lb (27 kg) rockets.
History: first flight (E.1/44 prototype) 27 July 1946; service delivery August 1951.

Designed to meet an RAF specification, the Attacker was schemed by Joe Smith's design team (which had managed the Spitfire programme following Mitchell's death in June 1937) to mate the Nene engine with the laminar wing of the piston-engined Spiteful. RAF interest waned, but in June 1947 a semi-navalised prototype was flown, with long-stroke main gears (the Attacker was one of the few jets to have a traditional landing gear, with twin tailwheels), spoilers and a hook.

After very protracted development the F.1 version entered service with 800 Sqn to give the Royal Navy its first jet equipment. Following 61 F.1 and FB.1, Supermarine's post-war plant at South Marston delivered 84 FB.2 with stiffer canopy, improved ailerons and other changes, and 36 land-based variants for the Royal Pakistan Air Force. The Attacker was far from being an outstanding aircraft and was poor at altitude, but it did at least enable the Fleet Air Arm to look and sound like a more modern force.

Supermarine Swift

Swift F.1, 2, 3, 4 and 7 and FR.5
Type: single-seat day fighter bomber; (FR.5) photo-reconnaissance.
Engine: one Rolls-Royce Avon single-shaft turbojet: (1, 2) 7,500 lb (3402 kg) thrust Avon 105; (3, 4) 9,500 lb (4310 kg) Avon 108 with afterburner; (5) 9,450 lb (4287 kg) Avon 114 with afterburner; (7) 9,950 lb (4514 kg) Avon 116 with afterburner.

wings; (2, 3, 4) as above but four 30 mm Aden; (5) two 30 mm Aden and increased external load; (7) two Blue Sky (Fireflash) air-to-air guided weapons.
History: first flight (Type 541) 5 August 1951; (production F.1) 25 August 1952; (FR.5) 24 May 1955; (F.7) April 1956.

Supermarine Swift FR.5 (79 Sqn, 2ATAF, Germany)

Dimensions: span (1–5) 32 ft 4 in (9·85 m); (7) 37 ft (11·28 m); length (1–4) 41 ft 5½ in (12·64 m); (5, 7) 42 ft 3 in (12·88 m); height 12 ft 6 in (3·8 m).
Weights: empty (1) 12,500 lb; (5) 12,800 lb (5800 kg); (7) about 13,200 lb (5900 kg); maximum loaded (1) 17,000 lb; (5) 21,400 lb (9706 kg); (7) not released.
Performance: maximum speed (1) 690 mph; (5) 685 mph (1100 km/h); (7) 700 mph (1127 km/h); initial climb and ceiling, not released; range (5) 480 miles (772 km) at low level.
Armament: (1) two 30 mm Aden cannon in lower fuselage, and structural provision for two 1,000 lb (454 kg) bombs, tanks or 16 rockets under outer

Despite the skill and devotion of Joe Smith's engineering team and the test pilots who operated from the short field at Chilbolton, the saga of the Swift is one of continual frantic battle against severe difficulty. Derived over many years from the Attacker by way of the Type 510 and 535, the 541 Swift was deficient in many respects and spring-tab ailerons prohibited supersonic dives. Later geared-tab surfaces did make transonic flight possible, but control was poor about all axes and dangerous above 25,000 ft. The F.1 and 2 equipped 56 Sqn from February 1954 to May 1955, but the afterburner-equipped 3 and variable-tailplane

4 were never released for use, though huge numbers were on the production line at South Marston and at Shorts, Belfast. Adding the two extra guns had required forward extension of the leading edge to accommodate ammunition, causing violent pitch-up which caused the programme to be abandoned, though an F.4 set a world speed record at 738 mph. Later the FR.5 (62 built) served with 2 and 79 Sqns in Germany, twice winning the NATO reconnaissance contest. The 12 F.7 had radar for their missiles, long span, slab tail and correct afterburning nozzle. They were superb aircraft and could have served with distinction.

Supermarine Scimitar

Type 544, Scimitar F.1
Type: single-seat carrier-based strike fighter.
Engines: two 11,250 lb (5105 kg) thrust Rolls-Royce Avon 202 single-shaft turbojets.
Dimensions: span 37 ft 2 in (11·33 m); length, excluding FR probe, 55 ft 4 in (16·87 m); height, 15 ft 3 in (4·65 m).
Weights: empty, 21,000 lb (9525 kg); maximum loaded 40,000 lb (18,144 kg).
Performance: maximum speed 710 mph (1143 km/h, Mach 0·95) or 650 mph at sea level; initial climb 20,000 ft (6100 m)/min; service ceiling 50,000 ft

(15,240 m); range, clean, 600 miles (966 km) at height.
Armament: four 30 mm Aden cannon under nose; four wing pylons for 96 air-to-air rockets, four Sidewinder missiles, tactical nuclear weapon, four AGM-12B Bullpup missiles or other large stores or tanks.
History: first flight (Type 508) 31 August 1951; (Type 525) 27 April 1954; (pre-production 544) 20 January 1956; (Scimitar F.1) 11 January 1957; service delivery June 1958.
The length of the gestation period of this big twin-engined aircraft is partly explained by the total lack of coherence of the procurement machine, which began

in 1945 asking for naval fighters without normal landing gear to land on a flexible deck. The 508, the first hardware, had thin straight wings and butterfly tail, changed in the 525 to conventional swept layout and progressing in the 544 to blown flaps, slab tail, area-ruled body and dog-tooth wings. Eventually 76 Scimitar F.1 were built, without radar but with an interchangeable camera nose and provision for an FR "buddy pack". They were good and popular aircraft, but shortly before withdrawal in 1965 the questionable decision was taken (but not implemented) to remove their guns.

Tupolev SB-2

ANT-40, SB-1, -2 and -2bis (ANT-41)
Type: medium bomber with usual crew of three.
Engines: two vee-12 liquid-cooled: (early -2 versions) 750 hp VK-100 (M-100) derived from Hispano-Suiza 12Y; (late -2 versions) 840 hp M-100A; (-2bis versions) 1,100 hp M-103.
Dimensions: span 66 ft 8½ in (20·34 m); length (with very few exceptions) 40 ft 3¼ in (12·29 m); height 10 ft 8 in (3·28 m).
Weights: empty (early -2) 8,267 lb (3750 kg); (M-100A) typically 8,820 lb (4000 kg); (-2bis) about 10,800 lb (4900 kg); maximum loaded (early -2) 13,449 lb (6100 kg); (M-100A) 13,955 lb (6330 kg), (-2bis) normally 17,196 lb (7800 kg); overload 21,165 lb (9600 kg).
Performance: maximum speed (early) 255 mph (410 km/h); (M-100A) 263 mph (425 km/h); (-2bis) 280 mph (450 km/h); initial climb (-2bis) 1,310 ft (400 m)/min; service ceiling (typical later version) 31,000–35,000 ft (9500–10,500 m); range with bomb load (typical -2) 746 miles (1200 km); (-2bis, max fuel) 994 miles (1600 km).

Armament: (normal for all versions) four 7·62 mm ShKAS machine guns, two manually aimed through vertical slits in nose, one from dorsal position and one from rear ventral position; internal bomb bay for six 220 lb (100 kg) or single 1,100 lb (500 kg).
History: first flight (SB-1) 7 October 1934; service delivery (-2) early 1936; (-2bis) probably late 1938; final delivery, probably 1942.

Like the TB-3, the SB-2 was built in great numbers in the 1930s and bore a heavy burden in "the Great Patriotic War" from June 1941 until long after it was obsolescent. Though built to a 1933 specification it was actually much superior to Britain's later Blenheim and it was the Soviet Union's first stressed-skin machine. The SB-1 prototype had M-25 radials, but performance was even better with the VK-100 in-lines

and service in the Spanish civil war in 1936–39 initially found the Nationalists lacking any fighters able to catch the speedy, high-flying SB. In speed and rate of climb even the first service versions surpassed contemporary fighters and, despite a considerable increase in fuel capacity and weight, performance was improved with the more streamlined M-103, without the original bluff frontal radiators. Total production exceeded 6,000 of all versions, and the type served against Japan in 1938–39, in Finland and against German forces until 1943, the last two years mainly in the role of a night bomber.

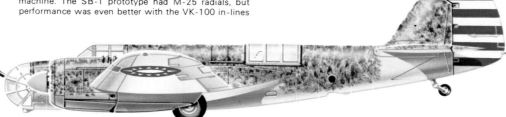

SB/M-100A (Chinese Central Government, northern Shansi)

SB-2 (Grupo de Bombardeo núm 24, Spanish Republican AF)

SB-2 bis (Soviet Frontal Aviation, found wrecked at Lvov, June 1941)

Tupolev TB-3

ANT-6, TB-3 Types 1932, 1934 and 1936
Type: heavy bomber with crew of ten (Type 1932)
and later six.
Engines: four vee-12 liquid-cooled: (1932) 730 hp
M-17; (1934) 900 hp M-34R (derived from BMW VI);
later 950–1280 hp M-34RN or RNF.
Dimensions: span 132 ft 10½ in (40·5 m); (1936)
137 ft 1½ in (41·8 m); length (early) 81 ft (24·69 m);
(1934 onward) 82 ft 8¼ in (25·21 m); height, not
available but about 18 ft.
Weights: empty, 22,000–26,450 lb (11,000–
12,000 kg); maximum loaded (1932) 38,360 lb
(17,500 kg); (1934) 41,021 lb (18,606 kg); (1936)
41,226 lb (18,700 kg), with overload of 54,020 lb
(24,500 kg).
Performance: maximum speed (M-17, 1932)
134 mph (215 km/h); (M-34R, 1934) 144 mph
(232 km/h); (M-34RN, 1936) 179 mph (288 km/h);
initial climb, not available; service ceiling (1932)
12,467 ft (3800 m); (1934) 15,090 ft (4600 m); (1936)
25,365 ft (7750 m); range with bomb load (typical of
all) 1,550 miles (2500 km).
Armament: (1932, 1934) five pairs of 7·62 mm DA-2
machine guns in nose, two dorsal mountings and two
underwing positions, all manually aimed; internal bomb
cells for maximum load of 4,850 lb (2200 kg); (1936)
five (later three or four) 7·62 mm ShKAS manually
aimed, by 1936 without wing positions; bomb load
up to 12,790 lb (5800 kg) carried on 26 fuselage racks
and 12 external racks under fuselage and wings.
History: first flight (ANT-6) 22 December 1930;
(production TB-3) probably late 1931; (M-34 prototype) March 1933; final delivery, probably 1939.

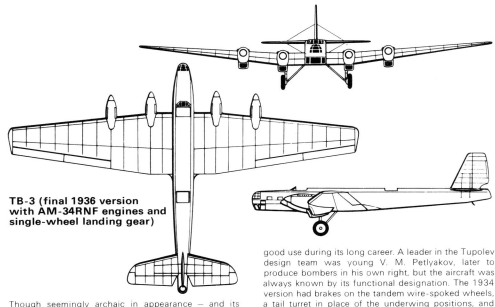

**TB-3 (final 1936 version
with AM-34RNF engines and
single-wheel landing gear)**

Though seemingly archaic in appearance — and its
basic design dated from 1926 — the TB-3 was a large
and formidable aircraft with capabilities outstripping
those of any other bomber in service in other countries.
Though not a stressed-skin design it was a cantilever
monoplane with corrugated metal skin using Junkers
technology and, thanks to generous stressing, had a
considerable "stretching" capability that was put to

good use during its long career. A leader in the Tupolev
design team was young V. M. Petlyakov, later to
produce bombers in his own right, but the aircraft was
always known by its functional designation. The 1934
version had brakes on the tandem wire-spoked wheels,
a tail turret in place of the underwing positions, and
geared engines, which in 1935 were supercharged RN
type. Altogether at least 800 of these fine machines
were built, final models having smooth skin, single-
wheel main gears and only three gunners in enclosed
manual turrets. TB-3s saw much action against Japan,
Poland, Finland and the German invader and served
until 1944 as freight and paratroop transports.

Tupolev Tu-2

ANT-58, Tu-2 (many sub-variants), Tu-6
Type: attack bomber with normal crew of four.
Engines: two 1,850 hp Shvetsov ASh-82FN or FNV
14-cylinder two-row radials.
Dimensions: span 61 ft 10½ in (18·86 m); length
45 ft 3¾ in (13·8 m); height 13 ft 9½ in (4·20 m).
Weights: empty 18,240 lb (8273 kg); maximum
loaded 28,219 lb (12,800 kg).
Performance: maximum speed 342 mph (550 km/h);
initial climb 2,300 ft (700 m)/m; service ceiling
31,168 ft (9500 m); range with 3,307 lb (1500 kg)
bombs 1,553 miles (2500 km).
Armament: typically three manually aimed 12·7 mm
Beresin BS, one in upper rear of crew compartment,
one in rear dorsal position and one in rear ventral
position, and two 20 mm ShVAK, each with 200
rounds, fixed in wing roots for ground attack (later,
often 23 mm); internal bomb bay for maximum load of
5,000 lb (2270 kg), later 6,615 lb (3000 kg).
History: first flight (ANT-58) October 1940; (production Tu-2) August 1942; final delivery 1948.

Tu-2 (example in FA service near Berlin, April 1945)

Though it was undoubtedly one of the outstanding
designs of World War II, the Tu-2 had the misfortune
to emerge into a Soviet Union teeming with the Pe-2,
and the older and smaller machine continued to be
produced at just ten times the rate of its supposed
replacement (much the same happened with German
bombers). It was formidable and reliable in service,
extremely popular and hardly needed any major

modification in the course of a career which extended
right through the nervous Berlin Airlift (1948), Korea
(1950–53, in North Korean service) and up to 1961
with several Communist nations. Known to NATO as
"Bat", the post-war variants included a close-support
type with 37 mm cannon, a radar-equipped (night
fighter?) variant and the high-altitude Tu-6 with long
span and bigger tail.

Tupolev Tu-16

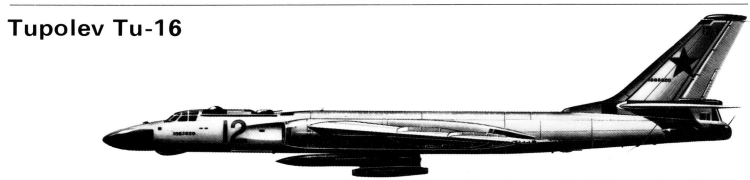

Tu-16 ("Badger C", AV-Morskaya [naval] Aviatsya)

**Sub-types known to West as "Badger A" to
"Badger G"; Tupolev bureau, Tu-88**
Type: designed as strategic bomber; see text.
Engines: believed in all versions, two Mikulin AM-
3M single-shaft turbojets each rated at about 20,950 lb
(9500 kg).
Dimensions: span (basic) 110 ft (33·5 m), (varies
with FR system). ECM and other features); length
(basic) 120 ft (36·5 m), (varies with radar or glazed
nose); height 35 ft 6 in (10·8 m).
Weights: empty, typically about 72,750 lb (33,000 kg)
in early versions, about 82,680 lb (37,500 kg) in
maritime/ECM roles; maximum loaded, about 150,000 lb
(68,000 kg).
Performance: maximum speed, clean at height,
587 mph (945 km/h); initial climb, clean, about
4,100 ft (1250 m)/min; service ceiling 42,650 ft

(13,000 m); range with maximum weapon load, no
missiles, 3,000 miles (4,800 km); extreme reconnaissance range, about 4,500 miles (7250 km).
Armament: in most variants, six 23 mm NR-23
cannon in radar-directed manned tail turret and remote-
aimed upper dorsal·and rear ventral barbettes; versions
without nose radar usually have seventh NR-23 fixed
firing ahead on right side of nose. Internal weapon bay
for load of 19,800 lb (9000 kg), with certain versions
equipped to launch missiles (see text).
History: first flight (Tu-88), believed 1952; service
delivery 1954; final delivery (USSR) about 1959,
(China) after 1975.

Representing a simple and low-risk approach to the
strategic jet-bomber requirement, the Tu-88 prototype
was generally in the class of the Valiant but incor-

porated heavy defensive arament. Technology
throughout was derived directly from the Boeing B-29,
which Tupolev's bureau had in 1945-53 built in large
numbers as the Tu-4. The first ("Badger A") version had
blind-bombing radar and glazed nose, and a few were
supplied to Egypt and Iraq. The B carried two "Kennel"
cruise missiles on underwing pylons and served the
AV-MF (Navy) and Indonesian AF. C carried the large
"Kipper" stand-off missile on the centreline, with
panoramic nose radar for ship search and missile
guidance. D is a maritime reconnaissance type, with
comprehensive radars and ECM. E is a photo and
multi-sensor reconnaissance type, F is an E with major
new ECM and ESM installations, and G is an updated
B which launched many missiles against Israel in 1973.
Total production exceeded 2,000, and production
(without Soviet aid) continues in China.

Tupolev Tu-20

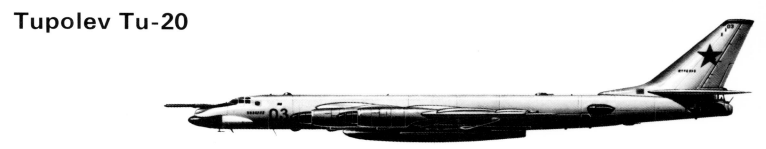

Tu-95 (Tupolev bureau designation) in versions known to West as "Bear A" to "Bear F" and "Moss" (Tu-126)
Type: designed as strategic bomber; see text.
Engines: four 14,795 ehp Kuznetsov NK-12M single-shaft turboprops.
Dimensions: span 159 ft (48·5 m); (Moss) 167 ft 8 in (51·10 m); length 155 ft 10 in (47·50 m), (certain versions differ by up to 6 ft, and Moss is much bigger); height 38 ft 8 in (11·78 m); (Moss) over 40 ft.
Weights: empty, probably about 160,000 lb (72,600 kg); maximum loaded (Bear and Moss, estimate) about 340,000 lb (154,000 kg).
Performance: maximum speed (typical Bear, clean) 540 mph (870 km/h); service ceiling, about 44,000 ft (13,400 m); range with 25,000 lb (11,340 kg) bomb load, 7,800 miles (12,550 km).

Armament: normally six 23 mm NS-23 in radar-directed manned tail turret and remote-aimed dorsal and ventral barbettes (defensive guns often absent from late conversions and from Moss); internal weapon bay for load of about 25,000 lb (11,340 kg); (Moss) no weapons.
History: first flight (prototype) mid-1954; service delivery, 1956; final delivery, probably about 1962.

Making use of identical systems, techniques and even similar airframe structures as the Tu-16, the Tu-95 (service designation, Tu-20) is much larger and has roughly double the range of its turbojet predecessor. The huge swept wing, forming integral tanks, was a major accomplishment in 1952–54, as were the monster turboprop engines and their eight-blade 18 ft 4½ in

(5·6 m) contraprops. The basic bomber called "Bear A" had a glazed nose, chin radar and gun-sight blisters on the rear fuselage. First seen in 1961, "Bear B" featured a solid nose with enormous radome, refuelling probe and centreline attachment for a large cruise missile ("Kangaroo"). C appeared in 1964 with a large new blister on each side of the fuselage (on one side only on B), while D was obviously a major ECM/ESM reconnaissance type with chin radar, very large belly radar, and from 12 to 21 avionic features visible from stem to stern. E is a multi-sensor reconnaissance conversion of A, while F is a recent further conversion with an array of ventral radars and stores bays in place of the ventral guns. "Moss" is an AWACS (Airborne Warning And Control System) with giant "saucer" radome and the larger airframe of the Tu-114 transport.

Tupolev Tu-22

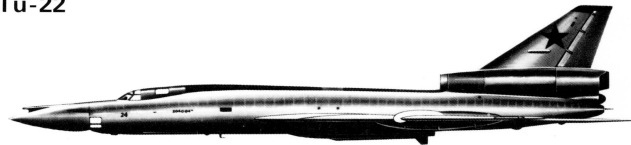

Tu-22 in versions known to West as "Blinder A" to "Blinder D"; Tupolev bureau, Tu-105
Type: originally bomber; see text.
Engines: two afterburning turbojets, of unknown type, each with maximum rating estimated at 27,000 lb (12,250 kg).
Dimensions: span 90 ft 10½ in (27·70 m); length (most versions) 132 ft 11½ in (40·53 m); height 17 ft (5·18 m).
Weights: empty, about 85,000 lb (38,600 kg); maximum loaded, about 185,200 lb (84,000 kg).
Performance: maximum speed (clean, at height) 920 mph (1480 km/h, Mach 1·4); initial climb, about

11,500 ft (3500 m)/min; service ceiling 59,000 ft (18,000 m); range (high, internal fuel only) 1,400 miles (2250 km).
Armament: one 23 mm NS-23 in radar-directed barbette in tail; internal weapon bay for at least 20,000 lb (9070 kg) of free-fall bombs or other stores, or (Blinder B) one "Kitchen" stand-off cruise missile semi-recessed under centreline.
History: first flight, well before public display in 1961; service delivery, probably 1960.

Having an efficient wing closely related to that of the Tu-28P, this supersonic bomber is a large aircraft with

a bigger body and higher gross weight than the USAF B-58 Hustler. Typical crew appears to be a pilot, upward-ejecting, and two more members in tandem at a lower level who eject downwards. "Blinder A" was a reconnaissance bomber, seen in small numbers. B carried the stand-off missile, had a larger nose radar and semi-flush FR probe. C is the main variant, used by Naval Aviation for oversea ECM/ESM surveillance, multi-sensor reconnaissance and with limited weapon capability. D is a dual trainer with stepped cockpits. Recent versions appear to have later engines (probably turbofans) with greater airflow.

Tupolev Tu-28P

Tu-28 versions of unknown designation; Tupolev bureau, Tu-102
Type: long-range all-weather interceptor.
Engines: originally, two large axial turbojets of unknown type, each with afterburning rating of about 27,000 lb (12,250 kg), probably similar to those of Tu-22; later versions, afterburning turbofans of about 30,000 lb (13,610 kg) each, as in later Tu-22.
Dimensions: (estimated) span 65 ft (20 m); length 85 ft (26 m); height 23 ft (7 m).
Weights: (estimated) empty 55,000 lb (25,000 kg); maximum loaded 100,000 lb (45,000 kg).
Performance: (estimated) maximum speed (with missiles, at height) 1,150 mph (1850 km/h, Mach 1·75);

initial climb, 25,000 ft (7500 m)/min; service ceiling (not gross weight) about 60,000 ft (18,000 m); range on internal fuel (high patrol) about 1,800 miles (2900 km).
Armament: no guns seen in any version; mix of infra-red homing and radar-homing "Ash" air-to-air guided missiles, originally one of each and since 1965 two of each.
History: first flight, believed 1957; service delivery, probably 1961.

Largest fighter known to be in service in the world, this formidable machine is essentially conventional yet has a interception radar known to exist. It was one of a

number of supersonic types produced by the Tupolev bureau with technology explored with the family of aircraft of the late 1950s known to NATO as "Backfin" (another is the Tu-22). Like the others the Tu-28P has a distinctive wing with sharply kinked trailing edge, the outer 45° panels being outboard of large fairings extending behind the trailing edge accommodating the four-wheel bogie landing gears. Two crew sit in tandem under upward-hinged canopies, and all armament is carried on wing pylons. Early versions had twin ventral fins and usually large belly fairings, but these features are absent from aircraft in current service. The Tu-28P would be an ideal strategic patrol fighter to operate in conjunction with the "Moss" AWACS.

Tupolev V-G bomber

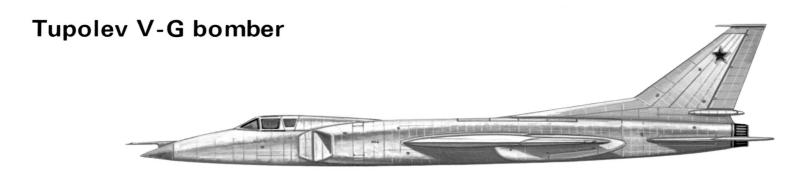

Two main versions with NATO code names "Backfire-A" and "-B"
Type: long-range bomber and missile platform with probable crew of four.
Engines: two afterburning turbofans, probably Kuznetsov NK-144 two-shaft engines each with maximum rating of 48,500 lb (22,000 kg).
Dimensions: (estimated) span (spread, about 20°) 110 ft (33·5 m), (swept, about 55°) 88 ft (26·8 m); length 135 ft (41·2 m); height 39 ft (11·9 m).
Weights: (estimated) empty 121, 250 lb (55,000 kg); maximum loaded 272,000 lb (123,350 kg).
Performance: (estimated, "Backfire B") maximum speed at altitude 1,520 mph (2445 km/h, Mach 2·3); speed at sea level, over Mach 1; service ceiling over 60,000 ft (18,290 m); maximum combat radius on

internal fuel 3,570 miles (5745 km); ferry range, about 8,000 miles (12,875 km).
Armament: internal weapon bay(s) for free-fall bombs up to largest thermonuclear sizes, with provision for carrying stand-off missiles of unknown types.
History: first flight ("Backfire-A" prototype) not later than 1969; ("Backfire-B") probably 1973; entry to service, probably 1974.
Owing to the obvious inability of the Tu-22 to fly strategic missions the Tupolev bureau designed this far more formidable aircraft, larger in size and fitted with a swing-wing. "Backfire-A" was apparently not a very successful design, with multi-wheel main gears folding into large fairings projecting in typical Tupolev fashion behind the only moderately swept wing. About half the gross wing area was fixed, just the outer

portions swinging through a modest arc. Today's "Backfire-B" has no landing-gear boxes and is improved in other ways, though the side view is still largely a matter for conjecture. The large engines are fed through wide inlet ducts which probably pass above the wing; a flight refuelling probe is fitted above the nose, but even without this "Backfire-B" has an endurance of some ten hours. The Chairman of the US Joint Chiefs of Staff said in 1974 "It is expected to replace some of both the current medium and heavy bombers and, when deployed with a compatible tanker force, constitutes a potential threat to the continental United States." The speed of development is also disquieting to the West, because these aircraft were being encountered on long oversea missions in early 1975.

Vickers F.B.5

F.B.5, F.B.9
Type: two-seat fighting scout.
Engine: standard, one 100 hp Gnome Monosoupape nine-cylinder rotary.
Dimensions: span 36 ft 6 in (11·13 m); length 27 ft 2 in (8·28 m); height 11 ft 6 in (3·51 m).
Weights: empty (typical F.B.5) 1,220 lb (553 kg); maximum loaded 2,050 lb (930 kg).
Performance: maximum speed 70 mph (113 km/h); initial climb 400 ft (122 m)/min; service ceiling 9,000 ft (2743 m); range, about 240 miles (386 km), (4 hr endurance).
Armament: one manually aimed 0·303 in machine gun in front (observer's) cockpit; initially, belt-fed Vickers or Maxim, later drum-fed Lewis (rarely, twin

Lewis). Often, light bomb load under wings.
History: first flight (EFB.1) 1913; (production F.B.5) October 1914; (F.B.9) December 1915; final delivery (F.B.9) late 1916.

Certainly one of the earliest combat aircraft in the world, the Vickers Type 18 Destroyer was built to designs of A. R. Low and G. H. Challenger to meet the 1912 Admiralty specification for an aircraft carrying a machine gun. Exhibited at the Olympia air show in 1913, it was redesignated EFB.1 (Experimental Fighting Biplane) and, by way of several intermediate proto-

Vickers F.B.5 (probably aircraft of 11 Sqn)

types, became the production F.B.5 "Gunbus" which went to France with 11 Sqn, RFC, on 25 July 1915, as a combat unit. Placing the engine at the back allowed the gunner to be in front, and though slow this sturdy machine did good work until it met Fokker scouts with synchronised guns. The F.B.9 had smaller rounded wings, a streamlined nacelle and all-round ball/socket gun mount. Vickers made 210 of both types and Darracq a further 99 in France.

Vickers Vimy

F.B.27A Vimy I to IV
Type: heavy bomber with crew of three.
Engines: (Mk I) two 207 hp Hispano-Suiza vee-8 water-cooled; (II) 280 hp Sunbeam Maori; (III) 310 hp Fiat A-12bis; (IV) 360 hp Rolls-Royce Eagle VIII vee-12 water-cooled; (late conversions) two 420 hp Armstrong Siddeley Jaguar 14-cylinder two-row radial or 460 hp Bristol Jupiter VIII nine-cylinder radials.
Dimensions: span 68 ft (20·73 m); length 43 ft 6½ in (13·27 m); height 15 ft (4·57 m).
Weights: empty (IV) 7,104 lb (3222 kg); loaded 10,884 lb; maximum loaded 12,500 lb (5670 kg).
Performance: maximum speed 103 mph (166 km/h); initial climb 360 ft (110 m)/min; service ceiling 12,000 ft (3660 m) (at 12,500 lb, 7,000 ft); range with bomb load 900 miles (1448 km).
Armament: two, three or four manually aimed 0·303 in Lewis machine guns in nose, rear upper and ventral or beam positions; internal bomb cells and underwing racks for total of (Mk IV) 4,804 lb (2179 kg), restricted in peacetime to 2,476 lb.

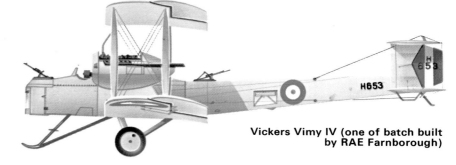

Vickers Vimy IV (one of batch built by RAE Farnborough)

History: first flight 30 November 1917; service delivery, October 1918 (combat ready July 1919); withdrawal, after 1930.

Designed by Rex Pierson as one of the new generation of Trenchardist bombers to attack Berlin with the Independent Air Force, the Vimy was relatively small and had an excellent performance. Chosen for production in Mk IV form it was too late for the war, but in the

immediate post-war era was the RAF's principal bomber, and gained major fame by being the type of aircraft to fly the Atlantic non-stop (Alcock/Brown, June 1919, in less than 16 hr) and from Britain to Australia (Ross and Keith Smith, November 1919, 136 hr). From 1926 the 80-odd surviving Vimys were re-engined with the more reliable and efficient post-war radial engines.

Vickers Virginia

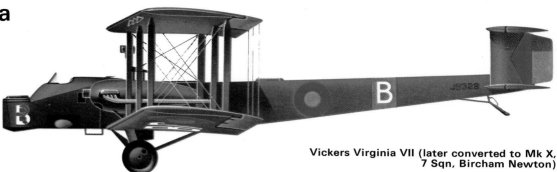

Vickers Virginia VII (later converted to Mk X, 7 Sqn, Bircham Newton)

Virginia I to X (Vickers type numbers from 76 to 167)
Type: heavy bomber with crew of four; later parachute trainer.
Engines: two Napier Lion W-12 (broad arrow) water-cooled; early marks, 450 hp Lion IIa or IV, all later marks 570 hp Lion V.
Dimensions: span 87 ft 8 in (26·72 m); length 62 ft 2¾ in (18·97 m); height 18 ft 2 in (5·54 m).
Weights: (X) empty 9,650 lb (4378 kg); maximum loaded 17,600 lb (7983 kg).
Performance: maximum speed 108 mph (174 km/h); initial climb 500 ft (152 m)/min; service ceiling

15,530 ft (4735 m); range with bomb load 985 miles (1585 km).
Armament: various, early version having three to five 0·303 in Lewis in nose, mid-upper (later tail) and (two only) upper-wing nacelles, and later marks one Lewis in the nose and a pair in the tail. Bomb load, originally nine 112 lb (50 kg) bombs internally but later marks fitted with external racks increasing total load to 3,000 lb (1361 kg).
History: first flight 24 November 1922; service delivery (Mk I) November 1924; final delivery (X) December 1932.

Though a traditional lumbering beast, whose snarling wooden screws driven by the direct-drive Lions could be heard for miles, the Virginia was the standard heavy bomber of the RAF from 1924 until 1937. Early marks were delivered silver, but the fabric was soon sprayed dark green and the white was removed from the roundels for night operations. Features included twin-wheel main landing gear, open cockpits, and, in the much-redesigned Mk X, metal structure, slats and an autopilot. Altogether 126 were built, all serving at home airfields and finishing their time as parachute trainers with jump-off platforms behind the engines.

Vickers Vincent

Vildebeest I to IV and Vincent (Types 267, 286 and 266)
Type: (Vildebeest) torpedo bomber with crew of three (IV, two); (Vincent) three-seat general purpose.
Engine: one 660 hp Bristol Pegasus IIM3 nine-

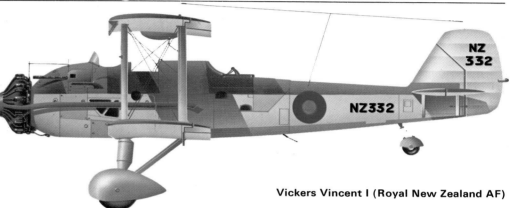

Vickers Vincent I (Royal New Zealand AF)

cylinder radial (Spanish CASA-built Vildebeest) 595 hp Hispano 12Nbr; (Vildebeest IV) 825 hp Bristol Perseus VIII nine-cylinder sleeve-valve radial.
Dimensions: span 49 ft (14·94 m); length 36 ft 8 in (11·17 m); (Vildebeest IV) 37 ft 8 in; height 17 ft 9 in (5·42 m).
Weights: empty 4,229 lb (1918 kg); (Vildebeest IV) 4,724 lb; maximum loaded 8,100 lb (3674 kg); (Vildebeest IV) 8,500 lb.
Performance: maximum speed 142 mph (230 km/h); (Vildebeest IV) 156 mph; initial climb 765 ft (233 m)/min; service ceiling 17,000 ft (5182 m); range 1,250 miles (2000 km).
Armament: one 0·303 in Vickers fixed firing forward, one 0·303 in Lewis manually aimed from rear cockpit; external bomb load of 1,000 lb (454 kg) or (Vildebeest) one 18 in (457 mm) torpedo.
History: first flight (Vildebeest) April 1928; service delivery (Vildebeest I) April 1933; (Vincent) late 1934; final delivery (Vildebeest IV) November 1937.

Designed to replace the Horsley as the RAF's coastal-defence torpedo-bomber, the Vildebeest (originally Vildebeeste) appeared with an uncowled Jupiter engine and two widely separated cockpits, the pilot being just ahead of the rectangular slatted wings and having a superb view. The production Mk I had a third cockpit and early Pegasus engine. After building 176, Vickers delivered 18 Mk IV with the first sleeve-valve engines ever cleared for service, fully cowled and

driving three-blade Rotol propellers. In 1939 the Vildebeest was the RAF's only torpedo carrier, and in 1941 Nos 36 and 100 Sqns at Singapore fought alone to try to hold back the Japanese, the last two aircraft surviving until March 1942 in Sumatra. The later Vincent, of which 171 were built between 1934 and 1936, served throughout the Middle East and Africa until 1942. One of its main replacements was the air-craft described below.

Vickers Wellesley

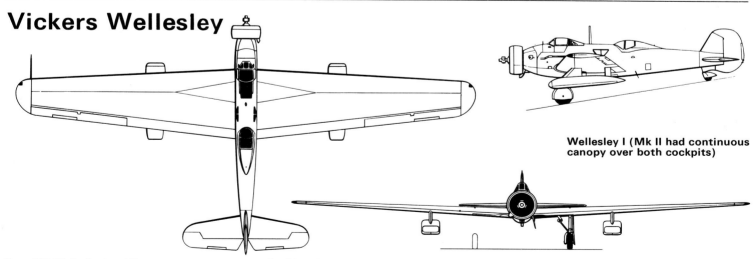

Wellesley I (Mk II had continuous canopy over both cockpits)

Type 287, Wellesley I and II
Type: two-seat general-purpose bomber.
Engine: one 925 hp Bristol Pegasus XX nine-cylinder radial.
Dimensions: span 74 ft 7 in (22·73 m); length 39 ft 3 in (11·96 m); height 12 ft 4 in (3·75 m).
Weights: empty 6,369 lb (2889 kg); maximum loaded (except record flight) 11,100 lb (5035 kg).
Performance: maximum speed 228 mph (369 km/h); initial climb 1,200 ft (366 m)/min; service ceiling 33,000 ft (10,060 m); range with bomb load 1,110 miles (1786 km).
Armament: one 0·303 in belt-fed Vickers in right

wing firing ahead, one Vickers K manually aimed from rear cockpit; four 500 lb (227 kg) or eight 250 lb bombs in streamlined containers, originally fitted with bomb doors, under wings.
History: first flight 19 June 1935; service delivery April 1937; final delivery May 1938.

Vickers built a large biplane to meet the RAF G.4/31 specification, but it was so humdrum the company board decided at their own risk to build a monoplane using the radical geodetic (metal basketwork) con-struction developed for airships by their structural wizard B.N. (later Sir Barnes) Wallis. The result was so

dramatically superior the Air Ministry lost its fear of monoplanes and bought 176 as the Wellesley. Distinguished by great span, high aspect ratio, extreme cruise efficiency and a most reliable engine (identical in size to the Jupiter but of virtually twice the power) it was natural to form a special Long-Range Develop-ment Flight. Three aircraft, with three seats, extra fuel and long-chord cowlings, took off from Ismalia, Egypt, on 5 November 1938; one landed at Koepang and the other two reached Darwin, 7,162 miles (11,525 km) in 48 hours non-stop. In World War II Wellesleys were extremely active in East Africa, Egypt, the Middle East and surrounding sea areas until late 1942.

Vickers-Armstrongs Wellington

Type 415 and 440, Wellington I to T.19

Type: originally long-range bomber with crew of six; later, see text.

Engines: variously two Bristol Pegasus nine-cylinder radials, two Rolls-Royce Merlin vee-12 liquid-cooled, two Pratt & Whitney Twin Wasp 14-cylinder two-row radials or two Bristol Hercules 14-cylinder two-row sleeve-valve radials; for details see text.

Dimensions: span 86 ft 2 in (26·26 m); (V, VI) 98 ft 2 in; length (most) 64 ft 7 in (19·68 m), (some, 60 ft 10 in or, with Leigh light, 66 ft); height 17 ft 6 in (5·33 m), (some 17 ft).

Weights: empty (IC) 18,556 lb (8417 kg); (X) 26,325 lb (11,940 kg); maximum loaded (IC) 25,800 lb (11,703 kg); (III) 29,500 lb (13,381 kg); (X) 36,500 lb (16,556 kg).

Performance: maximum speed (IC) 235 mph (379 km/h); (most other marks) 247–256 mph (410 km/h); (V, VI) 300 mph (483 km/h); initial climb (all, typical) 1,050 ft (320 m)/min; service ceiling (bomber versions, typical) 22,000 ft (6710 m); (V, VI) 38,000 ft (11,600 m); range with weapon load of 1,500 lb (680 kg), typically 2,200 miles (3540 km).

Armament: see text.

History: first flight (B.9/32) 15 June 1936; (production Mk I) 23 December 1937; service delivery (I) October 1938; final delivery (T.10) 13 October 1945.

It was natural that Vickers (Aviation), from October 1938 Vickers-Armstrongs (Aircraft), should have followed up the success of the Wellesley with a larger bomber using the geodetic form of construction. There were difficulties in applying it to wings, cut-out nacelles

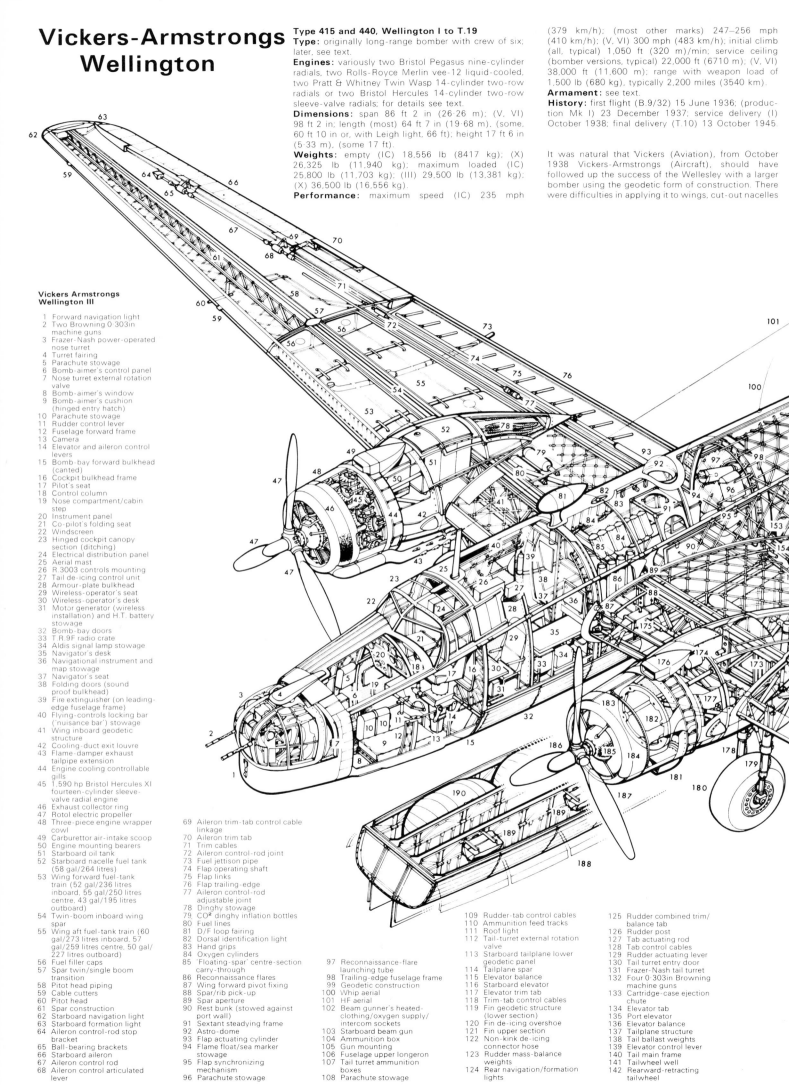

Vickers Armstrongs Wellington III

1 Forward navigation light
2 Two Browning 0·303in machine guns
3 Frazer-Nash power-operated nose turret
4 Turret fairing
5 Parachute stowage
6 Bomb-aimer's control panel
7 Nose turret external rotation valve
8 Bomb-aimer's window
9 Bomb-aimer's cushion (hinged entry hatch)
10 Parachute stowage
11 Rudder control lever
12 Fuselage forward frame
13 Camera
14 Elevator and aileron control levers
15 Bomb-bay forward bulkhead (canted)
16 Cockpit bulkhead frame
17 Pilot's seat
18 Control column
19 Nose compartment/cabin step
20 Instrument panel
21 Co-pilot's folding seat
22 Windscreen
23 Hinged cockpit canopy section (ditching)
24 Electrical distribution panel
25 Aerial mast
26 R.3003 controls mounting
27 Tail de-icing control unit
28 Armour-plate bulkhead
29 Wireless-operator's seat
30 Wireless-operator's desk
31 Motor generator (wireless installation) and H.T. battery stowage
32 Bomb-bay doors
33 T.R.9F radio crate
34 Aldis signal lamp stowage
35 Navigator's desk
36 Navigational instrument and map stowage
37 Navigator's seat
38 Folding doors (sound proof bulkhead)
39 Fire extinguisher (on leading-edge fuselage frame)
40 Flying-controls locking bar ('nuisance bar') stowage
41 Wing inboard geodetic structure
42 Cooling-duct exit louvre
43 Flame-damper exhaust tailpipe extension
44 Engine cooling controllable gills
45 1,590 hp Bristol Hercules XI fourteen-cylinder sleeve-valve radial engine
46 Exhaust collector ring
47 Rotol electric propeller
48 Three-piece engine wrapper cowl
49 Carburettor air-intake scoop
50 Engine mounting bearers
51 Starboard oil tank
52 Starboard nacelle fuel tank (58 gal/264 litres)
53 Wing forward fuel-tank train (52 gal/236 litres inboard, 55 gal/250 litres centre, 43 gal/195 litres outboard)
54 Twin-boom inboard wing spar
55 Wing aft fuel-tank train (60 gal/273 litres inboard, 57 gal/259 litres centre, 50 gal/227 litres outboard)
56 Fuel filler caps
57 Spar twin/single boom transition
58 Pitot head piping
59 Cable cutters
60 Pitot head
61 Spar construction
62 Starboard navigation light
63 Starboard formation light
64 Aileron control-rod stop bracket
65 Ball-bearing brackets
66 Starboard aileron
67 Aileron control rod
68 Aileron control articulated lever
69 Aileron trim-tab control cable linkage
70 Aileron trim tab
71 Trim cables
72 Aileron control-rod joint
73 Fuel jettison pipe
74 Flap operating shaft
75 Flap links
76 Flap trailing-edge
77 Aileron control-rod adjustable joint
78 Dinghy stowage
79 CO² dinghy inflation bottles
80 Fuel lines
81 D/F loop fairing
82 Dorsal identification light
83 Hand grips
84 Oxygen cylinders
85 'Floating-spar' centre-section carry-through
86 Reconnaissance flares
87 Wing forward pivot fixing
88 Spar/rib pick-up
89 Spar aperture
90 Rest bunk (stowed against port wall)
91 Sextant steadying frame
92 Astro-dome
93 Flap actuating cylinder
94 Flame float/sea marker stowage
95 Flap synchronizing mechanism
96 Parachute stowage
97 Reconnaissance-flare launching tube
98 Trailing-edge fuselage frame
99 Geodetic construction
100 Whip aerial
101 HF aerial
102 Beam gunner's heated-clothing/oxygen supply/intercom sockets
103 Starboard beam gun
104 Ammunition box
105 Gun mounting
106 Fuselage upper longeron
107 Tail turret ammunition boxes
108 Parachute stowage
109 Rudder-tab control cables
110 Ammunition feed tracks
111 Roof light
112 Tail-turret external rotation valve
113 Starboard tailplane lower geodetic panel
114 Tailplane spar
115 Elevator balance
116 Starboard elevator
117 Elevator trim tab
118 Trim-tab control cables
119 Fin geodetic structure (lower section)
120 Fin de-icing overshoe
121 Fin upper section
122 Non-kink de-icing connector hose
123 Rudder mass-balance weights
124 Rear navigation/formation lights
125 Rudder combined trim/balance tab
126 Rudder post
127 Tab actuating rod
128 Tab control cables
129 Rudder actuating lever
130 Tail turret entry door
131 Frazer-Nash tail turret
132 Four 0·303in Browning machine guns
133 Cartridge-case ejection chute
134 Elevator tab
135 Port elevator
136 Elevator balance
137 Tailplane structure
138 Tail ballast weights
139 Elevator control lever
140 Tail main frame
141 Tailwheel well
142 Rearward-retracting tailwheel

and fuselages with large bomb-doors and turrets, but the B.9/32 prototype was obviously efficient, and by September 1939 had been developed into Britain's most formidable bomber. The following were chief versions:

I Powered by 1,050 hp Pegasus XVIII and originally with twin 0·303 in Brownings in simple Vickers turrets at nose and tail; internal bomb load 4,500 lb (2041 kg).

Built one-a-day at Weybridge, later a further 50 per month at Chester and, later still, about 30 a month at Squire's Gate, Blackpool. Mk IA had Nash and Thompson power turrets, and the main IC version had two beam guns (some earlier had a ventral barbette). Production: 180+183+2,685.

II Had 1,145 hp Merlin X, otherwise as IC. Production: 400.

III Main Bomber Command type in 1941–2, with 1,375 hp Hercules III or XI, and four-gun tail turret. Production: 1,519.

IV Flown by two Polish squadrons, powered by 1,200 hp Twin Wasp R-1830-S3C4-G. Production: 220.

V Experimental pressurised high-altitude, turbocharged Hercules VIII. Three built, converted to VI.

VI Long-span pressurised, with 1,600 hp Merlin R6SM engines, no guns and special equipment. Used by 109 Sqn and as Gee trainers. Production: 63.

VII One only, Merlin engines, tested large 40 mm Vickers S gun turret for P.92 fighter, later with twin fins.

VIII Conversion of IC as Coastal reconnaissance version, with ASV radar arrays, Leigh light in long nose, and two 18 in torpedoes or anti-submarine weapons. Some, huge hoops for detonating magnetic mines.

IX Conversion of IC for special trooping.

X Standard bomber, similar to III but 1,675 hp Hercules VI or XVI. Production: 3,804.

XI Advanced Coastal version of X, no mast aerials but large chin radome, torpedoes, retractable Leigh light.

XII Similar to XI, with Leigh light ventral

XIII Reverted to ASV Mk II with masts, and nose turret.

XIV Final Coastal, ASV.III chin radome, wing rocket rails, Leigh light in bomb bay.

XV, XVI Unarmed Transport Command conversions of IC.

Total production of this outstanding type amounted to 11,461. After World War II hundreds were converted for use as trainers, the main variant being the T.10 which remained in service until 1953. The T.19 was a specialised navigation trainer. The Vickers successor to the Wellington, the bigger Warwick, was inferior to four-engine machines, and was used mainly in Coastal and transport roles.

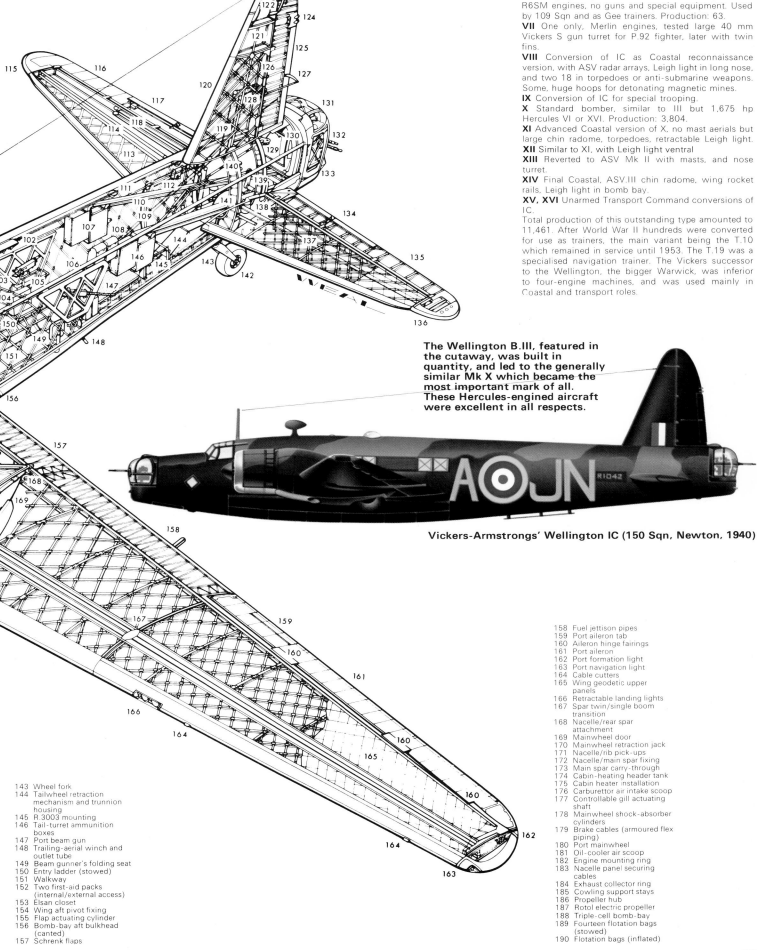

The Wellington B.III, featured in the cutaway, was built in quantity, and led to the generally similar Mk X which became the most important mark of all. These Hercules-engined aircraft were excellent in all respects.

Vickers-Armstrongs' Wellington IC (150 Sqn, Newton, 1940)

143 Wheel fork
144 Tailwheel retraction mechanism and trunnion housing
145 R.3003 mounting
146 Tail-turret ammunition boxes
147 Port beam gun
148 Trailing-aerial winch and outlet tube
149 Beam gunner's folding seat
150 Entry ladder (stowed)
151 Walkway
152 Two first-aid packs (internal/external access)
153 Elsan closet
154 Wing aft pivot fixing
155 Flap actuating cylinder
156 Bomb-bay aft bulkhead (canted)
157 Schrenk flaps
158 Fuel jettison pipes
159 Port aileron tab
160 Aileron hinge fairings
161 Port aileron
162 Port formation light
163 Port navigation light
164 Cable cutters
165 Wing geodetic upper panels
166 Retractable landing lights
167 Spar twin/single boom transition
168 Nacelle/rear spar attachment
169 Mainwheel door
170 Mainwheel retraction jack
171 Nacelle/rib pick-ups
172 Nacelle/main spar fixing
173 Main spar carry-through
174 Cabin-heating header tank
175 Cabin heater installation
176 Carburettor air intake scoop
177 Controllable gill actuating shaft
178 Mainwheel shock-absorber cylinders
179 Brake cables (armoured flex piping)
180 Port mainwheel
181 Oil-cooler air scoop
182 Engine mounting ring
183 Nacelle panel securing cables
184 Exhaust collector ring
185 Cowling support stays
186 Propeller hub
187 Rotol electric propeller
188 Triple-cell bomb-bay
189 Fourteen flotation bags (stowed)
190 Flotation bags (inflated)

Vickers-Armstrongs Valiant

Prototype (Type 660), B.1 (706), B(PR).1 (710), B(PR)K.1 (733) and B(K).1 (758).
Type: B.1, strategic bomber with crew of five; others, see text.
Engines: four 10,050 lb (4559 kg) thrust Rolls-Royce Avon 204 or 205 single-shaft turbojets.
Dimensions: span 114 ft 4 in (34·85 m); length (basic) 108 ft 3 in (33 m), (with FR probe) 116 ft 1 in or 111 ft 5 in; height 32 ft 2 in (9·8 m).
Weights: (B.1) empty 75,881 lb (34,419 kg); loaded 140,000 lb (63,500 lb); maximum loaded (drop tanks) 175,000 lb (79,378 kg).
Performance: maximum speed (sea level) 414 mph (666 km/h), (high altitude) 567 mph (912 km/h, Mach 0·857) clean, 554 mph (892 km/h, Mach 0·84) with tanks; initial climb 4,000 ft (1220 m)/min; service ceiling 54,000 ft (16,460 m); range (clean, dropping 10,000 lb, 4536 kg, bomb load half-way) 3,450 miles (5552 km); maximum range 4,500 miles (7242 km).
Armament: internal weapon bay for up to 21,000 lb (9525 kg) of nuclear or conventional bombs; no guns.
History: first flight (660) 18 May 1951; (pre-production 674) 22 December 1953; service delivery (706) August 1954; final delivery September 1957.

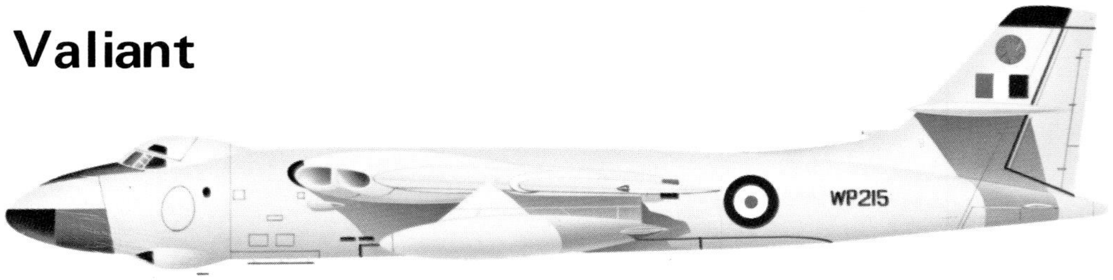

Vickers-Armstrongs Valiant B.1 (18 Sqn)

Though the Vickers 660 did not fully meet the "V-bomber" B.35/46 specification, it appeared so attractive on grounds of faster timing and lower risk than the more radical Vulcan and Victor that it was ordered to a reduced specification B.9/48. The Weybridge factory, already bursting with Viscount orders, developed this fine bomber swiftly and soon had it in production, the pressure cabin (forming the fuselage between wing and nose radar) being supplied by Saunders-Roe. The engines were buried in the wing roots, and the main gears comprised steel legs in tandem, each carrying one large wheel, retracted outwards into the wing. Almost all accessory services were operated by 112-volt electrics. Most production aircraft were finished in white anti-flash paint and had an extended tailcone housing avionics. Interspersed along the line were 11 B(PR) bomber-reconnaissance and 14 B(PR)K with a flight-refuelling hose-reel. The final 48, bringing the total to 107, were refined BK bomber-tankers with 5,000 gal of transfer fuel. Early Valiants dropped bombs on Egyptian airfields during the Suez campaign in 1956 and conducted all the live trials with British air-dropped nuclear weapons. In 1963 four of the six remaining squadrons were assigned to low-level missions, causing fatigue problems which led to the whole force being scrapped in 1964.

Voisin bombers

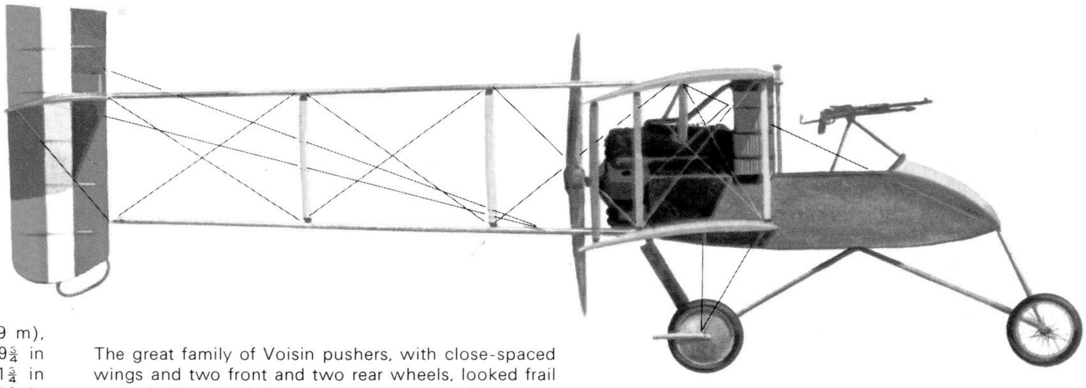

Type I (company designation Type L), III (LA and LAS), IV (LB and LBS), V (LAS), VIII (LAP and LBP) and X (LAR).
Type: most, two-seat bomber (see text).
Engine: (III, IV) one 120 hp Salmson (Canton-Unné) 9M nine-cylinder water-cooled (not air-cooled) radial; (V) 150 hp Canton-Unné 9P; (VIII) 220 hp Peugeot 8Aa vee-8 water-cooled; (X) 300 hp Renault 12Fe vee-12 water-cooled.
Dimensions: span (III, IV, V) 52 ft 4½ in (15·9 m), (some 48 ft 4¾ in, 14·75 m); (VIII, X) 58 ft 9¾ in (17·97 m); length (all) 31 ft 3¼ in to 36 ft 1¾ in (9·53–11·02 m); height (all) 12 ft to 12 ft 11¾ in (3·66–3·95 m).
Weights: empty (V) typically 1,650 lb (750 kg); (VIII) typically 2,645 lb (1200 kg); maximum loaded (V) 2,513–3,240 lb (1140–1470 kg); (VIII) 4,101 lb (1860 kg).
Performance: maximum speed (all) 74–82 mph (120–132 km/h); service ceiling 9,800–11,800 ft (2980–3600 m); range 205–310 miles (330–500 km).
Armament: see text.
History: first flight (I) early 1914; (III) February 1914; (IV) March 1915; (VIII) May 1916; (X) November 1917.

Voisin III (LA) (Aviation Militaire; pointed nose with pilot seated ahead of standing observer)

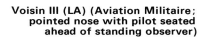

The great family of Voisin pushers, with close-spaced wings and two front and two rear wheels, looked frail and primitive, but in fact were tough and battleworthy. Their structure was mainly of steel, and with progressive development were made in great numbers throughout World War I. The 80 hp Voisin I (Type L) was built before the war for artillery observation, but the observer was soon throwing out light bombs and eventually a bomb load of 132 lb (60 kg) was being carried. The III, of which 2,162 were built by Voisin, REP, Breguet and Nieuport, served with the Aviation Militaire and with Belgium and Russia, while 112 were built in Italy. Most had a 7·7 mm Hotchkiss machine gun in the front cockpit and on 5 October 1914 one shot down the first enemy aircraft ever to fall in combat. Many were made in Britain, some being of the LAS type with higher, tilted engine. The IV often had a 47 mm cannon in the front cockpit. The VIII, of which 1,123 were built, had long-span wings with streamlined fuel tanks on the interplane struts. The powerful X carried 661 lb (300 kg) of bombs; like the VIII it often had a 37 mm cannon. Some versions with dual controls were for reconnaissance or training.

Vought V-166B Corsair

F4U-1 to -7, F3A, FG, F2G and AU.
Type: single-seat carrier-based fighter-bomber (sub-variants, see text).
Engine: (F4U-1) 2,000 hp Pratt & Whitney R-2800-8(B) Double Wasp 18-cylinder two-row radial; (-1A) 2,250 hp R-2800-8(W) with water injection; (-4) 2,450 hp R-2800-18W with water-methanol; (-5) 2,850 hp R-2800-32(E) with water-methanol; (F2G) 3,000 hp P&W R-4360 Wasp Major 28-cylinder four-row radial.
Dimensions: span 40 ft 11¾ in (12·48 m), (British, 39 ft 7 in); length 33 ft 8¼ in (10·27 m); (-1, -3) 33 ft 4 in; (-5N and -7) 34 ft 6 in; height 14 ft 9¼ in (4·49 m); (-1, -2) 16 ft 1 in.
Weights: empty (-1A) 8,873 lb (4025 kg); (-5, typical) 9,900 lb (4490 kg); maximum loaded (-1A) 14,000 lb (6350 kg); (-5) 15,079 lb (6840 kg); (AU-1) 19,398 lb.
Performance: maximum speed (-1A) 395 mph (635 km/h); (-5) 462 mph (744 km/h); initial climb (-1A) 2,890 ft (880 m)/min; (-5) 4,800 ft (1463 m)/min; service ceiling (-1A) 37,000 ft (11,280 m); (-5) 44,000 ft (13,400 m); range on internal fuel, typically 1,000 miles (1609 km).
Armament: see text.
History: first flight (XF4U) 29 May 1940; (production -1) June 1942; combat delivery July 1942; final delivery (-7) December 1952.

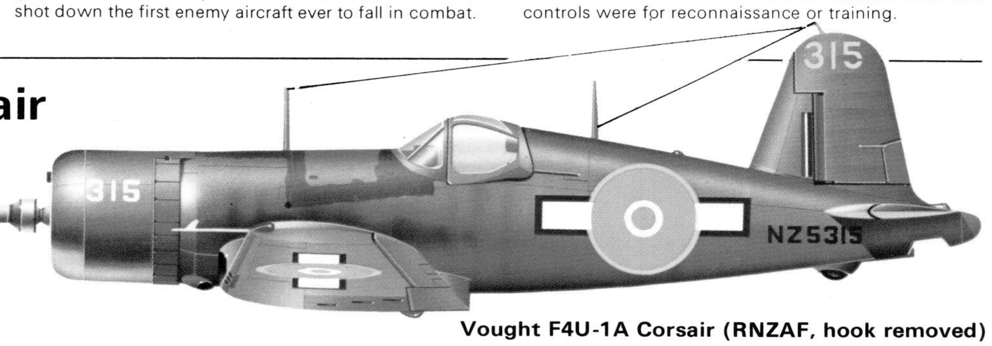

Vought F4U-1A Corsair (RNZAF, hook removed)

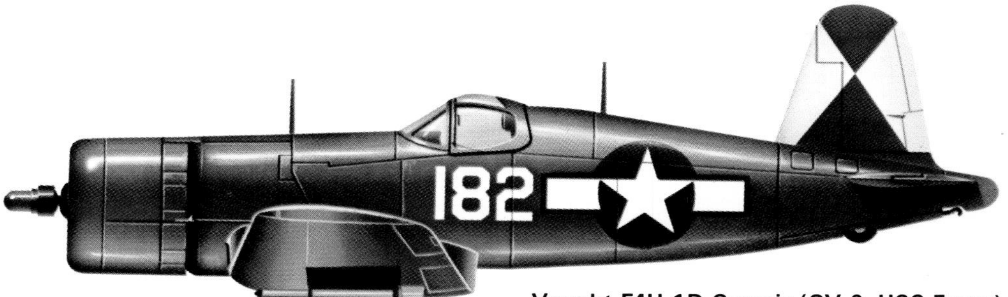

Vought F4U-1D Corsair (CV-9, USS Essex)

Designed by Rex Beisel and Igor Sikorsky, the inverted-gull-wing Corsair was one of the greatest combat aircraft in history. Planned to use the most powerful engine and biggest propeller ever fitted to a fighter, the prototype was the first US warplane to exceed 400 mph and outperformed all other American aircraft. Originally fitted with two fuselage and two wing guns, it was replanned with six 0·5 in Browning MG 53-2 in the folding outer wings, each with about 390 rounds. Action with land-based Marine squadrons began in the Solomons in February 1943; from then on the Corsair swiftly gained air supremacy over the previously untroubled Japanese. The -1C had four 20 mm cannon, and the -1D and most subsequent types carried a 160 gal drop tank and two 1,000 lb (907 kg) bombs or eight rockets. Many hundreds of P versions carried cameras, and N variants had an APS-4 or -6 radar in a wing pod for night interceptions. Brewster made 735 F3A, and Goodyear 4,008 FG versions, but only ten of the fearsome F2G. Fabric-skinned wings became metal in the post-war -5, most of which had cannon, while the 110 AU-1 attack bombers carried a 4,000 lb load in Korea at speeds seldom exceeding 240 mph! In December 1952 the last of 12,571 Corsairs came off the line after a longer production run (in terms of time) than any US fighter prior to the Phantom.

Vought V-346A Cutlass

Chance Vought F7U-1, -3, -3M and -3P
Type: single-seat carrier-based fighter-bomber; (P) reconnaissance.
Engines: (-1) two Westinghouse J34-32 single-shaft turbojets each rated at 4,200 lb (1905 kg) with Solar afterburner; (-3) two Westinghouse J46-8B each rated at 6,000 lb (2722 kg) with afterburner.
Dimensions: span 38 ft 8 in (11·78 m); length (-1) 39 ft 7 in; (-3, -3M) 44 ft 3 in (13·48 m); (-3P) 46 ft 4 in; height (-1) 9 ft 10 in; (-3) 14 ft 7 in.
Weights: empty (-1) 11,870 lb (5385 kg); (-3M) 15,900 lb (7212 kg); maximum loaded (-1) 16,840 lb (7640 kg); (-3M) 31,642 lb; (-3M) 32,954 lb (16,950 kg).
Performance: maximum speed (-1) 665 mph (1070 km/h); (-3M) clean 695 mph (1120 km/h), with missiles 648 mph (1043 km/h); initial climb (-1) 11,280 ft/min; (-3, clean) 17,600 ft (5380 m)/min; service ceiling (all) about 41,000 ft (12,500 m); range with maximum fuel (-1) 600 miles (966 km); (-3M, -3P) 1,400 miles (2250 km).
Armament: (-1) four 20 mm M-2 cannon under cockpit floor; (-3) four 20 mm M-2 above inlet ducts, plus four wing pylons for up to 5,500 lb (2495 kg) weapons; (-3M) as -3 but equipped to carry up to four Sparrow I air-to-air missiles; (-3P) none.

Vought F7U-3M Cutlass (VA-116, USS Hancock)

History: first flight (XF7U-1) 29 September 1948; (production -1) March 1950; (prototype -3) 12 December 1951; combat delivery (-3) June 1954.

Designed in 1946, when fighter aerodynamics were in turmoil, the unique Cutlass had a 38° swept wing carrying powered elevons and twin vertical tails. After building three prototypes and 14 production F7U-1 day fighters the whole aircraft was redesigned with more powerful engines. Westinghouse suffered severe engine problems and the first 16 F7U-3 had non-afterburning Allison J35-29 engines. Finally, by December 1955, Vought delivered 288 of the far more capable -3 series which equipped 13 Navy and Marine squadrons ashore and afloat. The last 98 were missile-armed -3M. Despite a poor accident record and excessive maintenance needs, the Cutlass was popular, being unbreakable in 16 g manoeuvres, exciting to fly and an excellent aerobatic machine. But the programme was stopped sharply once the Crusader flew.

Vought Crusader

Vought (LTV) F-8E(FN) Crusader (Flotte 12F, Aéronavale, with R530 missiles)

LTV Aerospace F-8A to F-8J, RF-8, DF-8 and QF-8
Type: originally single-seat carrier-based day fighter (see text).
Engine: one Pratt & Whitney J57 two-shaft turbojet with afterburner; (A, B, F, L) 16,200 lb (7327 kg) J57-12; (C, K) 16,900 lb (7665 kg) J57-16; others, 18,000 lb (8165 kg) J57-20A. About 100 F-8J re-engined with P&W TF30-420 afterburning turbofan, rated 19,600 lb.
Dimensions: span 35 ft 8 in (10·87 m); (E, J) 35 ft 2in; length 54 ft 3 in (16·54 m); (E, J) 54 ft 6 in; height 15 ft 9 in (4·80 m).
Weights: empty (C) about 17,000 lb (7710 kg); (J) 19,700 lb (8935 kg); maximum loaded (C) 27,550 lb (12,500 kg); (J) 34,000 lb (15,420 kg).
Performance: maximum speed, clean, at altitude (A, B, L. H) 1,013 mph; (RF-8A) 982 mph; (RF-8G) 1,002 mph; (C, K, J) 1,105 mph (1780 km/h, Mach 1·68); (E) 1,135 mph; (D) 1,230 mph; initial climb (typical) 21,000 ft (6400 m)/min; service ceiling, from 38,400 ft for J to 42,900 ft (13,100 m) for D; combat radius, from 368 miles for C, K to 440 miles (708 km) for J and 455 miles (732 km) for D.
Armament: (A, B, C) four 20 mm Colt Mk 12 cannon each with 84 rounds; one Sidewinder on each side and 32 folding-fin rockets in belly pack; (D) four 20 mm plus four Sidewinder; (E, H, J) four 20 mm plus four Sidewinder plus 12 Mk 81 bombs, or two Bullpups or eight Zuni rockets; (K, L) as J but 144 rounds per gun; RF versions, none.
History: first flight (XF8U-1) 25 March 1955; (production F-8A) November 1956; service delivery 25 March 1957; final delivery 1965.
This outstanding carrier-based fighter, notable for its variable-incidence wing, outperformed the F-100 on the same engine, besides having 1,165 gal internal fuel! Exceeding Mach 1 on the level on the first flight the F8U (as it then was) was rapidly developed for carrier service, and for 12 years was a popular combat aircraft of the US Navy and Marines. Altogether 1,259 were built, plus two prototypes, and in 1966–71 446 were rebuilt to a later standard (B to L, C to K, E to J and D to H). The continual process of improvement added all-weather radar, improved autopilot and weapon-delivery systems, air/ground weapons and, in the 42 F-8E(FN) for the French Navy, slower approach for small carriers. Variants include RF reconnaissance, DF drone RPV and QF RPV-control aircraft; a single dual trainer was also built. Many rebuilt versions remain in combat service, with long life ahead; total Crusader flight time exceeds 3,000,000 hr.

Vought Corsair II

LTV Aerospace A-7A to E and TA-7C
Type: single-seat attack bomber (carrier- or land-based); (TA) dual trainer.
Engine: (A) one 11,350 lb (5150 kg) thrust Pratt & Whitney TF30-6 two-shaft turbofan; (B, C) 12,200 lb (5534 kg) TF30-8; (D) 14,250 lb (6465 kg) Allison TF41-1 (Rolls-Royce Spey derivative) of same layout; (E) 15,000 lb (6804 kg) TF41-2.
Dimensions: span 38 ft 9 in (11·80 m); length 46 ft 1½ in (14·06 m); (TA) 48 ft 2 in (14·68 m); height 16 ft 0¾ in (4·90 m); (TA) 16 ft 5 in (5 m).
Weights: empty (A) 15,904 lb (7214 kg); (D) 19,781 lb (8972 kg); maximum loaded (A) 32,500 lb (14,750 kg); (D) 42,000 lb (19,050 kg).
Performance: maximum speed (all single-seat versions, clean) 698 mph (1123 km/h) at low level; climb and ceiling, not reported (seldom relevant); tactical radius with weapon load, typically 715 miles (1150 km); ferry range with four external tanks, typically 4,100 miles (6600 km).
Armament: (A, B) two 20 mm Colt Mk 12 in nose; six wing and two fuselage pylons for weapon load of 15,000 lb (6804 kg); (D, E) one 20 mm M61 Vulcan cannon on left side of fuselage with 1,000-round drum; external load up to theoretical 20,000 lb (9072 kg).
History: first flight 27 September 1965; service delivery October 1966; first flight of D, 26 September 1968.

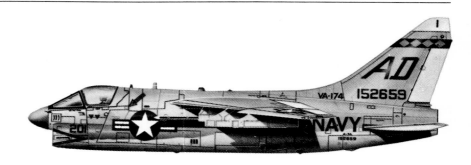

Vought (LTV) A-7A Corsair II (VA-174)

Though derived from the Crusader, the Corsair II is a totally different aircraft. By restricting performance to high subsonic speed, structure weight was reduced, range dramatically increased and weapon load multiplied by about 4. Development was outstandingly quick, as was production. Vought built 199 A-7A, used in action in the Gulf of Tonkin on 3 December 1967, followed by 196 B models. The C designation was used for the first 67 E models which retained the TF30 engine. In 1966 the Corsair II was adopted by the US Air Force, the A-7D having the superior TF41 engine, Gatling gun and more complete avionics for blind or automatic weapon delivery under all conditions, with head-up display and inertial/doppler navigation. By late 1975 over 380 had been delivered, with reduced production continuing. The Navy adopted the same model, with an even more powerful TF41, and by late 1975 about 490 E models had been built, bringing output to well over 1,250 within a decade. Vought funded development of a tandem-seat YA-7H, and later converted 40 B and C into the dual TA-7C. Greece is reviewing 60A-7H, costing $259·2 million.

Vultee 72 Vengeance

A-31 and -35, Vengeance I-IV
Type: two-seat dive bomber.
Engine: one Wright R-2600 Cyclone 14-cylinder two-row radial: (A-31, Vengeance I, II, III) 1,600 hp R-2600-19; (A-35, V. IV) 1,700 hp R-2600-13.
Dimensions: span 48 ft (14·63 m); length 39 ft 9 in (12·12 m); height 14 ft 6 in (4·40 m).
Weights: empty (typical) 9,900 lb (4490 kg); maximum loaded (A-31) 14,300 lb (6486 kg); (A-35) 15,600 lb; (A-35B) 17,100 lb (7756 kg).
Performance: maximum speed (all) 273–279 mph (440–450 km/h); initial climb, typically 1,200 ft (366 m)/min; service ceiling (typical) 22,000 ft (6700 m); range (typical) 600 miles (966 km).
Armament: (A-31, Vengeance I to III) four 0·303 in Brownings in wings and two manually aimed from rear cockpit; internal bomb load of up to 2,000 lb (907 kg); (A-35A, Vengeance IV) four 0·50 in in wings, one manually aimed from rear, same bomb load; (A-35B) same but six 0·50 in in wings.
History: first flight, July 1941; service delivery (RAF) November 1942; termination of production, September 1944.

Vultee Vengeance IV (7 Sqn, Indian AF, Arakan area)

Designed by a team led by Richard Palmer to a British specification passed to Vultee in July 1940, the Vengeance eventually became combat-ready in a different world. No longer was the dive bomber the unstoppable agent of destruction; by 1943 it was recognised to have value only in conditions of local air superiority, and even then to need fighter cover. Eventually 1,528 of all types were built, of which 1,205 were passed to the RAF (some purchased in 1940, others on Lend-Lease). Many served with the RAF,

RAAF and Indian AF in Burma and South East Asia, where they at least saw considerable active duty. In 1940 it had been thought vast numbers would be needed, and a second production line was opened at Northrop, while the US Army adopted the type as the A-31. In 1942 the Americanised A-35 was in production at Convair's Nashville plant, but the US Army soon dropped even this version. Many RAF aircraft were modified as target tugs, and the last batch went to Brazil.

Waco CG-4A

CG-4A Haig; RAF name Hadrian
Type: assault glider.
Engine: none.
Dimensions: span 83 ft 8 in (25·5 m); length 48 ft 3¾ in (14·7 m); height 12 ft 7½ in (3·84 m).
Weights: empty 3,790 lb (1721 kg); normal loaded 7,500 lb (3405 kg); overload 9,000 lb (4086 kg).
Performance: normal towing speed 125 mph (200 km/h); typical speed off tow 65 mph (105 km/h); minimum speed 38 mph (61 km/h).
Armament: none.
History: first flight, early 1941; (production CG-4A) April 1941; final delivery, December 1944.

Though the vast US aircraft industry produced many types of military glider during World War II, the entire production effort was concentrated upon this one type, which was the only US glider to see combat service. In sharp contrast to Britain's larger, all-wood Horsa, the CG-4A fuselage was constructed of welded steel tube with fabric covering, the entire nose being arranged to hinge upwards for loading/unloading vehicles up to Jeep size, or light artillery. The side-by-side pilot stations hinged with the nose, the two control wheels being suspended from the roof. In the main fuselage were benches for up to 15 fully armed troops or cargo up to 3,710 lb (5,210 lb as overload). The wing loading was very low; there were no flaps, but spoilers above the wing to steepen the glide. No fewer than 15 companies collaborated to build the

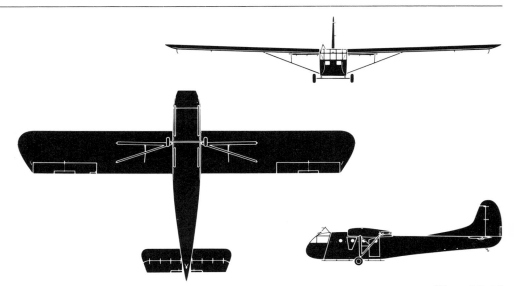

Waco CG-4A (typical; wheels jettisoned on operational mission)

CG-4A, and in two years more than 12,393 were delivered. In 1943 an RAF Hadrian was towed in stages from Montreal to Britain in a flight time of 28 hours. A few weeks later hundreds were used in the invasion

of Sicily. Several thousand were used in 1944 in Normandy and the Rhine crossing, while large numbers went to the Far East for the planned invasion of Japan.

Westland Wapiti

Wapiti I, II, IIA and sub-types
Type: two-seat general purpose.
Engine: one Bristol Jupiter nine-cylinder radial: (I) 420 hp Jupiter VI; (II) 460 hp Jupiter VI; (IIA, V and most later) 480 hp Jupiter VIII or VIIIF or 550 hp IXF or XFa. Some aircraft, 450 hp AS Jaguar IVS or 525 hp AS Panther IIA.
Dimensions: span 46 ft 5 in (14·14 m); length (short) 32 ft 6 in (9·90 m), (long) 34 ft 2 in (10·40 m); (seaplane, 33 ft 11 in); height 11 ft 10 in (3·60 m).
Weights: empty (typical IIA) 3,280 lb (1487 kg); maximum loaded 5,400 lb (2449 kg).
Performance: maximum speed (IIA) 140 mph (225 km/h); initial climb 1,140 ft (350 m)/min; service ceiling 20,600 ft (6280 m); range 360 miles (580 km).
Armament: one 0·303 in Vickers externally on left side, synchronised, and one 0·303 in Lewis manually aimed from rear cockpit; maximum bomb load 580 lb (263 kg) (two 250 lb plus four 20 lb) under wings and fuselage.
History: first flight, early 1927 (no record of date); service delivery August 1928; final delivery August 1932.

Westland Wapiti IIA (28 Sqn in India)

During World War I the Westland Aircraft Works at Yeovil (Petters Ltd) delivered 390 D.H.9A bombers, and over the next ten years gained its main income from reconditioning them for arduous service with the RAF overseas. The British government gradually came to understand that the aeroplane was a vital instrument in both administering and policing a far-flung empire, and in 1926 the Air Ministry issued a specification for a D.H.9A replacement, carrying a bigger load with better reliability but using as many "nine-ack" parts as possible. The winner of the competition was the

Wapiti, one of the most hard-used and well-loved aircraft to serve any air force. It also brought prosperity to Yeovil, for 512 were built for the RAF and well over 500 more for other customers, and many more were built in South Africa. The Mk II changed to metal structure, the army co-op version had a long fuselage, message hook, brakes and tailwheel, and there were Arctic, Long-Range, float and ski versions, target-tugs and dual trainers. About 80 survived in India well into World War II.

Westland Lysander

Lysander I, II, III and IIIA versions
Type: two-seat army co-operation; later, see text.
Engine: one Bristol nine-cylinder radial: (I) 890 hp Mercury XII; (II) 905 hp Perseus XII sleeve-valve; (III) 870 hp Mercury XX or XXX.
Dimensions: span 50 ft (15·24 m); length 30 ft 6 in (9·29 m); height 11 ft 6 in (3·50 m).
Weights: empty (typical I) 4,044 lb (1834 kg); normal loaded (I) 5,833 lb (2645 kg); maximum loaded (I) 7,500 lb (3402 kg); (IIISCW) 10,000 lb (4536 kg).
Performance: maximum speed (I, II) 237 mph (381 km/h); (IIISCW) 190 mph (306 km/h); initial climb (I) 1,900 ft (580 m)/min; service ceiling (I) 26,000 ft (7925 m); range (I) 600 miles (966 km); (IIISCW) 1,400 miles (2253 km).
Armament: when fitted, one 0·303 in Browning, with 500 rounds, above each wheel spat (outside propeller disc) and one 0·303 in Lewis or Vickers GO manually aimed from rear cockpit (IIIA, twin 0·303 in Browning in rear cockpit); bomb load up to two 250 lb (113 kg) on stub wings, or 16 20 lb (9 kg), four on fuselage carrier.
History: first flight 15 June 1936; service delivery June 1938; final delivery (Westland) January 1942, (Canada) late 1942.

One of the most distinctive military aircraft, the STOL Lysander was designed to A.39/34 as an army co-operation machine. When 16 Sqn at Old Sarum received the type in 1938 it practised sedate picking up

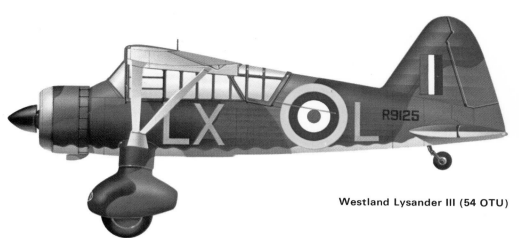

Westland Lysander III (54 OTU)

of messages and spotting for artillery. When war came, however, the well-liked "Lizzie" blossomed forth as a remarkable multi-role aircraft. The first He 111 to be shot down in BEF territory (in November 1939) fell to a Lysander's modest armament, and in June 1940 some served as night fighters whilst others spent their time in fierce ground attack on the German army and making precision supply-drops to the defenders of Calais. During the rest of the war Lysanders served as target tugs, overseas close support, air/sea rescue and,

memorably, in IIISCW form for dropping agents in Europe and recovering special passengers for Britain. The heavily loaded SCW had a belly tank, much special gear and a vital ladder to give access to the lofty cockpit. Production by Westland was 1,425, some of which were grotesque experimental versions; 325 more were built at Malton, Toronto, by National Steel Car. In 1974, after years of work, a Californian restored one to flying condition.

Westland P.9 Whirlwind

Westland Whirlwind I (263 Sqn, Exeter)

Whirlwind I, IA
Type: single-seat day fighter (later fighter-bomber).
Engines: two 885 hp Rolls-Royce Peregrine I vee-12 liquid-cooled.
Dimensions: span 45 ft (13·72 m); length 32 ft 9 in (9·98 m); height 11 ft 7 in (3·52 m).
Weights: empty (I) 7,840 lb (3699 kg); (IA) 8,310 lb (3770 kg); maximum loaded 10,270 lb (4658 kg); (IA) 11,388 lb (5166 kg).
Performance: maximum speed (clean) 360 mph (580 km/h), (with bombs) 270 mph (435 km/h); initial climb (clean) 3,000 ft (915 m)/min; service ceiling (clean) 30,000 ft (9144 m); range, not recorded but about 800 miles (1290 km).
Armament: standard, four 20 mm Hispano Mk I cannon in nose, each with 60-round drum; IA added underwing racks for bomb load up to 1,000 lb (454 kg).

History: first flight 11 October 1938; service delivery June 1940; final delivery December 1941.

At the outbreak of World War II the gravest deficiency of the RAF was in the field of twin-engined high-performance machines for use as long-range escort or night fighters. This was precisely the mission of the Whirlwind, designed to a specification as early as F.37/35. It was a fine and pleasant machine, and in its slender nose was an unprecedented punch. Yet its development was delayed by engine troubles, the

Peregrine being an unhappy outgrowth of the reliable Kestrel; another trouble was that, despite Fowler flaps, the landing speed was 80 mph which was incompatible with short grass fields. Eventually only 263 and 137 Sqns used the type, which in combat showed much promise. In August 1941 No 263 escorted Blenheims to Cologne in daylight! Only 112 were built, ending their days as "Whirlibombers" on cross-Channel "Rhubarb" sorties straffing and bombing targets of opportunity.

Westland W.35 Wyvern

Wyvern TF.2, T.3 and S.4
Type: single-seat carrier-based attack.
Engine: one 4,110 ehp Armstrong Siddeley Python 101 (ASP.3) single-shaft turboprop.
Dimensions: span 44 ft (13·41 m); length 42 ft 3 in (12·88 m); height 15 ft 9 in (4·80 m).
Weights: (S.4) empty 15,608 lb (7080 kg); maximum loaded 24,500 lb (11,115 kg).
Performance: (S.4) maximum speed (clean, low level) 383 mph (620 km/h), (about 440 mph at height); initial climb 7,000 ft (2135 m)/min; service ceiling 28,000 ft (8535 m); range with external weapons 900 miles (1450 km).
Armament: four 20 mm Hispano Mk 5 cannon, two in inner wing and two in folding outer wings; centreline attachment rated at 2,000 lb (907 kg) for torpedo, bombs, mines or depth charges, and underwing launchers for 16 60 lb (27 kg) rockets.
History: first flight (first prototype) 12 December 1946; (Clyde) 18 January 1949; (Python) 22 March 1949; service delivery May 1953.

Though it looked like an ordinary propeller-driven fighter, the Wyvern was heavier than most DC-3s and more than twice as powerful. John Digby's team designed it to meet N.11/44, a difficult Royal Navy specification for a day fighter carrying a torpedo. There followed five years of agonizing work using the 3,500 hp Rolls-Royce Eagle sleeve-valve driving large

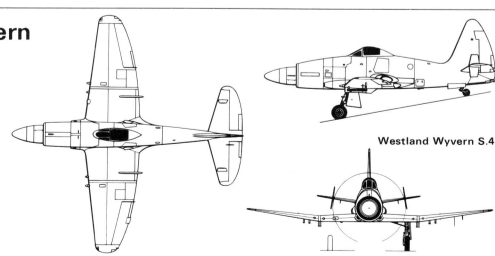

Westland Wyvern S.4

contra-rotating propellers, after which the "fighter" role had vanished and the turboprop become more attractive than the piston engine. In 1949 prototypes flew with Clyde and Python engines, and the latter — the final fruit of work begun by Griffith at Farnborough in 1925! — adopted for production. After more troubled and dangerous development the TF.2 went into production in 1950 and, when fitted with cut-back cowling, auxiliary fins, new aileron tabs and new

canopy, these became the S.4 which equipped four Fleet Air Arm squadrons. Altogether 107 production Wyverns were built, plus 15 with the aircraft carrier Eagle and a single dual T.3 which was a very enjoyable aircraft to handle but did not reach the Navy. Severe propeller-control problems and the fact the whole aircraft was breaking new ground greatly delayed this big and effective machine.

Westland Sea King and Commando

Sea King HAS.1 and Mks 41-50; Commando 1 and 2.

Type: (Sea King) either anti-submarine or search/rescue transport helicopter; (Commando) tactical helicopter for land warfare.

Engines: two Rolls-Royce Gnome (derived from GE T58) free-turbine turboshaft: past production, mostly 1,500 shp Gnome H.1400; current, 1,590 shp H.1400-1; future, 1,795 shp H.1400-3.

Dimensions: diameter of five-blade main rotor 62 ft (18·9 m); length overall (rotors turning) 72 ft 8 in (22·15 m); length of fuselage 55 ft 10 in (17·02 m); height (rotors turning) 16 ft 10 in (5·13 m).

Weights: empty (Sea King ASW) 15,474 lb (7019 kg); (Commando) 12,222 lb (5543 kg); maximum loaded (H.1400-1 engines) 21,000 lb (9525 kg).

Performance: maximum speed 143 mph (230 km/h); typical cruising speed 131 mph (211 km/h); maximum (not vertical) rate of climb (ASW) 1,770 ft (540 m)/min; (Commando) 2,020 ft (616 m)/min; approved ceiling 10,000 ft (3048 m); range (maximum load) about 350 miles (563 km), (maximum fuel) 937 miles (1507 km).

Armament: see text.

History: derived from Sikorsky S-61 (p. 198); first flight of Sea King 7 May 1969; (Commando) September 1973.

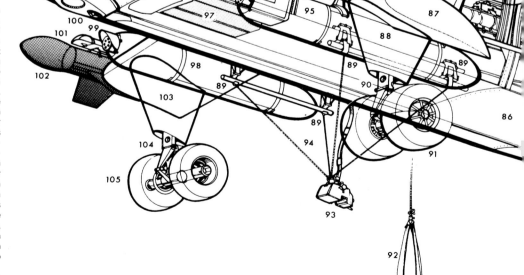

Sikorsky's S-61 was almost inevitably the subject of a licence agreement between that company and Westland Aircraft, continuing an association begun in 1947 when a licence was purchased to make the S-51. In the case of the S-61 the most immediate significant customer was the Royal Navy, which was searching for an ASW (anti-submarine warfare) helicopter to supplement and eventually replace the Wessex in operation from surface ships. Unlike the US Navy, which chose to regard its ASW helicopters as mere extensions of the all-important ship, the Fleet Air Arm concluded it would be preferable to allow the helicopter to operate independently. The Sea King HAS.1 was thus designed to carry sensors, weapons and a complete tactical centre to hunt down and destroy submerged submarines. The normal equipment for Sea Kings in the ASW role includes dunking sonar, doppler navigator, search radar and an autopilot and weapon system providing for automatic hovering at given heights or for a range of other automatic manoeuvres in all weather. The RN bought 56, with 13 more ordered in 1975; total Sea King sales are close to 150, many of them being for the much simpler SAR (search and rescue) version with seats for up to 22, apart from the crew, and special provision for casualties, cargo and slung loads.

Likely to find as large a market during the coming decade, the Commando is a purely land-based aircraft with fixed landing gear devoid of floats. It has been optimised to the range/payload needs of tactical operations, and carries much special equipment for use in a wide range of roles. The basic Commando provides accommodation for up to 28 troops in the transport role, or equivalent cargo payload (or 8,000 lb, 3630 kg, slung externally). Other roles include logistic support, casualty evacuation, search/rescue or, with any of a wide range of armament fits, air/surface strike. So far no armed Commandos have been ordered (the first sale was a large batch for Egypt, bought by Saudi Arabia in 1973), but various turrets and launchers, manually aimed guns, guided missiles and rocket pods can be fitted. Internal load can include a 105 mm gun or Shorland armoured car.

The cutaway drawing depicts a Commando assault helicopter for overland warfare. Points to note are the simple fixed landing gears, the roomy interior and wide range of external weapon options.

Westland Sea King Mk 41 (MFG.5, West German Marineflieger, Kiel-Holtenau)

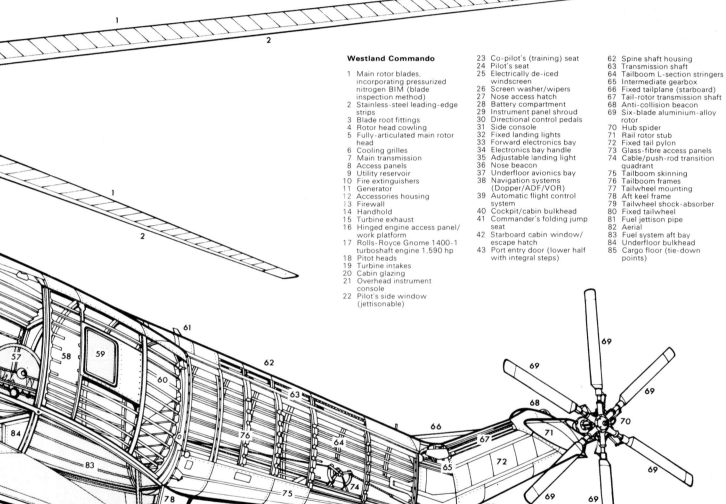

Westland Commando

1 Main rotor blades, incorporating pressurized nitrogen BIM (blade inspection method)
2 Stainless-steel leading-edge strips
3 Blade root fittings
4 Rotor head cowling
5 Fully-articulated main rotor head
6 Cooling grilles
7 Main transmission
8 Access panels
9 Utility reservoir
10 Fire extinguishers
11 Generator
12 Accessories housing
13 Firewall
14 Handhold
15 Turbine exhaust
16 Hinged engine access panel/work platform
17 Rolls-Royce Gnome 1400-1 turboshaft engine 1,590 hp
18 Pitot heads
19 Turbine intakes
20 Cabin glazing
21 Overhead instrument console
22 Pilot's side window (jettisonable)

23 Co-pilot's (training) seat
24 Pilot's seat
25 Electrically de-iced windscreen
26 Screen washer/wipers
27 Nose access hatch
28 Battery compartment
29 Instrument panel shroud
30 Directional control pedals
31 Side console
32 Fixed landing lights
33 Forward electronics bay
34 Electronics bay handle
35 Adjustable landing light
36 Nose beacon
37 Underfloor avionics bay
38 Navigation systems (Dopper/ADF/VOR)
39 Automatic flight control system
40 Cockpit/cabin bulkhead
41 Commander's folding jump seat
42 Starboard cabin window/escape hatch
43 Port entry door (lower half with integral steps)

62 Spine shaft housing
63 Transmission shaft
64 Tailboom L-section stringers
65 Intermediate gearbox
66 Fixed tailplane (starboard)
67 Tail-rotor transmission shaft
68 Anti-collision beacon
69 Six-blade aluminium-alloy rotor
70 Hub spider
71 Rail rotor stub
72 Fixed tail pylon
73 Glass-fibre access panels
74 Cable/push-rod transition quadrant
75 Tailboom skinning
76 Tailboom frames
77 Tailwheel mounting
78 Aft keel frame
79 Tailwheel shock-absorber
80 Fixed tailwheel
81 Fuel jettison pipe
82 Aerial
83 Fuel system aft bay
84 Underfloor bulkhead
85 Cargo floor (tie-down points)

44 Port entry door (upper half)
45 Engine/cabin firewall bulkhead
46 Strut/fuselage attachment fairing
47 Foothold
48 Door rail (starboard)
49 Fixed strut (emergency energy-absorbing)
50 Fuselage frame
51 Fuselage structure
52 Starboard sliding cargo door
53 Port missile shoe (optional)
54 Port cabin window/escape hatch
55 Door-mounted machine-gun (starboard)
56 Inflatable rubberized nylon troop seats (26)
57 Auxiliary internal fuel tanks
58 Fuselage stringers
59 Aft fixed window
60 Aft cabin bulkhead
61 UHF aerial

86 Ventral skinning
87 Undercarriage fixed sponson
88 Mainwheel leg fairing
89 Cargo sling frame
90 Mainwheel shock-absorbers
91 Port twin mainwheels
92 Personnel rescue hoist (winch above starboard cargo door)
93 Cargo sling
94 Sling wires
95 Port Minigun pod
96 Multi-barrel muzzle shroud
97 Fuel-system forward bay
98 Starboard gun pod
99 Muzzle shroud
100 Anti-collision beacon
101 Missile shoe
102 Starboard ASM (optional provision)
103 Starboard mainwheel leg fairing
104 Oleo shock absorbers
105 Starboard mainwheels

Westland Scout and Wasp

Scout AH.1 and Wasp HAS.1
Type: (S) multi-role tactical helicopter; (W) general utility and ASW helicopter for use from small surface vessels.
Engine: (S) one 685 shp Rolls-Royce Nimbus 102 free-turbine turbo shaft; (W) 710 shp Nimbus 503 (both engines flat-rated from thermodynamic output of 968 shp).
Dimensions: diameter of four-blade main rotor 32 ft 3 in (9·83 m); length overall (rotors turning) 40 ft 4 in (12·29 m); length of fuselage 30 ft 4 in (9·24 m); height (rotors turning) 11 ft 8 in (3·56 m).
Weights: empty (S) 3,232 lb (1465 kg); (W) 3,452 lb (1566 kg); maximum loaded (S) 5,300 lb (2405 kg); (W) 5,500 lb (2495 kg).
Performance: maximum speed at sea level (S) 131 mph (211 km/h); (W) 120 mph (193 km/h); maximum (not vertical) rate of climb (S) 1,670 ft (510 m)/min; (W) 1,440 ft (439 m)/min; practical manoeuvre ceiling (S) 13,400 ft (4085 m); (W) 12,200 ft (3720 m); range with four passengers and reserves (S) 315 miles (510 km); (W) 270 miles (435 km).
Armament: (S) various options including manually aimed guns of up to 20 mm calibre, fixed GPMG installations, rocket pods or guided missiles such as SS.11; (W) normally, two Mk 44 torpedoes.
History: first flight (P.531) 20 July 1958; (pre-production Scout) 4 August 1960; (production, powered-control AH.1) 6 March 1961; (Wasp HAS.1) 28 October 1962; final delivery (Wasp) 1974.

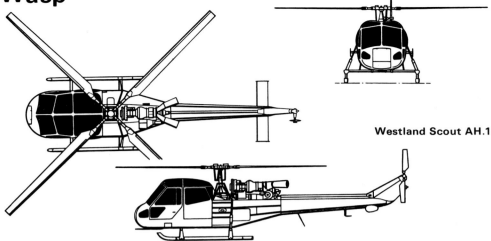

Westland Scout AH.1

Designed and originally developed by Saunders-Roe at Eastleigh, these neat helicopters were transferred to Hayes (the former Fairey works) on the merger with Westland and finally all helicopter work was concentrated at Yeovil. Westland built over 100 Scouts for the Army Air Corps, which has used them for every tactical purpose except heavy transport; small numbers were exported to overseas air forces, police, and even the Royal Australian Navy. The more specialised Wasp is used for liaison, ice reconnaissance, search/rescue and many other duties, but its basic task is ASW strike, operating from small destroyer or frigate platforms. Again well over 100 Wasps were built, and about 40 were exported to South Africa, the Netherlands, Brazil and New Zealand.

Westland WS-58 Wessex

Wessex HAS.1, HC.2, HAS.3, CC.4, HU.5 and civil/export versions.
Type: multi-role helicopter (see text).
Engine(s): (1) one 1,450 shp Rolls-Royce (Napier) Gazelle 161 free-turbine turboshaft; (2) Rolls-Royce Coupled Gnome 101/111 with two 1,350 shp power sections; (3) one 1,600 shp flat-rated Gazelle 165; (others) as Mk 2 except HAS.31 has 1,540 shp Gazelle 162.
Dimensions: diameter of four-blade main rotor 56 ft (17·07 m); length overall, (rotors turning) 65 ft 9 in (20·03 m); length of fuselage (2) 48 ft 4½ in (14·74 m); height overall 16 ft 2 in (4·93 m).
Weights: empty (1) 7,600 lb (3447 kg); (5) 8,657 lb (3927 kg); maximum loaded (1) 12,600 lb (5715 kg); (2, 5, 31) 13,500 lb (6120 kg).
Performance: maximum speed 133 mph (214 km/h); cruising speed 121 mph (195 km/h); maximum (not vertical) rate of climb (2) 1,650 ft (503 m)/min; service ceiling 10,000–14,000 ft (3048–4300 m); range with standard fuel (1) 390 miles (630 km).
Armament: see text.
History: first flight (rebuilt S-58) 17 May 1957; service delivery (HAS.1) April 1960; final delivery (civil) 1970.

In 1956 the Royal Navy dropped its plan to buy the twin-Gazelle Bristol 191 and opted for a cheaper and less risky solution with a Sikorsky S-58 (US Navy HSS-1) using a single Gazelle. Development was fast, and about 150 anti-submarine versions were used by the Fleet Air Arm, the HAS.1 being supplanted by the refined HAS.3, called "Camel" because of its hump-backed radome. The RAF bought a version with Coupled Gnome engines, over 100 HC.2 utility versions

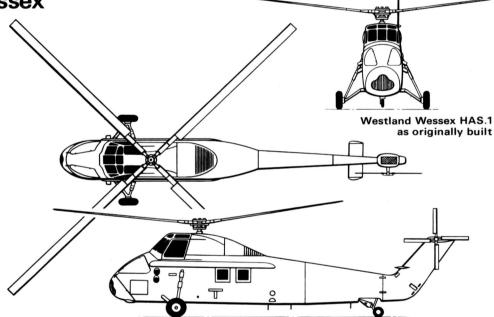

Westland Wessex HAS.1 as originally built

being followed by almost 100 HU.5 Commando assault machines. Two CC.4 VIP transport serve the Queen's Flight. HMAS *Melbourne* is main base afloat for 27 HAS.31 of the RAN which, like those in British service, have undergone progressive updating since 1965. Other military Wessex were supplied to Iraq, Ghana and Brunei. Many weapon fits have flown, the HAS marks carrying one or two homing torpedoes and all having capability to mount guns or a wide range of missiles and rockets.

Westland/Aérospatiale WG.13 Lynx

Lynx AH.1, HAS.2 and 2(FN), HT.3 and projects
Type: multi-role helicopter (see text).
Engines: two 900 shp Rolls-Royce Gem 10001 three-shaft turbines.
Dimensions: diameter of four-blade main rotor 42 ft (12·80 m); length overall (rotors turning) 49 ft 9 in (15·16 m); height overall (rotors turning) 12 ft (3·66 m).
Weights: empty weight (basic) 5,225 lb (2370 kg); empty (equipped for troop transport) 5,641 lb (2558 kg), (anti-tank) 6,313 lb (2863 kg), (dunking sonar search/strike) 7,218 lb (3274 kg); maximum loaded (army) 9,250 lb (4196 kg), (navy) 9,500 lb (4309 kg).
Performance: maximum speed 207 mph (333 km/h); continuous cruise 176 mph (284 km/h); single-engine cruise 164 mph (263 km/h); maximum (not vertical) rate of climb 2,370 ft (722 m)/min; ceiling, well over 25,000 ft (7600 m); range (army) 473 miles (761 km), (navy) 418 miles (673 km); ferry range with cabin tank 861 miles (1386 km).

Armament: see text.
History: first flight 21 March 1971; (HAS.2) 25 May 1972; service delivery (Royal Navy) May 1976.
Certain to be manufactured in very large numbers over a period greater than ten years, the Lynx is probably the outstanding example today of a military multi-role helicopter. Its agility is unsurpassed and its avionics and flight system provide for easy one-man operation in bad weather with minimal workload. Designed by Westland but built in 70/30 partnership with Aérospatiale of France, with contributions from certain other nations, the Lynx is sized to carry ten men (13 in civil versions) and has outstanding performance and smoothness, and early in development was looped, rolled at 100°/sec and flown backwards at 80 mph. The AH.1 is tailored to many battlefield duties, can carry almost all available helicopter sight systems, guns and missiles, and is proving a superior

Westland/Aérospatiale Lynx HAS.2

tank-killer. The HAS.2, with the Seaspray radar, performs virtually all shipboard roles including anti-submarine classification/strike, vertical replenishment, air/surface search/strike (using Sea Skua missiles), search/rescue, fire support and other duties. The (FN) for the Aéronavale has different sensors. The HT.3 is an RAF trainer. Contracts by late 1975 included 50 for the British Army, 30 RN, 18 FN, 13 RAF, 250 for Egypt (mainly to be built in that country), nine for Brazil and eight for the Netherlands; several are to be used by Argentina from frigates.

Weiss Manfred WM-21 Solyom

WM-21
Type: two-seat tactical reconnaissance.
Engine: one 870 hp WM (Gnome-Rhône licence) K-14 14-cylinder two-row radial.
Dimensions: span 41 ft 0¼ in (12·50 m); length 30 ft 10 in (9·39 m); height 11 ft (3·35 m).
Weights: empty, not known accurately; maximum loaded 5,180 lb (2350 kg).
Performance: maximum speed 199 mph (320 km/h); initial climb 1,800 ft (550 m)/min; service ceiling 26,250 ft (8000 m); range 420 miles (675 km).
Armament: two 7·9 mm Gebauer machine guns fixed above forward fuselage, single 7·9 mm manually aimed from rear cockpit; light bomb load (up to 551 lb (250 kg) total, carried on racks under fuselage and lower wing.
History: first flight (Budapest 1) 1931; (Budapest 9 prototype) 1936; (WM-21) probably 1937; service delivery 1938.

One of the least-known of the world's military aircraft, the Solyom (Falcon) is also the chief all-Hungarian type to have seen first-line service (though Austria–Hungary had a large and busy aircraft industry in World War I). The basic design was based on that of the Fokker C.VD (p. 83), but via several intermediate prototypes it was greatly altered. The final WM-21 had

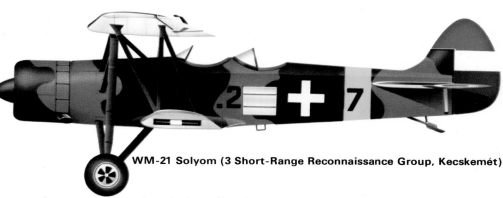

WM-21 Solyom (3 Short-Range Reconnaissance Group, Kecskemét)

a much more powerful engine, mixed wood/metal structure, a strut from each wheel to the upper wing, large windows in the sides of the rear cockpit, a larger rudder and other changes. Total production was 104, built by the Hungarian State Wagon Works at Györ, by the WM factory and by Mavag, the last being delivered

in early 1942. Several Solyom squadrons operated on the Eastern Front in 1941–43, including the example illustrated. Though extremely strong and reliable the basic obsolescence of the design resulted in its main use by 1943 being training, front-line liaison and supply, and patrols against partisans.

Yakovlev Yak-1

Ya-26, I-26, Yak-1, Yak-7
Type: single-seat fighter.
Engine: initially, one 1,100 hp VK-105PA (M-105PA) vee-12 liquid-cooled, derived from Hispano-Suiza 12Y; later, 1,260 hp VK-105PF.
Dimensions: span 32 ft 9¾ in (10 m); length 27 ft 9¾ in (8·48 m); height 8 ft 8 in (2·64 m).
Weights: empty (early I-26) 5,137 lb (2375 kg); maximum loaded 6,217 lb (2890 kg).
Performance: maximum speed 373 mph (600 km/h), 310 mph (500 km/h) at sea level; initial climb 3,940 ft (1200 m)/min; service ceiling 32,800 ft (10,000 m); range, 528 miles (850 km).
Armament: (I-26) one 20 mm ShVAK cannon, with 120 rounds, firing through propeller hub and two 7·62 mm ShKAS machine guns, each with 375 rounds, above engine. (Yak-1, late 1941) one 20 mm ShVAK, with 140 rounds, one or two 12·7 mm Beresin BS above engine, each with about 348 rounds, and underwing rails for six 25 lb (12 kg) RS-82 rockets. Some, wing racks for two 110 lb or 220 lb (50 or 100 kg) bombs.
History: first flight March 1939; service delivery (pre-production) October 1940; (production) July 1941.

In 1939 the Soviet government announced specifications for a new fighter. Surprisingly, the best of four rival prototypes was that from young Alexander S. Yakovlev, who had previously designed only gliders and sporting machines. His Ya-26 earned him fame and riches, and in June 1941 was cleared for production

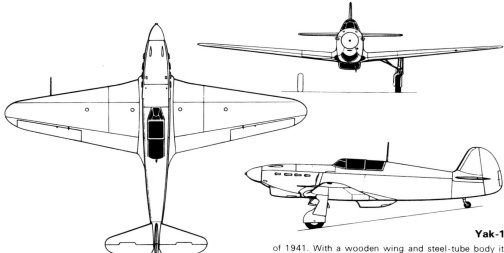

Yak-1

as the chief Soviet fighter. At this time the designation was changed from I-26 to Yak-1, in conformity with the new policy of designation by design bureau rather than by function. In the same month the German hordes swept in from the West and the entire production line was moved 1,000 miles eastwards to Kamensk-Uralsk. Despite this there was a delay of only about six weeks, and about 500 Yak-1 were in action by the end

of 1941. With a wooden wing and steel-tube body it was a solid and easily maintained machine, with excellent handling. In parallel came the UTI-26 trainer, with tandem seats, which went into production as the Yak-7V. In late 1941 this was modified with lower rear fuselage to improve view and this in turn led to the Yak-7B fighter which in early 1942 supplanted the Yak-1 in production. Such was the start of the second-biggest aircraft-production programme in history, which by 1945 had delivered 37,000 fighters.
Yak-3 see page 224.

Yakovlev Yak-9

Yak-9, -9D, -9T, -9U and -9P
Type: single-seat fighter (some, fighter-bomber).
Engine: (-9, D and T) one 1,260 hp Klimov VK-105PF vee-12 liquid-cooled; (U, P) one 1,650 hp VK-107A.
Dimensions: span 32 ft 9¾ in (10 m); length (-9, D, T) 28 ft 0½ in (8·54 m); (U, P) 28 ft 6½ in (8·70 m); height 8 ft (2·44 m).
Weights: empty (T) 6,063 lb (2750 kg); (U) 5,100 lb (2313 kg); maximum loaded (T) 7,055 lb (3200 kg); (U) 6,988 lb (3170 kg).
Performance: maximum speed (9) 373 mph (600 km/h); (D) 359 mph (573 km/h); (T) 367 mph (590 km/h); (U) 435 mph (700 km/h); (P) 416 mph (670 km/h); initial climb (typical 9, D, T) 3,795 ft (1150 m)/min; (U, P) 4,920 ft (1500 m)/min; service ceiling (all) about 34,500 ft (10,500 m); range (most) 520–550 miles (840–890 km); (D) 840 miles (1350 km); (DD) 1,367 miles (2200 km).
Armament: (most) one 20 mm ShVAK, with 100 rounds, and two 12·7 mm BS, each with 250 rounds, plus two 220 lb (100 kg) bombs; (B) internal bay for 880 lb (400 kg) bomb load; (T) gun through propeller changed to 37 mm NS-P37 with 32 rounds; (K) this changed for 45 mm cannon; certain aircraft had 12·7 mm BS firing through hub.
History: first flight (7DI) June 1942; (9M) about August 1942; (D, T) probably late 1943; (U) January 1944; (P) August 1945; final delivery (P) about 1946.

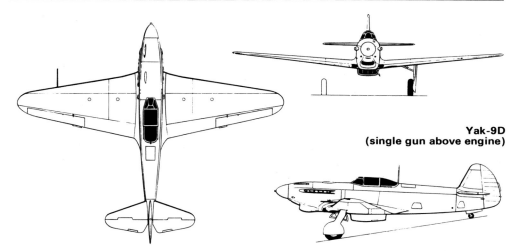

**Yak-9D
(single gun above engine)**

The Yak-7DI introduced light alloy wing spars and evolved into the Yak-9, most-produced Soviet aircraft apart from the Il-2. Able to outfly the Bf 109G, which it met over Stalingrad in late 1942, the -9 was developed into the anti-tank -9T, bomber -9B, long-range -9D and very long-range -9DD. The DD escorted US heavy bombers, and once a large group flew from the Ukraine to Bari (southern Italy) to help Yugoslav partisans. The famed Free French Normandie-Niemen Group and

both free Polish squadrons used various first-generation -9s. With a complete switch to stressed-skin structure and the VK-107 engine there was a dramatic jump in performance, the -9U entering service in the second half of 1944 and flying rings round the 109 and 190. The U could be identified by the smooth cowl, the oil coolers being in the wing root; the post-war -9P, encountered in Korea, had a DF loop under a transparent cover in the rear fuselage.

Yakovlev Yak-3

Yak-1M and -3
Type: single-seat fighter.
Engine: (-1M) one 1,260 hp Klimov VK-105PF vee-12 liquid-cooled; (-3) 1,225 hp VK-105PF-2; (final series) 1,650 hp VK-107A.
Dimensions: span 30 ft 2¼ in (9·20 m); length 27 ft 10¼ in (8·50 m); height 7 ft 10 in (2·39 m).
Weights: empty (VK-105) 4,960 lb (2250 kg); maximum loaded 5,864 lb (2660 kg).
Performance: maximum speed (VK-105) 404 mph (650 km/h); (VK-107) 447 mph (720 km/h); initial climb (105) 4,265 ft (1300 m)/min; (107) 5,250 ft (1600 m)/min; service ceiling (105) 35,450 ft (10,800 m); range (105) 506 miles (815 km).
Armament: one 20 mm ShVAK, with 120 rounds, and two 12·7 mm BS, each with 250 rounds.
History: first flight (-1M) 1942; (-3) spring 1943; service delivery (-3) about July 1943; (-3 with VK-107) not later than January 1944.

As early as 1941 Yakovlev was considering means whereby he could wring the highest possible performance out of the basic Yak-1 design. As there was no immediate prospect of more power, and armament and equipment were already minimal, the only solution seemed to be to cut down the airframe, reduce weight and reduce drag. In the Yak-1M the wing was reduced in size, the oil cooler replaced by twin small coolers in the wing roots, the rear fuselage cut down and a simple clear-view canopy fitted, the coolant radiator duct redesigned and other detail changes made. The result was a fighter even more formidable in close combat than the -1 and -9 families, though it landed faster. The production -3 was further refined by a thick coat of hard-wearing wax polish, and after meeting the new fighter during the mighty Kursk battle in the summer of 1943 the Luftwaffe recognised it had met its match. Indeed by 1944 a general directive had gone out to Luftwaffe units on the Eastern Front to "avoid combat below 5000 m with Yakovlev fighters lacking an oil cooler under the nose"! To show what the Yak-3 could do when bravely handled, despite its armament — which was trivial compared with that of the German fighters — on 14 July 1944 a force of 18 met 30 Luftwaffe fighters and destroyed 15 for the loss of one Yak-3. Small wonder that, offered all available Soviet, British or American fighters, the Normandie-Niemen Group changed from the Yak-9 to the Yak-3

and scored the last 99 of their 273 victories on these machines.

It was natural that the more powerful VK-107 engine should have been fitted to the Yak-3, though the designation was not changed. After prolonged trials in early 1944 the Soviet test centre judged the 107-engined aircraft to be 60—70 mph faster than either a Bf 109G or an Fw 190, but the re-engined aircraft was just too late to see action in World War II. As in the case of the Yak-1 and -9, there were various experimental conversions of the Yak-3, the best-known being the mixed-power Yak-3 ZhRD of early 1945, which reached at least 485 mph (780 km/h) on a VK-105 and a liquid-propellant rocket. A more radical installation was the Yak-7VRD with two large ramjets under the wings. Total production of the Yak-1, -3, -7 and -9 was not less than 37,000. These fighters may have been smaller and simpler than those of other nations in World War II but they served the Soviet Union well in its hour of great need. They conserved precious material, kept going under almost impossible airfield and maintenance conditions and consistently outperformed their enemies.

Yak-9 see page 223

The cutaway is typical of the Yak-3 as used in 1943. Later the more powerful VK-107 (M-107) engine was fitted, and many small changes were made to improve serviceability in harsh conditions.

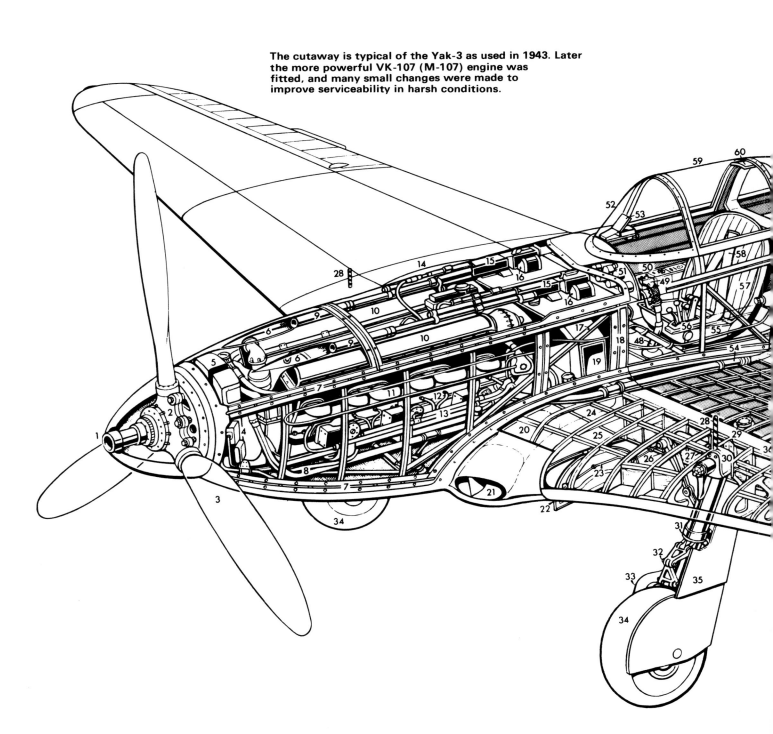

Yak-3 (aircraft of Hero of the Soviet Union Luganskii, central sector, 1944)

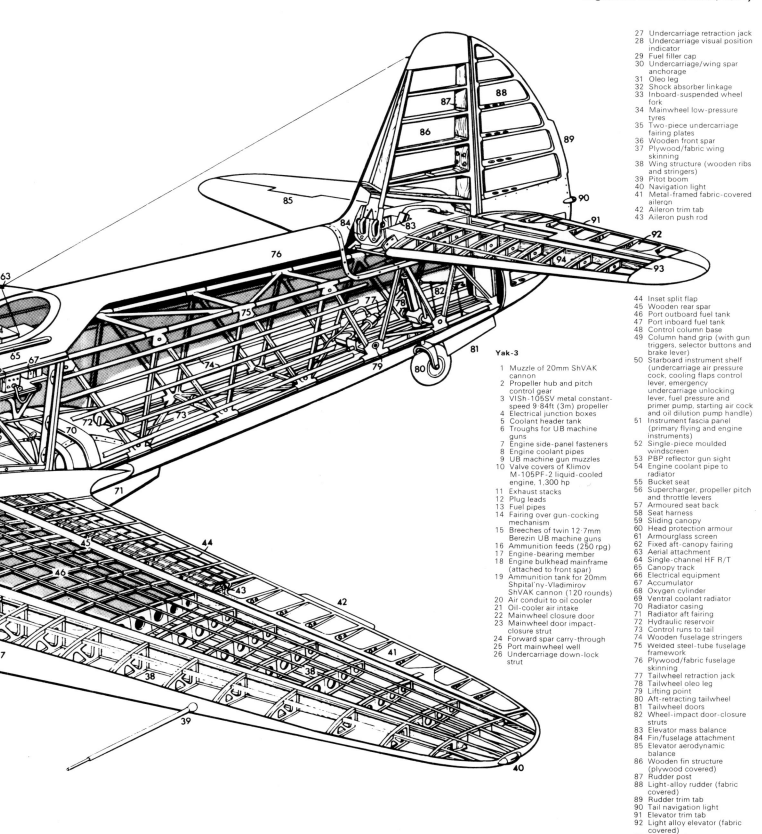

Yak-3

1 Muzzle of 20mm ShVAK cannon
2 Propeller hub and pitch control gear
3 VISh-105SV metal constant-speed 9·84ft (3m) propeller
4 Electrical junction boxes
5 Coolant header tank
6 Troughs for UB machine guns
7 Engine side-panel fasteners
8 Engine coolant pipes
9 UB machine gun muzzles
10 Valve covers of Klimov M-105PF-2 liquid-cooled engine, 1,300 hp
11 Exhaust stacks
12 Plug leads
13 Fuel pipes
14 Fairing over gun-cocking mechanism
15 Breeches of twin 12·7mm Berezin UB machine guns
16 Ammunition feeds (250 rpg)
17 Engine-bearing member
18 Engine bulkhead mainframe (attached to front spar)
19 Ammunition tank for 20mm Shpital'ny-Vladimirov ShVAK cannon (120 rounds)
20 Air conduit to oil cooler
21 Oil-cooler air intake
22 Mainwheel closure door
23 Mainwheel door impact-closure strut
24 Forward spar carry-through
25 Port mainwheel well
26 Undercarriage down-lock strut

27 Undercarriage retraction jack
28 Undercarriage visual position indicator
29 Fuel filler cap
30 Undercarriage/wing spar anchorage
31 Oleo leg
32 Shock absorber linkage
33 Inboard-suspended wheel fork
34 Mainwheel low-pressure tyres
35 Two-piece undercarriage fairing plates
36 Wooden front spar
37 Plywood/fabric wing skinning
38 Wing structure (wooden ribs and stringers)
39 Pitot boom
40 Navigation light
41 Metal-framed fabric-covered aileron
42 Aileron trim tab
43 Aileron push rod

44 Inset split flap
45 Wooden rear spar
46 Port outboard fuel tank
47 Port inboard fuel tank
48 Control column base
49 Column hand grip (with gun triggers, selector buttons and brake lever)
50 Starboard instrument shelf (undercarriage air pressure cock, cooling flaps control lever, emergency undercarriage unlocking lever, fuel pressure and primer pump, starting air cock and oil dilution pump handle)
51 Instrument fascia panel (primary flying and engine instruments)
52 Single-piece moulded windscreen
53 PBP reflector gun sight
54 Engine coolant pipe to radiator
55 Bucket seat
56 Supercharger, propeller pitch and throttle levers
57 Armoured seat back
58 Seat harness
59 Sliding canopy
60 Head protection armour
61 Armourglass screen
62 Fixed aft-canopy fairing
63 Aerial attachment
64 Single-channel HF R/T
65 Canopy track
66 Electrical equipment
67 Accumulator
68 Oxygen cylinder
69 Ventral coolant radiator
70 Radiator casing
71 Radiator aft fairing
72 Hydraulic reservoir
73 Control runs to tail
74 Wooden fuselage stringers
75 Welded steel-tube fuselage framework
76 Plywood/fabric fuselage skinning
77 Tailwheel retraction jack
78 Tailwheel oleo leg
79 Lifting point
80 Aft-retracting tailwheel
81 Tailwheel doors
82 Wheel-impact door-closure struts
83 Elevator mass balance
84 Fin/fuselage attachment
85 Elevator aerodynamic balance
86 Wooden fin structure (plywood covered)
87 Rudder post
88 Light-alloy rudder (fabric covered)
89 Rudder trim tab
90 Tail navigation light
91 Elevator trim tab
92 Light alloy elevator (fabric covered)
93 Wooden elevator spar
94 Wooden tailplane (plywood covered)

Yakovlev Yak-17

Yak-15, -17 and -17UTI
Type: single-seat jet fighter; (UTI) dual trainer.
Engine: (15) one 1,985 lb (900 kg) thrust RD-10 (Jumo 004B) single-shaft turbojet; (17) 2,205 lb (1000 kg) RD-10A.
Dimensions: span (15) 30 ft 2¼ in (9·20 m); (17) 31 ft 5½ in (9·60 m); length (15) 27 ft 10½ in (8·50 m); (17) 27 ft 2¼ in (8·29 m); height (15) 7 ft 2¾ in (2·20 m); (17) 6 ft 10 in (2·10 m).
Weights: empty, not known, but in both cases about 4,400 lb (2000 kg); loaded, reported to be close to 7,055 lb (3200 kg).
Performance: maximum speed (15) 503 mph (810 km/h); (17) 516 mph (830 km/h); initial climb, not known but probably about 4,000 ft (1200 m)/min; service ceiling (15) 41,010 ft (12,500 m); (17) 42,650 ft (13,000 m); range (15) 373 miles (600 km); (17) 460 miles (740 km).
Armament: (both) two 23 mm Nudelmann-Suranov NS-23 cannon above nose.
History: first flight (15) 24 April 1946; (17) early 1947.

At the close of 1945 Yakovlev was summoned to the Kremlin; one of the questions put to him was whether the Soviet Union should build the Me 262. He replied that it would frighten pilots away from jet aviation, whereas his own Yak-15, like the twin-engined MiG-9, would be simpler and safer. In fact, the -15 was only a hasty lash-up based on the Yak-3 and still retaining

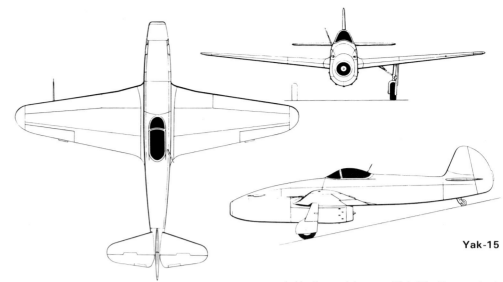

Yak-15

a tailwheel; but it won the designer a Stalin Prize. Mihail Ivanov, who flew it on the same day as Grinchik first flew the MiG-9, piloted the prototype at the Soviet Aviation Day display at Tushino on 18 August 1946. Subsequently about 200 were built before being suc-

ceeded by the much improved Yak-17 with nosewheel, redesigned tail and other changes. Code-named "Feather" by NATO, the -17 served with the VVS and with most Warsaw Pact countries. Probably well over 1,500 were built, a few being tandem-seat Yak-17UTI trainers (code name "Magnet").

Yakovlev Yak-23

Yak-23 (no variants known)
Type: single-seat day fighter.
Engine: one 3,527 lb (1600 kg) thrust Klimov RD-500 (Rolls-Royce Derwent V) centrifugal turbojet.
Dimensions: span 28 ft 6 in (8·69 m); length 26 ft 9¼ in (8·16 m); height 9 ft 10 in (3 m).
Weights: empty 6,395 lb (2900 kg); maximum loaded 10,990 lb (4985 kg).
Performance: maximum speed 550 mph (885 km/h) at sea level (slightly less at altitude); initial climb 5,740 ft (1750 m)/min; service ceiling 48,555 ft (14,800 m); range, about 870 miles (1400 km).
Armament: two 23 mm Nudelmann-Rikter NR-23 cannon in lower part of forward fuselage.
History: first flight, summer of 1947; service delivery, before May 1948.

A logical extension of the Yak-17 formula, the Yak-23 was a totally fresh design owing nothing to the piston-engined heritage. Though it was designed — very quickly indeed — around the imported British centrifugal engine, which was much more reliable and more powerful than the RD-10, the Yak-23 was actually smaller than its predecessor. The fat engine filled a complete fuselage bay ahead of the wing, fed by left and right inlet ducts served by a common nose intake. The jet pipe passed under the wing, flanked on either side by the bays for the mainwheels. The cockpit was

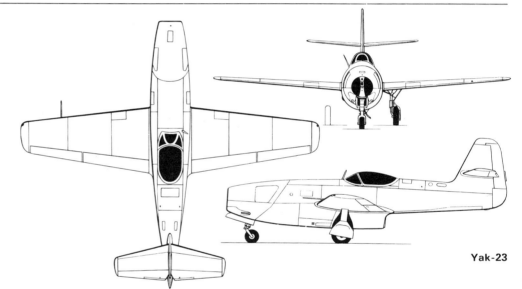

Yak-23

pressurised and equipped with an ejection seat, and manoeuvrability was outstanding. Many service examples carried tip tanks, and some were fitted with an

afterburner though this was not standard. Production certainly ran to some hundreds, and most were soon assigned to satellite air forces. The NATO code name was "Flora".

Yakovlev Yak-25

Yak-25, -25A, -25F and -25R
Type: two-seat all-weather interceptor; (R) reconnaissance.
Engines: (25) two 4,850 lb (2200 kg) thrust Mikulin AM-5 single-shaft turbojets; (A) 5,180 lb (2350 kg) AM-5D; (F) 6,175 lb (2800 kg) Tumansky RD-9, same layout; (R) AM-5, then RD-9.
Dimensions: span 36 ft 1 in (11 m); length (A, F) 51 ft 4½ in (15·66 m); (R) about 55 ft (16·75 m); height 12 ft 6 in (3·80 m).
Weights: empty (25) 16,095 lb (7300 kg); (F) about 16,500 lb (7500 kg); maximum loaded (25) 21,826 lb (9900 kg); (F) 23,150 lb (10,500 kg); (R) about 25,000 lb (estimate).
Performance: maximum speed (F, clean, low level) 630 mph (1015 km/h, Mach 0·83), (clean, at altitude) 594 mph (956 km/h, Mach 0·9); initial climb (F) 9,800 ft (3000 m)/min; service ceiling (F) 45,900 ft (14,000 m); range (F, at altitude) about 1,250 miles (2000 km), (R) over 2,000 miles (3220 km).
Armament: (25, 25A) two 37 mm Nudelmann cannon in quick-release pack under forward fuselage; flick-open box further aft housing 50 55 mm air-to-air rockets; (F) as above, plus wing pylons for four "Alkali" beam-riding missiles or four pods each containing 19 55 mm rockets; (R) probably none.
History: first flight, late 1952 or early 1953; (production Yak-25) late 1954; service delivery, early 1955.

Having a layout possibly inspired by the B-47, and

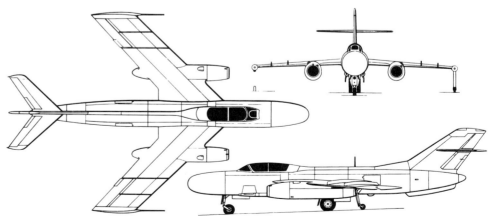

Yak-25A

very similar to that of the Vautour, the Yak-25 was the Soviet Union's first combat aircraft to carry radar and a radar observer. The radar was based on the American SCR-720, and the observer had two displays for seeing targets in an environment of chaff. The set was large and filled the whole of the capacious nose. At rest almost the whole weight of the aircraft was taken by a twin-wheel gear just aft of the c.g., there being a single-wheel nose gear (not steerable) and light tip outriggers.

All surfaces were swept, and the untapered mid wing had anhedral. Large numbers of the night fighter versions were built, and they remained in front-line service until 1973. The Yak-25 was first seen at the Soviet Aviation Day display of 1955, and received the NATO code-name "Flashlight". The Yak-25R was disclosed the following year; with the observer relocated in a pointed, glazed nose; it led to the Yak-26/27 family.

Yakovlev Yak-26

Yak-26, -27P and "Mandrake"
Type: two-seat reconnaissance (27P, interceptor).
Engines: (26, 27P) two Tumansky RD-9B or other RD-9 versions rated at from 7,165 lb (3250 kg) to 8,820 lb (4000 kg) with maximum afterburner; ("Mandrake") two non-afterburning turbojets, probably RD-9 rated at about 6,000 lb.
Dimensions: span (26 and 27P) 38 ft 6 in (11·75 m); (original 27) 36 ft 1 in; ("Mandrake") estimated at 71 ft (22 m); length (26) 62 ft (18·90 m); (27P) about 55 ft (16·75 m); ("Mandrake") about 51 ft (15·5 m); height (26, 27P) 14 ft 6 in (4·40 m); ("Mandrake") about 13 ft (4 m).
Weights: empty (all) about 18,000 lb (8165 kg); maximum loaded (26) about 26,000 lb (11,800 kg); (27P) about 24,000 lb (10,900 kg); ("Mandrake") possibly nearly 30,000 lb (13,600 kg).
Performance: maximum speed (26, 27P, at altitude) 686 mph (1104 km/h, Mach 0·95); ("Mandrake") about 470 mph (755 km/h); initial climb, about 15,000 ft (4600 m)/min ("Mandrake", less); service ceiling (26, 27P) 49,200 ft (15,000 m); ("Mandrake") about 62,000 ft (19,000 m); range at altitude (26) about 1,675 miles (2700 km); (27P) 1,000 miles (1600 km); ("Mandrake") possibly 2,500 miles (4000 km).
Armament: (26) one 30 mm NR-30 cannon in fairing low on right side of forward fuselage; (27P) small batches with cannon and rockets, then small

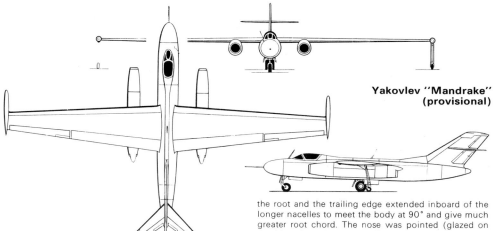

Yakovlev "Mandrake" (provisional)

batches with two missile pylons; ("Mandrake") none.
History: first flight (26) before mid-1956; (27P) before mid-1956; ("Mandrake") possibly 1957.

Stemming directly from the Yak-25, these aircraft introduced various changes, of which the most significant was afterburning engines in the Yak-26 and 27P. The leading edge was swept very sharply at the root and the trailing edge extended inboard of the longer nacelles to meet the body at 90° and give much greater root chord. The nose was pointed (glazed on the 26 and a radome on the 27P) and in the production aircraft the outer wings were extended beyond the outrigger gear and fitted with drooped extended-chord leading edges. Only the 26 was built in large numbers (NATO name "Mangrove"). The 27P was called "Flashlight C". The high-altitude, unswept "Mandrake", whose proper designation is not known, made overflights in Eastern Asia, the Middle East and along the borders of Communist territory in Europe before being retired in 1972 or 1973.

Yakovlev Yak-28

Yak-28 attack versions, -28P, -28R and -28U
Type: 28 (unknown designations) two-seat attack; (P) all-weather interceptor; (R) multi-sensor reconnaissance; (U) dual-control trainer.
Engines: two Tumansky RD-11 single-shaft afterburning turbojets each with maximum rating of 13,120 lb (5950 kg); certain sub-types have RD-11-300 rated at 13,670 lb (6200 kg).
Dimensions: (estimated) span 42 ft 6 in (12·95 m), (some versions have span slightly less than standard); length (except late P) 71 ft 0½ in (21·65 m); (late 28P) 74 ft (22·56 m); height 12 ft 11½ in (3·95 m).
Weights: empty (estimated, typical) 24,250 lb (11,000 kg); maximum loaded (U) 30,000 lb (13,600 kg); (others) 35,300–41,000 lb (16,000–18,600 kg).
Performance: (estimated) maximum speed at altitude 735 mph (1180 km/h, Mach 1·13); initial climb 27,900 ft (8500 m)/min; service ceiling 55,000 ft (16,750 m); range (clean, at altitude) 1,200–1,600 miles (1930–2575 km).
Armament: (attack versions) one 30 mm NR-30 cannon on both sides of fuselage or on right side only;

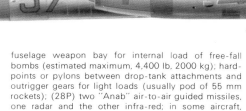

Yak-28P (IA-PVO, original short-nose version)

fuselage weapon bay for internal load of free-fall bombs (estimated maximum, 4,400 lb, 2000 kg); hardpoints or pylons between drop-tank attachments and outrigger gears for light loads (usually pod of 55 mm rockets); (28P) two "Anab" air-to-air guided missiles, one radar and the other infra-red; in some aircraft, two additional pylons for two K-13A ("Atoll") missiles, both "Anab" then being radar homers; (R) believed none; (U) retains weapon bay and single gun.
History: first flight, before 1961; (production attack and interceptor versions) before 1961; service delivery, not later than mid-1962; final delivery, before 1970.

Obviously derived from the Yak-25/26/27, the Yak-28 is a completely new aircraft, with high wing of different form, new engines, steerable twin-wheel nose gear and considerably greater weight. Early attack versions had slightly shorter fuselage and shorter nacelles ahead of the wing; many hundreds (possibly thousands) of glazed-nose attack 28s (code name "Brewer") were built, most having been rebuilt as ECM and other specialist tactical machines. The Yak-28P (code name "Firebar") remains a leading interceptor, its "Skip Spin" radar being enclosed in a much longer and more pointed nose from 1967. The 28U trainer (code name "Maestro") has a separate front (pupil) cockpit with canopy hinged to the right. Many 28R versions ("Brewer D"), with cameras and various non-optical sensors, may be converted attack aircraft. Flight refuelling is not fitted.

Yokosuka D4Y Suisei

D4Y1 and 1-C, D4Y2, 2-C and 2-S, D4Y3 and D4Y4.
Type: two-seat carrier dive bomber; (1-C, 2-C, reconnaissance; 2-S night fighter; D4Y4, single-seat Kamikaze).
Engine: (1) one 1,200 hp Aichi Atsuta 21 inverted-vee-12 liquid-cooled (Daimler-Benz 601); (2) 1,400 hp Atsuta 32; (3, 4) 1,560 hp Mitsubishi Kinsei 62 14-cylinder two-row radial.
Dimensions: span (1, 2) 37 ft 8½ in (11·493 m); (3, 4) 37 ft 9 in (11·50 m); length (all, despite engine change) 33 ft 6½ in (10·22 m); height (1, 2) 12 ft 1 in (3·67 m); (3, 4) 12 ft 3¼ in (3·74 m).
Weights: empty (1) 5,650 lb (2565 kg); (2) 5,840 lb (2635 kg); (3) 5,512 lb (2501 kg); (4) variable; maximum loaded (1) 9,615 lb (4361 kg); (2) 9,597 lb (4353 kg); (3) 10,267 lb (4657 kg); (4) 10,434 lb (4733 kg).
Performance: maximum speed (1) 339 mph (546 km/h); (2) 360 mph (580 km/h); (3) 356 mph (574 km/h); initial climb (1) 1,970 ft (600 m)/min; (others) 2,700 ft (820 m)/min; service ceiling (typical) 34,500 ft (10,500 m); range (2) 749 miles (1205 km); (3) 945 miles (1520 km).
Armament: normally, two 7·7 mm Type 97 fixed above engine, one 7·7 mm manually aimed from rear cockpit; internal bomb bay for single 551 lb (250 kg) bomb, plus one 66 lb (30 kg) bomb under each wing; (4) see text.
History: first flight November 1940; (production D4Y1) May 1941; service delivery, late 1941.

Designed to a challenging specification of the Imperial Japanese Navy of 1937, which called for a

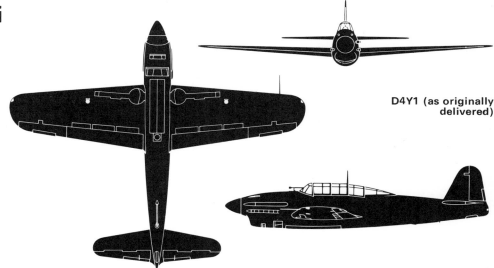
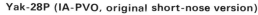

D4Y1 (as originally delivered)

long-range two-seat dive bomber as fast as the "Zero" fighter, the D4Y was one of the very few Japanese aircraft to go into production with a liquid-cooled engine. The supposed lower drag of such an engine had been one of the factors in meeting the requirement, but the Japanese version of the DB 601 had an unhappy history in carrier service. The first D4Y versions in combat were 1-C reconnaissance aircraft flying from the carrier *Soryu* during the Battle of Midway in June 1942. The carrier was sunk in that encounter, and soon most D4Y were being operated by unskilled crews from island airstrips. In 1943 the main problems with the aircraft – named Suisei (Comet), and called "Judy" by the Allies – were solved by switching to the smooth and reliable radial engine. During the final year of the war the D4Y4 appeared as a single-seat suicide attacker carrying 1,764 lb (800 kg) of explosives, while some dozens of Atsuta-engined examples were turned into 2-S night fighters with one or two 20 mm cannon fixed obliquely behind the rear cockpit. Total production was 2,319.

Yokosuka P1Y1 Ginga

P1Y1 Model 11, P1Y1-S, P1Y2 and 2-S
Type: three-seat multi-role attack bomber; -S, two-seat night fighter.
Engines: (1) two 1,820 hp Nakajima Ho-21 Homare 11 18-cylinder two-row radials; (2) 1,825 hp Mitsubishi Kasei 25 14-cylinder two-row radials.
Dimensions: span 65 ft 7½ in (20 m); length 49 ft 2½ in (15 m); height 14 ft 1¼ in (4·30 m).
Weights: empty (1) 14,748 lb (6690 kg); normal loaded (1) 23,148 lb (10,500 kg); maximum loaded (1) 29,762 lb (13,500 kg).
Performance: maximum speed (1) 345 mph (556 km/h); (2) 354 mph (570 km/h); initial climb (1) 2,100 ft (650 m)/min; service ceiling 33,530 ft (10,220 m); range (1) 2,728 miles (4390 km).
Armament: (1 and 2) one 20 mm Type 99-II cannon manually aimed from nose, one 20 mm or 12·7 mm manually aimed from rear cockpit (a few aircraft had dorsal turret with two 20 mm or 12·7 mm); internal bay for two 551 lb (250 kg) bombs, plus small bombs beneath outer wings; as alternative, one 1,764 lb (800 kg) or 1,874 lb (850 kg) torpedo externally, or two 1,102 lb (500 kg) bombs inboard of engines; (1-S, 2-S) two 20 mm fixed firing obliquely upward in centre fuselage, plus single 20 mm aimed from rear cockpit, or powered dorsal turret with two 20 mm.
History: first flight (Y-20 prototype) early 1943;

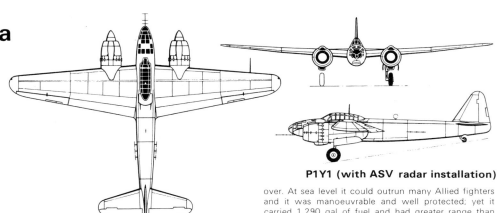

P1Y1 (with ASV radar installation)

(production P1Y1) August 1943; (prototype P1Y2-S) June 1944.
Similar to late-model Ju 88 aircraft in size, power and capability, this fine-looking aircraft was one of the best designed in Japan during World War II. The 1940 Navy specification called for a land-based aircraft capable of level and dive bombing, but by the time production began at the Nakajima factories at Koizumi and Fukushima it had already become a torpedo bomber, and it was to do much more before its brief career was over. At sea level it could outrun many Allied fighters and it was manoeuvrable and well protected; yet it carried 1,290 gal of fuel and had greater range than any other aircraft in its class. Called Ginga (Milky Way), and christened "Frances" by the Allies, this machine would have been a menace had it not been crippled by lack of skilled crews, lack of fuel and lack of spares. Nevertheless Nakajima built 1,002, of which some were used as suicide aircraft while a few were converted into the P1Y1-S night fighter. Kawanishi had meanwhile developed a completely new version, the Kasei-engined P1Y2, and delivered 96 P1Y2-S night fighters called Kyokko (Aurora), which saw little action.

Yokosuka MXY-7 Ohka

MXY-7 Model 11 and Model 22
Type: single-seat piloted missile for surface attack.
Engine: (11) one three-barrel Type 4 Model 20 rocket motor with sea-level thrust of 1,764 lb (800 kg); (22) TSU-11 jet engine, with piston-engined compressor, rated at 441 lb (200 kg) thrust.
Dimensions: span (11) 16 ft 4¾ in (5 m); (22) 13 ft 6¼ in (4·12 m); length (11) 19 ft 10¾ in (6·07 m); (22) 22 ft 6¾ in (6·88 m); height (both) about 3 ft 11¼ in (1·20 m).
Weights: empty (no warhead) (11) 970 lb (440 kg); (22) 1,202 lb (545 kg); loaded (11) 4,718 lb (2140 kg); (22) 3,200 lb (1450 kg).
Performance: maximum speed on level (11) 534 mph (860 km/h); (22) about 300 mph (480 km/h); final dive speed (both) 621 mph (1000 km/h); climb and ceiling, normally launched at about 27,000 ft (8200 m); range (11) 55 miles (88 km).
Armament: (11) warhead containing 2,645 lb (1200 kg) of tri-nitroaminol; (22) warhead weight 1,323 lb (600 kg).
History: start of design August 1944; start of quantity production (11) September 1944; service delivery, early October 1944.

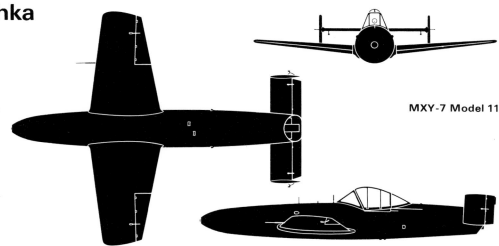

MXY-7 Model 11

Having accepted the principle of the Kamikaze suicide attack, the Imperial Navy was only logical in designing an aircraft for this duty instead of using inefficient and more vulnerable conventional machines having less devastating effect. Built partly of wood, Model 11 was carried aloft by a G4M ("Betty"), without bomb doors and specially modified for the task, and released about 50 miles from the target. The pilot then held a fast glide at about 290 mph (466 km/h), electrically igniting the rocket while pushing over into a steep final dive for the last 30 seconds of trajectory. Though nearly all these missiles failed to reach their objectives, the few that did wrought fearful havoc. Ohka (Cherry Blossom) was called "Baka" (Japanese for "fool") by the Allies, which was not very appropriate. Several manufacturers delivered 755, and some dozen unpowered versions were delivered for training. The Model 22, of which some 50 were delivered, was underpowered. Not completed by VJ-day, the Model 33 would have had the Ne-20 turbojet; Models 43A and 43B were for launching from submarines and land catapults, respectively, but these too failed to see service.

Zeppelin airships

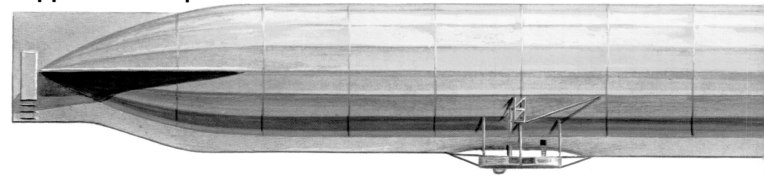

Types m, p, q, r, v and w
Type: airships for reconnaissance and bombing.
Engines: Maybach in-line water-cooled petrol engines (details, see text).
Dimensions: length (m) 518–520 ft (158–158·5 m); (w) 682 ft (208 m); diameter (m) typically 48 ft 6 in (14·78 m); (w) typically 78 ft 6 in (23·92 m); volume of gasbags (m) 794,500 cu ft (22,500 m³); (w) 2,418,700 cu ft (68,500 m³).
Weights: the most helpful parameter is the useful lift, the difference between the dead weight of the airship structure and engines and the gross lift of the gasbags, and thus available for fuel, crew and armament: (m) 20,250 lb (9185 kg); (p) 34,000 lb (15,420 kg); (q) 39,000 lb (17,700 kg); (r) 68,345 lb (31,000 kg); (v) 86,000 lb (39,000 kg); (w) 114,650 lb (52,000 kg).
Performance: maximum speed (m) 52 mph (84 km/h); (later types) 60–66 mph (96–106 km/h); operating ceiling (m) 11,500 ft (3500 m); (r) 17,200 ft (5250 m); (w) 21,000 ft (6500 m); range with bomb load, varied greatly with sub-type and with wind, but typically 800 miles (1290 km) in early ships and 3,100 miles (5000 km) in w-series, which had an endurance under power exceeding 100 hr.
Armament: (m) typically two or three 7·92 mm Parabellum machine guns, in control gondola; about 2,200 lb (1000 kg) of bombs. (r, v and w) nine or ten machine guns including two singles or pairs of guns manually aimed from the top of the hull; bomb load 11,000 to 15,500 lb (5000–7000 kg).
History: first flight (naval L.1) 7 October 1912; (m-series) 11 May 1914; (p) January 1915, delivered May 1915; (r) February 1916, delivered May 1916; (w) early 1917.

Yugoslavia/Romania Orao

"Jurom" Orao
Type: single-seat tactical fighter.
Engines: two 4,000 lb (1814 kg) thrust Rolls-Royce/Fiat Viper 632 single-shaft turbojets.
Dimensions: (estimated) span 28 ft (8·5 m); length 46 ft (14 m); height 12 ft (3·7 m).
Weights: (estimated) empty 11,000 lb (5000 kg); loaded (clean) 15,450 lb (7000 kg); maximum loaded 21,000 lb (9500 kg).
Performance: (estimated) maximum speed, equivalent to about Mach 0·95 over wide height band (thus, about 700–720 mph, 1150 km/h, clean at sea level; maximum speed with weapons, about 550 mph (885 km/h) at sea level; initial climb (clean) at least 9,800 ft (3000 m)/min; range on internal fuel (high altitude) about 900 miles (1450 km).
Armament: two guns (almost certainly of 30 mm calibre) in lower flanks of mid-fuselage; centreline and four wing pylons for external stores load of at least 4,400 lb (2000 kg) for rough-field operation, with possibility of heavier load from paved runway.
History: start of design, before 1973; photograph of completed prototype, June 1975; photograph of aircraft in flight, early September 1975.

Though no bilateral management organization has been announced, the governments of Yugoslavia and

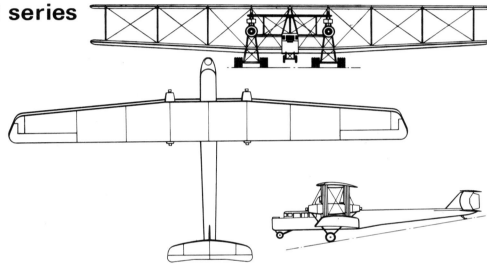

Orao (first prototype, as at roll-out)

Romania decided several years ago to collaborate in the design, development and production of a new light combat aircraft, which was later named Orao (Eagle). For lack of any other parent organization it has since been colloquially called "Jurom" (Jugoslavia-Romania) by outsiders. The chosen engine was the most powerful Viper, produced by Rolls-Royce in partnership with Fiat of Italy; Yugoslavia used earlier Vipers (p. 199) but has never announced a manu-

facturing licence and at present Orao engines are imported. The aircraft itself can be regarded as intermediate between the less powerful Fiat G91Y and the more powerful Jaguar. It is subsonic and is intended primarily for tactical attack from unpaved airstrips. The first of several prototypes was assembled in Yugoslavia and bears the markings of that country. No information on the work-split or the companies involved has yet been made public.

Zeppelin (Staaken) R series

V.G.O.I, II and III (R.II and III) and R.IV to XVI
Type: heavy bomber.
Engines: (R.VI) four 260 hp Mercedes D.IVa or 245 hp Maybach Mb.IV six-cylinder in-line water-cooled.
Dimensions: (VI) span 138 ft 5¾ in (42·20 m); length 72 ft 6¼ in (22·10 m); height 20 ft 8¼ in (6·30 m).
Weights: (VI) empty 15,210–16,200 lb (6900–7350 kg); maximum loaded 25,265 lb (11,460 kg).
Performance: (VI) maximum speed 81 mph (130 km/h) at sea level; initial climb 330 ft (100 m)/min; service ceiling, about 12,500 ft (3800 m); range, typically 500 miles (800 km) (endurance 7 to 10 hr depending on bomb load).
Armament: (VI) one or two 7·92 mm Parabellum machine guns manually aimed from nose cockpit, one or two aimed from dorsal cockpit and one from lower rear position; internal bay for up to 18 220 lb (100 kg) bombs, or single 2,205 lb (1000 kg) bomb carried semi-externally (maximum load, 4,409 lb, 2000 kg).
History: first flight (V.G.O.I) 11 April 1915; service delivery (I, II) late 1916; (R.VI) June 1917.

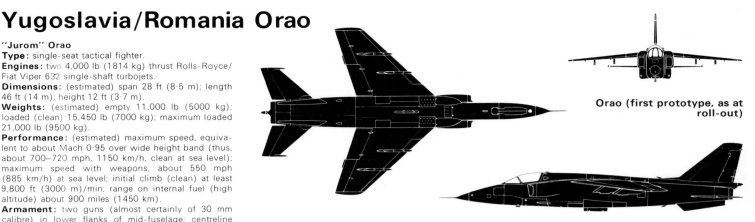

The largest aircraft used in World War I were the sluggish but capable Riesenflugzeug (giant aeroplane) series produced by the Zeppelin Werke Staaken. Originally this organization had been at Gotha, where the V.G.O.I, weighing 19,850 lb (9000 kg) first flew on the power of three 240 hp engines. Via several other one-off bombers, with three, four or five engines and different schemes of defensive armament, the design team of Baumann, Hirth and Klein eventually produced

the R.VI. Except for the crashed V.G.O.I, all the "Giants" had served on the Eastern Front or against Britain, and they far outperformed other bombers in range and bomb load. The VI now went into production, one by the Staaken works being followed by six from Aviatik, four by O.A.W. and seven by Schütte-Lanz. Three of the Aviatik machines had different noses and tails and

Maybach engines. Individual R.VI bombers wrought havoc over London in 1917–18, often dropping 1000 kg bombs. The VI was followed by an assortment of single aircraft or small batches, mainly powered by five 240 hp Maybach, with varied airframes and including three twin-float seaplanes.

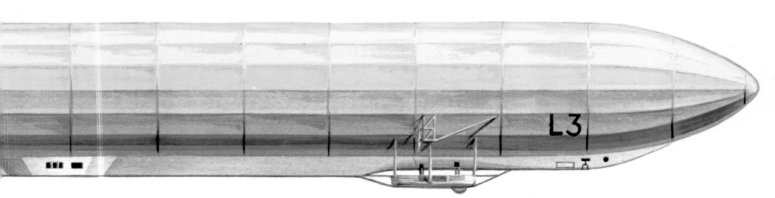

Zeppelin L3 (LZ23). This was one of the earliest operational bomber ships of the Imperial German Navy m-series

Count Ferdinand von Zeppelin, a former general, completed his first airship in July 1900. It was an advanced rigid ship, the gasbags being enclosed in an envelope of fabric covering a skeleton of aluminium girders. In 1910–14 Zeppelins maintained a regular civil airline throughout central Europe, laying the groundwork for the use of bigger ships in World War I. More than 100 Zeppelins were built during the war for the Imperial Navy (with numbers prefaced by L, for luftschiff = airship) and Army (numbers prefaced by LZ, for luftschiff Zeppelin). The Army also used many

Schütte-Lanz ships, with structures of wood. Between January 1915 and August 1918 the German airships, mainly navy Zeppelins, made 51 bombing raids over Britain, killing 557 and injuring 1,358. At first opposition was negligible and airship losses were due only to engine failure and storms. The early m and p ships had four 201–210 hp Maybach C-X engines and were able to escape before defending aircraft could reach them, though the army airships suffered severely in operations over the battlefields. Navy Zeppelins also did good work shadowing the Royal Navy and often

making attacks on submarines and seaplanes. All the later Zeppelins had five or six 240 hp HSLu engines and, though their ceiling was almost beyond the reach of defending fighters, Britain's defences at last became effective. The last major Zeppelin raid, called "the Silent Raid" because the w-ships flew at maximum height, took place on the night of 19 October 1917; five of the 11 raiders were shot down. All the Zeppelins had an appearance similar to the first wartime ship, illustrated, but most were much larger.

Index